DATE DUE

The Resurgence of the Radical Right in France
From Boulangisme to the Front National

This book attempts to account for the resurgence of the radical Right in France since the establishment of democracy in the country at the end of the nineteenth century. Taking to task historical treatments of the radical Right for their failure to specify the conditions and dynamics attending its emergence, and faulting the historical myopia of contemporary electoral and party-centric accounts of the Front National, it tries to explain the radical Right's continuing appeal by relating the sociostructural outcomes of the processes of industrialization and democratization in France to the persistence of economically and politically illiberal groups within French society. The book argues that, as a result of the country's protracted and uneven experience of industrialization and urbanization, significant pre- or antimodern social classes, which remained functionally ill-adapted and culturally ill-disposed to industrial capitalism and liberal democracy, subsisted late into its development.

Gabriel Goodliffe teaches international relations and international political economy at the Instituto Tecnológico Autónomo de México (ITAM) in Mexico City. He is also the author of the chapter on French politics for the fourth edition of *Europe Today* and a chapter on the Front National in *New Perspectives on European Right-Wing Extremism, Identity and Passions*, which is forthcoming. Goodliffe received his doctorate in international relations from the Johns Hopkins University School of Advanced International Studies in Washington, D.C., in 2008. He previously taught courses in comparative politics, international relations, and international political economy at American University and the Johns Hopkins University.

The Resurgence of the Radical Right in France

From Boulangisme to the Front National

GABRIEL GOODLIFFE

Instituto Tecnológico Autónomo de México

CAMBRIDGE
UNIVERSITY PRESS

CAMBRIDGE UNIVERSITY PRESS
Cambridge, New York, Melbourne, Madrid, Cape Town,
Singapore, São Paulo, Delhi, Tokyo, Mexico City

Cambridge University Press
32 Avenue of the Americas, New York, NY 10013-2473, USA

www.cambridge.org
Information on this title: www.cambridge.org/9781107006706

First published 2012

Printed in the United States of America

A catalog record for this publication is available from the British Library.

Library of Congress Cataloging in Publication Data
Goodliffe, Gabriel, 1971–
    The resurgence of the radical right in France : from Boulangisme to the Front
National / Gabriel Goodliffe.
        p.   cm.
Includes bibliographical references and index.
ISBN 978-1-107-00670-6 (hardback)
    1. Right-wing extremists – France – History – 20th century.   2. Right-wing extremists – France –
History – 21st century.   3. France – Politics and government – 20th century.   4. France – Social
conditions – 20th century.   5. France – Politics and government – 21st century.   6. France – Social
conditions – 21st century.   I. Title.
HN440.R3G66   2011
324.244′03–dc22   2011007908

ISBN 978-1-107-00670-6 Hardback

Pour Clara et Octave

Contents

Tables and Figures

Acknowledgments

Writing a book is perforce a collaborative effort – in this case doubly so, since the book as it now stands grew out of a Ph.D. dissertation begun nearly a decade ago. Accordingly, the end result, flawed as it may be, would not have been possible without the input and support of others: first, from those involved in supervising the dissertation and guiding it to its completion and, second, from colleagues and friends who, along the way, helped me to clarify and perfect the arguments set out in these pages. Among the former, my gratitude extends to my thesis adviser, David Calleo of the SAIS European Studies Department, whose thoughtful insights undoubtedly made the end result better than it would otherwise have been. Likewise, Ariane Chebel d'Appollonia, then of Sciences Po-Paris and now of Rutgers, also deserves a special mention. I would like to thank her for agreeing to work with me on this project from its inception and for her dedication in overseeing it through the dissertation stage. I benefited enormously from her extensive knowledge of the French Far Right, and I know the book would be much the poorer had she not assisted me. Third, I am indebted to Erik Jones of the SAIS Bologna Center, who was instrumental in helping give shape to my arguments and for offering invaluable advice and support when things – as they inevitably at times did – got rough. Finally, I am also grateful to Sunil Khilnani of SAIS and Martin Schain of New York University, whose insights were of great value to me as I distilled the dissertation into a book.

Beyond the contributions of my dissertation committee, the book has been immeasurably enriched by discussion with professors, colleagues, and friends. Conversations with Gérard Conac, Kendall Myers, Bruce Parrott, Gilbert Khadiagala, and Larry Diamond were invaluable in helping me to define this project and bring it into focus. Likewise, interviews with René Rémond, Nonna Mayer, Guy Michelat, Gérard Grunberg, and Jean-Luc Parodi enabled me to iron out some of the theoretical difficulties presented by this project and to specify the methodological approach I would adopt. Particular thanks go to Alain Lancelot who, as former director of Sciences Po-Paris, was extremely generous with his time and helped me to secure interviews with his colleagues.

More prosaically but no less importantly, I also greatly benefited from discussions with my peers in the SAIS European studies department and beyond, who turned out to be wonderful sources of both advice and moral support. Here, I would like to thank in no particular order of importance Jan-Martin Witte, Matthias Matthijs, Christopher Chivvis, Andy Wolfe, and Timo Behr. Likewise, I am grateful to Mitchell Orenstein, who offered great advice in terms of editing the dissertation and preparing it for submission to a university press. Finally, I want to express special gratitude to my colleagues in the ITAM International Studies department and thank them not only for their warm reception but also for their understanding and encouragement as the book entered the editing stage. Of course, despite the best efforts of the aforementioned, any inaccuracies, omissions, or distortions contained herein are my responsibility alone.

In turn, a project such as this would not have been possible without various forms of institutional support. A predoctoral research fellowship from the Florence Gould Memorial Foundation in Summer 2003 and a Bourse Chateaubriand from the French Ministry of Foreign Affairs in 2004–5 allowed me to conduct invaluable field research in France at the dissertation stage. Likewise, I was sustained for the first three years of the Ph.D. by a doctoral fellowship from SAIS, without which I would never have gotten to the point of writing the dissertation on which this book is based, let alone survived.

The institutional support I have received extends far beyond funding, however. First off, I should like to thank the respective staffs at the Library of Congress, the library of Sciences Po-Paris, and especially the SAIS library. The staff of the SAIS library in particular displayed exemplary patience in dealing with me and proved tireless in ferreting out obscure titles from libraries I never even knew existed. Similarly, I would like to express my gratitude to my editors at Cambridge University Press, Lewis Bateman, Anne Lovering Rounds, and Brian MacDonald, and to commend them for their advice and sensitivity in helping me to navigate the rigors of the publishing process. Finally, special thanks go to my research assistant, Arturo Mendoza, as well as to Jon Hopwood, for their assistance in helping me to negotiate the final harried stages of the editing process.

A very heartfelt thanks must also go to my family and especially to my parents. Their abiding support for and interest in this project cannot be overstated. *Merci, chers parents!!* By the same token, I should like to remember my late grandfather Eugène de Prat of Pont-de-Briques. He inspired me to write this book by exemplifying many of the political orientations and cultural traits that are its principal focus. And lastly, though he was not directly associated with it, I am deeply indebted to my old friend and *maître* Jacques Guicharnaud, who passed away while I was in France doing research for this project. I regret not having had a chance to tell him that, through his generosity of spirit and of mind, as well as the genuine affection he showed his students, he more than anyone traced out the academic path on which I would one day embark. I only hope I can follow in his example.

Last but not least, I should like to thank my own family, beginning with my wife, Natasha. Without her patience and support, I would never have been able to see this project through. She sustained me in good times and bad, and offered encouragement when I most needed it. For this I am deeply, truly in her debt. Also, I wish to thank my children, Clara and Octavio. By a series of fortuitous omens, Clara's arrival coincided with the finishing stages of the dissertation, while Octavio's barely preceded the manuscript's acceptance. In this sense, they guided the book's completion, and it is to them that it is dedicated.

1

Introduction

In May 2002 Jean-Marie Le Pen shocked the world by making it to the second round of the French presidential election. In that second round of voting, Le Pen received six million votes – 18 percent of the ballots cast – an unusually high number for the candidate of an overtly xenophobic party in a mature democracy. No doubt there was some truth to explanations that attributed Le Pen's first-round triumph to the fragmentation of the electoral field among a record sixteen candidates. Similarly, structural, economic, and social factors also surely played a role in his success. The themes of unemployment, immigration, and crime on which the Front National (FN) has campaigned for three decades now have incontestably emerged as the issues of greatest concern to French voters. In turn, the advent of similar sociostructural problems in other European countries has brought many analysts to view the FN as part of a broader, pan-European resurgence of the radical Right.

Yet, there is more to the present electoral success of the FN than the coincidence of rising unemployment with large non-European immigrant populations in Western European societies. These factors tell only half the story. If the FN is to be seen as part of a European-wide trend, how does one explain that its emergence predated that of radical right-wing parties in other European countries by at least a decade? Similarly, if its rise was attributable simply to economic factors, why did the FN remain popular through the boom period of the 1990s? And why did antisystem parties of the radical Left, which explicitly campaign on socioeconomic issues, not achieve the same electoral success? Likewise, why did support for the FN continue to increase even as the French immigrant population stagnated or even declined?[1] Subtending these explanations is the notion that the FN represents an exception or aberration in contemporary French political life.

---

[1] Census figures show that the proportion of immigrants in the total population has not substantially changed since the mid-1970s, remaining essentially steady at 7.4% of the total population from 1975 to 1999. This invalidates the direct causal relationship inferred by many researchers between the FN's rise and immigration, since it was not until the mid-1980s, that is, over a decade after the great wave of immigration the country experienced from 1956 to 1973, that Le Pen's party rose to political prominence. Similarly, the previous period of large-scale immigration, lasting through the

The Resurgence of the Radical Right in France

Even those accounts that highlight its continuities with previous radical right-wing movements in France emphasize its anachronistic and unnatural character. I would submit that the rise of the FN represents the reestablishment of the radical Right in its traditionally influential role within French politics. As a function of its pattern of social and political modernization, the country developed a peculiar class structure in which certain groups became significant sources of support for the radical Right. In addition to presenting socioeconomic interests and anxieties, these groups evolved particular cultural traits that disposed them favorably to it.

The foregoing suggests that prevailing theoretical interpretations inadequately account for the periodic – even cyclical – evanescence of radical right-wing movements and parties in the country since the advent of republican rule in 1875. These interpretations fall into one of two theoretical schools, each of which presents its own particular shortcomings. The first is the historical school, which identifies the ideological, programmatic, and discursive features of successive radical right-wing movements and describes their principals and rank-and-file members. These are situated in a coherent, autochthonous political tradition extending more or less far back in French history.[2] In their focus on the internal characteristics of radical right-wing movements and, in particular,

1920s and reaching a peak of 6.6% of the population in 1931, did not coincide with a surge of the radical Right. It was only in the following decade, as immigration rates paradoxically fell off, that radical right-wing movements gained political traction. Jacques Barou, "Immigration. Grandes tendances," in *L'état de la France. Un panorama unique et complet de la France 2005–2006*, ed. S. Cordellier and E. Lau (Paris: La Découverte, 2005), 39–40; Fabienne Daguet and Suzanne Thave, "La population immigrée. Le résultat d'une longue histoire," *INSEE Première*, no. 458 (June 1996), 1–4; and Gérard Noiriel, *The French Melting Pot: Immigration, Citizenship, and National Identity*, trans. G. de Laforcade (Minneapolis: University of Minnesota Press, 1996).

[2] This historical school subsumes a number of approaches and emphases. Some interpretations, for example, link the French radical Right to distinct political-philosophical traditions. For works that seek to tie it to fascism, see the trilogy by Zeev Sternhell, *Maurice Barrès et le nationalisme français*, 2nd ed. (Paris: Fayard, 2000), *La droite révolutionnaire, 1885–1914. Les origines françaises du fascisme* (Paris: Seuil, 1978), and *Neither Right nor Left: Fascist Ideology in France*, trans. D. Maisel (Berkeley: University of California Press, 1986); Robert Soucy, *Fascism in France: The Case of Maurice Barrès* (Berkeley: University of California Press, 1972); and Ernst Nolte, *Three Faces of Fascism: Action Française, Italian Fascism, National Socialism*, trans. L. Vennewitz (New York: Holt, Rinehart and Winston, 1966). Others link it to political traditions that emerged in the wake of the French Revolution, such as Bonapartism and Legitimism. In this vein, see René Rémond, *The Right Wing in France: From 1815 to de Gaulle*, 2nd ed., trans. J. Laux (Philadelphia: University of Pennsylvania Press, 1969). A third strain situates the contemporary radical Right in a populist tradition dating back at least to the Second World War. See Jim Shields, *The Extreme Right in France from Pétain to Le Pen* (London: Routledge, 2007); and Catherine Fieschi, *Fascism, Populism and the French Fifth Republic* (Manchester: Manchester University Press, 2004). Others still have chosen to emphasize the philosophical, programmatic, and leadership continuities presented by successive movements of the French radical Right. Contributions in this vein include Peter Davies, *The Extreme Right in France, 1789 to the Present: From de Maistre to Le Pen* (London: Routledge, 2002); Edward J. Arnold, ed., *The Development of the Radical Right in France: From Boulanger to Le Pen* (New York: St. Martin's Press, 2000); Michel Winock, *Nationalism, Anti-Semitism and Fascism in France*, trans. J. M. Todd (Stanford, CA: Stanford University Press, 1998); Ariane Chebel d'Appollonia, *L'extrême droite en France. De Maurras à Le*

on the intellectual and organizational elites who led them, such accounts have little to say about why ordinary French people have been periodically attracted to these movements. Historical accounts make no systematic attempt to elucidate the social causes that underlay their historical formation or to specify the sociopolitical dynamics by which they respectively emerged. At one level, they fail to establish the relationship between the fortunes of the radical Right and long-term processes of social and economic modernization. Second, they neglect the proximate socioeconomic and sociopolitical factors that fueled its resurgence at particular historical junctures. In short, they pay insufficient attention to the conditions of political "demand" that determined the success of the radical Right over the past one and a quarter centuries.

The second major school into which studies of the latter fall is the political-institutional school. If historical approaches tend to excessively concentrate on continuities in ideology and personnel without paying adequate attention to the structural causes and contexts that governed the emergence of particular radical right-wing movements, political-institutional ones tend to almost exclusively focus on these second types of factors. This is particularly evident in many contemporary analyses of the Front National, which examine the party strictly on its own terms and dismiss comparison with anterior parties of the French radical Right.

A raft of political-institutional approaches to studying the radical Right has emerged, particularly in its contemporary guise. The first, deriving from the field of electoral sociology, seeks to determine the "ecological" (class, religious, educational, income) attributes and strategic motivations (whether people vote in protest or for sincere ideological or interest-based reasons) of the FN's electorate. These are then related back to adverse developments affecting contemporary French society, such as structural unemployment, rising crime rates, and especially the presence of a large non-European immigrant minority.[3] Such factors are correlated with the sociological characteristics of the typical FN voter in order to explain his or her electoral choices. In a variant of this argument, the electoral impact of these sociostructural factors is magnified by the particularities of the

Pen (Brussels: Éditions Complexe, 1996); Winock, ed., *Histoire de l'extrême droite en France* (Paris: Seuil, 1993); Jean-Yves Camus and René Monzat, *Les droites nationales en France* (Lyon: Presses Universitaires de Lyon, 1992); and Pierre Milza, *Fascisme français, passé et présent* (Paris: Flammarion, 1987).

[3] Contributions in this vein include Nonna Mayer, "Pourquoi votent-ils pour le Front national?" *Pouvoirs*, no. 55 (1990), 163–81, "Du vote lepéniste au vote frontiste," *Revue française de science politique* 47(3–4) (1997), 438–53, and *Ces Français qui votent Le Pen* (Paris: Flammarion, 2002); Pascal Perrineau, *Le vote de crise* (Paris: Presses de Sciences Po, 1995), *Le symptôme Le Pen. Radiographie des électeurs du Front National* (Paris: Fayard, 1997), and *Le vote incertain: les élections régionales de 1998* (Paris: Presses de Sciences Po, 1999); Pierre Bréchon, "The National Front in France: Emergence of an Extreme Right Protest Movement," *Comparative Politics* 25(1) (1992), 63–82; Colette Ysmal, Philippe Habert, and P. Perrineau, eds., *Le vote sanction: les élections législatives des 21 et 28 mars 1993* (Paris: Presses de la FNSP, 1993); Jonathan Marcus, *The National Front and French Politics: The Resistible Rise of Jean-Marie Le Pen* (New York: New York University Press, 1995); Mayer and Perrineau, eds., *Le Front National à découvert* (Paris: Presses de la FSNP, 1989); and Ysmal and Perrineau, eds., *Le vote de tous les refus: les élections présidentielle et législatives 2002* (Paris: Presses de Sciences Po, 2002).

French political system. For example, in the late 1980s, the FN's rise was broadly imputed to the Socialists' introduction of proportional representation in order to divide the Right before the 1986 legislative elections. The result was that it was able to break onto the national political stage and assume a degree of visibility and prominence that it was never again to lose.

In both its sociostructural and political institutional variants, the FN vote is portrayed in these electoral sociological accounts as essentially a protest against current political institutions and elites, who are held to be unresponsive to voters' needs and concerns.[4] Yet neither stands up very well to empirical scrutiny, because sociostructural factors such as immigration and economic performance in and of themselves are not reliable predictors of the FN's popularity. Similarly, it is impossible to view the FN's rise as simply the byproduct of the introduction of proportional representation before the 1986 parliamentary elections because, had this been the case, the FN would have fallen back into obscurity once a first-past-the-post system was restored before the 1988 elections. Thus, although they are clearly part of the picture, these factors are better seen as intervening rather than causal variables in the party's emergence.

A second political-institutional approach analyzes the FN from a comparative perspective, conceiving of its rise as part of a broader trend toward the radical Right evident across a number of Western European democracies.[5] It attempts to elucidate the common sociostructural, economic, and political features that

---

[4] These sociostructural analyses are often accompanied by social psychological theories of authoritarianism to explain the present-day appeal of the radical Right. They take for granted the fact that, in the presence of socioeconomic insecurity, rising crime rates, and large numbers of nonwhite immigrants, growing numbers of Frenchmen evince an "authoritarian personality," which politically translates into support for the FN. At a proximate level of causality, such behavioralist accounts may well be accurate, but they have next to nothing to say about why certain groups of voters are more disposed to this kind of authoritarian reaction than others are, or why it was the FN that was most successful in politically harnessing their latent authoritarianism. Totally absent from the analysis is any consideration of the long-standing historical influence of the radical Right in shaping voters' political preferences and causing them to adopt authoritarian orientations. For accounts of the contemporary radical Right that deploy this concept of authoritarian personality, see Piero Ignazi, "Un nouvel acteur politique," and H. Lagrange and P. Perrineau, "Le syndrome lepéniste," in Mayer and Perrineau, *Front National à découvert*, specifically 69–70 and 236–9; and P. Perrineau, "The Conditions for the Re-emergence of an Extreme Right-Wing in France: The National Front, 1984–98," in Arnold, *Development of the Radical Right in France*, 266. For the original formulation of the concept, see T. Adorno, E. Fraenkel-Brunswick, D. Levinson, and R. Sanford, *The Authoritarian Personality* (New York: Harper and Row, 1950). For a revised and updated formulation, see Paul Sniderman, *Personality and Democratic Politics* (Berkeley: University of California Press, 1975).

[5] Cf. P. Ignazi, "The Silent Counter-Revolution: Hypothesis on the Emergence of Extreme Right-Wing Parties in Europe," *European Journal of Political Research* 22(1) (July 1992), 3–34; Hans-Georg Betz, *Radical Right-Wing Populism in Western Europe* (New York: St. Martin's Press, 1994); Herbert Kitschelt, *The Radical Right in Western Europe: A Comparative Analysis* (Ann Arbor: University of Michigan Press, 1995); Hans-Georg Betz and Stefan Immerfall, eds., *The New Politics of the Right* (New York: St. Martin's Press, 1998); Jean-Yves Camus, *Les extrémismes en Europe: état des lieux en 1998* (La Tour d'Aigues: Éd. de l'Aube, 1998); Pascal Perrineau, ed., *Les croisés de la société fermée: l'Europe des extrêmes droites* (La Tour d'Aigues:

hold across countries in which strong radical right-wing parties exist in order to explain their roughly simultaneous emergence within them. Most often, these parties are portrayed as the byproducts of sweeping sociocultural changes and the ensuing transformation of political competition in Western European countries as a result of their shift from a manufacturing-based industrial economy to a services-based postindustrial economy.[6] According to one variation of this argument, the processes of social fragmentation and individualization occasioned by this societal transition have eroded the communal ties and modes of social integration that underpinned political arrangements in industrial society, thereby undermining people's trust in those arrangements.[7] Alternatively, others have argued that the emergence of left-libertarian values in concert with the postindustrial transformation of society generated reactionary neoconservative values, which have been successfully repackaged by various European radical right-wing parties.[8]

A common thread running through these analyses of the contemporary radical Right is that the political landscapes of the advanced Western democracies have been fundamentally transformed by their transition from an industrial to a postindustrial form of society. This transformation is held to have opened up a space in the structures of political competition, which radical right-wing parties have been quick to occupy. Implicit in this spatial conception of contemporary European politics is the assumption that social classes have diminished in importance as a factor of political aggregation in postindustrial society, thereby transforming traditional class-based parties into catchall political formations seeking to broaden their appeal among all segments of the electorate.[9] Accordingly, formerly class-based parties are believed

Éd. de l'Aube, 2001); and Pierre-André Taguieff, ed., *Le retour du populisme: un défi pour les démocraties européennes* (Paris: Universalis, 2004). For a more sociologically grounded comparative study, see Michel Wieviorka, ed., *Racisme et xénophobie en Europe* (Paris: La Découverte, 1994).

[6] In this connection, see the contributions of Daniel Bell, Alain Touraine, Michel Crozier, and Herbert Marcuse, the first technocratic theorists to identify this fundamental evolution in the workings of the capitalist economy and to analyze its social and political implications: Bell, *The Coming of Post-Industrial Society: A Venture in Social Forecasting* (New York: Basic Books, 1973); Touraine, *The Post-Industrial Society: Tomorrow's Social History; Classes, Conflicts and Culture in a Programmed Society*, trans. L. Mayhew (New York: Random House, 1971); Crozier, *The Stalled Society* (New York: Viking Press, 1973); and Marcuse, *One-Dimensional Man: Studies in the Ideology of Advanced Industrial Society* (Boston: Beacon Press, 1968).

[7] Betz, *Radical Right-Wing Populism in Western Europe*, chs. 2 and 6. See also Michael Minkenberg, *Die neue radikale Rechte im Vergleich: USA, Frankreich, Deutschland* (Opladen: Westdeutscher 1998), and "The Renewal of the Radical Right: Between Modernity and Antimodernity," *Government and Opposition* 35(2) (2000), 170–88.

[8] Kitschelt, *The Radical Right in Western Europe*, ch. 2, particularly pp. 57–8, and Ignazi, "The Silent Counter-Revolution," 18–19. For a discussion of the causes and consequences of the emergence of left-libertarian values with the advent of a new 'postmaterialist' politics, see Ronald Inglehart, *Culture Shift in Advanced Industrial Society* (Princeton: Princeton University Press, 1990).

[9] Ignazi, "The Silent Counter-Revolution," 1–6; Kitschelt, *The Radical Right in Western Europe*, 14–19; and Betz, *Radical Right-Wing Populism in Western Europe*, 27–9, 36–41, and 174–80.

to have moved to the center of the political spectrum, effectively delinking voters from their traditional partisan attachments and thus ushering in a heightened electoral volatility among them. Leaving them increasingly dissatisfied with the choices offered to them as consumers in the electoral marketplace, this process supposedly translated voters' democratic disillusionment with mainstream political parties. Such partisan fragmentation created electoral openings on the extremes of the political spectrum, which both the radical Left and radical Right were well positioned to fill.[10] In short, the rise of the FN is seen to reflect the general "crisis of representation" resulting from the fragmentation of the French party system since the early 1980s.

There are significant problems with this postmaterialist politics argument, however. For one thing, it is unable to account for why radical left-wing or left-libertarian parties have failed to achieve the same degree of political popularity as parties of the radical Right. This incongruity is particularly striking in France, where parties that correspond to these appellations, the Greens and Trotskyist formations such as Lutte ouvrière and the Ligue communiste révolutionnaire, have remained endemically weak. A second question, with broader application, concerns why parties of the radical Right have failed to take root in other advanced capitalist nations, since the transition from an industrial to a post-industrial society is held to have similar political consequences in a substantial number of them. This has been particularly evident in the case of the Anglo-Saxon countries and, most notably, the United States. As the most advanced postindustrial society and economy, the United States would presumably best embody the political attributes imputed to the latter group. Instead, the failure of radical right-wing parties to take hold in these countries suggests that other, noninstitutional factors are at work.

More generally, the electoral success of the FN cannot simply be attributed to a crisis of representation reflecting the dysfunction of the French political system. Such an explanation mistakes the effect for the cause, the breakdown in political representation representing the symptom of a deeper societal crisis that has outstripped the capacity of the party system to give voice to the discontent that pervades the country today. Indeed, the FN might well be regarded as a logical institutional response to this crisis, proof of the continuing capacity of the political system to provide a voice to the discontented. However, the root

---

[10] On the dynamic of political dealignment imputed to the postindustrial transformation of contemporary European societies, see R. Inglehart, *The Changing Structure of Political Cleavages among West European Elites and Publics*, EUI Working Paper, no. 32 (Florence, 1982); and Russell Dalton, Scott Flanagan, and Paul Allen Beck, *Electoral Change in Advanced Industrial Democracies: Realignment and Dealignment* (Princeton: Princeton University Press, 1984). On the growing disillusionment of French voters with the choices open to them within the electoral marketplace and their resulting turn to the radical Right, see P. Perrineau, ed., *Le désenchantement démocratique* (La Tour d'Aigues: Ed. de l'Aube, 2003); and Pippa Norris, *Radical Right: Voters and Parties in the Electoral Market* (Cambridge: Cambridge University Press, 2005).

cause of their discontent lies elsewhere, at a more elemental structural and cultural level. As Michel Wieviorka has observed,

> If [the FN's] populism expresses a crisis of the political parties, it is that the latter give the impression of no longer being able to effectively process social demands. The political elites in this country are seen as a more or less corrupt clique, offering neither convictions nor projects for the future, driven by a thirst for money and personal power, and disconnected from the day-to-day realities of French people [and] unaware of their actual problems ... numerous are those for whom the political system has ceased being representative and capable of fulfilling their aspirations and addressing their claims ..., fuel[ing] the widespread feeling that the state is unable to communicate with the society and to manage its diversity. ... However, such an analysis has its limits. ... On the one hand, it fails to specify the principle of causality at work and to account for the how and the why of this crisis of the political system and of the state. On the other hand, it misses an important dimension of the populist phenomenon which, while it is profoundly reactive, also offers a means of interpreting social and political realities, simultaneously testifying to a loss of meaning and the attempt to compensate for this loss by reconstituting new forms of identification to orient political discourse and action.[11]

Most recently, there has been a movement away from broad sociostructural and institutional explanations that detail the political opportunity structure of the FN toward refocusing the analysis onto the party itself. Writing in this vein, some scholars have called for studying the party's internal discursive and organizational capacities in capturing the support of discontented voters and transforming them into a loyal base of support – namely its continued ability to disseminate its nativist ideology as a function of the persistence of a large, non-European immigrant presence in France as well as the dynamics of global economic competition and European integration.[12] Thus, the interpretive cycle has come full circle, with immigration returning to the fore of scholarly debate on the French and European Radical right.

Yet, by shunning the broader sociostructural and cultural context and focusing instead on the FN's discursive and organizational capabilities, internal supply-side explanations are unable to satisfactorily account for variations in the party's electoral fortunes over its thirty-seven-year history. Though its organizational and propagandistic capacities were certainly not as evolved in the 1970s compared to what they would become in the 1980s and 1990s, it seems far-fetched to assume that the party's breakthrough and subsequent consolidation had nothing to do with the social costs engendered by the fundamental transformation of the French economy during the 1980s and 1990s as a result of intensifying global competition and deepening European integration.

---

[11] Michel Wieviorka, "Les bases du national-populisme," *Le débat*, no. 61 (Sept.–Oct. 1990), 36–7.
[12] Cf. Cas Mudde, *Populist Radical Right Parties in Europe* (Cambridge: Cambridge University Press, 2007).

Finally, and more broadly, these various institutional approaches implicitly or explicitly assume that the FN and the radical right-wing movements that preceded it respectively derived from incommensurable social realities obviating any meaningful comparison between them. Consequently, little analytical importance is accorded to the radical Right as a coherent political tradition capable of influencing voters' preferences through its ideology and program. Along similar lines, no serious attempt has been made to tie the FN to previous formations of the French radical Right as a function of its ideological attractiveness to certain social or class groups. Thus, in contrast to historical analyses that overlook the conditions of political "demand" underlying the radical Right's appeal, such political-institutional approaches neglect the conditions of political "supply" attending its resurgence.

The purpose of this study is to move beyond this interpretive imbalance and show how these various factors of political supply and demand related to and articulated with one another in order to account for the radical Right's periodic political breakthroughs in France. Chiefly, it seeks to explain how its ideology and discourse expressed the hopes and harnessed the anxieties of certain class groups within French society, in particular those who lost out from the processes of economic modernization and saw their political capacity to halt their decline progressively diminish. As their social and political identities disintegrated under the impacts of the country's economic and social transformation, these groups latched onto alternative forms of collective identification through which they could sustain their sense of corporative worth. In modern industrial France, it was more often than not the radical Right that was able to supply a coherent sense of identity and purpose to these groups in crisis.

However, before one can show how such an outcome came about, a few remarks are in order regarding the continuing salience of class as an object of political analysis and of the importance of the political value and belief systems – in essence, the political cultures – that attach to it.

TOWARD A CLASS-CULTURAL ANALYSIS OF THE FRENCH
RADICAL RIGHT

Current political scientific analyses of the French radical Right suffer from two main theoretical weaknesses: the inadequacy of the postindustrial conception of society and the model of postmaterialist politics that such accounts take for granted, and the simplistic conception of political interest and action they assume. The portrayal of the Front National as a byproduct of the advent of a postindustrial society in France is contradicted by a substantial body of evidence that suggests that the social and political impact of this shift has been dramatically overstated. Chiefly, the assumption that class identification would decline in importance as a basis of political aggregation in postindustrial society has not been borne out. Despite the growth of service-sector employment and the rise in the general level of affluence, class conflict persists in advanced capitalist societies, along with its related modes of sociopolitical structuration.[13]

Those opposed to abandoning the concept of class in political analysis convincingly argue that the advent of a service-based postindustrial economy has not only generated a more complex class structure but also tended to preserve, if not widen, socioeconomic divides between social classes.[14] Citing a variety of indicators of class inequality such as earning and wealth disparities among social groups, the continuing preeminence of property as a basis of social differentiation, and the persistence of low social mobility, these authors show that class divisions remain as entrenched in contemporary postindustrial society as they were in industrial society.[15] First and foremost, they point to the growing underclasses in advanced capitalist societies to confute the argument that class no longer matters within them.[16] On the contrary, the ongoing differentiation of economic roles as well as persisting material and status differences among occupational groups "suggest conclusions about the impending death of class are premature."[17]

The persistence of class structuration within advanced capitalist societies invalidates the thesis of "de-alignment" or "unfreezing" of class-based political cleavages that has been advanced by many contemporary social scientists.[18] As

---

[13] By structuration is meant, *pace* Anthony Giddens, the process whereby "economic classes," as defined by the "market capacities" of their members, "are transformed into 'social classes'" that present common material, political, and cultural attributes and affinities. Giddens, *The Class Structure of the Advanced Societies* (New York: Harper and Row, 1975), 105, 107.

[14] For contemporary Marxist perspectives that posit the continuing salience of class in advanced capitalist society, see Erik Olin Wright, *Classes* (London: Verso, 1985) and "Rethinking the Concept of Class Structure," in *The Debate on Classes*, ed. E. O. Wright (London: Verso, 1989), 269–348, as well as Mike Hout, Clem Brooks, and Jeff Manza, "The Persistence of Classes in Post-Industrial Societies," *International Sociology* 8(3) (Sept. 1993), 259–77. For non-Marxist perspectives, see Giddens, *Class Structure*; and John H. Goldthorpe and Gordon Marshall, "The Promising Future of Class Analysis: A Response to Recent Critiques," *Sociology* 26(3) (Aug. 1992), 381–400.

[15] Hout et al., "The Persistence of Classes in Post-Industrial Societies," 261–3; Goldthorpe and Marshall, "The Promising Future of Class Analysis," 387–90; Giddens, *Class Structure*, chs. 14 and 15. For specific examples of persisting and even worsening wealth disparities within various advanced capitalist societies, see Kevin Phillips, *The Politics of Rich and Poor: Wealth and the American Electorate in the Reagan Aftermath* (New York: Harper Perennial, 1991); and John Gray, *False Dawn: The Delusions of Global Capitalism* (New York: New Press, 1998), chs. 2 and 5.

[16] Giddens, *Class Structure*, 219–20, 289; Hout et al., "The Persistence of Classes in Post-Industrial Societies," 262–3; and Gray, *False Dawn*, 30, 42.

[17] Hout et al., "The Persistence of Classes in Post-Industrial Societies," 263.

[18] Contributions that take this position include Terry Nichols Clark and S. M. Lipset, "Are Social Classes Dying?" *International Sociology: Journal of the International Sociological Association* 6(4) (Dec. 1991), 397–410; S. M. Lipset, T. N. Clark, and Michael Rempel, "The Declining Significance of Social Class" *International Sociology* 8(3) (Sept. 1993), 293–316; Jan Pakulski and Malcolm Waters, "The Reshaping and Dissolution of Social Class in Advanced Society," *Theory and Society* 25(5) (Oct. 1996), 667–691; and Mattei Doggan, "Classe, religion, parti: triple déclin dans les clivages electoraux," *Revue internationale de politique comparée* 3(3) (Dec. 1996), 515–40.

with the "death of class" thesis advanced by postindustrial theorists, this model
of political aggregation and competition does not stand up to empirical scrutiny.
Electoral studies of Western European countries have demonstrated the persistence and stability of class-based political cleavages throughout the period
equated with these countries' transitions to an advanced stage of capitalist
development.[19] Similarly, it has been shown that the postmaterialist issues and
values that are held to constitute novel sources of political aggregation in
advanced capitalist societies continue to be conceived in terms of a traditionally
class-based Left–Right antinomy.[20] In this sense, it would appear that the concept of social class is not as obsolete as postindustrial theorists would have us
believe and that, to the contrary, it remains useful for analyzing processes of
political aggregation and identification within advanced capitalist societies.

The failure of class divisions to disappear as a basis of social and political
differentiation underscores the speciousness of the universal vision of a class-
less and technocratic society toward which postindustrial theorists project
Western capitalist countries will converge. These have each evolved in their
own ways, as a function of their own specific experiences of social modernization and the particular economic and political institutions that grew up
within them. These societies have also developed distinctive class systems,
which present their own structural particularities and degrees of political
integration and conflict. Likewise, the institutional legacies of modernization
also differ across advanced capitalist countries. As a function of these varying
sociostructural and institutional outcomes, capitalist countries have developed distinctive political traditions, characterized by their own peculiar ideologies, movements, and rituals.

In turn, these varying outcomes of modernization raise the question of how
macrosocial developments inform people's political behavior. Political-institutionalists conceive this relationship in terms of more or less explicitly self-
interested models of political action according to which individual or collective
actors pursue wealth, power, or other advantages as a basis of their political
calculations and decisions. Such models come in two principal guises. First are

---

[19] Cf. Adam Przeworski and John Sprague, *Paper Stones: A History of Electoral Socialism* (Chicago:
University of Chicago Press, 1986), and Stefano Bartolini and Jeff Mair, *Identity, Competition
and Electoral Availability: The Stabilization of European Electorates, 1885–1985* (Cambridge:
Cambridge University Press, 1990). For the original elaboration of the "freezing" thesis, see
S. M. Lipset and S. Rokkan, "Cleavage Structures, Party Systems and Voter Alignments:
An Introduction," in *Party Systems and Voter Alignments*, ed. Lipset and Rokkan (New York:
Free Press, 1967), 1–64.

[20] Cf. Paul Sniderman, Richard Brody, and Philip Tetlock, *Reasoning and Choice: Explorations in
Political Psychology* (Cambridge: Cambridge University Press, 1991). For a similar analysis
pertaining to France, see Guy Michelat and Michel Simon, *Classe, religion et comportement
politique* (Paris: Presses de la Fondation nationale des sciences politiques, 1977), and
"Déterminations socio-économiques, organisations symboliques et comportement électoral,"
Revue française de sociologie 26(1) (Jan. 1985), 32–69.

economistic models of political behavior, which include but are not limited to those of (orthodox) Marxist inspiration.[21] These are most frequently employed in order to explain the collective behaviors of sectoral or class groups within society and to reduce their members' political preferences to clearly defined material interests. In their most extreme guises, they portray ideology, culture, religion, and any other belief system that may motivate political action as ideational expressions of the "objective" material interests that fundamentally drive the actors who hold them. From this standpoint, political beliefs and ideas are "nothing more than the ideal expression of the dominant material relationships ..., the dominant material relationships grasped as ideas."[22]

The second types of models favored by political-institutionalists are utility-based models of rational choice. Transposed from the field of economics, the latter posit that political actors will behave rationally in seeking to maximize their utility as defined by their particular preferences, tastes, or beliefs. Thus, these models assume that if political actors' preferences can be specified, their choices can be predicted given the contexts in which they operate and the constraints they face.[23]

The problem with utility-maximizing models of political behavior is that the processes they seek to explain are much more complex than the market processes from which they derive.[24] It is hardly worth pointing out that certain nonrational sources of agency, such as emotional or psychological motivations, bear on the preferences of political actors. Similarly, the latter cannot simply be reduced to the self-interested pursuit of wealth and power, because they also reflect a broad array of noninterested motivations. Individuals often engage in noninstrumental behaviors because of the psychic or emotive satisfaction they

[21] Cf., for example, Erik Olin Wright, *Class, Crisis and the State* (London: Verso, 1978). Non-Marxist contributions that also relate political action to the pursuit of more or less explicitly material or power-based interests include Barrington Moore Jr., *The Social Origins of Dictatorship and Democracy: Lord and Peasant in the Making of the Modern World* (Boston: Beacon Press, 1966); and Theda Skocpol, *States and Social Revolutions* (Cambridge: Cambridge University Press, 1979).

[22] Karl Marx, "The German Ideology: Part 1," in *The Marx-Engels Reader*, 2nd ed., ed. R. Tucker (New York: W. W. Norton, 1978), 173.

[23] In practice, for the purpose of theoretical generality and parsimony, most models of rational choice assume what Donald Green and Ian Shapiro have termed "thick" accounts of rationality, whereby agents across varying political and social contexts are held to value wealth, income, or power as the principal objects of utility maximization. In this sense, rational choice models of political behavior represent more theoretically conscious versions of the economistic models outlined in the text. See Green and Shapiro, *Pathologies of Rational Choice Theory: A Critique of Application in Political Science* (New Haven: Yale University Press, 1994), 17–18.

[24] As Jeffrey Friedman observes, rational choice accounts of politics treat "the *possibility* that people are as self-interested in their political as their economic behavior" as "the *assumption* that self-interest is always and everywhere the real fountainhead of politics." "Introduction: Economic Approaches to Politics," in *The Rational Choice Controversy*, ed. J. Friedman (New Haven: Yale University Press, 1996), 2.

derive from them, such as those motivated by a desire to fulfill certain political or social norms, or because they are considered as "good in themselves."[25]

The importance of noninterested motivations in political processes suggests the crucial role played by symbolic factors in influencing their outcomes. People evolve symbolic frameworks as means of interpreting the social world so they can effectively relate to and participate in it.[26] These provide the affective cues and shape the values and beliefs that condition people's relationships to the broader social and political worlds. In this sense, the symbolic representations evolved by the members of a given society or social group are key factors that define their political preferences and orient their political actions.[27]

The importance of symbolic systems in determining the affective motivations – norms, beliefs, and identifications – at the root of political behavior underscores the primacy of culture as the fundamental context within which these systems are constituted and reproduced.[28] Culturally determined symbolic

---

[25] Michael Taylor, "When Rationality Fails," and Robert Lane, "What Rational Choice Explains," in Friedman, *Rational Choice Controversy*, 229–30, 115. In this connection, theories of rational choice are particularly ill-equipped to account for protest voting, a phenomenon that must be addressed in analyzing the resurgence of the radical Right in France. It can hardly be argued that this mode of voting is rational in an economistic, utility-maximizing sense. Rather, it is a clear example of how psychically satisfying noninterested motivations deriving from voters' subjective frustrations play an important role in determining their political choices.

[26] Cf. Michelat and Simon, "Déterminations socio-économiques"; Lane, "What Rational Choice Explains"; David O. Sears and Carolyn Funk, "Self-Interest in Americans' Political Opinions," in *Beyond Self-Interest*, ed. J. Mansbridge (Chicago: University of Chicago, 1990), 147–70, and "The Role of Self-Interest in Social and Political Attitudes," in *Advances in Experimental Social Psychology*, vol. 24, ed. M. P. Zanna (New York: Academic Press, 1991), 1–91; Donald R. Kinder and D. O. Sears, "Public Opinion and Political Action," in *Handbook of Social Psychology*, 3rd ed., vol. 2, ed. G. Lindzey and E. Aronson (New York: Random House, 1985); and D. O. Sears, R. R. Lau, T. R. Tyler, and H. M. Allen Jr., "Self-Interest and Symbolic Politics in Policy Attitudes and Presidential Voting," *American Political Science Review* 74 (1980), 670–84.

[27] Michelat and Simon remark that the symbolic systems that condition people's norms and behaviors "include ... perceptions of the political world, strictly conceived, but do not reduce themselves to it." Instead, they write, these systems "structure" the totality of the individual's "perceptions, valorizations, convictions and behaviors, whether within the scope of the family, the professional setting or at the level of more or less explicit political attitudes, opinions and behaviors." "Déterminations socio-économiques," 32.

[28] The reliance on cultural modes of explanation in political science – and the social sciences in general – is nothing new. Nor are the theoretical debates opposing approaches drawn from a competing array of disciplines running the gamut from anthropology to cybernetics. For the sake of simplification, it is possible to distinguish between two broad kinds of culturalist explanation in the social sciences. In the first place, subjective approaches to culture can be traced back to the intellectual preeminence of behaviorism and structural functionalism in American political science during the 1950s and 1960s. The best-known theoretical exemplar of this approach is the civic culture tradition. Conversely, objective conceptions of culture derive from the importation into political science of the structuralist and poststructuralist theories that came to the fore during the 1970s in the fields of artistic and literary criticism, as well as symbolic or semiotic perspectives that originated roughly during the same period in the field of anthropology. More recently, after having been largely ignored during the 1980s and early 1990s, ideational explanations of political behavior have made a comeback in the field. Primarily focusing on the role of ideology in driving

influences play an autonomous role in conditioning people's social and political behavior, investing social objects with particular meanings that are collectively understood by members of a given group. Consequently, political behavior cannot be conceived as a mere epiphenomenon of general macroeconomic or institutional processes, with political actors pursuing their interests as defined by overriding material imperatives or in isolation from one another.[29] Rather, it is more apposite to conceive of political interests as aggregated bundles or packages that are bound up in political actors' cultural identities and which in turn are shaped and mediated by the social contexts in which they live.[30]

political change, these new accounts have the merit of shifting the analytical onus back to the beliefs and values held by political actors as independent variables explaining political outcomes, rather than simply reducing the latter to institutional choices and constraints.

Standard references in the civic culture tradition include Gabriel Almond and Sidney Verba, *The Civic Culture: Political Attitudes and Democracy in Five Nations* (Princeton: Princeton University Press, 1963); Lucian Pye and Sidney Verba, eds., *Political Culture and Political Development* (Princeton: Princeton University Press, 1965); Ronald Inglehart, "The Renaissance of Political Culture," *American Political Science Review* 82(4) (Dec. 1988), 1203–30; and Almond and Verba, eds., *The Civic Culture Revisited* (repr., Newbury Park, CA: Sage Publications, 1989). For examples of the application of structuralist or poststructuralist approaches to the social sciences, see Mary Douglas, *Natural Symbols* (New York: Vintage Books, 1970); Michel Foucault, *The Order of Things: An Archaeology of the Human Sciences* (New York: Random House, 1970) and *The Archaeology of Knowledge* (New York, Random House, 1972); and Jürgen Habermas, *Communication and the Evolution of Society* (Boston: Beacon Press, 1979). Works that set out symbolic or semiotic approaches to the study of culture include Peter Berger and Thomas Luckmann, *The Social Construction of Reality* (Garden City, NY: Doubleday, 1966), and Clifford Geertz, *The Interpretation of Cultures* (New York: Basic Books, 1973). For new ideational accounts that conceive of ideology and culture as independent variables in political science, see Mark Blyth, "'Any More Bright Ideas?' The Ideational Turn of Comparative Political Economy," *Comparative Politics* 29(4) (1997), 229–50; Stephen Hanson, "From Culture to Ideology in Comparative Politics," *Comparative Politics* 35(3) 2003), 355–76; and Sheri Berman, "Ideas, Norms, and Culture in Political Science," *Comparative Politics* 33(2) (2001), 231–50, and *The Primacy of Politics: Social Democracy and the Making of Europe's Twentieth Century* (Cambridge: Cambridge University Press, 2006), 8–12.

[29] Cf. Sears and Funk, "Self-Interest...," and "The Role of Self-Interest..."; Kinder and Sears, "Public Opinion and Political Action"; and Sears et al., "Self-Interest and Symbolic Politics." For a study that shows a correlation between self-interest and political behavior in respect to economic or "pocketbook" issues, see R. R. Lau and D. O. Sears, "Cognitive Links between Economic Grievances and Political Responses," *Political Behavior* 3 (1981), 279–302.

[30] Of particular importance for this study, this sociocultural conception of political interests makes it easier to explain instances of political change than institutional approaches that are better suited to analyzing the structural continuities underlying political processes. During periods of socio-political crisis in particular, formerly dominant ideologies and the regimes or parties that hold them are discredited by events, creating an ideational vacuum in which competing ideologies and the movements that hold them are able to assert themselves as the newly dominant forces structuring political life. In such periods of change, people's cultural orientations are crucial in determining which of these ideological alternatives they will choose. They make it possible to account for the newfound appeal of hitherto obscure ideologies and diminishing attraction of formerly prevalent ones at different historical junctures. In this sense, it could be argued that, whereas the ideologies held and circulated by political elites represent agents of political supply, cultural traits inherent in the broader society define the boundaries of political demand, effectively determining which ideologies will be accepted and rejected. Berman, *Primacy of Politics*, 9–10.

The symbolic systems mediating political life and the principles of action that derive from them are transmitted through processes of cultural learning or socialization. Through these processes, political agents internalize the symbolic representations that determine their dispositions toward the social world and solidify the values and beliefs that inform their behavior within it.[31] What these representations and ensuing cultural systems turn out to be – what Pierre Bourdieu summed up in his concept of the "habitus" – is determined by the particular social milieus to which they are exposed in the course of their lives.[32] In turn, the fact that individuals become politically acculturated as a function of their collective relationships and experiences as members of particular social groups makes it possible to relate their political preferences and behaviors to broader societal structures and forces. Because these collective milieus or loci of acculturation are themselves determined by the broader dynamics of social development, we can generalize across individual political behaviors and link them to the latter.[33] Thus, it becomes possible to explain people's

Cf. also Peter Gourevitch, *Politics in Hard Times* (Ithaca, NY: Cornell University Press, 1984), and Ernst Haas, *When Knowledge Is Power* (Berkeley: University of California Press, 1990).

[31] This relational or experiential conception of social roles and interests, which is in turn held to underpin the emergence and reproduction of distinct cultural systems within societies, has enjoyed particular prominence within the French school of sociology. Cf. Rogers Brubaker, "Rethinking Classical Theory: The Sociological Vision of Pierre Bourdieu," *Theory and Society* 14(6) (Nov. 1985), 745–75, as well as Michelat and Simon, "Déterminations socio-économiques," and "Classe sociale objective, classe sociale subjective et comportement électoral," *Revue française de sociologie* 12(4) (1971), 485–527.

[32] The bulk of the individual's socialization takes place during childhood and adolescence, the period when his or her personality is formed and he or she achieves the capacity for rational thought and develops a coherent worldview. Accordingly, the family serves as a lever of transmission for the influences of broader social affiliations, such as class or religious appurtenance, which impact on the individual's perceptions of society and the world. Cf. Herbert Hyman, *Political Socialization: A Study in the Psychology of Political Behavior* (New York: Free Press, 1969); Annick Percheron, "La socialisation politique: défense et illustration," in *Traité de science politique. L'action politique*, ed. J. Leca and M. Grawitz (Paris: Presses Universitaires de France, 1985), 165–235; and A. Percheron, ed., *Les 10–16 ans et la politique* (Paris: Presses de la FNSP, 1978).

[33] Two of the most important loci of political socialization in Western societies are social class and civil society. Class appurtenance, conceived as the bundle of social relationships and interactions determined by individuals' market-defined roles and communal experiences in the workplace, instills in its members particular values and representations that inform their political behavior. Defined by such factors as the "distance from necessity" people feel as a result of their material and status conditions, their life expectations, and the perspectives they develop on authority as a function of their economic and social roles, these values and representations give rise to a distinctive outlook on the social world that conditions the political preferences and actions of members of particular social classes. Similarly, the forms of political association and participation in which people become involved – for example, political parties, trade unions, professional associations, interest groups – are also key in shaping the orientations that underlie their political preferences and behaviors. The structures of authority they reflect, the norms governing decision making within them, the level of openness they display, not to mention the value systems they promote, all contribute to their members' political socialization. In short, the diversity and intensity of associational life as reflected in the peculiar practices and forms it assumes have a

"subjective" political actions in terms of "objective" macrosocial processes of modernization.[34]

What is needed, then, is a method of inquiry that makes it possible to identify the constitutive traits and social contours of politically determinative cultural systems and to trace their evolution over time. Historical sociology appears particularly well suited to this task because it focuses on the mid- or even micro-levels of analysis at which such cultures can be discerned.[35] From a long-run historical perspective, it can account for the evolution of people's cultural orientations as a function of objective structural economic and social forces.[36] From a short-run perspective, such an approach makes it possible to understand how cultural factors mediate between structural forces and sociopolitical processes to yield different outcomes. In particular, it facilitates our analysis of the role of conjunctural factors in enabling or activating the cultural dispositions that determine people's political actions within specific historical situations. In short, by relating how people's social and political experiences shaped their perspectives and orientations over time, we should be able to gain an understanding of how the cultural systems characterizing particular social constituencies predisposed their members toward certain political preferences and behaviors.

This study develops a historical and sociological analysis in order to advance a class-cultural explanation for the persistent resurgence of the radical Right in France. Its principal claim is that the radical Right is best understood as a continuous political tradition whose appeal can be traced to the modalities and consequences of the country's economic and political modernization since the mid-nineteenth century.[37] The latter generated a peculiar social structure and

singular impact on the political cultures of different societies and the social groups that compose them. On the connection between social class and political culture, see Bourdieu, *Distinction*, 53–56. On the linkages between the latter and civil society, see Ernest Gellner, "Civil Society in Historical Context," *International Social Science Journal*, no. 129 (1991), 495–510, and Robert Putnam, *Making Democracy Work: Civic Traditions in Modern Italy* (Princeton: Princeton University Press, 1993).

[34] Cf. P. Bourdieu, *Outline of a Theory of Practice*, trans. R. Nice (Cambridge: Cambridge University Press, 1977), and E. P. Thompson, "The Moral Economy of the English Crowd in the Eighteenth Century," *Past and Present* 50 (1971), 76–136.

[35] On the historical analysis of cultural systems, see Bertrand Badie, *Culture et politique* (Paris: Economica, 1983); Jean-François Sirinelli and Eric Vigne, "Des cultures politiques," in *Histoire des droites en France: cultures*, vol. 2, ed. J.-F. Sirinelli (Paris: Gallimard, 1992), i–xi, and Serge Berstein, "Nature et fonction des cultures politiques," in *Les cultures politiques en France*, ed. S. Berstein (Paris: Seuil, 1999), 7–31.

[36] Badie has remarked that "no culture can be traced back to a model that was created *ex nihilo*, but rather to precise historical contexts that allow us to understand the social conditions according to which particular patterns of interaction were able to constitute and eventually establish themselves as cultural systems." *Culture et politique*, 61.

[37] Among analysts of the contemporary radical Right, Mudde in particular has emphasized the appropriateness of political cultural analysis in order to explain the resurgence of radical right-wing parties in certain European countries while accounting for its absence in others. Curiously, however, he presents political culture as a supply-side political variable, though it seems more appropriate to view it as a factor of political demand because – as Mudde himself indicates – it

specific modes of political sociability and organization that in turn created cultural conditions favorable to this radical right-wing tradition. Specifically, as a result of their economic and sociopolitical evolution, certain groups in French society evolved antimodern and illiberal political cultures that facilitated their identification with the radical Right.[38] Historically, these included a large traditional sector composed of small tradesmen, craftsmen, and business owners – a group known in France as the *petits indépendants*. More recently, this base of support has broadened to include growing numbers of French industrial workers, particularly among the unskilled.

These groups are distinguished by their susceptibility – historical in the case of *petits indépendants*, contemporary in the case of industrial workers – to social crisis. Thanks to their support, the radical Right peaked during the most acute periods of economic and political dislocation experienced by the country over the past one and a quarter centuries. At a first level, such crises were structural in nature, the result of pronounced economic downturns following rapid techno-logical and social change that disproportionately impacted these groups. Thus, the first great wave of commercial and industrial concentration during the 1860s and 1870s and the revolution in production and consumption to which it gave rise meant that traditional shopkeepers and artisans suffered the brunt of the depression of the 1880s and 1890s. Similarly, the rapid industrial consolidation occasioned by World War I and continuing into the 1920s ensured that *petits indépendants* would be particularly hard hit by the Great Depression. The impact of the latter on *petits indépendants* was aggravated by their fear of revolution following the victory of the Popular Front and the ensuing wave of strikes and factory occupations in the summer of 1936. A similar dynamic characterized the postwar era, in which the country underwent its most pro-found economic and social transformation since the Second Empire, succeeded by a period of prolonged socioeconomic crisis. *Petits indépendants* and, increas-ingly, industrial workers have been particularly hard hit by this crisis, fueled by the chronically high unemployment that has gripped the country since the early 1980s.

Yet, the social crises that occasioned the resurgence of the radical Right were not limited to purely structural economic factors affecting the material well-being and social status of certain constituencies within French society. Such crises also reflected the subjective threats perceived by the members of these constituencies as well as objective, sociostructural factors or processes. From this

affects people's receptiveness to the discourse and ideas of the radical Right. *Populist Radical Right Parties*, 248–53, 297–303.

[38] The autonomy and resilience – or "stickiness" – of cultural orientations beyond the sociostructural conditions that initially gave rise to them explains how traditionalist and antimodern political forms can continue to survive in societies that ostensibly present the structural and institutional conditions for their disappearance. Cf. Harry Eckstein, "A Cultural Theory of Political Change," *American Political Science Review* 82(3) (Sept. 1988), 789–804, and Ewa Morawska and Wilfried Spohn, "'Cultural Pluralism' in Historical Sociology: Recent Theoretical Directions," in *The Sociology of Culture*, ed. D. Crane (Cambridge, MA: Blackwell, 1994), 45–90.

standpoint, the rise of the radical Right was as much a symptom of people's anxieties over an uncertain future as of their actual condition of material deprivation. *Petits indépendants* and other groups supportive of the radical Right often did not represent the poorest segments in French society. The latter, who were mainly drawn from the ranks of the industrial working class as well as the unemployed, lent until recently their support to the radical Left rather than the radical Right. In his recent study of the Front National, Erwan Lecœur observes that, "at root, those who vote for the [Radical Right] are not those who have nothing, but rather those who fear losing something"; through their vote, they "seek to resurrect a lost sense of self-esteem."[39] In this sense, one must be careful to take stock of the cultural, even psychological, components that enter into the phenomenon of crisis, particularly as these are reflected in a subjectively felt, yet socially generalized, loss of meaning or identity.[40]

In turn, this subjective conception of crisis places the analytical onus on understanding the cultural perspectives or worldviews of the *petits indépendants* and industrial workers who have suffered crises of identity in modern French society. Specifically, we should attempt to illustrate how these groups' respective experiences of economic and social modernization rendered them particularly susceptible to such crises and made them likely political clienteles for the radical Right. On the one hand, their members espoused norms and values that reflected their class function and position within the French economy and society. Because of the central role they occupied in an economy based until late in its development on petty production and commerce, French *petits indépendants* evolved a distinct, class-cultural system rooted in the working of small-scale economic property, the values of craftsmanship, and the implication of the family in the operation of their firms. This model of production engendered a traditionalist and patriarchal morality among these strata based on the respect for private property and authority and the values of hard work, frugality, and self-abnegation. As we shall see, this morality gave rise to feelings of frustration and resentment among *petits indépendants* that were ably exploited by the radical Right. Similarly, it translated into an economically conservative mind-set that ill-disposed *petits indépendants* as much toward

---

[39] Erwan Lecœur, *Un néo-populisme à la française: trente ans de Front national* (Paris: La Découverte, 2003), 238.

[40] This subjective conception of crisis implies a general dislocation of the individual's perspectives on the world and a fundamental questioning of his place and significance within it. Such a conception is particularly useful in explaining how, as a function of their culturally defined social identities and outlooks, the members of antimodern social groups come to conceive and react to their increasingly unsustainable economic role and marginal social position within advanced capitalist society. Cf. Alain Bihr, *Le Spectre de l'extrême droite: les Français dans le miroir du Front National* (Paris: Editions de l'Atelier, 1998), ch. 5; *Actualité d'un archaïsme: la pensée d'extrême droite et la crise de la modernité* (Lausanne: Page Deux, 1998), ch. 4, and, in condensed form, "Crise du sens et tentation totalitaire," *Le monde diplomatique*, May 1992, 16–17. For a similar formulation of sociocultural crisis, see also Lecœur, *Un néo-populisme à la française*, ch. 8, and Wieviorka, "Les bases du national-populisme," 37.

advanced, rationalized forms of capitalism as toward state-directed socialism or interventionist social democracy. In the case of industrial workers, the onerous character of factory work, as well as the collective conditions in which it was performed, became powerful markers of social identification. French workers staked out an oppositional class identity constructed around the struggle to improve their labor conditions and ameliorate their position in capitalist society. However, once the economic and social structures that underlay this collective class identity eroded, they also became increasingly receptive to the prescriptions of the radical Right.

On the other hand, the cultural worldviews of these groups were shaped by their respective sociopolitical experiences within modern French society, specifically their increasingly fraught relationship to the republican state. Their declining influence over the representative and administrative instances of the latter, particularly relative to other, economically and politically ascendant constituencies, fed their growing disillusionment with republican democracy. Thus, they each went from representing mainstays of the republican state – *petits indépendants* in the Belle Époque, industrial workers during the Trente glorieuses – to constituting significant sources of opposition to it. From the viewpoint of French *petits indépendants*, the republican state progressively abandoned, or even betrayed, the ideal of small producer democracy that underpinned their sociopolitical worldview. In turn, as it presided over the country's economic and social modernization, they came to blame it for their progressive political marginalization and socioeconomic decline. Even before the defeat of 1940, which shocked governing elites into embracing a comprehensive program of modernization, many *petits indépendants* had lost confidence in the ability of the French state to protect their interests. And as the postwar stigma of Vichy and the Occupation gradually faded, they were increasingly drawn to the political guarantees of petty production held out by the radical Right.

In recent times, this rejection of the republican state has spread to the growing number of industrial workers made redundant by the structural transformation of the French economy since the early 1980s. In particular, this transformation has had a catastrophic impact on the political and sectoral organizations, notably the Communist Party and trade unions, which had bound, from the 1930s on, the French working class to the republican order. Shorn of these agents of republican identification and participation, industrial workers became an increasingly listless and political constituency. Thus, as occurred with *petits indépendants* before them, many of them became receptive to the exclusionary and xenophobic message of the radical Right.

In short, the radical Right has successively harnessed the frustrations, anxieties, and resentments of *petits indépendants* and industrial workers who were increasingly functionally and culturally ill-equipped to overcome the economic and social dislocations to which they were confronted within a modernizing French society. The exclusionary conception of national appurtenance, misoneistic outlook, and order-affirming discourse that it deployed served to reassure them of their social validity and worth. By offering an alternative vision to a distressing present and a foreboding future, a powerful exclusive basis of identity, and ready scapegoats to blame for their decline, the radical Right restored a sense of collective purpose to these structurally and culturally embattled constituencies. Thus, it represented a factor of political supply that articulated with the political demands generated by such structural and cultural crises.

These conditions of political supply and political demand converged during the three periods in which the radical Right attained its greatest support: the late 1880s and 1890s, the 1920s and 1930s, and the 1980s to the present. A sociological analysis of the radical right-wing movements that emerged during each of these periods underlines the disproportionate presence of *petits indépendants* and, in the last case, industrial workers, in their followings. For the first period, Philip Nord has highlighted the strong support that Parisian shopkeepers and artisans brought to General Boulanger from 1887 to 1889 and to such nationalist and xenophobic formations as the Ligue des Patriotes and the Ligue Antisémitique throughout the 1890s.[41] These findings are confirmed by a more refined analysis of the results of the election of 27 January 1889, in Paris, which showed that Boulanger scored strongly in the city's central first, second, third, and fourth arrondissements, bastions of the Parisian petty bourgeoisie and traditional middle classes. Likewise, the substantial support lent by these constituencies to the anti-Dreyfusard ligues at the turn of the century has also been amply documented. Analyzing a random sample of 381 activists from the Ligue des Patriotes, Zeev Sternhell found that small shopkeepers and artisans represented the most important source of support, with 119 representatives, followed by 90 white-collar employees; 73 members of the liberal professions; 54 landlords, entrepreneurs, and wholesalers; and only 13 workers.[42]

---

[41] Nord has shown that shopkeepers and artisans figured prominently in the local Boulangiste committees not only in the heavily commercial central arrondissements, but also in some outer arrondissements such as the fifteenth, seventeenth, and nineteenth. Likewise, he shows that a number of the leading members of the Parti Commercial et Industriel, formed in 1901 to defend the interests of petty shopkeepers and artisans, as well as the leaders of several prominent federations within the Ligue syndicale du travail, de l'industrie et du commerce, which represented Parisian *petits indépendants*, figured prominently in the turn-of-the-century nationalist and anti-Dreyfusard movements. Finally, in the Paris municipal elections of 1900, which saw a right-wing majority elected for the first time, and the parliamentary elections of 1902, Paris's commercial arrondissements turned out strong majorities in favor of candidates from nationalist formations such as the Ligue des Patriotes. Of the sixteen municipal councilors elected in Paris, ten were nationalists, six of them coming from the latter federation. Similarly, in 1902, Nationalists won five of the six seats being contested in Paris (in the first, fourth, ninth, tenth, and seventeenth arrondissements), thereby highlighting the political salience of what Nord has termed "a shopkeeper/Nationalist alliance" during the 1890s and early 1900s. *Paris Shopkeepers and the Politics of Resentment* (Princeton: Princeton University Press, 1986), 314–15, 417–23, 443–4, and 465; or for a condensed version, Nord, "Le mouvement des petits commerçants et la politique en France de 1888 à 1914," *Le mouvement social*, no. 114 (Jan.–Mar. 1981), 35–55.

[42] Jacques Néré, "La crise industrielle de 1882 et le mouvement boulangiste" (Ph.D. diss., University of Paris, 1958), 2:541–2, 546, 556, and Sternhell, *Maurice Barrès et le nationalisme français* and *La droite révolutionnaire*, particularly chs. 2 and 5, and p. 118 for his sociological analysis of the

Similarly, studies of the nationalist and protofascist leagues of the 1920s and 1930s also attest to the preponderantly *petit indépendant* base of the radical Right historically. Buffeted by the inflationary wave of the early 1920s, rocked by the franc's collapse in 1925–6, then threatened in the early 1930s with proletarianization on the one hand and social revolution on the other, growing numbers of shopkeepers, artisans, and small businessmen sought refuge in the right-wing extraparliamentary *ligues* and paramilitary organizations that proliferated in France during this period. In his seminal study of the Action Française, Eugen Weber has demonstrated that, as the movement reached its zenith in the mid-1920s, its following, particularly its hard-core activists, the Camelots du Roi, were principally composed of lower middle-class elements.[43] In a similar vein, Georges Valois's self-proclaimed fascist organization, the Faisceau, as well as Pierre Taittinger's Jeunesses Patriotes, the third significant nationalist *ligue* in 1920s France, presented the same urban petit bourgeois base.[44]

The same preponderance of *petits indépendants* is to be noted in the extraparliamentary veterans' far-right and nationalist leagues of the 1930s. A national analysis of the membership records of the most significant among these, Colonel de la Rocque's Croix de Feu, shows that 41 percent of its members issued from the traditional middle classes, 28 percent from the white-collar sector (technicians, clerical and commercial employees, and other service-sector workers), 25 percent from corporate management (*cadres supérieurs*), and only 5 percent from agriculture. Thus, it presented a "strong underrepresentation of rural society, the

Ligue des Patriotes. Néré also underscores the vital support provided by workers to General Boulanger not only in Paris, where some of his best scores were recorded in the peripheral, predominantly working-class eleventh, thirteenth, fifteenth, eighteenth, and nineteenth arrondissements, but also in a number of other cities including Lyon, Bordeaux, and Lille-Roubaix-Tourcoing. His study is of particular import because it distinguishes Boulangisme as a historical precedent underscoring the considerable resonance that a populist, antiliberal, and nationalist discourse eventually to be identified with a novel strain of radical right-wing politics – what Sternhell has termed the revolutionary Right – could achieve, in an enabling context of socio-economic crisis, among French workers. The advance of revolutionary socialism in the form of Marxist parties, on the one hand, culminating in the formation of the French Socialist Party, the Section Française de l'Internationale Ouvrière (SFIO), in 1905, and of revolutionary syndicalism under the auspices of the anarchosyndicalist Confédération Générale du Travail during the 1890s, on the other, provided French workers with new class-based loci of identification through which they could express their frustrations with the functioning of the classical-liberal economy, and channel their hatred of the bourgeois elites responsible for its management and reproduction. "La crise industrielle de 1882," 543, 546–9, 556, and "Annexes" for results in Bordeaux, Lyon, and Lille.

[43] Working from police archives, Eugen Weber was able to establish a rough sketch of the sociological makeup of the AF's membership on the occasion of the organization's third national congress in December 1910. He surmised that 15% to 20% constituted titled persons, 15% to 20% issued from the clergy, and an overwhelming 60% to 70% came from the Third Estate. Within this last category could be found some army officers and members of the intellectual professions – lawyers, doctors, and the like – but the vast majority of recruits issued from the traditional petite bourgeoisie. *L'Action Française: Royalism and Reaction in Twentieth-Century France* (Stanford, CA: Stanford University Press, 1962), 64.

[44] Milza, *Fascisme français*, 101–3 and 110–14.

nearly total absence of factory workers (what workers were represented came from the traditional trades or small artisanal enterprises), and on the contrary an over-representation of small shopkeepers, white-collar workers and certain well-off urban social constituencies."[45] More plebian than the Croix de Feu was the constellation of protofascist *ligues* that proliferated during this period, such as François Coty's Solidarité française and Marcel Bucard's Franciste movement. Never numbering more than 10,000 dues-paying members and several thousand "active" members, these formations found recruits principally among déclassé *petits indépendants* and marginal elements of the Parisian proletariat.[46]

In contrast to these peripheral organizations, the Parti Populaire Français (PPF), founded by Communist apostate Jacques Doriot, forged the kind of "red-brown" alliance between the petite bourgeoisie and the working class that had formerly been envisioned by the advocates of an ideologically pure, preternatural fascism. Historians estimate that the PPF numbered between 60,000 and 100,000 rank-and-file members when it crested in late 1937 and early 1938. An analysis of the 740 delegates attending the PPF's first national party congress in November 1936 provides a fuller picture of the social provenance of its following. Working-class delegates represented the largest constituency with 49 percent of the whole, followed by white-collar workers (22 percent), small shopkeepers, businessmen, and members of the liberal professions (21 percent), and peasants (8 percent). However, by the PPF's second national congress in March 1938, the party's sociological makeup had substantially changed. The proportion of working-class delegates fell from 49 percent in November 1936 to 37 percent of the total, whereas the proportion of middle-class elements rose from 43 to 57 percent.[47] This slide in working-class support was intensified by the party's decision in March 1937 to establish a united front of the Right against the policies of the Blum government. As a result, the PPF came to reflect the more staunchly petit bourgeois profile that characterized other radical right-wing movements in France, as well as the larger fascist parties that had assumed power in Italy and Germany.[48]

---

[45] Ibid., 138. These general findings are confirmed at the local level by Kevin Passmore's study of the Croix de Feu and PSF in the Lyonnais. Cf. *From Liberalism to Fascism: The Right in a French Province, 1928–1939* (Cambridge: Cambridge University Press, 1997), particularly 239–43 and 274–87.

[46] Milza, *Fascisme français*, 146, 150.

[47] It appears that this already substantial percentage of working-class members may have underestimated the party's proletarian profile in some areas. For example, a study of the PPF in the Bouches-du-Rhône concluded that workers represented fully 78% of the party's membership within the department in November 1936. Ibid., 170–1.

[48] This shift in the social composition of the PPF is indirectly reflected in the changing political origins of the party's activists. At its first national congress in November 1936, fully a third (33.1%) of its delegates transited to the PPF from left-wing parties (among whom ex-Communists represented 21%), the second leading category of origin after previously nonaffiliated delegates (38.7%). Former members of other extreme right-wing groups and veterans organizations, such as the Croix de Feu and the Volontaires Nationaux, represent the third most important category of origin, with 23.6% of the total, meaning that less than 5% of them had come from parties of the

In turn, although support for Vichy was much more broadly based owing to the trauma of the *débacle* and despite the presence of modernizing elements within the regime, its strongest supporters were to be found – at least initially – among *petits indépendants*. The latter identified with Vichy's defense of traditional values and its glorification of a rural, artisanal France, enthusiastically greeting its corporatist designs and political and social authoritarianism.[49] At its inception, the regime even enjoyed a degree of support among French workers, attesting to its initial, "popular" legitimacy.[50]

The French radical Right did not, apart from such brief resurgences with the Poujade movement and during the Algerian crisis, again play a significant political role in France until the rise of the Front National in the mid-1980s.[51] Yet, despite this extended lapse of time, remarkable continuities subsisted between the FN and its predecessors in terms of the social composition of its following. However, the FN also presented a major evolution over its precursors since it was able to make inroads not only among the traditional middle classes that supported the radical Right historically but also among French workers. By the time of the 1995 presidential election, the FN had established itself as the single-most-popular party among working-class voters, a position it further consolidated in the 2002 presidential election (Table 1.1). This ability to preserve the radical Right's traditional following among the independent petite bourgeoisie on the one hand and to cultivate a substantive following among blue-collar workers on the other has given the FN a staying power that its predecessors conspicuously

mainstream Right. However, following the PPF's strategic shift six months later, its working-class support quickly melted away, an evolution confirmed by Doriot's defeat in the June 1937 mayoral race for Saint-Denis and the party's subsequent loss of its parliamentary seat there two months later. Ibid., 170, 176.

[49] Stephen Zdatny, *The Politics of Survival: Artisans in Twentieth-Century France* (New York: Oxford University Press, 1990), ch. 5, and Nonna Mayer, "Les classes moyennes indépendantes dans la vie politique: le cas des petits commerçants français" (Ph.D. diss., Institut d'Etudes Politiques de Paris, 1984), 738–9.

[50] Robert Paxton, *Vichy France: Old Guard and New Order 1940–1944*, 2nd ed. (New York: Columbia University Press, 1982), 273–9, and Jean-Pierre Le Crom, *Syndicats, nous voilà! Vichy et le corporatisme* (Paris: Éditions de l'Atelier, 1995), 111–21.

[51] The pedigree of Poujadism as a radical right-wing movement has not gone undisputed. Although the framing of its message in terms of the opposition between the *petits* and the *gros* and its use of anti-Semitic and racist tropes are not without recalling the discourse of a Doriot or a Le Pen, one must not overlook the movement's ideological evolution from its beginnings in late 1953 to its collapse in the second half of 1956. From its launch in the November 1953 to its first party congress a year later, the Union de Défense des Commerçants et Artisans (UDCA) evinced a populist egalitarianism that called not for overthrowing the Republic, but restoring the Jacobin ideal of small-proprietor democracy on which it had originally been founded. Following its November 1954 congress, however, the UDCA veered toward the radical Right. Through its increasingly violent defense of the French empire and denunciation of the trusts, the party came to espouse a brand of national populism mixed with Vichyiste traditionalism that attracted a number of notorious radical right-wing agitators – including a young Jean-Marie Le Pen – into its ranks. Cf. Mayer, "Classes moyennes," 298–309; Stanley Hoffmann, *Le mouvement Poujade* (Paris: Armand Colin, 1956); and Dominique Borne, *Petits bourgeois en révolte? Le mouvement Poujade* (Paris: Flammarion, 1977).

TABLE 1.1. *Election Results for Radical Right-Wing Parties under the Fifth Republic*

Election		Votes	% of Registered Voters	% of Votes Cast
1958	Parliamentary (1st rd.)	526,644	1.8	2.6
1962	Referendum	1,809,074	6.6	9.2
–	(Evian Accords)	–	–	–
1962	Parliamentary (1st rd.)	139,200	0.5	0.8
1965	Presidential (1st rd.)	1,260,208	4.4	5.2
1967	Parliamentary (1st rd.)	124,862	0.4	0.6
1968	Parliamentary (1st rd.)	18,933	0.1	0.1
1973	Parliamentary (1st rd.)	122,498	0.4	0.5
1974	Presidential (1st rd.)	190,921	0.6	0.7
1978	Parliamentary (1st rd.)	210,761	0.6	0.8
1979	European (1st rd.)	265,911	0.8	1.3
1981	Parliamentary (1st rd.)	71,345	0.2	0.3
1984	European (1st rd.)	2,227,837	6.0	11.0
1986	Parliamentary (1st rd.)	2,727,870	7.3	9.7
1986	Regional (1st rd.)	2,682,654	7.2	9.6
1988	Presidential (1st rd.)	4,375,894	11.5	14.4
1988	Parliamentary (1st rd.)	2,391,973	6.3	9.8
1989	European (1st rd.)	2,154,005	5.7	11.9
1992	Regional (1st rd.)	3,423,176	9.0	13.8
1993	Parliamentary (1st rd.)	3,229,462	8.3	12.7
1994	European (1st rd.)	2,050,086	5.2	10.5
1995	Presidential (1st rd.)	4,656,107	11.6	15.3
1997	Parliamentary (1st rd.)	3,827,544	9.7	15.0
1998	Regional (1st rd.)	3,297,209	8.4	15.1
1999	European (1st rd.)	1,568,315	3.9	9.0
2002	Presidential (1st rd.)	5,471,739	13.3	19.2
2002	Presidential (2nd rd.)	5,525,034	13.4	17.8
2002	Parliamentary (1st rd.)	3,159,199	7.7	12.5
2004	Regional (1st rd.)	3,913,325	9.4	16.1
2004	European (1st rd.)	1,738,553	4.2	10.1
2007	Presidential (1st rd.)	3,834,530	8.6	10.4
2007	Parliamentary (1st rd.)	1,223,570	2.8	4.7
2009	European (1st rd.)	1,220,870	2.8	7.1
2010	Regional (1st rd.)	2,397,069	5.5	12.3

Note: Aggregated results for candidates from radical right-wing parties, including Poujadistes, Alliance républicaine, and, from 1972 on, the Front National plus other small parties – Parti des forces nouvelles, Parti ouvrier européen, Mouvement national républicain, Parti de la France, Parti antisioniste, Alliance royale, and Citoyenneté-culture européennes.
Source: P. Perrineau, "Le vote d'extrême droite en France: adhésion ou protestation?" *Futuribles*, no. 276 (June 2002), 9, and French Government, Ministère de l'Intérieur [online], available from http://www.interieur.gouv.fr/sections/a_votre_service/elections/resultats, accessed 23 Nov. 2010.

lacked. As a result, it has proved the most influential and durable radical right-wing movement to emerge in France since the establishment of democracy in the country in 1870.

From a sociological standpoint, the electoral progression of the FN can be broken down into three phases. From its establishment in October 1972 to the cantonal and municipal elections of 1982 and 1983, it remained a fringe party incapable of garnering support among any category of the electorate.[52] However, following its initial emergence in the June 1984 European parliamentary elections to the 1988 presidential election, the FN gleaned growing support from notably middle-class and lower-middle-class voters alarmed by the economic and social policies of the Socialist government. Likewise, these strata were angered by what they saw as the acquiescence of the parties of the mainstream Right in these policies, particularly during the first period of *cohabitation*, which lasted from March 1986 to May 1988. Accordingly, in the 1984 European parliamentary elections the FN accounted for 21 percent of the total shopkeeper and artisanal vote versus 15 percent of the white-collar worker vote (employees and midlevel executives), 12 percent of that of professionals and executives, and only 8 percent of the worker vote. By the 1988 presidential election, these proportions had shifted to 31 percent of the shopkeeper and artisan vote, 13 percent of the white-collar vote, 19 percent of the liberal professions and executive vote, and 19 percent of the working-class vote. Thus, during this phase in its development, the FN was principally supported by a coalition of petit bourgeois and bourgeois interests. However, put off by Le Pen's rhetorical excesses and reassured by the mainstream Right's co-optation of the FN's campaign themes, by the March 1993 parliamentary elections many of these bourgeois and petit bourgeois voters had dutifully returned to the fold of the RPR and UDF. They were replaced in large measure by working-class voters, many of whom had been former supporters of the Left.[53] Whereas 15 percent of small shopkeepers and artisans, 13 percent of white-collar workers, and only 6 percent of members of the liberal professions and corporate executives cast their votes in favor of the FN in the 1993 parliamentary elections, the proportion of workers who voted for it rose to 18 percent (Table 1.2).

---

[52] In this period, the FN received only 0.6% of the vote in the first round of the 1974 presidential election, while failing to secure the 500 signatures from elected officials required to compete in the 1981 election. Similarly, the party managed to secure only 0.4%, 0.6%, and 0.2% respectively in the parliamentary elections of 1973, 1978, and 1981. P. Perrineau, "Les étapes d'une implantation électorale (1972–1988)," in Mayer and Perrineau, *Le Front national à découvert*, 59. On the organizational and ideological evolution of the FN during this period, see J.-Y. Camus, "Origine et formation du Front national (1972–1981)," in ibid., 17–36.

[53] On this evolution in the social composition of the FN's electorate, see Bihr, *Spectre* 21–3; Perrineau, *Le symptôme Le Pen*, 107–10; and Nonna Mayer, "Le vote FN de Passy à Barbès," in Mayer and Perrineau, *Le Front national à découvert*, 256–61, and "Le vote Front national au pluriel," *Le Banquet*, no. 10 (Jan.–Jun. 1997), 71. On former left-wing voters' attraction to the FN, see Perrineau, *Le symptôme Le Pen*, 80–4, 218–19, and 230–2.

TABLE 1.2. *Electorate of the Front National by Socioprofessional Category (%)*

	Euro. 1984	Parl. 1986	Pres. 1988	Parl. 1993	Pres. 1995	Parl. 1997	Pres. 2002[a]	Pres. 2007
Farmers/agricultural workers	10	17	13	13	16	4	22	10
Shopkeepers/artisans	21	14	31	15	24	18	20	9
Liberal professionals/ management executives	12	9	19	6	7	4	13	7
Midlevel executives/ employees	15	11	13	13	19	16	23	12
Industrial workers	8	11	19	18	30	24	24	16
Unemployed	–	–	12	–	25	15	20	11

[a] Results for the first round of the 2002 presidential election.
Sources: Alain Bihr, *Le spectre de l'extrême droite. Les Français dans le miroir du Front national* (Paris: Éditions de l'Atelier, 1998), 18; Pascal Perrineau, *Le symptôme Le Pen. Radiographie des électeurs du Front national* (Paris: Fayard, 1997), 102, and "La surprise lepéniste et sa suite législative," in *Le vote de tous les refus. Les elections présidentielle et legislatives de 2002*, ed. C. Ysmal and P. Perrineau (Paris: Presses de Sciences Po, 2002), 210; and Nonna Mayer, "Comment Nicolas Sarkozy a rétréci l'électorat Le Pen," *Revue française de science politique* 57(3–4) (2007), 436.

In this sense, the 1993 parliamentary elections marked a fundamental departure in the evolution of the FN's electorate. From that point on, the proportion of *petits indépendants* who voted for the FN would remain constant around 20 percent (it was never again to reach the high of 31 percent attained in the 1988 presidential race), whereas the percentage of workers who did so continued to increase, leveling out at between 20 and 25 percent by the end of the1990s. This trend is borne out by a more recent comparative study running up to the presidential election of 2002. In the first round of the 1995 presidential election, the first round of the 1997 parliamentary election, and the first round of the 2002 presidential election respectively, the FN garnered 24 (1995), 18 (1997), and 20 percent (2002a) of the vote among shopkeepers and artisans; 19, 16, and 23 percent among commercial and clerical employees; and 30, 24, and 24 percent among industrial workers. Even in the 2007 presidential election in which it lost nearly a million votes from the high attained in April 2002, 59 percent of workers and *employés* who had voted for Le Pen in 2002 remained loyal to the FN (versus only 23 percent of cadres and members of the *professions intermédiaires*), testifying to the resilience of the party's lower-class base of support.[54]

[54] Jérôme Fourquet, "L'échec de Jean-Marie Le Pen à la présidentielle de 2007: les causes d'une hémorragie," *Baromètre politique français: élections 2007* (Paris: CEVIPOF), available from http://www.cevipof.msh-paris.fr/bpf/analyses/Fourquet_Le%20pen2007.pdf, 9–10, accessed 16 Oct. 2007. The INSEE defines as *professions intermédiaires* those socioprofessional

This *déclassement* of the FN's electorate was also reflected in the party's traction among France's growing constituency of unemployed, most of them former workers turned out of their jobs as a result of the wave of factory closures that hit the country beginning in the late 1970s and early1980s. Thus, whereas the FN accounted for only 12 percent of the total ballots cast by unemployed voters in the first round of the 1988 presidential election, this proportion rose to 28 percent in the 1994 European parliamentary election, 25 percent in the first round of the 1995 presidential election, 15 percent in the first round of the 1997 parliamentary election, 20 and 30 percent in the two rounds of the 2002 presidential election, and 22 percent in the first round of the 2002 parliamentary election. By the end of the1990s, the FN had emerged as the leading recipient of votes among not only French workers but the unemployed as well.[55]

By the close of the1990s, then, the Front National had built its support on a lasting alliance between the traditional petite bourgeoisie and industrial working class – something which its predecessors on the radical Right had been unable to achieve. By successfully forging this alliance between *la boutique* and *l'atelier*, and thus preserving the radical Right's historic *petit indépendant* core of support and grafting onto it a substantial working-class following on the

categories occupying "an intermediate position between *cadres* and other upper-level managers and *fonctionnaires* and industrial workers and service employees," including midlevel administrators and managers, and service and industrial technicians, foremen, and supervisors. In addition, this category also includes "primary and secondary school teachers, health and social workers, clerical *fonctionnaires*, and members of the clergy." "Professions Intermédiaires," *INSEE Nomenclatures-Définitions-Méthodes: Professions et catégories socioprofessionnelles*, http://www.insee.fr/fr/nom_def.met/nomenclatures/prof_cat_soc/html/4_N1.HTM, accessed 21 Oct. 2007.

[55] The growing electoral support cultivated by the FN among workers and the unemployed is reflected in the declining electoral fortunes of the principal parties of the Left – PS and PC – among these social constituencies. Concerning the working-class vote, one study estimates that the proportion of French workers who cast votes for the Communist Party fell from 39% in 1978, to 24% in 1981, to only 6% in 2002. Similarly, the proportion of workers who voted for the Socialist candidate declined from 41% in the 1988 presidential elections, to 24% in 1995, to only 13% in 2002. Overall, the proportion of workers who voted for left-wing parties, including the Greens, has fallen from 70% in the first round of the parliamentary elections of 1978 to 43% in the first round of the presidential election of 2002. Likewise, the number of unemployed Frenchmen who cast their votes for parties of the Left also substantially declined. The proportion of unemployed who voted Socialist fell from 41% in the 1988 presidential race, to 20% in 1995, to only 13% in 2002.

This dual evolution suggests that the principal parties of the Left – in particular the PS – have undergone a general process of *embourgeoisement* over the past three decades, shedding their traditional working-class base while making inroads among social constituencies that had hitherto been more favorable to the Right, such as professionals and corporate managers and executives. This implies that the radical Right has become the principal beneficiary of this progressive abandonment of the Left by the workers – or, as some have put it, of the workers by the Left. Bernard Dolez and Annie Laurent, "Marches et marges de la gauche," in Ysmal and Perrineau, *Le vote de tous les refus*, 256; Jérôme Jaffré, "Comprendre l'élimination de Lionel Jospin," in ibid., 226; Nonna Mayer and Bruno Cautrès, "Les métamorphoses du vote de classe," in *Le nouveau désordre électoral: les leçons du 21 Avril 2002* (Paris: Presses de Sciences Po, 2004), 150, 152; and Perrineau, *Symptôme Le Pen*, 230.

other, the FN is an agent of both continuity and departure from previous movements of the radical Right.

THE PLAN OF THE BOOK

The purpose of this study is to account for these continuities and evolutions in ideology and support that characterize the French radical Right, both past and present. Chapter 2 identifies the factors of political supply that underlie its periodic resurgence. It demonstrates that successive radical right-wing movements, from Boulangisme in the late 1880s to the present-day Front National, cohered around a common ideology of "closed nationalism" presenting doctrinal, symbolic, and programmatic attributes that particularly appealed to antimodern social groups. It argues that the members of these strata latched onto the exclusionary and organic conception of identity that was held out by the radical Right as a means of salvaging their own sense of collective belonging in modern French society.

Chapters 3 through 8 specify the factors of political demand that account for the enduring appeal of the radical Right by analyzing the cultural systems evolved by *petits indépendants* and industrial workers as a function of their economic roles and political experiences in French society. They illustrate that these groups were culturally ill-adapted to the structural and normative conditions of advanced industrial and postindustrial capitalism. Chapter 3 argues that, as a function of their self-employed and intermediary status within French society, *petits indépendants* developed an economically Malthusian mind-set that brought them to resist the advances of modern industrial capitalism.[56] In turn, Chapters 4 through 7 clarify how their cumulative political experiences reinforced the illiberal, antimodern sensibilities of these strata, detailing how French *petits indépendants* went from representing the strongest base of support for the French republican state to increasing ambivalence in their attachment to that state and the liberal democratic principles it enshrined. Specifically, as modernization progressed, these strata felt increasingly aggrieved by the progressive downgrading of their interests by the republican state and the abandonment of the petty proprietary ideal on which it was founded, thus rendering them

---

[56] Coined by the interwar French economist Alfred Sauvy, the term "economic Malthusianism" is here used to denote an overly cautious and restrictive economic mind-set privileging stability over growth, savings over investment, and collusion over competition. Because its highest aim is to maximize firm profits as opposed to enhancing firm productivity and efficiency, this mentality is diametrically opposed to that driving the modern – Schumpeterian – capitalist entrepreneur. Cf. respectively David Landes, "French Business and the Businessman: A Social and Cultural Analysis," in *Modern France: Problems of the Third and Fourth Republics*, ed. E. M. Earle (Princeton: Princeton University Press, 1951), 334–53; Henry Ehrmann, *Organized Business in France* (Princeton: Princeton University Press, 1957), 208; Dean Savage, *Founders, Heirs and Managers: French Industrial Leadership in Transition* (Beverley Hills: Sage Publications, 1979), 27–8; and Richard Kuisel, *Capitalism and the State in Modern France: Renovation and Economic Management in the Twentieth Century* (Cambridge: Cambridge University Press, 1981), 29–95.

increasingly receptive to antirepublican movements of the radical Right. This was particularly the case during periods of rapid economic change and intense social dislocation in which *petits indépendants* sought new ways of defending the petty producer vision that underpinned their sociopolitical worldview.

Chapter 8 extends the preceding analysis to the industrial working class. First, it argues that, as a result of their collective experience of industrial labor, French workers historically evolved a strong class identity that shaped their social and political worldview. As the sociostructural foundations of their identity were progressively eroded by deindustrialization, they too became agents of resistance to capitalist modernization. In turn, as the French economic structure was transformed from the 1970s on and institutions of working-class defense collapsed, French workers progressively grew disaffected with the institutions and policies of the post-Gaullist state. As they fell deeper into economic and social crisis, they thus proved increasingly receptive to the program and discourse of the radical Right.

Finally, in Chapter 9, we reflect on the historical experience of the radical Right in France as compared to other countries and then, in conclusion, seek to ascertain its impact on French politics and society. Keeping in mind the class-cultural framework, we assess the radical Right's prospects and correlative effects on French democracy, as well as the broader theoretical implications these hold for our understanding of the processes of social and political modernization.

2

Defining the Radical Right in France, Past and Present

> Que Dreyfus est capable de trahir, je le conclus de sa race.
>
> Maurice Barrès, *Scènes et doctrines du nationalisme*[1]
>
> La démocratie, c'est le mal. La démocratie, c'est la mort.
>
> Charles Maurras, *Enquête sur la monarchie*[2]
>
> établissement, qu'il s'agit de renverser par une révolution du salut public, désigne la classe dirigeante qui impose aujourd'hui son pouvoir. Les droits de l'homme sont ses tables de la Loi. Il a ses évangiles selon saint Freud et saint Marx. Il a son clergé, son architecte et ses maçons. Son lieu de culte, le Panthéon républicain, ses rites, dont il prêche la morale. Le Front national a pour devoir d'assurer le retour au pouvoir des vraies élites, après avoir dépouillé la société française des corps parasitaires qui l'enserrent et l'asphyxient.
>
> Jean-Marie Le Pen, *Identité*, January 1990[3]

Attempts to define the radical Right in France have produced a raft of interpretations over the years. As most students of French politics would attest, it is not an easy political construct to pin down. In the words of Michel Winock, it is "a 'hard' political current but a 'soft' political concept."[4] This difficulty can be attributed to several factors. In the first place, it stems from the strategic rejection of the label "radical," "far," or "extreme Right" on the part of figures and parties who actually belong to this political current. In concealing their real ideological affiliations and programmatic intentions, they hope to enhance their democratic credentials or, alternatively, to present a nonideological stance that transcends partisanship and to espouse a pragmatic agenda for governing the country. Second, this confusion stems from a lack of conceptual exactness defining the radical Right, specifically as a result of the indiscriminate ascription of

---

[1] Quoted in P. A. Taguieff, *La couleur et le sang. Doctrines racistes à la française*, 2nd ed. (Paris: Mille et une nuits, 2002), 170.

[2] *Enquête sur la monarchie*, 10th ed. (Paris: Nouvelle Librairie Nationale, 1924), 121.

[3] Quoted in I. Cuminal, M. Souchard, S. Wahnich, and V. Wathier, *Le Pen. Les mots* (Paris: La Découverte, 1998), 124.

[4] Introduction to Winock, *Histoire de l'extrême droite en France*, 14.

related but inappropriate labels, such as fascism, to political formations to which they do not ultimately apply. Third, conceptual dissonance follows from the debate over whether the radical Right is to be considered a unitary or plural phenomenon, and whether it descends from singular or multifarious ideological and organizational strands. Finally, it reflects the ambiguous relationship of parties of the radical Right to other formations within the French political system. By obscuring where they lie on the political spectrum, the ambivalence of inter-party relationships blurs the conceptual lines by which the radical Right comes to be distinguished from other political parties. Accordingly, some historians have portrayed the radical Right as part of the French conservative tradition. For them, it displays more similarities than differences in respect to more moderate forma-tions on the right because of their common attachment to the values of tradition and order.[5] Conversely, other historians have viewed the radical Right as a kind of revolutionary left-wing heresy whose hatred of political and economic liberalism was ideologically and politically closer to the radical Left than to the mainstream, conservative Right.[6] Given this array of conceptual interpretations, it should come as no surprise that a singular, concise, and commonly acceptable definition of the French radical Right – an "'identikit' extreme right" to use Peter Davies's phrase – has yet to emerge.[7]

The task of the present chapter cannot be to arrive at such a categorical definition. Rather, it will seek to flesh out the broad contours and uncover the common properties presented by political formations identified historically with the radical Right. In particular, special analytical emphasis is given to the discursive properties presented by successive radical right-wing movements and parties. It is argued that their discourse articulated with this mind-set and addressed the concerns of economically and socially vulnerable antimodern constituencies within French society. Specifically, this discourse became a source of reassurance and identification for these crisis-ridden social groups – petits

[5] This is notably the thesis defended by René Rémond and Robert Soucy. Whereas the former conceives of the radical Right as an ultraconservative incarnation of Bonapartism, the latter portrays it as an indigenous form of fascism deriving from the traditional conservatism of the nineteenth-century French Right. According to this view, this new fascist Right was to be distin-guished from its conservative forerunners not so much in terms of having invented a new ideo-logical corpus or worldview but rather because of the novel ways in which it combined the reactionary and authoritarian ideas of the traditional Right. Soucy, Fascism in France, 313–15, and Rémond, The Right Wing in France, 223–5, 276–7, 281.

[6] This is the conclusion reached by Zeev Sternhell, who traces the emergence of an indigenous and "phenomenologically pure" French fascism to revisionist revolutionary socialism. First appearing with Boulangisme and its offshoots during the 1880s and 1890s, the latter was doctrinally refined by syndicalist theorists such as Georges Sorel and Édouard Berth during the first two decades of the new century and finally came of age during the 1930s, with the planist ideas of Henri de Man and the high-profile conversions to fascism of leftists such as the neosocialist Marcel Déat and Communist deputy and Central Committee member Jacques Doriot. Cf. Sternhell's trilogy, Maurice Barrès et le nationalisme français, La droite révolutionnaire (1885–1914). Les origines françaises du fascisme, and Neither Right nor Left.

[7] The Extreme Right in France, 12.

indépendants historically, industrial workers today – thereby sustaining the radical Right's appeal throughout the course of modern French social and political development.

IDEOLOGY AND PROGRAM OF THE FRENCH RADICAL RIGHT

La France aux Français. Parliamentary campaign slogan of Maurice Barrès, 1893[8]

La France aux Français. Presidential campaign slogan of Jean-Marie Le Pen, 1988[9]

At root, in both its historic and contemporary guise, the French radical Right must be considered the product of the central conflict underlying post-Revolutionary French political history: namely, the conflict opposing the republican defenders of the philosophical and political legacy of 1789, the champions of political and economic liberalism, to the opponents of that legacy, the proponents of antiliberalism and antirepublicanism. By the close of the nineteenth century, this conflict had evolved into a fundamental struggle between the ideologies of open and closed nationalism. "Open" nationalism refers to the republican nationalism that was inherited from the Revolution and, in the words of one historian, "asserted the liberty and equality of a sovereign people."[10] The triumph of the universal ideals of individual rights, political equality; and popular sovereignty that had been consecrated by the Revolution – all concepts deriving from the application of Enlightenment rationalism and scientism to politics, notably in the form of social contract theory – gave rise to a nation-building movement, a *mouvement nationalitaire*, which conceived of France as the model for republican self-government across Europe. Thus was born a form of French nationalism founded on the myth of France's historical vocation to defend universal republican ideals and spread them throughout the world. "It endowed," observed Winock, "the principle of the French nation with an affective content and transfigured its history into a destiny, infusing the cult of patriotism with the mythology of a chosen people."[11]

Such a nationalism bound the individual to the nation as the primordial political collectivity from whence he derived his rights as a citizen and conversely conferred upon the republican state the principle of sovereignty by which it could legitimately speak for the nation and its people. In one sense, open nationalism was inclusive insofar as it conceived of national belonging solely in terms of the sociopolitical contract that existed between the individual and the state as a function of the (imputably) voluntary choice of citizenship. Since national belonging was thereby defined in terms of the rights and obligations of republican citizenship, it theoretically extended to all manner of peoples,

---

[8] Quoted in Soucy, *Fascism in France*, 235.
[9] Quoted in Davies, *The Extreme Right in France*, 148.
[10] Winock, *Nationalism, Anti-Semitism and Fascism in France*, 6.
[11] Ibid., 7.

races, and collectivities. Accordingly, open nationalism remained the preserve of
the Left in post-Revolutionary France. In its Jacobin and, later, Radical and even
socialist incarnations, it was with the Left that the broadly universalist, inclusive
sweep of open nationalism resonated most strongly. By the same token, open
nationalism was of necessity externally oriented, sometimes fiercely so. Defense
of the nation as the conferrer of citizenship and guarantor of the political rights
attaching to it became the single highest duty of the citizen-patriot.[12] In this light,
it should come as no surprise that the loudest cries for *revanche* in the decade
following the Franco-Prussian War were to be heard on the republican and
socialist Left.

   However, by the late 1880s and 1890s, a novel – and essentially antithetical –
form of nationalism had appeared on the French political scene. The latter
marked the culmination of the progressive shift away from the inclusive and
universalist republican nationalism that had issued from the tradition of 1789
toward a nationalism based on an exclusive and particularistic definition of the
nation and national appurtenance. This new "closed" nationalism – what Raoul
Girardet has termed *le nationalisme des nationalistes* – appeared on the backdrop of the profound technological, social, and intellectual transformations that
overtook the country during the closing decades of the nineteenth century.[13] The
destruction of traditional social and economic structures due to the pressures of
industrialization and urbanization fundamentally altered people's consciousness
and had a profoundly disorienting effect on how they defined their social roles
and identities. At the same time, accelerating industrialization and urbanization
heralded the progressive "massification" of French society. Uprooted by sweeping economic and social change from the traditional structures that had ordered
its existence for generations, a growing proportion of the population was
crowded into cities where it was put to work in the alienating confines of the
factory. The institution of universal (manhood) suffrage under the Third
Republic transformed virtually overnight these new and growing masses into a
potent political force. Foreclosed from any real possibility of improving their
social and economic position, they quickly became one of the greatest factors of
instability within industrial society.

   In effect, industrial society had generated conditions that would fuel an
intellectual, cultural, and, ultimately sociopolitical backlash against the ideological and societal structures of economic and political modernity. At the ideational level, this backlash came in the form of a movement of revolt against the
rationalism, positivism, and materialism that were associated with the industrial

---

[12] The potential virulence of republican nationalism is well captured by an officer of the Ancien
     Régime who witnessed the defeat of the Prussian and Austrian armies by revolutionary conscripts
     at the Battle of Valmy on 20 September 1792. The battle turned, he writes, on the "hellish tactic"
     consisting of "fifty thousand savage beasts foaming at the mouth like cannibals, hurling them-
     selves at top speed upon soldiers whose courage has been excited by no passion." Quoted in John
     Merriman, *A History of Modern Europe*, vol. 1 (New York: W. W. Norton, 1996), 526.
[13] "Présentation," in *Le nationalisme français 1871–1914*, ed. R. Girardet (Paris: Armand Colin,
     1966), 10.

age. In the social and political spheres, it translated into an attack on bourgeois society and liberal democracy. Within this fluid intellectual and societal context, the great political crises that shook France in the 1880s and 1890s, the Boulangiste crisis and Dreyfus affair, crystallized these diffuse antirationalist and antimodernist sentiments into an explicitly antiliberal political doctrine. Within the span of a decade, the campaign of a certain Radical and Socialist Left to reclaim the egalitarian legacy of the French Revolution by extending the political rights bequeathed by the republic into the socioeconomic sphere, combined with the growing disenchantment of the Right over the regime's unwillingness to take back the lost provinces of Alsace-Lorraine, translated into an outright rejection of the principles and institutions of the Third Republic. By the end of the Dreyfus affair, *revanchisme* and this radical aversion to the liberal republican order had grafted itself onto a defensive or closed form of nationalism. Positing a virulent xenophobia and anti-Semitism, this new antirepublican nationalism sought to unite and mobilize hitherto antagonistic social classes under the aegis of an exclusive definition of the nation – what one author has termed "the nationalization of the masses."[14] At the same time, it categorically rejected the trappings of liberal democracy in favor of an authoritarian and hierarchical model of politics, which took its cues from ideas and institutions antedating the advent of republican rule in France. Thus, tenants of this new brand of authoritarian and nationalist politics believed they could, if not replicate the sociopolitical structures of pre-Revolutionary France, then at least return to the principles that underlay them in order to recast the French body politic.

This new authoritarian politics based on an exclusionary or closed definition of the nation came in two guises. The first, a national populist version representing a xenophobic perversion of the Jacobin tradition of direct (i.e., plebiscitarian) democracy, can be traced to the ideas of Maurice Barrès. Barrès's principal contribution to the definition of closed nationalism lay in discarding the universalist conception of the nation based on the republican ideal of the general will and grounding it instead in an organicistic, indeed physiological, determinism. For him, the nation and its people drew their essential physical and spiritual traits from their land of origin. Their history was the tale of their collective rootedness in that land, as most powerfully symbolized by the ritual return of the dead to it so that the land, in turn, represented the organic repository of the nation's identity. Barrès's essentialist definition of the nation reflected the intrusion of a specifically French romanticism, with its exaltation of nature as fundamentally graspable only through sentiment, into politics. It signaled the wider rejection of Enlightenment rationalism in favor of emotion and instinct as the primary bases of national identification, "reducing," in Michel Winock's phrase, "nationalism to a patch of meadowland."[15]

---

[14] Sternhell, *La droite révolutionnaire*, 24.
[15] *Nationalism, Anti-Semitism and Fascism in France*, 12.

The second incarnation of this new closed nationalism was under the guise of a revised counterrevolutionary tradition. In contrast to its national populist counterpart, the latter wholly repudiated the republican legacy of 1789, combining an exclusive definition of French identity with a conservative and elitist restorationist program. The intellectual progenitor for this counterrevolutionary nationalism was Charles Maurras. Whereas Barrès had served as the romantic progenitor of closed nationalism, Maurras emerged as its "doctrinaire positivist." An erstwhile republican who had become disillusioned with republicanism during the Dreyfus affair, Maurras was convinced that the only way to preserve the country's cohesion was through a return to the strong social and institutional frameworks – the family, guild structure, aristocracy, Catholic Church, unitary state – that had defined the pre-Revolutionary order. He pinned his hopes on a monarchist restoration as the institutional prescription most capable of or integral to safeguarding the vital interests of the nation. Accordingly, the body of ideas with which he was identified came to be known as the doctrine of *nationalisme intégral* and gave birth to a political and intellectual movement, *l'Action Française*, to pursue his monarchist aim. Like Barrès, Maurras repudiated the universal ideals of individual rights and political equality that had issued from the French Revolution. He did so, however, on rationalist empirical grounds, embracing in their stead the conception of a hierarchically ordered, inegalitarian society that would replicate the stratified corporative order of the Ancien Régime.[16] His positivist dissection of French society thus became the basis for a conservative nationalism that sought to root out all elements foreign to its conception of France. As Winock put it, such a nationalism "resolutely eliminated from French patrimony and national wealth everything foreign to [its] own classicism: the Revolution and all that followed, Protestants, Jews, Freemasons, foreigners."[17]

Therefore, although it was couched in a different intellectual demarche, Maurras's nationalism merged with that of Barrès in its domestic focus and exclusionary intent. Like the Barrèsian conception that rooted national belonging in a pedigreed affiliation with the land, Maurras's conservative nationalism, equating the preservation of national identity with the traditional collectivities of absolutist French society, was an essentially negative nationalism. By definition, both targeted for expulsion from the national body those political institutions and social groups that fell afoul of their exclusive definitions of the nation. Given this shared exclusionary emphasis, it was only a matter of time before the traditionalist conception of the nation that had been arrived at by Maurras

---

[16] Highlighting the rationalistic basis of his neoroyalism, Maurras famously wrote in *Enquête sur la monarchie*: "Once the will to save our French fatherland has been accepted as a postulate, everything else unfolds like a chain, and is deduced in an indisputable sequence. There is no room for choice or fantasy . . .: if you have resolved to be a patriot, you must compulsorily be a royalist . . . *La raison le veut.*" Quoted in Samuel Osgood, *French Royalism under the Third and Fourth Republics* (The Hague: Martins Nijhoff, 1960), 60.

[17] *Nationalism, Anti-Semitism and Fascism in France*, 13.

on positivistic, rationalist grounds came to be infused with the organicistic determinism of Barrès. In combination, their respective ideas yielded a synthetic conception of closed nationalism that advocated the return to the sempiternal structures and values associated with a mythical, primordial France, ethnically pure and socially harmonious.[18]

The successive movements of the radical Right that have come to the fore since its eclosion in the 1880s and 1890s have followed closely in the line of the closed nationalist ideology first elaborated by Barrès and Maurras. Some of these movements, such as the *syndicalistes jaunes* in the decade preceding World War I, the protofascist leagues of the interwar period, and the Poujadiste movement following World War II, clearly descended from the national populist current that can be traced to Barrès and first came to the fore with Boulangisme and the anti-Dreyfusard *ligues*. Conversely, Action Française and its latter-day descendants squarely fell into the counterrevolutionary, neoroyalist tradition inaugurated by Maurras.[19] However, the substantial fluidity that existed between these dual currents of the closed nationalist Right militates against considering them separately. For example, some nationalist Republicans who had begun their intellectual and political careers as radical Jacobins under the aegis of Boulangisme gravitated to the Action Française by the turn of the century.[20] Likewise, a significant number of the fascist intellectuals of the interwar period received their initial political education in the ranks of the AF.[21]

---

[18] For a comprehensive treatment of Barrès's ideas, see respectively Soucy, *Fascism in France*; Sternhell, *Barrès*; and Bihr, *Actualité d'un archaïsme*, ch. 4. For an exposition of Maurras's political philosophy and program, see respectively Eugen Weber, *Action Française*; Nolte, *Three Faces of Fascism: Action Française, Italian Fascism, National Socialism*, part II; Victor Nguyen, *Aux origines de l'Action Française* (Paris: Fayard, 1991); and Bruno Goyet, *Charles Maurras* (Paris: Presses de Sciences Po, 2000). On the conceptual bases of closed nationalism and its opposition to open nationalism, see notably P.-A. Taguieff, "Le 'nationalisme des nationalistes.' Un problème pour l'histoire des idées politiques en France," in *Théories du nationalisme*, ed. G. Delannoi and P.-A. Taguieff (Paris: Kimé, 1991), 47–124, as well as Winock, introduction, and *Working paper: Les nationalismes français* (Barcelona, 1994), available from http://www. recercat.net/bitstream/2072/1370/1/ICPS97.pdf.

[19] Sternhell, *Droite révolutionnaire*, and *Neither Right nor Left*; Milza, *Fascisme français*, chs. 2–3; Chebel d'Appollonia, *L'extrême droite en France*, 145–58, 182–90, and Weber, *L'Action Française* chs. 29–30.

[20] Indeed, starting with Maurras himself, the founding cadre of the AF had almost all been nationalist republicans before becoming monarchists. Most prominent among them perhaps was Léon Daudet, who would second Maurras in editing the movement's newspaper. Issuing from a prominent republican family – his father was the famous republican politician and author, Alphonse Daudet – he transited from Radicalism to anti-Semitism and anti-Dreyfusism before ending his political trajectory in the ranks of the AF. Weber, *Action Française*, 25.

[21] Georges Valois, founder of the first self-proclaimed fascist party in France, the Faisceau, as well as nearly the entire editorial staff – including Robert Brasillach, Lucien Rebatet, and Pierre Gaxotte – of the fascist and ultimately collaborationist newspaper *Je suis partout*, come most obviously to mind. Similarly, Pierre Drieu La Rochelle, though never actually belonging to the AF, underscored

By contrast, the sole governmental formation in which the radical Right would wield significant influence, the Vichy regime, and its most notable contemporary incarnation, the Front National, represent syntheses of these national populist and counterrevolutionary currents. The strong Maurrassian affiliations of Vichy's leading cadre combined with nationalist populist tendencies in inflecting the policies and rhetoric of the regime. Thus, the traditionalist, counterrevolutionary emphases on hierarchical principles and on church and family as the primordial organic structures underpinning French society cohabited with institutional prescriptions, such as plebiscitarianism and cæsarism, as well as symbols and locutions – the *tricolore*, the *Marseillaise*, and the Révolution Nationale – which remained more closely identified with the national populist tradition.[22] By the same token, as exemplified by its view of itself as unifying the various strands of the "authentic" (i.e., Far) Right, the FN also presents an ideological and programmatic synthesis of these national populist and counterrevolutionary currents. On the one hand, its includes advocates of a plebiscitarian and antiparliamentary populism ranging from avowed republicans such as Le Pen to, in their most radical guise, figures deriving from the neofascist movements of the 1960s and 1970s such as Ordre Nouveau and the GRECE. On the other hand, the FN has become a home for the denizens of a small but vocal counterrevolutionary current identifiable with the Maurrassian political tradition. Foremost among these are Catholic *intégriste* formations such as the Comités chrétienté-solidarité and holdovers from the traditionalist Vichyiste Right close to the journals *Présent* and *Itinéraires*.[23]

---

the intellectual debt he owed to Maurras in framing his political ideas. Cf., for example, his *Journal: 1939–1945*, ed. J. Hervier (Paris: Gallimard, 1992), 84.

[22] It is important to note, however, that Vichy represented an amalgam of political and philosophical traditions of which the radical Right, though significant, was but one element. Alongside populist and conservative nationalists, Vichy, particularly in its early incarnation, also incorporated prewar elites who had formerly been loyal to the republic, as well as technocratic modernizers whose vision for developing the country conflicted with the traditionalist agenda of the regime's far-right supporters. But as the war progressed and collaboration with Germany deepened, the influence of radical right-wing and even fascist elements over the political-administrative apparatus of the Vichy state disproportionately grew compared to other factions within the regime. For the various political-cultural tendencies represented at Vichy, see Jean-Pierre Azéma, "Vichy," in Winock, *Histoire de l'extrême droite*, 191–214. On the continuities in personnel between Vichy and the prewar period and the heterogeneous intellectual and ideological influences on the regime, see Philippe Burrin, "The Ideology of the National Revolution," in Arnold, *The Development of the Radical Right in France*, 135–52. On its progressive fascization or totalitarianization, see Julian Jackson, "Vichy and Fascism," in *The Development of the Radical Right*, 153–71; Milza, *Fascisme français*, ch. 4; and Paxton, *Vichy France*, chs. 3 and 4. On the modernizing ambitions of Vichy technocrats, see Kuisel, *Capitalism*, ch. 5.

[23] Milza, *Fascisme français*, 348–50, and Pierre-André Taguieff, "Biopolitique de l'identité et ordre moral: l'orthodoxie du Front national," *Raison présente* 127 (July–Sept. 1998), 43–58. For a comprehensive analysis of the various political "families" coexisting under the umbrella of the FN, the reader is directed to Jean-Yves Camus, "Political Cultures within the Front National: The Emergence of a Counter-Ideology on the French Far-Right," *Patterns of Prejudice* 26(2) (1992), 5–16, and *Le Front national. Histoire et analyses*, 2nd ed. (Paris: Laurens, 1997), particularly

From a general standpoint, then, the successive formations of the French radical Right possessed elements of both newness and continuity about them. Although each of them presented certain novel aspects, reflecting the socio-political context that conditioned its emergence and the specific constellation of issues around which it crystallized, these parties also display notable ideological and programmatic likenesses that are traceable to the radical Right, considered as an analytically distinct and historically continuous political tradition. Despite the variations they present, these reflect their fundamental adherence to the conception of closed nationalism outlined here.

Specifically, five ideological and programmatic features have characterized radical right-wing movements in France historically.[24] First, they are united in their more or less open disdain toward political and economic liberalism. At one level, they express an uncompromising hostility toward representative democracy and, specifically, toward parliamentarism. The latter are viewed as synonymous with ineffectual government and institutional corruption and, because of their grounding in the erroneous precept of equality, as fundamentally in conflict with nature. Similarly, radical right-wing parties oppose the tenets of modern finance capitalism, viewed as the vehicle of exploitative "cosmopolitan" (i.e., Jewish or foreign) feudalities that would destroy the internal cohesion of the nation for their own economic and political gain.[25] Second, and conversely, parties of the radical Right express an abiding hatred for the ideologies of socialism and communism. These are excoriated not only for most fully enshrining the principle of equality but also for professing a class-based internationalism. Third, radical right-wing parties envision the installation of a strong leader and, by extension, the concentration of executive power in an authoritarian guise. The leadership principle conforms, in the political sphere, to the laws of authority and hierarchy that are held by the Radical Right to reflect the fundamental principle of inequality obtaining in the natural world. Fourth, radical right-wing parties have unanimously advocated closing the national frontiers. Evincing a deep-seated wariness or even hatred of foreigners

125–70 and 231–9; Gilles Ivaldi, "Conservation, Revolution and Protest: A Case Study in the Political Cultures of the Front National's Members and Sympathizers," *Electoral Studies* 15(3) (1996), 339–62; and P. Milza, "Le Front national: droite extrême ... ou national-populisme?" in *Histoire des droites en France*, vol. 1, ed. J.-F. Sirinelli (Paris: Gallimard, 1992), 691–729, and "Le Front national crée-t-il une culture politique?" *Vingtième siècle. Revue d'histoire*, no. 44 (Oct.–Dec. 1994), 39–44.

[24] Thoughtful syntheses of the ideological and programmatic features of the French radical Right since the end of the nineteenth century are to be found in Girardet, "Présentation," in *Le nationalisme français*, 7–34; Winock, introduction; J.-F. Sirinelli, "L'extrême droite vient de loin," *Pouvoirs*, no. 87 (1998), 5–19; E. J. Arnold, preface to *The Development of the Radical Right in France*, xi–xxi; and Davies, *The Extreme Right in France*, ch. 1.

[25] Regarding the anticapitalist biases of the radical Right during the interwar period, see Sternhell, *Droite Révolutionnaire*, introduction and ch. 1, and *Neither Right nor Left*, chs. 3–6. For a recent appraisal of the economic illiberalism of the radical Right, see notably Steve Bastow, "Front National Economic Policy: From Neo-Liberalism to Protectionism," *Modern and Contemporary France* 5(1) (1997), 61–72, and "The Radicalization of Front National Discourse: A Politics of the 'Third Way'?" *Patterns of Prejudice* 32(3) (1998), 55–68.

that reflects the radical Right's organicistic conception of national identity, they advocate exclusionary measures in the form of restrictions on immigration and access to citizenship in order to defend the nation from unwanted foreign influences. Historically, such proposals targeted Jews as the so-called agents of cosmopolitanism. More recently, these have been redirected against immigrants of non-European – particularly North and sub-Saharan African – origin. Fifth, and finally, parties of the French radical Right express the singular desire to rebuild *la maison française*, that is, posit a project of national renewal in order to remedy the social, political, and cultural ills wrought by the Revolution and the subsequent evolution of republican rule. This renovative project is deemed essential to purge the country of the pernicious effects of individualism and egalitarianism in undermining the cohesion of the French nation and to reduce the influence of foreign, anti-French elements that benefited from these principles at the expense of the authentic French people. Thus, by doing away with representative democracy and installing an authoritarian regime to achieve this national renovation, radical right-wing parties hope to restore the unity of the nation through the reimposition of social, cultural, and racial homogeneity within it.

THE DISCOURSE OF THE RADICAL RIGHT: AN APPEAL TO THE LOSERS OF MODERNITY

> Comme toujours et plus que jamais, la politique [est] d'abord et avant tout une guerre de langage, une guerre des signes, une guerre des modèles, des symboles. Jean-Marie Le Pen, *Aspects de la France*, October 10, 1991[26]

Central to the political presentation of the French radical Right is its discourse. Through this discourse, it has proved particularly adept at harnessing the fears and frustrations of antimodern social groups – *petits indépendants* historically and industrial workers today – in modern industrial society. The symbolic motifs or myths that it deployed strongly appealed to the members of these crisis-ridden groups who respectively lost confidence in the norms and institutions governing social and political life. In such periods of crisis and uncertainty, these myths made sense of the complex sociostructural evolutions that were a source of profound disorientation and anxiety to these antimodern groups.[27] Through these myths, the radical Right was able to explain and condemn the economic and social decline of *petits indépendants* and industrial workers, thereby rendering the social world

---

[26] Quoted in Lecœur, *Un néo-populisme à la française*, 218.

[27] In this sense, as the social psychologist Murray Edelman put it, such myths serve to "channel individual anxieties and impulses into a widely shared set of expectations and a widely shared scenario to guide action." *Politics as Symbolic Action: Mass Arousal and Quiescence* (New York: Academic Press, 1971), 54. On the psychically ordering and socially mobilizing function of myth – and, more broadly, of symbolism – in politics, see Raoul Girardet, *Mythes et mythologies politiques* (Paris: Seuil, 1986), and Christopher Flood, *Political Myth: A Theoretical Introduction* (New York: Garland Publishing, 1996).

intelligible to them while delineating their rightful place within it. In turn, by tying their social roles and interests to an exclusive and organicistic identity, the radical Right invested the members of these antimodern groups with a renewed sense of purpose and belonging. Thus, it both validated and reassured these respective constituencies as they suffered social demotion and cultural estrangement within modern French society.

The discourse of the radical Right takes the form of a general "meditation on decadence."[28] By situating the social crises that successively enveloped *petits indépendants* and industrial workers within a broader dynamic of national decline, this meditation projected the return to a primordial, socially harmonious, and morally unblemished "community of destiny" that had been adulterated by the modern world. In turn, by basing this primordial vision of community on an exclusive and organicistic conception of national appurtenance, the radical Right set out an array of internal enemies on whom this national decline could be blamed. As such, it provided ready targets against whom the anxieties, frustrations, and resentments of the losers of economic and social modernization could be projected.[29] This "meditation on decadence" is structured around three thematic components. First is the acknowledgment of the social, political, and moral decline into which the country has fallen – the "diagnosis of decadence" that serves as the thematic starting point for this discourse. Proceeding from this diagnosis, the radical Right derived a powerful rationale that reduced the complex reasons for the economic and social decline of particular groups to a simple, easily apprehended order of causality.

At base, the radical Right's diagnosis of decadence springs from an intense sentiment of misoneism.[30] It entails an unequivocal rejection of a modern world held to have destroyed the values and institutions associated with a primordial and authentic France and replaced them with the corrupting and debilitating – in a word, decadent – influences identified with a baneful present.[31] Foremost among the blights wrought by economic and social modernity were the loss of respect for authority and general lawlessness and permissiveness viewed by the radical Right as synonymous with modern urban society and culture. Similarly, it held up the social divisions and conflicts that characterized modern industrial

---

[28] Girardet, "Présentation," 17.

[29] In this sense, as a number of analysts have pointed out, the discourse of the radical Right fulfills an essential cathartic, even psychotherapeutic function on behalf of declining groups in modern French society. By offering them a mechanism for projecting these negative affects, it provides them a measure of psychic relief from the increasingly acute crisis of identity that they respectively face in industrial and postindustrial society. Birgitta Orfali, *L'adhesion au Front national. De la minorité active au mouvement social* (Paris: Kimé, 1990), 278, and Bihr, *Spectre*, 142.

[30] Defined as the "hatred of anything new," misoneism translates a basic fear of the present as the vehicle for changes that one is powerless to control, and which are therefore perceived to be all the more threatening. *Collins Dictionary of the English Language*, ed. P. Hanks (repr., London and Glasgow: Collins, 1979), 943.

[31] Cf. Arnold, preface, xiii–xv, and Winock, introduction, 15.

40 *The Resurgence of the Radical Right in France*

society as proof of the fundamental immorality and illegitimacy of the latter. Finally, theorists of the radical Right deplored the dissolution of the strong collective attachments and solidarities that bound French society in the past, the principal cause in their eyes of the mounting social alienation and anomie afflicting advanced industrial society. This anomie reflected the rampant individualism and materialism of the latter and the consequent erosion of the collective values of mutual obligation and trust that formerly underpinned the social order.[32] In particular, the debilitating effect of these factors of moral and cultural decadence was reflected for the radical Right in the country's demographic decline. The social and moral blights that it associated with social and economic modernity were held to have a quasi-physiological impact on the health of the nation and to sap it of its vital dynamism.[33]

The diagnosis of decadence is expressed at two symbolic levels. First and foremost, it is asserted in the form of a deep-seated fear of national death, often conveyed through "tragic and crepuscular" utterances that articulate a pronounced sentiment of cultural pessimism and historical foreboding.[34] In turn, the fact of decadence is expressed through the trope of a physical, organic process of decomposition, leading to a rendering of decadence in essentially biological terms.[35] Society is cast as a holistic, living organism, so that decadence comes to represent the literal symptom, evident within the nation as a whole, of its sickness or physical dysfunction.[36] The tragic utterances of the radical Right,

[32] In a representative passage, Maurras deplored the absence of the sense of collective obligation that characterized the liberal political and economic order, prefiguring its moral and social collapse, noting that "the obtaining social order does not require that one make any sacrifices in order to ... support it. Politically, economically, and morally it is ugly, it is base, it is stupid, it is mediocre, it is vile, it is useless, it is evil.... Nothing within it means anything nor has any purpose whatever." Quoted in Nguyen, *Aux origines de l'Action Française*, 893.

[33] On this motif, see Davies, *The Extreme Right in France*, 149, and *The National Front in France: Ideology, Discourse and Power* (London: Routledge, 1999), 120–4, and P. A. Taguieff, "Un programme 'révolutionnaire'?" in Mayer and Perrineau, *Le Front national à découvert*, 217–20.

[34] This fear is to be seen in declarations of Barrès – for example, "I can feel our French nationality, that is to say the substance that sustains us without which I would pass away, diminishing, disappearing"; and "We have been stricken in the depths of our lives, in our true reality, in our energy." It was similarly echoed by Maurras in his pessimistic appraisal of "the sure and tragic likelihood of having to look upon ourselves as the last of the French" (Girardet, "Présentation," 17). More recently, this same fear of national extinction shows through in the discourse of the FN. The following excerpt from a speech given by Le Pen in September 1994 is indicative. "France," he declaims, "has continued ... to regress and, following in the path of the Western and Northern world generally, has fallen into such a grave crisis that, at the economic, social, political, but also the cultural and moral levels, her very existence, and with it that of the French people as a whole, finds itself threatened with death." Cuminal et al., *Le Pen. Les mots*, 108.

[35] Thus, as Alain Bihr has put it, the radical Right elevates the life sciences to "a privileged, even exclusive, mode of explanation of social and human phenomena." "Identité, inégalité, pugnacité: courte synthèse sur l'idéologie d'extrême droite," *Raison présente*, no. 99 (1991), 97.

[36] Not surprisingly, particular prominence is given within this biologized framework to hygienic and medical metaphors having to do with sickness, infection, and disease. As E. J. Arnold points out, Barrès was already comparing in his novels the effects of parliamentarianism on the French people to those of alcoholism, syphilis, or lead poisoning. Similarly, Georges Valois claimed in the 1920s

which serve to amplify the process of national decline, give substance to the deep anxiety felt by the victims of economic and social modernization. This rendering of social processes in naturalistic or organicistic terms reinforces the misoneist tenor of its discourse, enhancing the radical Right's appeal to anti-modern groups. Its use of biological, sanitary, or epidemiological metaphors to evoke the opposition between a pure and healthy past and a tainted and corrupt present strongly resonates with the respective losers of modernity. In this sense, the symbolic representation of decadence by the radical Right underlines the plight and offers much needed validation to these strata in periods of economic and social crisis.[37]

Following from this general diagnosis of decadence identified with economic and social modernity, the radical Right introduced a second important theme that has resonated with antimodern social groups: the myth of diabolical causality.[38] It imputed the general condition of decadence with which it associated their decline to the noxious influence of the agents of what Maurras famously termed *l'anti-France*.[39] Resorting to a classic conspiratorial framework that reduces complex social phenomena to a Manichaean order of causality and responsibility, the radical Right offered members of these groups a simple explanation for their decline in modern French society. The agents of decadence were most often identified with specific groups who, as a function of their

that parliamentarianism had "sterilized" the French people, symbolically associating impotence or the loss of virility with democracy, a motif that was to be amplified upon by interwar fascist intellectuals such as Pierre Drieu la Rochelle and Robert Brasillach. In turn, closer to our time, the motifs of disease and infection are constantly evoked by spokesmen for the FN as representations of the physical corruption and moral degeneration of the nation. An essay entitled "Exclusion: A Law of Nature," which appeared in the September–October 1990 issue of *Identité*, is particularly revealing of this reliance on medical and organic imagery to depict social and political processes. Portraying society as a biological organism, the article likens immigrants to foreign "cells" infecting the body politic and casts the nation's immigration policy as the immune system by which these are to be combated. A stricter immigration regime is equated with a stronger immune system, a more lax regime with a weaker one. Thus, within this symbolic schema, the immigrant is identified and eliminated from the social body in literally the same way that pathogens are identified by the human body and antibodies created to destroy them. The following passage is illustrative: "Within the organism, each cell must carry its own 'identity card' and present it to the immunity barrier: 'customs.' ... In general principles the system is simple: the intruders are recognized and rejected ... the invading virus will be identified as a 'foreigner' and destroyed by the 'brigades' of the defensive immune system." Quoted in Peter Davies, *The National Front in France: Ideology, Discourse and Power* (London: Routledge, 1999), 136, and see Arnold, preface, xiv–xv.

[37] Bihr writes: "in the symbolic dereliction of the contemporary world" that was adumbrated by the radical Right, these groups "found the amplified echo, raised to the level of a historical, even ontological drama, of the loss of their former positions in the social and political spheres." *Spectre*, 143.

[38] The term is derived from Léon Poliakov: cf. *La causalité diabolique. Essai sur l'origine des persécutions* (Paris: Calmann Lévy, 1980).

[39] "*L'Action Française* of 6 July, 1912," in Girardet, *Nationalisme français*, 209–10.

ethnic or racial makeup, remained irreducibly alien to French values and traditions. These were portrayed as having advanced the economic, social, and cultural decline of the nation for their own economic and political advantage and to facilitate their domination and exploitation of it.

Until well into the postwar period, this function of diabolical causality was principally ascribed to the Jew, though other elements such as Freemasons and Protestants were also seen by theorists of the radical Right as facilitating national decadence.[40] More recently, however, the discrediting of anti-Semitism in the wake of the Holocaust and the dissolution of the French empire, which brought large numbers of migrants from former colonies to the *métropole*, saw the stock figure of the Jew replaced by that of the immigrant – particularly of North African origin – as the primary agent of diabolical causality in the discourse of the radical Right. The immigrant, held to be supported by occult cosmopolitan forces, was cast in identical terms to the way the Jew had traditionally been as the purveyor of national decadence.[41]

Proof of the irreducibly alien character of these groups was to be ascertained for the radical Right in the modern economic and political ideas and institutions that they were held to have introduced in the country. Going back to 1789, they were identified as revolutionary agents who fomented the social dislocation and moral dissolution of the country. Accordingly, from the end of the nineteenth century up through the interwar period and into the 1950s, Jews in particular were blamed for spreading foreign collectivist ideologies that

---

[40] The following passage attributable to Urbain Gohier, a disciple of the notorious anti-Semitic propagandist Édouard Drumont, is illustrative: "Despite their being dispersed across the surface of the earth, the twelve million Jews constitute the most homogeneous and resolutely nationalistic of all the nations. Their dispersion does not prevent them, in the modern world, from asserting a narrow community of interests, an extraordinary discipline directed towards the purpose of universal conquest and domination." Quoted in Chebel d'Appollonia, *L'extrême droite en France*, 81. On the anti-French designs imputed by radical right-wing thinkers to Protestants and Freemasons, see, for example, Barrès, "Scènes et doctrines du nationalisme"; Maurras, "Romanticism and Revolution," in *The French Right: From de Maistre to Maurras*, ed. J. S. McClelland (London: Jonathan Cape, 1970), 179–81, 240–7; Nguyen, *Aux origines de l'Action Française*, 858, 909, 929, 943; Chebel d'Appollonia, *L'extrême droite en France*, 73–80, and Cuminal et al., *Le Pen. Les mots*, 70–1.

[41] It is important not to overstate this shift, however. Anti-Semitism has not disappeared from the thematic arsenal of the contemporary radical Right but rather been euphemized, conveyed in its everyday discourse under the guise of code words such as "cosmopolitanism" and "statelessness" (*apatridie*). And, indeed, it continues to fulfill the same dialectical function within the radical Right's discourse, the obscure forces of cosmopolitanism being cast by the FN and others as weakening the country by opening it to Third World immigration under the banner of a multicultural humanitarianism. Cuminal et al., *Le Pen. Les mots*, 73–7, and Herbert Simmons, *The French National Front: The Extremist Challenge to Democracy* (Boulder, CO: Westview Press, 1996), 129, 227. On the parallels between the FN's anti-immigrant discourse and program and the anti-Semitic rhetoric and prescriptions of the interwar radical Right, see Ralph Schor, "L'extrême droite française et les immigrés en temps de crise: Années 1930–Années 1980," *Revue européenne des migrations internationales* 12(2) (1996), 241–60.

threatened to plunge the country into anarchy and civil war.[42] Conversely, as the themes of a plutocratic Judeo-Masonic conspiracy suggest, these alien forces were held by the radical Right to exercise an unhealthy dominion over the levers of economic and political power. Specifically, they were portrayed as controlling international high finance and, through it, as having corrupted the republican political elites charged with governing the country. Through their plutocratic influence, these agents manipulated the republican state for their own economic and political ends, inevitably at the expense of the authentic French people. Thus, they represented an illegitimate and oppressive oligarchy that, in a political system so susceptible to financial influence, effectively controlled the political leadership and agenda of the country. In this sense, the radical Right was able to recast in ethnic terms the revolutionary imagery of the people's struggle against an immoral and exploitative aristocracy.[43]

At a symbolic level, the myth of diabolical causality articulated closely with the dichotomy between the *petits* and the *gros* central to the political imagination of social groups threatened by capitalist modernization.[44] While it cast the *gros* as nefarious and corrupting agents of oligarchy and cosmopolitanism, this dichotomy also underscored the meritorious traits and oppressed condition of the average *petits Français* who were exploited by them. Contrary to the former, to whom negative, often racialized traits were attributed, *le petit* was portrayed within this symbolic economy as a sympathetic and attractive figure.[45] Whereas

[42] Thus, the portrayal of the Bolshevik Revolution as a Jewish conspiracy was a major theme of radical right-wing propaganda throughout the interwar period. More recently, with the decline of the French Communist Party beginning in the late 1970s and the collapse of the Soviet Union a decade later, the motif of Jewish-inspired revolution has given way, with the emergence of the North African immigrant as a new agent of diabolical causality, to the evocation by the radical Right of the threat of the progressive Islamicization of the country under the nefarious influence of "cosmopolitan" multiculturalism.

[43] Accordingly, in the late nineteenth and early twentieth centuries, the radical Right "reworded," as Philip Nord has put it, "the traditional dichotomy of people vs. aristocracy to read people vs. Freemasons, Jews and Protestants." By the end of the twentieth century, these traditional figures of oppression of the "little people" had been replaced by the trope of the Arab immigrant who, encouraged by unspecified but supremely powerful "cosmopolitan" (i.e., Jewish) interests, was seen to have perverted the republican social compact. By appropriating to themselves the largesse of the social welfare state, *les arabes* were seen to defraud the overburdened French taxpayer while depriving the authentic French people of the social benefits to which they alone were legitimately entitled. *Paris Shopkeepers*, 373, and Cuminal et al., *Le Pen. Les mots*, 62–3.

[44] This political myth has assumed a number of forms over the course of modern French history – *les deux cent familles*, *la synarchie*, more recently *les 600 familles*. It has been an integral part of the rhetorical and symbolic arsenal of populist movements from the Boulangistes and the anti-Dreyfusards of the late nineteenth century, through the extraparliamentary leagues of the 1930s and Poujadism in the early fifties, down to the present-day Front National. Cf. in particular Pierre Birnbaum, *Le peuple et les gros* (Paris: Grasset, 1979), and Davies, *The Extreme Right in France*, 150–1.

[45] For example, the negative figure of the cosmopolitan financier is easily overlaid with the negative ethnic or racial traits that were ascribed to the Jew in the symbolic economy of the radical Right. The multiple levels of signification at which the agents of diabolical causality were portrayed by

the *gros* was exploitative, rapacious, and cynical, the *petit* was hardworking, generous, and naive. He was meritorious for both his elemental honesty and the heroic resignation with which he endured his lot in life. And contrary to the rootless cosmopolitan forces that were arrayed against him, he continued to believe in his country and in its future, daring to hope that tomorrow would bring better things. In this sense, the opposition between *les petits* and *les gros* serves as an evocative framework for a populist discourse linking, respectively, the antiliberal, specifically anticapitalist, emphases of the ideology of the radical Right with its closed nationalist content. As such, it explicitly connects the grievances of antimodern social groups with the radical Right's ideology and program.

The figures of the Jew, the Freemason, and the "Arab" immigrant that have been successively cast by the radical Right as agents of diabolical causality are overlaid with a mix of negative associations and images that surmises everything *petits indépendants* and then industrial workers came to despise about the modern world and could identify with their respective declines within it. As part of this dynamic, the radical Right posited racialized antinomies between these stock figures and the average "authentic" Frenchman, which in turn were invested with offsetting moral qualities and character traits.[46] Whereas the real Frenchman was cast as immovably rooted in and loyal to his country, the Jew or immigrant, as a function of his elemental rootlessness, was loyal to nothing or no one. Likewise, whereas the former was portrayed as fundamentally honest and moral, the latter was depicted as irretrievably corrupt and amoral.[47] From this standpoint, the alien agent of decadence provided the symbolic linkage

the radical Right, allowing it to create new symbolic associations while reinforcing existing ones, became a powerful means of conveying its exclusionary political message.

[46] Specifically, the imputation of the spread of decadence to these conspiratorial actors continued to be cast in terms of a strongly organicist or biologized rhetoric within the radical Right's discourse. The medical or hygienic symbology that first appeared as a means of depicting the symptoms of decadence was now employed to evoke its transmission, and the foreign or alien elements on which it was blamed are portrayed as pathogenic agents responsible for the "infection" or "diseased" state of society. These representations constituted the foundational images for what one author has called a "national-racism à *la française*," combining biological or racial determinism with the motif of Jewish conspiracy as the universal key to interpreting modern political history. Taguieff, *La couleur et le sang*, 138.

[47] This figurative reduction of the evils of modernity to certain racial or ethnic groups was further advanced by the representation of the latter in the form of certain highly recognizable stock figures or personalities within French society. For example, during the Belle Époque, the figures of Rothschild and Perreire became ciphers for a Jewish oligarchy responsible for the ruinous advance of economic and social modernization. By the end of the twentieth century, though the Rothschild family remained a trope in its symbolic repertoire, the figurative onus was increasingly placed on the representatives of a new cosmopolitan multiculturalism. Including such figures as the progressive human rights lawyer and one-time Justice Minister Robert Badinter, or the founder of the immigrant defense association SOS-Racisme, Harlem Désir, these were blamed for advancing the "cause" of Third World immigration. Nord, *Paris Shopkeepers*, 297, 378; Cuminal et al., *Le Pen. Les mots*, 73–4, 110–11; and Milza, *Fascisme français*, 426.

subtending the collective imagery by which the radical Right focalized the *ressentiment* of its target audience.[48]

These racialized antinomies inherent in the discourse of the radical Right served to shore up the flagging sense of self-worth and legitimacy of the declining social groups that represented its target audience. As Nonna Mayer observed in her study of Parisian shopkeepers, its symbolic appeal to "racism, anti-Semitism or nationalism ... made it possible for many [*petits indépendants*] to forget the reality of their own failures and to place the responsibility for them squarely on others."[49] For the members of declining groups, these symbolic motifs offered important sources of identification and affirmation in a society in which they felt increasingly superfluous and disoriented. As Alain Bihr put it, they could "find no other way out than in the fetichization of a communitarian, national or social identity" that was offered by the radical Right.[50] In this light, the theoretical significance of the myth of diabolical causality resides in rendering the decline of *petits indépendants* and industrial workers intelligible to them. By underscoring the illegitimacy and unnaturalness of this decline, it assuaged – if only temporarily – the crisis of identity they respectively suffered in modern French society. Thus, it restored to members of these groups a sense of purpose and belonging within it.

Following this deconstruction of the causes and agents of national decline, the third principal theme that structures the discourse of the radical Right is the overcoming of decadence through a campaign of national renovation. Defined in contradistinction to a blighted and baneful modernity, such a campaign aims to re-create a traditional social order identified with an immemorial past. It posits a return to a happy and harmonious golden age that, in stark contrast to the general alienation and anomie characteristic of advanced capitalist society, presents "a privileged bond, constantly present, of collective intimacy and mutual aid."[51] In particular, the radical Right envisioned the return to a closed, autarkic, and self-sustaining society in which the imperative of collective solidarity trumped that of individual liberty.[52] Highlighting the need to eradicate the political and social forms that it equated with an abhorrent modernity, it thus

---

[48] In this sense, the myth of diabolical causality assumed an important cathartic social function. By providing them with a scapegoat on whom all their economic and social troubles could be blamed, it allowed the members of crisis-ridden social groups to exorcise their pent up fears and resentment of a changing world. Alluding to this important social-psychological function of the scapegoat, Emile Durkheim famously wrote: "When society suffers, it feels the need to find someone to whom it can impute its pain, on whom it can avenge itself of its disappointments." Quoted in Girardet, *Mythes*, 54.

[49] "Les classes moyennes," 342.

[50] *Spectre*, 116–17.

[51] Girardet, *Mythes*, 119.

[52] On the rejection by the radical Right of the principle of economic and social openness characteristic of liberal societies, see Pascal Perrineau, "L'extrême droite en Europe: des crispations face à la société ouverte," in *Les croisés de la société fermée*, 1–11.

called for reestablishing traditional values and institutions in order to re-create this happy society of the past.[53]

Predictably, the radical Right's projection of a mythical golden age strongly resonated with antimodern groups who felt less and less at home within modern French society. *Petits indépendants* identified this harmonious social order with a preindustrial society overwhelmingly composed of petty tradesmen and artisans.[54] Conversely, industrial workers identified it with a pre-postindustrial order, when the virtues of working-class unity and solidarity ostensibly reigned supreme. In short, such a vision was bound up in the collective remembrance – or invention – of a past that recalled the prosperity and contentment of these respective losers of economic and social modernity. By casting modern French society as structurally unsustainable and morally indefensible, and positing in its

---

[53] Dissecting this myth of a primordial, organic community synonymous with a lost, paradisiacal state of social unity and harmony, Raoul Girardet has written: "Considered in its mythical configuration ... the organic community knows in principle no divisions and schisms or any conflict of interest, of caste or of generation. It sustains a fundamental equilibrium between the activities of the human group that it unites and the essential order of the world. It guarantees on behalf of its members their defense against foreign threats. But it also preserves each of those who compose it from the dangers of solitude: it keeps them from the disorientation of the senses and the tumult of antisocial passions. It is the very image of wellness, of shelter, of refuge." *Mythes*, 126.

[54] In particular, the hereditary, quasi-organic conception of property that was advanced by the radical Right articulated closely with that evolved by French *petits indépendants*. Following from its organicist model of society, the radical Right viewed property, particularly in a traditional landed sense, as the basis for the social identity and continuity of the individual and his family. It represented the concrete bond rooting the latter within their natural collectivities – their town, region, and ultimately, nation – of origin. Economic property was similarly conceived by *petits indépendants*, who saw their accession to it as the characteristic trait underlying their peculiar social status and differentiating them from wage earners and particularly industrial workers. Thus, given the importance they accorded to private property as a factor of economic and social differentiation, it is not surprising that many *petits indépendants* should have embraced the rationale offered by the radical Right for its defense and espoused the organicist vision of society the latter built around it. In turn, on the basis of this organic conception of property, the radical Right also evolved a limited and benign view of economic wealth that articulated well with the distinction drawn by *petits indépendants* between "legitimate" small or middling property and "illegitimate" large-scale capital. Stipulating that the individual and his family could become rooted within the community only through the acquisition and fructification of economic property – in the form of land or family enterprise – by their own labor, the radical Right saw as morally illegitimate and socially ruinous those more modern forms of wealth that derived from the accumulation of rootless or vagabond (i.e., financial) capital. Such a conception dovetailed with the contrast that was drawn by *petits indépendants* between what they considered to be the legitimate property acquired through the fruits of their personal labor and illegitimate capital amassed by immoral speculative means. Thus, for many *petits indépendants*, the radical Right's organicist conception of property provided a powerful ideological legitimation of small-scale economic property as the structural corollary of the cultural model of *indépendance* that underpinned their social identity and worldview. For a comprehensive account of the sociocultural worldview of French *petits indépendants*, see Chapter 3. On the radical Right's conception of private property as a factor of communal rootedness and the distinction it drew between legitimate and illegitimate property, see Soucy, *Fascism in France*, 248–50; Nguyen, *Aux origines de l'Action Française*, 900–2; and Taguieff, "Un programme 'revolutionnaire'?" 207–11.

stead the return to a sheltered and benign social order, the radical Right spoke to the deep-seated anxieties of these declining social groups. Consequently, as the latter respectively fell into crisis within capitalist society, their members gravitated to it in ever-increasing numbers.

For the radical Right, the key to returning to this harmonious society of the past lay in restoring the natural foundations of the French national community. In effect, this meant replacing the universal, rights-bound conception of citizenship that had been inherited from the Revolution with an organicistic, racialized basis of political appurtenance. It implied supplanting the open conception of nationhood and nationality identified with the former with an essentially closed conception based on rootedness in the land and purity of blood. This projection of a closed social order based on a mythical past provided declining groups a common imaginary space in which they could redefine their collective identity and purpose. Holding out the prospect of their resocialization by offering them, in Bihr's phrase, "the means to be reborn into a great family," the radical Right became a source of emotional and psychological succor for the members of crisis-ridden groups.[55]

Two prerequisites are laid out in the radical Right's discourse for attaining the goal of national renovation. The first is a totalizing campaign of national cleansing or purification: the extirpation of those foreign agents responsible for plunging the nation into decadence by precipitating the decline of traditional authorities and groups. Following from its organicistic conception of French history and society, the radical Right has sought to reestablish the cultural and racial homogeneity of the nation as a means of restoring the order and harmony that characterized the country before its fall into decadence. Accordingly, it has consistently tried to impose an exclusionary definition of national identity, defined either in racial terms or according to similarly exclusive cultural criteria. Such a definition of national identity underlies the restrictions on citizenship and nationalization as well as the draconian anti-immigration measures that have been proposed by successive radical right-wing movements in the aim of purging the nation of the agents of decadence.[56]

[55] *Spectre*, 145. Birgitta Orfali makes a similar point in her psychological study of the adherents of the Front National, when she emphasizes the resocializing function fulfilled by the latter vis-à-vis the "losers" of modern society. "While social deviance had been the lot of its activists prior to joining the party," she writes, "their adhesion endows them with the means to demarginalize themselves: they are henceforth 'happy' and speak of their 'contentment' (*bonheur*) at having found people who think as they do." Thus, she concludes, "by becoming members of the FN, the individual can finally situate himself in the world and acquire a social dimension." *L'adhésion au Front national*, 129–30.

[56] The principal objects of these measures have shifted over time, as the agents of diabolical causality responsible for national decadence evolved in tandem with socioeconomic and demographic trends. From the 1880s through the end of World War II, Jews were cast as the principal alien agents targeted for elimination from French society. From the 1970s on, the exclusionary onus of these policies increasingly focused on Third World immigrants, and particularly those of North African origin. For a comparison of the exclusionary slogans and proposals of the radical Right

This reconstitution of French society based on a closed, exclusionary conception of national appurtenance inevitably shaded over into the radical Right's conceptualization of social and economic policy. Its vision for restoring an ethnically and culturally homogeneous society has been accompanied by a host of proposals to create an autarkic and self-regulating economy and society. These include sweeping trade restrictions in order to protect French producers from foreign competition, as well as various corporatist proposals to regulate domestic economic competition and defuse social conflict.[57] From Barrès and Maurras through Vichy down to the Front National, successive theorists and movements have striven to harmonize class relations in French society by trying to establish intermediary bodies to represent individual productive sectors and institutionalize mechanisms for moderating socioeconomic conflicts. In so doing, they sought to strike the right balance between the imperatives of social justice and of wealth and status differentiation within a largely static, hierarchically defined social order.[58]

At the same time, successive radical right-wing movements have also advocated social programs in the form of "welfare chauvinism." Figures as disparate as Maurras and Doriot, Barrès and Le Pen respectively espoused the concept of national preference *(préférence nationale)* – the delimitation of civic and social rights to only pure or authentic Frenchmen – as the overriding criterion governing the provision of social services and assistance. Aside from denoting

during the interwar period and the 1980s, see Schor, "L'extrême droite française et les immigrés en temps de crise."

[57] On the protectionist proposals of Barrès and Maurras, see Sternhell, *Barrès*, 226–8, and *Droite révolutionnaire*, 70; Soucy, *Fascism in France*, 248–50; Maurras, "*L'Action française* of 6 July, 1912," 211. On the FN's protectionist agenda, see respectively Peter Fysh and Jim Wolfreys, *The Politics of a Racism in France* (London: Macmillan, 1998), 119–20, 125–6; Davies, *National Front*, 24–5; Marcus, *The National Front and French Politics*, 110–11; and Bastow, "Front National Economic Policy."

[58] In practice, these sectorally defined intermediaries were to be organized at a national level into a council or assembly of producers (along the lines of, for example, the Organization and Social Committees created by Vichy, or the *comités professionnels* envisioned by the FN) in order to arrive at major economic decisions regarding production, working conditions, and the distribution of revenues among various subsets of producers. These were then to be approved, as in the case of Vichy, by the national leader or, in the FN's version, by a sectorally elected "assembly of producers." In essence, these corporatist prescriptions envisioned the establishment of a harmonious and hierarchical social order in which competition would be replaced by cooperation and antagonistic class groupings would be supplanted by "natural" sectoral units sharing common economic and social interests. Following from the Social Catholic ideas of Albert de Mun and the Marquis de La Tour du Pin, they could be traced back to a precapitalist model of society in which occupational groups kept their place in the social hierarchy in exchange for a guaranteed economic role within it. For the corporatist prescriptions of Barrès and of Maurras and the Action Française, see Soucy, *Fascism in France*, 245–6; Sternhell, *Barrès*, 303; Nguyen, *Aux origines de l'Action Française*, 932–3; and Weber, *L'Action Française*, 69–70, 205–7. For corporatism at Vichy, see Paxton, *Vichy France*, 216–18. For the FN's corporatist prescriptions, see Bastow, "Front National Economic Policy," 67, 70; Davies, *National Front*, 24; and Christiane Chombeau, "Le Front national tente de réinvestir le monde du travail," *Le Monde*, 3 April, 2007, 13.

the exclusion of undesirable others from the social body, these welfarist policies were designed to serve an equilibrating social function. At a first level, they were meant to reduce the inequalities and defuse the social tensions fostered by the operation of speculative finance capitalism within French society.[59] In turn, such measures were also designed to encourage the rootedness of the lower classes in the national body by facilitating their accession to small-scale economic property. Through the promotion of a policy of *morcellement* that would inculcate among these classes a taste for petty property, the radical Right looked to resolve class conflicts by turning French workers into aspiring *petits indépendants*.[60]

The program of national cleansing outlined by the radical Right, articulated according to the principle of *préférence nationale* and pursued through a policy of social defense combined with the promotion of small-scale economic property,

---

[59] From the earliest, theorists of the radical Right had advocated welfarist policies to lessen the negative effects of economic change on the most vulnerable segments of the French population. For example, the Boulangiste program of 1886 to 1888 contained a host of socialist measures, including nationalizing the mines, railroads, and Banque de France and Crédit Foncier; progressive tax reform; and the authorization of producer cooperatives. However, such socially reformist measures were increasingly married with exclusionary prescriptions. In his 1889 parliamentary election campaign, for example, Barrès proposed that a state-run pension plan for French workers be established that would be funded by taxing foreign workers. To complement this scheme, he also called for emergency legislation to protect French producers against competition from foreigners, advocating the preferential hiring of French workers for state or municipal works projects. By the time of his 1893 reelection campaign, the chauvinistic basis of Barrès's social program had considerably broadened. Claiming that the "influx of foreign workers" endangered "the economic harmony of the nation" and calling for "the introduction of patriotism into the political economy," he advocated heavily taxing employers who hired foreign workers, assessing foreign workers the equivalent of the fine charged French citizens for foregoing their military service, prohibiting the employment of foreign workers for all public or military contracts, and expelling all foreigners who received public assistance. In turn, if we fast-forward a hundred years, we find the same welfare chauvinism at the heart of the FN's social program. Alongside protectionism, progressive social policies predicated on an exclusive conception of national identity undergirded the party's social and economic proposals. For example, in the run-up to the 1997 parliamentary elections, the FN campaigned on the promise to raise the minimum wage to 7,000 francs per month, introduce a state parental wage, strengthen workers' organizations, protect public-sector jobs, preserve state control over nationally vital sectors, and restore full employment by ending free trade and immigration. Sternhell, *Barrès*, 123–4, 191, 251, 255, 256, and Bastow, "Radicalization," 63.

[60] In this sense, in addition to reinforcing the cultural and ethnic homogeneity of French society through its espousal of the principle of *préférence nationale*, the economic and social program of the radical Right also assumed an important order-preserving function. On the one hand, by promoting the diffusion of petty property, it sought to prevent the excessive concentration of wealth that fueled class conflict within capitalist society. On the other hand, by holding out the prospect of property ownership and social advancement to the working classes, it sought to weaken the appeal of socialism among them. In short, the radical Right conceived – much like the Radicals during the Belle Époque – the promotion of independent petty property as a universal answer to the dual evils of plutocracy and revolution, which were held to characterize advanced capitalist society. Correlatively, it regarded – again much as the Radicals before them – the *petits indépendants* and *petits patrons* who incarnated this form of property as natural bulwarks of the social order, which explains why the radical Right has sought to re-create a society based upon these strata since the end of the nineteenth century.

was successively embraced by *petits indépendants* and industrial workers as a solution for arresting their social and economic decline. For *petits indépendants*, such a program was synonymous with the recovery of the social and political consideration they had enjoyed at the outset of the Third Republic, but which progressively eroded with the advance of industrial and commercial rationalization. For industrial workers, it addressed the rapid economic and social demotion that they had suffered during the last quarter of the twentieth century as a function of intensifying global competition and the ensuing transition of the French economy away from manufacturing toward services.

As a corollary to recasting the French state and society according to the principle of *préférence nationale*, the second major condition stipulated by the radical Right for attaining the goal of national renewal was the reaffirmation of political authority. At an institutional level, this presupposed the restoration of a strong and centralized executive power, under either the guise of direct plebiscitarian democracy (Barrès) or the institution of an autocratic or monarchical regime (Maurras).[61] Coextensive with this establishment of a powerful – if not all-powerful – executive was the substantial diminution if not elimination of representative elected bodies, held to be particularly susceptible to the corrupting influence of anti-French special interests. The radical Right viewed the concentration of executive power, usually under the auspices of a charismatic leader, and the curtailing or abolition of parliamentary assemblies as indispensable to the task of national renewal. Similarly, a strong hand was held to be of paramount importance for restoring internal order and discipline within French society. In particular, successive leaders of the radical Right called for a strong executive to repress the social conflicts that inevitably spun out of control under democratic regimes, as well as to stamp out criminality and other expressions of social deviance resulting from the slackening of mores in modern society.

This call for reestablishing a strong political authority morphed into a broader appeal for the restoration of traditional social authorities within French society. Accordingly, successive thinkers of the radical Right sought to reaffirm the traditional principles and structures of authority that obtained within the patriarchal family. Conceiving of the family as the primordial natural community enshrining the principles of hierarchy and authority, they saw its strengthening as an essential vehicle for maintaining order within French society.[62] In the same vein, these thinkers envisioned restoring a prominent role to the (traditionalist or *intégriste*)

---

[61] On the plebiscitarian prescriptions of Barrès, see Sternhell, *Barrès*, ch. 3, and Soucy, *Fascism in France*, 220–6. On Maurras's vision of monarchic authority, see Charles Maurras, "Dictator and King," in McClelland, *French Right*, 227, and "*Le Soleil* of March 2, 1900," in Girardet, *Le nationalisme français*, 202–3. On the FN's adoption of the institutional prescriptions associated with plebiscitarian or direct democracy, see Taguieff, "Programme 'révolutionnaire?'" in Mayer and Perrineau, *Front national*, 221–6.

[62] This conceptualization of the family as the wellspring for a hierarchical and inegalitarian social order, most recently taken up by the FN, is outlined in Maurras's "The Politics of Nature," (preface to *Mes idées politiques* [1937]). McClelland, *French Right*, 280ff., and Milza, *Fascisme français*, 438.

church, viewed as a crucial vehicle of socialization as well as an agent of social and political control.[63]

The radical Right's affirmation of the need to restore the bases of political and social authority within French society was bound to appeal to economically and socially vulnerable constituencies such as the *petits indépendants* of yesteryear and industrial workers of today. Such a restoration heralded a return to a happier "France that was" in which they recognized themselves and with the core values and institutions of which they identified. Given the acute crises of identity that they respectively suffered in modern capitalist society, the authoritarian prescriptions of the radical Right were tailor-made to resonate with these declining groups. By holding out the promise of strong national leadership and restored bases of social authority, the radical Right's authoritarian blueprint would eventually appeal to members of these crisis-ridden constituencies who longed to restore morality to the political-economic arena and order to the social sphere.

This call for strengthening political and social authority is figuratively conveyed through the myth of the providential leader in the image of whom leaders of radical right-wing movements and parties have successively portrayed themselves. Charged with overseeing the task of national *redressement*, this figure is simultaneously cast as an exceptional and representative being to whom the French people should defer and identify. Evincing the qualities of clairvoyance, self-sacrifice, and charisma, he is both prophet and savior, committing himself to identifying the evils that plague the nation and leading the campaign for its renewal. In short, he is cast as the natural head of the authentic French people, the only one capable of grasping their true concerns and of marshaling them in a great effort of collective transcendence. At the same time, the providential leader is also cast as a highly representative figure in whom ordinary Frenchmen can recognize themselves. Capable of speaking directly to the common people in their language, he establishes a more primal and abiding connection with the *petit peuple* than could ever be achieved by any mainstream elitist politician.[64] In this sense, the providential leader is able to achieve "a strange communion whereby," as Raoul Girardet put it, "by ... addressing himself to the masses, the masses in turn come to express themselves in him, through him."[65]

---

[63] On the socially and politically integrating function imputed to Catholicism by radical right-wing thinkers, see Sternhell, *Barrès*, 305–8; Nguyen, *Aux origines de l'Action Française*, 932–44; and Lecœur, *Un néo-populisme à la française*, 224–5.

[64] The most successful leaders of the French radical Right – men such as Boulanger, Doriot, and Le Pen – owed their success to this ability to establish themselves through their oratory as "authentic plebeian tribunes." Through the recourse to forceful and direct rhetoric, frequently interspersed with popular slang, they distinguished themselves in the eyes of the common people from a dissembling and self-serving political class by appearing to speak truthfully to them, as one of them. Likewise, the dramatic, often apocalyptic tone that they employed resonated strongly with the members of economically and culturally afflicted groups who increasingly felt like they were teetering on the brink of a personal and collective catastrophe. Bihr, *Spectre*, 136–42.

[65] *Mythes*, 79. Since its beginnings, the qualities imputed to the providential leader by the radical Right have most often been exemplified by the mythical figure of Joan of Arc. The salvational role that is imputed to her, consisting in reuniting France behind her rightful king and liberating the

From both a cultural and a psychological standpoint, the providential leader symbolizes not only, as the foremost exemplar of an authentic communal identity, the paradigmatic son of the nation but also, as the supreme agent of national stewardship, a father figure for the latter.[66] By relating this figure back to the national community of which they were a part, the members of crisis-ridden groups find in this motif an additional source of identification and affirmation. Thus, it allows them to maintain a sense of collective purpose and belonging even as their social identities are increasingly under threat in modern French society.

The discursive mechanisms outlined here – the symbols, themes, tropes, and rhetorical strategies by which these are conveyed – underscore the proselytizing and propagandistic vocation of the French radical Right. Through these discursive elements, successive radical right-wing movements were able to harness the grievances of declining groups threatened by economic and social change. In this sense, the radical Right has consistently been able to tap into certain key sociopolitical myths embedded in the French collective unconscious. Reflecting the country's political-institutional and sociocultural development as well as the dictates of human psychology, such myths were most easily exploited by it in periods of social and cultural crisis.[67]

country from the yoke of foreign occupation, has been seized upon by successive movements of the radical Right as both a historical precedent and a moral parable highlighting the imperative of national renewal and calling for the expulsion of foreign invaders from the nation's midst. As the French national savior par excellence, Joan enshrines the prophetic and heroic traits ascribed to the charismatic leader by the radical Right. However, she not only symbolizes a kind of leadership personality but also exemplifies the defining traits of the traditional society to be opposed to a baneful modernity as the guiding principles of national restoration. Accordingly, she is often contrasted to the figure of the Jew, the quintessential exemplar of social and political modernity within the symbolic economy of the radical Right. Whereas Joan symbolizes rootedness in the land and France's fundamentally rural character, the Jew personifies rootlessness and urbanity. Similarly, although she embodies the characteristics of spirituality, racial purity, and French national identity, the Jew is portrayed as the agent of materialism, racial inferiority, and anti-French cosmopolitanism. In short, the figure of Joan is deployed by the radical Right both past and present as a metonym for the moral, homogeneous, and traditional France that it seeks to re-create in the face of a corrupt and decadent modernity. On the symbolic use of Joan of Arc by the French radical Right, see Winock, *Nationalism, Anti-Semitism and Fascism in France*, ch. 8; Cuminal et al., *Le Pen. Les mots*, 98–100, and Davies, *National Front*, 112–16.

[66] This figure narrowly corresponds to the patriarchal conception of authority that has been historically evolved by *petits indépendants*. It articulates with the authority structure and value system of the traditional family, which in turn define the moral universe that subtend productive and social relations within the small family firm. In this sense, as Girardet has put it, the myth of the providential leader serves as "a kind of revealing ideological agent . . . the reflection of a system of values or a type of mentality" that historically lent itself to the development of what French political scientists and historians have termed "a Bonapartist political sensibility." Consequently, the general appeal of the myth of the salvational hero within French society could be said to reflect certain specific 'models of authority' that were prevalent among certain socially and culturally distinct segments of it. Underscoring this point, Girardet remarked that, "through a certain style of authority, it is the long process of fashioning social attitudes and behaviors, of certain reflexes of respect and adhesion whose imprint fully reveals itself" to the student of French history and society. *Mythes*, 83, 86.

[67] See in particular the conclusion in ibid.

The ideological, programmatic, and discursive features of the radical Right specified in this chapter represent the conditions of political *supply* that it has historically presented in the political marketplace of ideas and policies. Now, following this analogy, it remains for us to determine the features of political *demand* inherent in French society that account for its recurrent resurgence over the past 125 years. The rest of this study is directed to this task. Specifically, it seeks to uncover the particular susceptibility of *petits indépendants* and industrial workers to crisis within modern French society and to explain why, during such crisis, they so readily identified politically with the radical Right. As was stipulated at the outset, a class-cultural analysis is advanced to this end. In the first place, we examine the cultural systems or worldviews evolved by the members of these groups as a function of their respective economic and social roles within French capitalist society. It is argued that these roles translated into particular values, attitudes, dispositions, and perspectives that, at different stages in the country's development, put them at intractable loggerheads with its course of modernization, thus condemning them to structural and cultural crisis. In turn, we try to determine how the cumulative political experiences of these groups shaped their political-cultural outlooks in such a way as to favorably dispose them to the radical Right. Here, the study of their relationship to the state and to other social classes – and, paradoxically, to one another – is crucial for identifying their cumulative political "memories" that, passed down over time, reinforced the illiberal cultural proclivities that derived from their functional position and role in the French economy and society.

3

The Class-Cultural Roots of the Radical Right

Structures and Expressions of *Indépendance*

A class is aware of its identity as a whole, sublimates itself as such, has its own peculiar life and characteristic "spirit." ... Class members behave toward one another in a fashion characteristically different from their conduct toward members of other classes. They are in closer association with one another; they understand one another better; they work more readily in concert; they close ranks and erect barriers against the outside; they look out into the same segment of the world, with the same eyes, from the same viewpoint, in the same direction.

Joseph Schumpeter, *Imperialism and Social Classes*[1]

Le métier suppose non seulement une certaine technique de production et de rationalité économique, mais tout un ensemble d'attitudes, de perspectives, de sensibilités et de mentalités, liées à la base à la place qu'ils occupent dans le procès de production et à leur interaction sociale commune au sein ou en fonction de celui-ci. ... Le métier a une histoire et des traditions, à la fois objectivées dans des outils, des instruments, des productions, des livres et des institutions incorporées aux individus dont les gestes, les attitudes, le jargon, la mise vestimentaire, les expressions du visage et le mode relationnel sont d'autant mieux reconnaissables que le métier est plus ancien, son histoire plus riche, sa qualification intrinsèque plus haute et son apprentissage plus difficile.

Bernard Zarca, *L'artisanat français: du métier traditionnel au groupe social*[2]

The petit bourgeois and, more recently, working-class bases of support on which the French radical Right has depended confound many of the standard explanations offered by political scientists for its appeal. On the one hand, the support for the radical Right evinced by these socially and economically distinct groups discredits postmaterialist models of politics that downplay class variables in accounting for political outcomes in Western societies.[3] On the other hand, the

---

[1] *Imperialism and Social Classes*, trans. H. Norden (New York: A. M. Kelly, 1951), 107, 110.

[2] *L'artisanat français: du métier traditionnel au groupe social* (Paris: Economica, 1986), 16–17.

[3] Postmaterialist analyses of the French and European radical Right include Kitschelt, *The Radical Right in Western Europe*; Betz, *Radical Right-Wing Populism in Western Europe*; and Ignazi, "The Silent Counter-Revolution: Hypotheses on the Emergence of Extreme Right-Wing Parties in

substantial historical support afforded the radical Right by the petite bourgeoisie and, more recently, industrial workers undercuts strategic electoral explanations that equate voters' support for the latter with a protest against sitting political elites in response to adverse sociostructural conditions such as crime, immigration, and unemployment. From this perspective, casting one's vote for the radical Right is seen as little more than a short-term electoral calculus on the part of voters to gain the attention of and exact concessions from mainstream political leaders, rather than the expression of a genuine commitment or attraction to its message.[4] The ideological and discursive stability the radical Right has displayed for over a century, combined with the consistently plebeian – *petit indépendant* and, more recently, working-class – composition of its following, militate against these ahistorical, predominantly political-institutional readings of its success. Indeed, these continuities suggest that deeper, more elemental cultural factors are at work, namely that people came to support the radical Right on the basis of more primordial, subterranean realms of feeling and cognition, reflecting irrational affective impulses to action, rather than the rational calculus to – as the strategic notion of protest voting implies – maximize their political utility.

From this standpoint, class-cultural factors – in a word, the dispositions, feelings, values, attitudes, and norms that inform people's social and political perceptions and perspectives, along with the social identities in which these are inextricably bound up – present a more promising field of inquiry than standard postmaterialist and political-institutional explanations for understanding the radical Right's perennial appeal in France. I argue that its historical attraction for the traditional lower middle class and, more recently, industrial workers can be traced to the class-cultural systems that underpinned their economic roles and defined their social and political identities within French society. In the case of French *petits indépendants*, role and identity were bound up in the class-cultural model of *indépendance* and the sociopolitical colorations that it assumed as a function of their evolution as a distinct social group or class since the French Revolution.[5] In the case of industrial workers, these were subtended by a strong sense of class consciousness that, in contrast to *petits indépendants*, was defined in contradistinction to the nature and conditions of their work. In the following chapter, I focus on the class-cultural model of *independance* animating French

Europe." For a broader theoretical exposition of the 'postmaterialist' politics thesis, see Inglehart, *Culture Shift in Advanced Industrial Society*.

[4] For a recapitulation of the principal explanations that have surfaced in the political science field in order to account for the emergence of the French and European radical Right over the past two decades, as well as of the attendant critiques of them, see the Introduction.

[5] The French word *indépendance* has a meaning distinct from its English equivalent, possessing a more strongly cultural connotation than the latter and in particular relating the individualistic economic outlook or mind-set that characterizes petty shopkeepers and artisans – the *petits indépendants* – who will be the principal focus of enquiry in the following chapters. Hence, although for the sake of convenience I interchangeably use the labels small independent sector and *petits indépendants* to designate the members of these social groupings, I usually employ the French term *indépendance* to identify the sociocultural system that defines them, as opposed to the English "independence."

shopkeepers and artisans.[6] I plan to argue that this model bred certain ways of thinking and feeling and translated into certain social and economic behaviors that made *petits indépendants* particularly ill-suited to the structures and processes of modern industrial capitalism. Consequently, as the latter advanced in France, these strata increasingly suffered from a crisis of function and identity within French society on which the radical Right was well placed to capitalize.

THE *PETIT INDÉPENDANT* SECTOR FROM 1870 TO THE PRESENT

> Il y a une marge inférieure, plus ou moins épaisse, de l'économie. Appelez-la comme vous voudrez, mais elle existe et elle est faite d'unités indépendantes. Alors ne dites pas trop vite que le capitalisme est l'ensemble social, qu'il enveloppe nos sociétés entières. ... Les grandes firmes industrielles ... ont besoin de plus petites unités qu'elles-mêmes ... pour se décharger de mille besognes plus ou moins médiocres, indispensables à la vie de toute société et dont le capitalisme n'a cure. Fernand Braudel, *Le temps du monde*[7]

> It is a fact that everyone knows that there never has been, nor does there exist at present, a country with exclusively capitalist production, where there are only capitalists and wage earners. Rosa Luxemburg, *The Accumulation of Capital: An Anti-Critique*[8]

Before we lay out the principal elements of the class-cultural model underlying the social and political outlooks of French *petits indépendants*, it is first necessary to spell out what or whom we mean by this term and to give a sense of the historical salience of this category in French society – a salience that, though *petits indépendants* have substantially declined in number since the 1950s and 1960s, continues to this day to distinguish France from most other advanced Western countries. By dint of the cultural system it developed, the petty independent sector represented a substantial reservoir on which successive movements of the radical Right have been able to draw over the past 120 years.

By *petits indépendants* or the petty independent sector, we mean small producers and traders, artisans and petty shopkeepers, who simultaneously own and work their instrument of production.[9] As François Gresle put it,

---

[6] We save our analysis of the model of class consciousness animating French industrial workers for Chapter 8.

[7] *Civilisation matérielle, économie et société. Le temps du monde*, vol. 3 (Paris: Armand Colin, 1979), 546–7.

[8] *The Accumulation of Capital: An Anti-Critique* trans. R. Wichmann (New York: Monthly Review Press, 1972), 64.

[9] In contrast to these largely urban and semiurban independent lower-middle-class elements, petty, land-owning agricultural producers have been excluded from the purview of this study because, owing to a variety of factors associated with their own particular social evolution, they have not constituted an important source of support for the radical Right historically. (This too, however, may be in the process of changing. Whereas in the first round of the 1988 and 1995 presidential elections, only 10% of active and former farmers voted for Le Pen, in the 2002 presidential contest this proportion had jumped by 12 percentage points to 22%. Similarly, the proportion of the vote

"Notwithstanding agricultural producers, *indépendants* can be defined as non-salaried workers registered with the board of commerce, the board of trades, or both at the same time, who exercise on their own account an artisanal or commercial profession, employ a restricted number of paid workers, and personally control the finances and manage the affairs of their businesses."[10] Historically, we find that the shopkeepers and artisans who compose this mass of *petits indépendants* have gone from constituting the principal agents of production and commerce in the middle and even during the latter third of the nineteenth century to representing an ever-declining proportion of total commercial and industrial revenues and workforce by the close of the twentieth century. As in other advanced industrial societies, they have been the victims of the industrial and commercial concentration and rationalization that progressively gained strength with the advance of industrial and postindustrial capitalism in France.

Yet, with the possible exception of Italy, two differences must be borne in mind when comparing the historical experience of French small producers and traders to that of their counterparts in other industrialized countries. In the first place, the process of concentration was much more fitful and drawn out in France than in most other developed countries. Second, even today, shopkeepers and artisans continue to represent a greater proportion of the active workforce and account for a larger percentage of national revenues in France than in other industrialized countries.[11] Hence, the disproportionate political

reaped by Le Pen in the smallest communes of less than two thousand inhabitants rose steadily during the period, from 12% in 1988 to 19% in 2002, suggesting that the FN was making serious inroads in rural areas, despite the historical impermeability of these areas to radical right-wing politics and the absence of the sociostructural conditions – for example, a large immigrant presence, high rates of petty crime – traditionally considered to be strongly correlated with the FN vote. See Mayer, *Ces Français qui votent Le Pen*, 345.

[10] *Indépendants et petits patrons: perennité et transformation d'une classe sociale*, Vol. 1. (Lille: Presses de l'Université de Lille III, 1980), 227. In France, these socioprofessional categories have been given a more or less precise judicial meaning or identity as a function of the separate fiscal obligation – until very recently known as the *patente* (or business licensing fee) – under which artisans and petty shopkeepers fell as a function of the small size of their enterprises. The most precise judicial definition of this fiscal identity applied to qualified artisans who, from 1938 until the late 1970s, ran businesses counting no more than five salaried employees, not withstanding unpaid family help and a specified number of apprentices. Starting in 1977, this was extended to ten salaried workers including the owner, a juridical qualification that still applies today. In the case of the judicial identity of small shopkeepers, the definition is less precise. In her thesis on Parisian shopkeepers, Nonna Mayer has taken up the INSEE definition of the *petit commerçant* as the small shopowner employing no more than two salaried employees. At the same time, as Gresle has noted, integral to the identity of artisans and shopkeepers is the requirement that they be registered with their respective, state-sanctioned professional associations or boards of trade or commerce. On the evolution of the judicial identity of the *artisanat*, see Zarca, *L'artisanat français*, ch. 2. Regarding the functional definition of the *petit commerçant*, see Mayer, "Les classes moyennes," 30–3.

[11] Suzanne Berger and Michael Piore, *Dualism and Discontinuity in Industrial Societies* (Cambridge: Cambridge University Press, 1980), 94–8; Berger, "D'une boutique à l'autre: Changes in the Organization of the Traditional Middle Classes from the Fourth to the Fifth Republics," *Comparative Politics* 10(1) (Oct. 1977), 122–3; and François Caron, *An Economic History of Modern France*, trans. B. Bray (New York: Columbia University Press, 1979), 163–7,

clout they have exercised in the country, and the enduring appeal of their cultural model of *indépendance* in French society.

A general periodization of the development of French *petits indépendants* can be broken down into two broad phases: from the late nineteenth century to the 1950s, and the 1950s to the present. The first of these is characterized by a marked trend of dualism, whereby the processes of industrial and commercial growth coincided with the subsistence and even consolidation of a thriving sector of *petits indépendants*. Conversely, during the second phase, the process of industrial and commercial modernization became progressively decoupled from the preservation of the artisanal and petty commercial sectors, such that the latter entered into an inexorable if gradual decline. However, far from proceeding in a smooth and linear fashion, each of these broad phases of development proceeded fitfully and intermittently. Until fairly recently, intensive bursts of concentration were followed by prolonged periods of inertia or even rediffusion of economic structures.

Considering the eighty-year span stretching from 1870 to 1950, we find that the *petit indépendant* sector expanded significantly during the Belle Époque, followed by a substantial contraction in the decade following World War I, only to surge again in the 1930s and the immediate aftermath of World War II. (See Figure 3.1 below.) The first of these periods, running roughly from 1880 to 1914, represents the heyday of small business in France, the latter continuing, despite the onset of industrial and commercial concentration, to dominate the French economic structure in the decades leading up to World War I. The statistics amply convey the scope of this phenomenon. Adeline daumard has estimated that the number of business licenses or *patentes* issued to French firms rose from 1,353,000 in 1845–6, to an average of 1,753,000 between 1866 and 1869, 2,006,000 in 1890, 2,138,000 in 1900, attaining a mean of 2,359,750 for the years 1910 to 1913.[12] Licensing revenues attaching to the "A" schedule of the *patente* paid by shopkeepers and artisans increased from almost 26 million francs in 1845 to 45.5 million francs between 1869 and 1871, 55 million francs around 1900, to finally settle at between 50 and 52 million francs between 1906 and 1910.[13] This would suggest that, in this period when the country was embarking on its "second" industrial revolution and new forms of commercial

---

278–81, and 293–5. For a national comparison, see D. Savage, *Founders, Heirs and Managers: French Industrial Leadership in Transition*, 53–5. For more contemporary findings that confirm these trends, see Benoît de Lapasse and Hervé Loiseau, "Panorama des petites entreprises industrielles," *INSEE Première*, no. 667 (July 1999), 1–4; Nathalie Blanpain and Dominique Rouault, "Les indépendants et dirigeants dans les années quatre-vingt-dix," in *Données sociales: la société française 2002–2003* (Paris: INSEE, 2002), 427–38; and Bruno Lutinier, "Les petites entreprises du commerce depuis 30 ans. Beaucoup moins d'épiceries, un peu plus de fleuristes," *INSEE Première*, no. 831 (Feb. 2002), 1–4.

[12] Though they also include supplemental commercial licensing fees levied on larger and more diversified retailers and producers, these figures overwhelmingly represent single payers of the *patente*, that is, petty shopkeepers and artisans.

[13] Adeline Daumard, "L'évolution des structures sociales en France à l'époque de l'industriali-sation (1815–1914)," *Revue Historique*, no. 502 (Apr.–June 1972), 326–7n. The same trend

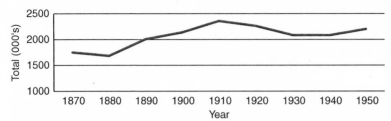

FIGURE 3.1. *Petits Indépendants* from 1870 to 1950. *Sources:* A. Daumard, "L'évolution des structures sociales," 326–7n, and "Puissance," 404; M. Lévy Leboyer, "Le patronat français a-t-il été malthusien?" *Le mouvement social*, no. 88 (1974), 6; Didier and Malinvaud, "La concentration de l'industrie," 7; S. Zdatny, *Politics*, 68, 140, and "The Artisanat in France: An Economic Portrait, 1900–1956," *French Historical Studies* 13(3) (1984), 420–1; and Mayer, "Classes moyennes," 86, 96.

concentration were becoming increasingly prevalent within it, France continued to feature an unusually large number of small producers and traders, which even grew until the years immediately preceding World War I.[14] In short, the country experienced a dualistic pattern of economic development during the Belle

toward a mostly diffuse yet tendentially concentrating economic structure is confirmed if we examine the proportion of *patrons* or employers within the active workforces of the industrial and commercial sectors for this period. Relying on studies from the interwar years, Maurice Lévy-Leboyer has calculated that, in the industrial, transportation, and commercial sectors, employers – the vast majority self-employed artisans or shopkeepers with no paid workers – represented respectively 44% of the total male workforce in 1851, 41% in 1866, 38% in 1881, 29% in 1896, and 31% in 1906. A further analysis of *petits patrons* considered as a proportion of the total workforce occupied in firms of all sectors yielded similar findings. Out of a total workforce of 14,688,000 employed in French firms in 1896, Lévy-Leboyer found that roughly 4,342,900 or 29.6% were workerless *patrons* and self-employed workers. Ten years later, this number had risen to 5,669,500, representing 34.4% of a total workforce of 16,495,000. For his part, Gresle estimates that on the eve of World War I (1911), the total active French workforce still counted two *patrons* for every three salaried workers. Maurice Lévy-Leboyer, "Le patronat français a-t-il été malthusien?" *Le mouvement social*, no. 88 (July–Sept. 1974), 6; Gresle, *Indépendants*, 70.

[14] Given the foregoing, it is perhaps easy to forget that, on the whole, a significant part of the country's industrial and commercial structure underwent consolidation and concentration during this period. A number of indicators clearly show this. For example, a parliamentary enquiry found in 1912 that, on the basis of the number of *patentes* levied within the industrial sector, the number of industrial firms had declined by 0.2% between 1881 and 1905. Simultaneously, *patente* revenues linked to larger-scale industry more than tripled from 7 million francs in 1845 to between 23 and 25 million francs – that is, approximately half the revenues generated by the *patente* on artisans and shopkeepers – between 1906 and 1910. This suggests that industrial production was substantially increasing at the same time that the number of industrial firms was shrinking. Similarly, the *patente* revenues ascribable to *haut commerce* and the banking sector increased by a factor of eight over the period under examination, from approximately 2 million francs in 1845 to between 15 and 17 million francs from 1907 to 1910. Finally, the substantial growth of the industrial workforce during the Belle Époque, coinciding with the stagnation of the firm population, suggests that in some sectors at least, significant concentration was taking place, particularly as a result of the growth of capital-intensive methods of production. Caron

Époque. Following the slump of the 1880s and early 1890s, the rapid expansion that lasted from the second half of the 1890s until 1914 impelled greater industrial and commercial concentration, while simultaneously fueling the growth of small independent producers and tradesmen.[15]

estimates that from 1896 to 1913, the French industrial workforce increased annually by 2%, while Daumard places this increase at 43% from 3,303,000 industrial workers in 1891 to 4,726,000 in 1911. During this same period, capital investment rose significantly: by 3.3% over the period from 1890–4 to 1910–13, 3.7% from 1900–4 to 1910–13, and 5.2% from 1905–9 to 1910–13. Thus, even though, unlike other industrialized countries such as Germany and Great Britain, France remained on the eve of World War I "a country of very small enterprises," this situation coincided with a definite movement toward concentration that would intensify as the twentieth century progressed. A. Daumard, "Puissance et inquiétudes de la société bourgeoise," in *Histoire économique de la France. L'ère industrielle et la société d'aujourd'hui (siècle 1880– 1980). Ambiguïtés des débuts et croissance effective (années 1880–1914)*, vol. 4, part 1, ed. F. Braudel and E. Labrousse (Paris: Presses Universitaires de France, 1979) 404, 457; Daumard, "L'évolution des structures sociales en France," 327n; Caron, *Economic History*, 146; and Gresle, *Indépendants*, 71.

[15] Sector-specific analyses of French industry and commerce during this period bear out these general findings. Both saw a proliferation of small establishments in the run-up to World War I. Considering the industrial sector first, according to T. J. Markovitch and Maurice Lévy-Leboyer, employers constituted 35% of the total industrial workforce in 1886 (versus 38.9% in 1866), a proportion that diminished to 31.7%, that is, 1,350,000 employers out of a total industrial workforce of 4,265,000, by 1896. However, by 1906, this trend toward industrial concentration had substantially reversed itself, as the proportion of employers in the industrial workforce climbed back up again to 36.9%, or 1,760,000 out of a total of 4,770,000, to a level exceeding that attained twenty years earlier. In a similar vein, another study found that more than half (53%) of the French industrial workforce was employed in firms counting less than five employees in 1906, fully 27% of which worked in firms employing no paid workers. This compares to only 25% of the French industrial workforce that was employed in firms counting more than 100 workers, and only 12% in those counting over 500. Lévy-Leboyer, "Le patronat français a-t-il été malthusien?" 6; Caron, *Economic History*, 136; and Michel Didier and Edmond Malinvaud, "La concentration de l'industrie s'est-elle accentuée depuis le début du siècle?" *Économie et statistique*, no. 2 (June 1969), 7.

The evolution of the commercial sector during this period reflects similar trends. If anything, the structure of French commerce remained even more diffuse than that of French industry, despite experiencing, like the latter, certain new forms of concentration, such as the growth of *grands magasins* starting in the 1850s and 1860s, the emergence of consumer cooperatives during the 1880s and 1890s, and the appearance of retail store chains beginning in the first decade of the twentieth century. Basing ourselves upon the figures given by the 1912 parliamentary enquiry on the state of French business, we find that from 1881 to 1905, the number of *patentes* paid on ordinary retailing businesses (i.e., small shopkeepers and commercial *artisans*) rose by 0.4% from 1,353,000 to 1,521,000. Correspondingly, the proportion of primary or ordinary *patentes* represented by small shops increased from 86% of the total number of *patentes* in 1881 to 87.7% in 1905, suggesting a proportional increase in the number of small retailers operating within the French commercial structure as a whole. In turn if we compare, as in the case of industry, the number of employers working in the commercial sector to the commercial workforce as a whole, we find that, out of a total of 1,980,000 people in 1906, 1,079,000 (i.e., 54.5%) were *patrons*, 901,000 (45.5%) were wage-earning employees, of which 495,000 were *isolés*, or self-employed workers in the commercial sector. Finally, assessing the level of sectoral concentration in terms of quantity and size of commercial firms, Mayer estimates that a total of 878,000 commercial establishments existed in France in 1906, 609,000 – 69.3% – of which had no paid

In turn, the interwar and immediate post–World War II periods, running roughly from 1919 to the early 1950s, saw vigorous economic growth and substantial concentration in the decade following the First World War, succeeded by a renewed tendency toward dispersion during the 1930s and 1940s. The decrease in the number of small independent producers and tradesmen during the 1920s followed primarily from the rationalization of French industry during the Great War. However, as increasing numbers of unemployed workers sought refuge in the independent sector during the 1930s and then wartime restrictions on accession to the *petit commerce* and the *artisanat* were lifted at the end of World War II, there followed a new trend of firm dispersion that resulted in an upsurge in the number of *petits indépendants*. As Lucienne Cahen has shown, during the 1920s and 1930s the number of *isolés* and establishments without employees (including agricultural smallholdings) globally dwindled from 4,730,900 in 1921 (compared to the peak of 7,475,000 in 1906) to 4,359,700 in 1926, 4,290,100 in 1931, and 4,258,500 in 1936.[16] However, she estimates that, after initially falling from 67.9 percent in 1921 to 67.2 percent in 1926, the proportion of the smallest firms (i.e., those employing no workers) in the aggregate firm population rose again to 68.5 percent in 1931 and 69.9 percent in 1936. Similarly, after declining from 92.2 percent of the total in 1921 to 90.0 percent a decade later, the proportion of firms counting zero to five salaried workers edged back up to 91.3 percent in 1936.[17] In turn, as wartime restrictions on the establishment of new businesses were lifted, a glut of ex-soldiers, former workers, and the unemployed, encouraged by the postwar inflationary environment, flooded into the independent sector. According to one estimate, 125,000 new independent businesses were constituted in 1945 alone, whereas 300,000 new enterprises were established between 1938 and 1949. Similarly, according to figures published in the *Bulletin officiel de la propriété industrielle*, there were approximately 2 million small independent enterprises in France in 1952, divided roughly evenly between artisans and small shopkeepers. "At the midpoint of the twentieth century," according to Gresle, "France remained a country dominated by a traditional

---

employees (were run by the owner in conjunction with a spouse or associate owner) and 250,000 – 28.5% – of which counted one to five paid employees. Only 19,000 of these establishments – that is, 2.1% of the total – had more than five employees. Daumard, "Puissance," 404, and Mayer, "Les classes moyennes," 86.

[16] Quoted in Zdatny, *Politics*, 66. It must be noted that in her estimates Cahen includes agricultural smallholdings as small enterprises, which invariably tend to overestimate the weight of small enterprises in the French economy. However, the figures she provides remain instructive as an indication of the broader structural trends characterizing the evolution of the economy and, more specifically, of the relative weight of such firms within it.

[17] Conversely, the percentage of firms in the economy drawn from the size bracket that experienced the greatest proportional increase over this period, those counting from 11 to 50 employees, rose from 2.9% of the total in 1921 to 3.5% in 1926, and to 4.1% in 1931, before falling back to 3.5% in 1936. Ibid., 66–7.

and provincial petite bourgeoisie symbolized by the small neighborhood *épicerie* and the small-time peddler scouring the countryside."[18]

[18] *Indépendants*, 92–3. Again, individual analyses of the industrial and commercial sectors confirm this general trend. According to Lévy-Leboyer, there were 1,425,000 employers operating in the industrial sector for 3,945,000 wage-earning employees in 1921 compared to 1,760,000 employers for 3,010,000 wage earners in 1906. Composed in vast majority by *artisans isolés* or the owners of small artisanal enterprises, the proportion of the total industrial workforce represented by self-employed *petits indépendants* fell from 36.9% in 1906 to 26.5% in 1921. These figures largely comport with subsequent studies based on the 1921 and 1926 censuses, which respectively enumerated 466,066 artisanal workshops and 1,199,511 persons involved in artisanal production (including masters, journeymen, and apprentices) in 1921, and identified 995,000 artisanal businesses in 1926, comprising 435,000 licensed firms of which 35,000 had no employees, 400,000 between one and five employees, and 560,000 *artisans isolés*. Though not perfectly comparable because they do not rely on the same exact bases of categorization of the *artisanat*, these studies nevertheless give a rough idea of the concentration that occurred in this period in the industrial sector, marking a roughly 7% drop in the number of registered firms. This dynamic of concentration was cut short by the onset of the Depression, as the number of artisanal firms – and more specifically, of *artisans isolés* – dramatically increased as large numbers of unemployed workers attempted to recast themselves as small independent tradesmen. In 1931 the Chamber of Trade of Alsace estimated that in 1931 there were 1,300,000 artisanal workshops in France, of which 960,000 employed up to one assistant and a further 325,000 from one to ten. Eight years later, Didier-Jean, president of the Chamber of Trade of the Marne, stipulated that there were 1,707,000 *artisans isolés* in the country, 977,536 masters and journeymen working in establishments with one assistant, 735,010 in shops with two to four, 54,513 in workshops with five assistants, and 98,021 in establishments counting from six to ten employees.

This trend toward relative concentration during the 1920s, followed by a period of considerable deconcentration in the 1930s, is particularly underlined if we examine the distribution of the industrial workforce according to firm size during the interwar period. According to one study, the proportion of the industrial workforce represented by self-employed artisans fell from 27% in 1906 to 14% in 1926, and 12% in 1931. However, attesting to the swing back toward deconcentration that was precipitated by the Depression, the percentage of the industrial workforce represented by employee-less firms and artisans *isolés* had shot back up to 17% by the time of the 1936 census, a greater proportion than ten years earlier. Correlatively, after falling from 21% in 1926 to 16% in 1931, the proportion of industrial workers employed in the smallest firms, that is, those counting one to four paid employees, remained the same five years later whereas the proportion represented by firms counting more than ten salaried employees declined from 66% to 61% of the workforce. In turn, this pattern of deconcentration literally exploded in the immediate aftermath of the Second World War. The abrogation of the 1939 decree restricting entry into the trades, combined with the return of prisoners of war and conscripted workers to France, translated into the registration of 210,000 new artisanal enterprises with the Chamber of Trades between 1946 and 1952 (59,000 of these representing changes in activity by existing firms.) Basing itself on the tax rolls of the Chambers of Trades for the immediate postwar period, another study calculated that the number of artisans reached a peak of 1,011,633 in 1948 – as compared to 998,082 the year before – before falling back to 992,379 in 1949, 950,653 in 1950 and then dropping steadily after that.

The commercial sector underwent a similar evolution during the interwar and immediate postwar periods, with the caveat that the initial pattern of concentration was less marked during the 1920s, while the reciprocal movement of deconcentration experienced during the 1930s and the second half of the 1940s was even more pronounced than in industry. The pattern of piecemeal concentration that had characterized French commerce endured in the interwar period, with an increase in the number of chain stores – *magasins à succursales* – in the 1920s and the development of discount or "five-cent stores" – *magasins à prix uniques* – during the 1930s. As a function of this movement

In short, the French industrial and commercial sectors were characterized by considerable firm diffusion from 1870 to 1950. For the duration of this period, *petits indépendants* accounted for a sizable proportion – more than half in the case of commerce – of the country's industrial and commercial workforces. As

toward commercial concentration, the proportion of the commercial workforce employed in establishments of one to five employees fell from 81% in 1906 to 65% in 1931, whereas those working for establishments counting more than ten employees increased from 13% of the total in 1906 to 28% in 1931. In absolute numerical terms, out of a total commercial workforce of 2,116,000 in 1921, 1,020,000 (48.2%) were salaried employees, and 1,096,000 (51.2%) were employers, of which 483,000 were *isolés* (i.e., *patrons* without employees). In 1926, these proportions had roughly reversed themselves, with the number of salaried employees – 1,144,000 or 50.4% of a total commercial workforce of 2,270,000 – exceeding that of *patrons* – 1,126,000 (including 518,000 *isolés*) or 49.6% of the total – for the first time. This marked nearly a 9% proportional fall in the share of the commercial workforce represented by *petits patrons* as compared to 1906. The same tendency is borne out if one considers the changing distribution of commercial firms in terms of size over this period. Although from 1906 to 1931 the proportion of the smallest commercial establishments – that is, those with zero employees – increased by 0.7% from 69.3% of the total in 1906 to 70.0% in 1931, that of the largest commercial firms – that is, those counting over five employees – rose by a comparatively greater margin, from 2.1% of the total in 1906 to 3.4% in 1931.

Finally, as in the case of the industrial sector, the Depression and the immediate postwar period saw a significant upsurge in the number of the smallest firms operating within the commercial sector. By 1931 the number of *patrons* had once again come to exceed – though barely – that of salaried employees, the former numbering 1,257,000, or 50.2% of a total commercial workforce of 2,506,000, versus 1,249,000 for the latter. By 1936, this reversal had been strongly reinforced, with the number of employers having increased to 1,319,000 or 51.4% of a total commercial workforce of 2,564,000, while the number of paid commercial employees fell under the previous census level for the first time, to 1,246,000. Of particular note was the rise during this period of the number of self-employed shopkeepers relying exclusively on themselves and their families to run their businesses. After stagnating at 22.8% of the commercial workforce from 1921 to 1926 and falling to 20.6% in 1931, by 1936 the proportion of *isolés* had nearly risen back up to 1926 levels, accounting for 22.4% of the commercial workforce. Similarly, after stagnating at 70% of the aggregate commercial firm population between 1926 and 1931, the proportion of the smallest retailers – those having no paid employees – increased to 70.9% of the total in 1936. Conversely, the proportion of commercial establishments counting more than five salaried employees fell from the peak of 3.4% attained in 1931 to 3.0% of the total in 1936. As in the case of the *artisanat*, the prospect of economic improvement held out by small-scale, independent retailing attracted large numbers of unemployed. As several authors have pointed out, the small amount of financial and cultural capital necessary to start up a small *épicerie*, requiring little by way of initial investment and qualification, made petty commerce an attractive refuge for those worst hit by the Depression. In turn, the number of small shopkeepers dramatically increased in the immediate aftermath of the Second World War. According to one estimate, 350,000 more commercial enterprises were in operation in 1947 compared to 1938. Taking as a base of 100 the number of retailers existing in France in 1928, the study found that the aggregate size of the commercial sector had reached an index of 150 by 1946. By 1954, the commercial firm population had reached approximately 1,006,500 establishments, counting 715,900 retail stores and 290,500 cafés, hotels, and restaurants. Mayer offers an even higher estimate, putting the number of commercial establishments at 1,252,000 in 1954, an increase of approximately 21% from 1936, 37% from 1926, and 43% from 1906. On these trends for the artisanal sector, see Lévy-Leboyer, "Le patronat français a-t-il été malthusien?" 6; Zdatny, *Politics*, 68, 140, 207, 212, and "The Artisanat in France," 420–1; Didier and Malinvaud, "La concentration de l'industrie s'est-elle accentuée depuis le début du siècle?" 7; and Gresle, *Indépendants*, 93. On these trends for the commercial sector, see respectively F. Caron and J. Bouvier, "Structure des

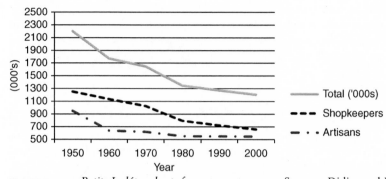

FIGURE 3.2. *Petits Indépendants* from 1950 to 2000. *Sources:* Didier and Malinvaud, "La concentration de l'industrie," 7; Zdatny, *Politics*, 140; Mayer, "Classes moyennes," 96, 100, and *La boutique contre la gauche* (Paris: Presses de la FNSP, 1986), 28; Gresle, *Indépendants*, 93; Jaeger, *Artisanat*, 104; Zohor Djider, "Les categories socioprofession-nelles: Étude des milieux sociaux," in *Données Sociales* 1990 (Paris: INSEE, 1990), 31; Michel Louis Lévy, "Population active et catégories sociales au recensement de 1990," *Population et Sociétés*, no. 270 (July–Aug. 1992), 3; Thomas Amossé, "Recensement de la population de 1999: L'espace des métiers de 1990 à 1999," *INSEE Première*, no. 790 (July 2001), 2; and Blanpain and Rouault, "Les indépendants et dirigeants dans les années quatre-vingt-dix," 428.

such, they continued to constitute a significant economic and social force in France well after World War II, thereby representing a nonnegligible factor in the country's postwar political development.

In similar fashion, the second principal period in the economic and social evolution of the *petit indépendant* sector, running from the 1950s to the present, also followed a fitful course. On the one hand, it was marked by the resumption of rapid industrial and commercial concentration, particularly under the strategy of state-led economic planning pursued by the country from the late 1940s through the 1960s. On the other hand, though the number of shopkeepers and artisans significantly diminished during this period, they nevertheless continued to repre-sent a sizable component of the French productive and commercial structures, particularly in comparison to other industrialized countries (Figure 3.2).

Seeing the most intensive spurt of economic modernization and firm concen-tration experienced by the country since the nineteenth century, the initial postwar decades presided over *petits indépendants'* most significant and rapid decline to date. In the industrial sector, the number of artisanal firms registered with the Chamber of Trades fell from a total of 883,000 enterprises in 1954 to

firmes, emprise de l'État," in *Histoire économique et sociale de la France. L'ère industrielle et la société d'aujourd'hui (siècle 1880–1980). Le temps des guerres mondiales et de la grande crise (1914–vers 1950)*, vol. 4, part 2, ed. F. Braudel and E. Labrousse (Paris: Presses Universitaires de France, 1980), 777, 778; Mayer, "Classes moyennes," 86, 96, 100; J. Gaillard, "La petite entreprise en France au XIXe et au XXe siècle," in *Petite entreprise et croissance industrielle dans le monde au XIXe et XXe siècles*, vol. 1, ed. M. Fauvel-Diouf (Paris: Eds. du CNRS, 1981), 138–9; and Gresle, *Indépendants*, 77–8.

765,000 in 1966 and 749,899 in 1974, an overall decline of 15.1 percent.[19] Another study concluded that between 1954 and 1975, the number of artisanal firms excluding the commercial and service *artisanat* (e.g., bakers, butchers, and café, restaurant, and hotel owners) had fallen from 757,000 in 1954 to 638,000 in 1962, 620,000 in 1968, and 533,000 in 1975, a roughly 30 percent decline.[20] Correspondingly, the median French enterprise grew in size during the 1960s and 1970s, the proportion of the total workforce employed in firms counting less than ten employees falling from 25 percent in 1954 (compared to 39 percent in 1936) to 21 percent in 1962 and 20 percent in 1966. Among juridically defined artisanal firms – that is, those counting from zero to four employees, excluding the firm owner – this proportion decreased from 19 percent in 1954 (versus 33 percent in 1936) to 16 percent in 1962 and 14 percent in 1966. In turn, within these smallest firms, the proportion of self-employed artisans accounted for 6 percent of the industrial workforce in 1954 and 4 percent twelve years later, compared to 17 percent in 1936.[21]

By contrast, because it had progressed far less than in industry up to that point, the dynamic of concentration was even more pronounced in commerce during the 1950s and 1960's.[22] The general rise in living standards and consequent emergence of a mass market, combined with the growing capacity to mass-produce consumer goods, created the conditions for much more concentrated forms of commerce under the guise of supermarkets and *hypermarchés*.[23] Such

---

[19] We note that this decline was more rapid for the first period from 1954 to 1966, during which the number of firms fell by 13.4%, than between 1966 and 1974, when it declined by only 2%. Gresle, *Indépendants*, 143, and Christine Jaeger, *Artisanat et capitalisme: l'envers de la roue de l'histoire* (Paris: Payot, 1982), 104.

[20] Mayer, "Classes moyennes," 96.

[21] Although this process of industrial concentration substantially reduced the number of artisanal firms in operation and led to a significant reduction in the proportion of the industrial workforce employed in them, one must not overstate the decline of the *artisanat*. Even though the smallest artisanal firms continued to decline throughout the 1960s, those in the second smallest tier of industrial enterprises, comprising six to nine workers, actually saw their numbers rise during this period. In 1970 artisanal enterprises numbering zero to five employees still represented 82.7% of the total of French industrial firms and those with zero to nine employees, 88.3%. A year later, it was estimated that the proportion of enterprises with fewer than ten employees constituted 87.1% of the total of industrial firms (excluding construction), with fully 40.8% counting zero employees, 30% one to two employees, 11% three to five, and 5.3% six to nine. This suggests that, although many artisans went out of business during the 1950s and 1960s, a great many others managed to reconvert themselves into new areas in which they were able to work in concert with large-scale industry. Correspondingly, certain branches of activity, such as repair services, food, and beauty and care services remained almost exclusively the preserve of artisans. Didier and Malinvaud, "La concentration de l'industrie s'est-elle accentuée depuis le début du siècle?" 7; Berger and Piore, *Dualism and Discontinuity*, 95, 97; Gresle, *Indépendants*, 141; Jaeger, *Artisanat et capitalisme*, 102–3.

[22] On the differential rate of concentration in the commercial and industrial structures, see Gresle, *Indépendants*, 159.

[23] Supermarkets designate commercial spaces comprising an area of between 400 and 2,500 square meters, and *hypermarchés*, those having an area greater than 2,500 square meters. The first supermarket opened in France in 1957, the first *hypermarché* in 1963. This process of large-scale

commercial concentration led to a substantial reduction in the size of the traditional *petit commerce*, the number of shopkeepers falling from 1,252,000 in 1954 to 1,134,000 in 1962, 1,026,000 in 1968, and 913,000 in 1975, a total decrease of 27.1 percent.[24] As in the case of the *artisanat*, the effects of concentration were also seen in the shifting composition of the commercial workforce and, specifically, the falling proportion of nonsalaried workers – primarily family aides – within it. The latter went from representing nearly one-half of commercial workers in 1954 to little more than a quarter in 1975.[25]

The small independent sector continued to shrink from the mid-1970s through the 1980s and 1990s, albeit at an attenuated rate owing to the slowdown in industrial and commercial concentration.[26] After benefiting during the

commercial concentration gained particular momentum during the 1960s. From 1966 to 1974, the number of *hypermarchés* increased from 5 to 292, while that of supermarkets jumped from 1,441 to 2,719. Over roughly the same period, the total surface area accounted for by supermarkets and *hypermarchés* rose from 830,000 square meters in 1968 to 3,087,000 square meters in 1972. By the early 1970s, these mass-scale forms of retail broadly extended to nonfood sectors, including home appliances, home improvement, and gardening goods, in effect coming to dominate the commercial structure in its totality. If we examine the respective market shares attaching to the different retailing categories, we find that, in the food sector, the propagation of total sales accounted for by small shopkeepers fell progressively from 89.3% in 1950 to 79.8% in 1960, 64.2% in 1970, and 58.7% in 1972. Conversely, the proportion of food sales imputable to the *grand commerce* (i.e., supermarkets and *hypermarchés*) increased from 10.7% in 1950 to 14.4% in 1960, 27.7% in 1970, and 32.5% in 1972. In the nonfood sector, a similar picture emerges. The market share accounted for by the *petit commerce* progressively declined from 88.4% of sales in 1950 to 82.1% in 1960, 70.1% in 1970, and 69.5% in 1972, while that imputable to the *grand commerce* rose from 11.6% of nonfood sales in 1950, to 15.9% in 1960, 26.7% in 1970, and 25.9% in 1972. Finally, it has been estimated that the proportion of total commercial revenues accounted for by *petits commerçants* fell from 89% in 1950 to 65% in 1972, while that accounted for by mass retailers rose from 11% to 29% over the same period. F. Caron and J. Bouvier, "Les agents: les entreprises," in *Histoire économique et sociale de la France. L'ère industrielle et la société d'aujourd'hui (siècle 1880–1980). Années 1950 à nos jours*, vol. 4, part 3, ed. F. Braudel and E. Labrousse (Paris: Presses Universitaires de France, 1982), 1156, and Gresle, *Indépendants*, 149–50, 152, 467.

[24] Mayer, "Classes moyennes," 96. This general decline in the size of the petty independent commercial sector masks substantial internal variation in the negative impact of the process of commercial concentration. Indeed, the brunt of the effects of concentration fell upon petty retailers in the food sector, the latter experiencing a decline of 17.7% and falling from a total of 316,000 enterprises in 1960 to 260,000 in 1975. Conversely, small shopkeepers in the nonfood sector fared much better, seeing their numbers actually increase by 15.3% during the same time period from 270,500 in 1960 to 311,800 in 1975. Correspondingly, food retailers went from representing a majority (53.9% in 1960) to a minority (45.5% in 1975) of commercial establishments with respect to nonfood retailers over this time period, attesting to the unequal effects of the emergence of mass retailing structures on the commercial sector considered as a whole. Ibid., 94.

[25] Once again, the area that suffered the greatest losses of nonsalaried employees was the general food retail sector, which saw its proportion of nonsalaried workers fall by 43.9% from 1960 to 1975 versus a decline of 17.4% for all retail trades combined. This precipitous drop was attributable to the closure en masse of *épiceries* because of increased competition from supermarkets and *hypermarchés* during this period. Ibid., 95, 90.

[26] This period coincided with a relative trend toward deconcentration that reflected a shift away from the imperative of consolidation and "bigness" that characterized state planning and which placed a renewed emphasis on smaller firms as agents of flexibility in an age of increasing

late 1970s and early 1980s from a temporary lull in economic concentration (or even, in some cases, a resumption in deconcentration), the number of shop-keepers and artisans began to drop off again from the late eighties on. In the artisanal sector, the pattern of decline slowed considerably during the 1970s, even experiencing a fillip in the second half of the decade into the early 1980s before resuming an extremely gradual rate of decline. If we tabulate the number of artisans (including family aides) on the basis of the INSEE Population Surveys for this period, we find that their number increased from 865,000 in 1975 to 904,000 in 1982 – a rise of approximately 4.5 percent – before gradually decreasing to a total of 853,000 in 1990 – a decline of nearly 6 percent – and 691,000 in 1999 – a drop of 19 percent from 1990 and 23 percent from 1982.[27]

economic uncertainty and competition. Within all commercial and industrial sectors combined, the proportion of the total workforce employed in the smallest firms – that is, those counting less than ten employees – rose from 18.4% in 1975 to 23.2% in 1985, to a peak of 26.1% in 1996, before falling back to 25.9% in 1998. Conversely, from 1975 to 1996, the proportion of the total workforce employed in the largest enterprises fell, all sectors included, from 14.1% to 11.5% for firms employing 200 to 499 workers, and from 20.7% to 10.8% for those employing 500 workers or more. This relative deconcentration coincided with the campaign initiated by the French state under the Seventh Plan (1975–81) to move away from the policy of national champions that had created enormous but inefficient plants during the 1960s and early 1970s toward a policy of decentralization as a means to enhance the competitiveness of French firms. However, a more finely tuned analysis reveals that the trend toward concentration has continued unabated among the smallest enterprises. Thus, the mean number of workers employed by firms counting one to ten employees increased from 3.6 in 1985 to 5.0 in 1997, reflecting the continuing erosion of the tiniest artisan and commercial firms. *Annuaire retrospectif de la France. Séries longues. 1948–1988* (Paris: INSEE, 1990), 61; *Annuaire retrospectif de la France 2000* (Paris: INSEE, 2000), 133; Karim Moussallam, "Le poids des grandes entreprises dans l'emploi: Baisse dans l'industrie, augmentation dans les services et le commerce," *INSEE Première*, no. 683 (Nov. 1999), 3; Malinvaud and Didier, "La concentration de l'industrie s'est-elle accentuée depuis le début du siècle?" 7; and S. Berger, *Dualism*, 97.

[27] An alternative tabulation, based on the INSEE Employment Surveys that began in 1982, renders a similar overall picture, if slightly different figures. According to studies based on these surveys, the number of artisans (including family aides) fell from 915,000 in 1982 to 842,000 in 1989, a decline of 8% during the 1980s. This tendency became more pronounced throughout the 1990s, the total number of artisans falling to approximately 803,000 in 1993, 782,000 in 1996 and 726,000 in 1999, before settling at 687,000 in 2001, marking a total drop of approximately 18% from 1989 and 25% from 1982. A similar trend is borne out if we examine the evolution of the quantity of artisanal firms in operation since the 1970s, rather than simply the number of persons categorized as artisans, which includes familial helpers, *isolés*, and self-employed work-ers. Basing itself on a restrictive definition of the *artisanat* that equates the quantity of firms exclusively with the number of *patrons* working within the artisanal trades and excluding from the purview of the latter the commercial – primarily food-preparation-based – *artisanat*, a study of the independent sector conducted during the 1980s and 1990s found that, starting at a peak level of 584,000 in 1983, the number of artisanal enterprises progressively fell back to 572,000 in 1988, 551,000 in 1993, and finally 547,000 in 1998. These figures comport with those provided by Mayer, who posited that after falling to a low point of 533,000 in 1975 (compared to 620,000 in 1968), the number of *patrons artisans*–and, hence, artisanal firms – had risen in the course of the latter half of the 1970s to 573,000 in 1982. Thus, if we jointly consider these data, from 1975 to 1983 the number of artisanal firms increased by roughly 10%, confirming the initial fillip experienced by the sector during the second half of the 1970s and early 1980s,

The shopkeeper sector essentially replicated this pattern of development during the last quarter of the twentieth century. The erosion of the *petit commerce* since the 1960s ground to a halt in the mid-seventies, the sector essentially stabilizing during the 1980s before resuming a much slower rate of decline in the 1990s. According to the INSEE Population Surveys, there were 792,000 *petits commerçants* (including family aides) in 1975, a number that rose slightly throughout the 1980s to 797,000 in 1982 and 799,000 in 1990, before falling again in the 1990s to 664,000 in 1999, a drop of 17 percent since 1990 and of 16 percent since 1975.[28]

In short, following their consolidation during the late seventies and early eighties, the artisanal and shopkeeping sectors resumed their pattern of decline in the late 1980s and throughout the 1990s.[29] However, despite this decline, the *artisanat* and *petit commerce* continue to occupy a significant niche in the French industrial and commercial structure.[30] From an economic and social standpoint,

before starting to undergo a period of gradual decline (–6% over the period studied) from the mid-1980s through the 1990s. Djider, "Les catégories socioprofessionnelles," 31; Lévy, "Population active et catégories sociales," 3; Amossé, "Recensement de la population de 1999," *INSEE Première*, no. 790 (July 2001), 2; Blanpain and Rouault, "Les indépendants et dirigeants dans les années quatre-vingt-dix," 428; Marc-Antoine Estrade and Nathalie Missègue, "Se mettre à son compte et rester indépendant: des logiques différentes pour les artisans et les indépendants des services," *Economie et Statistique*, nos. 337–8 (July–Aug. 2000), 160.; and Mayer, "Les Classes moyennes," 96, and *La boutique*, 28.

[28] Levy, "Population active et catégories sociales au recensement de 1990," 3; Amossé, "L'espace des métiers," 2; and Djider, "Les categories socioprofessionnelles," 31. If we base ourselves on the INSEE Employment Surveys, we find that the number of *commerçants* rose slightly from 772,000 in 1982 to 774,000 in 1989, before falling to 721,000 in 1993, 699,000 in 1996, and 652,000 in 1999, and settling at 621,000 in 2001, an overall decline of 20% since the 1980s. Blanpain and Rouault, "Les indépandants et dirigeants dans les années quatre-vingt-dix," 428.

[29] Predictably, this decline is unevenly distributed across occupations. Within the artisanal sector, those hardest hit have been the *artisans de fabrication* – tailors, printers, and carpenters – as well as cobblers and locksmiths. Conversely, some sectors, such as food preparation and processing, and building and construction as a whole, have been relatively spared by the contraction that has impacted the sectors as a whole since the 1980s, some, such as hairdressers and manicurists, even seeing their aggregate number rise since the early eighties. The same holds true for the shopkeeper sector. *Petits commerces* hardest hit by commercial concentration during the 1980s and 1990s include home improvement stores (–69%), *épiceries* (–49%), clothing retailers (–42%), and butcher shops (–39%). Conversely, the smallest commercial outlets in certain sectors have managed to sustain themselves, including bakeries and pastry shops, bookstores, and news vendors. Finally, some petty commercial fields have even managed to thrive in the midst of this general movement toward concentration. These include florists, pharmacies, and goods and services in the hygienic, cultural, and leisure fields. Amossé and Olivier Chardon, "La carte des professions (1982–1999): le marché du travail par le menu," in *Données sociale: la société française 2002–2003*, 223; Lutinier, "Les petites entreprises du commerce depuis 30 ans," 2–3; and Mayer, "Classes moyennes," 93–4. On the variable fortunes of the *artisanat* during this period, see notably Amossé, "L'espace des métiers," 1–2, and Amossé and Chardon, "La carte des professions (1982–1999)," 222–3.

[30] In 1998, petty commercial enterprises – defined as employing at most two paid employees – continued to account for 74% of the total number of enterprises, 24% of the total employment, and 13% of the total revenues within the commercial sector. Similarly, artisanal enterprises – that is, those counting five paid employees or less – represented fully 67% of the total number of

they remain a key constituency within the French body politic. In this sense, it is important not to underestimate the enduring economic and social salience of the petty independent sector within French society. Even today, if one were to count the number of workers employed in artisanal enterprises – 78 percent of whom continue to employ five or less people – in addition to *petits patrons* and family aides, one would arrive at a total workforce of 3,523,000, or 14.2 percent of the total French workforce.[31] These figures are roughly the same as estimates of the proportional size of the artisanal workforce that were advanced by Jaeger for 1978 (14 percent) and Zarca for 1973 (13.8 percent).[32]

The substantial proportion of the workforce and of revenues for which they account underscores the crucial position that *petits indépendants* continue to occupy in the French economy. Therefore, rather than conceiving of the dualistic structure of the latter as a desultory byproduct of the country's pattern of economic development since the end of the nineteenth century, it is more apposite to view it as a simultaneously complementary and integral feature of that development. As Christine Jaeger put it, French "capitalism evolved while creating around it zones that escaped it," shopkeepers and artisans constituting in effect "a non-capitalist world on the fringes of capitalism."[33]

In turn, the survival of a significant petty independent sector also testifies to the continuing appeal of the socioeconomic relations and cultural attributes that characterize French *petits indépendants*. For a long time, this appeal could be seen in the high rate of reproduction of petty shopkeepers and artisans among themselves.[34] Similarly, the status of *petit indépendant* has long been sought after by members of other social groups as a pathway to social mobility.

enterprises, 6.2% of the total employment, and 2.2% of the total revenues of French industry. (If the firm size is increased to include all enterprises counting under twenty employees, these respective proportions increase to 86% of the industrial firm population, 15% of industrial employment, and 6% of sectoral turnover.) Lutinier, "Les petites entreprises du commerce depuis 30 ans," 1, and Jean-Michel Charpin, "Les petites entreprises industrielles en 2001," *INSEE Résultats. Économie*, no. 10 (Sept. 2003), 11, 15.

[31] INSEE, "Enquête Emploi 2004," available from http://www.insee.fr/fr/ppp/ir/accueil.asp? page=EEC04/synt/synthese.htm, accessed Sept. 2006. This proportion may in fact be an understatement of the true size of the petty independent sector and its attendant workforce, since it does not take into account salaried workers in the small commercial sector.

[32] Jaeger, *Artisanat et capitalisme*, 13, 106, and Zarca, *L'artisanat français*, 1.

[33] Jaeger, *Artisanat et capitalisme*, 285, 6–7. Indeed, some authors have gone so far as to assert that it is precisely the anti- or noncapitalist modes of behavior and forms of production that characterize the petty independent sector that have made it possible for it to survive within an otherwise fast-evolving capitalist system. For example, Jaeger has observed that artisanal enterprises were able to survive economically because of their total or partial renunciation of the profit margins required by ordinary capitalists in order to make good on their investment – hence, their persistence in areas in which the gains on capital were low or virtually nil and those on labor comparatively higher. She writes: "The chief function of enterprises in the petty independent sector consists in undertaking a certain number of activities of no economic value or interest . . . to bigger enterprises, as a function of the peculiar processes of production that characterize them and which make it possible for them to sell their services below the marginal costs of capitalist production." Ibid., 208.

[34] Gresle, *Indépendants*, 260; Gaillard, "La petite entreprise," 141n; and Estrade and Missègue, "Se mettre à son compte et rester indépendant," 172.

This is particularly the case during periods of economic recession and rising unemployment, such as during the 1930s or since the early 1980s, when the *petit indépendant* sector served as a refuge for the economic victims of depression.[35] Accordingly, it is to analyzing these socioeconomic relations and the cultural system that came to characterize French *petits indépendants* that we now turn.

THE ROOTS AND AGENTS OF *INDÉPENDANCE*

À chaque propriété qui se crée, c'est un citoyen qui se forme; car la propriété, dont on nous présente comme les ennemis, la propriété est, à nos yeux, le signe supérieur et préparateur de l'émancipation morale et matérielle de l'individu. Ce n'est pas de la propriété que nous sommes les ennemis, à coup sûr, mais plutôt de sa raréfaction qui diminue heureusement de jour en jour, la propriété passant à des mains nouvelles. Ce que nous demandons, ce qui se fait, ce qui est une loi sociale de la démocratie, c'est que la propriété se divise, c'est qu'elle aille à celui qui l'exploite et qui la féconde de tous ses efforts pour lui faire produire chaque jour davantage, à son avantage personnel, mais aussi au plus grand avantage social. Léon Gambetta, 1 June, 1874[36]

---

[35] For example, during the 1930s, the petty independent sector attracted numerous industrial workers and *employés*. As a function of the low capitalization requirement to start a small shop or establish oneself as an *artisan isolé*, all manner of new businesses, specializing in the most incongruous of occupations, proliferated during this period, contributing even more to the marginal and ephemeral character of the smallest enterprises. Accordingly, at the height of the Depression, the Lyon registry of commerce listed an incongruous assortment of occupations, which read more like temporary expedients for riding out the crisis than as viable, long-term business establishments in their own right: "In the area of maintenance and repair and sale of used goods: repair of portable stoves, of umbrellas, of clogs, of velocipedes, and salesmen of used tires, empty bottles and used crates. In the area of petty retail (often street vending): a seller of brooms of all types, peddlers of collectors' stamps, a salesman of pearl flower and leaf motifs (he's an Italian, born in Murano), pawn brokering of clocks and jewelry. And, in no apparent order: a builder of bird cages, of muzzles for dogs, of specialized brushes for dentures, of new articulated toys, or, still, a fake-wood painter and an accordion tuner." Correspondingly, recent studies for which more precise numerical data are available have shown that growing numbers of artisans and shopkeepers are former blue-collar or clerical workers deriving from working-class or similarly non-*indépendant* backgrounds. For example, 300,000 of the *petits patrons* who set up shop from 1980 to 1985, accounting respectively for 87% of newly established shopkeepers and 89% of new artisans, belonged to the industrial and service-sector workforce in 1980. This compares to more than half (51.2% or 151,000) of *petits patrons* who established their own small businesses from 1965 to 1970 who had been industrial workers in 1965, a ratio that similarly held for the period 1959 to 1964. Mayer, "Classes moyennes," 102–3; "Une filière de mobilité ouvrière: l'accession à la petite entreprise artisanale ou commerciale," *Revue française de sociologie* 22(1) (1977), 28, 33; and "L'atelier et la boutique: deux filières de mobilité sociale," in *Le modèle républicain*, ed. S. Berstein and O. Rudelle (Paris: PUF, 1992), 271, 273.

[36] Quoted in *Les fondateurs de la Troisième république*, ed. P. Barral (Paris: Armand Colin, 1968), 232.

N'es tu pas l'avenir de tous les souvenirs qui sont en toi? L'avenir d'un passé?
Paul Valéry[37]

The survival of a large traditional lower middle class composed of petty producers and shopkeepers reflects the distinctive pattern of economic and social modernization that was followed by France from the middle of the nineteenth century on.[38] As we saw, this pattern was characterized by periods of intense industrial concentration interspersed with spells of relative stasis, or even deconcentration, of industry and commerce – a dynamic resulting in a persistent diffuseness of the French firm structure relative to other industrial countries. Two orders of causes account for this persistence of firm diffusion in France. The first are largely structural causes, including the nature of French consumer and labor markets, the character of the economic institutions that evolved in the country, and the impact of particular policies that, by forestalling the process of economic concentration, prolonged the survival of a disproportionately large *petit indépendant* sector in France. In the second place, cultural factors tied to the social consequences of French economic development account for this longstanding economic dualism. By preserving significant sociological reservoirs by which the cultural model of *indépendance* was transmitted and preserved, these factors indirectly sustained the *petit indépendant* sector while facilitating the diffusion of its cultural system within the broader French society.

[37] Quoted in Claude Thélot, *Tel père, tel fils? Position sociale et origine familiale* (Paris: Dunod, 1982), xiii.
[38] The historical reproduction of this sociocultural model among *petits indépendants* is readily explained by standard theories of socialization, applied to two principal settings or "loci" of social interaction. The first, and most obvious, is the family. The synergy between the structure and workings of the petty independent enterprise and those of the family render the latter a powerful vehicle for transmitting the values and affinities characteristic of *petits indépendants*. In this regard, it should come as no surprise that a much higher proportion of this group has been historically constituted of heirs compared to other socioprofessional categories – that is, the sons and daughters of petty independent producers or tradesmen who, either in taking up the reins of the family enterprise or in creating their own new businesses, sought to realize for themselves the ideal of *indépendance* that had been passed on to them by their parents.
In the second place, the model of *indépendance* is also replicated through socialization processes intervening within the workplace. As a result of the social relations that evolve between them through their shared participation in a common work process, workers – both salaried and unpaid – employed in petty independent establishments "come to share," in the words of Bechhofer and Elliott, "many of the predilections and values of their employers." Consequently, it should come as no surprise that the ideal of *indépendance* is most strongly grounded among workers in petty independent enterprises, particularly those employed in artisanal firms. This transmission of the ideal of *indépendance* is particularly pronounced among artisans as a result of the institution of apprenticeship, inculcating the cultural values and practical know-how attending a particular trade. Frank Bechhofer and Brian Elliott, "Petty Property: The Survival of a Moral Economy," in *The Petite Bourgeoisie*, ed. F. Bechhofer and B. Elliott (London: Macmillan, 1981), 195, and Zarca, *L'artisanat français*, 184, 208. On the transmission of the values of *indépendance* within the family, see in particular Thélot, *Tel père, tel fils?* 47; Mayer, "Classes moyennes," 205; and Zarca, *L'artisanat français*, 211.

Turning to the first, structural order of causes, the diffuseness of the French firm structure could be ascribed in part to the specific character of French consumer and labor markets and the particular economic institutions that evolved in the country as a result. These can be broken down into factors of demand and of supply. On the demand side, considerable market segmentation endured at the national level until fairly late on in the country's development, ensuring the survival of large numbers of small firms that continued to cater to local and regional markets.[39] On the supply side, first and perhaps most fundamentally, the failure of an integrated and efficient financial system to emerge in France until the beginning of the twentieth century impeded the processes of capital formation required to drive industrial and commercial rationalization across the economy.[40] The weakness of the French financial system coupled with

[39] Two causes in particular have been adduced for this segmentation of French market structures. In the first place, the belated integration of transportation and distribution systems, compounded by the country's large size by European standards, reinforced until fairly late on in its development the preponderance of diverse regional markets over a unitary, national market. In particular, the slow development of the French railroad network during the second half of the nineteenth century retarded the emergence of this national market – first, by failing to connect rural areas, particularly in the West and Southwest, to the industrial centers of Paris and the Northeast, and second by delaying the urbanization required to unify demand and hence integrate the national consumer market. In turn, the impact of this structural shortcoming was magnified by the traditional insistence of French consumers on quality and the individualism of taste that they habitually displayed. These factors impeded the standardization of production and attendant rationalization of French firms that, in order to serve the fissiparous tastes of their clienteles, continued to focus on the inefficient, quasi-artisanal production of small quantities of individualized goods, rather than the mass production of standardized goods that was customary of industry in other advanced countries. Charles Kindleberger, *Economic Growth in France and Britain: 1851–1951* (New York: Clarion, 1969), 171–3, and Landes, "French Business and the Businessman, 345.

[40] The historic weakness of the French financial sector held back the country's economic development in three principal ways. First and most importantly, the inadequate number and uneven distribution of banks throughout the country from the mid-nineteenth century until the end of the First World War meant that firms in most regions outside of Paris and other large cities were unable to secure the financing necessary to modernize and grow their operations. Lack of access to an adequate level of capital condemned them to remain small, the overwhelming proportion of firms having to rely on family assets as their principal sources of capital. The following figures give some idea of the relative backwardness of the French banking sector during the second half of the nineteenth century, when the country was completing its first great wave of industrialization. According to one estimate, in 1863, just as the Bank of France's monopoly on credit was being broken and separate banking institutions were coming into being, fully three-quarters of the French territory lacked access to credit facilities. In 1870 the Bank of France had 60 branches in operation, compared to only 37 in 1857 and 13 in 1848. This left twenty-five departments totally bereft of its services, at a time when the large deposit banks that had been established during the late 1850s and early 1860s had only a few branches each. If we put these figures into relative perspective, in 1870 France had approximately the same bank density (i.e., banks per inhabitant) as Scotland in the middle of the eighteenth century. Likewise, the country had fewer bank assets per inhabitant in the mid-nineteenth century than had England and Scotland in 1770. It was only after 1880, with the expansion of deposit banks and the emergence of other types of financial institutions, that the number of "bankable places" finally began to grow more quickly, from 115 in 1881, to 205 in 1885, to 479 in 1908, to 583 in 1913. However, even by the eve of the First

the conservatism of financial authorities left the vast majority of French industrial and commercial enterprises without ready access to short- and medium-term credit during the periods of industrial takeoff experienced by the country during the 1860s and 1870s and then from the mid-1890s to World War I. The

World War, and despite this growth in size and the undeniable industrial and commercial concentration that accompanied it, the banking sector in France remained substantially underdeveloped compared to that in evidence in other industrialized countries, and hence, the access of French entrepreneurs to credit remained comparatively limited.

In the second place, compounding the dearth of banks was the insufficient variety of specialized financial institutions to help meet the increasingly diverse credit needs of firms in a rapidly evolving economy. Beginning in the late 1850s and early 1860s, four or five joint-stock banks that operated on a national scale had emerged. However, though initially conceived as industrial banks with the purpose of providing investment credit to manufacturing, these institutions increasingly turned to making short-term loans and especially toward speculation in higher-yield domestic and especially foreign obligations, effectively privileging *les affaires* (i.e., speculation in French and, later, foreign securities) over industrial enterprises as the principal objects of their investments. Thus, they sought to establish branches in towns and regions that had excess savings rather than in areas with the greatest need of credit so they could accumulate pools of capital, which they in turn could direct toward foreign investments. At the same time, banking and credit facilities during this period became increasingly centralized in Paris, so that regional industry found itself further deprived of local sources of financing and capital. Finally, the investment banks (*banques d'affaires*) during the closing decades of the nineteenth century were specifically geared to supply capital to commerce and industry on a large scale. However, because they limited their lending and purchasing of securities to new industrial sectors, such as electricity, steel, and gas, their investment strategies rarely extended to firms in more traditional sectors, forcing them to rely on more limited and localized sources of credit as well as self-financing to fulfill their capital needs. In short, despite the emergence of regional banks and informal local lending institutions, the availability of credit remained extremely uneven across the country, with regional and local firms enjoying much more limited access to capital than the largest national firms, which could turn to the Bank of France or Parisian joint-stock banks and investment houses for their financing needs.

In turn, despite the precocious launch of the Paris Bourse in the 1820s, the country's financial markets remained largely embryonic for much of the nineteenth century, thus depriving French firms of another potential source of external financing. This was the result of the belated introduction of true joint-stock or publicly limited companies (*sociétés anonymes*) that made it possible to raise capital through the selling of shares to the public in 1863 and 1867. In consequence, the vast majority of firms were forced to employ modes of incorporation that offered much less initial access to capital: the *commandite par actions* (partnership limited by shares) or *commandite simple* (mixed liability company) for the largest among them, while the mass of remaining enterprises represented either simple partnerships or individual proprietorships. Thus, as France was entering its most intensive period of industrialization to date in the 1850s and 1860s and setting down the institutional bases that would determine the future character of its industry and commerce, the relative backwardness of the country's financial markets and the legal limitations placed on firms' access to public capital were significant factors contributing to the relatively low rate of firm capitalization and consequently small average size of French enterprises.

Finally, the dearth of private banking institutions and relative underdevelopment of the French financial markets accorded a preeminent role to the Bank of France as the principal source of lending and credit within the country from the mid-nineteenth century through the 1890s, and even up to 1914. However, the bank's glacial conservatism made it a significant impediment to industrial and commercial modernization and only very sparingly provided short-term credit to principal legacy of France's financial backwardness was that many of these enterprises remained smaller and economically less efficient than they might otherwise have been, thus sustaining a pattern of economic dualism whereby a highly advanced and concentrated industrial sector emerged alongside a large and diffuse traditional sector. In this sense, the retardation of the country's financial system doubtless contributed, to use Cameron's phrase, to the "schizophrenic development of French industry" and helped to account for its relative industrial and commercial backwardness compared to the situation in other industrialized countries.[41]

In turn, another no less important supply-side factor accounting for the diffuseness of the French firm structure is the highly skilled, craft-proficient – in short, artisanal – character of the French workforce. The quasi-artisanal values and skills of French workers, implying their engagement in all stages of the production of a given good, made it difficult for them to adapt to the scientific division of labor and specialization of tasks characteristic of the modern industrial workplace.[42] Finally, and more generally, the subsistence of a diffuse firm structure in France can be related to the important functions fulfilled by small enterprises within the particular form of industrial capitalism that evolved in the country, implying that, far from representing an impediment to it, structural dualism was an integral feature of French economic modernization.

firms for the purpose of development. The conditions the bank imposed for admission to discount were so severe and the rules for issuing credit so rigid that the vast majority of enterprises remained simply ineligible to receive loans from it. Similarly, the overly restrictive monetary policies that it pursued up until World War I exacerbated the regressive impact of this tight credit policy, the ensuing liquidity crunch and rise in interest rates effectively deterring firms from borrowing to expand their operations. In short, combined with the high cost of credit, the dearth of adequate financial institutions, the reticence of what banks there were to offer loans to the vast majority of firms, and the basic unwillingness of the Bank of France to supply credit to business meant that most enterprises were forced to rely on self-financing and family connections in order to meet their capitalization needs. On the evolution of French financial institutions and the elements of relative backwardness that it presented, see in particular Rondo Cameron, *Banking in the Early Stages of Industrialization: A Study in Comparative Economic History* (New York: Oxford University Press, 1967), 100–28, as well as Charles Kindleberger, *A Financial History of Western Europe* (London: George Allen and Unwin, 1984), ch. 6; Kindleberger, *Economic Growth*, 53–4; and Alain Plessis, "Le 'retard français': la faute à la banque?" in *Le capitalisme français au XIXe–XXe siècle: blocages et dynamismes d'une croissance*, ed. P. Fridenson and A. Straus (Paris: Fayard, 1987), 204, 209–10.

[41] *Banking*, 115. Comparing the French and British cases, Kindleberger observed that "France lagged a hundred years behind Britain in money, banking and finance, and ... this was both a reflection and a cause for its economic retardation." *Financial History*, 115.

[42] Three causes have been adduced for the highly skilled character of French workers: the early historical diffusion of compulsory education throughout the country; the widespread opportunities for technical training offered historically to French workers; and, most fundamentally, the deeply ingrained respect for artisanal traditions that long remained prevalent among them. As Maurice Lévy-Leboyer has put it, these factors instilled among French workers "a very real desire for autonomy, for self-realization through work, which are both the vehicle and the engine of small enterprise." "Le patronat français a-t-il été malthusien?" 13. On the sociocultural proximity between French industrial workers and artisans, see also Zarca, *L'artisanat français*, ch. 4.

At a primary, functional level, *petites enterprises* assumed a complementary role with respect to large firms in the performance of certain economic tasks, effectively giving rise to a division of labor between the two that guaranteed the survival of small, traditional enterprises alongside large, advanced ones.[43]

Second, petty independent firms also helped to preserve the integrity of the capitalist system by serving a vital socially stabilizing function. On the one hand, they provided an important measure of economic flexibility to the capitalist economy – an increasingly important function as social and labor regulation intensified under the auspices of the post–World War II welfare state – by keeping a significant proportion of the French workforce employed in firms that, for largely cultural reasons, presented low rates of unionization and thus lower wage costs.[44] On the other hand, because of their labor-intensive character, small traditional firms assimilated workers who had been laid off during periods of economic stagnation and recession, effectively acting, as Berger has put it, as "sponges that absorb[ed] the workers that the modern economy c[ould]

---

[43] In the first place, small enterprises occupied zones of activity unprofitable to capitalists who needed to generate greater revenues than artisans or petty shopkeepers in order to amortize their initial capitalization and ongoing operational costs. In contrast to large-scale capitalists, because they essentially live, like workers, on a salary defined by their trade, *petits indépendants* could survive by selling their goods or services at an intermediate price between the selling price set by larger capitalist enterprises and their cost of production, an outcome only possible in sectors in which the gains on capital are extremely low or virtually nil – hence, the concentration of petty producers in primarily labor-intensive trades, which allow them to survive by essentially scrimping on their own labor costs. Second, traditional *petites entreprises* were able to continue specializing in goods and services that remained ill-adapted to the standardized modes of production that characterized the modern industrial firm. At one level, they traded in goods and services over the production of which they had complete control and which required only limited amounts of fixed capital, while satisfying a demand for customized goods reflecting the individualistic tastes of French consumers. Finally, as industrial concentration progressed as a result of the mobilization of ever greater amounts of capital, the impact of new techniques and technologies of production, and the emergence of ever-larger markets for standardized goods, firms in the petty independent sector increasingly took on ancillary subcontracting or servicing functions in respect to the advanced sector. In short, though their function within the French economy may have changed as they shifted out of primary production into an auxiliary support role to large industry, their enduring complementarity with the modern sector continued to ensure a place for many *petits indépendants* within the structure of French industrial capitalism. As such, predictions of their impending death over the past century or more have proved premature, if not wrongheaded. Jaeger, *Artisanat et capitalisme*, 206, 210–11, and Berger and Piore, *Dualism*, 106.

[44] Specifically, because they were unable to absorb or shed labor as easily in response to the vicissitudes of the business cycle, modern firms increasingly resorted to transferring work out of their own heavily capitalized plants, which were constrained by the value-adding costs of advanced technology, a high wage bill, and an inflexible labor supply, to the much smaller, lower-cost, more flexible firms in the traditional *petit indépendant* sector. By allowing modern firms to subcontract production and services that would have been unprofitable for them to carry out, traditional firms provided an essential factor of flexibility that helped to ensure the stable functioning of industrial capitalism in France, the traditional sector functioning, to use Jeanne Gaillard's phrase, as "a reserve serving alternatively as a reservoir and a refuge for the concentrated sector." "La petite entreprise," 138. See also Berger and Piore, *Dualism*, 101–3, 106–7.

not employ."[45] By historically serving as a "refuge activity" that made it possible to maintain employment in the face of cyclical downturns, the *petit indépendant* sector thus performed a vital shock-absorbing function within the French economy.[46]

In short, far from opposing one another, in many respects the modern and traditional sectors evolved a complementary, even symbiotic relationship as a result of the particular process of capitalist development that unfolded in France. Whereas the modern sector relied on the traditional sector to provide it with wage and labor flexibility and absorb its excess workforce during economic downturns, the traditional sector in turn received "support, protection and new life" from its linkages with the modern sector.[47] This would suggest that, in the French case at least, far from constituting an impediment to the development of modern capitalism, the persistence of the traditional sector and of economic dualism represented an integral feature of that development.

At a second, structural level of analysis, the survival of a diffuse firm structure in France can be ascribed to the protective policies put in place by the French state since the end of the nineteenth century in order to shield small producers from the effects of economic competition and concentration. At base, these policies were rooted in the petty proprietary ideal of the *sans-culottes*, which conceived the accession to small-scale property as the prerequisite of political equality and envisioned its diffusion as a precondition for the development of a harmonious social order.[48] This ideal was first enshrined in the Décret d'Allarde of 1791, which, by abolishing corporatist restrictions on entry into the trades, effectively consecrated the principle of free accession to small economic property. In turn, this principle was central to the Napoleonic Civil Code of 1804 and provided the legal basis for the simultaneous concentration and diffusion of

---

[45] Berger and Piore, *Dualism*, 107. Acting out of a sense of mutual obligation rather than according to the tenets of economic rationality, these firms provided jobs to family and friends in order to shield them from the worst of the economic depression. In Berger's words, "as employers, ... independent, small owners are likely to absorb more labor than their firm requires and ... to acknowledge the claims of family members to employment in the small family enterprise"; as a result, "in hard times, shops, farms and small industry open their doors to let in family members that have lost jobs elsewhere." Ibid., 104–5.

[46] In an echo of the pre–World War II era in which political figures of all stripes glorified the small enterprise and farm as the bedrock of economic and social stability within the country, the economic and social value of petty enterprises has increasingly come to be reaffirmed within certain political circles, leading to their portrayal as a viable antidote for offsetting the deleterious effects of the structural unemployment that took hold of the country from the early seventies on. Ibid., 107–8.

[47] Ibid., 106.

[48] A petition addressed to the members of the Convention in 1793 articulated this ideal thus: "that each citizen be able to have his own field, his own workshop or shop, that is the ideal of the *sans-culottes*." In the aim of preserving social equality, however, limitations were called for on the amount of property each individual could own, such "that no one would be able to rent out more land than that which could be worked by a set number of ploughs," a measure "that would make disappear bit by bit the too great inequality of wealth and increase the number of proprietors." Quoted in N. Mayer, "L'atelier et la boutique," 264n.

property and capital that accompanied the country's economic development.[49] However, it was in the ideas and program of the founders of the Third Republic that economic and social dualism found its most complete expression and legitimization. Men such as Léon Gambetta and Jules Ferry sought to achieve the ideal of a republic of small property holders by facilitating the advent of and politically empowering the *couches nouvelles* of small property owners, who came to represent the social backbone of the new republican order. Thus, they updated the *sans-culotte* conviction that small-scale economic property, limited to that which could be directly worked or fructified by the individual and his family, was the material guarantee of economic opportunity, political equality, and social advancement under the new republic.[50]

For largely politically strategic motives, this ideal was initially directed to the peasantry. Republican politicians understood that its atavistic desire to accumulate land made the latter the natural champion of the small proprietary ideal.[51] This conviction was borne out by the massive peasant turnout in favor of republican candidates in the elections of 1876, which, by producing a large republican majority in the National Assembly, definitively defeated the bid of monarchist forces to turn the clock back to before 1830, if not 1789. In turn, as the Third Republic was consolidated in the 1880s and 1890s and successive groups of conservatives rallied to it, the pandering of the Republic's founders to the proprietary interests of the French peasantry became the basis for an *agrariste* ideology that came to be shared by Left and Right alike in France.[52] They espoused common policies in defense of peasants' interests, and thus came to conceive of the latter as the vital sectoral backbone of the French nation and society.[53]

---

[49] Jacques Capdevielle, *Le fétichisme du patrimoine* (Paris: Presses de la FNSP, 1986), 146.

[50] In a speech delivered at Auxerre on 1 June 1874, Gambetta famously asserted that petty property simultaneously laid the basis for and guaranteed the effective exercise of republican citizenship, casting it as the foundational principle for a radical republic of small property holders: "With each property that is created, it is a citizen that is formed; because property, of which we are falsely accused of being the enemies, is, in our eyes, the superior and annunciatory sign of the moral and material emancipation of the individual. It is not of property that we are the enemies, this much is sure, but of its increasing scarcity which happily is diminishing every day as property passes into new hands. What we demand, what is being done, what is a social and democratic law, is that property be divided, that it go to the person who exploits and who renders it fecund through his efforts in order to make it produce more each day, not only for his own personal benefit, but also for the greater social benefit." Quoted in Barral, *Les fondateurs de la Troisième république*, 232.

[51] In the two decades spanning the years 1862 and 1882, during a period when the rural population as whole had begun to decline, the number of small agricultural properties increased from 1,802,000 in 1862 to 2,132,000 in 1882. Capdevielle, *Fétichisme*, 173.

[52] For a historical synopsis, see Pierre Barral, "Agrarisme de gauche et agrarisme de droite sous la Troisième République," in *L'univers politique des paysans dans la France contemporaine*, ed. Y. Tavernier, M. Gervais, and C. Servolin (Paris: Cahiers de FNSP, 1972), 243–53.

[53] For the original republican Left, the peasants represented, as we saw, the epitome of the *couches nouvelles* on which the new republican order was founded. They were the incarnation of the idealized citizen upheld by Jacobin ideology, who, following their liberation from the bonds of feudalism, could achieve political empowerment and social advancement through their accession

Despite differences in how they conceived of the peasantry in their respective visions of French society, the fact that both regarded it as the foundation on which that society should rest united Left and Right in favoring the preservation, artificially if need be, of a large class of small peasant holders. For the Opportunist politicians who presided over the founding of the Third Republic and the Radicals who succeeded them, these small property owners represented a crucial political base whose interests could not be ignored if they hoped to retain power. For conservative elites and the large agricultural landowners who supported them, a small peasantry was seen as a bulwark against the revolutionary ideologies of Jacobinism and later socialism and offered a useful social justification for keeping agricultural prices high.[54] At a policy level, this general commitment to defend the interests of the peasantry implied the conservation of a mixed economy in which industrialization would be effectively managed and even impeded through measures to protect a large rural sector composed essentially of small and middling peasants.[55] In turn,

to small property. For the formerly Orleanist or Legitimist Right, the small landed peasant served a quite different ideological and symbolic function, being essentially conceived as the linchpin for an organicistic conception of society that bound rural small property holders into a harmonious, hierarchically ordered social whole. Striving to "re-create the image of a mythical and harmonious feudalism," conservative thinkers projected the mythologized figure of the peasant who, living as he always had since time immemorial, became a symbol of permanence and stability in the face of increasingly rapid and disruptive social change. As such, the peasant symbolized for the Ralliés and their descendants "the basis of social life, of man rooted in the land, of man integrated in his community, whose life is in itself an order, the model for any viable social order." Nicole Eizner, "L'idéologie paysanne," in Tavernier et al., *L'univers politique des paysans dans la France contemporaine*, 319, 320.

[54] An eloquent testament to this global commitment to safeguarding peasant interests that characterized French political elites regardless of political affiliation during the course of the Third Republic is the fact that even the extreme Left and radical Right rallied to the defense of small peasant landholders in this period. Thus, in 1892, the French Socialists abandoned the orthodox Marxist prescription of land collectivization, coming to advocate in its place a policy of small-peasant preservation and protection that would later essentially come to be emulated by the French Communist Party during the interwar period. Likewise, throughout this era, the Action Française also sought to defend French peasants as the basis for reestablishing a traditional and corporatist social order, even attempting to organize them into a Corporation française de l'agriculture geared toward more effectively defending their interests. Gordon Wright, *Rural Revolution in France: The Peasantry in the Twentieth Century* (Stanford, CA: Stanford University Press, 1964), 22, and Barral, "Agrarisme de gauche et agrarisme de droite," 251.

[55] In the first place, a mixed economy was held by figures on both the left and the right to guarantee the continued economic solvency of the country once the process of industrialization lost momentum. According to this line of thinking, a crisis of overproduction would inevitably follow the explosion of manufacturing that had been wrought by industrialization. This, peasant advocates argued, would provoke a drastic cutback in industrial output and employment, thereby precipitating a significant return to the land as a guaranteed source of economic productivity and wealth. It is a real testament to the grip of this image of a perennially agricultural and rural France among the political elites of the Third Republic that they were incapable of seeing industrialization as an irreversible process that would spell the end of France as a predominantly rural society.

In the second place and perhaps more importantly, advocates of *agrarisme* argued that a mixed economy would preserve French society from the social ravages and political turmoil that were sure to ensue from industrialization, thereby guaranteeing the prospective harmony and stability

defense of small peasant property inevitably morphed into a generalized defense of small property *tout court*, the latter being alternately portrayed as a source of stability and order by the Right and an agent of equality and leveling by the Left. This tendency of politicians of all stripes to defend small property in all its manifestations became increasingly widespread as the rural exodus began in earnest and substantial pockets of urban petty property emerged in the country.[56]

Thus, as the foregoing suggests, the history of the French Republic is inextricably linked to policies designed to defend small property holders and producers. These have been perceived as the principal social foundation and political bulwark of the French republican state in its successive guises, going all the way back to L'An Un down to the Gaullist Fifth Republic. Similarly, at Vichy the authoritarian and corporatist designs of the Révolution Nationale sought to preserve petty rural and urban property under much the same terms as the reviled Third Republic. In turn, policies defending the traditional middle classes (i.e., small farmers, shopkeepers, and artisans) have endured down to the present day despite the successful postwar drive to rationalize and modernize French agriculture and industry. In this sense, rather than simply reflecting the political importance of these groups, the episodic resurgence of such policies also expressed the lingering appeal of prewar, petty proprietary ideologies among postwar policy makers, who continued to identify small-scale property and production not only with the economic well-being and social peace of the country but with its true values and character as well. Thus, even in the present era of technological innovation and economic globalization, defense of smallness remains widespread in France, reflecting a deeply ingrained, atavistic respect for the

of French society. Proponents of this view argued that because it had been able to preserve a large agricultural base, France would essentially be spared the social and political dislocations that wracked more fully industrialized countries. Writing at the turn of the century, the French historian Henri Sée neatly encapsulated this view: "France remains at the beginning of the twentieth century a rich agricultural nation which does not have to sell the products of its factories, like England, to live. It has lost relatively to the rest of Europe since the end of the eighteenth century, when it was the richest and most populated country, distanced by Germany. But the equilibrium which it has maintained at home between agriculture and industry, this sort of harmony, assures it a strong stability and an enviable situation. It is this equilibrium which renders the class struggle less bitter." Quoted in Kindleberger, *Economic Growth*, 196n.

[56] The roots of this identification of the political potential of urban small property holders stretch farther back, to the Revolutions of 1830 and especially of 1848, which saw significant mobilizations on the part of petty producers and traders. As the direct heirs of the *sans-culottes* who preceded them, the latter came to identify their interests with a sociopolitical vision not far removed from the petty-property-based ideal that would be advanced by the future founders of the Third Republic, seeing in it a means of socioeconomic advancement and political empowerment. This "conception of democratic liberalism, associating the idea of liberty to that of equality," as Francis Demier has put it, "became the principal demand of a nation of petty independent producers" throughout the course of the Third Republic and beyond. "Libéralisme à la française et synthèse républicaine," in *L'univers politique des classes moyennes*, ed. G. Lavau, G. Grunberg, and N. Mayer (Paris: Presses de la FNSP, 1983), 29.

values of *indépendance* not just among petty producers and traders but throughout French society as a whole.[57]

Protective policies enacted by successive French governments to preserve the *petit indépendant* sector fall into three categories. First and most obvious are measures that directly protected small producers and traders and promoted conditions that ensured their economic survival. At the forefront of these was a lenient tax regime that exempted *petits indépendants* from the more onerous tax schedules that applied to their larger competitors. Initially traceable to the tax legislation that governed petty property during the Second Republic, it was with the establishment of the Third Republic, and its commitment to the defense of the *couches nouvelles*, that a fiscal regime favorable to *petits indépendants* became entrenched. Beginning with the *patente* law of 15 July 1880, an extremely lenient tax schedule was instituted for small proprietors that drastically decreased their tax dues from the previous fiscal regime, resulting in many cases in a full tax exemption.[58] In turn, a law passed in 1909 on the hereditary transmission and sale of businesses stipulated for the first time the comprehensive judicial identity of small enterprises, providing a clear legal definition for firms to which the *patente* was to be applied.[59] This preferential fiscal regime for the smallest enterprises remained essentially unchanged until 1977, when it was replaced by a "professional tax" that was still advantageous in comparison to the tax paid by larger firms.[60]

As a corollary to this favorable fiscal regime, the solicitude displayed by political elites toward *petits indépendants* also led them to craft unfavorable tax regulations on big business as a means of shielding them from competition. In the case of industry, the stipulation of a special juridical status for artisans – the status of *artisan fiscal* applying to craftsmen counting no more than five salaried employees – provided the basis for subjecting larger industrial concerns to much higher tax rates than their artisanal counterparts. The differences in their tax obligations were significant enough that, from the 1920s on, when this special fiscal status was first introduced, French industrialists regularly groused about what they considered the unwarranted fiscal advantages extended to artisans by the French state.[61]

---

[57] Writing in the late 1970s, François Caron made the following observation that continues to remain valid today: "The solicitude shown toward small- and medium-sized enterprises today expresses the belief that they are a necessary counterpoise to the concentration and multinationalization of economic power – a manifestation of some sort of 'authenticity' which is threatened by the bureaucracy of the state and of big business." *Economic History*, 366–7.

[58] From this period up until 1880, the *patente* was equivalent to a fixed tax calculated as a fixed proportion of the rental value of the locale or place of business. Mayer, "Classes moyennes," 104. Gaillard, "La petite entreprise," 50.

[59] Capdevielle, *Fétichisme*, 191.

[60] Caron, *Economic History*, 366. In fact, some researchers have concluded that the new professional tax was even more fiscally advantageous to petty entrepreneurs than the *patente*. *Le Monde* reported on 21 January 1977 that 29% of artisans and 39% of shopkeepers paid a tax equivalent to less than 25% of the amount they had owed under the old patente. S. Berger, "D'une boutique à l'autre," 133.

[61] Zdatny, *Politics*, 50–1, 91, and Ehrmann, *Organized Business in France*, 312–13.

A similar dynamic could be observed in the commercial sector where, if anything, the fiscal divide between large retailers and shopkeepers was even more pronounced. Indeed, perhaps as a result of the political influence of lobbies representing the *petit commerce*, the French state long imposed proportionately greater tax obligations on large commercial concerns than on shopkeepers.[62] In addition, the state introduced fairly early on prohibitive fiscal measures to deter new concentrated forms of commerce.[63] By lessening the degree of economic competition to which shopkeepers were subjected and thereby impeding further commercial concentration, such laws helped to ensure the survival of a large *petit indépendant* sector in France.

The second type of policies promulgated by the state to protect *petits indépendants* involved trade tariffs. Whereas the fiscal advantages conferred upon small firms were primarily designed to shield them from the competition of more concentrated and advanced domestic firms, tariffs defended these small enterprises against foreign competition. Originally, such tariffs were instituted to protect peasant producers but soon came, particularly from the 1890s on, to include a broad range of manufactured goods as well.[64] The effect of these protectionist measures was to sustain small, marginal producers in both industry

---

[62] Such lopsided fiscal arrangements favoring small retailers and penalizing large ones could be traced back to the very beginnings of republican government in France. The original *patente* law of 15 July 1880 imposed a much higher *patente* schedule on retailers and service businesses counting more than ten employees. This higher schedule was based on a variable tax rate proportional to the rental-space costs of these concerns, as well as a fixed rate determined according to city population and the number of employees over five appearing on their payroll. These tax rates were subsequently increased in August 1890. In turn, a new law in April 1893 imposed additional tax levies based on the number of specialties exercised by a particular business – that is, the variety of products it sold. Department stores counting over two hundred employees were made to pay a separate tax on each of sixteen stipulated specialties that were specified by the new commercial tax code, in addition to the fixed *patente* schedule to which they were already subjected as a function of their size and the dimension of the city in which they operated. In 1905 a stricter law still reduced the maximum number of employees of stores that were made to pay this specialty tax from 200 to either 50, 25, or 15. Correspondingly, it increased the number of specialties on which larger retailers were taxed from 16 to 24. Mayer, "Classes moyennes," 105.

[63] Laws passed in 1905, 1910, and 1912 extended the *patente* to, respectively, consumer cooperatives, discount stores, and chain stores, each outlet of which was subject to a separate tax. Then, in 1917, a special tax on revenues exceeding a certain ceiling was applied to the *grands magasins* as a function of the new income tax code that was introduced in that year. This tax was in turn extended to consumer cooperatives in 1933. Ibid.

[64] Shortly following the establishment of the Ministry of Agriculture in 1881, the first tariff was levied on wheat in order to counteract the fall of grain prices provoked by the glut of cereals that flooded the world market during the 1870s. In 1882 the first industrial tariff was passed, targeting woolens and protecting the French textile sector. These measures prefigured the Méline tariff of 1892 which, placing comprehensive duties on agricultural products, raw materials, and industrial goods, would anchor French trade – and, by extension, agricultural and industrial policy over the following half century. The Méline tariffs were strengthened in 1910 and again during the 1930s, in response to the global raising of tariffs that characterized the interwar period. Kindleberger, *Economic Growth*, 279.

and agriculture, allowing them in effect to cling to outdated, autarkic, and subsistence-based forms of production that were disappearing in most other industrialized countries. Indeed, one would have to wait until well after World War II and the country's entry into the European Economic Community for France to liberalize its trade regime. And even thereafter, the agricultural sector in particular would remain protected under the provisions of the Common Agricultural Policy, slowing its rationalization into even the 1970s and 1980s.

Finally, a third manner in which the French state protected small business was through credit policies and institutions that aimed to sustain petty independent enterprises in the face of intensifying competition and concentration. For example, in the interwar period, mutual or cooperative banks (*banques populaires*) were created with government support in order to help channel credit at preferential rates to small farmers, artisans, and shopkeepers who were unable to gain access to loans from large, national deposit banks or the Bank of France. The Crédit Agricole was revived in this period and eventually successfully established itself as the principal lender to French farmers during the course of the twentieth century. Similarly, the government established a credit institution, the Caisse centrale du crédit hôtelier, commercial et industriel, to distribute 35 million francs worth of credits to small artisanal and commercial enterprises at preferential rates of interest, in order to assist them in modernizing their capital stock.[65] Though less widespread than fiscal and tariff policies, such institutions and policies played an important role in prolonging the life of small, unviable enterprises in the face of economic concentration and rationalization until well after World War II.

At a second level, in addition to shielding small producers from the impacts of competition and rationalization, French governments also pursued interdictory policies that aimed either to deter concentration or to restrict alternative forms of commerce and production that competed with small enterprises. These were particularly evident in the commercial sector, where measures barring concentration were much more prevalent than in industry, in which the fiscal advantages extended artisans were deemed sufficient to protect them. For example, in the 1930s, a series of laws was enacted that restricted the number of sales trucks (*camions bazars*) and prohibited the establishment or expansion of "nickel" or "dime" stores (*magasins à prix unique*). These measures were extended by Vichy and again renewed following a short hiatus after the war.[66] In turn, even the great postwar dynamic of liberalization and concentration, resulting in the wave of supermarket and hypermarket creations that swept the country from the late 1950s to the early 1970s, was cut short by restrictions on commercial concentration. In December 1973 the most restrictive measure to be enacted

---

[65] André Gueslin, "Dynamisme et lenteur d'un secteur abrité: banques mutualistes au XXe siècle," 221, and Michel Lescure, "L'état, l'investissement et la petite entreprise: l'expérience des bonifications d'intérêts (1937–1939)," 225–38, both in Fridenson and Straus, *Le capitalisme français au XIXe–XXe siècle.*

[66] Mayer, "Classes moyennes," 106.

against commercial concentration in recent times, the Royer Law, passed unanimously.[67] Though supermarket and hypermarket construction gained renewed momentum in the 1980s and 1990s, this law has never been struck from the books, attesting to the continuing importance accorded to small business interests by the French political elite. In short, even though restrictions on commercial concentration were considerably loosened, impediments to it persisted, reflecting the residual political influence of the *petit commerce* throughout the postwar era.[68]

Finally, this analysis of the relationship between government policy and the survival of a large *petit indépendant* sector in France would be incomplete if we failed to underline the consistency with which the French state has selectively applied and enforced general social and economic regulation to the benefit of the small business sector in order to help it survive in an increasingly open and competitive economy. As Suzanne Berger has written, "different norms, institutions, and modes of state intervention have been developed to regulate the activities of the small independent property holders on the one hand, and those of the large capitalist sector on the other."[69] Exceptions were frequently made for small businesses in the drafting and interpretation of social laws, effectively exempting them from having to provide the same salaries and benefits to their workers as their larger counterparts. Correlatively, laws that applied to them were often not as forcefully enforced as those regulating the advanced sector.[70] The willingness of the state to turn a blind eye to *petits indépendants'* infringements of social laws undoubtedly also contributed to their resilience in the face of ongoing economic rationalization.

---

[67] Officially titled the Law on the Orientation of Commerce and of the *Artisanat* but more commonly named after the minister of commerce who conceived it, it increased the representation of the *petit commerce* and *artisanat* on the local commercial zoning commissions that were charged with authorizing the construction of new supermarkets in local communes. In many cases, this amounted to *petits indépendants* being granted an effective veto on the construction of new supermarkets, a fact pointedly underscored by the rapid drop in the number of new supermarkets that were built once the law came into force in 1974. Ibid., 108–9, 111.

[68] Thus, in reaction to their renewed decline, the government has most recently introduced new measures protecting *petits commerçants* against the depredations of concentrated forms of commerce. Most notably, the so-called Galland Law passed by the Juppé government in 1996 stiffened the penalties on businesses caught selling at a loss – a practice outlawed since 1960 – while lifting the prohibition imposed by the Fontanet Circular of 1960 on wholesalers to refuse sale to retailers. Hence, the latter were able to more effectively combat the deflated prices imposed upon them by large supermarket chains, thereby indirectly benefiting small retailers. Marie-Laure Allain and Claire Chambolle, "Les relations entre producteurs et distributeurs: conflits et réglementations," *Recherches en économie et sociologie rurales* 6(3) (Mar. 2004), 2.

[69] "D'une boutique à l'autre," 123.

[70] In Berger's words, the former benefited from "the state's willingness to overlook violations of social security, minimum wage, and working conditions legislation," the implication being that, had the state enforced these regulations as judiciously in respect to *petits indépendants* as the advanced sector, many small firms would not have been able to bear the higher costs entailed by compliance with these regulations. Ibid.

In short, there is considerable evidence to suggest that state policy since the end of the nineteenth century did little to hamper the operation of small business and force it to modernize itself. On the contrary, one could easily conclude that the French state enabled *petits indépendants* to resist modernization by providing them with various protections, means of assistance, and special privileges that shielded them from the level of competition that consigned their counterparts in other countries to economic oblivion. Before World War II, state-led efforts to modernize the French economy were timid at best. These involved the nonsensical pursuit of redistributive policies that aimed to make all of the country's social constituencies happy, rather than its merchants and producers more competitive and efficient. And as we have seen, policies to modernize the economy continued to coexist with measures to protect small producers even after World War II.[71] At the same time, postwar planners continued to advocate as economically sound and socially desirable a contradictory mix of policies that sought to simultaneously protect small producers and streamline the economy.[72] Notwithstanding the dubious compatibility of economic dualism with the necessity of national specialization in an increasingly integrated global marketplace, such recommendations remind us of the central role accorded until quite recently by French policy makers to *petits indépendants* in the economic life of the nation. From this perspective, postwar attempts at economic modernization and industrial and commercial rationalization never succeeded in fully displacing the traditional sector. Berger has observed that, "throughout the postwar period, the grand schemes for industrialization and modernization of the economy and society never entirely supplanted a second set of policies that were pursued to protect the small firms that the first set of policies were designed to eliminate."[73]

Finally, the structural and institutional modalities of French capitalist development, combined with the protective policies shielding the traditional sector from domestic and foreign competition, generated a social structure that facilitated the renewal and replenishment of the *petit indépendant* sector. Specifically, by allowing a substantial peasant sector to persist until late on into its development, France's dualistic pattern of modernization sustained an abiding reservoir for *petits indépendants* within French society. In many ways, small peasant

[71] Witness, for example, the Chavannes Report and the crusade of Finance Inspector Michel Albert during the 1960s and 1970s, which, through their advocacy of a program of decentralization aiming to develop industry in rural areas, effectively framed, seventy-five years after Méline, the return to the countryside as a sociopolitical imperative for the Fifth Republic. Nicole Eizner and Bertrand Hervieu, *Anciens paysans, nouveaux ouvriers* (Paris: L'Harmattan, 1979), 62–5, 76–7.

[72] This, for example, was the gist of the Seventh Economic Plan that guided French economic policy through the second half of 1970s into the 1980s. While continuing to stress the need for industrial and commercial concentration, this plan also included measures that would encourage the growth of "small and average-sized firms." Such firms, its authors argued, were "by no means a relic of the past, doomed to disappear" or consigned to "become only the subcontracting infrastructure of big firms." Instead, "technical production and changes in the organization of labor often point[ed] to a reduction in the optimum size of units of production." Quoted in Caron, *Economic History*, 362.

[73] Berger and Piore, *Dualism*, 109.

farmers originally embodied the cultural system of *indépendance* built around the principles of small property, the *métier*, and the family that conditioned the economic and social outlook of French shopkeepers and artisans.[74] As a result, the peasantry became a steady source of replacement for French *petits indépendants*.

The abiding attachment to the values of *indépendance* displayed by rural migrants meant that, short of recovering the family farm and the socioprofessional autonomy that went with it, many of them would strive to replicate their status as *petits indépendants* within the urban setting.[75] The lucky few who disposed of sufficient financial and professional capital were able to set up shop on their own directly after leaving the countryside.[76] Usually, however, the social trajectory by which rural migrants recovered their original condition of *indépendance* was a more protracted and graduated one.[77] Most of them were

---

[74] A cursory examination of the economic habits and perspectives evolved by the peasantry highlights the fundamental sociocultural affinities that exist between this historically dominant demographic group in French society and the *petit indépendant* sector. In the first place, like the *petit indépendant* in respect to his shop or workshop, the peasant comes to view his land not just as an instrument of production but more importantly as the structural and symbolic linchpin of his social identity. The structural guarantee of both his financial and professional autonomy, that is, of "being one's own boss," his land represents the fundamentally concrete, organic reality that defines the nature of the work around which his identity is structured. It is the notion of agrarian individualism based on this small-scale, personally worked parcel of land that underlies the powerful tendency toward autarky traditionally evinced by the French peasant. By extension, this agrarian individualism constitutes the primordial model for the overriding attachment of *petits indépendants* to their own social and professional autonomy, the atavistic mold for the ideal of *indépendance* as it came to be defined by successive generations of French shopkeepers and artisans since at least the nineteenth century. On the specific nature of work in the agrarian setting and its suffusion with the ideal of small property, see "L'evolution du travail agraire," in Placide Rambaud, *Société rurale et urbanisation* (Paris: Seuil, 1969), 41–86, and Monique Vincienne, *Du village à la ville: le système de mobilité des agriculteurs* (Paris: Mouton, 1972), ch. 1.

[75] Eizner and Hervieu note that "the desire to reclaim the autonomy of the free entrepreneur and to win back a zone of autonomy in one's work became the central preoccupation" for these migrants. As such, they would "try to escape the world of salaried work by becoming an artisan or a shopkeeper, [or be] attracted to solitary and responsible work positions." *Anciens paysans, nouveaux ouvriers*, 122.

[76] The small number of rural migrants acceding directly to professions in the petty independent sector is suggested by an INSEE study of social and professional mobility undertaken between 1959 and 1965 – that is, during the period when the rate of rural migration reached its historical peak. It found that only 5% of urban petty independent artisans or tradesmen in 1965 had been agricultural migrants in 1959. Gresle, *Indépendants*, 268.

[77] That the prospect of social advancement, even if spaced out over two generations, holds deeper appeal for workers of rural origin than others is underscored by a study undertaken during the 1950s that showed that, in response to the question, "If your children could have your job, would you be happy about that?" only 16% of the former did not answer in the negative (i.e., "yes," or "that it depends on them, they must be allowed to choose on their own") compared to 31% of skilled workers, 34% of unskilled workers, and 53% of skilled workers who had completed a technical training course that would give them access to a lower management position. Alain Touraine, "Les ouvriers d'origine agricole," *Sociologie du travail*, no. 3 (July–Sept. 1960), 236.

forced to become industrial workers, even if they did not want to remain so.[78] In marked contrast to workers of urban origin, many rural migrants proved incapable of adapting to factory work.[79] They consequently sought to escape the industrial condition and, if this proved unfeasible in their own lifetime, to ensure that their children would not be subjected to it.[80] This incapacity to adapt to factory life, rooted in the diametrically opposite experiences, values, and perspectives associated with agricultural work, was reinforced by the fact that many new workers continued to maintain strong ties to rural society.[81] Not

---

[78] According to a study also conducted at the height of the rural migration in France, in 1957, nearly half the industrial workers of agricultural origin (i.e., former farmers) who expressed the desire to change jobs did not wish to remain working in the factory setting, as opposed to 20% of unskilled workers, 5% of skilled workers, and 18% of young qualified workers on the point of completing an advanced technical training program and ready to accede to a lower management (foreman) position. In turn, fully two-thirds of them affirmed that they wished to "set up shop" on their own when directly asked the question but felt that they would be unable to do so (compared to only half of the workers of other categories). Ibid., 241.

[79] This is not really surprising, since industrial labor represented in almost all aspects a complete antithesis to the agricultural work experience. Thus, for example, factory work is undertaken in a closed space in which the production process is rigidly segmented and controlled, whereas agricultural work is carried out in the open, and is subject to constant flux and much less procedural rigidity and segmentation. Second, factory work is undertaken collectively, whereas agricultural work remains on the whole a solitary endeavor. Third, factory work is performed according to a fixed time schedule, whereas in agriculture the temporality of work is principally determined by the duration of the tasks themselves. Fourth, factory work is characterized by an endless repetition of tasks, whereas agricultural work is much more varied and irregular in character. Fifth, the social and professional relations obtaining within the factory are rigidly hierarchical, whereas those obtaining on the small farm, based principally on the family, remain largely informal. Sixth, and last, within the factory the individual comes to feel like a small part of a totalistic process of production, whereas in agriculture he or she retains quasi-total initiative and control over the productive process. Nicole Eizner and Bertrand Hervieu eloquently captured the antinomous character of industrial and agricultural work and the consequently dislocating experience of the factory for many rural migrants in pointing out that "the work of the farmer is a work of creation; the [agricultural] worker masters from one end to the other the process of production. He sows, and he collects his harvest. The finished product is his work in its entirety. By contrast, in the factory, placed before a kind of predetermined labor, the upstream and downstream processes of production escape him. At no moment does he have in front of him an object created by himself. He is an element, incidentally replaceable, of a process that escapes him. It is clear that this analysis of the alienation of industrial work is not specific to the worker of agricultural origin. Perhaps, however, the concrete and lived experience of this new kind of relationship to work renders even more oppressive for the former farmer the working-class condition. . . . For him, the entrance into the industrial world is first and foremost a loss of liberty and of the joy of work." *Anciens paysans, nouveaux ouvriers,* 106–7. Regarding these experiential antinomies between industrial and agricultural work, see Vincienne, *Du village à la ville,* ch. 1; Rambaud, *Société rurale et urbanisation,* 50–66; and Eizner and Hervieu, *Anciens paysans, nouveaux ouvriers,* 105–7.

[80] On the strategies pursued by workers of rural origin to enable their children to escape the proletarian condition and the premium they placed on their education, see Eizner and Hervieu, *Anciens paysans, nouveaux ouvriers,* 120–1.

[81] Guy Barbichon, "Aspects psychologiques et sociaux du transfert des agriculteurs de l'agriculture vers l'industrie," *Economie rurale,* no. 77 (1968), 46, and Eizner and Hervieu, *Anciens paysans, nouveaux ouvriers,* 70–1, 85.

surprisingly, then, most workers of rural origin continued to express the desire of one day being able to recover the status of *indépendance* that they had lost in migrating to the city and factory. They developed, in effect, schizoid economic and social personae, in which their attachment to the ideal of *indépendance* remained the dominant social-psychological trait. According to a study from 1957, fully two-thirds of rural migrant workers answered in the affirmative when they were asked whether they hoped to one day establish their own businesses.[82] This figure comports with subsequent findings that show that many workers of rural origin – that is, those whose father was a farmer – became *petits indépendants* later in life.[83]

In turn, the diffusion of the ideal of *indépendance* among rural migrants helps to explain the conservative social and economic values evinced by a sizable proportion of French workers. Of the latter, 20 percent in 1970 and 32 percent in 1978 expressed the hope of one day being able to set up shop on their own – figures strongly at odds with the standard representation of French industrial workers as a homogeneously class-conscious far-left constituency in French

[82] Touraine, "Les ouvriers d'origine agricole," 241.

[83] A study on social and professional mobility from the 1960s found that among 745,200 artisans and petty tradesmen born after 1917 and plying their trades between 1959 and 1964, the leading socioprofessional category of origin, after petty artisan or shopkeeper, was that of farmer. Specifically, within the ranks of practicing *petits indépendants* during these years, 16.9% of the men (out of a total of 423,600) and 22.8% of the women (out of a total of 321,600) had farmers as fathers, as compared to 37.9% of men and 28.6% of women whose fathers were themselves petty shopkeepers or artisans. The upshot of these figures has also been borne out by regionally localized studies of the petty independent sector. Thus, in his study of 570 retired petty shop-keepers and artisans in the department of the Nord in the early 1970s, François Gresle found that more than one-third (36.5% of men, 36% of women) had been born in rural communes or small towns numbering less than 5,000 people. Finally, this finding is confirmed by Vincienne's 1964 study of the industrial Alpine town of St. Jean-de-Maurienne, which experienced a heavy influx of rural migrants during the 1950s and 1960s. She found that high school students who were the children of rural migrants showed a marked preference for pursuing a petty commercial or artisanal career, compared to those of a working-class or even a *petit indépendant* background. Gresle, *Indépendants*, 265, 255, and Vincienne, *Du village à la ville*, 146–8.

This professed interest of the children of farmers or of workers of rural origin in setting up shop in turn underscores in turn the various paths by which people of rural backgrounds hope to recover the primordial status of *indépendance* that was originally bound up in the petty property and work experience of the peasantry. A first path is one that could be termed of intragenerational mobility, whereby, after a more or less prolonged stint of work in the factory, the rural migrant is able to develop the skills and accumulate the capital to establish his own small business. Conversely, a second trajectory is that of intergenerational mobility, whereby it is the sons or daughters of the rural migrants who, having internalized the model of *indépendance* characteristic of their milieu of origin, accede once again to the condition of *petit indépendant* in their parents' stead. In this context, education often serves as the principal means by which, in opening the prospects for social mobility, rural migrants are able to vicariously recover their lost status of *indépendance* through their children and thereby, to escape the fate of proletarianization to which they were in great majority initially subjected upon moving to the city. On this specific point, see Eizner and Hervieu, *Anciens paysans, nouveaux ouvriers*, 121.

society.[84] By contrast, these figures underscore the enduring salience of the cultural system of *indépendance* among French workers recently transplanted from the countryside.[85]

In this sense, the dualistic course of development that was followed by France and resulted in its belated urbanization not only ensured the reproduction of a large *petit indépendant* sector but also sustained the diffusion of the cultural system of *indépendance* within the broader French society. The diffusion of this cultural system in turn served as a brake on the process of modernization, reinforcing the impact of the structural factors of economic retardation described earlier. This cultural attachment to *indépendance* impeded economic modernization at two levels. First, it instilled a Malthusian mind-set among the country's mass of small entrepreneurs, while inculcating among peasants and even some workers an antiquated, economically regressive ideal of individual autonomy based on petty property. At the same time, the culture of *indépendance* also bred ancillary social and economic behaviors that impeded development and growth.[86] As such, the diffusion of *indépendance* helped to sustain the sociostructural conditions for its very persistence. It provided a crucial impetus behind the perpetuation of economic dualism, forestalling the country's adoption of a rational and efficient model of capitalism as a basis for organizing its economy and society. Charles Kindleberger has observed that, "if anything is to be blamed" for the country's perennial dualism and belated industrialization, "it is the insistence on the independent life of an artisan or shopkeeper by a people too bound up in *égalité* and too conscious of their individual worth to be happily engaged in factory work."[87]

THE CULTURAL ANATOMY OF *INDÉPENDANCE*

Ne pas monter bien haut, peut être, mais tout seul. Cyrano de Bergerac[88]

Moi je vais vous dire, ce qu'il leur faut aux Français, c'est un nouvel Hitler! A Parisian *fromager* in 1978[89]

---

[84] Gérard Adam, Frédéric Bon, Jacques Capdevielle, and René Mouriaux, *L'ouvrier français en 1970. Enquête nationale auprès de 1116 ouvriers d'industrie* (Paris: Armand Colin, 1970), 247–9, and Mayer, "L'atelier et la boutique," 266.

[85] For an analysis of the economic and sociopolitical behaviors and outlooks characteristic of this particular segment of the French working class, see in particular Jacques Capdevielle and René Mouriaux, *L'ouvrier conservateur* (Paris: Laboratoire d'Etudes et de Recherches Sociologiques sur la Classe Ouvrière, 1983).

[86] For example, it translated into a love of the *rente foncière* and an atavistic penchant for investing in the land (*la terre*) and, beginning in the twentieth century, real estate (*la pierre*), which, as many students of French economy and society have pointed out, undercut entrepreneurship and obviated the efficient allocation of resources to the most productive areas of the economy. Capdevielle, *Fétichisme*, 367.

[87] *Economic Growth*, 237.

[88] Edmond Rostand, *Cyrano de Bergerac* (Paris: Gallimard, Coll. Folio, 1983), 142.

[89] Quoted in Mayer, "Classes moyennes," 455.

At base, the survival of a substantial *petit indépendant* sector can be seen as the sociostructural expression of the individual's atavistic desire for economic and social autonomy. It implies the simultaneous ownership and working of productive property on a small scale by the individual and his family. According to this minimalist conception of economic production and organization, outside labor is employed by the small firm owner only as a last resort, as an extension of his own labor. As one author put it, the *petit indépendant* "is first and foremost a worker ... [who] is at the same time part of the proprietary class."[90]

Petits indépendants thus represent an intermediate form of production that translates into their ambiguous position and status within industrial capitalism. Although they may not be counted as proletarians because of their ownership of their own instrument of production, they cannot be defined as bourgeois on account of the personal – often manual – character of the labor by which they work their petty property, often earning an income similar to an industrial worker's salary. In *Das Kapital*, Karl Marx identified this fundamental ambiguity at the heart of the functional and social identity of *petits indépendants*:

> The independent peasant or handicraftsman is cut up into two persons. As owner of the means of production, he is a capitalist, as laborer he is his own wage-laborer. As capitalist he therefore pays himself his wages and draws his profit on his capital; that is he exploits himself as wage-laborer, and pays himself in the surplus-value, the tribute that labor owes to capital.[91]

Their ambiguous position within the capitalist economy reflects the peculiar status of *petits indépendants* as functional holdovers from a bygone era. They enshrine modes of production associated with both a precapitalist handicraft industry and small-scale peasant agriculture. Alluding to the persistence of these antiquated modes of production within industrial capitalist society, Marx writes that "within capitalist production there are always certain parts of the productive process that are carried out in a way typical of *earlier modes of production*, in which the relations of *capital and wage-labour* did not yet exist and where in consequence the capitalist concepts of *productive* and unproductive labour are quite inapplicable."[92]

Petits indépendants' functional ambiguity within industrial capitalism, reflecting economic and social relations rooted in a precapitalist past, bred a peculiar mix of perspectives, attitudes, and values, or "class culture," among them. Considered as a whole, these traits constitute the cultural system – in E. P. Thomson's phrase, the "moral economy" – of *indépendance* underpinning the

---

[90] F. Gresle, "L'indépendance professionnelle: actualité et portée du concept dans le cas français," *Revue française de sociologie* 22 (1981), 488–9.

[91] "Productivity of Capital. Productive and Unproductive Labour," in *Theories of Surplus Value*, vol. IV of *Capital*, part I (London: Lawrence and Wishart, 1969), 408.

[92] "Appendix: Results of the Immediate Process of Production," in *Capital: A Critique of Political Economy*, vol. I, trans. B. Fowkes (New York: Penguin Books, 1981), 1042 (emphasis in the original).

worldview of these strata in France.[93] This cultural system was sustained by the survival of a significant artisanal and shopkeeper sector alongside modern industry and commerce, holding important implications not just for the country's economic development but for its social and political evolution as well.

Three principal cultural correlates of *indépendance* define the economic and social identity of French *petits indépendants*: the ideal of economic and social autonomy, the spirit of craft or *métier*, and the primacy of the family. These underpin *petits indépendants'* economic and social relations, conditioning their worldview and informing their social and political behavior. The first of these motifs, the ideal of economic and social autonomy, is rooted in the precapitalist agrarian individualism characteristic of the French peasantry. Implying ownership of one's own means of production and the provision through one's labor of the output associated with it, such petty producer individualism translates a basic desire to "be one's own boss" and the consequent refusal of salaried employment. As Nonna Mayer found in her interviews of Parisian shopkeepers, *petits indépendants* uniformly recoiled before the regimentation of office and factory work, characterized by one of her interlocutors as "paid slavery." They depicted the working-class condition in particular as synonymous with economic and social subjugation.[94]

By contrast, *petits indépendants* pursue occupations that give free rein to their individual initiative. Artisans and petty shopkeepers conceive "their enterprise as their creation, which they made according to their idea, investing in it a part of themselves."[95] For them, self-employment represents the path to a higher social status, a vehicle for escaping the economic hardship and social inferiority associated with wage labor.[96] In turn, their conception of economic liberty, closely identified with small business ownership, broadened into a

---

[93] Quoted in Bechhofer and Elliott, "Petty Property," 182. In the words of François Gresle, the notion of *indépendance* emerges as the "unifying psycho-sociological principle" according to which petty producers and tradesmen are able to constitute themselves as "a social class … the keystone of a social philosophy deeply anchored in the collective unconscious of shopkeepers [and] artisans." *Indépendants*, 217, 242.

[94] "Classes moyennes," 272.

[95] Ibid., 273.

[96] This notion was clearly articulated by Gérard Nicoud, leader of the CID-UNATI, the principal sectoral formation advocating on behalf of *petits indépendants* during the late 1960s and early 1970s. He maintained that, by holding out the prospect of social advancement through the exercise of individual initiative, the petty independent sector effectively guaranteed social stability by reinforcing the principles of liberty and upward mobility that preserved the social order. In *Les dernières libertés, menottes aux mains*, a tract in which he argued for the preservation of the petty artisanal and commercial trades, he asserted that "petty shopkeepers and artisans, members of the independent professions, MUST NOT disappear. First because we represent that human contact so necessary to the "client," and that does not exist in those great anonymous [commercial] structures, second because we have an intimate knowledge of our trade that the ephemeral, unspecialized employee so lacks but which nevertheless remains essential. … But especially, because we represent the possibility of ADVANCEMENT, the potential that every man must feel of becoming one day his own master, with all the opportunities that this implies, but also the satisfaction of being able to give totally free

comprehensive social vision. They conceived of a society based on individual small business as quintessentially free, fluid, and supportive of individual creativity and potential.[97]

The structural correlate of the ideal of *indépendance* is the commitment to smallness. Stemming from their limited financial capacity to launch anything but the most rudimentary of enterprises, this commitment also reflects *petits indépendants'* desire to safeguard their economic autonomy and the distinctive social status they derive from it. They prefer to remain small and independent to expanding their profits but foregoing control over their enterprises.[98] Perhaps as an ex post facto rationalization of the economic marginality of their firms, shopkeepers and artisans appear to place greater importance on preserving their independent economic and social status than on achieving a higher income, particularly if the latter implies joining the ranks of wage earners. In the final analysis, they are content with keeping their enterprises small because such is the price for managing them on their own. Privileging autonomy over wealth,

---

rein to one's initiative, one's intelligence, one's work. . . . A journeyman, an employee, a wage earner must, if they are willing, have the possibility, the means to try their luck, to have one day their own enterprise, which will emancipate them and allow them to fully realize all their intellectual and manual faculties. . . .

"[Thus] once our social class disappears, never will the worker, the employee, the wage earner be able to aspire to this [social] advancement. In particular, with its disappearance, it is liberty itself that will be disappearing, because even though it costs us dear at the moment, either financially or in terms of labor expended, it is the love we display for this liberty, the love of *indépendance* that has driven a number of us to leave the office or the factory behind in order to set up shop on our own. It is this love of liberty that pushes us today to fight in order to save it, because we are, when all is said and done, the 'final keepers of individual freedoms.'" Quoted in C. Baudelot, R. Establet, and J. Malemort, *La petite bourgeoisie en France* (Paris: Maspero, 1974), 272.

[97] The professional autonomy sought by *petits indépendants* corresponded to a deep-seated desire for social respectability and status that was most often posited in contradistinction to the proletarian condition. In this context, the assertion and defense of individual liberty were both a normative legitimization of this desire for social advancement and a means by which the *petit indépendant* could couch his normative superiority to the wage earner, despite the gradual deterioration of his socioeconomic position relative to the latter. In turn, because of the normative and social superiority it implied vis-à-vis wage labor, the status of *indépendance* came to be regarded by petty artisans and shopkeepers as an end in itself, the guarantee of a worthwhile social identity and existence. It represents the consummation of an upward social trajectory that is jealously safeguarded upon attainment and clung to even more fiercely in the face of ever-increasing economic volatility and social instability. Summarizing this sentiment, Gresle has remarked that "the social advancement that is symbolized by the fact of having one's shop on the high street [*avoir pignon sur rue*] does not represent an intermediary and temporary stage in the expectation of achieving a higher social destiny; it marks a culmination, and translates the *petit bourgeois* conviction that by opening up shop, one has won a haven offering protection from the fiercest economic struggles and greatest social tensions." *Indépendants*, 63. On this point, see also Mayer, "Classes moyennes," 274.

[98] Hence, the wariness evinced by *petits patrons* historically against appealing to outside capital in order to increase the size of their enterprises and their fear that such growth would subject them to an unacceptably onerous regulative and fiscal regime. Mayer, "Classes moyennes," 484, 950.

control over growth, the motto resuming the attitude of the artisan or petty shopkeeper tenaciously remains *ça me suffit.*[99]

The second cultural component of the system of *indépendance* is the strong attachment of *petits indépendants* to their craft (*métier*). Insofar as this "spirit of the craft," to use Bernard Zarca's phrase, gives concrete form and specific content to their economic function, it constitutes a primordial element in shopkeepers' and artisans' social identity.[100] Traceable historically to the corporative guilds – the Chambres des métiers – which controlled access to the crafts from the late Middle Ages up to the French Revolution, the notion of *métier* implies a mastery of the productive skills and of the technical know-how underlying the profession of the small trader or producer. Overlaid with shared cultural identifications and resonances, this attachment to the *métier* subtends the common cultural outlook distinguishing shopkeepers and artisans as a group or class within French society.[101]

The nature of self-employed or independent labor, presenting attributes that underlie a common experience and conception of work, in turn functionally unites *petits indépendants* and facilitates their development of a common cultural outlook and psychology. The latter evince a totalistic versus specialized approach to work, the artisan, in marked contrast to the industrial worker, being involved in all stages of the conception, production, and sale of a particular good or service. Correlatively, *petits indépendants* also evolve a different sense of time in performing their work, laboring until a particular job or task is completed rather than for a preordained number of hours, irrespective of

---

[99] A fishmonger from Paris's tenth arrondissement perfectly captured this contentment with remaining small. "Even if someone were to propose to me, for instance, something much more ... er, fabulous, much more ... in which I would be almost certain to make more ... I would make much more money, to be quite honest about it ... well, frankly, no ... I am happy in my trade where I can stay at the maximum of my possibilities ... and in the *petit commerce* ... this big stuff, it doesn't interest me at all. I say no to all that. It doesn't appeal to me at all. I prefer the small-scale thing." Ibid., 365. For the sake of brevity, let us note that, throughout the remainder of this chapter, reproduced extracts from the interviews of *petits indépendants* refer back, unless otherwise attributed, to the aforementioned study by N. Mayer.

[100] Zarca, *L'artisanat français*, 20.

[101] Obviously, this general attachment to the *métier* allowed for considerable variation in the definition of the economic and social identities of petty traders and producers. The practical and technical dimensions of various trades, the specific nature of the work they commanded and materials they involved, reflected a broad array of productive relations that underpinned the economic roles of *petits indépendants*, thereby leading them to develop differentiated and nuanced social identities between them. Despite their common adherence to a *métier*, *petits indépendants* were sufficiently diverse that it would be overly reductionist to conceive of them as culturally or sociopolitically homogeneous in the same way that, say, unskilled industrial workers could be said to be culturally homogeneous. Instead, it might be more apposite to say that, by virtue of their universal exercise of a particular craft, *petits indépendants* evolved a common sensibility and certain shared dispositions and perspectives that fashioned a certain general mentality or "turn of mind" among them. On the internal differences manifest within the *artisanat* in particular and the independent sector in general, see ibid., 234–5.

output.[102] In short, the structural and temporal attributes and constraints of the *métier* inculcate certain attitudinal and behavioral dispositions among *petits indépendants* that together laid the basis for a distinct socioeconomic mind-set or culture. The requirements of the *métier* presupposes, as Bernard Zarca put it, "the reproduction of both a technical and social division of labor" that is "subordinated to the adherence ... to specific values, constituting a veritable culture that produces norms of behavior."[103]

The third component of *indépendance* is the primacy accorded to the family as the locus of the economic as well as social existence of *petits indépendants*. As was previously noted, the *petit indépendant* sector was characterized historically by a low ratio of wage-earning labor to unremunerated family work.[104] This reflected the primacy of family help to the economic activity and survival of *petits indépendants*. Unpaid family labor was often the functional guarantee of socioprofessional independence, the institution of marriage representing "the necessary if not sufficient condition for the existence of a craft."[105] In many

---

[102] Writing on the temporality of agricultural work that, as we saw, is very similar to that of artisans and even shopkeepers, Monique Vincienne has adduced that, in the context of independent labor, "time has no value in and of itself; what counts is its contents in work and in production, which is why the product of labor is at least approximately measured, but not the duration of labor." *Du village à la ville*, 53–4.

[103] *L'artisanat français*, 19. In this sense, the organic evolution of the trades over the centuries served to progressively build up and harden the distinct sociocultural orientations of *petits indépendants* by firmly grounding them in the notion of *métier*. This was particularly true in the case of the *artisanat*, where a strong *métier*-based culture was intergenerationally transmitted through the age-old institutions of *apprentissage* (apprenticeship) and *compagnonnage* (journeyman training). In turn, this cultural salience of the *métier* was often just as important in defining the economic and social identity of shopkeepers. As several studies have shown, this was mainly due to the fact that historically, the productive or transformative function of most small shopkeepers in preparing their goods for sale was as significant a component of their work as the actual sale of those goods to their clientele. Alain Faure, "L'épicerie parisienne au XIXme siècle ou la corporation eclatée," *Le mouvement social*, no. 108 (July–Sept. 1979), 115–17.

[104] Mayer estimates that in 1975, family help in the commercial sector accounted for 685,100 persons, a number that fell steadily in the 1980s and especially the 1990s, reflecting the general decline in the number of *petits indépendants* as well as the commensurate rise in the female, wage-earning workforce. In 1990, considering the nonagricultural independent sector as a whole, this number had declined to 279,000 (424,000 if one includes salaried family members) and in 2001, to 176,000 (335,000 including salaried family members). "Classes moyennes," 90, and Blanpain and Rouault, "Les indépendants et dirigeants dans les années quatre-vingt-dix," 427–8.

[105] Gresle, *Indépendants*, 291. An overwhelming proportion of such informal familial labor comprised wives assisting their husbands in the day-to-day operations of their artisanal workshop or store. According to one study, 86% of the wives of petty shopkeepers between 1965 and 1970 were themselves *indépendants*. This situation had not substantially changed by 1990, when the majority of the spouses of *indépendants* could also be counted as such. This functional primacy of marriage to the survival of petty independent enterprises helps to explain the greater durability of marriages – translated by lower rates of divorce – among *petits indépendants*. Divorce was avoided at all costs by the latter, because in most cases it spelled the end of their businesses. In this light, marriage represented as much a "social-economic strategy as a symbol of traditional moral values that serve in effect to legitimize this strategy." Ibid., 295–6, 298.

cases, the obligations of *indépendance* extended to the entire family, children as well as wives being enlisted in the daily running of the family store or workshop. In these conditions, the nuclear family became the structural surrogate – a reservoir of labor spelling the difference between solvency and bankruptcy – for the small self-owned firm. It thus represents an intrinsic and essential component of *petits indépendants'* relations of production, the practical guarantee of their economic and social existence.[106]

Thus, it is hardly surprising that of all the socioprofessional categories comprising French society, shopkeepers and artisans are among the strongest defenders of traditional family values in French society.[107] Indeed, the normative principles and relations of authority underlying the traditional nuclear family are ideally suited to the operation of the small independent firm. The paternalistic relations that prevail in the artisanal workplace can be seen as the natural extension of the patriarchal relations obtaining in the traditional family. Just as the husband is held to command the family, so the *petit patron* commands his firm. In turn, just as the operation and solvency of the business comes to depend on the family's contributions, the status and well-being of the family is inextricably linked to the performance of the business. The wealth and prestige devolving to the family from the business becomes the principal justification for the existence of the latter. The upshot is that it is increasingly difficult to distinguish the firm from the family as separate economic and social entities. The values and prerogatives attaching to the family effectively become imbricated with those of the firm, reflecting a unitary cultural system encompassing the spheres of both work and private life.[108]

The cultural system of *indépendance* predicated on small-scale economic property and subtended by the imperatives of the *métier* and the defense of the family translates into a peculiar morality that sets *petits indépendants* apart from

[106] Writing in 1926 on the social conditions of the *artisanat*, the social commentator Jean Delage ably captured this totalistic engagement of the family in the functioning of the small independent business: "The artisan works at home. He has his shop, his home. Marriage for him is the foundation of his trade. His wife will be his helpmate; his children, too. The more children, the more assistants, and the more his enterprise will prosper." Quoted in Zdatny, *Politics*, 43.

[107] Accordingly, a poll from June 1980, found that 63% of *petits indépendants* were fully in agreement with the statement that "preserving the family 'as it has always existed' is one of the most important priorities for our society," versus 59% for the French population as a whole. Mayer, "Classes moyennes," 495.

[108] This merging of the affairs of the family with those of the firm was specific not only to the group of *petits indépendants*, though they provided the primordial model for it. It also extended to larger, family-owned enterprises – what David Landes has called the model of the French "bourgeois firm" – and thus came to characterize certain, traditionalist segments of the greater French bourgeoisie. On the spillover of this petty bourgeois cultural model to larger family-firm owners, see in particular John Sawyer, "Strains in the Social Structure of Modern France," and Landes, "French Business and the Businessman," both in Earle, *Modern France: Problems of the Third and Fourth Republics*, 293–312 and 334–53. For a relatively recent statistical analysis of the prevalence of this family-firm model among larger industrial and commercial enterprises in France, see Dean Savage, *Founders, Heirs and Managers: French Industrial Leadership in Transition*.

other socioprofessional groups. This petit bourgeois morality is constructed around the three interrelated values of hard work, frugality, and self-abnegation, each of which serves a vital normative function in the operation of the small independent firm. In addition to sustaining the *petite entreprise*, the ethos of hard work affirms the primacy of the *métier* that underpins the professional and social identity of *petits indépendants*. In turn, the value of thrift becomes the principal means of preserving the financial viability and social status of their families. Finally, these twin imperatives come together in a powerful ethic of self-abnegation that, as several authors have pointed out, lies at the heart of the moral system of *petits indépendants*. Such an ethic implies both a sacrifice of leisure through hard work and a foregoing of consumption through frugality. Thus, it confers a sense of moral superiority upon the *petits indépendants* who follow it, particularly as compared to the consumerism and ostentation displayed by their alleged social betters.

From this standpoint, the principles of hard work, frugality, and abnegation that drove *petits indépendants* are not simply a reflection of the functional necessities and material constraints faced by the latter but are cast as proof of their moral superiority to both an indolent and untalented *salariat* and an undeserving and spoiled *grand patronat*.[109] Together, they serve as powerful normative justifications for the role and position of *petits indépendants* within the French economy and society. By buttressing the institutions of petty economic property, the *métier*, and the traditional family, this rigorist moral system legitimizes the economic function of the *petit indépendant* sector and the social relations that characterize it. At the same time, this exacting moral system, preventing them from enjoying the fruits of their labor and subjecting them to near permanent privation, became a powerful source of *ressentiment* for *petits indépendants*.[110] Alternately directed at *gros patrons* and wage earners, undeclared workers and the "professional" unemployed, and, increasingly, at immigrants, this animus was exploited by the radical Right to growing effect as the economic and social position of the latter progressively deteriorated.

This cultural model of *indépendance* and the rigorist morality to which it gives rise constitute important interfaces or "filters" by which social and political events are apprehended by *petits indépendants*. These subtend certain

---

[109] Pierre Bourdieu has ably captured the sense of moral superiority developed by *petits indépendants* as a result of their rigorist economic and social ethos. Describing an updated Protestant Ethic of sorts transposable to the modern-day petite bourgeoisie, he writes: "In the context of social exchanges in which others are able to advance concrete guarantees, money, culture or social connections, [the petite bourgeoisie] can only offer moral guarantees; (relatively) poor in cultural, economic and social capital, it can only 'justify its pretensions,' as they say, and thereby give itself the possibility of realizing them in terms of paying for them in sacrifice, privation, and renunciation, in a word, of paying for them in virtue." "Avenir de classe et causalité du probable," *Revue française de sociologie* 15(1) (Jan.–Mar. 1974), 23.

[110] Mayer, "Classes moyennes," 337–42. Cf. also P. Bourdieu, "Condition de classe et position de classe." *Archives européennes de sociologie* 7(1) (1966), 201–23, and "Avenir de classe et causalité du probable," 18–28.

fundamental attitudes that are harbored by *petits indépendants* toward contemporary society, which in turn structure their economic and political outlooks and beliefs. This complex of attitudes is ably surmised by the concept of misoneism, which, defined as the "hatred of anything new," implies a strong nostalgia for a bygone social and economic order.[111]

Arising from the conflict between the cultural system of *indépendance* and the guiding principles of industrial society, these attitudes amount to a general repudiation of social and economic modernity, perceived as both physically threatening and morally debilitating by *petits indépendants*. By contrast, the latter come to see themselves as the last remaining defenders of timeless and authentic French values against the pernicious evolution of modern industrial society. Perhaps because it affirms their social superiority and utility, the critique of economic and social modernity that is advanced by these strata has displayed a remarkable continuity over time. As witnessed by their cultivation of essentially the same motifs and themes today as fifty or even one hundred years ago, this critique continues to color their social and political convictions and perspectives down to the present day.

This critique of modernity is advanced at two distinct yet interrelated thematic levels. First, it involves the denunciation of the concrete, physical manifestations of modernity, portrayed as a hostile and oppressive environment in which the individual finds himself alienated. Initially, such a critique is bound up in a negative deconstruction of the big city, which is held to distill the most dehumanizing effects of modern life on the individual. In the impersonal and alienating environment of the city, the individual's identity is dissolved in an amorphous mass of similarly alienated individuals.[112] Communication with

---

[111] See Chapter 2, note 30.

[112] In the words of a confectioner from Paris's seventh arrondissement: "And so we ... we are moving towards bigness. For example, just a little while ago, my daughter came by, we were talking about Roissy [Charles-de-Gaulle airport], the things, er ... Before I was telling her, listen, the RER, I come from ... from the Boulevard Saint-German often, I said at Etoile [RER station] there's too many escalators, I said, um, we should put these, anyway, these things to walk, I said ... you have these mechanical walkways, so they make you go into this steel tube, it seems like you're being sucked into it, well, all that is inhuman, it's inhuman ." And relating her general recoil before the mechanical coldness and gigantism of the modern world specifically to the setting of the large-scale supermarket, she adds: "And me, I think that ... we're going towards too much. ... See, not so long ago they built another supermarket in Poissy, where I live, that's called Continent.... We went there once with my husband to see.... Well I said: you won't catch me going there again! You get lost in there, you get lost! Between the pepper and the other thing, well you'll waste a lot of time, anyway, it's, it's ... awful ... you can't help asking yourself, why?" In turn, alluding to the frenetic pace of life in the city, a clockmaker from Paris's tenth arrondissement complains about the "craziness" of life – *la vie de dingue* – that is coextensive with modern urban and industrial society: "Try not to run! If you take the métro, me I see, it sometimes still happens to me at six in the evening, if you want to go home gently, well you're not going to be able to go home gently! You'll have a tidal wave pushing you, you'll have a thousand people taking the métro as well and who want to get home quickly; if you're on the street and you want to go slowly, there'll still be people to knock into you ... who'll say 'Well what's going on, he's not moving?' etc. If you're in your car, try to go slowly, to drive at twenty [kilometers] an hour.

others becomes impossible. The modern culture of work and leisure, the latter subtended by the mind-numbing ubiquity of the television, effectively replaces the culture of conversation and storytelling that underpinned social relations in the village.[113] In this sense, the advent of the city – and of the mass society that it represents – marks the tearing asunder of the close interpersonal bonds that characterized social life in the village. It gives rise among *petits indépendants* to a nostalgic yearning for a rural past in which life was both simpler and healthier and which, by contrast to the modern city, was synonymous with their social and material security.

As a corollary to this negative rendering of the city as a metonym for industrial society, *petits indépendants* also inveigh against the depredations of the modern workplace. Portrayed as the locus of individual dehumanization and collective alienation, man is reduced to being a cog in the industrial machine, forced to repeat day after day and hour after hour the same stultifying tasks within a highly segmented and compartmentalized process of production. By virtue of its near absolute rationalization and mechanization, the industrial workplace replicates in microcosm the stultifying environment and infernal cadence of the modern city. At the same time, the individual is subordinated to the primeval functioning of the machine as the principal agent of production within the factory. As such, the critique of the industrial workplace translates a broader wariness of the technological progress celebrated by the champions of industrialism in particular and modernization in general.[114]

You'll see what happens [laughs]. They'll be saying: this guy's nuts, he's not going fast enough, he's wasting time, he's ... In fact, you don't have that luxury anymore, you've got to go faster. So you go through the motions, the rhythm you get it, it's ... it's the rhythm, the rhythm of the age. On the other hand, back in the old days you could afford to go slowly! Now you can't afford to do it. You have to go faster, faster, faster, faster! You have to go faster for everything, everything, everything!" Quoted in Mayer, "Classes moyennes," 318.

[113] Romanticizing the pace of life and sense of community obtaining within the countryside, a Parisian fishmonger from the tenth arrondissement deplores the fundamental incommunicativeness that has come to subtend social relations in the urban setting: "It's wonderful, the country folk, they're all there together. In Paris, it's that ... well nowadays, the 'me' doesn't exist anymore. We are machines. I'll tell you, we get up in the morning, we go to work, and we come home. That's it. We turn on the television and it's all over. In the countryside they take time to live. They see each other, they talk about things. They try to understand each other's problems. And that's what we need more of in Paris." Ibid., 319.

[114] This critique is redolent of the suspicions expressed by one artisan as long as a century ago, at the turn of the beginning of the twentieth century, regarding the liberating potential of new machines and technology. Rather than welcoming the installation of electricity in his house, he denounced it as the harbinger of subjugation and alienation: "Never! I don't want anything to do with your so-called progress. Progress is going to kill you all. It'll cut off your arms; you won't be able to work anymore. Machines will do everything. They'll replace you and you'll be worthless." No less apocalyptic in its assessment of the effect of technology was the newspaper *L'Artisan* of Le Puy, which thundered in February 1932: "The triumph of the machine will lead to worldwide disaster." And in no way was this an outdated sentiment. According to a survey conducted in 1972, such attitudes toward the forms and processes attaching to modern production and consumption endured among *petits indépendants* despite the much-heralded passage from an

Finally, *petits indépendants* also blame the alienation of the individual on the plethora of consumer goods that have inundated French society as a result of economic progress and technological innovation in the modern industrial era. The standardization of goods due to the mechanization and rationalization of production translates into a stultifying uniformity of consumption, inevitably debasing personal taste and individuality. People become increasingly indistinguishable from one another as they consume the same goods in ever greater quantities.[115] Similarly, the new materials used in industrial production are held to herald the triumph of the chemical, the synthetic, and the artificial over the natural, the organic, and the authentic. As Mayer remarks: "To the frozen vegetables, to the cellophane-wrapped meat available at the supermarket, [*petits indépendants*] contrast the honey from the farm, the wine from the *terroir*, the earth-encrusted heads of lettuce. A whole litany of stereotypical images of the countryside, green, fresh, odoriferous, invigorating, is opposed by them to the colorlessness, odorlessness, the deathly coldness of the supermarket."[116]

At a second level, *petits indépendants* overlay their critique of the concrete, ecological manifestations of industrial modernity with a denunciation of the moral corrosion that they see as synonymous with the latter. Three aspects of modern life in particular come in for their excoriation. First, they denounce the dominant ethos of consumerism and the search for immediate gratification that

industrial to a postindustrial society. Out of a field of six socioprofessional categories, petty shopkeepers and artisans proved the most unfavorably disposed toward the advances of science and technological progress. Tellingly, only 23% of petty artisans and shopkeepers agreed with the notion that technological progress was on balance "more good than bad," versus 56% of Frenchmen as a whole. Likewise, 52% of them (versus 42% of the general French population) were totally in agreement with the statement that modern life "had transformed people into robots," 44% (versus 36%) believed that the development of science and technology had a "rather unfavorable" effect on relations between people, and 47% of *petits indépendants* (as against 37% of the whole) judged that science and technology had an "absolutely unfavorable" effect on public morals. Zdatny, *Politics*, 46, 45, and Mayer, "Classes moyennes," 477–8.

[115] As Philip Nord has shown in his study of Paris shopkeepers at the end of the nineteenth century, such sentiments became widespread among *petits indépendants* as soon as standardized, mass-produced consumer products made their appearance on French markets beginning in the 1860s. In turn, a half century later during the interwar period, the president of the butchers' federation and future Vichy functionary Georges Chaudieu expressed a similar concern when he equated modern industrial production and consumption with "monotony, standardized taste . . . and lack of human contact." Nord, *Paris Shopkeepers*, 282–5, and Zdatny, *Politics*, 46.

[116] "Classes moyennes," 321–2. In addition to contributing to this social alienation and uniformization, the modern era of production and technology came to be associated by *petits indépendants* with a slow, inexorable process of poisoning as the empire of unnatural foods and goods supplanted the natural ecology of consumption that had characterized life in the past. In this sense, the mass production of goods was perceived not only as a fundamental debasement of natural quality, but represented for them a substantial health hazard warranting the concern of all. One Parisian *petite commerçante* articulated this concern in this way: "The biggest abattoir in Limoges, they say that everything now is falsified and unnatural, they receive animals that are more or less, that have been reared on [bone] meal and all that. Everything is shipped to the Inno [supermarket chain], you know, and people end up not knowing what they're buying, they get sick, but you have to see what kind of bad meat was being sent to these supermarket chains, you understand?" Ibid., 321.

it betrays as one of the principal sources of individual and collective degradation within modern capitalist society. Likewise, they condemn the superlative primacy accorded to money within modern society on the grounds that it reduces individual existence to a relentless pursuit of wealth and ostentatious consumption.[117] Flying in the face of their ethic of frugality and self-abnegation, consumerism and materialism are portrayed by *petits indépendants* as futile attempts by people to compensate for the vacuity of modern life itself.[118]

Similarly, the search for facility and the renunciation of effort implied by the materialism and consumerism of modern society run counter to the ideals of hard work and self-abnegation that mark *petits indépendants'* worldview.[119] As people renounce effort in the search for easy pleasures, the quality of work and production inevitably suffers, thereby contributing to a general condition of *laisser-aller* within contemporary society.[120] By contrast, *petits indépendants* view themselves as the last remaining guardians of the virtues of effort, hard work, and quality that are universally flouted in modern society, underscoring further the intractable conflict between their traditional morality and the core values and processes of advanced capitalist society.

This denunciation of the search for gratification, resulting in the abandonment of the values of hard work and self-abnegation, broadens into a general condemnation of the relaxation of mores evident in contemporary French society. Central to this critique is the condemnation of the increase of licentious and immoral behavior that has allegedly been wrought by economic and social modernity. Once again, the modern city comes in for special criticism

---

[117] Ibid., 328.

[118] Hence, the frequent allusions by the *petits indépendants* interviewed by Mayer to the Christian admonition, drawn from the Gospels, that man cannot live on bread alone and that wealth does not in itself bring happiness. In the words of the owner of a cheese and dairy shop: "When people say 'life is hard,' when you see all this merchandise, when you see people eating [in restaurants], when you see them going out all the time but ... they're not happy, even when you see them there, maybe they're stuffing themselves but from a moral point of view, that isn't really nourishment, is it?" Ibid., 329.

[119] In particular, *petits indépendants* deplore the habituation of the young to a life of easy comfort and leisure, synonymous in the eyes of many with their pursuit of a university education and consequent adoption of a cushy student lifestyle, devoid of rigor and discipline. As a butcher's wife from Paris's seventh arrondissement observed: "Now [the young people] don't want to work anymore. They want to become unemployed right away [and receive unemployment benefits]. They work much less and then they become unemployed ... because they always start working too late. ... Most of them always take too long. ... The majority of students, they finish [their studies] at twenty-five, they are still studying. ... So then, when it comes to work, they don't want to anymore!" Ibid., 330.

[120] In the words of a hardware store owner from Paris's tenth arrondissement: "I think that in the past people put a lot more heart into their work than they do now. I don't know. ... You get your merchandise delivered to you and, well. ... It's not well packaged or ... people do whatever the hell they like. Um, that's true for a lot of things. ... And it always creates a lot of problems for other people. But anyway ... er, people, they just don't care. It's sort of a time when people don't give a damn ... that's it, monsieur, people just don't give a damn anymore, that's where we're at today." Ibid., 332.

as a seedbed of immorality, starting with the onset of rural migration during the final quarter of the nineteenth century. As social commentators in the interwar era opined, the city was to be condemned not just as a dehumanizing physical and work environment but as a center of "cinemas, dancehalls, and other dens of germs and distractions" that exercised a "deleterious influence" on the nation's mores.[121]

Such sentiments are in no sense confined to the prewar era. An equal vehemence could be deciphered in the denunciations leveled by contemporary *petits indépendants* against the moral laxity of present-day popular culture. Central to this rigorist moralizing is the excoriation of the loose sexual mores identified with today's urban and youth culture. Reminiscent of interwar social commentary deploring the moral corruption of country girls upon their arrival to the city, contemporary *petits indépendants* rail against the "ravages of pornography," express indignation that (young) people today are "having sex with several partners at the same time," and are outraged that girls as young as fourteen are taking the birth-control pill so they can "sleep around."[122] By contrast, contemporary *petits indépendants* portray themselves as the guardians of sexual propriety, displaying "the respect, the instinct to restrain themselves" and channeling their urges into the "desire to build a home."[123] They stand as the last defenders of a traditionalist morality diametrically opposed to the social permissiveness and cultural freedom characteristic of advanced capitalist society.

Their condemnation of social and cultural modernity in turn leads *petits indépendants* to envision the return to a happier past in which the socially dehumanizing and morally corrosive aspects of contemporary modernity are absent. It translates into their own myth of a golden age constructed around structural and moral attributes quite opposed to those identified with social and economic modernity. In the first place, the environment and processes decried in the critique of urban and industrial modernity find their antidote in the forms and habits associated with a mythologized rendering of a precapitalist – specifically rural – society. In contrast to the hellish environment of the city, *petits indépendants* envision the return to an idealized conception of rural life as the basis for reconstituting French society. Fondly evoking the beauty of its landscapes and the freshness of its air, they portray the countryside as an ideal physical setting in which to live compared to the dank and polluted confines of the city.

---

[121] In a similar vein, Lucien Gelly, a longtime advocate of artisanal interests and one of the principal exponents of Vichy's *agrariste* philosophy, deplored the flight of young women from rural areas to the city, where they were bound to succumb to the temptations of rank consumerism and "the possibility of an easier promiscuity." Quoted in Zdatny, *Politics*, 45.

[122] Commenting specifically on the morally corrosive effects of the pill, one Parisian café owner averred: "As far as I'm concerned, I don't know, but that thing brings decadence into the society. It destroys one's will, it destroys everything, its *laisser-aller*, it's ... let's just say it, puts our well-being into jeopardy. ... What do you think it's going to bring when these people live like that? Then people shouldn't be surprised if there are more divorces, when it's time for them to get married or some such thing." Mayer, "Classes moyennes," 330.

[123] Ibid.

In turn, this idealized natural setting becomes a metonym for the spiritual and normative superiority of country life for *petits indépendants*. Spared the dehumanizing conditions of industrial work and the generalized anonymity of city life, country folk are held to lead a much more personally and collectively rewarding existence than their urban counterparts. They offer a social ideal to which *petits indépendants* continue to aspire, on the basis of restoring the strong interpersonal bonds characteristic of the small country village.[124] Similarly, in contrast to the dehumanizing setting and stultifying character of industrial work, *petits indépendants* defend the virtues of creativity and individuality inherent in artisanal craftsmanship, itself a throwback to an earlier, simpler time when France was a rural country.[125] As we saw, the *métier* encapsulates the values of human creativity, skill, and individuality that subtend the artisan's – and, to a lesser degree, the shopkeeper's – economic persona and social identity. In contrast to the plethora of standardized goods that roll off the industrial production line and end up on supermarket shelves, *petits indépendants* aspire to produce high-quality goods, natural products connected to the country setting rather than artificial ones whose authenticity and freshness have been fundamentally debased.[126] Thus, just as they envision the countryside to be the antithesis to the city as an ideal environment in which to live and to work, they contrast handcrafted goods to the standardized ones churned out by

[124] *Petits indépendants* adopted various strategies in order to replicate the physical and social atmosphere of village life. Some sought to reestablish themselves in the *banlieue*, where trees and the possibility of having a garden remind them of the countryside. Others, for want of ever being able to return to their village of origin, elected to vacation there (a strategy that is incidentally also characteristic of industrial workers of recent rural origin). Finally, *petits indépendants* tried to re-create the atmosphere of their village of origin within the gray confines of the *quartier* by sprucing up their own stores, erecting themselves as the preservers through the close rapport they entertain with their clients of the close social relations typical of village life. As one Parisian *petit commerçant* recently put it, small shopkeepers offered "a kind of merchandise that is more and more rare, *le contact humain*." Quoted in ibid., 319–20. On the compensatory strategies adopted by former rural émigrés to recover the physical reality and social atmosphere of life in the countryside, see Eizner and Hervieu, *Anciens paysans, nouveaux ouvriers*, 118–19.

[125] Capturing these values and contrasting them to the rigid organization and numbing repetition of factory work, a Parisian cobbler from the tenth arrondissement told Mayer: "Us, we tinker, we build things, we're artisans, you know. Us, we can make things that others can't make for you, you understand? And it depends on the temperament of . . . of the person that makes them, you understand? It's always the same question in all our work. In whatever work he's doing, [an artisan] needs to be somewhat of an artist, he needs to have an idea, he needs to have a certain taste, he's got to be able to get around something that's insoluble! He's got to be able to manage! While in the big factories it isn't the same. They put one person here, one person there, and then he always does the same thing and that's the end of it! You understand, when he goes home in the evening it's, it's over. He doesn't try to think more deeply about it." Ibid., 322.

[126] This sentiment was echoed by the aforementioned cobbler who, in defense of his fellow *petit commerçant*, extolled to Mayer the freshness of the meat on offer at the local butcher shop while condemning the blandness of that to be found at the supermarket: "For example, in the supermarkets like that they put things in fridges . . . it's not . . . you can't say that it's nice and warm, that it's fresh. While at the local butcher's, slices of liver, a slice of [beef] heart, fresh tongue, you see, it's just been fresh picked, it's alive, it arrived that morning." Ibid.

modern industry as exemplifying the true values of French production. In so doing, they project the values of a bygone, rural, and precapitalist order, their nostalgia for which inspires them to resist the encroachments of economic and social modernity.

Not surprisingly, as an antidote to the moral depredations of the modern age, *petits indépendants* oppose their own traditionalist morality built around family values and the principles of hard work, thrift, and abnegation. They continue to idealize the small proprietor-producer who was predominant during the Belle Époque and interwar periods and cast as the moral backbone and spiritual hero of French society in the literature of the day.[127] Similarly, *petits indépendants'* nostalgia for a return to these traditional values easily shades into nostalgia for the social institutions that historically enforced them. In particular, contemporary *petits indépendants* are unanimous in calling for the restoration of law and order, calling for a time when respect for the law was normal and widespread – particularly as opposed to a lawless present in which the latter is regularly, indeed wantonly, flouted.[128]

This call for a greater respect for the law is accompanied by an increasingly repressive disposition on the part of *petits indépendants*. Such an inclination can be seen in a number of areas, exceeding – in some cases substantially – the repressive inclinations of the general population.[129] Correspondingly, *petits*

---

[127] Attesting to the resilience of this trope, contemporary shopkeepers and artisans identify as much today with the image of the "craftsman as independent, hard-working, and disdainful of the materialism of urban, industrial culture" as when the literary glorification of small producers and shopkeepers reached its zenith during the 1920s and 1930s. They would no doubt echo the June 1925 issue of the *Artisan* newspaper that endowed the figure of the artisan with all the virtues, depicting him in effect as the ideal Frenchman. "An artisan is honest," it quipped, "he's a man of courage in the fullest sense of the word. He is absolutely incapable of cheating anyone out of even a centime. ... The artisan is the Frenchman most admired in the world." Zdatny, *Politics*, 45.

[128] Such nostalgia shows through particularly strongly in the following remarks by a cobbler from Paris's tenth arrondissement: "In the old days we had ... it was ... we held ourselves back more than [people do] today. That is to say we had a greater respect for the law. Now there is no more respect. There's no more ... there's no respect for the law. And that's the case wherever you go. Yesterday even, you know, I almost got in a fight with two young guys who were going up a one-way street on their mopeds, you know, the wrong way. They wanted to go up it the wrong way. But so as not to be in the street they were riding on the sidewalk, you had to get out of the way to let them through! In the old days people wouldn't have done that, that kind of thing, in the old days. It was innate. You weren't supposed to do that, you knew you weren't supposed to do it, so you didn't do it. Nowadays, they know they're not supposed to do it, but they do it anyway." Mayer, "Classes moyennes," 333–4.

[129] Accordingly, 52% of *petits indépendants* surveyed in 1981 placed themselves on the side of the "partisans of the strictest authority and discipline," versus 46% of the French public as a whole. With respect to specific issues, their repressive biases were respectively expressed in the overwhelming belief found among them (72% versus 60% for the French as a whole in 1978) that the function of schooling was to inculcate "the values of discipline and effort" rather than "to train people to have an inquisitive and critical mind" (24% versus 35%). Similarly, 32% of *petits indépendants* versus 19% of the French as a whole in 1981 were absolutely in agreement with the statement "that you can't bring up your children effectively without giving them a good hiding once in a while." Ibid., 498–9.

indépendants express the highest degree of confidence in the legal and justice systems among socioprofessional groups, placing the greatest faith in the police, the army, and the *gendarmerie*. Unsurprisingly, it is among this social constituency that the justice system is most widely seen as too lax.[130] In addition to expressing the strongest desire for restoring law and order, *petits indépendants* also favor pursuing the most repressive policies in order to ensure that respect for the law is properly maintained. Thus, in 1979, 73 percent of *petits indépendants* (versus 53 percent of the French as a whole) considered that the sentences handed down by French Criminal Courts were too lenient, and 77 percent of them (versus 59 percent among the general population) believed that it was wrong to grant leaves to prison inmates. Finally, 75 percent of *petits indépendants* (versus 56 percent) declared themselves personally in favor of the death penalty.[131]

Broadly speaking, then, the general sentiment of misoneism evinced by French *petits indépendants* translated into a fundamental dislike of the manifestations of economic and social modernity and the attendant transformation of the values that was wrought by it. Harkening back to a rural past in which the small proprietor reigned supreme and traditional values governed people's behavior, it was the principal attitudinal corollary of the cultural system of *indépendance* developed by shopkeepers and artisans in France. From an affective or psychological standpoint, such misoneism provided the latter with a defense mechanism against their increasingly precarious economic and social position within industrial society. Legitimizing the economic and social role of *petits indépendants* in advanced capitalist society, it should come as no surprise

---

[130] These repressive sentiments were articulated in the following way by the cobbler interviewed earlier: "Nowadays, you know, it's, it's, it's ... it's really shocking, now, the police, if they want to do something or whatever, they can't do anything anymore. If they have the misfortune, in the line of duty, if they have the misfortune of killing somebody, it's a huge scandal! Yet, what do you want, those are the risks of the [criminal] trade, that's absolutely clear. If someone wants to go outside the law, there's no doubt he knows, he has to know [the risks]. He has to know he's risking his life, that he's risking something whatever it is, he's risking prison, he's risking everything. These days, however, he doesn't risk anything any more, since we're giving them these ... these four-star prisons, and this and that!" Ibid., 385.

[131] Ibid., 498–501. The desire of many *petits indépendants* to restore traditional moral precepts to the center of social and personal life was frequently accompanied by an affirmation of the church as the principal agent of traditional values within the country. Indeed, many of them deplored the state of the contemporary church in France, arguing that it had become too liberal and lax to stand as an effective guardian of traditional mores and principles. Accordingly, numerous – particularly older – *petits indépendants* nostalgically recalled "their old priests," some even going so far as to call for the restoration of the most traditional wing of the church in France, perceived as the sole organizational incarnation of the Catholic faith capable of adequately defending traditional values. This appeal of traditionalist Catholicism to a significant segment of *petits indépendants* reflected not so much doctrinal concerns over the evolution of the church, but rather the conviction that this form of Catholicism best fulfilled the vocation of the latter as an instrument of social control and source of moral authority. In this case as in others, *petits indépendants* were thus, as Mayer surmised, "instinctively inclined toward tradition against progress." Ibid., 333, 507–8.

that this misoneism found its most extreme expression at times when their role and status were most gravely threatened.

Inevitably, the misoneism deriving from the cultural system of *indépendance* conditions the economic and political behavior of shopkeepers and artisans in a number of ways. Touching first on the economic sphere, the wariness evinced by these strata toward the contemporary workplace is overlaid by a precapitalist economic mind-set dramatically at odds with the imperatives of rationality and efficiency characteristic of the most advanced forms of industrial production. As we saw, this mind-set is colored by the attachment felt by *petits indépendants* to their craft, which they conceive as a life-defining vocation, as well as to their families, enlisted in the service of their firms. It necessarily gives rise to an affective approach to doing business that is incompatible with the rationalist precepts of profit and share-price maximization upon which decision making in the advanced capitalist firm is predicated.[132] Hence, *petits indépendants'* adoption of what one observer has termed a "noneconomic approach to the economy."[133]

As such, the traditional economic mentality developed by *petits indépendants* is in diametrical opposition to that of the modern capitalist entrepreneur. In the first place, whereas the latter seeks to enhance the economic performance of his business, the former perceive it first and foremost as a vehicle for exercising their craft. Accordingly, the entrepreneur aims to expand his business, enlarge his market share, and maximize his profit; the *indépendant* seeks merely to generate enough income to be able to exercise his trade while taking care of his family's needs. In essence, the *petit indépendant* strives to maximize the freedom to pursue his *métier* and run his enterprise as he sees fit. He prefers to preserve his independence to the possibility of growing his enterprise should this mean relinquishing control or accepting outside interference in it.[134] In this sense, the

---

[132] In a passage whose main point could apply just as well to petty shopkeepers as to artisans, Bernard Zarca has adroitly underlined the analytical vacuity bound up in trying to understand the economic behavior of *petits indépendants* according to the abstruse, absolutist schemata of economic rationality that today dominate much economic theorizing and overlook the important psychological, cultural, and historical factors that inevitably intrude upon and inform their economic behavior. He asserts that "any informed study of the economic rationality of artisans must not limit its field of inquiry to that of the rationality of means and that there are good reasons to take into consideration a ... manifold and complex 'material rationality.' Their [economic] objectives reflect different kinds of imperatives that can be extremely varied, even contradictory, in their motivations. The individual does not choose his tastes; the actions he undertakes, the objectives he sets for himself, depend on values that experience has forged for him without his assent. Is it really still possible to speak of rationality in this case? ... any economic decision is not taken in as schematic a manner as the microeconomic theory of the utility maximizing agent would have us suppose." *L'artisanat français*, 138.

[133] Mayer, "Classes moyennes," 377.

[134] Gresle, *Indépendants*, 484. In this connection, growing the firm was contemplated only if it remained in keeping with the moral and functional strictures imposed by the *métier*. As one researcher has written, "The development of the firm can only be permitted if it marks the end-product of a real and lasting activity, the expansion of which would in some sense be self-sustained and morally transfigured by love of *métier* and voluntary abandonment of the self to

economic mentality of *petits indépendants* is explicitly Malthusian in the French use of the term and encapsulated by the motto: "It is better to be a small *patron* than a big lackey." Shunning growth in favor of stability, the possibility of greater profit in favor of independent control, French *petits patrons* condemn their firms to remain small. It is this outlook that contributed to the profusion of small and inefficient firms that have clogged the country's industrial and commercial structures down to the present day.

Such a Malthusian approach to business implies that the management principles and business practices of the small independent firm are structured around habit and custom, rather than the rationality characteristic of the modern capitalist entrepreneur. The firm is conceived as an instrument of production rather than a capital investment, the *petit patron* running it as an immediate "breadwinning" activity rather than a means of capitalizing his investment over the long term.[135] In turn, such a visceral and immediate approach toward managing their firms brings *petits indépendants* to develop a strongly conservative business outlook that is fundamentally incompatible with the risk-taking disposition that defines the modern Schumpeterian entrepreneur. Instead, his business principles are best resumed by the admonition "to sell little, but expensively, what he already has," to employ the smallest personnel possible, and to calculate as "meanly" as possible. In this light, the *petit indépendant* is "the man of small savings and of small profits."[136] And when he does generate profits, he rarely channels them to his firm but instead invests in traditionally safe, low-yield assets, such as real estate and, historically at least, government-backed treasury bonds. In essence, then, the typical *petit indépendant* has evolved defensive economic strategies both in running his business and in his approach to investing that are reminiscent of the *petits rentiers* of old. Representing the cultural antithesis of the Schumpeterian entrepreneur, "all of his choices betray," as Mayer has observed, "the search for security [and] the fear of risk."[137]

one's work." Thus, following in the image of Jean Marbréry, the hero of an interwar novel that exalts the social status and moral stature of the *artisanat*, the *petit indépendant* "is someone who prefers to quietly perform his job rather than to expand his enterprise and make more money." Zarca, *L'artisanat français*, 147. On the figure of Jean Marbréry, see Zdatny, *Politics*, 45.

[135] The absence within the *petit indépendant* mind-set of any long-term approach toward making money, subordinated to the rational economic calculus implicit in investing in and expanding one's business, translated into a concrete and immediate relationship to money. Upon being earned, the latter was "either spent or put aside." Rather than seeing them as a means of maximizing their future utility and earnings potential, *petits indépendants* conceived of their receipts as palpable and immediate "cash in hand" – an accumulation of bills and coins to be counted at the end of each working day, instead of potential profits that could be reinvested in their businesses. As Mayer points out, such an unsophisticated approach reflected a basic lack of business training on the part of the vast majority of *petits indépendants*, betraying their ignorance of the most elemental business practices such as basic accounting, the tracking of sales in relation to inventory, and so on. Mayer, "Classes Moyennes," 365, 374–7, and 380ff.

[136] Ibid., 367.

[137] Ibid., 368. The refusal to invest in the financial markets has long translated into the distinction drawn by *petits indépendants* between "legitimate" economic gains, acquired through hard

The aversion to risk characteristic of *petits indépendants* translated in turn into a broader repudiation of the principle of competition. Many petty producers and traders hold the latter to be immoral and unjust, particularly when it opposes small firms to large ones. Hence *petits indépendants'* postulate that "each small business has 'the right to live' and 'each person must be able to exercise his craft.'"[138] In particular, in contrast to advocates of unfettered free markets, *petits indépendants* advance the concept of "loyal competition": the belief that competition is justified only if it opposes adversaries of equal size on a "level playing field."[139] Because supermarket chains and large industrial firms are not only much larger than the small enterprises run by *petits indépendants* but are also held by them to benefit from unjustifiable fiscal advantages and political protections from the state, this admonition rules out as patently unfair their competing against small, self-owned firms. Accordingly, the notion of loyal competition becomes the principal moral justification legitimizing the entry of *petits indépendants* into sectoral alliances against supermarkets and other large retailers.[140] Finally, it translates into a protectionist ethos that is irreducibly at odds with the principles of free trade defended by classical-liberal economists and the advocates of unfettered market capitalism. Thus, this notion constitutes yet another element reinforcing *petits indépendants'* precapitalist or even anticapitalist mind-set, which, in turn, is a fundamental component of the rearguard struggle that they have been waging against the forces of social and economic modernity. Like their misoneistic perceptions, it serves to legitimize the resistance of petty artisans and traders against the structures and processes of

work and economy, and "illegitimate" economic gains, acquired not by means of individual effort but through speculation. As Jacques Capdevielle reminds us, it was not until the interwar period, which saw what he terms the "democratization" of the financial markets, that there was an evolution on the part of *petits indépendants* toward regarding speculative investing as an acceptable means of making money. The moral stigma attached by this constituency to financial investing prevented them from engaging in more profitable investment practices that would have resulted in their more rapid enrichment and facilitated their accession to the ranks of the bourgeoisie. Thus, this factor substantially contributed to the persistent economic and social fragility that was to plague *petits indépendants* throughout the course of the twentieth century. Capdevielle, *Fétichisme*, 230–4, 210–11.

[138] Mayer, "Classes moyennes," 369.

[139] A luxury food store owner in Paris's seventh arrondissement articulated this notion in the following terms: "No, I think that competition is a good thing but only provided that it be ... on an equal footing. In that case, it's okay, it's a struggle, er, that's fair ... but otherwise no ... and unfortunately ... that everybody be on the same level, er, defend themselves you know through their personal abilities, fine, but I don't see why some should be given certain advantages." Ibid.

[140] In practice, the affirmation of *petit indépendant* unity in the face of unfair competition extended to reducing competition among themselves within the *quartier*. Shopkeepers and artisans contracted informal ententes with one another, effectively precluding competition – even of the loyal variety – from becoming too strong between them. As a fishmonger from the tenth arrondissement put it, "We get each other to work, we send each other our clients ... we're obligated among ourselves as shopkeepers to help each other out ... so that people won't take their business to the neighborhood next door. ... It's all part of the game, and besides, it helps stimulate business." Ibid., 370.

modern capitalism by offering an essentially moral justification for their survival in industrial society.

At a second level, the cultural model of *indépendance* also leads shopkeepers and artisans to develop certain specific political dispositions. In the first place, their total absorption in their occupations translates into a general ignorance of political issues that brings *petits indépendants* to view politics as the exclusive preserve of politicians and parties from which they are far removed. At the same time, their individualistic experience of work precludes them from developing the collective identifications and attachments necessary for sustained political action. As François Gresle has put it, "Believing that he is living out a singular destiny with respect to his peers as well as to society as a whole, the *indépendant* has difficulty transcending the fundamental egocentrism to which he is inevitably led by the particularistic pursuit of his trade."[141] Thus, he evinces – at least in periods of relative economic and social stability – what another author has termed a "refusal of politics," the unwillingness to engage on a quotidian basis with political processes and issues.[142]

This refusal of politics is articulated around certain basic themes. First, it translates *petits indépendants*' fundamental wariness of the state and its agents, a proclivity most obviously expressed in their abiding opposition to state intervention in the economic sphere. The opposition to state intervention in turn leads them to criticize the two principal incarnations of the modern French state: the welfare state (*L'État providence*) and the bureaucratic state (*L'État fonctionnaire*). The welfare state is guilty of killing off personal initiative and breeding generations of indolent recipients of state aid who would rather remain unemployed and continue to receive benefits rather than actively find a job.[143] By the same token, *petits indépendants* also direct their ire against the state bureaucracy, in their eyes an agent of wastefulness and inertia whose agents – the

---

[141] Ibid., 392. Arno Mayer couches this point somewhat differently, arguing that the traditional lower middle classes only displayed a sense of class identity or consciousness in periods of political and economic crisis when they felt their economic interests to be seriously threatened. Conversely, in periods of relative calm, he suggests, they expressed only a diffuse sense of class awareness, insufficient to constitute the basis for a common political program or project. "The Lower Middle Class as Historical Problem," *Journal of Modern History* 47, no. 3 (Sept. 1975), 434.

[142] As a baker from Paris's seventh arrondissement put it, "Politics? It doesn't interest me at all. I absolutely don't understand it. It's the last person who speaks who says the best thing. Anyway they all speak well. They're all right." Mayer, "Classes moyennes," 393.

[143] As a Parisian cobbler put it, "Nowadays, I think that they've succeeded in killing the ... I don't know the ... They just don't give people a taste for pulling themselves up by their own bootstraps anymore. They're being given the means, all the means they need, falling right in their lap. I was going to say ... that's it, everything's given to them in advance! ... And then they're not being given a taste for work, they're being given a taste for ... doing nothing, it's true! These days, a taste for what are they being given? A taste for not doing anything. We're paying them not to do anything. In the old days there was no unemployment. The person who wanted, who felt like having enough to eat, well he had to work, you know, there's no question about that!" Ibid., 385.

hated *fonctionnaires* – they deem to be as lazy as they are incompetent.[144] In short, the bureaucratic welfare state is seen by *petits indépendants* to be a grossly inefficient source of economic and social paralysis, whose functions are better left to private initiative. Correlatively, they also oppose the modern state on the grounds that they are disproportionately taxed in order to pay for it, while benefiting least from its assistance. In this sense, the economic liberalism professed by this constituency most frequently takes the form of a denunciation of the encroachments – whether fiscal or otherwise – of the state upon their lives. It is essentially in this negative sense, through their excoriation of government intervention, that *petits indépendants* can be said to be economically liberal.

In turn, this defensive liberalism and the refusal of governmental intervention politically translate into a refusal of the ideologies of socialism and communism. Not only are the latter synonymous for them with revolutionary disorder, but they conflict at a more fundamental level with the prerequisite of individual economic property underlying the condition of *indépendance*. From their perspective, the only true form of liberty resides in the work ethic and the prospects for social advancement that it offers – that, by working hard, industrial wage earners or service-sector *employés* could one day aspire to set up shop as they did. In this sense, *petits indépendants* reject the principle of social equality that underpins socialism and communism and instead place their faith in meritocracy as a basis for determining economic and social outcomes.[145] They view social inequality as naturally warranted, the logical outgrowth of innate differences in ability and talent that separate individuals. Consequently, they unconditionally reject the leveling prescriptions of left-wing parties and trade unions on the grounds that they hinder the freedom of initiative and enterprise celebrated by the *petit patron*.[146]

Yet, the notion of loyal – i.e., restricted – competition defended by *petits indépendants* in practice diminishes the force of their commitment to economic liberalism because it often leads them to espouse inconsistent, if not contradictory, political and economic prescriptions. The most flagrant example is their

[144] Ridiculing the standard-bearers of all *fonctionnaires*, the French postal workers, one *petit commerçant* derided them by playing on the widespread stereotype that people from the South of France are lazy: "I still wouldn't sit around with my butt in a chair, even if it was for thirty five thousand francs! I'm not from the *Midi*, you know, because in the PTT [French postal service], well you can just tell from their accents, they're all from the Midi. [laughs]. Just to stamp a letter, and this and that ... half-an-hour you have to wait. Well, those people aren't over exerting themselves, that's for sure!" Ibid., 386.

[145] Justifying the economic inequalities separating the *patron* from the worker, a Parisian vegetable vendor made this point in the following terms: "But who is a capitalist? He who is willing to become it! Therefore we take risks, therefore it totally makes sense that a *commerçant*, even a small one, or a certain type of capitalist, among others, make more money than a worker, given that ... he invests his own money. He can lose this ... this money. Me, I'm not preventing, you know, the worker from setting up his own business! On the contrary! If there is no *patron*, there are no workers. You could say, that it's the other way. ... But anyway I think that you still need both. Not everyone can be a *patron*." Ibid., 418.

[146] On *petit indépendant* views of trade unions and assorted quotes, see ibid., 396–7.

demand that, given their virulent criticism of the welfare state, the latter provide them financial assistance and regulatory protection in the face of economic competition from large-scale commerce and industry.[147] And when they deem the state to not be doing enough on their behalf, they direct their ire against the political class as a whole, accusing it of being deaf to the plight of the common hardworking Frenchmen they claim to represent.[148] In short, *petits indépendants* come to feel increasingly disconnected from and unrepresented by the nation's political leaders, the perceived failure of the latter to protect them translating into their abiding distrust of politicians and rendering them potentially favorable to oppositional movements and parties.[149]

What the foregoing suggests is that, as a function of their cultural mind-set, French *petits indépendants* have evolved a passive yet negative view of political processes, institutions, and elites. Indeed, it is this basic orientation that has periodically disposed them toward movements of the radical Right. In turn, one cannot but be struck by the commonalities between the cultural model of *indépendance* that characterizes *petits indépendants*' mind-set and the discourse of the radical Right. Both place the same emphasis on the family as the

---

[147] Specific state policies to assist *petits indépendants* would presumably include providing them with funds to support their installation, giving financial incentives and (even greater) tax breaks to small business, even compensating *petits patrons* if they go bankrupt – that is, the very kind of policies that are virulently attacked by *petits indépendants* on liberal economic grounds when they benefit large industrial and commercial concerns. Ibid., 390.

[148] Their anger at the supposed inaction or indifference of the political elite comes through in the following statement from a butcher from Paris's seventh arrondissement: "The [government] ministers, that's great, they're there, they're there, um ... they're the ones who make the laws, they do everything, they make their ... the laws to their own advantage anyway, they're not making laws to their disadvantage, are they? And we need to be able to discuss it with them, but for me, I don't understand, the law nowadays is [made] by ministers who only discuss it among themselves. Okay, there's the minister of the interior, the minister of this, the minister of that, they tell each other this stuff, you know, but they don't ask the opinion of ... of the people. You can say that again. They don't ask the opinion of the people! ... Why is it that when there is a cabinet meeting only the ministers get to take part and discuss things? That shouldn't be the case. What they should do is talk to all the shopkeepers, since it's the shopkeepers that [through their taxes] support the state, you know, talk with the shopkeepers to see, um, why something isn't working, and why this and why that, um. When there are [cabinet] meetings it's only them that are there, that ... fight it out or talk forever, and shop ... shopkeepers, they're never invited!" Ibid., 388.

[149] This sentiment comes through particularly emphatically in the virulent attack launched on politicians by a Parisian stationer: "I think that a human being who begins to get involved in politics is a rotten man. And I'm not kidding you, right? He can be of any political current, from the extreme Left to the extreme Right, they're all the same, they're all as bad one as the other, they should all be put in a sack with a weight and thrown into the Canal Saint-Martin, because it's closest to here. Me, I find ... all politicians, I find that they're all horrible men. Everything has got to be for them, whoever they are. When they are ... when they are sitting. ... They'll feed you any old bullshit in order to get elected. The day they're elected, they sit behind their desk and say: 'It's time for me to make some money.' You could be dying next to them they wouldn't lift a finger to help you." Ibid., 394.

fundamental social unit at the center of their respective worldviews. Each professes the same attachment to a primordial archaeoliberal conception of economics based on the sanctity of private property, loyal competition, and limited state intervention.[150] Finally, each posits a traditionalist ethic and rigorist morality while evincing a common aversion to modern industrial society. Projecting by contrast the vision of a mythical past each glorified both the French countryside and rural life as reflected in their shared philosophy of rusticism.[151] In short, one might conclude that the cultural model characterizing *petits indépendants* and the discourse of the radical Right in many ways reflected one another, a likeness reinforced by their mutual emergence at the end of the nineteenth century and their often intersecting evolution since then.

More broadly, as a result of the sweeping transformation of the French economy and society, *petits indépendants* were increasingly subject to crises of identity – what the French sociologist Alain Bihr has termed cultural crisis – which in turn rendered them amenable to the discourse of the radical Right.[152] At a first level, new methods of organizing production entailing the ever-greater expansion, rationalization, and automation of the workplace sounded the death knell for the ancient values of the craft or *métier* that is typical of their professional and social identities.[153] These new ways of organizing production were subtended by principles of economic rationality that, positing purely financial criteria of performance and achievement, were anathema to the economic Malthusianism of French *petits indépendants*.

In turn, the intervention of new structures, practices, and norms in the economic life of the country reflected broader shifts in the general social and cultural environment that made *petits indépendants* feel increasingly less at home within modern French society. Their unease underscored the growing incompatibility between their petty-producer-based conception of society and the increasingly pervasive modern industrial milieu, heralding the dissolution of the familiar and comforting surroundings of the *quartier* of which they had been the traditional economic and social linchpins. In this sense, the deleterious impact of commercial and industrial concentration upon *petits indépendants*, whether it be the *grands magasins* of the 1880s and 1890s or the *supermarchés* and *hypermarchés* of the 1960s and 1970s, was to be measured not only in their deteriorating economic posture but also in the dislocation of the social

---

[150] I have borrowed this term from Patrick Fridenson, "L'idéologie des grands constructeurs dans l'entre-deux-guerres," *Le mouvement social*, no. 81 (1972), 52.

[151] Zdatny, *Politics*, 45.

[152] On this point, see note 40 in the Introduction.

[153] As Gresle has put it, this radical reconfiguration of production under the conditions of advanced industrial capitalism resulted in "the despecialization of certain skills and gestures . . ., stripping the [*petit indépendant*] of that which he holds most dear: his professional competence." Thus, "the trade . . . lost the central importance that it had commanded only a few short years before," translating a general "lack of social consideration and recognition from which independent craftsmen were bound to suffer." *Indépendants*, 187, 190–1, 192.

environments and relationships that had shaped their sociopolitical world-view.[154] In particular, the advent of concentrated industry and commerce was held to threaten the two social institutions of greatest import to *petits indépendants*: the petty producer republic and the traditional patriarchal family. At one level, because no group had welcomed the republic more fervently than petty producers, their progressive extinction as a result of industrial and commercial concentration was portrayed as a mortal danger to the republican order in its primordial and authentic guise. Second, by ruining small enterprises, considered as the sociostructural corollary of the traditional family, the large factory and *grand magasin* were seen as attacking the latter. In short, the progressive extinction of the *petit commerce* and artisanat and the ensuing deliquescence of the *quartier* heralded a political and normative catastrophe, signaling the death of a sempiternal France that was identified with the petty producer vision of *morcellisme* and the perpetuation of traditional family values.[155]

Likewise, *petits indépendants* blamed industrial society for hastening the destruction of the natural rural setting and corrupting the traditional ways of life historically associated with it.[156] The despoiling and emptying of the countryside as a result of industrialization was in turn a symbol for the general moral

---

[154] Thus, deploring their effect on the social vitality of the *quartier*, *La Crise commerciale*, a newspaper close to *petit indépendant* interests, opined in October 1887: "Behind a facade of anonymity [the *grands magasins*] cynically monopolize everything for themselves ... already they have overrun their neighborhoods, indeed entire streets; it's a veritable invasion." Similarly, a year later, Eugène Delattre, a Radical deputy close to the Ligue syndicale, declaimed in its official organ that, as a result of the nefarious influence of department stores on local commerce in Paris, "certain *quartiers* were like a desert" and that consequently "the city [was] in decay."

In her study of Parisian shopkeepers almost a century later, Nonna Mayer uncovered essentially the same sentiments and concerns among *petits indépendants*. Notably, she recorded how the introduction of new, more concentrated forms of commerce were held by *petits indépendants* to have precipitated the destruction of *quartier* life through their obliteration of *petit commerce*, considered the essential functional backbone and sinew of city neighborhoods. "In each street, in each *quartier*," she writes, "small shops recreate a 'small village,' that is 'bustling' and 'alive.' They know each other, they know their clients, they call them by their names, people chat while they wait in line. ... And their displays, their storefront windows, bring a note of joy to the grayness of the city. They represent warmth and life, by contrast to the mortal frigidity of the supermarket and of modern life in general." Nord, *Paris Shopkeepers*, 266, and Mayer, "Classes moyennes," 320.

[155] Regarding *petits commerçants* during the Belle Époque in terms that would still apply today, Philip Nord observed that "the shopkeeper occupied a strategic position in the moral life of the community. His enterprise and authority assured the continued existence of *quartier*, workshop and family. Without him neighborhood life would disintegrate, the Republic crumble, and society sink into anarchy and sexual disorder." Nord, *Paris Shopkeepers*, 265, and chs. 7 and 8.

[156] Such sentiments were particularly evident in the rusticist literature that came to the fore in *fin-de-siècle* France and experienced a revival during the interwar period. Within this literature, the city, and Paris in particular, was cast as a den of promiscuity, disease, and sexual depravity. Likewise, in her study of Paris shopkeepers, Mayer found the same outlook to be pervasive among contemporary *petits indépendants*, the latter tending to mythologize or romanticize country life as both a practical and a normative foil to the immoral and dehumanizing influences of

collapse that had been wrought by economic and social modernity. As we saw, for *petits indépendants* the latter ushered in a pernicious relaxation, even perversion, of mores that was evident in the steep rise of antisocial forms of behavior: burgeoning criminality, prostitution and pornography, the advent of a hypersexualized and drug-ridden youth culture, the erosion of the work ethic, and the creation of ever greater numbers of *assistés* through welfare policies that effectively rewarded laziness. In turn, this moral dissolution was seen to be accompanied by a creeping loss of respect, particularly among the young, for traditional sources of authority – in particular the patriarchal family and the Catholic Church.[157] Amid this universal moral degradation, *petits indépendants* saw themselves as the sole remaining bulwark for the defense of traditional values. Cultivating a deeply felt sense of moral superiority based on their respect for such values, the latter portrayed themselves as the last bastion on which the moral redemption and social *redressement* of the country ultimately depended.[158]

modern urban life. On these assorted images and motifs, see Nord, *Paris Shopkeepers*, 269–70, and Zdatny, *Politics*, 45.

[157] The importance accorded by *petits indépendants* to the dislocation of the traditional sources of familial and religious authority and the profound concern it elicited among them shows through in the responses of many of the Parisian shopkeepers who were interviewed by Mayer for her study. For example, identifying the disastrous consequences of the breakdown of *l'éducation traditionnelle*, a stationer from the tenth arrondissment intoned: "Since we are talking about the family, still about the education of the family, well why are there so many louts [*voyous*] on this earth? It's incredible at the moment, all the ... the terrorists that there are. But if ... if there are so many louts in the world, what is it due to? It's due to the absence of the parents when the children come home from school. At the age of ten, twelve they start to hang out in the streets, they put each other up to no good, the problem starts there. If the mother was there ... well especially the mother, but the father as well, if they were at home more often [then you wouldn't have the same problems.]" Similarly, a Parisian candy-store owner deplored the grave social consequences of the growing secularization of French society: "Well, there needs to be a [moral] support! Everyone needs a support. If there's no more religion. ... You need a support. People had religion before. It was a mystification you might say. ... Right now, we demystify everything, that's serious you know, for society, very serious, you understand? The abolition of religion has been a serious ... a very serious [development.] "Classes moyennes," 331, 333.

[158] This general sense of impending moral collapse and social disintegration was accompanied for many *petits indépendants* by an equally universal sentiment of the degradation of cultural, particularly aesthetic, norms. Such a critique saw in the impersonal materials and forms that defined the urban and industrial environment telling symbols of the dehumanizing coldness of the modern age. Quintessentially modern materials such as steel, concrete, and glass were contrasted in the aesthetic idiom of the *petit indépendant* with time-worn, traditional substances such as wood and stone that had been the sempiternal objects of artisanal craftsmanship. In short, the ecological, aesthetic, even sensory dislocation to which *petits indépendants* were subjected in the modern urban setting transformed it into an increasingly hostile and unrecognizable environment for them. As such, it symbolized their own decline in an age of ever quickening technological innovation and economic modernization. For example, drawing this connection between the structures and materials of industrial civilization and the general process of moral and social deliquescence afflicting French society during the Belle Époque, the proshopkeeper and pro-artisan organ *La Revendication* portrayed the iron construction of the Eiffel Tower as broadly evocative of the moral turpitude and social injustice of the modern age. Thus did it proclaim, in a February 1889 article recording the start of the world's fair for which the

By any measure, then, the reconfiguration of the French economy and society throughout the era of capitalist development was a traumatic experience for *petits indépendants*. It induced a permanent state of cognitive dissonance among them, the result of the intractable antagonism between their petty producer vision of society and economy and the structures and values accompanying industrial civilization. At one level, the advance of capitalist economic and social relations served to delegitimize and discredit the ethos of *indépendance* on which they had based their social identity. In turn, the singular absence of a new collective ethos by which they could make sense of the social order and define their place within it made life in modern industrial society increasingly inhospitable and unintelligible for these strata. Thus, as French society underwent ever more rapid mutation, individual *petits indépendants* found it more and more difficult to impart conceptual and affective coherence to their experience of modernity. As one writer surmised, they increasingly lacked a symbolic order that was "capable of furnishing and unifying the existential points of reference that g[a]ve meaning to their lives."[159] Hence, the crisis of meaning suffered by the members of these antimodern groups within advanced industrial society, fundamentally bringing into question their relationship to the social world and basic identity and role within it.[160] In turn, their inability to find meaning in modern industrial society and consequent search for new forms of identity drew

tower had been built: "That rude metal has given its name to an age in which the strong physically crush the weak. It's only natural that iron has reached its apotheosis in a century and in a country ... where the wealthy have all the advantages and the little people all the sufferings." Likewise, the same denunciation of the inhumanity of the modern urban environment continued to characterize the outlook of *petits indépendants* during the closing decades of the twentieth century. They deplored a modern setting where "everything is too big: the factories, the avenues, the skyscrapers where one 'gets lost' and where everything is cold: the steel, the glass which have replaced the familiarity of stone and wood." In such an inhuman setting, "communication itself becomes impossible," the material and structural environment synonymous with the modern age adding to and exacerbating the general alienation experienced by the individual within it. Nord, *Paris Shopkeepers*, 278, and Mayer, "Classes moyennes," 317.

[159] Bihr, *Spectre*, 130. On the concept of cognitive dissonance and its application to the social and political spheres, see Orfali, *L'adhésion au Front national*, 222–4.

[160] In this sense, the crisis afflicting *petits indépendants* extends well beyond "objective" structural processes and material indicators pertaining to their professional function or socioeconomic condition as a group. Rather, it is felt by them first and foremost at a "subjective," affective level, as a function of their culturally fraught and symbolically discordant experience of the modern world. This subjective crisis of meaning, linked to the loss of individual signification and identity within contemporary society, calls to mind the "hysteresis of the habitus" described by Pierre Bourdieu, whereby "the schemas of perception, of appreciation and of action that have been internalized by the individual ... as a function of his routine confrontation with social reality" are rendered increasingly impracticable and irrelevant by their unsustainable contradiction with the "objective exigencies" of the sociostructural and sociocultural environment. According to Bourdieu, such situations of disjuncture or conflict between the subjective orientations that are bound up in the individual habitus and the objective conditions characterizing the external environment typically give rise to "a gamut of adaptive behaviors" that range from "simple resignation" to "extreme revolt." Quoted in Michel Dobry, *Sociologies des crises politiques. La dynamique des mobilisations multisectorielles* (Paris: Presses de la Fondation Nationale des Sciences Politiques, 1986), 241, 243.

petits indépendants to identify en masse with the radical Right at certain junctures in recent French history. The thematic and symbolic likenesses between its ideology and the ethos of *independence*, not to mention its provision of easy scapegoats on whom their troubles could be blamed, made it an ideal source of reassurance and identification for these strata.

However, despite these likenesses, it is important to emphasize that there was nothing inherent in the cultural model of *indépendance* that automatically predisposed *petits indépendants* to the radical Right. To put it in a different way, it was not simply as a function of the class-cultural mind-set that they evolved as a result of their peculiar economic role and social position that *petits indépendants* came to constitute the principal source of support for the radical Right historically. A lot of history needed to unfold and many political developments to occur before this could come to pass. If anything, it could be said that the cultural system of *indépendance* did little to insulate shopkeepers and artisans against the discourse and the program of the French radical Right. Only in conjunction with *petits indépendants*' cumulative political experiences and memories, and only in the conditions of social and cultural crisis just outlined, did this cultural mind-set help favorably dispose them to the radical Right.

4

The Age of Contentment

Petits Indépendants during the Belle Époque

Ils n'allaient guère au-delà de la pauvre pensée de Robespierre: une démocratie politiquement souveraine faite de petits propriétaires paysans et de petite bourgeoisie artisane.

Jean Jaurès, *Histoire socialiste de la Révolution française*[1]

The political behavior of French *petits indépendants* cannot simply be imputed to the cultural model of *indépendance* they have evolved as a function of their economic and social role in French society. It also reflects the cumulative political experiences of these social segments, which translated into a collective memory replete with preferences and prejudices that informed their political outlook and actions. This collective memory gave an affective political content to the motif of *indépendance*, thereby shaping the political orientations and dispositions – or political culture – evolved by French *petits indépendants* over the past one and a quarter centuries.

At the root of this collective political memory is what could be termed the primordial republicanism of French *petits indépendants*. As we have seen, this republicanism envisioned a sociopolitical order made up of independent, small-property-owning producers and tradesmen, Léon Gambetta's famous *couches nouvelles*. Harkening back to the small-property-based Jacobin ideal, this ideology was enshrined at the outset of the Third Republic by republican Modérés such as Jules Ferry and Gambetta, who would lead the Opportunist Republic of the 1880s, and Radical Socialists in the mold of Georges Clemenceau, who anchored the turn-of-the-century governments of republican defense. At the same time, in the 1890s and early 1900s, petty proprietor republicanism was reconciled with Social Catholic thought, and the emphasis placed by the latter on small property as the basis for a harmonious and moral social order. In its conception of a polity constituted of self-employed, small-property-owning producers and traders, this primordial republican ethos became a vital ideological corollary to the cultural model of *indépendance* that underlay the economic

---

[1] Quoted in Henri Hatzfeld, *Du paupérisme à la sécurité sociale* (Paris: Armand Colin, 1971), 313.

and social identity of French shopkeepers, artisans, and small firm owners from the end of the nineteenth century on.

Yet, the political identity of French *petits indépendants* was not invariably fixed to this primordial, small-producer-based republicanism. It also developed as a function of the evolving relationship of the French traditional middle classes to the republican state and the degree to which they influenced and were impacted by its policies. The latter reflected the capacity of *petits indépendants* to shape policy making relative to other sectoral constituencies and social groups, that is, big business, industrial workers, peasant farmers, *fonctionnaires*, white-collar employees, and the burgeoning segment of *cadres* (industrial managers, engineers, and technicians) thrown up by the modern industrial economy. In this sense, state policy was a revealing gauge of the relations of power that developed among various class and sectoral interests, reflecting the respective "winners" and "losers" of the broad course of policy making since the end of the nineteenth century.

The policy outcomes of intersectoral or interclass competition depended in large part on the evolving institutional framework of the republican state and of the instances by which economic and social interests were politically aggregated and mediated within it. At a first level, these included the political parties, the agents of representation through which these interests were articulated and which, depending on their influence over the levers of executive and legislative power, fashioned policies that were congruent with their demands. At a second level, they involved the ability of these different constituencies to influence, through pressure or lobbying organizations, the instances of state administration responsible for implementing policy. As the state's scope and competencies grew, partly in response to the challenges raised by the ongoing evolution and transformation of the French economy and society, the ability of various interests to act upon and become embedded in its bureaucracy was an increasingly important feature of the dynamics of interest competition. Under the Third Republic, in which political parties occupied a position of both executive and legislative authority, interest organizations effectively became stand-ins for the legislative committees set up by the various parliamentary groups to debate and legislate policy. Simultaneously, interest groups also "colonized" the administrative agencies of the evolving French state. Under the Fourth Republic and especially the Fifth, the state administration's power as the arm of the executive increased considerably at the expense of the parliament, enhancing the influence of interests with access to the bureaucracy while reducing the sway of those who were shut out from it.

From this political-institutional standpoint, French *petits indépendants* experienced a gradual erosion in influence over the policy-making and administrative instances of the French state. Exacerbated by the rising fortunes of their sectoral, economic, and social competitors, this decline provoked their mounting displeasure, if not outright hostility, toward the personnel and institutions of the republican state. These were seen to have betrayed the primordial republican compact by which small producers and traders had been the original progenitors and rightful benefactors of the early republic.

Consequently, they grew increasingly frustrated and resentful of state policies that ran counter to their social and economic interests, feelings that morphed at times into a wholesale rejection of the republican regime and principles of representative democracy. It was this growing ambivalence toward the workings of the republican state, combined with the traditionalist morality and misoneistic outlook deriving from their culture of *indépendance*, which rendered small traders and producers in France politically susceptible to the radical Right.

The decline in influence suffered by *petits indépendants* under successive republican regimes and their consequent ambivalence toward the republican state reflected the gradual shift in state policy from the unconditional defense of petty producer interests in the final quarter of the nineteenth century to the intentional neglecting of and even active opposition to those interests in the 1950s and 1960s. A function of broader economic and social changes and the burgeoning commitment of state and societal actors to industrial and commercial modernization, this declining influence could be seen at the three levels of the industrial, social, and macroeconomic policies that were enacted by successive governments since the establishment of republican government in 1870. The object of this and the following three chapters is to trace the evolution of interest competition since that time and map the declining influence of *petits indépendants* over the representative and administrative instances of the French state as reflected at each of these policy levels. Thus, they show how these strata went from representing the staunchest defenders of the republican state to constituting its greatest detractors in the name of "authentic" republican ideals, which they accused it of betraying and of which they remained the last bulwark in an increasingly debased and illegitimate sociopolitical order.

PETITS INDÉPENDANTS AND POLITICS IN THE BELLE ÉPOQUE: FROM 1870 TO 1914

> [La petite industrie et le petit commerce] constituent comme de nécessaires anneaux de la chaîne entre les puissants potentats de l'industrie et du commerce et ceux qui vivent de leur travail manuel ... ce sont des personnes dont la fonction dans l'industrie et le commerce est d'être à la fois de petits capitalistes et des travailleurs. ... Il faut à tout prix les conserver entre la très grande industrie, le très grand commerce, qui sont nécessaires, et ceux qui ne sont appelés à vivre que de leur salaire ... si ces petits industriels, si ces petits commerçants ne restaient pas vivants et bien organisés pour la production dans notre pays, nous laisserions face à face deux puissances qui se chargeraient peut-être de nous détruire ou, dans tous les cas, d'amener une lutte dont on ne peut pas envisager, sans une sorte de terreur, les conséquences pour la paix du pays. Édouard Aymard, president of the *Société internationale d'économie sociale*, 1910[2]

As we saw in the preceding chapter, the political identity of *petits indépendants* was rooted in the primordial republican ideal of petty producer democracy.

---

[2] Quoted in Capdevielle, *Fétichisme*, 208.

Traceable to the Jacobin revolutionary ideology cultivated by urban artisans and shopkeepers during the Revolution and later incorporating the peasantry, such an ideal married political equality with the defense of private property and freedom of enterprise, projecting the accession to small property as the precondition and guarantee of democratic citizenship. Thus, it remained coextensive with a preindustrial social and economic order subtended by petty production and commerce. As Maurice Agulhon observed, this primordial republicanism presupposed the "anteriority of democracy to modernity," a conception that ineluctably placed *petits indépendants* at loggerheads with the advocates of economic concentration and rationalization.[3] Correspondingly, because they constituted the majority of the citizenry within this sociopolitical dispensation, petty producers and traders came to conceive of themselves as the essential functional and moral glue holding together the democratic republican order. In the words of another historian, many shopkeepers and artisans became convinced that without them, "the Republic [would] crumble, and society sink into anarchy and ... disorder."[4]

This primordial republicanism was given programmatic shape by republican dissidents in the waning years of the July Monarchy and, following the overthrow of the Second Republic, during the Second Empire. Their political platform, most completely expressed in the Belleville Program of 1869, articulated three basic demands: the institution of universal suffrage, the diffusion of private property, and state intervention as an instrument of social progress. Whereas the first two demands respectively enshrined and guaranteed the principle of political equality, the third was cast as the agent of the popular weal embodied in the republican state. Central to this program was its evolutionary and progressive conception of the social order. The Radical republicans responsible for drawing up the Belleville Program refused to accept the fixed, hierarchical view of a society divided into hermetic and stratified social ranks that characterized traditionalist (Legitimist) and constitutionalist (Orleanist) monarchists. At the same time, they rejected the antagonistic conception of class struggle that characterized the revolutionary teleology posited by socialists such as Jules Guesde. On the contrary, they saw social mobility as the key not only to transcending the archaic social divisions that were attributable to feudalism but also to attenuating the deleterious effects of class conflict.[5]

---

[3] Quoted in Gaillard, "La petite entreprise," 146.

[4] Nord, *Paris Shopkeepers*, 265.

[5] Hence Gambetta's famous admonition that the *couches nouvelles*, drawn from the "world of petty proprietors, small businessmen, [and] petty shopkeepers driven forth by the movement of the economy," break the hold of the traditional aristocratic and bourgeois notables who had held political sway since the Restoration and constitute the basis for new structures of local representation and authority throughout the country. In the thinking of Gambetta and other Radical republicans, the political accession of these new strata would provide the surest bulwark for creating and consolidating a nascent republican social and political order, since it could only serve to entrench the primordial republican ideal of small-property-based democracy and broaden its appeal. Barral, *Les fondateurs de la Troisième république*, 232. On the origins and early

From the mid-nineteenth century on, this Radical republican program became synonymous with the defense of the sociopolitical aspirations of small property holders.[6] In this sense, Radicalism was more than just a political manifesto or set of policy proposals corresponding to a particular conception of republican democracy. It also captured the psychological state of the traditional middle classes in *fin-de-siècle* France, feeding on the ambitions and fears of the small propertied strata that would become the dominant force in French society with the establishment of the Third Republic. In the words of Senator Joseph Caillaux, one of the principal leaders of the Radical Party in the first half of the twentieth century: "Radicalism was not a party but a state of mind, the state of mind of the petty bourgeoisie and the majority of the rural population."[7]

In its initial guise, Radicalism belonged on the left of the political spectrum. It corresponded to the demands for political enfranchisement and social advancement expressed by the small-property-owning strata, appealing to the egalitarian principles of 1789 to defend the latter against the encroachments of the economic elite, whether in the guise of traditional large landowners or the *parvenue* aristocracy of finance and industry. Cultivating a *culte du petit* vis-à-vis its petit bourgeois denizens, it lambasted these agents of "gigantism" who impeded the advancement of small property holders and called for overthrowing the new parafeudal order that denied them their political and economic rights.[8] Yet, despite its initial positioning on the left, Radical republicanism also presented conservative, even reactionary, elements. Most notably, it defended a conception of the social order that was based on the sanctity of private property and individual economic liberty, thereby reflecting the attachment of petty producers to their farm, store, or workshop. Radicalism sought a middle way between revolutionary collectivism, which threatened to do away with all

development of the ideology of Radicalism, see Serge Berstein, *Histoire du parti radical. La recherche de l'âge d'or, 1919–1926*, vol. I (Paris: Presses de la Fondation nationale des sciences politiques, 1980), 24–8, and Jean-Thomas Nordmann, *Histoire des radicaux, 1820–1973* (Paris: La Table Ronde, 1974), chs. 1–4.

[6] In time, the Radical Party (which was officially founded in 1901) would indeed fulfill this injunction, coming in the first half of the twentieth century to be identified with the France of the *juste mesure* and representing what the Radical deputy Albert Thibaudet aptly described as the "middling ideas of France, anchored in petty and middling property." The strong identification of small and middling property owners with the principles of Radicalism was reflected at the local level in the composition of the party committee for Chalon-sur-Saône during the 1920s and 1930s. Almost half (47%) of the committee was constituted of *petits indépendants* (37% were shopkeepers and traders and 10% artisans), compared to 25% who were civil servants, 15% white-collar workers, 7% industrialists and entrepreneurs, 4% members of the liberal professions, and 2% farmers. If we add to the shopkeepers and artisans the proportion of farmers, industrialists, and entrepreneurs, we find that well over half – 56% – of the Chalon Radical committee was composed of what could broadly be termed the independent middle classes. Barral, *Fondateurs de la Troisième république*, 45; Nordmann, *Histoire des radicaux*, 324; and Berstein, *Histoire* (I), 259.

[7] Quoted in R. D. Anderson, *France, 1870–1914: Politics and Society* (London: Routledge and Kegan Paul, 1977), 98.

[8] S. Berstein, "La culture républicaine dans la première moitié du XXe siècle," in Berstein and Rudelle, *Le modèle républicain*, 169. On the initial identification of *petits indépendants* with the Left, see Gaillard, "La petite entreprise," 147–52, and Mayer, "Classes moyennes," 709–21.

private economic property, and unrestrained "monopolistic" capitalism, which benefited the *gros* at the expense of the *petits*. Combining the tenets of political equality and of the respect for private property, it provided the dual ideological foundations of the nascent Third Republic.[9]

Accordingly, the "Republican Revolution" that gave birth to this new regime strove to enshrine the ideal of political equality without threatening the economic and social foundations that had characterized the preexisting sociopolitical order. Undergirding it was a class alliance between the progressive, economically dominant strata of the bourgeoisie and petty urban and rural producers, the republican synthesis famously identified by Stanley Hoffmann of the bourgeoisie and either its "preserves," the mass of *petits indépendants*, or its "reserves," the peasantry.[10] Under the terms of this synthesis, a crucial division of labor emerged between the grande and petite bourgeoisie. The former functioned as the caretaker of republican society and steward of the republican state. Meanwhile, the latter operated as "shock troops" of the republic, serving first as a prophylactic against aristocratic reaction and subsequently as a foil to working-class revolutionism. In exchange for retaining control over the levers of political and economic power, the grande bourgeoisie pledged to guarantee the economic interests of petty producers, often to the detriment of modernization – a process from which, as the most advanced economic group, it most stood to benefit. In effect, as a function of its alliance with the traditional middle classes, the advanced bourgeoisie was "blocked from undertaking a thoroughgoing program of capitalist concentration."[11] Instead, it was forced to adopt a slew of protectionist policies to safeguard the economic interests of petty producers, laying the foundation for the economic dualism that would characterize the country's subsequent development and providing the social bases for the "stalemate society" that would come to define the Third Republic.[12]

Crucial to the regime's republican synthesis was the democratic myth that ideologically legitimized "the union of the bourgeoisie and the people."[13] This myth posited that the introduction of universal suffrage and the provision of free, universal education under the new republic would vastly increase social mobility by allowing "the people," that is, petty property holders and propertyless workers, to expand their existing holdings or accede to property ownership in their own right. As a function of the diffusion of property, conflict between worker and *bourgeois* would become baseless because the possibility of acceding to property meant the former could join the ranks of the latter. Similarly, the opposition between the grande and petite bourgeoisie no longer

[9] In this sense, Radicalism constituted, as Sanford Elwitt has put it, a "party of both 'movement' and 'order.'" *The Making of the Third Republic: Class and Politics in France, 1868–1884* (Baton Rouge: Louisiana State University Press, 1975), 14.

[10] "Paradoxes of the French Political Community," in *In Search of France*, ed. S. Hoffmann (Cambridge, MA: Harvard University Press, 1963), 5–6.

[11] Elwitt, *Making of the Third Republic*, 58.

[12] Hoffmann, "Paradoxes," 3.

[13] The phrase is from Henri Allain-Targé. Quoted in Elwitt, *Making of the Third Republic*, 22.

made sense within a society characterized by a high degree of social mobility and property diffusion, because the bourgeoisie now formed a fluid whole characterized by movement from its lower to its higher strata.[14] In short, the framers of the Third Republic took it for granted that enhanced social mobility and the diffusion of property for which it provided would not conflict with the social and economic relations that had been inherited from the July Monarchy and Second Empire. It would only be with the emergence of a substantial industrial working class, and its subsequent organization into a socialist party and union movement, that these property relations, and the democratic myth that legitimized them, would fundamentally be brought into question.

The commitment of the new regime to a social order that respected the sanctity of private property and defended existing economic and social relations explains the ease with which former conservatives – that is, Legitimists and Orleanists – joined moderate republicans, particularly following Pope Leo XIII's advocacy of *Ralliement* in 1890, in sincere adhesion to the republic. The ranks of the moderate republicans or Opportunists who had split from the Radicals and Radical-Socialists over social and constitutional questions were swollen by erstwhile conservatives who formed their own republican groupings on the right.[15] Their adhesion was not simply a cynical ploy to defend the

---

[14] Waxing poetic as to its moral and social virtues, Gambetta lauded the role of this bourgeoisie as an essential agent of stability in French society: "Nothing is ever lost with the French bourgeoisie. It is in fact impossible to say where begins and where ends this bourgeoisie, to whom the nation owes so much after all its missteps, its errors, despite all its unfeeling and selfishness. It is impossible to deny the services it has rendered throughout our history, to contest its qualities, which it could put to such noble use for the greater good of the country." Quoted in Barral, *Les fondateurs de la Troisième république*, 46.

[15] Throughout the 1890s, the parliamentary Right was composed essentially of the Progressistes, former Opportunists and Orleanists, and of Ralliés, former Legitimists. The turn of the century saw a further ramification of the political formations of the Right, and their attempted crystallization into organized parliamentary parties. In 1901 the Alliance démocratique was formed out of the Dreyfusard left wing of the Progressistes, who had supported Waldeck Rousseau's largely Radical Bloc Républicain government. Conversely, in 1902 former Ralliés, won over to the ideas of Social Catholicism, formed the Action libérale populaire, while in 1903 the Fédération républicaine was established by right-wing Progressistes and some Legitimist Ralliés who had opposed Waldeck-Rousseau's decision to reopen the Dreyfus case. By the eve of the First World War, the two principal formations on the Right were the staunchly right-of-center and clericalist Fédération républicaine, which had absorbed most of the membership of the Action libérale populaire in 1906, and the center-Right Alliance démocratique, which in 1911 had absorbed more moderate elements of the Fédération républicaine after the party split over the church-state question. The Alliance was also close to the Républicains de gauche of Poincaré, with whom it would often combine in the postwar period to form governments. The only right-wing contingent whose loyalty to the republic remained suspect was the Nationalists, some of whose members (such as from the Ligue de la patrie française) sat in the Chamber of Deputies under the aegis of the Groupe nationaliste républicain. On the political makeup and origins of the parliamentary Right in the Belle Époque, see R. D. Anderson, *France, 1870–1914*, ch. 7; Malcolm Anderson, *Conservative Politics in France* (London: George Unwin, 1974), ch. 3; and Eugen Weber, *The Nationalist Revival in France, 1905–1914* (Berkeley: University of California University Press, 1968).

privileges and safeguard the interests of the former aristocracy and the grande bourgeoisie. As in the case of the Radicals – and even to some extent, the Socialists – rightists at the turn of the century also projected the vision of a society and polity based on small property owners and producers. The latter were cast by the Right as exemplars of the conservative virtues of the family, thrift, and hard work. Meanwhile, others on the right evoked the individualism of *petits indépendants* in order to mobilize support for their economically liberal prescriptions. Some rightist elements, such as Christian Democratic activists who had issued from the ranks of Social Catholicism, attempted to counter the influence of the Radical Party among small artisans, shopkeepers, and other *petits patrons* and farmers by actively targeting these groups for proselytization.[16] Thus, by the eve of the First World War, a broad consensus had emerged that extended from the Radical Party on the center Left to the parties of the mainstream and extreme Right that France should remain a country of small, independent producers and tradesmen. Each of these political currents internalized and articulated in its own way the primordial republican vision of small proprietor democracy that ideologically conditioned the social outlook of the Third Republic.

Until at least the First World War, the Third Republic's social and political system showed itself to be remarkably resilient. The latter successfully weathered the storms of Boulangisme and Nationalism that had come from the right, while keeping at bay the challenges of socialism and anarchism that had emerged on the left. There was a striking coherence between the social structure of the country and its representation and articulation in the political institutions of the Third Republic and its underlying economic framework.[17] The class alliance between the grande and petite bourgeoisie that initially supported the republic's

---

[16] Chief among these groups was the Christian Democratic Union nationale, established in 1893 by Abbé Théodore Garnier, founder of the Action sociale catholique close to the Social Catholic Cercles ouvriers of Albert de Mun, and the Union fraternelle du commerce et de l'industrie, launched in 1891 by Léon Harmel, a small textile employer. Christian Democratic attempts to recruit *petits indépendants* were vigorously supported by the Assumptionist daily *La Croix*, which also enjoyed close ties to small employer interests. A decade later, in 1907, the Social Catholic activist Maurice Colrat attempted to enlist *petits indépendants* into a broadly based Association de défense des classes moyennes, comprising an alliance between the traditional middle classes of shopkeepers, artisans, and small and middling employers and the nascent "new" middle class of white-collar employees and *cadres* – industrial technicians, engineers, and managers. The goal of the new formation was to "contribute to the organization of all social forces desiring to work in an orderly and legal manner toward the elevation of their social condition, to study all the questions concerning the middle classes, to combat against all measures damaging to their freedoms, and to take in hand their interests and to defend them against all manner of usurpation or encroachment whatever their origin." Quoted in Capdevielle, *Fétichisme*, 207. On the links between Social Catholicism, Christian Democracy, and *petits indépendants* during this period, see ibid., 205–7, and Nord, *Paris Shopkeepers*, 392–406, 474–5.

[17] As a young Antonio Gramsci noted at the time, pre–World War I France remained one of the most stable, homogeneous, and conservative societies in Europe – a society that, under the superficial appearance of instability, had effectively resolved the internal contradictions that had developed within French society in the wake of the Revolution. In the words of another contemporary

social and political order largely held firm. On the right, the urban petty bourgeoisie that had been tempted by nationalism in the 1880s and 1890s was drawn back into the republican fold – if not by the Radicals, then by the *Modéré* Right – as many of them were put off by the militancy and violence of the nationalist leagues.[18] At the same time, representatives of large and small capital also joined forces to combat the emergent bogeyman of socialism and block the first legislative attempts at social reform.[19] Thus, this period consecrated the conversion of many urban *petits indépendants* to a strategy of class collaboration with the larger employers with whom they had been at political loggerheads in the 1880s and 1890s.[20] This dynamic culminated in the decade preceding the First World War when *petits* and *grands patrons* came together and formed organizations – the Confédération des groupes commerciaux et industriels (1903), the Association de défense des classes moyennes (1907) – that were committed to a broad agenda of bourgeois defense. This period bore "witness," in the words of Jeanne Gaillard, "to a new political orientation and ... the victory of a strategy of envelopment of small by large-scale [business]."[21] In turn, the "pilgrimage" of

observer, France during the Belle Époque presented the "spectacle of a tranquil people with agitated legislators." Quoted in R. D. Anderson, *France, 1870–1914*, 30.

[18] On the diminishing popularity of the most radical nationalist and anti-Semitic formations among the turn-of-the-century petite bourgeoisie, see Nord, *Paris Shopkeepers*, 391, and Z. Sternhell, *La droite révolutionnaire*, 138, 144–5, 224.

[19] These first social reform proposals included the introduction of a progressive income tax and the establishment of compulsory medical insurance and workers' pension systems. On the debate surrounding these proposals and the conditions leading to their defeat, see Hatzfeld, *Du paupérisme*, chs. 2–3.

[20] Central to this shift was the growing influence of Social Catholic and Christian Democratic corporatist ideas among artisans, shopkeepers, and small and middling industrialists, which called for them to establish producer associations as a means of pursuing their economic and social interests. At a first level, these associations sought to assist small and medium-sized businesses in organizing purchasing cooperatives in order to obtain better prices from suppliers, secure credit on more favorable terms, and provide technical and management training to their members. Concurrently, they were created to counter threats to private property, that is, Socialists and later Communists, as well as to resist attempts by the state to intervene in the affairs of private firms through the imposition of social reforms and an income tax. On the evolution of Social Catholic associationism, see Jean-Marie Mayeur, "L'Église Catholique: les limites d'une prise de conscience," in Lavau, Grunberg, and Mayer, *L'univers politique des classes moyennes*, 125–39, and Jean-Luc Pouthier, "Émergence et ambiguïtés de la culture politique démocrate chrétienne," in Berstein, *Les cultures politiques en France*, 285–314.

[21] "La petite entreprise," 155. This softening in the stance of petty producers and tradesmen toward big business translated into a newfound solicitude on the part of large capitalists with respect to their petty entrepreneurial brethren. It was as if, faced by the common threat posed by an increasingly militant workers' movement, the interests of large and small businesses effectively dovetailed and the divisions that separated them in the past were now forgotten. Similarly, some large capitalists had come to feel a certain responsibility toward the *petit patronat*, now deemed vital to the health and stability of the nation because it exemplified the possibility of social and economic advancement that made socialist agitation superfluous. In this vein, the head of the Comité des forges, Robert Pinot, wrote in March 1924: "Landed proprietors, *petits patrons*, and artisans constitute one of the great social strengths of our country as well as great economic strength. The diversity of our industrial production, the power of its inventiveness appropriate to

numerous *petits indépendants* from the left to the right before World War I did not go unnoticed on the Radical left.[22] Following its failure to legislate social reforms and the shift of its base of support from the politically volatile urban centers to more conservative bases of support in the provinces, the Radical Party toned down its reformist rhetoric and program. Largely abandoning the agenda of social reform that it had vigorously pursued immediately following its founding in 1901, the Radicals emulated their political rivals on the right by committing themselves to a strategy of middle-class defense. Specifically, they sought to promote the identification of *petits indépendants* with large employers within pressure groups that were close to the party, such as the Comité républicain du commerce et de l'industrie.[23]

On the whole, then, during the run-up to the First World War *petits indépendants* remained indispensable to the stable economic and political functioning of the republic. Economically, though their preponderance had already begun to decline, artisans continued to represent a significant force in manufacturing, while shopkeepers retained a virtual stranglehold over commerce. Politically, the primordial republican ideal of small producer democracy to which these strata aspired continued to be guaranteed by the republican synthesis underlying the regime. Thus, the political and social standing of small producers and tradesmen remained high within French society, as the latter were effectively shielded from the impacts of industrial and commercial concentration and more rapid economic modernization was forestalled in the name of preserving social stability and bourgeois class rule.

Yet the class alliance between the grande and petite bourgeoisie that subtended the French political economy under the Third Republic produced a pattern of industrial retardation and social stagnation that was pregnant with future class and political conflict, however. As the pressure built up to modernize the country and outside shocks destabilized the French economy, the republican synthesis progressively eroded until it became unsustainable. According to one historian, the Third Republic's founders and their Radical and *modéré* heirs had "purchased political and social stability at the cost of stagnation and of structural weaknesses in the French economy that showed up later in the twentieth century."[24]

the tastes of every day, its incomparable originality and imagination, are they not in large part the work of these individual workers in whom the spirit of invention is overexcited by personal effort and the legitimate desire to succeed? From their advancement, the fruit of their own personal labor, there has resulted in France a continual intermixing of social milieus and backgrounds, in which the most dignified always manage to elevate themselves above their present situation and to constitute a constantly renewed elite." Quoted in Hatzfeld, *Du paupérisme*, 140.

[22] Nord, *Paris Shopkeepers*, 486.

[23] Founded in March 1899 by the Radical senator Alfred Mascuraud to promote the collaboration between the Radical-dominated Waldeck-Rousseau "government and the vital forces of commerce and industry," the CRCI (also known as the Comité Mascuraud) constituted until well after the First World War the principal pressure group representing the interests of French business within the Radical Party. Gaillard, "La petite entreprise," 162.

[24] R. D. Anderson, *France, 1870–1914*, 31.

Indeed, despite the stability displayed by the Third Republic through the Belle Époque, premonitory fissures appeared in the sociopolitical structure of the regime that pointed to its unsustainability over the long term. As the country underwent increasingly rapid economic and social change, burgeoning sectoral and class antagonisms emerged that threatened the alliance between the grande and petite bourgeoisie on which the regime was predicated. This incipient class conflict was of essentially two types. In the first place, it testified to the broadening divide between the most advanced strata of the bourgeoisie tied to powerful commercial, industrial, and financial interests and the small-property-owning bourgeoisie attached to antiquated forms of production and trade. This conflict was complicated by the emergence of new class and social constituencies, principally a growing industrial working class as well as a wage-earning white-collar middle class. These new strata also vied for economic and political influence, thereby entering into competition with the republic's original bourgeois founders and placing a further strain on the class alliance that supported it. Thus, even the course of controlled development that was followed by the country during the Belle Époque saw the interests of *petits indépendants* come under increasing attack from other, more economically advanced and better politically organized class and sectoral groups.

The fissures that appeared in the alliance between the petite bourgeoisie of small producers and traders and the grande bourgeoisie of large industrial and commercial employers and financiers were best reflected in the dynamics of interest representation that increasingly pit the former against the latter. During the republic's opening decades, this dynamic was bound up in the opposition that divided the republican camp between Radicals and Radical-Socialists, who were perceived as the representatives of the petite bourgeoisie, and the Opportunists, who were identified with the grande bourgeoisie. Following Pope Leo XIII's call for *Ralliement* in 1890, the latter were joined by conservative Catholic landowners and industrialists, who had hitherto rejected the republic to form a new parliamentary group, the Progressistes.[25] Accordingly, by the turn of the century, the republican Right was closely allied to sectoral organizations and pressure groups representing big business, such as the Comité national républicain du commerce et de l'industrie, the Union des intérêts économiques, and the most powerful industrial associations, such as the Comité des forges, the Union des industries métallurgiques et minières, and the Union textile.[26]

Given these linkages, *petits indépendants* saw the Opportunists and later, the Progressistes, as unprincipled defenders of monopoly, especially of the big department stores that drove growing numbers of small shopkeepers and artisans out of business. Their opinion of the parliamentary Right or Modérés was

---

[25] On the sectoral and geographical implantation of conservative republican politics during the Third Republic, see M. Anderson, *Conservative Politics*, ch. 2, and R. D. Anderson, *France, 1870–1914*, ch. 2.

[26] Kuisel, *Capitalism*, ch. 1, and Ehrmann, *Organized Business in France*, 19.

little improved by the refusal of the latter to acknowledge the commercial crisis affecting petty producers and tradesmen. Instead, Modéré politicians disparaged them as "incompetents" and cast their struggle against the forces of industrial and commercial concentration as futile and unworthy of sympathy.[27] Consequently, through the 1880s and the first half of the 1890s, the sectoral representatives of petty commercial interests, such as the Ligue syndicale, mounted concerted campaigns against Opportunist and Progressive candidates.[28] They most often identified in these early years with Radical politicians, although they were capable even at this stage of empathizing with authoritarian and antiparliamentary movements, such as Boulangisme, which sought to harness their discontent. In these campaigns, *petit indépendant* activists adopted the revolutionary rhetoric of the *sans-culottes* of 1793, denouncing commercial "monopolies" as "capitalist bastilles" to be demolished and the "bourgeois aristocracy" as a new "feudality" to be overthrown. For these activists, big business and their Modéré defenders represented "a new class of seigneurs ..., who, like their forebears, treated the people with high handed contempt."[29] By contrast, they preached the doctrine of *morcellement*, the diffusion of petty property through the breakup of large economic units into smaller ones, as fulfilling the revolutionary ideals of liberty and equality. For these militant shopkeepers and artisans, defense of their economic interests neatly dovetailed with the vision of small producer democracy they identified with the Revolution and the primordial republicanism that derived from it. Correspondingly, in their opposition to large producer and commercial interests, *petits indépendants* sought in the late 1880s and early 1890s to ally with industrial workers in combating the forces of monopoly, with certain members of the Ligue syndicale even going so far as to call themselves "socialists" in order to gain their support.[30] In short, by the turn of the century, the class alliance between *petits* and *grands bourgeois* of the Third Republic had already begun to fray. In this sense, the increasingly *strident* opposition of *petits indépendants* to republican Modérés foreshadowed the political conflicts that would oppose these two groups in the new century.

Yet, *petits indépendants* were not just in conflict with Modéré republicans and their big business allies during the opening decades of the regime. They were also increasingly estranged from certain elements of the traditional party of small producer defense, the Radicals themselves. At one level, this development

---

[27] Nord, *Paris Shopkeepers*, 315–16.

[28] For example, in the 1890 municipal elections, the Ligue syndicale pursued a vigorous campaign to unseat the Opportunist candidate Jacques Ruel, owner of the hated department store, the Bazar de l' Hôtel de Ville, from the municipal council seat for the quartier Notre-Dame. Ibid., 316.

[29] Ibid., 262, 274, 275.

[30] One of the most fervent Ligue militants, Louis Gazon, wrote in 1893 in *La Revendication*, the organization's official organ: "If among us – the humble, the little folk of the commercial world – there are people too stuck up, too inflated with pride to make alliance with the workers, ... they are false friends. We must let them smother themselves in the flab of the overstuffed bourgeoisie." Quoted in ibid., 290.

reflected a shift in orientation among a growing number of Radicals who, out of opportunism or in the interest of governing, elected to work with the Modérés and hence accepted the pro-big-business policies of the latter.[31] At a second level, despite having cultivated a reputation as the political bastion of a middling France constituted of petty producers, tradesmen, and small businessmen, big business interests were solidly – if not overtly – represented among the Radicals. In the first place, the party contained within its ranks, particularly among its senatorial delegation, members of the high industrial bourgeoisie.[32] Likewise, it also fell under the influence of powerful organized interests that were dominated by big business. For example, the Comité républicain du commerce et de l'industrie included some large-scale industrialists and retailers as well as representatives of small and middling businesses, to the extent that petty producer organizations that had formerly supported Radical candidates became overtly hostile to the party.[33] In turn, by the eve of the First World War, the CRCI had been supplanted by the Union des intérêts économiques as the principal pressure group representing business interests within the Radical Party. The latter was even more hidebound to big business than its predecessor (though like the latter it claimed to represent the interests of all businesses), and it enjoyed particularly close ties to conservative senators such as Joseph Caillaux who belonged to the party's economically classical-liberal wing.[34] Thus, the fact that even the traditional party of small producers and shopkeepers, the Radicals, found itself torn

---

[31] These represented principally rightist currents within the party, the Gauche radicale and Gauche démocratique blocs that perpetuated the moderate, early Radicalism of Gambetta, and especially the Union progressiste, which contained those *radicaux de gouvernement* who had broken away from the party in order to participate in Opportunist and, later, Progressist-dominated ministries during the 1880s and early 1890s. These more moderate and rightward-leaning elements contrasted with the Radical-Socialist Left, led by such figures as Georges Clemenceau and Camille Pelletan, who claimed the progressive democratic heritage of the Radical opposition of the Montagne during the short-lived Second Republic, and continued to adhere in spirit to the progressive Belleville Program. As time went on, these more conservative factions found a particular home in the Senate, whose members tended, as a function of their selection by provincial notables, to reflect the more traditionalist and order-bound proclivities of their rural constituents. On these and other divisions within early Radicalism, see Berstein, *Histoire* (I), 28–32, and Nordmann, *Histoire des radicaux*, chs. 6–7.

[32] Berstein, *Histoire* (I), 287.

[33] Thus, in the wake of the 1902 elections, *L'Ami des petits commerçants*, a newspaper close to the Ligue syndicale, denounced the CRCI as an instrument of "big business interests," comparing big department store owners such as Jules Jaluzot and Georges Dufayel in France to the "trusteurs" Rockefeller, Gould, or Vanderbilt in the United States. Similarly, an *étalagiste* poster in Paris accused the "capitalist feudality" controlling the CRCI of having bought the 1902 elections and of bringing the Waldeck-Rousseau administration, considered overly sympathetic to big business, to power. Nord, *Paris Shopkeepers*, 429.

[34] The disproportionate influence of big business among the Radicals is confirmed by the fact that, in addition to the party's centrist senatorial delegation, the UIE also supported the Alliance démocratique, which was unabashedly close to the more advanced sectors of industry as well as high finance. Charles Maier, *Recasting Bourgeois Europe: Stabilization in France, Germany, and Italy in the Decade after World War I* (Princeton: Princeton University Press, 1975), 101–4; Marcus Kreuzer, *Institutions and Innovation: Voters, Parties, and Interest Groups in the*

in its policy deliberations between its historical allegiance to small producers and the influence exerted by big business highlighted the weakening political clout of *petits indépendants* as the Belle Époque drew to a close. It reflected in microcosm the broader fissures that had appeared between the petite and grande bourgeoisie and bode ominously for the future.

One issue in particular emphasized the cracks between the *petite* and the grande bourgeoisie during the Belle Époque: the controversy over *patente* reform. Most notably, the latter underscored the ambivalence of the Radicals – not to speak of the Opportunists/Progressistes – toward the plight of *petits indépendants*.[35] The failure of small producer groups to push through *patente* reform in line with the demands of their constituents illustrated the lessening importance accorded to their concerns by the ruling republican coalition when they collided with big business interests. As Philip Nord put it, "in the event of conflict within the republican alliance, it was the *petit indépendant* who was sacrificed to big business." Deploring the growing influence of the financial and economic oligarchy over the republican regime, one contemporary political commentator drove home this point when he wrote that "the Republic which triumphed in 1878 was the Republic of Schneider, Dubouchet and Boucicaut," scions of the most powerful industrial and commercial families in *fin-de-siècle* France.[36]

Consolidation of Democracy: France and Germany, 1870–1939 (Ann Arbor: University of Michigan Press, 2001), 95; and Capdevielle, *Fétichisme*, 201.

[35] Claiming that the original *patente* law of 1880 unfavorably favored large commercial interests, petty producer groups such as the Ligue syndicale clamored during the following two decades for its revision. Wary of the consequences of inaction following Boulangisme's tapping of *petit indépendant* discontent in the late 1880s, a parliamentary commission was established in June 1890 under the Radical deputy Gustave Mesureur to study the possibility of reforming the *patente*. The Mesureur Committee did indeed find the existing tax provisions to be unfairly skewed toward big business. For example, after comparing the effective taxes paid by large versus small establishments, the Bon Marché had paid only 0.37% of its revenue in taxes in fiscal year 1890, whereas small shops in the sixth arrondissement that grossed no more than 100,000 francs per year, had ended up paying as much as 2% or 2.5%. However, the prospect of reform mobilized a powerful array of economic interests in opposition to the Ligue's proposals, including the heads of all the *grands magasins* (deputy Jules Jaluzot, the owner of Le Printemps, even obtaining a seat on the committee), factory owners who depended on contracts with the latter, and powerful organized business groups, such as the Comité central des chambres syndicales, the Syndicat général du commerce et de l'industrie, and the provincial Chambers of Commerce. The result was a very limited reform proposal, which would leave the *patente* essentially intact. Only two changes were envisaged by the committee, which would have forced large retailers to pay greater tax in proportion to the types of goods they sold – the so-called specialization clause – and increased their tax obligation in proportion to the number of workers they employed. Yet, even these provisions were watered down by the Radical-dominated Senate, so that the *patente* reform bill that was finally passed in April 1893 limited the specialization clause only to establishments counting over two hundred employees, while considerably reducing the tax per number of supplemental employees. In turn, subsequent attempts at reform, such as those undertaken by the ex-Boulangist deputy Georges Berry in the mid- and late 1890s, also failed, underscoring the inability of shopkeepers and artisans to secure a more favorable tax regime as big business progressively strengthened its hold over the republic. Nord, *Paris Shopkeepers*, 354–61.

[36] Ibid., 361.

From this standpoint, it is interesting to note that the cause of *petits indépendants* was embraced by members of the ex-Boulangiste, nationalist, and Social Catholic Right, that is, those very elements that had swollen the ranks of the radical Right and of neotraditionalists recently rallied to the republic. This evolution spelled the first major decoupling of petty producers and traders from the Radicals, who in 1901 constituted themselves into a formal political party. By the time World War I broke out, the rupture of the republican synthesis had already been prefigured by the economic and political conflicts opposing the grande and petite bourgeoisie during the Belle Époque.

These premonitory fissures in the republican synthesis were aggravated by the rise of new sectoral and class groups that threatened the bourgeois alliance that sustained it. The burgeoning workers' movement had an especially destabilizing effect on the Third Republic during this period. Not only did it directly threaten the interests of the grande and petite bourgeoisies, but it elicited contradictory reactions – of outright opposition from *petits patrons* and qualified cooperation from large-scale employers – which became a further source of antagonism between them. The 1890s in particular saw a substantial increase in the size of the industrial working class, as the country, following the slump of the 1880s, experienced its most intensive period of industrialization since the Second Empire. Worker organization considerably grew during these years, and wage earners gained political representation through the nascent Socialist Party. According to one estimate, the number of unionized workers tripled from 140,000 in 1890, the year of the first May Day celebration, to more than 420,000 in 1895, the year the Confédération générale du travail (CGT) was founded. Similarly, Socialist representation in the Chamber of Deputies increased fourfold from ten to forty deputies in the elections of 1893.[37] The workers' movement became increasingly politically radicalized under the stewardship of Marxist leaders such as Jules Guesde, Édouard Vaillant, and Jean Jaurès, who embraced the tenets of class struggle, social revolution, and collectivism.

Outward agreement within the business community on the dangers of socialism masked considerable tension between large and small employers on how to deal with this rapidly expanding workers' movement. *Petits patrons* and their sectoral representatives quickly forewent their temporary commitment to socialist struggle once workers in the small business sector began to threaten their economic property and excoriate them as bosses. At a philosophical level, *petit indépendant* unease in the face of socialism was compounded by its prediction that petty producers and traders were condemned to disappear as a result of industrial and commercial concentration. Socialist leaders welcomed the proletarianization of small, self-employed proprietors because it would hasten the historic showdown between the working class and the bourgeoisie.[38] At a more immediate, practical level, *petits indépendants* were also put off by the determination of socialist leaders to

---

[37] Ibid., 362.
[38] Ibid., and Alain Bergounioux, "La SFIO ou les classes moyennes impensées (1905–1939)," in Lavau, Grunberg, and Mayer, *L'univers politique des classes moyennes*, 94–8.

implement their collectivist ideas in practice. Such initiatives represented a concrete threat to the interests of the *petit commerce and artisanat* and thus were strenuously opposed by their sectoral representatives.[39] Finally, the growing militancy of the union movement set workers into conflict not only with large employers but with small ones as well.[40] Both refused to pay a minimum wage to their employees, imposed disciplinary fines on them, and relied on the hated *bureaux de placement* (daily work-placement agencies), which allowed employers to bid down wages by interchangeably hiring workers on an ad hoc basis. This new radicalism was comforted by anarchist and Allemanist influences, which gave an increasingly revolutionary-syndicalist imprint to the labor movement.[41]

Thus, by the turn of the century, the growing social and political radicalization of French workers brought *petits indépendants* to view the latter as a greater threat than large commercial and industrial concerns. Accordingly, the onus of petty producer defense shifted from the resistance to monopoly to the struggle against socialism, *La Revendication* exclaiming in June 1896 that "the petit commerce is our last rampart against the invasion of socialism."[42] Accordingly, the first decade of the new century saw the sectoral representatives of shopkeepers, artisans, and small industry embrace a unitary policy of middle-class defense that sought to unite large and small business in a common defense of private economic property against socialism.

Yet, this political unity of business concealed divergent conceptions of "the social question" that would become a looming source of conflict between large and small employers. Although both viewed the socialist movement as a threat not only to their own businesses but to civilization itself, each offered very different solutions for how to confront and neutralize it. *Petits indépendants* made no real practical prescription beyond appealing to the traditional values of work, thrift, and the accession to small property as means for workers to improve their socioeconomic condition. By contrast, large employers espoused a much more active approach, enacting a variety of prophylactic measures to improve the material and moral condition of their workers. In so doing, they believed they could reduce the economic and social frustrations that drove workers to embrace socialism. Thus, as early as the 1890s, big employers

---

[39] For example, in 1893 Vaillant submitted a proposal to the Paris city council calling for the establishment of a collectively run municipal *boucherie*. In 1894 Guesdists on the Roubaix town council successfully organized a municipal pharmacy to be run by the city. More broadly, Socialists supported the creation of consumer cooperatives, "an institution feared and reviled" by *petits indépendants* because it combined the threat of commercial concentration with collectivist principles. Nord, *Paris Shopkeepers*, 363.

[40] Thus, whereas in 1892 the Chambre syndicale des employés, the principal trade association of sales employees, had supported shopkeepers in their endorsement of *patente* reform, by the end of the 1890s it regarded the latter as no less exploitative than the *grands magasins*. Similarly testifying to the progress of socialist ideas, from 1893 on the Chambre syndicale de l'alimentation in which *petits indépendants* were preponderant demanded no less than the total suppression of the employer class. Ibid.

[41] Ibid.

[42] Ibid., 364.

began to put in place worker insurance schemes to assist their employees if they fell sick or suffered an accident, and they introduced pension plans to help provide for their needs upon retirement.[43] In addition to health and accident insurance and retirement plans, large employers also extended other economic and social benefits to their workers, including ownership of their houses and small plots of land and subsidies for the education of their children, as well as nurseries, dispensaries, and discount stores for their benefit.[44] In short, they sought to secure under a paternalist guise their workers' allegiance by offering them tangible material benefits without surrendering any of their authority over the operation of their firms. In this sense, as Henri Hatzfeld put it, the large employer came to view such benefits as an essential "source of leverage permitting him to keep his workforce well in hand."[45]

These divergent conceptions of workers' needs and of how they should be addressed reflected the different conditions and experiences that shaped the respective outlooks of large employers and *petits patrons* on economic and social issues. First and most obviously, the great differences in wealth that distinguished them meant that the former could afford to grant such benefits to their employees whereas the latter could not. In turn, other situational and cultural differences conditioned their respective views of their workers' demands in more subtle but no less significant ways. The quasi-familial setting of the small enterprise, in which employees were more likely to share the same cultural outlook as their employer, was far removed from the stratified and compartmentalized milieu of the large enterprise, in which enormous cultural differences existed between wage earners and the *patronat* and managers who oversaw them. Thus, as Hatzfeld has pointed out, workers and employers in large, advanced firms came to "think in terms that are impossible to conceive between *patrons* and workers in small enterprises," large employers proving much less inclined than *petits patrons* to resist reforms at the level of their enterprises.[46]

---

[43] In some sectors, such as metallurgy, the existence of such plans extended back to the eighteenth century if not before. Hatzfeld traces the earliest instance of such a plan back to the seventeenth century, when Jean-Baptiste Colbert established a compulsory pension scheme for volunteers of the French merchant marine. Such plans were the private precursors for the comprehensive public social security system that was to be established immediately following the Second World War. *Du paupérisme*, 109.

[44] Ibid., 110, and Sanford Elwitt, *The Third Republic Defended: Bourgeois Reform in France, 1880–1914* (Baton Rouge: Louisiana State University Press, 1986), ch. 5.

[45] Hatzfeld, *Du paupérisme*, 110.

[46] Summarizing these fundamental structural and cultural differences distinguishing large and small firms, and the variable capacities to adapt to social reforms they evolved as a result, Hatzfeld has written: "To a world made up of customs and of contracts (which often represented no more than 'good manners' or tacit agreements) has succeeded a world which is more and more narrowly codified. This development of the regulatory framework in which we are caught in no way frightens large enterprises. ... They create, they develop their own regulation and bureaucratic habits. By contrast, small enterprise cannot live in this world. It finds itself constantly limited, constrained, impeded in all the forms of initiative which it would like to be able to freely undertake." Ibid., 264.

These different outlooks and responses suggest that *petits indépendants* and large firms were motivated by drastically different considerations in attempting to block the socialist aspirations of French workers at the dawn of the twentieth century. The principal calculus of the small *patronat* was simply to keep wage costs down and fashion a common front with big business to beat back the threat of socialism. Conversely, the goal of the *grand patronat* was to preserve the facade of employer unity to maximize their economic and political influence while developing private institutions that would allow them to continue "to dominate the workforce while doing it good."[47] In short, the latter was disposed to take a more conciliatory line toward workers than the former, proving willing in essence to buy them off with the promise of social benefits that small businesses neither could afford nor were inclined to grant.

Thus, as industrial and commercial concentration progressed and the wage-earning workforce rapidly grew, large and small employers increasingly diverged in their attitudes toward the transformation of the economy and its social and political ramifications. While many of the representatives of small business called for turning the clock back to an archaeoliberal petty producer capitalism, a growing minority of big employers accepted the need for greater economic organization and regulation, some even going so far as to accept social reform in principle in order to preempt social strife. Hence, even as they joined small employers in a politics of antisocialist defense, the willingness of larger employers to accept state intervention in the economy and limited social reforms placed them increasingly at odds with *petits indépendants*, most of whom viewed any state intrusion in the economy as socialism in a new guise.[48]

These divergent approaches to the social question played out politically in ways that highlighted the growing divisions between small and big business, and ultimately prefigured a reconfiguration of class relations in French society as a whole. Among the principal political formations of the republic, there was growing recognition of the need for authoritative and effective social management, subtended by a mutual conviction that there could be "no progress without order, no social peace without class collaboration."[49] Yet, within this broad consensus, there was considerable variation among the various political parties on how to achieve this goal. Republican Modérés and their descendants who, at the turn of the century, flocked to the newly formed Alliance démocratique and Fédération républicaine generally shared in the paternalist outlook of big business. The moderate Right advocated voluntary solutions by which employers designed and controlled the mechanisms to improve the condition of the workers so that their authority over the operation of their firms was not brought into

[47] Ibid., 110.
[48] On these divergences between small and big business and their political and policy manifestations, see Elwitt, *Third Republic Defended*, ch. 5; Hatzfeld, *Du paupérisme*, 126–41; and Kuisel, *Capitalism*, 8–20.
[49] Elwitt, *Third Republic Defended*, 295.

question.[50] For their part, many representatives of the traditionalist *rallié* Right – affiliated at the turn of the century with the Action libérale populaire – were influenced by Social Catholicism in their approach to resolving the social question. Reflecting the concerns of a smaller, traditionalist, and provincial *patronat* who strongly resisted any encroachment upon its authority over the workplace, they placed a strong emphasis on corporatist associations and consensual decision making within the various economic sectors as the means to defuse class conflict in French society. The commitment of the Social Catholic Right to combat socialism was accompanied, particularly following the *Rerum Novarum* encyclical in 1891, by a concern to ameliorate the conditions of the working class and curb the excesses of industrial capitalism – hence, its adhesion to corporatist formulae that affirmed patronal authority over the firm while acknowledging worker grievances.[51]

Whereas such attitudes were predictable among the republican Right, a more surprising evolution was to be seen in Radicals' attitude to the social question. In an attempt to halt the progress of socialism, they espoused at the turn of the century a reform program that was seen by many *petits indépendants* as threatening. Influenced by the Solidarist philosophy of the Radical thinker Léon Bourgeois, they attempted to tailor republicanism to meet the challenges of industrialization and the growth of wage labor by facilitating the workers' accession to petty property.[52] To achieve this goal, Radical advocates of Solidarism called for greater state intervention in certain areas while fundamentally preserving the liberal foundations of democratic capitalist society. Bourgeois argued that it was up to "positive law [to] ensure through the sanctions it imposes the acquittal of the social debt, the fulfillment of the obligation resulting for each among men from his state of indebtedness to all."[53]

Accordingly, building on the piecemeal social legislation of the early and mid-1890s, the Radicals introduced a whole series of reformist proposals.[54] In 1898

[50] Ibid., ch. 4, as well as M. Anderson, *Conservative Politics*, 158–62, and William Irvine, *French Conservatism in Crisis: The Republican Federation of France in the 1930s* (Baton Rouge: Louisiana State University Press, 1979), ch. 1.
[51] Pouthier, "Émergence et ambiguïtés de la culture politique démocrate chrétienne," 292–4; Émile Poulat, *Église contre bourgeoisie. Introduction au devenir du catholicisme actuel* (Paris: Casterman, 1977); and Jean-Marie Mayeur, *Catholicisme social et Démocratie chrétienne. Principes romains, expériences françaises* (Paris: Cerf, 1986).
[52] For a thorough exposition of the philosophical underpinnings of Solidarism and of its programmatic offshoots, see Elwitt, *Third Republic Defended*, ch. 5, and Hatzfeld, *Du paupérisme*, 268–81.
[53] Hatzfeld, *Du paupérisme*, 274. In this sense, Solidarism can be seen as a turn-of-the-century reincarnation of the statist Jacobin orientations at the root of early Radicalism, representing their extension to the social and economic spheres. It strove to temper the bourgeois principles of individual freedom and competition identified with the primordial liberalism that had issued from the Revolution and to square them with the universal ideals of political equality and social solidarity that represented the other political-philosophical correlates of 1789.
[54] Most important among these preexisting measures was the institution of free health care for workers in 1893, as well as the guarantee of (extremely) minimal retirement benefits to workers, based on either private company funds or newly established state-run retirement funds. Ibid., 57.

the first law establishing a compulsory system of workers' disability insurance was passed. The following year, the newly elected Waldeck-Rousseau government resurrected legislation to introduce the progressive income tax, only to see it defeated in the Chamber.[55] Then, in 1901, the Waldeck ministry presented a bill to create the first, state-run universal pension system for wage earners, paid for with obligatory contributions from employers and employees.[56] Although the measure that ended up being passed was modest in its impact – the minimum contribution levels prescribed in the original bill having been gutted by the Senate – it represented an important symbolic step because it stipulated for the first time the principle of compulsory retirement contributions.[57] The succeeding Combes government continued on the social-reformist tack of its predecessor. During its three-year life, it pursued an ambitious program of fiscal reform, tabling proposals that, in addition to the progressive income tax, would have introduced a capital gains tax and increased the inheritance tax.[58] Thus, it strove to provide, by means of limited legislative intervention, a modicum of social equality that would allow propertyless workers to accede to small-scale economic property and thus diminish the attraction of socialism.

These Solidarist proposals continued to inform the policies of the Radical Party up to the eve of the First World War. The party's policy platform during this period, the Nancy Program of 1908, strove to ameliorate the condition of the working class while combating excessive capitalist concentration and control.[59] Its principal aim was to secure the allegiance of the workers as wage labor

[55] This proposal had been initially submitted by the Bourgeois ministry four years earlier, but was almost immediately withdrawn in the face of quasi-universal business and public opposition. It was eventually represented by Caillaux and passed the Chamber in 1907, but dilatory maneuvering by the Senate allowed it to become law only in 1914. Nordmann, *Histoire des radicaux*, 111, and Hatzfeld, *Du paupérisme*, 315.

[56] The proposal was enthusiastically supported by Bourgeois at the foundational congress of the Radical Party in 1901. He exclaimed that such a program was essential for giving workers a stake in the society and thereby keeping them from acceding "to the revolt, to the violence, to the chimeras" of revolutionary socialism. Berstein, *Histoire* (I), 42.

[57] Hatzfeld, *Du paupérisme*, 62–3. However, even this principle was temporarily abandoned, as successful court challenges to the law in effect rendered such contributions optional. Thus, it was only in 1930 that comprehensive and compulsory retirement legislation was finally passed.

[58] Berstein, *Histoire* (I), 53.

[59] In the area of social and economic policy, the Nancy Program reads like an anthology of Solidarist prescriptions, some of which appear remarkably far-sighted in retrospect and would eventually become law. These can be broken down into five general areas: progressive social reforms, including the provision of state assistance to the indigent, pensions for retired workers, financial aid to state-assisted children and poor pregnant women, and maternity leave for working women; the institution of legislation regulating working conditions and outlining the responsibilities of employers toward their employees, as enshrined in a legally binding Code of Work and Social Security; progressive labor-relations measures, such as the establishment of a system of arbitration and the substitution of collective bargaining for individual contracts, thereby recognizing the right of trade unions to negotiate on behalf of their members; fiscal reform, in the form "of a universal and progressive income tax" and a more progressive inheritance tax; and, finally, the nationalization of certain key sectors, such as the railroads and the insurance industry. Ibid., 61–3.

overtook independent labor as the preponderant form of economic activity. For largely this reason, Radical proposals of limited government intervention in the economy were grudgingly accepted by Modéré politicians. Indeed, by the outbreak of the Great War, most politicians on the right as well as the left had accepted the need for an income tax and even universal social security.[60]

Needless to say, despite the avowed commitment of Radicals and the parties of the Right to the diffusion of property and the defense of the middle classes, such social reforms elicited considerable alarm among *petits indépendants* and small business owners. Although the Radical Party progressively distanced itself from such interventionism and sought to reclaim its standing as defender of the traditional middle classes, its advocacy of these policies in the early years of the new century doubtless pushed *petits indépendants* to the right during this period.[61] Groups representing shopkeepers and artisans such as the Comité de l'alimentation parisienne viewed such measures as threats not only to their economic well-being but, ultimately, to their very way of life. Conversely, these policies were much more acceptable to large employers, who in many cases had introduced their own social benefit system, often at a higher cost than the state-sanctioned regime that was to replace it.[62]

The growing unease of *petits indépendants* in respect to these social policies, and the increasing dissonance *between* small and large business on how to address the social question, prefigured the eventual breakup of the alliance between the grande and petite bourgeoisie that had presided over the birth of the Third Republic. Though this alliance, fashioned under the rubrics of "middle-class defense" and sanctity of private property, remained basically intact on the eve of the war, the divergent motives of each of these constituencies in entering into it rendered it increasingly untenable. Industrialization and the expansion of wage labor put growing pressure on business and the state to meet the challenges posed by the ever-greater organization and collectivization of economic and social life.

At the same time, rival ideologies such as socialism, corporatism, and *étatisme* emerged to challenge the classical liberalism that had guided economic and

---

[60] M. Anderson, *Conservative Politics*, 43.

[61] Capdevielle, *Fétichisme*, 209–10.

[62] Taking for example the social security law of 1910, it spelled at a purely economic level the ruin of the smallest, most marginal firms, which were unable to keep up with even the modest retirement contributions demanded of them. At a deeper, existential level, by heralding the universal advent of wage labor through regulations geared principally to wage earners and the large firms that employed them, the new law underscored the growing irrelevance of *petits patrons* and foreshadowed their passing as a socioeconomic group. In turn, their sense of vulnerability was exacerbated by the difficulties they faced in adapting their work practices to conform to the law – adaptations that large modern firms, by dint of their bureaucratic nature, had no trouble implementing. For example, many of them had difficulty incorporating a rational accounting system in order to keep track of their own and their employees' social security contributions as required by the new law. Precisely because it seemed to signal their impending demise, the social security law that placed a financial, procedural, and cultural burden on *petits patrons* incited them, as Hatzfeld put it, "to judge the contributions that were being imposed ... to be much more onerous than they in actual fact were." *Du pauperisme*, 138, 295, 298.

political elites during the Belle Époque. Shunning the classical liberal paradigm of minimal state intrusion in the economy, these alternatives preconized an increased organization of the economy by the public power.[63] Correspondingly, as we just saw, big business and its political representatives progressively came round to accepting an expanded role for the state in coping with the challenges of industrialization, principally in the form of fiscal and social reform.[64] This shift in outlook suggests that, among the high industrial, commercial, and financial bourgeoisie of the time, the traditional dogma underlying the republican synthesis, namely, that petty producers and traders needed to be protected in order to preserve social and political stability, no longer enjoyed the same unanimity. Thus, though there still was, on the eve of World War I, general agreement that some kind of interbourgeois alliance between big business and small proprietors was necessary, one observer remarked that "the concept of the bourgeois–small producer axis ... was unstable and open to a multitude of conflicting interpretations."[65]

Even before World War I, then, substantial structural changes occurring within the French society and economy were causing the outlooks and interests of big and small business to diverge. Considered in conjunction with the emergence of new, ascendant social and economic constituencies – industrial workers, white-collar workers, civil servants – vying for economic and political power at the expense of established groups, this suggested that the small producer democracy that came into being with the Third Republic was being progressively outstripped by fundamental changes in the makeup of French society. A growing diversity of interests pulled the republic in different directions, resulting in policy outcomes that did not necessarily favor *petits indépendants*.[66] Therefore, though they continued to predominate both demographically and

---

[63] Kuisel, *Capitalism*, ch. 1.

[64] Some leading industrial groups went even further. Thus, the Comité des Forges petitioned the government to enact an industrial policy copied on the German model during the decade before World War I. Specifically, it called on the state to take the lead in steering industrial development and giving priority to economic expansion. Prefiguring in a sense a planist model of economic management, this proposal called for an economic program based on consultation between the state and industry through institutionalized advisory bodies. Ibid., 25.

[65] Kevin Passmore, "The French Third Republic: Stalemate Society or Cradle of Fascism?" *French History* 7(4) (1993), 422.

[66] For example, the single-most significant piece of trade legislation of the Third Republic, the Méline tariff passed in 1892 and then reinforced in the following years, mainly benefited large agricultural interests and import-competing sectors such as textiles rather than, as is often claimed, small agricultural and industrial producers. The higher supplier and consumer prices resulting from the tariff generally hurt the small peasants, artisans, and shopkeepers who made up the French traditional middle classes. This could be seen in their lack of support for the representatives of the policy. For example, the Radical Party initially opposed trade protection on the grounds that it benefited big business to the detriment of small producers and consumers. Only in 1929 did the party reverse this line on trade issues and adopt protectionism in its program. And even thereafter, shopkeepers, artisans, and industrialists complained of the import quotas on agricultural goods that were introduced after 1931 and steeply increased the price of raw materials and manufactures. On the differential impacts of protectionism on various social constituencies and their political

culturally, *petits indépendants* were confronted with growing economic and social uncertainty as their model status within the French polity increasingly came under attack.

consequences during the Third Republic, see respectively Kuisel, *Capitalism*, 17–19; G. Wright, *Rural Revolution in France*, 17; Passmore, "French Third Republic," 422; Serge Berstein, "Les conceptions du Parti radical en matière de politique économique extérieure," *Relations internationales*, no. 13 (Spring 1978), 76–7, 85; and Kreuzer, *Institutions and Innovation*, 108.

5

The Fateful Transition

Petits Indépendants *in the Interwar Period*

C'était pas assez de m'avoir ruiné par la stabilisation Poincaré ... c'est toujours sur le petit rentier qu'on s'en prend, c'est toujours lui qui paie les pots cassés ... nous voilà presque ruiner [*sic*], je dis bien ruiner Monsieur le Ministre.

Letter from a seventy-six-year-old *petit rentier* to Finance Minister Georges Bonnet, March 1933[1]

La jeunesse bourgeoise française ne pouvait plus ... avoir le sentiment que la France était son domaine. ... Le choc de 1936 le fit pénétrer en eux à une profondeur irréparable. On ne leur avait fait aucun mal; mais ils avaient eu peur; ils avaient été humiliés, et, crime impardonnable à leurs yeux, humiliés par ceux qu'ils regardaient comme leurs inférieurs.

Simone Weil, *L'enracinement*[2]

The First World War represents a crucial watershed in the structural transformation of the French economy because it lent tremendous organizational and political impetus to the forces of modernization that had appeared in the country. It brought to the fore the imperative of state control over the economy in order to meet its astronomical costs and production requirements. In turn, state intervention was required to rebuild the economy after the war, especially since the greatest damage had been sustained in the North and Northeast, the country's most industrialized and natural-resource-rich regions. The war established precedents that, though quickly erased from the surface of economic life, would have abiding institutional and intellectual ramifications. As such, it marked a seminal moment at which a line was drawn under previous French economic development and a new period of development began.

In parallel, the structural and intellectual changes occasioned by the war had profound sociopolitical consequences. It accelerated the political as well as economic rise of new class and sectoral actors, while hastening the decline of

---

[1] Quoted in Julian Jackson, *The Politics of Depression in France, 1932–1936* (Cambridge: Cambridge University Press, 1985), 167.

[2] *L'enracinement. Prélude à une déclaration des devoirs envers l'être humain* (Paris: Gallimard, Coll. Espoir, 1949), 131–2.

established groups that had benefited from the prewar status quo. Most notably, as they were confronted with the challenge of both a forward-looking industrial bourgeoisie and increasingly dynamic middle and working-class groups, French *petits indépendants* and *petits patrons* gradually forfeited the privileged economic and political position that had been theirs during the Belle Époque. This chapter traces the demotion of these constituencies and how they went from representing the most dependable defenders of the Third Republic to becoming conditional supporters and even outright adversaries of it. As a result of their economic and sociopolitical experiences in the interwar period, *petits indépendants* would evolve increasingly ambivalent attitudes toward the French republican state, attitudes that under conditions of social and economic duress would make them ready supporters for the radical Right.

THE 1920S: *PETITS INDÉPENDANTS* AND THE SEARCH FOR POSTWAR STABILITY (1918–1932)

> Tout le programme économique du radicalisme consiste à majorer sous une auréole mystique une épithète, l'épithète petit, le petit agriculteur, le petit commerçant, la petite propriété, la petite épargne, les petits porteurs. Albert Thibaudet, *Les idées politiques en France*, 1932[3]

> Ce qui s'est effondré en juillet [1926], c'est tout un système de pensée, rebâti après le conflit sur les bases et les fondements des catégories d'avant-guerre et qui s'est avéré sans prise sur la réalité des années 20. Serge Berstein, *Histoire du radicalisme*[4]

At root of this transformation of the French sociopolitical landscape during the interwar period were the momentous changes occasioned in the French economy and society by the experience of the First World War. The latter impressed unprecedented responsibility upon the state for marshaling the French economy and society in order to meet the staggering material and human requirements of war in the industrial era. From 1916 to 1919, state control and intervention affected most areas of economic life. State-operated consortia were created for the purpose of buying and allocating resources, and the state assumed quasi-total control over industrial output and the distribution of goods. Overseen by Étienne Clémentel, minister of commerce from October 1915 until the end of 1919, the French economy was run in virtually *dirigiste* fashion for at least three years.[5] However, it was universally understood that, following the end of

---

[3] Quoted in Nordmann, *Histoire des radicaux*, 324.

[4] *Histoire* (II), 29.

[5] Seeking to achieve an "étatiste-corporatist realignment of liberal capitalism" through the implementation of producer agreements that would lessen market uncertainty, Clémentel hoped to create an overarching corporatist network consisting of consortia, employers' associations, and regional economic bodies that could serve as the institutional framework for the postwar French economy. At the peak of this corporatist structure would preside a powerful Ministry of the National Economy, which was in turn to be constituted around a Production

hostilities, statist management of the economy would be ended and prewar economic structures and processes reestablished.

Within weeks of the armistice, a stream of measures was enacted to relax wartime controls, with market processes being fully reestablished in June 1919. This reversion to economic liberalism continued under the Bloc national government that came into office in November 1919, and which sought to hasten the restoration of a market economy through a policy of liberal "decontrol and retrenchment."[6] Clémentel's successors at the Ministry of Commerce, Louis Dubois and Lucien Dior, removed the last vestiges of state control (though they remained trade protectionists, restoring tariff barriers from before the war). Policywise, they followed the prescriptions of orthodox liberal economists such as Paul Leroy-Beaulieu, who advocated discharging the state of almost all economic functions and returning to private management those public services that had been assumed by it. They saw their charge as a mandate "to shrink state economic activities or at least bring them into line with the best practice of private enterprise."[7] Similarly, the new postwar framers of economic policy adhered to restrictive, financially orthodox formulae. They enacted substantial budget cuts in an effort to improve the position of the Treasury, burdened with the debt occasioned by the war and reconstruction.

Yet, despite this attempt to return the French economy to its prewar state, the institutional, structural, and legislative legacies of the war made such a gambit impossible. Reflecting the need for centrally coordinating postwar reconstruction, these legacies redefined the relationship of the state to the economy. First, at an institutional level, many of the administrative innovations introduced by Clémentel survived in truncated or attenuated form. Most notably, in the place of many of the state-directed consortia that had been created during the war to buy and sell raw materials and oversee industrial production, there emerged an unregulated network of private cartels or ententes that were only incompletely dismantled by postwar liberals.[8] Even at the firm level, a remnant of state control persisted in certain sectors, the state even extending its "direct participation" in the management of some firms. Correlatively, "mixed" companies emerged in certain branches in which both

---

Office that would be charged with drafting "plans of action" for the economy in a manner similar to a modern planning agency. In this sense, this vision of a planned economy was a harbinger of the dirigiste structures that would oversee the French economy after World War II. Kuisel, *Capitalism*, 44–6.

[6] Ibid., 52–4, 62–6.

[7] Ibid., 63.

[8] Casting "producer agreements" as the "way of the future" that "would stabilize existing markets and win new ones," Clémentel made the case for producer agreements in the following terms: "Freed from prejudice and taught by hard experience we can say: individualism and collectivism are doctrinal quarrels. We must undertake a national policy which will not obstruct free and fruitful initiatives; it will result from the coordination of individual efforts and from collective effort. It will assure simultaneously the development of our national wealth and private wealth. This is the policy of groups, unions, and federations." Ibid., 45.

the state and private interests were shareholders, marking the advent of what Richard Kuisel described as a "disguised étatisme."[9]

At the same time, the postwar economy was singularly influenced by the fiscal and social legislation that was inherited from the war. The income tax, passed in 1914 and first levied in 1916, had become an indispensable source of government financing. As German reparation payments dried up, a substantial increase in the income tax was proposed to help pay for the costs of reconstruction.[10] Similarly, social legislation that had been enacted to encourage the wartime collaboration of industry and labor was maintained after the war ended. The eight-hour workday, which had existed in government enterprises before the outbreak of hostilities and in coal mines since 1913, was extended to all firms in April 1919. In March 1919, though it would long remain unenforced, collective bargaining was extended from government suppliers to industry as a whole.[11] Carrying these social measures over into peacetime was geared to secure industrial peace for the task of reconstruction. However, it also meant that, once reconstruction was complete, it would be extremely difficult for employers and the state to reverse the gains to which workers and their unions had become habituated.

In short, the new institutional, structural, and legislative environment that emerged from the postwar period marked out a greater role for the state in the country's economic life. It occasioned a sea change in the development of the French society and economy, which, despite repeated attempts to turn back the clock to 1914, heralded a momentous evolution in the thinking of both policy makers and social actors about the economy. As Kuisel has put it, the imbrication of the structures of the state with those of the economy, and the broadening

---

[9] These became particularly prominent in areas requiring rapid reconstruction or that were considered vital to national defense, such as mining and petroleum, or, to a more limited extent, hydroelectricity and high-tension networks. Accordingly, in 1919 mines became part of the private domain, with the state claiming a share in their profits. In the electricity sector, utility companies were jointly owned and operated in the war-scarred Northeast. In 1921 the mixed Compagnie nationale du Rhône was created with a mandate to develop navigation, irrigation, and hydroeclectric projects on the Rhône River. Similarly, the mixed company formula was frequently employed to operate commercial properties confiscated by the Germans, the most notable instance being the absorption of confiscated German shares in the Turkish Petroleum Company into the French-owned Compagnie française des pétroles. The state in turn extended its stake in the latter and its affiliate, the Companie française de raffinage, in the late 1920s and early 1930s. Most conspicuously, however, the state poured investment into the railroads to close the gaping deficits and repair the extensive damage sustained by the latter during the war. A bill passed in 1921 gave the state a stake in the railroad companies and made it responsible for managing them and distributing their profits. Ultimately, their continued deterioration and crippling debt burden – not to mention the fact they were guaranteed by the state – made the outright nationalization of the railroads inevitable. Ibid., 66–9.

[10] The most notorious was the *double décime* tax introduced by the Poincaré government in March 1924, which proposed a 20% across-the-board increase including the income tax, sales taxes, and new turnover tax on commercial and artisanal business. C. Maier, *Recasting Bourgeois Europe*, 462–3.

[11] Ibid., 77.

of its managerial and regulative competencies over the latter, signified that "slowly and reluctantly the liberal republic eased toward economic dirigisme."[12] Correlatively, though far from marking the demise of the small-producer-based, archaeoliberal order of the Belle Époque, this new economic primacy of the state prefigured the obsolescence of that order in the face of the deep-seated structural transformations occasioned by the war.

These changes were not limited to extending the economic structures and competencies of the state. They also reflected a fundamental recasting of the structures of interest representation in the country. In the first place, a new peak organization, the Confédération générale de la production française (CGPF), was established in July 1919 to represent French business. Conceived by Clémentel as part of his corporatist-dirigiste blueprint for organizing postwar French industry, the CGPF was initially met with suspicion by French employers who saw in it an attempt to assert state control over the economy.[13] By the early 1920s, however, it had recast itself as the organizational spokesman for the country's most powerful industrial interests, which had reconstituted themselves into cartels. These included the steel, mining, railroad, chemical, electrical, and insurance industries, the sectoral associations of which furnished the employer confederation's "informal directorate."[14] Accordingly, though it claimed to speak in the name of French business as a whole, the CGPF was not representative of the small employers and *petits indépendants* constituting the mass of French businesses in this period. Its principal objective, advancing the cause of cartelization, did not concern them and indeed, by promoting the rationalization of industry, may well have run counter to their interests.[15]

At a second level, the principal organization representing industrial workers, the CGT, emerged strengthened from the war. Under the stewardship of reformist leaders such as Léon Jouhaux, it had proved reliable at the hour of national peril and emerged from the conflict with its prestige enhanced, having abandoned its prewar brand of revolutionary syndicalism for a more moderate discourse that accommodated itself to the capitalist system. As a result, the CGT enjoyed a new legitimacy among mainstream political forces, particularly

[12] Kuisel, *Capitalism*, 31.

[13] The new federation was composed of twenty basic trade associations that were granted a consultative role in Clémentel's Ministry of Commerce following the war. Subsequently, these would increase to twenty-one by the end of 1919 and twenty-seven by 1936. On the conditions surrounding the formation of the CGPF, see Kuisel, *Capitalism*, 55–7, and Ehrmann, *Organized Business in France*, 19–22.

[14] The fact that the staff-work of the CGPF was carried out by the head office of the Union des industries métallurgiques et minières, the branch of the Comité des forges that dealt with social questions, highlights the extent to which the organization's agenda was dictated by the priorities of big business. Ehrmann, *Organized Business*, 25, 26, and Maier, *Recasting Bourgeois Europe*, 76.

[15] According to one estimate, from 1919 to 1936, no more than 15% to 20% of the totality of French employers could be counted as dues-paying members of the CGPF. Ehrmann, *Organized Business in France*, 24.

the Radicals and even certain centrist politicians.[16] The social legislation that came out of the war, such as the eight-hour law, testified to this new legitimacy. Even the CGT's call for a far-reaching reorganization of the economy, preaching the virtues of industrial concentration, class collaboration, and statist economic direction, failed to raise the same alarm in elite circles as they would have before the war.[17] Certain advanced business sectors, particularly concentrated heavy industries, even shrugged off their reservations and were willing to deal with the CGT.[18]

Conversely, compared to the gains achieved by the principal organizational representatives of big business and industrial workers, the organizational spokesmen for small employers and *petits indépendants* emerged from the war severely weakened. Though they remained economically and socially significant in postwar French society, these strata, and the political and sectoral entities that represented them, saw their capacity to steer policy dramatically diminished, particularly relative to big business and organized labor.[19]

This diminished influence of *petits indépendants* over the policy process was tellingly reflected in the respective programs of the principal political parties in the immediate postwar years. On the moderate right, the centrist elements that were the dominant force behind the Bloc national were unabashed supporters of big business. Of all the political formations of the time, they maintained the strongest connection to the most advanced industrial and financial sectors. The principal formation identified with these interests in the 1920s, the Alliance

---

[16] For example, although they expressed their disapproval of the general strike organized by the CGT in the spring of 1920, the Radicals objected to the Millerand government's proposal to dissolve the union federation. Berstein, *Histoire* (I), 329.

[17] The centerpiece of this program of economic reorganization was a National Economic Council that was to oversee the nationalization of vital resources and set postwar reconstruction policy. Although it was rejected by the Clemenceau government as excessively dirigiste and economically illiberal, one cannot but be struck by the conceptual and institutional similarities presented by this program and that outlined by Clémentel for restructuring the postwar French economy. Through the emphases they placed on industrial organization and growth, the institutional moderation of class conflict, and mechanisms for state direction and planning, they both testified to the growing influence of dirigiste ideas among certain elites after the war. Kuisel, *Capitalism*, 59–62.

[18] Maier, *Recasting Bourgeois Europe*, 77–8, and Passmore, *From Liberalism to Fascism*, 75.

[19] The only organization moderately successful in defending *petits indépendants* following the war was the Confédération générale de l'artisanat français. Constituted in March 1922 in order to get artisans exempted from the turnover tax and new tax on business profits, the CGAF was initially successful in securing state recognition of a distinct corporate identity for artisans, as enshrined in the status of *artisan fiscal* that was conferred to them in June 1923. Yet, fairly early on, the political effectiveness of the CGAF was diluted by divisions between its corporatist and syndicalist wings. By the mid-1920s, the CGAF had undergone a first schism, the corporatist Union des fédérations régionales de France (which subsequently changed its name to the Union des artisans français) breaking away in 1924. This fragmentation continued into the late 1920s and 1930s as new rivals to the CGAF appeared on the scene, such as the Confédération de l'artisanat familial in the mid-thirties. Consequently, though its success in securing a distinct fiscal status for artisans testified to a certain degree of parliamentary influence, in the end the artisanal movement proved way too fractured to mount an effective challenge to big business and the union movement among the parties and bureaucracy of the Third Republic. Zdatny, *Politics*, chs. 1–2.

démocratique, enjoyed the support of the powerful Union des intérêts économiques (UIE), which on the eve of the war had eclipsed the CRCI as the most influential pressure group in France and essentially represented big business.[20] As such, one contemporary observer qualified it as the partisan incarnation of "organized capitalism."[21]

As a function of their proximity to big business interests, politicians of the center Right increasingly espoused policies celebrating the imperatives of industrial concentration and rationalization. Though they claimed to be economic liberals, many of them affirmed the right of big business to form cartels and accepted a certain degree of state intervention provided it encouraged economic rationalization and productivity.[22] On social policy, the center Right was willing to accept social legislation such as the eight-hour law, as well as consult with labor in economic decision making.[23] Finally, in the area of financial policy, the center Right advocated fiscal restraint and maintaining a balanced budget in order to keep interest rates low and thereby maintain business confidence. In order to contain the deficit, its members were even willing to raise taxes, reflecting the greater willingness of big business to pay taxes than *petits indépendants* and small employers.[24] Thus, though they were couched in terms designed to propitiate the latter, the economic and social policies of successive Bloc national governments and of the Alliance démocratique seemed to have been designed with the aims of big business in mind and, hence, generally enjoyed its support.

By contrast, among the conservative Right, the Fédération républicaine, heir of the Ralliés of the 1890s and the nationalist and Social Catholic Action libérale populaire of the early 1900s, explicitly appealed to traditional small and middling employers. The party shed its initial, more moderate and business-friendly Progressiste constituency and shifted markedly to the right, coming to espouse the orthodox liberalism and clerical nationalist outlook representative of the more traditionalist provincial *patronat*.[25] The strong influence on the Fédération of such nineteenth-century Social Catholic thinkers as Frédéric Le Play and

---

[20] The UIE chose to support to the center Right – including certain conservative Radicals – and largely ignored the conservative traditionalist Right because of its strong ties to Social Catholicism, which looked unfavorably on unregulated, laissez-faire capitalism. Maier, *Recasting Bourgeois Europe*, 103.

[21] Quoted in Passmore, *From Liberalism*, 129. On this point, see also his "French Third Republic," 429, and Jackson, *Politics*, 16–17.

[22] Accordingly, the party program of the Alliance démocratique for 1927 called "for increased production as the best social policy, encouragement of business mergers and industrial rationalization." Passmore, *From Liberalism*, 45n.

[23] In this vein, the Bloc national proposed to establish arbitration tribunals in order to settle industrial disputes, in addition to measures to combat bad housing, tuberculosis, and worker "demoralization." M. Anderson, *Conservative Politics*, 50.

[24] Maier, *Recasting Bourgeois Europe*, 469.

[25] This turn became especially pronounced following the succession of the traditionalist nationalist Louis Marin to the moderate Lyon silk manufacturer Auguste Isaac as party president in 1924. The ensuing emphasis placed by the Fédération on the concerns of the small and middling *patronat* was reflected in the socioprofessional makeup of the party's elected representatives.

Albert De Mun infused the party with the same paternalist conception of patronal authority and conservative ethic of hard work, thrift, and sober living that characterized the traditional family firm. Its clientele evinced the same belief in the righteous and moderate accumulation of property, cautious economic practices, and social conservatism that were typical of the turn-of-the-century, petit bourgeois *rentier*.[26]

Given its strong identification with this economically conservative clientele, the Fédération adhered to the most antiquated liberalism, refusing to countenance any economic intervention (except, of course, in the case of protectionism) or social regulation on the part of the state. By extension, it opposed economic concentration and rationalization – that is, cartelization – on the grounds that these would harm its small-employer base.[27] Following from these archaeoliberal convictions, the party's proposals in the areas of social and fiscal policy tended to be much more reactionary than those advanced by the center-right Alliance démocratique or the Radical Party. It virulently opposed any measure diminishing patronal authority – whether in the form of regulating working conditions within the firm, such as the eight-hour law, or arrangements granting workers a greater say over their wage and work contracts. Similarly, Fédération members viewed trade unions – particularly the CGT – as little more than agents of social revolution. Finally, in respect to fiscal policy, the party was opposed to taxes on principle, viewing them as an unacceptable impingement on the economic liberty of the individual. This opposition was strongest when taxes went to funding social welfare programs, which it saw as rewarding indolence and creating a society of *assistés*.[28]

Yet, despite the proximity in outlook that it shared with *petits indépendants* and its commitment to defending small producers and employers, the Fédération did not enjoy as much support among these constituencies as one might presume. In the first place, it was seen as too far to the right by many of them, its

Although it included in its ranks the representatives of large-scale industrial and landed interests – the most famous of these being the steel magnate François de Wendel – most of the deputies it counted with ties to the business world were the heads of small or middling family firms. Thus, they shared similar economic and cultural outlooks to many French *petits indépendants* and *patrons*. On the sociological and sectoral bases of the Fédération républicaine, see notably Irvine, *French Conservatism in Crisis*, 18–21, and Maier, *Recasting Bourgeois Europe*, 469.

[26] In this sense, as Charles Maier has noted, the Fédération's political clientele was most proximate in both an economic and a cultural sense to that of the Radical Party. In his words, the former "was separated from the Radicals more by temperament or regional habits or fear of collectivism than by social composition." *Recasting Bourgeois Europe*, 506.

[27] Evoking this quasi-artisanal depiction of the ideal French firm and its cultural and moral blessings, a spokesman for the party stated: "Our policy seeks to divide and disperse the large factory into a group of small workshops, ... removing forever the possibility of social upheaval through the wisdom that comes with property. ... We are for the family workshop, the family house, where husband, wife, and children work together, preserved from the temptations of the street and powerfully woven to each other." Quoted in ibid., 470.

[28] Accordingly, in the years immediately following the First World War, they sought first and foremost the repeal of the income tax that had finally been ratified in 1914. Maier, *Recasting Bourgeois Europe*, 469–70, and Irvine, *French Conservatism in Crisis*, 3–4.

strong clericalism proving particularly unsettling for the more secular elements among them. Second, due to its _rallié_ roots and the visibility of representatives of the grande bourgeoisie and landed aristocracy within its ranks, the Fédération continued to be identified by many of these would-be recruits with "les gros."[29] Consequently, despite the solicitude it showed them, the feeling grew among the traditional middle classes and the small and middling _patronat_ that their interests were not being adequately represented.

If on the right the Fédération failed to secure as broad a base of support among _petits indépendants_ as it hoped, on the center left, the Radical Party, the political formation historically identified with small producers, also saw its hold over this constituency weaken during the postwar period. As was previously noted, the Radicals shared with the Fédération a belief in the diffusion of small-scale property, appealing to secular _petits indépendants_ wary of the clericalism of the latter.[30] Yet, as French economic and social structures began to change, the Radical Party's base of support grew more diverse and its appeal to the traditional middle classes became increasingly vague and diffuse. In order to defend a growing array of middle-class interests of which _petits indépendants_ were just one part, the party advocated conflicting policies to secure the allegiance of these constituencies.[31] By attempting to fashion itself as a catchall party catering to the middle classes writ large, it ended up pursuing incoherent economic and social policies that damaged its credibility among its traditional constituencies of support. Specifically, in its effort to cater to newly ascendant groups such as _fonctionnaires_, white-collar employees, and even blue-collar workers, the Radical Party increasingly alienated the traditional middle-class base on which it had historically depended.

In short, even a party as strongly identified with the _petits indépendants_ as the Radicals could appear to have fallen under the sway of interests inimical to them. This is precisely what began to occur after World War I, when

---

[29] In this vein, the contemporary political observer Emmanuel Berl observed in 1932 that "they are the party of the petite bourgeoisie who hoped to be saved by the grands bourgeois." Quoted in Maier, _Recasting Bourgeois Europe_, 470. On the upper-class origins of many of the leading deputies within the Fédération, see Irvine, _French Conservatism in Crisis_, 18–21.

[30] The Radical Party's desire to continue to present itself after the war as first and foremost the party of _petit indépendant_ producers is reflected in the guiding resolutions of its postwar electoral programs. In its program for 1919, it called on petty farmers to "return to the land" and promised them massive aid in the hope of reversing the large-scale rural migration that had begun around the turn of the century and intensified as a result of the war. Likewise, in its program for 1923, the party laid out a series of measures to protect the interests of farmers, shopkeepers, artisans – the staple constituencies subtending the vision of small producer democracy that the Radical Party was still committed to defend. Berstein, _Histoire_ (I), 127, 328–9.

[31] For example, in 1919 the Radicals simultaneously called for fiscal retrenchment in order to defend the incomes of holders of fixed-revenue government-bonds and for raising taxes in order to increase subsidies to small farmers. Similarly, the Radicals' commitment in their 1923 party platform to support the right of _fonctionnaires_ to organize and to upwardly revalue their pensions was bound to be negatively received by fiscally conservative _petits indépendants_ who continued to represent the party's core constituency. Ibid.

"anti-middle-class" interests were perceived to have assumed an undue influence over the party and become a divisive force within it. On the one hand, big business interests such as the UIE and, to a lesser extent, the Comité Mascuraud were thought by the *petit indépendant* rank and file to have co-opted the party's leadership (i.e., the executive committee and parliamentary and senatorial delegations) and pushed it to adopt policies favoring the *gros* over the *petits*. In a scenario reminiscent of the 1890s debate over *patente* reform, the perceived pandering of the Radicals to moneyed industrial and financial interests was a source of growing discontent among their *petit indépendant* followers, some of whom bolted the party to join parties further on the left.[32] On the other hand, the party's new advocacy of state intervention to resolve the social question rankled with some *petits indépendant*, who felt it was increasingly neglecting them in order to secure the allegiance of their "social inferiors."[33] This emerging middle-class discontent was reminiscent of the first decade of the century, when many – in particular urban – *petits indépendants*, angered by the Solidarist policies of the party, had shifted their allegiance to the Right under the aegis of a common front of middle-class defense. *Petit indépendant* disquiet over policies deemed either too friendly to big business or excessively sympathetic to industrial workers became a burgeoning source of division in the party, pitting its conservative, orthodox-liberal wing against its progressive, Solidarist-inspired wing. Whereas the former remained close to big business and committed to a conservative strategy of middle-class defense based on fiscal responsibility and budgetary retrenchment, the latter advocated an increasingly inclusive agenda that aimed to fuse new middle-class strata – *fonctionnaires*, white-collar employees, industrial technicians – and upwardly mobile workers with the party's traditional middle-class base.

[32] This development is attested to by the emergence of the SFIO as a serious competitor to the Radicals in areas traditionally dominated by the latter, such as the Southwest, the Massif Central, and the Rhône valley. Berstein, *Histoire* (I), 310–11. On the influence of organized business on the Radical Party in the decade following the war, see Maier, *Recasting Bourgeois Europe*, 102–4.

[33] This reformist tenor adopted by the party following the war and envisioning the incorporation of the working class into the property-owning middle class through social reform, was articulated by the long-standing Radical deputy Ferdinand Brinon in a speech delivered before the 1920 party congress: "We are not a party of bourgeois, nor of the middle class, but a party of work, of all the workers. And, for this reason, we cannot abide the principle of class struggle, of the oppression of the workers by other workers. The *salariat* is a transitional regime that will need to disappear and give way to the free association of workers. No more underprivileged, no more inferiors. We are all equal! We view as necessary and certain this disappearance of classes and we must put into place reforms that will make it possible to avoid a revolution as a result of inevitable social transformations." Accordingly, the program agreed on at the congress defended maintaining the eight-hour law, opposed the Millerand ministry's proposal to dissolve the CGT, and called for workers who had been fired for participating in the general strike of the spring of 1920 to be reinstated. Similarly, the Radical program for the 1924 national elections contained several measures designed to improve the social and economic standing of French workers, including worker consultation on firm management and profit distribution, as well as the introduction of a more progressive income tax in order to lessen wealth inequality in the country. Berstein, *Histoire* (I), 172–3.

These new tensions within the Radical Party, mirrored by their growing neglect by the republican Right, marked a signal decline in the influence of *petits indépendants* following World War I. They were symptomatic of profound social and economic changes that, beginning in the final third of the nineteenth century, had been intensified by the war and recalibrated the social and political balance within the country. Given their diminished position within this new dispensation, it is not surprising that *petits indépendants* felt a growing sense of social and economic foreboding. Correspondingly, they became increasingly frustrated with the republican state and political elite, blaming the latter for their declining stature and heightened vulnerability in postwar French society.

This diminished stature and declining influence of *petits indépendants* could especially be seen in the financial policies that were pursued by governments of both the Right and the Left during the 1920s. Successively enacted by the Bloc national (1919–24) and then the Cartel des gauches (1924–6), these policies culminated in the official devaluation of the franc at one-fifth of its prewar value in June 1928. They were a response to the tenuous financial situation of the country as a result of the debt burden it had incurred to meet the costs of the war and finance postwar reconstruction.[34] The balance of these costs was financed through domestic government debt – that is, the sale of war bonds to the public – as the low income tax rate introduced in 1914 precluded taxation as an adequate means of sustaining the war effort. The costs of reconstruction generated further foreign and domestic borrowing in the form of U.S. loans and the government's issuing of Victory Bonds. In order to service this foreign and domestic debt, the government planned to rely on the war reparations agreed on at Versailles, predicating the country's economic and financial position on Germany's fulfilling its treaty obligations.[35] As it became apparent that Germany would not pay the reparations demanded of it, the French government was forced to incur ever-larger deficits in order to finance the country's

---

[34] By the end of the conflict, French governmental expenditures reached a total of $9.3 billion. Of that, $7 billion were covered through foreign debts contracted with the United States ($4 billion) and the United Kingdom ($3 billion). Stephen Schuker, *The End of French Predominance in Europe: The Financial Crisis of 1924 and the Adoption of the Dawes Plan* (Chapel Hill: University of North Carolina Press, 1976), 9, and C. Kindleberger, *The World in Depression, 1929–1939*, rev. ed. (Berkeley: University of California Press, 1986), 24.

[35] Accordingly, from almost the end of the war, interest payments on these loans were counted by the government against expected German reparation payments. In turn, as war and reconstruction bonds came due, the government opted to replace them with a series of new bond issues bearing even higher interest rates. The government's interest obligations quickly piled up so that, once German reparation payments dried up, deficitary spending exploded in the early to mid-1920s. Maier estimates that in 1922 alone, although the "ordinary" budget (i.e., that assuming Germany's fulfillment of its reparations obligations) was held to be in balance, the government had spent 7 billion francs in "recoverable expenses" for reconstruction. For his part, Jackson estimates that between 1918 and 1924, the French national debt jumped from 173 billion francs to 428 billion francs. Correlatively, he puts the amount represented by outstanding short-term Treasury bonds alone at the end of June 1923 at nearly 60 billion francs. Maier, *Recasting Bourgeois Europe*, 233, 274, and Jackson, *Politics*, 10.

reconstruction. This in turn fed an inflationary spiral that was exacerbated by the Bank of France putting ever-larger supplies of money into circulation.[36]

The bankruptcy of French financial policy, based on the erroneous assumption that Germany would respect its reparation obligations, was underlined by the failure of the January 1923 occupation of the Ruhr to force Germany to pay what it owed, and the subsequent easing of reparations under the Dawes Plan of 1924. The French government's failure to foresee Germany's defaulting on its reparations until it was too late, combined with the unwillingness of American bankers and politicians to forgive French war and reconstruction debts, plunged the country into a vicious circle of mounting deficitary spending and rising inflation. According to one estimate, by 1924 the cost of living had nearly doubled since 1918 and increased almost fourfold since 1913. Another study found that by 1926 retail prices in Paris had more than doubled since 1919 and risen by roughly a factor of five and a half since 1914, while those in the provinces increased even more rapidly, jumping almost sixfold between 1914 and 1926.[37] This inflationary spiral brought downward pressure to bear on the franc, which lost nearly 70 percent of its value within a year of the armistice.[38] Aggravated by the prospect of Germany defaulting, the mounting budget deficit, and spiraling debt obligations, this pressure on the franc forced the government to contract further foreign loans in order to defend it, rendering the French currency increasingly vulnerable to speculative attack.

The spiral of inflation and the pressure it put on the franc had significant redistributive effects that underscored the increasingly precarious economic status of the traditional middle classes. The burden of the costs associated with inflation and a weakening franc fell primarily on middle-class savers, the pro- verbial *rentiers*, many of them former *petits indépendants* who had invested their life savings – often the proceeds from the sale of their enterprises – in government-backed treasury bonds.[39] Conversely, considered from the stand- point of big business, inflation and devaluation were preferred for two reasons. In the first place, they allowed governments to pay off wartime bonds and

---

[36] Maier, *Recasting Bourgeois Europe*, 462–3, and Schuker, *End of French Predominance*, 40–2.

[37] According to Angus Maddison, taking 1914 as a base of 100, the cost of living index for France increased from 213 in 1918, to 268 in 1919, 371 in 1920, 333 in 1921, 315 in 1922, 344 in 1923, and 395 in 1924. Relying on another set of data, Schuker arrived at similar results. Basing himself also on the year 1914 (= 100), he found that retail prices in Paris rose from 260 in 1919 to 371 in 1920, falling back to 337 in 1921 and 301 in 1922, before spiking again to 332 in 1923, 380 in 1924, 424 in 1925, and 554 in 1926. Correspondingly, he found that, on average, prices in provincial towns and cities fluctuated from 291 in 1919 to 386 in 1920, 374 in 1921, 317 in 1922, 349 in 1923, 406 in 1924, 450 in 1925, and 571 in 1926. *Dynamic Forces in Capitalist Development: A Long-Run Comparative View* (New York: Oxford University Press, 1991), 300, and Schuker, *End of French Predominance*, 73.

[38] According to Jackson, by the end of 1919, the franc had depreciated from its prewar level of 25 francs to the pound to 42. A year later in December 1920, it had further fallen to 59 francs to the pound. *Politics*, 10.

[39] Capdevielle, *Fétichisme*, 180n, 231, 234–5, and Maier, *Recasting Bourgeois Europe*, 513–14.

foreign debts with devalued money, thereby reducing pressures to increase corporate tax rates as a means of fulfilling these obligations. Second, inflation or a weak franc made it possible for business to use devalued money to pay off its debts and year-end taxes while also effectively lowering labor costs, since unions were still too weak at this point to fight for wage indexation. So long as inflation did not exceed certain bounds and spiral out of control, big business representatives had no real reason to support a deflationary policy that would restrict demand and negatively impact their bottom lines.[40]

Conversely, finding themselves hardest hit by inflation and a weakening franc, traditional middle-class groups wished for the adoption of deflation and the return to the prewar gold standard. Holders of government-backed fixed-income securities, as well as individuals deriving the bulk of their income from liquid assets such as pensions, were adversely impacted by inflation and the devalued franc, which reduced the real value of their savings and coupon payments.[41] Similarly, white-collar workers and other members of the salaried middle classes were also hurt because they too were insufficiently organized to force their employers to index their wages. Finally, inflation or devaluation proved deleterious to shopkeepers, who needed to pay their wholesalers in cash but often were required to extend credit to their customers.[42] Thus, as Maier has written, "vexing redistributive questions . . . lay underneath the issues of inflation and revaluation."[43] On the one hand, the latter were strongly opposed by middle-class savers and, in particular, by traditional petit bourgeois *rentiers*, a large number of whom were *petits indépendants*. On the other, policies leading to moderate levels of inflation and devaluation were supported by large producer interests, that is, large-scale industry and commerce and those sectoral groups employed in the most advanced and concentrated branches of production, including industrial workers.

---

[40] On the favorable effects of inflation or devaluation from the standpoint of big business and its ensuing political calculations, see Kreuzer, *Institutions and Innovation*, 95, and Maier, *Recasting Bourgeois Europe*, 361.

[41] If we bear in mind the vertiginous spiral of inflation that hit the country in the immediate postwar period, a comparison of the returns on fixed-income securities to those of other financial assets underscores the precipitous fall in income suffered by *petits rentiers* in the postwar era. Equating the value for 1913 with a base of 100, the value of fixed-revenue securities equaled 83 in 1919, 74 in 1920, 72 in 1921, 77 in 1922, 75 in 1923, 67 in 1924, 58 in 1925, and 60 in 1926. When we consider that retail prices in Paris (1914 = 100) spiraled from 260 at the beginning of this period to 554 at the end of it, while those in the provinces rose from 291 in 1919 to 571 in 1926, we can appreciate the extent to which the poor performance of these securities eroded the incomes of small middle-class savers in the decade following World War I. In effect, of all the categories of financial assets, only the returns on foreign securities caught up with and eventually overtook the rise in inflation – an asset category that only sophisticated (i.e., wealthy) investors were likely to specialize in. Schuker, *End of French Predominance*, 73.

[42] On the negative consequences of inflation and devaluation on these various middle-class strata, see ibid., 73, and Kreuzer, *Institutions and Innovation*, 96.

[43] *Recasting Bourgeois Europe*, 503.

The policy choices revolving around inflation and pressure on the franc became a major locus of competition between various sectoral interests and their organizational and political representatives during the 1920s. As far as *petits indépendants* are concerned, we see that their interests were increasingly ignored by policy makers relative to those other sectoral and class actors. Indeed, the Bloc national government manifested quite early on in its tenure a willingness to live with inflation or a devalued franc. This reflected the proximity of the moderate and conservative politicians who led it to large-scale industrial and financial interests. Heeding the advice of the latter, Bloc politicians "were discounting reparations and beginning to think about the unthinkable, living with inflation."[44]

However, as inflation continued to climb and middle-class discontent increased, most political leaders began to see the necessity of adopting a deflationary policy. By 1923 there was widespread agreement on the need for spending cuts and tax increases, the question being which social segments would bear the brunt of these measures. In January 1924 Poincaré, following the failed occupation of the Ruhr and the Dawes Plan, opted for a radical austerity program. The centerpiece of the latter was a 20 percent across-the-board tax increase.[45] Not surprisingly, the latter encountered particularly stiff opposition among *petits indépendants* and small employers, who were more adversely impacted by the regressive flat tax rate it entailed than were larger concerns.[46]

Politically, the *double décime* law translated significant divisions within both the Left and Right that opposed the defenders of petty producers to those of big business. Many in the Radical Party joined the Fédération républicaine in attacking the new measures, whereas moderates from the Alliance démocratique as well Poincaré's Républicains de gauche and some

[44] Maier, *Recasting Bourgeois Europe*, 274. For example, Maurice Bokanowski, rapporteur of the powerful Finance Commission of the Chamber of Deputies under the Bloc national, advocated a monetary policy that would prevent the franc from rising above its level of thirteen to the dollar in November 1921, arguing that revaluation to the prewar level of five francs to the dollar would make debt charges and pension obligations – which were disproportionately held by large-scale industry – an insupportable burden to their holders. Likewise, Maier notes that even the notoriously cautious Briand, who was prime minister at the time, was also beginning to lean in the direction of not returning the franc to its prewar value, for fear of the negative impact this might have on the most dynamic sectors of industry. Ibid., 274–5.

[45] Complementary measures were introduced to maintain the appearance that the costs of balancing the budget were being fairly distributed, including giving the government decree powers to reduce the number of *fonctionnaires*, divesting the state from the recently nationalized match monopoly, and instituting new controls on the income generated by certain types of securities. However, there was no doubt that the 20% general tax increase, or *double décime* as it came to be known, remained the principal means for balancing the budget. Ibid., 465, and Schuker, *End of French Predominance*, 60.

[46] In addition to increasing their fiscal burden, shopkeepers and artisans also opposed the new tax because it required them to adopt accounting practices that impinged on their freedom to run their businesses, not to mention represented an extra burden in terms of time and effort. Maier, *Recasting Bourgeois Europe*, 469.

conservative Radicals proved much more willing to accept the new tax.[47] The failure of the *double décime* to halt inflation, coupled with the anger it produced among *petits indépendants* and other middle-class constituencies, precipitated the defeat of the Bloc national by the Cartel des gauches in the 1926 elections. Rather than signaling the electorate's approval of a new left-wing program, this defeat reflected the revolt of the "little man" against inflation and the draconian tax regime enacted by the preceding government in order to deal with it.[48]

The Radical-dominated Cartel des gauches under Édouard Herriot that succeeded the Bloc was nominally as committed as its predecessor to fiscal retrenchment and to increasing taxes in order to reduce the deficit, rein in inflation, and lessen pressure on the franc. However, divisions soon appeared between Radical and Socialist supporters of the new government, as well as among the Radicals themselves, regarding who should bear the brunt of spending cuts and tax increases. The left wing of the Radical party, representing the party rank and file and more socially progressive deputies in the Chamber, agreed with the SFIO that the wealthy should assume a greater proportion of the costs of retrenchment. The Right of the party, led by orthodox economic liberals such as Senator Joseph Caillaux, sought to perpetuate many of the Bloc's policies. Chief among these was the *double décime*, which conservative Radicals wanted preserved as the cornerstone of the new government's financial policy.[49]

---

[47] On these internal cleavages dividing both Left and Right at this time, see ibid., 469–72.

[48] Ibid., 477.

[49] These intraparty divisions first came into the open when Étienne Clémentel, the finance minister in the first Herriot ministry, outlined a budget that reflected the liberal orthodoxy of his Radical colleagues in the Senate. Clémentel refused to repeal the *double décime* tax, while opting to maintain other controversial measures introduced under the Bloc national such as the turnover tax. This tax grouped *petits indépendants* with larger merchants and industrialists under a common schedule applying to commercial profits, taxing them all – regardless of the magnitude of revenues – at a flat rate of 8%. Artisans were effectively exempted from the law when a separate fiscal status was established for them in June 1923, but it continued to apply to small shopkeepers as well as larger commercial and industrial enterprises until its repeal in 1954. Similarly, he was unwilling to increase the salaries of *fonctionnaires* – an increasingly important constituency among the party rank and file – despite the rising cost of living, in the name of preserving orthodox monetary principles. These proposals met with the opposition of the Socialists and from the Finance Committee of the Chamber of Deputies, which had evolved into a bastion of left-wing Radicals and represented the views of the *cartelliste* majority in the Chamber. The committee proposed a more expansionary and socially oriented budget, seeking in particular to push through certain spending increases on behalf of *fonctionnaires*, and especially to secure the abrogation of the hated *double décime* tax as well as of the turnover tax on shopkeepers. Its budget proposal also sought to raise the inheritance tax as well as expand state monopolies in oil, insurance, and other sectors. In effect, the committee sought to shift the burden of fiscal retrenchment away from *fonctionnaires* and *petits indépendants* toward the wealthiest economic and social segments within French society. On these divisions plaguing the Radical Party upon assuming power, see Berstein, *Histoire* (I), 396–7, 406–7. On the taxes affecting *petits indépendants*, see Zdatny, *Politics*, 10–11, 168.

These conflicts between the Left and the Right of the Radical Party paralyzed the Cartel, limiting its effectiveness in tackling the country's economic and financial problems. The new government's inability to agree on a coherent financial and tax policy, combined with its continuous borrowing to pay for the interest on previous bond issues, spurred a further growth of the money supply, fueling new inflation and greater downward pressure on the franc. The situation reached a critical point when the Bank of France refused to exceed the ceiling on monetary advances to the government, forcing the latter to resort to twenty-four-hour stopgap loans in order to service its outstanding debt. It fell in April 1925, when Senate Radicals voted against Herriot's proposal to institute a modest capital gains tax in order to improve the government's finances. The conditions of Herriot's overthrow underscored the deepening rift between the business-friendly Radical establishment and the party rank and file who wanted to shift the burden of restoring the country's budgetary balance more squarely to the rich.[50]

The failure of the Cartel cannot be blamed on just the inability of its participants, especially the Radicals, to rectify the country's worsening financial situation. It was also in large measure attributable to the unwillingness of big business to back a program of fiscal retrenchment that would have fallen more equitably on moneyed interests as well as the middle classes. Happy to support spending cuts targeting *fonctionnaires* as well as the *double décime* tax that disproportionately hit *petits indépendants*, big business and its political advocates refused to countenance any measure, such as the capital gains levy, that would have placed a greater share of the burden for retrenchment on them. In this sense, the experience of the Cartel, checked at every turn by the representatives of large-scale industry and high finance, testified to the greater influence wielded by big business over the leadership of the Radical Party than the *petits indépendants* and *petits rentiers*, who constituted its traditional base of support. Consequently, it represented a critical point in the decoupling of the traditional middle classes from the Radical Party in the interwar period, a process that was

---

[50] Not that the fall of the Herriot government succeeded in breaking the deadlock between the Left and the Right of the Radical Party. It was followed by fifteen months of parliamentary paralysis reflecting the standoff between Herriot, who continued to lobby for a capital gains levy, and Caillaux, who advocated a strict policy of deflation based exclusively on spending cuts. In turn, this paralysis precipitated mounting speculation against the franc, which fell to an all-time low of 240 to the pound in July 1926 (compared to 60 in January 1924). Pressure on the franc reached its paroxysm following the failure of the second Herriot ministry to gain parliamentary approval to increase the ceiling on advances from the Bank of France to service the debt. In order to calm the financial and currency markets, Herriot was once again forced to stand down, and Poincaré was reinstated at the head of a new government of Union nationale in order to save the faltering franc. An eloquent testament to how low the credibility of the Cartel had fallen even among its erstwhile supporters, he reassumed power with the blessing of a majority of Radical deputies. Underlining the Radicals' own responsibility in burying the Cartel, no less than four Radical ministers joined the new government, including Herriot himself. Berstein, *Histoire* (I), 408–10, 414–21, and (II), 17; and Maier, *Recasting Bourgeois Europe*, 497–8, 500, 504.

ultimately consummated by the party's adhesion to the Popular Front in the spring of 1936.

In contrast to its predecessor, the new Union nationale government formed by Poincaré was able to successfully stabilize the franc because it gained the assent of the Bank of France to pursue the very policies that the latter had denied the Cartel. Namely, Poincaré obtained its consent to sell francs below the official 1914 rate, thereby making it possible to reconstitute the country's foreign reserves by engaging in open market operations while pressure on the franc declined. At the same time, the bank allowed the government to establish an amortization fund in order to help it pay back its debts. Finally, a new budget was passed that, enjoying the support of moderate Radicals as well as the Bank of France, would reduce the deficit by levying new taxes.[51]

The combined effect of these measures was to bring inflation under control and stabilize the franc. In terms of their distributive costs, however, they came largely at the expense of the middle classes. In the first place, the financial adjustment implicit in the new taxes disproportionately fell upon these strata. As Pierre Saly has indicated, they effectively decreased the tax burden on the wealthiest since they reduced the taxation of financial assets, while diminishing the progressiveness of the income tax. Only a steep tax increase on industrial and commercial revenues, including those of *petits indépendants*, could reduce the deficit without substantially cutting spending.[52] Remarking on the regressiveness of the new income tax and on the increase of the turnover tax, Saly concludes that this balancing of the budget by Poincaré's Union nationale government was achieved largely at the expense of traditional middle-class savers.[53]

The succeeding devaluation of the franc by Poincaré, which was officially stabilized at one-fifth of its prewar value in June 1928, also had a deleterious effect on traditional middle-class groups. It primarily hurt *petits rentiers* as well as other holders of government paper and liquid assets, who saw the real value of their savings fall by 80 percent. Conversely, this lower level of stabilization proved a major boon to producer interests – that is, big business and their dependents. Not only did it effectively reduce their corporate debt but, even more importantly, it also stimulated a vigorous demand for exports from which they were the first to benefit. Consequently, the Poincaré devaluation generated substantial growth among advanced exporting firms, proving a fillip not only

---

[51] Maier, *Recasting Bourgeois Europe*, 505, and Berstein, *Histoire* (II), 18–19.

[52] In fact, as Saly points out, the Poincaré government even increased government expenditure by instituting a pseudo-Keynesian public investment scheme. This suggests that the increased taxation of commercial and industrial revenues must have been substantial indeed, given that it was able to cover this rise in spending while significantly reducing the deficit. "Poincaré Keynesien?" in Fridenson and Straus, *Le capitalisme français au XIXe–XXe siècle*, 33–46.

[53] He writes: "Yet again the middle classes, stirred to action in the name of the defense of the rights of savers, found themselves sacrificed to the very large-scale interests on behalf of which they served as the political reserves." Ibid., 38.

for their shareholders and managers but also for their workers, who saw their wages rise.[54]

The revaluation debate that preceded the franc's stabilization highlighted the growing political weakness of small creditors and, more generally, of middle-class interests relative to big business. Until stabilization was officially decreed and the franc pegged at one-fifth of its prewar value, the *petits rentiers* who had traditionally backed the Radical Party and the Fédération républicaine clamored in vain for its upward revision. By contrast, the political muscle of big business in getting the government to stabilize the franc at a low level was all too apparent as the latter quickly rose against the pound in 1926–7.[55] Big business was in turn joined by other producer interests, including the moderate faction of the CGT, making for an unlikely assemblage of bankers, businessmen, and *cégétistes* demanding the franc's stabilization at a lower exchange rate.[56]

Thus, the introduction of the *franc Poincaré* created the basis for novel economic alliances between formerly antagonistic interests that continued to be otherwise politically opposed. On the one hand, a certain fraction of the working class, represented by the nominally anticapitalist CGT, was combining with big business and large financial interests connected to the party of *grand capitalisme*, the Alliance démocratique, to support stabilizing the franc at a lower exchange rate. On the other hand, advocacy of a strong franc strengthened economic ties between *petits rentiers* and *indépendants* across the still-antagonistic center-left Radical Party and the conservative Fédération républicaine. In this sense, the debate over devaluation testified to the emergence of a new economic divide between producers and savers that lay at cross-purposes with the political divisions that traditionally demarcated the parliamentary Right and Left.[57]

This growing incongruity between socioeconomic and political forces in the country reflected the dislocating impact of industrialization upon the structure of French society and its representative institutions. It had thrown up new, advanced categories of workers and employers who were attached to the most dynamic and concentrated sectors of the economy, while reinforcing the backwardness of the traditional middle-class *petits indépendants*, who not so long before had been portrayed as the inalterable bedrock of the French society and

---

[54] Maier, *Recasting Bourgeois Europe*, 484, 507–9, and Kreuzer, *Institutions and Innovation*, 95–6.

[55] Enjoying the active backing of the head of the Bank of France, Émile Moreau, these interests prevailed upon Poincaré to stabilize the franc at a value of around 120 to the pound. This was in stark contrast to speculators who, exuding renewed confidence in the French currency following Poincaré's emergency financial measures in the second half of 1926, were wagering in the spring of 1927 that the franc would increase in value to 80 or even 60 to the pound. Maier, *Recasting Bourgeois Europe*, 507.

[56] Faced with this alliance of diverse producer interests, Louis Marin, the newly appointed president of the Fédération, charged that the stabilizers wanted "to favor the big banks while he and his friends intended to safeguard the interest of the lowly and the humble." Similar sentiments were voiced by Radicals on the left of the Party, some even attempting to reconstitute the Cartel in order to block stabilization at the low exchange rate agreed by Poincaré. Ibid., 508.

[57] This point is developed by Maier, *Recasting Bourgeois Europe*, 510–11.

economy. Now these constituencies were increasingly viewed by political and economic elites partly as an obstacle, partly as the victims of the great transformation overtaking the country. In turn, the powerlessness these strata came to feel in attempting to resist this transformation was cruelly underscored by their inability to secure their interests by parliamentary means. In this sense, the policy debates of the 1920s gave rise to mounting disillusionment among the traditional middle classes, laying the foundations for their turn against parliamentarism in the 1930s.

The financial and monetary instability that plagued the country in the aftermath of the First World War, combined with the upsurge of labor unrest and emergence of the Communist Party in the early 1920s, awakened more progressive elements of the business community to the need to render the structures of production more efficient and to better integrate the working classes within them.[58] Seeking an organizational solution to these problems, they encouraged greater economic rationalization, concentration, and coordination. Though they believed these goals should be pursued by private means, these business leaders were ready to concede an active, even interventionary role to the state in order to achieve them. Thus, these business leaders arrived at the novel vision of a technologically advanced and organizationally streamlined economy composed of large, rationalized units of production and distribution, coordinating among themselves to marshal the innovative and productive capacities of society. Predictably, such a neocapitalist vision of economic reorganization had little time for the mass of petty producers and traders who had represented the country's prewar economic base.

Such plans for restructuring the economy had already been aired in the immediate aftermath of World War I but did not gain traction among the nation's business elites until the mid-1920s when they were given organizational and programmatic focus by the Redressement français.[59] Founded in 1925, the Redressement enlisted the leaders of the most advanced sectors who questioned the adequacy of nineteenth-century liberalism for managing the French economy and society in the wake of the Great War. Deploring the ineffectual responses of

---

[58] According to historians, the general strikes called by the CGT in the springs of 1919 and 1920 dwarfed in both magnitude and organization the strike movements that it had mobilized before the war. See ibid., 94, 135, 156-7, and Claude Willard, "Les couches populaires urbaines," in Braudel and Labrousse *Histoire économique et sociale de la France. L'ère industrielle et la société d'aujourd'hui*, vol. 4, part 2, 925.

[59] These were the brainchildren of figures as diverse as the Radical Étienne Clémentel, who envisioned an "étatiste-corporatist realignment of liberal capitalism," the Socialist Albert Thomas, who called for "industrial concentration and renovation, industrial democracy, class collaboration, and selective nationalization," and the CGT leader Léon Jouhaux, who posited a neosyndicalist program of technocratic management embracing key nationalized industries and credit institutions, as respective bases for grounding the postwar economic order. What these political and corporative leaders shared was a common commitment to economic renovation, combined with a strong willingness to resort to interventionist, if not *dirigiste* or statist, means in order to achieve it. On these respective figures and their ideas for reorganizing the French economy in the immediate postwar period, see Kuisel, *Capitalism*, 34-48, 77-84.

governments to the chronic social unrest, ballooning deficits, and out-of-control inflation of the postwar period, the tenants of neocapitalism called for a recasting of the liberal paradigm that defined the relationship of the state to the economy and of the agents of production to each other. Accordingly, they advocated the cooperation and consolidation of businesses rather than the anarchic competition between firms that had obtained before, as well as an active role for the state in managing the economy. Invoking the mantra of "rationalization," leading industrial managers such as Ernest Mercier and Auguste Detoeuf – both *polytechniciens* employed in the electricity sector – launched the Redressement in order to pursue a program of "national regeneration under the guise of technocracy."[60] They professed a kind of updated Saint-Simonianism that projected the creation of an advanced economy and harmonious society made possible through the seamless interaction and mutual entente of producers.

As a testament to its transformative ambitions, the Redressement simultaneously advocated economic, social, and political reform. In the economic realm, it sought to make the economy more efficient by establishing "modern ententes" (cartels) that would create economies of scale without interfering in the functioning of the market.[61] In addition, the Redressement's leaders also advocated measures to enhance productivity within the firm, namely by applying the principles of scientific management – the standardization of production and introduction of labor-saving machinery – in the workplace. Reflecting the

---

[60] Ibid., 88. The spokesmen for capitalist rationalization came primarily from industries that had experienced rapid growth and undergone substantial structural reordering during the war. The greatest number derived from the electricity sector, but other advanced branches of industry were also represented, including automobiles and metallurgical engineering. Firms in these sectors had experienced extensive concentration through cartelization, organized their workplaces and production according to Taylorist principles, and shared the engineering outlook increasingly common among the managers of the largest French firms. Regarding this latter point, the influx of engineers into the industrial and business elite reflected the discarding by the top French firms of the model of dynastic capitalism that had long held sway in the country and its replacement by managerial capitalism. Needless to say, the experiences of these leaders made it difficult for them to comprehend the social and economic outlook of petty producers or sellers, and empathize with their predicament. On the social and professional provenance of the adherents to the new neocapitalist thinking, see respectively Richard Kuisel, *Ernest Mercier: French Technocrat* (Berkeley: University of California Press, 1967), 68; Fridenson, "L'idéologie des grands constructeurs dans l'entre-deux-guerres"; and Passmore, *From Liberalism*, 75–6.

[61] This imperative reflected the movement's conviction that the chief impediment to economic modernization was the extremely fragmented structure of the French economy. Inveighing against the myriad small firms producing a wasteful diversity of goods as well as the legions of shopkeepers clogging the distribution network and keeping prices high to the detriment of consumers, the Redressement deplored the ideal of economic autonomy to which it attributed this firm overpopulation. Leading neocapitalists were convinced that encouraging firm concentration "would correct fundamental irrationalities" in the economy and increase firm efficiency by stimulating rationalization and mechanization on the one hand and encouraging research and development on the other. Kuisel, *Mercier*, 53, and "Auguste Detoeuf, Conscience of French Industry: 1926–47," *International Review of Social History* 20 (1975), 154.

technological bias of the neocapitalists, such rationalization and automation were well suited to the huge, manager-run firms from which most of them came. By contrast, such prescriptions were ill-adapted to the mass of small, quasi-artisanal firms specializing in the production of labor-intensive goods. The latter stood to benefit only marginally from mechanization, since they did not employ sufficient numbers of workers to achieve the economies of scale that justified the introduction of labor-saving technology.

In turn, in the social realm the Redressement broke with past employer practices by accepting trade unions and inviting them to participate in rationalizing the firm so long as managerial authority was preserved. In keeping with their call for economic concentration, the movement's leaders believed that cooperation between labor and capital would be facilitated by the advent of big corporations.[62] In this sense, the economic and social program of the neocapitalists could be viewed as a precursory form of Fordism, whereby social conflict would be allayed through firms paying their workers high enough wages to fuel the demand for the goods they produced. Underlying this vision was a basic compact whereby workers agreed to augment their output within an increasingly standardized process of production, while employers consented to pass on to them some of the cost savings of standardization by raising their wages. Hence, economic prosperity was to be indefinitely ensured through this functional solidarity between workers and employers, and social peace preserved by their mutually sharing in this prosperity.[63]

Finally, in the area of political reform, the Redressement aimed to streamline the republican regime in order to facilitate the crafting and implementation of policy. The principal institutional change underlying this reformist blueprint was a proposal to expand the powers of initiative and decision of sitting governments while curbing those of the legislature and political parties. To help in this task, the Redressement also proposed expanding the authority and autonomy of the state administration and – in the economic ministries especially – enlisting technocrats in a policy-making role. Thus, though the neocapitalist movement stopped short of advocating dirigisme or planning, it did call upon the state to help fulfill part of its economic and social agenda, urging it to promote economic

---

[62] They based this belief on the technocratic principle according to which the class struggle could be defused by making the employer into a salaried manager who shared the employee status of other workers, while giving workers an ownership stake in the company by allowing them to purchase shares in it. Thus, in an effort to rally the workers to the Redressement's program of modernization, Mercier's own professional association, the Union d'électricité, extended a variety of these kinds of benefits to its workers in the hope of strengthening their loyalty to their firms. And, although the effectiveness of these measures must not be exaggerated, they did achieve a certain popularity among workers, particularly among reformist members of the CGT, and even on the left with certain Socialists. On the conceptualization of these measures and their effectiveness, see Kuisel, *Mercier*, 54, 78.

[63] Ibid., 54, and Kuisel, "Auguste Detoeuf," 153.

concentration, on the one hand, and to institute measures of social concertation to reconcile workers to industrial capitalism, on the other.[64]

The impact of the Redressement remained fairly limited among French employers, the movement counting no more than ten thousand members when it peaked between 1926 and 1928.[65] Its principal influence lay not so much in the concrete reforms that it achieved but in the intellectual sway it was able to exert on economic and political leaders who would be in a position to undertake such reforms in the future.[66] Similarly, though the Redressement was not a properly *dirigiste* movement, its advocacy of economic rationalization and technocracy set an important precedent for subsequent interwar attempts at modernization and, ultimately, for the political and economic reformers who would embrace state planning after World War II. As Richard Kuisel observed, the originality and importance of the Redressement français lay in the "special reforming spirit [and] technocratic zeal" that it impressed upon a growing fringe of French political and business leaders "to modernize the government and the economy by introducing efficiency, productivity, and rationality."[67]

Though the Redressement was their most visible exemplar, these modernizing ideas were by no means the exclusive preserve of the Right during the 1920s. They also fed minority currents among the Left in this period. As we saw, certain elements in the CGT were not indifferent to the call for concentration and rationalization issued by the Redressement. Such conceptions dovetailed with the neosyndicalist ideas of the labor confederation's reformist leadership, whose goal was to reorganize economic and social life based on the coordination of autonomous groups of producers. Accordingly, in 1928 the CGT officially endorsed rationalization on the condition that it be accompanied by wage increases, worker controls, and collective bargaining.[68]

However, it was in another, less anticipated direction that the most systematic impetus toward economic modernization and reorganization emerged on the left: the Young Turk movement that arose within that historical bastion of petit bourgeois defense, the Radical Party. Launched after the collapse of the Cartel des gauches, the Young Turks comprised a new generation of Radical leaders who sought to modernize the party by endowing it with the intellectual and

[64] On the specific proposals for political reform that were advanced by the Redressement, see Kuisel, *Mercier*, 57–63.
[65] Thus was it rejected by the Paris Chamber of Commerce, which remained unconvinced about the applicability of its ideas in France. Similarly, René-Paul Duchemin, head of the CGPF, the new employers' federation created in the immediate aftermath of the war, expressed his wariness of the "mystique of modernization" with which he equated the Redressement's program and which he felt might lead to overproduction and international industrial conflict. Jackson, *Politics*, 12, and Kuisel, *Mercier*, 74.
[66] In particular, the movement came to have a strong influence over the party closest to big business, the center-right Alliance démocratique. The leader of the party, André Tardieu, would take up the Redressement's productivist mantra and attempt to put its ideas in practice upon succeeding Poincaré as premier in 1929.
[67] Kuisel, *Mercier*, 51.
[68] Ibid., 78.

organizational means to operate effectively in the post–World War I era. In an intellectual *démarche* similar to that which brought advanced industrialists to embrace the tenets of neocapitalism, the Young Turks were impelled by the realization that the traditional doctrine of the Radical Party was inadequate to address the sociopolitical realities that had been wrought by the war. Of primary concern to them was the intensification of the social conflicts that wracked postwar French society, and which, if left unresolved, they believed would lead to revolution.

As the centerpiece of this renovative enterprise, the movement incorporated a technocratic, even dirigiste outlook similar to the economic and social perspectives of the neocapitalists. Many Young Turks, particularly figures on the left of the Party such as Bertrand de Jouvenel, Gaston Bergery, and Georges Boris, came to advocate "the control of the nation over its economy."[69] They prescribed state planning as the principal vehicle by which the latter could be made to work toward the general interest, without threatening private property or suppressing private initiative.[70] In turn, these theorists adopted a technocratic conception of the responsibilities and competencies of the dirigiste state. The role of the latter would be to take stock of the possibilities of production through a statistical accounting of past and projected economic performance, and then to allocate credit to the various branches of production in conformity with certain preset social and economic goals. In this respect, the dirigiste conceptions of the Young Turks prefigured the mechanisms of state planning that would be established at Vichy and under the Fourth Republic.[71]

[69] Berstein, *Histoire* (II), 106.
[70] As de Jouvenel proclaimed: "The state provides guidance, but the individual acts. Liberty is exercised in a framework set down by authority." Ibid., 107.
[71] Beyond their general commitment to accord a greater role to the state over economic and social affairs, however, the Young Turks were far from a unitary and consistent movement. Considerable disagreements existed among them as to what the overarching economic and social goals of dirigisme should be, with contrary leftist and rightist currents soon emerging within the movement. Among the most urgent questions dividing these various currents was the place to be accorded petty production and commerce in postwar French society. Figures on the left of the Young Turks, such as de Jouvenel and Bergery, felt nonprofitable small producers were condemned by economic progress to either disappear or be made more efficient with the help of the state. Indeed, when faced with the question of how the fate of marginal small producers, who represented the political base of the Radical Party, was to be reconciled with the technocratic conception of economic modernization that he advanced, de Jouvenel resorted to unsatisfactory institutional expedients, such as the creation of agricultural cooperatives regrouping the smallest farmers, or the incorporation of artisans and shopkeepers as subcontractors by large industrial concerns, in order to reconcile the preservation of a large petty independent sector with industrial and commercial rationalization and concentration. Conversely, figures on the right of the Young Turk movement, such as André Sauger, advocated state intervention in order to protect petty producers from the monopolistic ambitions of "powerful coalitions of interests." To this end, they proposed revising the legislation governing *sociétés anonymes* to defend the interests of small versus large shareholders, and earmarking additional state aid to assist small artisanal, commercial, and industrial enterprises. However, despite these differences in objective and prescription, the Young Turks were unanimous in advocating for the collective organization of the economy by

Alongside calling for a greater role for the state in managing the economy, the Young Turks also sought to reform the republican state. In marked contrast to the orthodox Radicals who represented the parliamentary party par excellence, these Radical reformers did not automatically equate the republic with the parliamentary regime and condemned the inertia and inefficiency of the latter. Accordingly, they envisioned several important institutional revisions, including strengthening the power of the cabinet, reforming the instances of parliamentary representation – notably by suppressing the Senate and replacing it with a corporatist Economic Chamber – and reinforcing the competencies of high civil servants over economic and social policy.[72]

One cannot but be struck by the resemblance of this program to the proposals outlined around the same time by reform movements of the Right such as the Redressement. It testified to the broad appeal of modernizing ideas among reformers on both sides of the political spectrum. The momentum behind these ideas would continue to build in the 1930s, as prescriptions for reorganizing the economy and society – notably planism – spread across the political spectrum. More immediately, however, the rationalization movement directly inspired the social and economic program of the center-right government that came to power in November 1929, under the stewardship of André Tardieu.

The centerpiece of Tardieu's modernization program was a national retooling plan (*plan d'outillage national*), an ambitious effort to modernize the country's infrastructure through public works, rural electrification, water purification, and the improvement of communication networks.[73] What set this plan apart from past initiatives was the attribution of exclusive responsibility for its

---

the state. All of them foreswore on this basis the tenets of the classical, individualistic liberalism that still characterized the traditional wing of the Radical Party. Ibid., 108.

[72] Charged with representing the various sectoral and class interests in the economy and society, the Young Turks called for granting this body veto power over any law passed by the Chamber of Deputies. On this and the other political-institutional reforms envisaged by them, see ibid., 109–11.

[73] The influence of technocratic thinking in general and of neocapitalism in particular so completely suffused Tardieu's economic and social program that one historian would remark that the two ministries over which he presided from November 1929 to December 1930 "epitomized the neo-capitalist movement for renovation." This ideological proximity is confirmed by the fact that, in early 1930, Redressement français leader Ernest Mercier was admitted into Tardieu's inner circle of advisors and kept in "constant contact" with him during the formation of his second cabinet. On the issue of economic reform, Tardieu agreed with the neocapitalists that the proliferation of small businesses in the country represented a major impediment to economic development. And on the political front, he shared their belief in strengthening the power of the executive to enact requisite economic and institutional reforms and mediate between the manifold economic and social interests that had arisen since the war. Finally, like his neocapitalist acolytes, Tardieu posited the need to enlist the support of wage earners, particularly industrial workers, for the new economic regime. He proposed – and succeeded in passing – what in its day was a sweeping program of social reform. In many ways, then, the modernization program pursued by Tardieu was a faithful replica of the reformist blueprint set out by the Redressement. As such, his ministries represented the first significant instance when the advocates of technocratic economic and social renovation were able to exercise a dominant influence over state policy. Kuisel, *Capitalism*, 90, and *Mercier*, 85; Passmore, "French Third Republic," 433–4, and *From Liberalism*, 119–20.

implementation to the state. The latter was to act as a powerful lever that would encourage the rationalization of production and guide private enterprise toward greater efficiency in the aim of optimizing production and improving living standards.[74] At the same time, Tardieu promoted the collaboration of trade unions and employers' associations under the auspices of the state to ensure social peace and further economic prosperity.[75] In short, the principal objective of Tardieu's ministries was to empower the state to help the "vital forces of the nation" arbitrate and resolve the social conflicts that had plagued the country since the end of the war. By combining this conciliatory role with a quasi-dirigiste prosperity policy, the state would restore national unity by, as Passmore put it, "shifting attention from political divisions to the economic domain, where distribution of the fruits of progress would bind all classes to the nation."[76]

An essential aspect of this effort at class reconciliation was the social welfare measures introduced by Tardieu to address the grievances of French industrial workers and reintegrate them into industrial capitalist society. The keystone of these measures was the Social Insurance Act of 1930, which instituted a compulsory system of retirement and health benefits to be funded equally by workers and employers. Other reforms included a measure extending the principle of free schooling to include secondary education and a Family Allowances law providing child support to large families and those in need. These progressive social measures, combined with *étatiste* policies to boost output and improve living standards, were devised to conciliate a heretofore hostile working class to a process of technocratic modernization to be pursued in the interests of all. As one historian observed, "In sum, Tardieu's reforms were designed to use economic prosperity and social reform to integrate wage earners into a broad conservative consensus led by progressive businessmen and politicians."[77]

This program of economic and social modernization elicited a mixed reaction from the social and sectoral actors that were impacted by it. Within industry, it was well received only by the most advanced sectors, such as metallurgy, mechanical engineering, and electricity – that is, sectors characterized by the largest and most efficient firms. This was hardly surprising, since these sectors were to implement the national retooling plan and could most easily absorb the costs of Tardieu's social legislation. Similarly, many of the leaders of these sectors – who, as we saw, had been prominent in the Redressement français – were increasingly sensitive to the inadequacy of orthodox liberal prescriptions for running an industrial economy and resolving the class conflicts to which it

---

[74] Kuisel, *Capitalism*, 91–2, and Jackson, *Politics*, 32–3.
[75] Notably, by heightening its representation at the level of the state, he hoped to win the CGT to the cause of productivism and thus transform it into a bulwark against communism. Passmore, "French Third Republic," 434.
[76] *From Liberalism*, 119.
[77] Passmore, "French Third Republic," 434. On the particular social and political conditions attending the passage of these social reforms, see Hatzfeld, *Du paupérisme*, 150–4.

gave rise.[78] Meanwhile, the representatives of other business sectors warmed to some of Tardieu's proposals but remained reticent about others. This was notably the case within the CGPF, where some federations approved certain aspects of his program – dropping, in particular, their opposition to the new social insurance laws – but remained frankly unreceptive to other aspects of it, notably state attempts to organize or direct production.[79]

Petty producers and traders, by contrast, remained implacably opposed to Tardieu's modernization program. They were particularly incensed by the social insurance law and the contributions it imposed, which threatened to kill off the most marginal among them. Beyond its financial impact, *petits patrons* and *indépendants* opposed this measure on normative or cultural grounds, the compulsory contribution on which it was premised impinging on their patronal authority and autonomy. Ultimately, they viewed the new law as confirmation of their diminishing economic and political importance in a society whose guiding values, institutions, and processes were increasingly alien to them.

Tardieu's neocapitalist program proved as divisive politically as it was economically and socially. It was opposed on the center-left by the Radicals, who contended that allying with a right-wing government would drive some of their voters into the arms of the Socialists. This reflected the wariness of traditional – and even reformist – Radicals toward a program celebrating concentration at the expense of "smallness" when petty producers constituted the principal social base of the party.[80] More significant were the divisions provoked by Tardieu's program among the parliamentary Right. Predictably, it was supported in his own Alliance démocratique, the party most closely allied to big business. However, it met with stiff opposition from the conservative Fédération républicaine, the party to which traditionalist *petits patrons* most naturally gravitated. The Fédération was particularly exercised over the social insurance law and the compulsory contributions it imposed on employers.[81] This split in the majority was ultimately to prove unbridgeable. In December 1930 Fédération deputies broke with the majority and joined the Left in opposition, bringing down Tardieu's ministry after little more than a year in power.

The failure of the Tardieu experiment, not to mention the general absence of support for modernizing movements such as the Redressement français and the Young Turks, testified to the unwillingness of the country and, by extension, its political elite to contemplate the far-reaching economic and social reforms they envisioned. In this sense, the latter were ahead of their time. Yet, their emergence in the decade following World War I was no coincidence. The profound structural and conceptual transformations that had been wrought by the war and the

---

[78] Passmore, *From Liberalism*, 76–7.
[79] Hatzfeld, *Du paupérisme*, 151–2.
[80] Berstein, *Histoire* (II), 154–7, 160–4.
[81] On the opposition of the Fédération to Tardieu's modernization schemes in general, and the social reforms he enacted in particular, see Passmore, *From Liberalism*, 121–3.

daunting economic, social, and political challenges these entailed ensured that thereafter the modernization issue would remain at the center of the French political debate. At the same time, even if they only faintly resonated in the public square, these modernizing movements and programs seemed to confirm the passing of the prewar republican order – an order in which the traditional middle classes reigned supreme, democracy was equated with small property, and technocracy and nationalization were the whimsical buzzwords of a few utopians. Indeed, the erosion of the orthodox liberal consensus heralded by their appearance would come to a dramatic head with the economic crisis of the 1930s, and the republic's inability to solve it.

THE 1930S: *PETITS INDÉPENDANTS* AND THE POLITICS OF DEPRESSION (1932–1939)

> On propose la déflation, c'est-à-dire la compression des prix en France pour réduire la marge entre les prix français et les prix mondiaux. Est-ce possible? Oui, il suffit de sacrifier la petite industrie et le petit commerce. Il suffit d'imposer les prix les plus bas qui ne pourraient être pratiqués que par les plus grandes entreprises ayant derrière elles des capitaux importants. Les petites sauteront. Voilà la déflation. Cela a été fait par M. Brüning en Allemagne, et il a précipité les petits commerçants, les petits industriels dans les rangs hitlériens. . . . Point de capitaux nouveaux, point d'industries nouvelles! C'est l'accroissement du chômage. Depuis deux ans, les grandes usines ont congédié un ouvrier sur cinq. Et je demande a M. le ministre du Travail: combien aurez-vous de chômeurs cet hiver? Le chômage est en baisse aux États-Unis. Il est en baisse en Allemagne. Il sera en hausse en France. Bertrand de Jouvenel, Speech to the 1933 Radical Party Congress[82]

> Un cri monte de nos campagnes et de nos villes: c'est le cri des classes moyennes. . . . Ces hommes, qui crient leur détresse, sont des fabricants; des artisans; des commerçants; des paysans. Ils représentent les huit dixièmes de la nation, son armature séculaire et, dans le total des tués de la dernière guerre, au moins 80%. C'est ce qu'on appelle les classes moyennes. La présente détresse des classes moyennes, d'où vient-elle? Elle vient de cet Accord Matignon du 7 juin 1936, qui fut le don de joyeux anniversaire de M. Blum et le fait le plus désastreux des cinquante dernières années; de l'Accord Matignon où les trois quarts du patronat français, c'est-à-dire les petits et moyens patrons qui emploient moins de cent personnes, qui n'étaient ni représentés, ni défendus, ont été livrés, par la capitulation des deux cent familles, à la dictature cégétiste. André Tardieu, *La note de la semaine, 1936*[83]

If World War I and the 1920s shook to its core the small-producer-based, archaeoliberal system of production that had been inherited from the Belle

---

[82] Quoted in Berstein, *Histoire* (II), 227.
[83] Quoted in Capdevielle, *Fétichisme*, 247.

Époque, the Depression of the 1930s underscored the deficiencies of this system and set the stage for its eclipse after World War II. The Depression highlighted the basic inability of classical liberal economic institutions and policies to deal with the challenges posed by large-scale industrialization, the emergence of a large class of wage earners, and rapid urbanization and rural depopulation. This was especially the case in a sustained economic recession brought on by the fall in domestic and world demand, ensuing oversupply, and a steep rise in unemployment. The failure of classical liberalism to remedy the situation underscored the need for a new economic model in which the state and industry – and, to an increasing extent, labor – could achieve consensus to move the economy forward. In many ways, the experience of 1930s France is the story of how the intellectual and structural rudiments of this model were fitfully set down, prefiguring the economic transformations that would be wrought by World War II and its aftermath. The principal benefactors of the orthodox liberal order, the traditional middle classes of *petits indépendants* and *petits patrons* found themselves increasingly excluded from this model of development, and their interests and practices ill-suited to the requirements of the new industrial economy that emerged after the First World War. Similarly, these groups were put off by statist economic initiatives, which they felt favored big business and labor, and fed broader processes of economic rationalization and social reform from which they stood to lose.

The onset of the Depression in France, the full impact of which was felt later than elsewhere, triggered a singular response from the governments that ruled the country during the first half of the 1930s: the recourse to the classical liberal policy of deflation. The Radical governments that held office from May 1932 to February 1934, and those of the Right that lasted from February 1934 to April 1936, shared a common devotion to deflation as the surest means of extricating the country from its economic paralysis. There were several reasons for this consensus. First and foremost, many Radicals, particularly in the conservative wing of the party, as well as members of the two principal formations of the Right, the Alliance démocratique and Fédération républicaine, favored deflation on political grounds. Chastened by the experience of the Cartel des gauches, the Radicals who held power when the Depression broke out were keen to demonstrate that they could govern responsibly, which in macroeconomic policy terms meant strictly adhering to the tenets of financial orthodoxy and restraint.[84] In turn, the rightist political leaders who succeeded the Radicals embraced deflation in order to create a propitious investment environment that would propitiate the financial interests to which they were beholden.

Second, deflation was also defended on its economic merits. It was widely felt by economic and political elites that this policy was necessary to shake out the disequilibria between the factors of demand and supply that they held to have

[84] On the impact of the experience of the Cartel on the Radical leadership and particularly on Édouard Herriot, whose memories of the overthrow his previous two ministries – the second lasting only a day – remained vivid, see Jackson, *Politics*, 19, and Berstein, *Histoire* (II), 217–18.

caused the Depression and to restore a functioning free market. By dampening aggregate demand, its advocates argued, deflation would bring down French prices and production costs until they eventually equalized with world prices and costs, at which point domestic demand would pick up again, supply surpluses fall, and the economy begin on a new cycle of growth. For orthodox liberals, the key to reducing demand lay in reducing the government spending that they believed had exploded in the late 1920s and early 1930s as a result of costly public works programs and social legislation. Accordingly, the deflationary policies enacted by both Radical and right-wing governments up until the spring of 1936 primarily consisted of budget reduction measures, though with very different sectoral consequences. Determined to rein in spending, successive governments disparaged the "folly" and "extravagance" of the recent past and tried to prepare their constituents for leaner times ahead, invoking a spirit of collective sacrifice – what the conservative Radical Georges Bonnet would term *la grande pénitence* – vital for returning the country to prosperity.[85] As Julian Jackson surmised, "to conservative economists and politicians, the economic crisis required no innovatory reform but, on the contrary, a return to 'wisdom,' a repudiation of the 'facility' of the 'era of illusions.'"[86]

Finally, the initial support for the policy of deflation was psychologically or emotively rooted. Deflation was equated across the political spectrum with a sacrosanct commitment to defend the franc.[87] At one level, political considerations lay beneath this refusal to countenance devaluation, since a stable franc was seen as the bulwark of *petits rentiers* and, by extension, the middle classes as a whole. Politicians wanted at all costs to avoid a repeat of the calamitous collapse of the franc that had wiped out their savings in 1925 and 1926. Yet, defense of the franc also corresponded to a deeply ingrained equation of national power and well-being with the strength of the national currency for many Frenchmen. Attacks on the franc came to be perceived in martial, quasi-existential terms, its defense portrayed as the monetary equivalent of military victories such as the Marne or Verdun that had saved the nation from disaster.[88]

---

[85] Berstein, *Histoire* (II), 226, and Jackson, *Politics*, 33–4.

[86] Jackson, *Politics*, 35.

[87] Even within the SFIO and the PCF, belief in maintaining the franc preempted politicians from advocating devaluation, even though such a course fit into their conviction that the best way to overcome the Depression was through policies that stimulated, rather than suppressed, demand. Ibid., 192–3.

[88] The daily *Le Matin* involuntarily captured this deeply felt, irrational identification when it sanctimoniously intoned in April 1935 that "the religion of the franc is none other than the religion of France." Such irrational and emotive arguments were far from confined to the economically benighted masses and popular press, but could also be detected in elite business and political opinion. Thus, portraying the defense of the franc in the same quasi-existential terms as those just outlined, no less an important financial figure as the director of the French Treasury, Wilfrid Baumgartner, would opine in November 1933, "Far from coinciding with the recovery of the economy and state finances of a country, [devaluation] can lead to total ruin." Quoted in Kenneth Mouré, *Managing the Franc Poincaré: Economic Understanding and Political*

However, the common commitment to deflation evinced by the principal parties of government during the first half of the 1930s masked important differences in emphasis that reflected the social and sectoral constituencies to which they appealed. Large and small business, labor, white-collar employees, *cadres*, peasants, and *fonctionnaires* jockeyed for influence over successive Depression-era governments, the leverage of these interests within the governing parties often determining economic policy. Sometimes, certain interests succeeded in shaping policy to their advantage, but frequently to the detriment of the higher objective of deflation. More often, the pressures of competing interests produced contradictory policies that canceled each other out, so that their overall effect was negligible. Indeed, neither Radical nor right-wing governments were able to rise above the special interests that dominated the parties on which they relied. Thus, their ability to implement a cogent and effective deflationary program, whether by means of budget cuts or price reductions, was severely compromised. Correspondingly, the concerns of *petits indépendants* and small businessmen were increasingly drowned out by the cacophony of interests seeking to influence economic policy in this period. Until the summer of 1936, their complaints would fall on more or less deaf ears, testifying once again to how far their political star had fallen, especially compared to the status they had enjoyed not so long before.

The third Herriot government that assumed power in June 1932 enacted a deflationary program that broke spectacularly with the expansionary policies of its predecessors.[89] The painful memories of 1925–6 doubtless not far from his mind, Herriot sought to reassure the financial establishment by naming economic conservatives to key financial posts who, convinced that the Depression was the result of the prodigal expenditures of the 1920s, would strive to balance the budget through the imposition of "severe economies."[90] Conversely, the

Constraint in French Monetary Policy, 1928–1936 (Cambridge: Cambridge University Press, 1991), 212, 219.

[89] According to one estimate, for example, government expenditures increased from 42 billion francs in 1926 to 55.7 billion in 1930, with the result that the proposed budget for 1930–1 showed a deficit despite the tax increase instituted by Poincaré in 1926. By the end of 1931, this deficit stood at approximately 5.5 billion francs. In turn, the budget proposed for 1932–3 by the first Laval government was theoretically in balance. However, its voting of 41.4 billion francs in credits to soften the impact of the Depression left no doubt as to the speciousness of this claim and to the fact that the new Radical-led government would be confronted with a sizable deficit. Jackson, *Politics*, 26–7.

[90] Hence, the economically orthodox figures appointed by Herriot to the key posts responsible for financial policy: the Radical moderate Maurice Palmade as minister of the budget, and the centrist independent deputy and former finance minister of Tardieu, Louis Germain-Martin, as minister of finance. That he succeeded in allaying any potential concerns within the financial establishment about the economic seriousness of the new government was underlined by the favorable reaction of spokesmen for big business. For example, financial commentator and editor of the conservative *Journal des Finances*, Gaston Jèze, congratulated Herriot on the judiciousness of the new appointments: "I wish to convey to you all my congratulations for the composition of your ministry. This time, you have chosen worthy collaborators. In particular, I rejoice at seeing Germain-Martin at [the Ministry of] Finance. [And] Palmade is a very serious man. . . . [Y]ou could not have chosen

composition of the new government and its commitment to a policy of budgetary retrenchment dissatisfied more left-leaning constituencies that had voted it to power.[91] As in 1924, the opposition of the Radical Left came to be focalized within the party's executive committee, which represented the rank-and-file departmental federations, and in the Finance Committee of the Chamber of Deputies. The latter, which also counted several Socialist deputies, tried to block retrenchment proposals that penalized *fonctionnaires*, one of the key constituencies for the Left of the party.[92]

The resistance elicited among rank-and-file Radicals and left-wing dissidents in the party's executive committee and parliamentary delegation made it extremely difficult for the Herriot government to impose its deflationary program. Initial proposals to substantially cut *fonctionnaire* salaries had to be abandoned in the face of the uproar they provoked in the party.[93] The ensuing reduction in spending cuts, combined with a shortfall in tax revenues, caused the deficit to explode, convincing the government of the need for even more stringent budget reduction measures, once again primarily targeting *fonctionnaires*.[94] As before, these proposals caused a storm of protest among the Radical majority. This time, however, such protest came not just from the Left of the party, which pilloried the government for being the puppet of moneyed financial and business interests, but from the Right as well.[95] Moderate Radicals in the Senate found these proposals too timid and were put off by the government's separate

better ministers within the whole of Parliament, the opposition included. You have, this time, reassured capitalist opinion, which is not to be overlooked. It is a force which broke you six years ago and which could break you again like glass." Quoted in Berstein, *Histoire* (II), 218–19. See also Jackson, *Politics*, 57.

[91] Thus, despite the fact that 109 of the 157 Radical deputies who entered the new parliament in 1932 had campaigned in support of budgetary retrenchment, many of them owed their election in the second round of voting to the support of voters who had previously cast their ballots for the SFIO in the first round of the 1932 elections. The leftist deputy Gaston Bergery expressed the dismay felt by many of them at the composition of the new government and the policies it proposed to pursue: "This is not a government in the image of our victory, this is not the government that the people had wanted during the first days of May." Berstein, *Histoire* (II), 201, 208–9, 218.

[92] Ibid., 242–3.

[93] The final budget bill that passed the Chamber in July 1932 instituted only minor economies in the form of cuts to military expenditure, in addition to tax increases, which were considerably watered down as well. On the debate surrounding the initial budget proposal, see ibid., 242–4, and Jackson, *Politics*, 58–61.

[94] According to the government's own estimates, the budget deficit at the end of 1932 was of 8 billion francs. In order to reduce this shortfall, the government proposed to increase taxation and take measures against tax fraud (F2.5 billion), cut *fonctionnaires'* salaries and benefits, reduce state pensions by 1.3 billion francs, and transfer 1.5 billion worth of previous spending to a 3.4 billion franc out-of-budget public works program intended to stimulate new growth. Jackson, *Politics*, 60–1.

[95] Giving voice to this critique at the 1932 Radical Party Congress, Bergery accused the government of betraying the trust of the French people and undermining the legitimacy of French democracy in order to do the bidding of high finance and big industry: "It is the second time since the war that [the Radical Party] is in power, and that French democracy, which accepted that the [Radical government] could be broken in 1924 on the wall of money, would tolerate, eight years later, that it refused

inclusion of spending for a public works program whose costs were discounted from the budget on the grounds of its projected expansionary effects. Caught in a crossfire of criticism from both the Left and Right in the Radical Party as well as from the opposition, the government fell of its own volition in December 1932 once it realized that its budget would not pass.

The collapse of Herriot's third ministry ultimately reflected a failure to conciliate the contradictory interests within the Radical Party. Though it strove to enact budget cuts in order to preserve the support of financial and business interests, his government was forced by the outcry these cuts provoked among other key constituencies to attenuate their severity or restrict their application. Not surprisingly, the result was a halfhearted deflationary program that satisfied no one. These conflicts between contradictory interests and the inability of Depression-era governments to manage them would be a persistent hallmark of the 1930s. They go a long way to explaining the dramatic erosion of legitimacy suffered by the parliamentary regime during this period.

The pseudo-*cartelliste* Daladier government that succeeded the Herriot ministry was plagued by the same conflicts as those that had brought down its predecessor. On the one hand, Daladier proved to be just as reticent about taking on the financial establishment as Herriot had been.[96] On the other, he was increasingly caught between the contradictory demands of angry *fonctionnaires* protesting cuts in their pay and of *petits indépendants* advocating spending and tax cuts.[97] The government's ability to adjudicate between these interests was severely hampered by the worsening state of the Treasury.[98]

to take on this symbolic obstacle, or, worse, that it accommodated itself with it to the point of making that wall into a foundation of its own house." Quoted in Berstein, *Histoire* (II), 246.

[96] Affirming his unwillingness to stand up to the "power of money," even the moderate Lucien Lamoureux, who had been appointed minister of the budget alongside the new economically conservative Treasury Minister Georges Bonnet, was struck by the supineness with which Daladier acceded to the financial sector's demands that he install orthodox liberals to key financial posts in the government. Describing the atmosphere that prevailed at the Hôtel Matignon the day Daladier decided on the composition of his new government, Lamoureux observed: "The truth is that Édouard Daladier was harassed all day long by the 'emissaries of confidence.' At six o'clock in the evening, he was a defeated man, crushed by the responsibility that he no longer dared to assume, to hold fast against the powers of money. He was a man who had resigned himself no longer to fight, but to reassure. Therein lies the tragedy and nowhere else. He invoked to justify his decision the situation of the Treasury, the necessity to call upon the banks to float new bonds, the need for the banks to reassure their clientele." Quoted in ibid., 258.

[97] Indeed, it was under the first Daladier ministry that the disquiet of the traditional middle classes over taxes materialized into significant extraparliamentary protest for the first time. Thus, the Fédération des contribuables, formed in the 1920s to defend *petits indépendants* and small employers against the fiscal intrusion of the state, organized street protests and tax strikes across the country to highlight the anger of the *classes moyennes*, culminating in the riots of 6 February 1934, which brought the Daladier government down. See Jackson, *Politics*, 66; Passmore, *From Liberalism*, 218; and William Hoisington Jr., *Taxpayer Revolt in France: The National Taxpayers' Federation, 1928–1939* (Stanford, CA: Hoover Institution Press, 1973), ch. 2.

[98] By the end of January 1933, it was running a 350 million franc deficit and, in a climate of growing financial uncertainty, the government was finding it increasingly difficult to renew its floating debt through the issue of new Treasury bills. In April 1933, the government's difficulty in renewing

Recalling the suicidal attempt of the short-lived Paul-Boncour government to eliminate the deficit in one fell swoop, however, it proposed in the winter and spring of 1933 a series of measures to gradually reduce the deficit rather than eliminate it entirely. Such incremental reductions were made easier by the improvement of the financial situation following a mild economic upturn in 1932 and the government's defense of the convertibility of the franc into gold at the London Economic Conference in July 1933.[99] Yet, at the same time that it was enacting these budget cuts, the Daladier government found itself under growing pressure to raise spending on behalf of another key constituency, small farmers. In the face of violent protests in the countryside, it established a minimum price for wheat in order to slow the fall of peasant incomes. However, this new measure worked at cross-purposes with the objective of deflation since it was likely to increase bread prices.[100] In this sense, the wheat-pricing law was a good example of how certain electoral constituencies were able to force Depression-era governments into compromising the deflationary programs to which they were officially committed, and which other constituencies – *petits indépendants* included – expected them to pursue.

As in the case of Herriot, the financial proposals enacted by Daladier proved unsatisfactory to both the Left and the Right of his party, not to mention within the Chamber. At one level, the apparent financial orthodoxy of his proposals rankled with left-wing Radicals – all the more so because Daladier had come to power on the reputation of being one of them.[101] His credit among the Radical Left was diminished further by the Socialists' decision to officially withdraw their support for his government in May 1933. Similarly, the failure of the London Monetary Conference to come to an agreement on currency stabilization lent added urgency to reducing the budget deficit following Daladier's commitment to continue tying the franc to gold. Thus, the government was forced to push even further down the path of budgetary deflation, in order to maintain the capital inflows that had lessened pressure on the franc following the decision to maintain convertibility.[102]

     even old bills had grown so serious that it was forced to appeal to the London money market in order to obtain the necessary credit to fund its expenditures. Jackson, *Politics*, 66–7.

[99] These measures included a one-monthly provisional appropriation bill (*douzième provisoire*) that instituted new taxes on *fonctionnaires* earning over 15,000 francs a year, and a "special crisis tax" on all incomes that had not fallen by over 10% between 1930 and 1932. In turn, a budget bill was passed in May that instituted a new national lottery, the proceeds from which completed the 5.5 billion franc budget reduction objective the government had set itself for the year, leaving an outstanding deficit of 3.5 billion francs by the fall of 1933. Ibid., 67–8, 73. For the political debate surrounding these measures, see also Berstein, *Histoire* (II), 263–4.

[100] Jackson, *Politics*, 69–70.

[101] Indeed, among all the leading figures in the party, it had been Daladier who had given cover to the largely left-of-center Young Turk movement, and who had been the chief exponent within the party leadership of renewing the Cartelliste formula of joint Radical and Socialist rule. Berstein, *Histoire* (II), 93–4, and ch. 3.

[102] Jackson, *Politics*, 74. On the domestic and international monetary issues surrounding the currency stabilization negotiations at the London conference and their outcome, see Mouré, *Managing the Franc Poincaré*, ch. 3.

Needless to say, this course was anathema to left-wing Radicals such as Bergery, de Jouvenel, and Boris, who saw it as a callous sacrifice of the French middle and working classes to the interests of big business.[103] At the same time, Daladier's financial program proved equally unsatisfactory to fiscal conservatives and orthodox liberals on the right of the party. These elements criticized his deflationary policies for being too timid, charging that the problem lay in the government's desire to propitiate the demands of certain constituencies by either raising spending on their behalf or failing to cut it by enough.[104] Therefore, caught as Herriot had been between the contradictory demands of the Left and the Right of the Radical Party and stripped of Socialist support, Daladier was unable to pass a budget that was acceptable to all parties.[105] Whereas the SFIO saw the government's budget proposal for 1934 as too financially orthodox and refused to countenance any further taxes on *fonctionnaires*, the Right and center Right viewed it as fiscally irresponsible. Deprived of the support of the Socialists, the proposal was defeated in the Chamber, precipitating the government's fall on 24 October 1933 amid heightened speculation against the franc.[106]

The fall of the Daladier government triggered a cycle of parliamentary instability that, culminating in the riots of 6 February 1934, ended the Radical interregnum that had begun in June 1932. The two governments that assumed power in the interim – the third, Daladier's abortive attempt to form a new ministry after Chautemp's resignation, lasting only six days – proved even less adept than their predecessors at dealing with the vexing questions of financial and economic policy. Because of its improbable attempt to reduce the deficit through spending cuts while seeking to lessen impositions on *fonctionnaires*, the Sarraut government proved equally incapable of attracting the support of either the moderate Left or moderate Right. It was overthrown only one month after taking office. The ensuing Chautemps government fared little better. Though it

---

[103] Berstein, *Histoire* (II), 227.

[104] During the debate over the *douzième provisoire*, for example, or the wheat pricing legislation, some conservative Radicals – particularly in the Finance Committee of the Senate – believed that the government was sacrificing the overarching goal of deflation on the altar of illegitimate special interests, whether these be *fonctionnaires*, farmers, or even war veterans. Jackson, *Politics*, 67–8, 70.

[105] On the one hand, given the easier financial situation and improved ability of the government to float debts following the London conference, the government sought to regain the support of the Socialists by proposing an expansionary 13.5 billion franc spending program over four years that was intended to stimulate domestic consumption. On the other hand and in somewhat contradictory fashion, in order to raise the funds necessary to pay for this program, the government proposed a series of offsetting budget cuts that it hoped would be satisfactory to the moderate Right as well as to conservatives in its own party. In a variation on the *douzième provisoire*, these included a 6% tax on all state payments to individuals (war veterans, state pensioners, *fonctionnaires*) as well as on all other incomes that had not fallen by more than 10% since 1930. Although these potentially contradictory measures were sufficient to keep the Left and the Right of the party on the side of the government's position, they failed to attract sufficient support among the broader Left and Right within the Chamber as a whole. Ibid., 76.

[106] Ibid., 77.

managed to pass a budget-reduction bill, its inability to fashion a *cartelliste* majority with the Socialists or a government of "concentration" with moderate conservatives condemned it from the start. In turn, the fall in economic output and rise in unemployment following the devaluation of the dollar in the spring of 1933, combined with the intensification of the financial crisis due to renewed concern about the government's ability to service the debt, raised questions about the government's economic competence.[107] The discredit cast by the Stavisky scandal was the final straw. In a climate of mounting social tension and growing financial volatility, Chautemps resigned at the end of January 1934, setting in motion the events that led on 6 February to the instauration of a conservative "national union" government under the stewardship of former president Gaston Doumergue.

The modalities of the deflationary programs put in place by these successive Radical governments testified to the dynamics of interest competition playing out both within the Radical Party and society at large. First, largely out of fear of repeating the disastrous experience of the Cartel, they pursued deflation to propitiate high finance and big industry. The former favored deflation in order to preserve a strong franc and stable economic environment, the necessary conditions for attracting foreign and domestic capital. Meanwhile, the latter stood to benefit from the lower production and wage costs that deflation would bring about. The principal consequence of this policy, however, notably the continuing drop in consumer demand, ended up disproportionately impacting – as de Jouvenel and Bergery predicted – *petits indépendants* and small employers. Fearful of upsetting the financial and business establishment, Radical governments had pursued financial and economic policies that hurt the traditional middle classes of farmers and *petits indépendants* on which they had historically depended for support. Berstein has observed that, "because they felt vulnerable on economic and financial grounds and because, the experience of 1925–1926 fresh in their minds, they intended not to do anything that might upset the financial sector and provoke capital flight, the Radicals would apply a policy of deflation desired by the latter which ran against the interests of their political base."[108]

Yet, although they primarily suffered from a policy designed first and foremost to placate big business, *petits indépendants* persisted in believing that their interests were being downgraded to benefit other social groups. First and

---

[107] On the financial side, the situation dramatically worsened in the months following the fall of Daladier. With 7 billion francs worth of Treasury bills coming due for renewal in November and December 1933, and only 2.4 billion francs available to the Treasury as of mid-November, confidence in the government's capacity to meet its obligations rapidly deteriorated. Individuals offloaded their treasury notes in order to buy gold or foreign currency, provoking a liquidity crunch that forced banks to trade in their own bonds, thereby diminishing the Treasury's reserves even further and casting greater doubt on the government's creditworthiness. In just six weeks from mid-October through the end of November, the Bank of France lost 6.5 billion francs in gold. Ibid.

[108] *Histoire* (II), 236.

foremost, they resented the favors they felt were being unfairly bestowed on peasants and *fonctionnaires* – this despite the spending cuts and tax levies imposed on the latter by Herriot and Daladier. In short, the policies by which these Radical governments pursued deflation appeared not to favor *petits indépendants*. And when such policies were combined with protectionist measures that benefited farmers and large industrialists while negatively impacting middle-class consumers, it is not surprising that petty producers and traders felt increasingly frustrated and betrayed.[109] Accordingly, it is around this time that *petits indépendants* began to abandon the Radical Party and to shift their allegiance to the parliamentary and, increasingly, the extraparliamentary Right.

The return of the Right *aux affaires* signified the continuation of deflation but in a markedly different guise. The string of right-wing ministries that ran from February 1934 to the spring of 1936 would all claim (with the partial exception of the Flandin government) to pursue deflation with a single-mindedness of purpose that their Radical predecessors had lacked. Yet, the coherence and effectiveness of their deflationary policies were quickly no less blunted by particularistic interests. The Doumergue government that took over in February 1934 found itself confronted not only with a critical financial situation – the Bank of France lost 2.6 billion francs in gold during the first two weeks of February alone – but with a yawning trade deficit due to the devaluation of the dollar in the spring of 1933.[110] In order to improve the country's financial and commercial position, stop the hemorrhaging of gold, and preserve the franc, it determined that it was necessary to close the trade and budget deficits. The objective of bringing down French prices into line with world prices consequently became doubly important and, according to Germain-Martin, Doumergue's finance minister, could be achieved only by acting on the two factors that kept French costs high: high interest rates and excessive taxation. Interest rates were to be reduced by eliminating the budget deficit and, hence, through substantial cuts in spending. Taxes were to be brought down through tax reform, which in turn required even more severe budget cuts.[111]

At the same time, however, the Doumergue government employed the decree powers that were granted to it following the February crisis to placate certain

---

[109] The negative effect of these protectionist policies on petty traders and producers was captured by the president of the Commission of Commerce and Industry within the Radical Party's executive committee, Salomon Hirsch. Citing their deleterious impact on the independent middle classes, he called for an end to trade quotas and the revision of tariff policy at the party's annual conference in September 1932. Berstein, "Les conceptions du parti radical en matière de politique économique extérieure," 85.

[110] Jackson, *Politics*, 80.

[111] Measures to accomplish these aims were introduced by the government in two stages. The first were the budget-reduction measures decreed in April 1934, including cutting *fonctionnaires'* salaries by 5% to 10% and war veterans' pensions by 3%, which represented savings of 2.7 billion francs. These were followed by a sweeping tax reform law that instituted reductions in direct – corporate and income – taxes in order to spur new investment and reduce industrial costs. However, these tax cuts were offset by an increase in indirect (i.e., sales) taxes – a policy seemingly at odds with the stated goal of price reduction. Ibid., 82–3.

constituencies judged crucial to its survival – a strategy that essentially nullified price deflation. Most prominently, it enacted policies to address grievances in the countryside, where peasant discontent had continued to mount through the summer of 1934.[112] Similarly, in a course seemingly at odds with its commitment to fiscal retrenchment, the government also earmarked spending for military expenditure and, more importantly, for a plan of *outillage national* devised by the neo-Socialist Labor Minister, Adrien Marquet.[113] Thus, as in the case of the Radical ministries that preceded it, the Doumergue government's deflationary program was conditioned by certain essential interests and strategic political calculations. As a consequence, it was no less halfhearted – or "financially lax or irresponsible" – than earlier programs for which the current leadership had brought preceding governments so severely to task.

The fall of Doumergue following the refusal of the Radicals to support his constitutional reforms to strengthen the executive gave way to a more centrist ministry under the leadership of Pierre-Etienne Flandin. Because it incorporated elements from the center Left and center Right that reflected divergent political objectives, the new government found itself in a delicate position from the start. It needed to settle on an economic formula that would satisfy both of these constituencies, hardly an optimal scenario for tailoring effective policy. Flandin's economic program was based on the assumption that deflation had run its course and that prices had fallen as low as they would go so that further spending cuts would have only a marginal effect. Accordingly, the new government set about trying to stimulate an economic revival, proposing a series of measures that, it hoped, would inject new life into the economy while satisfying its supporters on both the left and the right. As a sop to the Left, the government put in place a more liberal credit policy. By lifting government restrictions on borrowing, it hoped to spur a fall in interest rates that would encourage new investment and generate new growth. Correspondingly, to propitiate the Right, Flandin sought to correct for the distorting effects of previous government interventions and restore the free functioning of the market by implementing a series of "counterinterventionary" measures, including repealing the minimum wheat price and authorizing provisional cartels in sectors in which a majority of firms demanded them. The reasoning behind this proposal – the so-called Marchandeau law – was that, through their "free" association, firms would be able to more quickly surmount the economic crisis.[114]

As with previous attempts to propitiate too many different interests, Flandin's program ran into trouble from the start. The repeal of the minimum wheat price

---

[112] Notably, these included extending the minimum wheat-price law introduced by the Daladier government the year before through the end of 1935. Ibid., 85–6.

[113] That such a measure was adopted, over the objections of Finance Minister Germain-Martin, was principally attributable to the desire of the government to portray itself as a veritable government of national unity, extending beyond the Right and embracing elements of the "reasonable" Left. Ibid., 86–7.

[114] Ibid., 93–9.

predictably ignited a storm of protest in the countryside. The Radicals, whose small farmer base was the worst affected, tried to pressure the government to restore the minimum price, marking the first, significant strain within the majority.[115] The Marchandeau law proved similarly unpopular, especially among small businessmen – another key constituency of the Radicals as well as the Right – who viewed it as an attempt to encourage industrial and commercial concentration at the expense of small enterprises such as their own.[116] Yet it was the government's loose credit policy that proved most controversial and led ultimately to its undoing. From an economic standpoint, it was ineffective in stimulating growth in an environment characterized first and foremost by lack of demand. In addition, it aroused the hostility of powerful institutional and political foes, effectively condemning it from the start. Indeed, the policy failed to win the support of either the Treasury or the Bank of France – bastions of liberal economic orthodoxy close to the financial establishment – the respective heads of which, Wilfrid Baumgartner and Jean Tannery, advocated that Flandin abandon his policy of cheap money and return to one of strict deflation. This position was largely echoed by the government's supporters on the right as well as by conservative Radicals.[117]

Pressure to resume a deflationary course mounted through the first half of 1935 as the country reached the nadir of the Depression, with both industrial production and agricultural prices falling to their lowest points. The resulting shortfall in tax revenues and growth in government spending for the military, unemployment insurance, and the purchase of excess grain stocks made a new round of budget cuts indispensable.[118] This pressure to resume a deflationary course further intensified in May 1935, as the franc weathered the most serious speculative attack upon it since 1926 following the successive devaluations of the pound and the belga and the strong gains by the Left in municipal elections. In the ensuing run on the franc, panic-stricken *rentiers* and small investors joined foreign speculators in trying to convert their francs into gold, translating into a calamitous fall in the nation's reserves.[119] Only at this point did Flandin resolve to revert to the deflationary policy of his predecessors, but it was too late. The government's request for decree powers to stabilize the franc and institute

---

[115] Ibid., 100–1.

[116] Resistance to the measure extended beyond this constituency, however. The bill also generated opposition on the grounds that it was likely to restrict growth as well as lead to an increase in industrial prices. Even certain large business circles, such as the CGPF and the Paris Chamber of Commerce, objected on the grounds that it would increase supplier prices. Consequently, no one was particularly sorry when the bill became mired in the Senate and subsequently died in committee. Ibid., 96, and Passmore, *From Liberalism*, 171, 182–3.

[117] Mouré, *Managing the Franc Poincaré*, 220.

[118] At the end of April 1935, Germain-Martin predicted that without further cuts, the government deficit would swell to 6 billion francs in 1935 and 7 billion for the following year. Jackson, *Politics*, 101–2.

[119] As an indication of the magnitude of this run on the franc, whereas the Bank lost approximately 1 billion francs in gold between 1 May and 17 May, from 18 May to 26 May it lost 5.8 billion, and then 1.2 billion on 27 May, 1.2 billion on 28 May, and 940 million on 29 May. Ibid., 103.

significant budget cuts was denied by the Chamber's Finance Commission, and the government fell on May 31. In short, Flandin was condemned by his refusal to revert to deflation until his allies on the right and among the Radicals deserted him during the May currency crisis. In the interim, his government had been widely discredited throughout the country, not only among *petits rentiers*, who had been traumatized by the attack on the franc, but by big business, which questioned his financial judgment despite his ostensibly being, as leader of the probusiness Alliance démocratique, "one of them."

Drawing on the lessons of the Flandin ministry's collapse, the succeeding center-right government of Pierre Laval announced a policy of extreme deflation in order to save the franc. To put this policy into effect, Laval persuaded the Bank of France and the Chamber of Deputies to grant him the decree powers that they had refused his predecessors, and which he put to immediate use in instituting a series of draconian spending cuts.[120] Alongside these financial measures, however, Laval also introduced initiatives to revive economic activity, some of which offset the deflationary impact of the latter. These included introducing price supports in the wine, wheat, and sugar markets; hastening the implementation of the Marquet public works plan; increasing defense spending; and intervening in labor markets to reduce unemployment. At the same time, the government introduced measures to reorganize certain industrial sectors (i.e., silk), lessen trade restrictions, and enhance protections for investors in order to spur investment and stimulate growth.[121] In short, the Laval government's economic program presented a mélange of budgetary deflation combined with "Malthusian" pricing measures protecting certain special interests.[122] That the government's policies were at least as ambiguous in their effects as those which had gone before was underlined by the resumption of the loose credit policy that had brought Flandin's government to grief earlier in the year.

Owing to persistent shortfalls in government receipts and increased spending on defense, wheat, and unemployment benefits, the deficit persisted, and the

---

[120] The centerpiece of these cuts was a 10% reduction in all expenditures by the government, municipalities, colonial authorities, and state concessions (i.e., railways) – including the payment of yields to the holders of fixed-interest Treasury notes – unemployment benefits and other social allowances excepted. Combined with various tax increases, the government planned to reduce total spending by 10.9 billion francs, 6 billion of it national government expenditure. In order to make these cuts easier to accept, the government declared an equivalent 10% reduction in the price of essential goods, such as gas, coal, and electricity, as well as in noncommercial rents and mortgage payments. Ibid., 106.

[121] Ibid. On the compulsory ententes sought by the Laval government in the silk industry, see Passmore, *From Liberalism*, 170–1.

[122] Jackson, *Politics*, 107. A flagrant example of the contradictory tenor of these policies was that, at the same time that twenty-three industrial quotas were abolished, agricultural quotas were strengthened. Some decrees even ran against the sacrosanct imperative of cutting down the size of the *Administration*: a decree of 31 October 1935 provided for the creation of three thousand new government jobs resulting in an increase of 60 million francs in new spending. Ibid., 106, 105.

Treasury was forced to appeal to the Bank of France to rediscount its bills.[123] As the nation's financial position failed to improve, the government came under increasing criticism not just from the Left but also from certain segments of conservative opinion, notably the Alliance démocratique and the Christian-Democratic Parti démocrate populaire. As deputies on both sides of the *hémicycle* were quick to point out, though the flurry of 549 decrees enacted by the government had achieved the immediate objective of saving the franc, this had brought no sign of economic recovery. The Radicals in particular harbored growing doubts about the effectiveness of deflation as they found themselves under mounting pressure from their core middle-class constituencies to improve the economic situation. Accordingly, in January 1935, the Radical Party withdrew its support for the government and joined with the SFIO and PCF (Parti Communiste Français or French Communist Party) in preparing a common program for the 1936 general election, precipitating Laval's fall.[124]

In short, as in the case of their Radical predecessors, the Doumergue and Laval governments' commitment to deflation, and the attempt of the intervening Flandin ministry to move beyond it, concealed contradictory policies that detracted from the effectiveness of their economic programs. In turn, their contradictory nature reflected the competing influences of the particularistic economic and social interests that were vying for political access through the various parties of government. Within this dynamic of interest advocacy, *petits indépendants* increasingly lost out, which suggests that their interests were less important to conservative policy makers than those of other social and economic constituencies. For example, the Doumergue government's attempt to repeal fiscal exemptions for shopkeepers and artisans in order to increase tax receipts, while instituting price supports for wheat to placate farmers and earmarking spending for public works programs, was easily construed by *petits indépendants* as a betrayal of their interests.[125] Farmer interests were also at the forefront of the Laval government's preoccupations, whose price supports for certain agricultural goods conflicted with the price deflation it decreed in other sectors. Consequently, while deflation stifled demand for the goods and

[123] By September 1935, these amounted to 2.1 billion francs in new government debt. The parlous state of the budget was starkly underlined by the Senate Finance Committee's rapporteur who concluded that, despite the 5.1 billion francs of savings to be achieved through budget cuts in 1936, the government still needed to borrow 10 billion francs in order to cover its expenditures on defense, price supports, public works programs, and debt reimbursements for the year. Ibid., 107–8.

[124] On the political factors and developments surrounding the break of the Radicals with the government and its subsequent fall, see Berstein, *Histoire* (II), 403–13, and Jackson, *Politics*, 126–33.

[125] Although the privileged fiscal status of artisans was restored in 1935 following the intense lobbying of deputies by the Comité d'entente et d'action artisanales and especially the Confédération générale de l'artisanat français, the fact that the government could have pushed through such a proposal in the first place illustrated the lesser priority accorded by the Right to the concerns of *petits indépendants* as compared to other social and sectoral constituencies, especially farmers. Zdatny, *Politics*, 91.

services offered by *petits indépendants*, they also suffered as consumers from the higher food prices entailed by agricultural price supports, a situation that led them to call for an end to deflation. By the summer of 1935, *petits indépendants'* discontent had grown so strong that they even joined with *fonctionnaires* in protest against the policy.[126]

At the same time, right-of-center governments in the first half of the 1930s were also seen to unfairly favor large-scale financial and business interests to the detriment of *petits rentiers*, many of them *petits indépendants*. Certainly, Laval's 10 percent reduction on fixed-interest-bearing treasury bonds, especially when juxtaposed with the measures instituted by his government to protect large-scale investors, could not be viewed in any other light. Through these decrees, the government strove to regain the confidence of foreign investors in the domestic financial establishment, in part by reducing government expenditures at the expense of small traditional middle-class savers. Similarly, the policy of favoring large versus small business also extended to manufacturing. The Marchandeau cartelization law introduced by Flandin and then resubmitted by Laval could only be seen by small producers as favoring their bigger competitors at their expense. This impression was strongly reinforced by the enthusiastic support these measures received from the representatives of the largest and most advanced sectors of business.[127] Though they ultimately failed to pass, the fact that they were proposed at all underscored the declining importance accorded to *petits indépendants* and small businessmen by the mainstream Right in this period.

Thus, considered as a whole, the experience of deflation during the first half of the 1930s signally underscored the fact that the response of the Right to the Depression was just as contradictory as that of the Radicals had been. On the one hand, right-wing governments claimed to preserve the advantages of middle-class and large-scale capital holders by transferring resources from subordinate

[126] Noting the emergence of this improbable alliance, the Commissaire spécial of Pau reported that *petits indépendants* "no longer attack the *fonctionnaires* as they did previously." Jackson, *The Popular Front in France* (Cambridge: Cambridge University Press, 1988), 46.

[127] For example, the Marchandeau bill was strongly supported by the Redressement français, which saw cartelization as an essential precondition for rationalizing and streamlining the French productive structure. Likewise, in his study of the Lyonnais during the interwar period, Kevin Passmore notes that the Lyon Chamber of Commerce, dominated by the largest textile and weaving firms, was among the leading supporters of the Marchandeau law and the ensuing Laval decree. According to him, it was the request originally emitted by the Syndicat des fabricants, the leading silk weavers' association based in Lyon, that the government take measures to protect the silk industry, which was at the origin of the Marchandeau Bill and the proposal to create a compulsory entente in the silk sector. Artisans and small industrialists essentially saw these measures for what they were: attempts to rationalize the country's productive structure through a state-backed process of industrial concentration that would undercut the market position of small producers. In the words of a spokesman for small and medium-sized Lyonnais textile producers, Victor Perret, these would make "small family-based concerns disappear in order to serve the needs of the trusts and cartels." Kuisel, *Mercier*, 96, and Passmore, *From Liberalism*, 170–1.

groups (i.e., workers) through recourse to a policy of deflation presented as being in the national interest. On the other hand, various constituencies that were deemed electorally and politically indispensable were given fiscally irresponsible subsidies.[128] Within this constellation of interests, spokesmen for *petits indépendants* were unable to compete against more financially powerful and better-connected interests, such as high finance and large industry, or groups, such as farmers, whose support was considered vital by both the parliamentary Left and Right. Consequently, by the middle of the decade, small producers must have been increasingly conscious of their relative decline in status among the different interests competing for influence within the French polity.

The worsening of the Depression during the first half of the 1930s underscored the failure of deflation to resolve the economic crisis. At one level, this represented a failure of implementation, the undermining of deflation by continuous government borrowing, which in turn was precipitated by antideflationary expenditures or pricing measures designed to placate certain social and sectoral constituencies. At a second level, the failure of deflation also reflected its unsustainability in terms of its economic and social costs for certain segments of society. As a study of the Depression's impact on different social categories reveals, shopkeepers and small businessmen saw their real incomes fall by 18 percent from 1930 to 1935.[129] Conversely, the effects of the Depression were much less severe for advanced producer groups, that is, large industrial and commercial concerns and their workers. Statistics published in the *Revue d'économie politique* in December 1935 showed that the profits and dividends of semipublic service industries and the largest cartelized sectors had either increased or not declined to the same extent as across the rest of the economy.[130] This unequal distribution of costs reinforced the conviction among small producers that big industry was being unfairly protected. Likewise, other groups linked to large-scale industry also saw their fortunes decline relatively less than those of small producers and traders. These included the burgeoning class of *cadres* and technicians as the proportion of shareholder-owned enterprises

---

[128] As Jackson observes, perhaps the greatest difference between the periods of Radical and rightist rule lay in the manner in which expenditure cuts were carried out and particular deflationary policies enacted. From June 1932 to February 1934, the brunt of deflation was achieved by cutting capital and military expenditures and converting part of the debt. From February 1934 to January 1936, the burden of deflation shifted to those who received payments from the government – *fonctionnaires*, state pension holders, war veterans, and, ultimately, *rentiers* – in order to facilitate capital expenditures as well as to ease the financial pressures attributable to persisting budget deficits. However, both programs featured inconsistent policies, which contravened the objective of deflation so as not to alienate constituencies crucial to the survival of sitting governments. *Politics*, 218.

[129] Jackson, *Popular Front*, 20.

[130] Jackson, *Politics*, 115. This differential impact is borne out locally by Passmore's study of the Lyonnais, where highly capitalized and concentrated firms, such as in the electricity sector, fared much better than firms in traditionally dispersed sectors, such as the textile, shoe, and building trades. Passmore, *From Liberalism*, 166–7.

markedly increased in the wake of the Great War.[131] Similarly, industrial workers, particularly those employed by the most advanced industrial sectors, were
comparatively insulated from the impact of the Depression. France did not experience the same levels of unemployment as Germany or the United States did, and
workers saw their purchasing power fall by only 5 percent – much less than the 18
and 30 percent declines suffered by *petits indépendants* and farmers, respectively.[132] As one historian remarked, the French working class became "homo-
genized and stabilized" during the 1930s, shedding its most marginal elements
while increasingly organizing itself in the various branches of industry.[133]

Given the fact that they had been rendered worse off than most, French *petits
indépendants* began to lose trust in their traditional sectoral organizations,
particularly as against the representatives of big industry and organized
labor.[134] At the same time, *petits indépendants* became convinced that the
political parties that they had historically supported – particularly the Radicals
but also, since the early 1900s, those of the parliamentary Right – had abandoned them in order to propitiate other groups – big business, farmers, *fonctionnaires, cadres* – whose interests were at odds with theirs. Sensing the social and
economic tide turning against them, and feeling increasingly organizationally
and politically isolated, *petits indépendants* saw their sociopolitical situation in
the mid-1930s as bleak. Growing numbers of them became disillusioned with
the parliamentary politics of the Third Republic, in some cases precipitating their
outright revolt against it.

The deteriorating economic situation and increasing social and political
turmoil during the first half of the 1930s precipitated a sweeping *remise en
cause* of the deflationary programs pursued by successive governments on the
part of dissenters from both the Left and the Right. At base, such doubt
proceeded from a questioning of the classical-liberal economic ideology that
had inspired these programs in the first place. Accordingly, in early 1933 a few
solitary voices on both the left and the right had started to call for the unthinkable – namely, devaluing the franc. Doing so, they argued, would relieve the
ultimately unsustainable pressure that was being brought upon it by growing
budget and trade deficits. Likewise, devaluation would also eliminate the need

---

[131] On the development of a sectoral consciousness among the group of *cadres* during the 1930s, see
Luc Boltanski, *Les cadres. La formation d'un groupe social* (Paris: Éditions de Minuit, 1982), ch. 1.

[132] Capdevielle, *Fétichisme*, 242.

[133] Passmore, "French Third Republic," 437.

[134] This is suggested by the eclipse of traditional business lobbies, such as the Comité Mascuraud or
the Union des intérêts économiques, which represented the interests of small as well as large
producers, as well as by new organizations that were entirely beholden to big business, such as
the CGPF. Similarly, the relative organizational weakness of *petits indépendants* vis-à-vis big
business was magnified by divisions among the former, which blunted their effectiveness in
defending petty producers and traders. Within the artisanal movement, for example, confes-
sional, strategic, and philosophical differences resulted in acrimonious splits between the various
artisanal organizations – one could count four nationally representative federations by the end of
1936 – a situation that considerably reduced their ability to collectively advance, let alone agree
on, the interests of artisans. Cf. Zdatny, *Politics*, chs. 2–4.

for the economically and socially debilitating policies, namely prohibitive interest rates and draconian spending cuts, required by its defense.[135] Any possibility of devaluation still lay in the future, however, and its advocates remained a tiny minority within their respective formations.

Conversely, a broader minority consensus was forming around another current of thought that advocated an increasing role for the state in organizing and managing the economy. The inability of classical liberalism to redress the economic situation ushered in the vogue of "planism" on both the left and the right. First coined by the revisionist Marxist theorist Henri de Man, planism sought to replace free-market capitalism and the orthodox liberal economic dogma that subtended it with a voluntaristic model of state intervention. Only through state planning, de Man argued, would it be possible to resolve the socioeconomic crisis deriving from the dysfunction of capitalism and forestall fascism by uniting the middle and working classes in common cause against monopolistic capitalism. In this sense, planism as initially conceived by de Man was an attempt to achieve socialism not through redistributive policies, that is, by diverting to the lower classes a larger share of the national income, but by expanding it through a rational and scientific management of the economy.[136]

Though planism as a corpus of economic thought was born on the radical left, its call for "some form of permanent, rational, economic management" came to pervade the whole of the political spectrum. Within the Radical Party, planist ideas were enthusiastically taken up among the Young Turks.[137] Similarly, they also neatly dovetailed with neocapitalism and corporatism on the right.[138] By

---

[135] On the left, advocates of devaluation included several left-wing Radicals such as de Jouvenel, Bergery, and Boris, neosocialist dissidents from the SFIO, such as Marcel Déat and Adrien Marquet, and the independent politician Raymond Patenôtre. They advocated devaluation because they believed it would raise domestic prices and hence wages, thereby increasing the purchasing power of the working class, as well as put an end to the country's credit shortage, making more money available for investment. Conversely, on the right, the only serious advocate of devaluation was the future finance and prime minister Paul Reynaud. He considered this policy the only means of closing the increasingly unsustainable gap between wholesale prices and wages, which were falling as a result of deflation, and continuously high retail prices. Only devaluation, he argued, could arrest the decline in purchasing power suffered by the average Frenchman as a result of the ongoing deflation to which the country had been subjected since 1932. See Jackson, *Politics*, 180–6, and Mouré, *Managing the Franc Poincaré*, 43–4.

[136] On de Man and his ideas, as well as the intellectual underpinnings of planism, see respectively Jackson, *Politics*, 137–45; Kuisel, *Capitalism*, 98–100; and Sternhell, *Neither Right nor Left*, ch. 4.

[137] For example, in addition to advocating expansionary fiscal and monetary measures, de Jouvenel presented his own version of the *économie ordonnée* at the 1934 Radical Party conference. He proposed a plan to reorganize the state based on two principal ideas: first, the creation of a corporatist system of representation in the form of an "economic assembly" responsible for formulating economic policy; and, second, the empowerment of government technocrats to directly manage key sectors of the economy, principally by determining the allocation of credit to them. Berstein, *Histoire* (II), 213–14.

[138] Planism appealed to managerial advocates of economic organization such as Auguste Detoeuf and other members of the *polytechnicien* managerial elite such as Jacques Branger, Jean Coutrot, and Robert Gibrat, who had lost faith in the self-correcting mechanisms and inherent stability of

the middle of the 1930s, two strains of planism had emerged. The first was a neocapitalist strain, which advocated planist organization as a means of reforming capitalism without overthrowing it. Second, there was a socialist or syndicalist variant of planism, which sought – as in de Man's original – to build a socialist society according to its principles. Whether of the neocapitalist or socialist-syndicalist variety, however, all forms of planism shared the goal of grounding the economic order in, as Kuisel put it, a "a rational, man-made economic budget and an institutional system of direction at odds with the market economy."[139] Within this system, market functions, such as the pricing mechanism, were to be replaced by forecasting and controls as the principal means of allocating resources and tailoring production to meet economic and social needs. Accordingly, the institutional proposals put forward by planists typically included a forecasting agency, a supervisory economic council, and a "plan" to serve as a blueprint for economic activity by stipulating production targets within the various branches of industry. Likewise, most plans envisioned a mixed economy and placed a particular emphasis on the need for democratic participation in the formulation and execution of economic policy.[140]

the market economy. They shared with Detoeuf the belief that Liberalism had been "killed by an irresistible internal evolution," making state planning necessary for restoring economic productivity and growth. Likewise, the Redressement français adapted planist doctrine to its conception of an "organized capitalism" or *économie orientée*. Repeating old calls for economic reorganization in the form of concentration and strengthening of professional bodies, the Redressement also called for economic councils to be established in order to advise parliament on economic legislation and help oversee its implementation. By attempting through such extraparliamentary bodies to institutionalize cooperation between big business and the government, the Redressement set down the formula for joint economic planning that was to be adopted under Vichy and after the war. Finally, planism also made inroads in Christian Democratic circles, which saw in it a means of curbing the economic chaos of free market capitalism and of attenuating the social inequalities associated with it. The Christian Democratic trade union, the Confédération française des travailleurs chrétiens (CFTC), announced a plan in 1936 "to remake the economy along Christian principles," while the nonconformist Catholic intellectuals of the thirties also saw in planism a tool for curbing the individualistic excesses of liberal capitalism and thereby restoring a more spiritually worthy social order. See Kuisel, *Capitalism*, 101–2, 105–6, and *Mercier*, 96–7.

[139] Kuisel, *Capitalism*, 99.

[140] This call for a rational reorganization of the economy was often joined with high-minded appeals for the moral or spiritual renewal of the nation's political life. Such an orientation was certainly discernible in perhaps the most famous plan to be issued during the interwar period, that of 9 July 1934. Conceived to help lift the country out of the economic and political crisis that had culminated in the 6 February riots, activists, economists, intellectuals, civil servants, and firm managers from across the political spectrum united around a call for replacing the anarchy and dysfunction identified with liberal capitalism with a "self-conscious economy" in which the state would act as a neutral arbiter and the profit motive be supplanted by social service and pride in one's work as the imperatives guiding economic life. Despite these often vague and naive proposals for reform, planism acquired a serious audience during the first half of the 1930s. The intellectual momentum it was able to marshal opened the way for planists to accede to an important policy-making role after 1935. For example, syndicalist planism was to inspire some of the institutional reforms mooted under the Popular Front. Likewise, even more telling

The rapid advance of planist ideas in the second half of the 1930s underscored the erosion of the petty-property-based liberalism of the nation's *petits indépendants* and small employers. Not only did it represent a philosophical attack on their archaeoliberal ideals, but it also called for their replacement as social and economic interlocutors by the ascendant constituencies of big business and labor, whose input was deemed more important in economic planning. In this sense, the upsurge of planism was yet another indication of the weakening socio-political position of *petits indépendants* and heralded the displacement of small producer republicanism as the defining ideological paradigm of French politics.

Yet, despite the growing appeal of planism in certain political and economic circles, one must not exaggerate its impact on broader French society in the mid-1930s. Essentially restricted to an intellectual and political elite, it remained a minority current far removed from the beliefs and preoccupations of the average shopkeeper, artisan, or small employer. The advent of the Popular Front in June 1936 was an entirely different matter. The newly elected Blum government was perceived by these constituencies as representing grave a threat to their livelihoods as any they had previously known. They viewed the new governing coalition of Socialists and Communists as heralding the takeover of the Republican state by a radical working class hostile to the existence of small business.

At one level, the blizzard of social legislation that was enacted by the Blum government as soon as it came into office was perceived by *petits patrons* as a direct threat to their viability. At a second level, the wave of strikes and factory takeovers that swept the nation in the summer and fall of 1936 was seen by many of them as the harbinger of a socialist revolution. *Petits indépendants'* sense of vulnerability was further reinforced by the acceptance by big business of these new social laws and, crucially, its conclusion with labor of the July 1936 Matignon Accords. In this sense, the advent of the Popular Front substantially aggravated the economic and social insecurity wrought by the Depression among *petits indépendants.*

The economic and social program introduced by the Blum government start-ing in June 1936 marked a radical departure from what had gone before. It reversed the commitment to deflation evinced by previous administrations and sought to spur growth through reflationary means by rekindling consumer demand. The core of this program was the Matignon Accords signed by the CGPF and the CGT to put an end to the generalized labor unrest occasioned by the May elections. The accord instituted mandatory 7 to 15 percent wage increases in all industrial sectors, compulsory collective bargaining in firms of more than ten employees, a forty-hour workweek without reductions in pay, and paid vacations for all workers. A new minister of the national economy was also established to "unify and revitalize policy," and the powers of the Conseil national économique (CNE) – first commissioned as a consultative body by Herriot in 1925 – were extended to enlist a broader array of social and sectoral

trappings of the *économie dirigée* were adopted by the third Daladier government in 1938, before being taken up in earnest by Vichy. Ibid., 101, 126, as well as Jackson, *Politics,* 154–5.

actors in the formulation of economic policy.[141] In addition, the new government introduced a series of measures that increased state intervention in the economy and moved away from the classical liberal orientation, under the auspices of deflation, of its predecessors. These included revising the statutes of the Bank of France in order to sever its ties to the financial and business establishment, reintroducing price supports for grain through the creation of a wheat marketing board, and nationalizing the armaments industry. Finally, because they cumulatively raised production costs, these social and economic reforms rendered devaluation inevitable. Thus, on 26 September 1936, to the horror of French savers and *petits rentiers*, the Blum government signed the Tripartite Agreement, which devalued the franc by between 25 and 35 percent relative to the pound.[142]

Needless to say, these reforms and the resulting devaluation occasioned considerable trepidation and anger among *petits indépendants*. In the first place, because they subsisted on thin profit margins, the higher production costs implied by these measures threatened to drive them out of business.[143] These costs were compounded by the devaluation, which undercut the purchasing power and reduced the savings of *rentiers*, life insurance policyholders, and pensioners, many of them former artisans, shopkeepers, and small firm owners. Capturing the disquiet of many Radicals, the deputy from the Nièvre Georges Potut excoriated the downward adjustment of the franc as "contrary to the Radical doctrine that you have constantly affirmed, to the promises of the government, and, in sum, against all the principles of political probity and honesty."[144]

---

[141] The most overtly planist reform introduced by Blum, the upgrading of the CNE prefigured the Ministry of the National Economy and Commissariat général du plan that would be charged with economic planning after the war. Likewise, the emphasis it placed on social consultation and coordination heralded the tripartite Fordist model of industrial relations that emerged after World War II and which institutionalized contract negotiations between the representatives of labor and the various branches of industry under the auspices of the state. Kuisel, *Capitalism*, 119–25; Zdatny, *Politics*, 98–9; and Jackson, *Politics*, 202–3, and *Popular Front*, 9.

[142] Jackson, *Popular Front*, 9.

[143] Salomon Hirsch, president of the Commission of Commerce and Industry within the Radical Party, estimated that the new laws represented a cost increase of 35% to 40% for small business owners. Commenting on the general incapacity of petty shopkeepers and producers to cope with such an increase, he observed: "The new social laws, in fairness, had given legitimate satisfaction to the working class. ... The question for us then became – and it is still valid – to find out how the *petit patronat* would be able to support the weight of these new costs, especially when, today, it often finds itself in a more precarious and less profitable situation than its own personnel. Indeed, it is not rare to currently see *petits patrons* having to pass up their own vacations so as to be able to grant them to their employees, having to work ten hours a day in order to apply the forty-hour law to their employees, and even to forgo the most basic necessities in order to be able to respect the stipulated wage increases." Other reactions were far less even-headed. *L'Artisan de l'Ouest*, the leading professional organ of the *artisanat* in Brittany, titled an article outlining the new social laws: "La fin de tout" (The End of It All). It then went on to liken the new social obligations imposed by the new laws as "a volley of *coups de bâtons*" mercilessly falling on the backs of *petits indépendants*. Berstein, *Histoire* (II), 461, and Zdatny, *Politics*, 97.

[144] Berstein, *Histoire* (II), 478.

On the backdrop of these redistributive social and economic measures, the wave of factory occupations that followed the Popular Front's victory was perceived by many *petits indépendants* and small employers as an existential threat. Henry Ehrmann remarked that the occupation of plants and the ensuing Matignon Accords portended for them a "gathering storm that would destroy altogether the rights and privileges of ownership."[145] In this sense, the summer of 1936 not only brought significant social and economic changes but also had a profound psychological impact on small businessmen in particular and the French bourgeoisie in general. It became synonymous with a sense of collective fear and humiliation that they would not quickly forget – or forgive.[146] In turn, for many small employers, the Matignon Accords that ended the factory occupations were an abject surrender, "amount[ing]" in Ehrmann's phrase, "to nothing less than a capitulation before the enemy."[147] The fear of expropriation provoked by the factory occupations was all the more traumatic for small owners in that it not only threatened their economic interests but also was a direct affront to their cultural values.[148]

This sense of crisis felt by *petits indépendants* following the advent of the Popular Front was compounded by their perceived betrayal by the political and sectoral formations charged with defending their interests. At a first level, the decision of the Radical Party to participate in the Popular Front alongside the Socialists and the Communists generated considerable dismay among *petits indépendants*. It was seen by many of them as an unpardonable betrayal on the part of the party identified with the vision of a small-property-based society and democracy that they upheld. Accordingly, petty producers and traders deserted the Radical Party en masse for the Right, precipitating what Nonna Mayer has termed the *grande rupture* – the great break – of *petits indépendants* with Radicalism.[149] At the same time, the Popular Front and its aftermath

[145] *Organized Business in France*, 5, 13. Representing an unprecedented revolt by the workers against patronal authority, these occupations were akin for traditional *petits patrons* to the *grande peur* that had so profoundly marked the consciousness of French peasants following the Revolution of 1789.

[146] Figures as disparate as the stodgy Radical deputy Lucien Lamoureux and the radical social commentator and activist Simone Weil commented on the traumatic impact the factory occupations had on many middle-class Frenchmen. Evoking the atmosphere of June 1936, Lamoureux wrote in his memoirs, "The terror was great in the milieu of the French bourgeoisie. People believed that the revolution was impending and that a communist regime was on the way." Similarly, Weil would write several years later that "for ... the bourgeoisie, the shock of 1936 penetrated to irreparable depths. Nobody had done them harm. But they had been afraid, they had been humiliated by those they regarded as their social inferiors, in their eyes an unpardonable crime." Quoted in Berstein, *Histoire* (II), 456, and Ehrmann, *Organized Business in France*, 14.

[147] Ehrmann, *Organized Business in France*, 10.

[148] As Luc Boltanski has suggested, the mobilization of *petits indépendants* against the Popular Front cannot be construed in terms of purely economic motives, but must also be seen as part of a greater normative or cultural struggle "for the defense of the values to which the group is attached." *Les cadres*, 115.

[149] "Classes moyennes," 732, and also Gaillard, "La petite entreprise," 163–4.

spelled the end of the historic identification of Radicalism with the *sans culotte* republicanism that had subtended the party's political program and discourse since the inception of the Third Republic.

In turn, the factory occupations and their ending with the Matignon Accords were viewed by *petits indépendants* and small employers not only as a frontal assault on their rights as *patrons* but also as a class betrayal by big business of small and middling employers. The latter felt that the CGPF, which, as the sectoral body empowered by the Blum government to represent all employers, was the principal signatory to the accords alongside the CGT, had sold out small and medium-sized firm owners by making concessions to labor that only the largest firms could hope to respect. This suspicion was reinforced by the fact that the CGPF's leadership, from its president René-Paul Duchemin down, represented the largest firms and the most advanced industrial sectors. Thus, small businessmen remained convinced of the CGPF's insensitivity, even hostility, to their needs and concerns.[150]

The divergent reaction of large and small employers to the Popular Front and the strikes and factory occupations helps to explain the divisions that emerged between them following the Matignon Accords. Whereas big business had little difficulty finding its bearings after the initial shock of the Popular Front's victory and the May and June strikes, small family firm owners never really overcame the trauma of seeing their patronal authority come under such direct attack. Consequently, big firms were much less uncompromising in their hostility to the Blum government's reforms than smaller ones. Indeed, large firms were not so much concerned about having to comply with the new social laws and to assume the higher costs these implied, but worried that the latter would exclusively fall on them while smaller enterprises would be exempted. Some big firms even agreed with the general thrust of the Popular Front's policies, supporting its rejection of deflation and adoption of demand-boosting expansionary policies to get out of the Depression.[151] Similarly, larger employers might also have felt less

---

[150] As Ehrmann has pointed out, four of the five leaders of the CGPF who agreed to the terms of the accords were the heads of very large, Paris-based enterprises. Although their factories were also occupied by striking workers, they were too far removed from the workplace to feel as threatened and humiliated as small, provincial employers would be by the occupation of their enterprises. This domination of the CGPF by big business was replicated at the regional and local level, where the largest firms tended to accept the accords negotiated by the leadership, whereas smaller, more traditional ones did not. *Organized Business in France*, 7–8, and Passmore, *From Liberalism*, 252.

[151] Indeed, some of the largest employers, such as the automakers Louis Renault and André Citroën, even prefigured some of the Blum government's policies when they countenanced the limiting of working hours in order to help reduce unemployment and supported the creation of firm-level tripartite commissions that would give workers a say over the social benefits offered them by the firm. Although these *grands patrons* remained paternalists at heart in the sense that they would not accept encroachments on their managerial authority, their progressive social outlook and search for innovative solutions to secure the loyalty of their workers dovetailed in some respects with the Popular Front's social reforms. Fridenson, "L'idéologie des grands constructeurs dans l'entre-deux-guerres," 61ff.

aggrieved by the social provisions of the Matignon Accords because they were given a representative voice in the new instances of interest intermediation, such as the Conseil national économique, which attempted to enlist various sectoral actors in the elaboration of economic and social policy. In stark contrast, small firms were given only nominal representation in these instances, making them feel even more aggrieved in respect to large enterprises.[152]

Inevitably, small firm owners became increasingly convinced that, in the words of one historian, "a sheltered sector of large firms had been able to avoid the consequences of Matignon."[153] Excluded from the instances of sectoral and economic representation and unheeded by a government that they viewed as irreconcilably hostile to their interests and beliefs, many petits patrons and their representatives concluded that they were the victims of an alliance forged between the *grand patronat* and the CGT at their expense. Many of them denounced what they viewed as this supposed collusion between the *grand patronat* and the Popular Front government, lending credence to the conspiracy theories that emerged in some circles that presented the latter as a plot between the *deux cent familles* and the forces of Bolshevism to take over the state and plunder the country.[154] Ill feeling between large and small business in the wake of Matignon became so intense that it caused associations representing branches in which small firms were prominent (e.g., textiles) to split away from the CGPF.[155]

---

[152] Accordingly, within the representative council of the CNE, the Chambers of Trades representing *petits indépendants* received only four seats, while twenty seats were given to the big business–dominated chambers of commerce and a further twenty to the representatives of the agricultural sector. Despite attempts to broaden representativeness of the CNE in June and November 1938 to include more representatives of small business, the latter continued to remain marginalized within the instances charged with overseeing contract negotiations and the elaboration of social policy. Zdatny, *Politics*, 99–100.

[153] Passmore, *From Liberalism*, 253–4.

[154] No less a figure as the former prime minister André Tardieu succumbed to this kind of thinking when he portrayed the Matignon Accords as "the capitulation of the two hundred families to the tender mercies of the *cégétiste* dictatorship." Capdevielle, *Fétichisme*, 247.

[155] As a result, the CGPF attempted to reform itself and become more representative of business as a whole. Duchemin was replaced by Claude Gignoux, an industrial journalist favorable to small business, as president of the employers' confederation. Similarly, the organization changed its name from the generic-sounding Confédération générale de la production française to the more occupationally precise Confédération générale du patronat français, rewrote its bylaws, and rejiggered its internal structure in an attempt to draw small employers back into its fold. The new CGPF's general council was expanded to make room for sectors with a high proportion of small firms. Likewise, the business associations that made up the confederation were reconfigured to represent both industry and trade within a same branch in order to better combine their respective interests.

Yet, despite the new leadership's best efforts, the CGPF was never able to confer any real internal cohesion and discipline to the employers' movement. Divisions between small and large employers continued to persist, hampering its organizational effectiveness. (For example, the new CGPF was unable to bring the textile industry association back into its fold.) Likewise, the continuing concentration and rationalization of the more advanced capital-intensive branches of industry further alienated small business, eroding the new CGPF's legitimacy despite its best efforts

This fundamental divide between large and small business would endure beyond the Blum government's collapse in June 1937, and despite the repeal of many of the social laws enacted during its tenure by the succeeding Chautemps and Daladier ministries. The primary lesson gleaned by employers in the most-advanced business sectors from the Popular Front experience was for them to treat workers as social equals within the firm. By giving their employees a consultative role in decision making, these employers believed, it would be possible to inoculate them against the affliction of socialism and class struggle.[156] These progressive employers were openly critical of the paternalist attitudes espoused by *petits indépendants* and small firm owners, seeing in them a source of resentment that promised to alienate workers instead of conciliating them to the capitalist order. They insisted that employers treat their workers as equals in order to promote the "assimilation and the fusion of the classes," the sole means of exorcising the demons of revolution and preserving industrial capitalism over the long term.[157] In short, progressive employers envisioned the institutionalization of more egalitarian industrial relations as a prerequisite for better managing production. Only through structured and formalized worker-employer relations, they argued, would it be possible to end the economic and social anarchy that had been wrought by the dysfunction of the liberal economy during the interwar period. As Ehrmann surmised, "To them more orderly industrial relations, based on the mutual respect of the partners and of their respective interests, were the complement of a high degree of economic organization."[158] In this sense, in both their philosophical outlook and institutional prescriptions, these employers prefigured the tripartite, Fordist system of industrial relations and economic organization that was to emerge after World War II.

to represent French business as a whole. Jackson, *Popular Front*, 264, and Ehrmann, *Organized Business in France*, 32–5.

[156] The chief exemplar of this progressive thinking was the Nouveaux Cahiers group launched by Auguste Detoeuf in spring 1937. Pursuing "a progressive agenda of rational economic planning and class collaboration" in order to heal the social and political rifts that had opened in French society during the 1930s, the Nouveaux Cahiers enlisted leaders from industry, banking, and the professions; high-level members of the *Administration*; intellectuals; and reformist trade unionists in devising constructive solutions to the sectoral and class antagonisms and disorganization of production that plagued the country in the interwar period. First and foremost, the Nouveaux Cahiers group implored French employers to accept organized labor as a necessary, even constructive partner at all stages of economic decision making, from the microeconomic level of the firm all the way up to the macroeconomic level of the state. As Detoeuf proclaimed in January 1938, "I believe that syndicalism is necessary and that it must be unitary, compulsory and apolitical. ... Wage earners must be defended. It is indispensable that those who organize, direct, and defend the workers be not only tolerated, but respected by the *patronat*." Ehrmann, *Organized Business in France*, 46; Georges Lefranc, *Les organisations patronales en France, du passé au présent* (Paris: Payot, 1976), 258–9; and Kuisel, "Auguste Detoeuf," 158ff.

[157] Kuisel, "Auguste Detoeuf," 167.

[158] *Organized Business*, 48. It seems that in their institutional prescriptions, Detoeuf and others in the Nouveaux Cahiers group looked to the Swedish system of industrial relations, based on mutual respect, the institutionalization of collective bargaining, and social welfare programs, as an exemplary model of labor-employer relations to try to emulate in France. Kuisel, "Auguste Detoeuf," 166.

In diametrical contrast to this current, traditionalist and paternalist *patrons* sought to muzzle the material and political aspirations of workers and of organized labor. In June 1936 a political advocacy group, the Comité de prévoyance et d'action sociale, was formed within the newly reconfigured CGPF and placed under the stewardship of erstwhile finance minister Louis Germain-Martin in order to enlist public opinion against organized labor and the Left. Presenting vague authoritarian and corporatist prescriptions for reorganizing labor-employer relations, its program was specifically tailored to appeal to small firm owners keen to restore their authority within their shops and factories.[159]

Despite the best efforts of the Comité, however, the vast majority of *petits patrons* did not flock back – if they had ever belonged at all – to the CGPF. Many deserted the employer movement altogether to join the plethora of movements of "middle-class defense" that made their appearance in this period. According to one estimate, there were no less than sixteen such movements before World War II, reflecting the general angst of the French middle classes following the May 1936 labor explosion and the conclusion of the Matignon Accords in the face of sustained worker militancy. At one level, these included organizations dedicated specifically to defending *petits patrons*, such as the Confédération générale du commerce et de l'artisanat, the Bloc du petit commerce, the Confédération française des professions commerciales, industrielles et libérales, the Confédération du petit commerce, the Syndicat de la petite et moyenne industrie, and the Groupement de l'industrie moyenne. In turn, certain movements, following the historical example of the pre–World War I Association de défense des classes moyennes, strove to unite both the old and new middle classes into a common antilabor front. Chief among these was the Confédération générale des syndicats des classes moyennes (CGSCM), which assembled, alongside the sectoral representatives of *petits indépendants*, professional groups representing farmers, members of the liberal professions, and the growing segment of *cadres*, and the Confédération générale des classes moyennes (CGCM), founded by parliamentarians committed to a program of middle-class defense.[160]

The broad-based middle-class coalition envisioned by these organizations proved unsustainable over the long term. Brought together by economic crisis and the threat of labor radicalism, the uneasy relations that formerly obtained between their various constituencies quickly reasserted themselves once the

---

[159] Some of the Comité's spokesmen even went so far as to advocate the kind of compulsory corporatist framework that had been established in fascist Italy and Nazi Germany, in which workers and employers were organized according to industrial branch and forced to accept state-sanctioned wage contracts. Though its influence remained relatively circumscribed throughout the 1930s, many of its ideas and prescriptions prefigured the authoritarian-corporatist model of social and economic organization that Vichy would try to put in place during the war. On the ideas and influence of the Comité, see Ehrmann, *Organized Business in France*, 43–6.

[160] By the end of 1936, the CGSCM claimed a membership of 2.5 million adherents. Meanwhile, counting 350 deputies in 1938, the CGCM numbered 400,000 members on the eve of the war. Mayer, "Les classes moyennes," 734–5.

economy improved and worker militancy subsided. This was especially true in regard to the relationship between the old and new middle classes, *petits patrons* on the one hand and *cadres* on the other, whose divergent interests made any lasting entente impossible.[161] Thus, despite the appearance of middle-class unity against it, by the time the Popular Front drew to an end the traditional middle classes found themselves substantially isolated and weakened as a sociopolitical force. Long gone were the days when they could shift on their own the economic and political balance of the Third Republic and force the state to fashion policies on their behalf.

This loss of influence was confirmed following the collapse of the Popular Front. Although the Radical governments that succeeded the Blum ministry took measures to address the most pressing concerns of small business and to curb the rights of labor, they preserved institutions from the Blum period that confirmed that the era of the traditional middle classes had passed. The preservation by the succeeding Chautemps and Daladier ministries of such dirigiste organs as the CNE and Ministry of National Economy set the stage for the state-directed process of modernization that would be initiated at Vichy and then expanded after the Liberation. Likewise, in its final days the Third Republic restored a mix of market forces and state intervention – notably in the form of increased spending on armaments and incentives to encourage new plant investment, higher output, and higher returns on capital – that harkened not so much back to the Popular Front but to the end of the First World War.[162] Though they claimed to do so under a liberal guise, post–Popular Front governments, in particular the three Daladier ministries from April 1938 to March 1940, pursued state-led growth strategies under the auspices of a "managed capitalism." This dirigiste departure intensified with the approach of hostilities with Germany and the placing of the economy on a war footing.

By the eve of World War II, then, the second Daladier ministry had accepted the inevitability and even desirability of an *économie orientée*. Even as formerly staunch a classical liberal as Paul Reynaud, Daladier's new finance minister, was now arguing that "the state is responsible for the general orientation of the economy" and calling for "a guided economy within the framework of liberty."[163] This conceptual shift among the nation's economic and political elites reflected that, following the Depression and with the imminence of war, "many

---

[161] The basic functional and cultural incompatibility between the small, traditional family-run firms with which *petits indépendants* identified and the large, shareholder or state-owned firms that employed *cadres* made such a rift ultimately unavoidable. Whereas *petits patrons* had joined the movement of middle-class defense to fight for their economic and social survival, the *cadres* had done so to secure recognition of their distinct socioprofessional status by employers and the state. They evinced contrary economic rationalities and cultural outlooks that, respectively, identified with archaeoliberal and technocratic visions of organization, which doomed the effort to maintain the unity of the middle classes to failure. Boltanski, *Les cadres*, 110–12.

[162] Kuisel, *Capitalism*, 126–7.

[163] Quoted in ibid., 127. The increasingly dirigiste tenor of the second Daladier ministry before the war was evocatively reflected in the mix of personnel occupying positions of authority in

Frenchmen had come to accept ... the neo-liberal practice of stimulating production and coordinating government intervention ... as the shape of the
nation's future political economy."[164] The conversion of key elites to dirigisme
sounded the death knell of the traditional "balanced" or "dualistic" economy,
based on a multitude of small agricultural, commercial, and industrial producers
shielded from competition by a battery of Malthusian policies. This evolution
also marked the intellectual and institutional displacement of the primordial
Jacobin vision of republican democracy that had presided over the establishment
of the Third Republic, projecting a society of small producers as the surest
sociostructural bulwark for the regime. Thus, this philosophical and institutional shift toward dirigisme rendered the *petits indépendants* who sustained this
atavistic, petty producer republicanism increasingly redundant not only economically but politically as well.

In a fundamental sense, then, the evolution of the Third Republic entailed a
progressive erosion of the primordial republican ideal of small producer democracy and economy in which the state played almost no role and the only mechanism for resolving class antagonisms was through the projection of social mobility
out of the proletarian condition to the status of *indépendance*. Predictably, this
erosion of petty producer republicanism coincided with the diminution of *petits
indépendants'* economic and political clout. As their role in the nation's productive
structure declined, *petits patrons* found themselves increasingly shut out of the
principal policy-making instances of the Third Republic in favor of more powerful
and better-connected sectoral and class groups. Alongside the *deux cent familles*,
the trusts, and the monopolies against whom they had inveighed historically, new
sectoral threats to their sociopolitical position emerged in the form of an increasingly organized working class and the growing mass of *fonctionnaires* generated
by the expansion of the state bureaucracy, not to mention the new middle classes –
white-collar *salariés*, *cadres*, and technicians – who were thrown up by the
increasing concentration, rationalization, and bureaucratization of industry.
Amid the growing pluralism of the Third Republic, it is perhaps not surprising
that better-organized and more financially powerful interests, such as big business
associations or trade unions, proved more effective in pressing their demands than
did *petits indépendants*. In short, the dominant position of petty producers in
social and political life was progressively eroded until they were supplanted by
these new groups as key deciders of government policy.

As a testament to the sense of powerlessness that they came to feel in this
changing republican order, *petits indépendants* periodically adopted extraparliamentary methods to make themselves heard. Increasingly shut out from the
instances of political representation, such as the Radical Party, or established

---

Reynaud's Finance Ministry. Alongside Jacques Rueff, an orthodox liberal, cohabitated such
convinced dirigistes as Yves Bouthillier, who would become finance minister in the first Vichy
government, and Michel Debré, future prime minister and economy and finance minister under
de Gaulle.
[164] Ibid.

pressure groups such as the Comité Mascuraud or the UIE before World War I and the CGPF after it, they resorted to extrainstitutional forms of protest in order to press their demands on the state. During the Belle Époque, the Ligue syndicale did not shy away from street demonstrations, occupational stoppages, and tax boycotts – all of which contained the potential for violent confrontation – when the government failed to accede to its wishes, such as on *patente* reform or the regulation of external shop displays. Ligue activists embraced the rough style and confrontational tactics of the nationalist leagues during the 1890s and early 1900s, some of them even espousing the antiparliamentary and antirepublican designs of the latter.[165]

During the interwar period, the most prominent extraparliamentary formation to harness *petit indépendant* protest was the Fédération des contribuables. Akin to the nationalist and right-wing *ligues* that proliferated during the 1920s and 1930s, the Fédération was the only extraparliamentary group composed of *petit indépendant*s and small businessmen that succeeded in reaching a national audience.[166] Relying on tax strikes, mass protests, and other extrainstitutional actions, the Fédération's tactics were not far removed from those employed by explicitly fascist or antirepublican *ligues*.[167] Yet, not unlike the Poujadiste movement two decades later, the Fédération did not seek to overthrow the republican order. Rather, it looked to amend the latter in order to make it more responsive to the economic needs and political concerns of its *petit indépendant* constituency.[168] Thus, despite flirting with the radical Right and borrowing from its methods, when push came to shove, the Fédération was wary of the revolutionary aspects of fascism and the threat it posed to the social and political order. It would probably be closer to the mark to argue that it expressed in conservative guise the Radical belief in direct, plebiscitarian democracy that had formerly underpinned the revisionist program of Boulangisme and many turn-of-the-century nationalist leagues. In this sense, the Fédération was

---

[165] Nord, *Paris Shopkeepers*, 349–50, 407.

[166] Cf. Hoisington, *Taxpayer Revolt in France*. Similar national initiatives, such as the Bloc du petit commerce of Armand Pugi, failed to achieve a comparable following. Extraparliamentary movements of *petit indépendant* protest more frequently sprang up on a more local level. In his study of interwar conservative politics in the Rhône, for example, Passmore notes the emergence of an antiparliamentarian *petit indépendant movement*, the Union fédérale des commerçants, artisans et petits industriels de la Croix Rousse, in the old center of Lyon throughout the first half of the 1930s. Zdatny, *Politics*, 104, 215 n. 48, and Passmore, *From Liberalism*, 174–5.

[167] Indeed, beyond sharing in their tactics, some of its leaders enjoyed close ties to the far-right *ligues* and extreme right-wing circles as well. Most spectacularly, the head of the Fédération, Jacques Lemaigre Dubreuil, would be implicated in the Cagoule affair in the winter of 1937. Hoisington, *Taxpayer Revolt in France*, 90.

[168] That it remained committed to republican ideals is suggested by the fact that the Fédération also heavily relied on imagery and symbolism recalling the French Revolution in its discourse. In a rhetorical motif that would also later be taken up by Poujadism, it drew a parallel between the situation of the Tiers État on the eve of the Revolution and the situation of the traditional middle classes during the 1930s. Ibid., 165.

a latter-day reflection – much like Poujadism twenty years later – of the illiberal potential of the primordial Radicalism traceable to the beginning of the Third Republic, if not before.

Yet, despite its refusal to repudiate republican democracy altogether, the Fédération des contribuables inculcated among its *petit indépendant* constituents a taste for conflictual methods and a radical sensibility that remained largely incompatible with the practices of civil debate, compromise, and acceptance of contrary electoral outcomes – the so-called principle of "contingent consent" – that are the preconditions of liberal democracy.[169] In this sense, the Fédération might well have served as an incubator for an antidemocratic political culture that ended up reinforcing the ambivalence of its petty producer subscribers in regard to the republican state. This would suggest that the values that accompany certain forms of association come to shape the political outlook and beliefs of the people involved in them.[170] From this standpoint, the extraparliamentary tenor of some of the sectoral groups that mobilized on behalf of *petits indépendants* under the Third Republic contributed to the ambivalence of many of the latter toward parliamentary democracy and thus facilitated their attraction to the radical Right.

By the same token, *petits indépendants'* adoption of extraparliamentary means also reflected the brittle commitment of the mainstream political parties, particularly on the right, to parliamentary democracy during the Third Republic. This was particularly true in the 1930s when, for example, the Fédération républicaine clamored for constitutional revisions that would have substantially strengthened the executive power at the expense of the parliament.[171] Following the departure of the party's more moderate elements and the installation of Louis Marin as its leader in 1924, the Fédération's commitment to the Republic was brought into question by its incorporation of reactionary monarchist and Catholic elements, prompting one historian to remark that, by the mid-1930s, the Fédération was effectively situated on the extreme right.[172] As proof of this extremist drift, the party developed close ties to the extraparliamentary *ligues* in the run-up to the riots of 6 February 1934. And by 1937 and 1938, it was the only parliamentary party that had subscribed to the Front de la liberté, the

---

[169] Cf. T. Karl and P. Schmitter, "What Democracy Is ... and Is Not," *Journal of Democracy* 2(3) (Summer 1991), 75–88.

[170] P. Nord, introduction to *Civil Society before Democracy: Lessons from Nineteenth Century Europe*, ed. Nancy Bermeo and Philip Nord (Lanham, MD: Rowman & Littlefield, 2000), xv.

[171] We might recall that the first mainstream political figure to float this idea was none other than the leader of the ostensibly centrist and moderate Alliance démocratique, André Tardieu, who viewed it as a vital institutional corollary for pushing through and implementing his general program of social and economic reform during the late 1920s.

[172] Among the most notable reactionaries to enter the party was the ex-Action Française activist Xavier Vallat, who became the first commissioner of the Commissariat-General for Jewish Affairs under Vichy, and the extreme nationalist and future Nazi collaborator Philippe Henriot. Irvine, *French Conservatism in Crisis*, 6.

umbrella organization launched by the proto-fascist Parti populaire français to combat the Popular Front.[173]

In a similar vein, the Parti social français created by Colonel François de la Rocque in 1936 mooted a program of authoritarian constitutional reforms. It envisioned strengthening executive authority, reducing parliamentary power, and establishing a corporatist system of sectoral organization and intermediation.[174] That there was considerable support for these proposals was underscored by the fact that, on the eve of the war, the PSF had developed into the most popular party on the right, if not the country as a whole.[175] Much of this support was attributable to *petits indépendants* and small and middling employers, underscoring the extent of their disaffection with the parliamentary republic and translating their defection from the traditional parties of middle-class defense, the Radicals and the Fédération républicaine.

This hardening of rhetoric and programs during the 1930s was limited not only to the Right, however. Even the Radical Party, the political formation most closely identified with the parliamentarism of the Third Republic, displayed its own authoritarian proclivities as it moved toward neoradicalism under the stewardship of Daladier and the right wing of the Young Turk movement in the late 1930s. The latter developed a youth organization, the Jeunesses radicales, which adopted the martial accoutrements and penchant for direct action that was typical of the extraparliamentary ligues in order to intimidate its rivals and silence critics both inside and outside the party.[176]

In general, then, these authoritarian tendencies that increasingly permeated French politics during the thirties, and that were visible not only in the extraparliamentary *ligues* but also – and more worryingly – among the principal parliamentary parties, helped lay the groundwork for what was to follow. Indeed, it seems beyond dispute that the spread of these new antiparliamentary sensibilities in the twilight years of the Third Republic facilitated the constitutional overthrow of the regime and the attribution of full executive and legislative powers to Marshal Pétain in July 1940.[177] As with some of the sectoral organizations with which they identified during the Third Republic, the authoritarian proclivities of the mainstream parties strengthened *petits indépendants'* ambivalence toward the republican state. In turn, the disproportionate influence assumed by their social and economic rivals over the representative and administrative instances of the regime made *petits indépendants*

---

[173] Ibid., 146–9.

[174] M. Anderson, *Conservative Politics*, 205–6, and Passmore, *From Liberalism*, ch. 9.

[175] Malcolm Anderson, for example, calculated that the PSF claimed two million members in 1938 and three million in 1939, making it the largest political formation in France. Accordingly, historians agree that had the 1940 general election gone ahead, La Rocque's party would have garnered the greatest number of parliamentary seats. *Conservative Politics*, 205.

[176] Berstein, *Histoire* (II), 582–90.

[177] On the ideological continuities between certain elements of the latter-day Third Republic and the Vichy regime, see Jean-Pierre Azéma, "Vichy face au modèle républicain," in Berstein and Rudelle, *Le modèle républicain*, 337–56.

all the more susceptible to antiparliamentary and authoritarian initiatives in the 1930s.

These illiberal proclivities fully manifested themselves following the installation of the Vichy regime, which was initially well received by *petits indépendants* and their sectoral representatives. These strata identified with the regime's traditionalist values as well as its pledge to revert to social and economic forms associated with the virtues of small-scale independent property, artisanal craftsmanship, and family enterprise. Indeed, for many *petits indépendants* the advent of Vichy was, to use Maurras's phrase, "une divine surprise," one artisanal commentator asking in October 1940: "Who would dare hope that the defeat could be beneficial and that it would have a more salutary effect on the country's destinies than the victory of 1918?" As Stephen Zdatny put it, Vichy and the Révolution Nationale "offered a social conservatism rooted in the values of the peasant and artisan," which, distilled in the slogan *Travail-Famille-Patrie*, was seemingly tailor-made to appeal to French *petits indépendants*.[178]

Accordingly, in marked contrast to the interwar years in which they saw themselves as victims of both a revolutionary labor movement and a financial and industrial oligarchy, *petits indépendants* believed that their interests would be safeguarded under Pétain's new regime. In particular, many of them put great store in the corporatist vision held out by the Maréchal that promised to allay the class conflict that had wracked the country in the thirties and restore economic prosperity and social harmony. *Petits indépendants* – artisans in particular – were held by Vichy traditionalists to embody the principles underpinning their corporatist vision of society. As a function of the quasi-familial relations they evolved with their workers in their workshops, petty producers and tradesmen were cast as shining exemplars of the ideal of class collaboration that Vichy corporatists hoped to replicate on a national scale.[179] Given the special

---

[178] Zdatny, *Politics*, 128–9, 128. Pétain himself echoed these sentiments, celebrating the virtues of the *artisanat* in a speech delivered on May Day 1942, in which he affirmed that "the *artisanat* is one of the vital forces of our nation and ... attach[ed] special importance to its development, its conservation, and its perfection." Portraying the *artisanat* as indispensable to the renaissance of the countryside and a precious auxiliary to French industry, he cast it in turn as "one of the vital elements of our economic policy of tomorrow ..., a seedbed of good workers ... united by a common ideal: that of a work well done" as well as "one of the most solid supports of social peace [because] no class struggle was possible in the artisan's workshop." Ibid. and Zarca, *L'artisanat français*, 54.

[179] Thus, the *Charte du travail* (Labor Charter), the foremost legislative and institutional articulation of Vichy corporatism, stated in its preamble that the corporatist "system" that it sought to put in place "is, in the thinking of the *Maréchal*, the most complete and ideal system for organizing work, to which all the professions must progressively adhere. But it can only be immediately applied to those professions that have already achieved a perfect internal balance, that have attained the age of reason at which point they become emancipated and can be left to govern themselves. This condition has already been attained in certain industries and more particularly in those small-scale, or artisanal, industries, in which narrow contacts exist between employers and workers. It is in order to facilitate the accession of all the professions to such a stage in their moral development that this system and the stages it lays out for the organization of work are being instituted and confirmed." Ibid.

consideration apparently granted them by the regime, *petits indépendants'* sectoral organizations adhered en masse to the Révolution Nationale. Enthusiasm was particularly strong within the *artisanat*, which presented the most developed corporative identity.[180]

Thus, as their political trajectory in the 1930s illustrates, the assumption that *petits indépendants* remained ideologically and culturally committed to parliamentary democracy under the Third Republic appears questionable. It is far from clear that this commitment was as solid throughout the life of the regime as Hoffmann and others have supposed, particularly as economic and political challengers to their primacy emerged and the republican state began to shed the protections it had historically afforded petty producers. If fascism and right-wing authoritarianism failed to materialize in France, it seems that this had more to do with the strength of the working class and the Left – a condition distinctly lacking in prefascist Germany and Italy – than of an atavistic cultural commitment to democracy on the part of the French traditional middle classes.[181] Indeed, one might argue that it was *petits indépendants'* fundamental ambivalence toward parliamentary democracy, combined with the traditionalist and authoritarian proclivities of their class-cultural system of *indépendance*, that favorably disposed so many of them to the radical Right in this period.

---

[180] Predictably, traditionalist artisanal organizations such as the Comité d'entente et d'action artisanales (CEAA) and the Confédération de l'artisanat familial (CAF) immediately rallied to Vichy's project. Yet, it was an eloquent testament to the appeal of Vichy's corporatist designs and, more generally, of its projection of a return to a small-producer-based economy and society that even the traditionally center-left Confédération générale de l'artisanat français (CGAF) enthusiastically greeted the advent of the regime. Ibid., 128–37.

[181] For an instructive summary of this argument, see Passmore, *From Liberalism*, 309–10.

6

The Eclipse of the Petty Producer Republic

Petits Indépendants *from Vichy through the Fourth Republic*

[Il] faut créer dans le public, dans l'industrie et parmi les techniciens, un mouvement d'idées, une mentalité de l'économie, tant par l'enseignement que par la presse et l'action directe, pour empêcher – une fois la crise passée – les usagers de retomber, comme après la dernière guerre, dans l'indifférence à l'égard de ce problème vital pour le pays.

Mission statement for the exposition, "Les économies de matière et de produits de remplacement," Summer 1943[1]

You can no longer think of the future in the context of the past. We Europeans are still haunted by past notions of security and stability. Today the principal idea is that of expansion.

Jean Monnet, December 1949[2]

Il est bien vrai que le dernier malheur qui pourrait nous arriver serait de revoir cette France de boutiquiers que des générations de politiciens professionnels nous ont fabriquée. . . . Ces hommes, petits dans leurs vertus comme dans leurs vices, graves dans leurs propos mais légers dans leurs actions, satisfaits d'eux-mêmes mais mécontents des autres, non décidément, nous ne voulons pas les revoir.

Albert Camus, *Combat*, 25 August 1945[3]

The postwar era marked the demise of petty producer society and politics in France. It presided over the declining economic fortunes of French *petits indépendants* and *petits patrons* as well as their loss of influence, particularly over the determination of economic and social policy. This economic and political decline reflected a dramatic intensification of industrial and commercial concentration. During the 1950s and 1960s in particular, the French economy underwent as profound a transformation as any the country had seen since the Second Empire. This period of intensive modernization contracted the structural divide between the smallest and biggest firms as the former saw their numbers

---

[1] Quoted in Henri Rousso, "Les paradoxes de Vichy et de l'Occupation. Contraintes, archaïsmes et modernités," in Fridenson and Straus, *Le capitalisme français au XIXe–XXe siècle*, 77.

[2] Quoted in Kuisel, *Capitalism*, 244.

[3] Quoted in Nordmann, *Histoire des radicaux*, 340.

dramatically decline as a result of their heightened exposure to commercial and industrial competition in the immediate postwar decades.

In turn, their rapid economic decline translated the inability of French small business to slow or arrest the process of modernization, testifying to their precipitous loss of influence relative to other social groups. Whether in favor of the new dynamic sector of cadres and technicians, or the old dynamic constituencies of advanced employers, managers, and industrial workers, this socioeconomic and political debasement of *petits indépendants* could only fuel their mounting frustration with the postwar economic and political order. When it combined with their cultural traditionalism and illiberalism, this frustration drove many *petits indépendants* to join petit bourgeois extraparliamentary movements, such as Poujadism and the CID-UNATI in the 1950s and 1970s, and, beginning in the 1980s, to embrace the Front National.

The dwindling postwar influence of *petits indépendants* can be surmised at three levels of analysis. At a first, ideological level, a new primacy was given to economic modernization by political and economic elites as the urgent goal toward which the vital forces of society needed to be marshaled and directed. This imperative reflected the conviction that France needed to modernize economically if it was to regain the great power status it had lost in the *débâcle* of May 1940. For its proponents, modernization meant discarding the commitment to a mixed or balanced economy, which subtended the *agrariste* philosophies of the Third Republic and Vichy, and setting by contrast a course that would speed urbanization.[4] In addition to heralding the demise of the rural *petit commerce* and *artisanat*, this commitment to modernization envisioned a totalizing process of economic rationalization that bodes ill for *petits indépendants* as a whole.

The practical corollary of this modernizing imperative was the primary role assumed by the state as the principal agent or steward of economic development. In the first place, the relationship of the state to the economy was radically redefined, heralding the advent of dirigisme whereby the state planned and controlled the modernization process. Accordingly, it was left to the state to specify the priorities of economic development; oversee the allocation of investment to key sectors; and set performance criteria, specifically output targets within the various branches of production. Correlatively, dirigisme also implied a much more proactive role for the state in fashioning macroeconomic policies that would support industrialization and growth. As the postwar period unfolded, a Keynesian fiscal and monetary framework was adopted by French policy makers in order to fuel growth through expansionary spending and loose credit policies.[5] Finally, the third component of the postwar state's modernizing

---

[4] Regarding the influence of *agrarisme* or "peasantist" doctrine among the political elites of the Third Republic and at Vichy, see respectively, P. Barral, "Agrarisme de gauche et agrarisme de droite," and Eizner, "L'idéologie paysanne," as well as G. Wright, *Rural Revolution in France*, chs. 2, 5.

[5] Kuisel, *Capitalism*, 251–2, 255, and Peter Hall, *Governing the Economy: The Politics of State Intervention in Britain and France* (Cambridge: Polity Press, 1986), 244–5.

ideology was its commitment to social reform. In order to attenuate the social tensions likely to follow from the economic and social transformations envisioned by postwar planners, the state strove to enlist the working class in the modernization process by guaranteeing the latter a greater share in postwar prosperity. Beginning in the immediate aftermath of the war, a series of legislative measures was passed that aimed to improve workers' social insurance and strengthen their position in the workplace. These included laws establishing a universal social security regime (1945–6), collective bargaining (1950), and *comités d'entreprises* (works councils) and *délégués du personnel* (workers' delegates) to enhance worker participation in firms counting more than fifty employees.[6]

The commitment of postwar elites to modernization, stipulating state direction of the economy, was bound to conflict with the economic and social values of *petits indépendants*. Chiefly, it clashed with their archaeoliberal philosophy, which posited a market free from state intervention or interference (except, of course, when these strata were themselves faced with "disloyal" competition from monopolists and trusts). The hostility of *petits indépendants* toward state control was all the more pronounced when it promoted dynamic industrial and commercial sectors at their expense. Similarly, reflecting their fiscal conservatism, *petits indépendants* rejected increases in government spending to fund economic expansion and welfare programs, particularly when these benefited constituencies – the advanced capitalist sector on the one hand, industrial workers on the other – by which they felt threatened. In general, the postwar commitment to state-driven processes of economic and social modernization testified to the downgrading of *petits indépendants'* interests and concerns in promoting economic development and managing its sociostructural impacts.

At a second, institutional, level of analysis, *petits indépendants* saw their influence dramatically decline as a function of the sweeping transformation of the French state in the postwar period. The latter saw the emergence of a technocratic state bureaucracy more centralized and insulated from the representative instances of government than anything that had gone before. Starting at Vichy and continuing under the Fourth and Fifth Republics, the executive organs of the state grew increasingly autonomous from the sectoral and class interests that had dictated, with often incoherent results, economic policy under the Third Republic. The institutional downgrading of parliament, combined with the decline of traditional notable-based political parties under the Fourth and Fifth Republics, significantly curtailed the influence of *petits indépendants* over social and economic policy. Similarly, the emergence of broad-based, national political formations in the postwar era restricted the political capacity of small producer groups, which found themselves increasingly unable to get deputies to do their bidding at the local level. Accordingly, petty producer interests found themselves increasingly marginalized by the organizational representatives of

---

[6] Jacques Fournier and Nicole Questiaux, *Traité du social: situations, luttes, politiques, institutions*, 5th ed. (Paris: Dalloz, 1989), 278, 498, 522.

200 *The Resurgence of the Radical Right in France*

ascendant economic groups including *cadres*, big business, and labor in the new postwar catchall parties.

Finally, *petits indépendants'* postwar decline was evidenced at an organizational level, namely in the inability of their sectoral spokesmen to adapt to the new bureaucratic rules of the game established under the Fourth and Fifth Republics. Their organizational weakness was particularly underscored in comparison to the ability of other economic groups to press their interests within the new administrative organs charged with formulating social and economic policy. In turn, their incapacity to accede to the levers of power through institutional channels explains the growing recourse of *petits indépendants* to extrainstitutional means in the postwar period. Unable to effectively press their interests through entreaties to the parliament and the state bureaucracy, more and more *petits indépendants* increasingly resorted to shouting their displeasure in the streets.

This and the following chapter analyze the intersection of these ideational, institutional, and organizational dimensions. They endeavor to explain how, as a function of their collective experiences under successive postwar regimes, so many *petits indépendants* became alienated from the political mainstream and grew tired of the republican state and liberal democracy. Combined with the traditionalist illiberal values these strata evolved as a function of their economic and social roles in French society historically, these sentiments drew them to protest movements extolling a small-property-based society and economy and, ultimately, to the radical Right.

PETITS INDÉPENDANTS UNDER VICHY

> The *économie dirigée* is destined to place a powerful means of action at the service of the economy ... and, in this respect, it must continue after the war is over. ... Instead of the disorder of the prewar years, the peace will bring coordination and rational management. Jean Bichelonne, Speech at the École des Sciences Politiques, spring 1942[7]

> We do not doubt that the government of the Maréchal will make into reality what for the past twenty-five years has been only a dream and a slogan. Robert Tailledet, President of the *Confédération générale de l'artisanat français*, October 1941[8]

The foundations for the country's postwar modernization were laid by the Vichy regime during World War II. The principles, institutions, and methods underpinning this process were conceived at Vichy and subsequently taken up by the leaders of the Resistance who assumed power in the summer of 1944. These flowed from their shared disdain for parliamentarism and common critique of the prevailing form of French capitalism. Deploring the Malthusianism of the

---

[7] Quoted in Zdatny, *Politics*, 151.
[8] Ibid., 128.

latter, they condemned its wastefulness and disorderliness, its privileging of powerful financial interests, its celebration of social egotism, and its poor economic performance.

Though they were fundamentally politically divided, leading figures at Vichy and in the Resistance were united in their refusal to revert to the prewar stalemate society. According to Richard Kuisel, both "looked ahead, not to reconstituting prewar conditions but to overhauling the structure of the economy. . . . They sought an industry competitive in world markets, a modernized rural sector, a higher standard of living, and a people who embraced technology."[9] Similarly, Vichy and the ensuing Provisional Government enacted reforms that had much in common: "nationalist revival, social reconciliation, moral rehabilitation, a planned and more just economy, and a more dynamic state."[10] In this sense, Vichy and the Resistance simultaneously represented antagonistic but parallel forces that lent great impetus to the country's economic and social modernization.

The similarities between Vichy and the Resistance also extended to the ambiguities, even contradictions, of their respective projects of national restoration. In both cases, the commitment to economic modernization found itself offset by the imperatives of social conservation and stability. At Vichy, the objective of modernization and rationalization conflicted with the regime's attempt to reorganize French society along corporatist lines. Likewise, after the Liberation, the pursuit of modernization was threatened by the return to prewar parliamentary pluralism and particularism following the restoration of liberal democracy. The tension between these aims was exacerbated by the extreme circumstances facing both regimes – military occupation and the privations of war under Vichy, the task of reconstruction for the postliberation Provisional Government – and it quickly suffused the policy debates opposing modernizers and conservatives.[11] *Petits indépendants* and their representatives were soon caught up in these debates and predictably aligned themselves with the latter. However, as their powers of resistance against economic and social change waned, they increasingly found themselves on the losing end of a structurally and culturally dislocating course of modernization.

Indeed, the hope *petits indépendants* placed in Vichy that it would fulfill their economic and social aspirations was quickly dashed. Almost from the outset, the vision of an ordered and harmonious society projected by Vichy corporatists clashed with the modernizing ambitions of technocratic reformers who had acceded to positions of greatest influence within the regime. The widescale economic rationalization and restructuring envisioned by the latter

---

[9] Kuisel, *Capitalism*, 148.
[10] Ibid., 128.
[11] Alluding to the former, Henri Rousso remarked that the paradox of Vichy "resided in its willingness to effect reforms in the long term, as a function of the making of lucid decisions, in a climate marked by extremely brutal constraints and large-scale instability." "Les paradoxes de Vichy," 69.

generated significant social disequilibria and revived latent class and sectoral tensions, thereby undermining the new corporatist dispensation in which *petits indépendants* had put their trust. In this sense, the history of Vichy is the story of the antagonistic evolution and divergence of these corporatist and modernizing projects. To small producers' growing frustration and dismay, the latter progressively supplanted the former in informing the economic and social policies of the regime.

By and large, the program of national modernization envisaged by Vichy reformers was coextensive with dirigisme. It presided over a major conceptual, even cultural shift among French political elites, marking their acceptance of greater state intervention in the workings of the economy than ever before. Though its precursors could be traced to the First World War and the interwar period, it was at Vichy that state economic management, specifically in the form of indicative planning, was pursued for the first time.[12] Economic policy became the exclusive preserve of the technocratic state, run by a neutral, rational, and technically competent elite occupying the highest echelons of the state bureaucracy.[13] The primary task of reorganizing the economy fell to Jean Bichelonne's Ministry of Industrial Production, which introduced a system based on *comités d'organisation* (organization committees or COs) as the institutional framework of dirigisme within the state. Initially conceived as part of Vichy's corporatist program, the mandate of the COs was to overcome the structural backwardness of the economy by rationalizing key sectors of production and optimizing their innovation and efficiency. Accordingly, the COs were tasked with the following dirigiste functions: drawing up inventories of production facilities, raw materials, and manpower in their respective sectors; setting down sectoral production targets; organizing the purchase and distribution of raw materials; developing production and quality standards; and fixing prices in each sector.[14] Correspondingly, an Office central de répartition des produits industriels (OCRPI) was created in order to allocate raw materials and primary industrial goods to the various productive sectors. This new office was divided into a dozen sections that "regulated the acquisition, storage, distribution, sale and use of

---

[12] In a sense, Vichy's dirigisme marked a qualitative extension of the growth of state oversight over the economy that could be traced to the Popular Front and, especially, to Daladier's National Unity government (November 1938 to September 1939), which pursued statist policies to mobilize the nation's economic capacities for war with Germany. Kuisel, *Capitalism*, 125–7, 135–6.

[13] Emblematic of these technocratic state managers were such figures as Yves Bouthillier, finance minister for the regime from 1940 to 1942, and Jean Bichelonne, the new minister of industrial production. In the interwar period, Bouthillier had been an upper-level manager at the Messine electricity syndicate affiliated with the Société lyonnaise des eaux et de l'éclairage and, as such, been a subordinate of Ernest Mercier, director of Messine during the 1920s and 1930s. For his part, widely considered as the brightest *Polytechnicien* of his generation, Bichelonne was the paragon of the modernizing French technocrat and civil servant. Professing, according to one observer, a "religious trust in the virtues of economic organization," he became "one of the masterminds of [Vichy's] economic organization, and its most influential administrator ... of business and industry." Ehrmann, *Organized Business in France*, 71, 70, and Kuisel, *Mercier*, 146.

[14] Ehrmann, *Organized Business in France*, 77–8.

rationed products" in areas key to future economic development, such as coal and steel production.[15] Given the sweeping competences and controls it assumed over these economic tasks and processes, the CO-OCRPI system was the institutional expression par excellence of Vichy's modernizing ambitions. According to Richard Kuisel, it represented nothing less than "the most far-reaching attempt at managing industry in modern times."[16]

Perhaps the greatest symbol of Vichy's modernizing and technocratic impulse was its recourse to indicative planning.[17] In March 1941, the country's first planning agency, the Délégation générale à l'équipement national (DGEN) was established and placed under the direction of François Lehideux. A prototype for the postwar Commissariat général du plan, its mandate was to coordinate the activities and assess the information provided by the COs in order to direct investment to areas deemed essential for the country's modernization. In 1942 the DGEN was augmented by the Conseil supérieur de l'économie industrielle et commerciale, which was commissioned to analyze how planning might be most effectively implemented after the war. These innovations testified to the importance that Vichy policy makers accorded to planning not just in wartime but in peacetime as well.

Over its three-year existence, the DGEN drafted two economic plans, the primary purpose of which was to expand and improve the nation's capital stock. The first, dating from May 1942, was the Plan d'équipement national, which earmarked credits, raw materials, and labor in order to renovate and expand the nation's capital stock through domestic production and a recourse to imports. Although it set no production targets, this ten-year plan proposed investment and works programs in a number of crucial sectors, including agriculture,

---

[15] In practice, these OCRPI sections overlapped considerably with the COs within these advanced sectors. In a number of instances they even shared the same directors and officers, hence giving the latter effective authority not just over the organization of production within these sectors but over the allocation and distribution of resources as well. Kuisel, *Capitalism*, 136, 137.

[16] Ibid., 144. The modernizing impetus exemplified by the Vichy technocrats charged with formulating economic policy was clearly reflected in the staff selected to head the COs. These included a disproportionate number of firm managers from the most advanced sectors, such as former Redressement français leader and Nouveaux Cahiers founder Auguste Detoeuf in the electrical equipment field; the mining engineer Aimé Lepercq in coal; the leading Messine managers Raoul de Vitry, Roger Boutheville, and Joseph Thuillier in aluminum, electric power, and gas; and Robert Cayrol, an associate of Ernest Mercier's at the Compagnie française des pétroles during the 1930s, in liquid fuels. In a number of instances, the COs essentially replicated the largest prewar cartels, their function extending to the promotion of industrial specialization and standardization and to the setting of production targets, in addition to the prewar practice of determining sales quotas. Thus, though the COs – along with the OCRPI – were theoretically meant to be both insulated (i.e., state-controlled) and corporatist (i.e., compulsorily consultative) institutions acting in the best interests of society as whole, they marked the de facto turning over of industrial governance to large-scale, advanced business interests, effectively drowning out the voice of small employers and *petits indépendants* within them. Ibid., 137, 138, 142; Kuisel, *Mercier*, 147; Ehrmann, *Organized Business in France*, 78, 82; and Zdatny, *Politics*, 131.

[17] Unless otherwise noted, the following account of economic planning under Vichy is drawn from Kuisel, *Capitalism*, 144–56.

communications, and urban development. In addition, it was also novel in abandoning the classical-liberal imperatives of monetary stability and balanced budgets, its drafters advocating a loose credit policy and deficitary spending to spur renovation and growth.

The second plan, based on input from the Conseil supérieur de l'économie, was the Tranche de démarrage published in summer 1944. Anticipating the economic and social dislocations that would likely follow the end of hostilities, the *Tranche* set down economic and planning priorities for after the war. The principal assumption underlying it was that it was necessary to expand the nation's capital stock in order to increase output, stimulate consumption, and raise living standards. Accordingly, it aimed to modernize the country's industrial output by emphasizing the development of synthetic primary goods, especially in leading sectors such as automobiles and chemicals.[18] The Tranche called for disregarding the tenets of monetary and fiscal orthodoxy when these impeded investment in developing sectors, positing that the object of macroeconomic policy should be "to promote the full employment of the nation's working capacities."[19] Finally, its commitment to more modern forms of planning was accompanied by the establishment of an enabling judicial framework designed to encourage investment and growth. This included reforming the banking sector in order to facilitate the provision of credit to firms, as well as revising the legal status of shareholder-owned firms to stimulate investment in them.[20]

The experience of planning at Vichy and its creation of new institutions to administer the economy presided over a seminal change in outlook among not only high civil servants but the economic elite as a whole. As Hoffmann noted in the early 1960s, "'new men' of business" emerged under Vichy who held "a less parochial and less compartmentalized view of the economic problems of their professions and of the nation than their predecessors."[21] As a function of their oversight of the COs, Vichy habituated this advanced fraction of the *patronat* to exercising economic and even political power. Their influence over the economy imbued them with the conviction that they should "assert themselves as the nation's elite through the kind of 'industrial self-government' that the CO had instituted and which would eventually lead to the rule of the managers in the political field as well."[22] In short, by leaving economic decisions to the representatives of the most advanced and powerful industrial sectors, Vichy encouraged an unprecedented interpenetration between big business and the Administration d'État, thereby laying the groundwork for the close cooperation

---

[18] For example, it was symptomatic of the new emphasis that was placed by Vichy planners on technological innovation during the final stages of the war that the first television set to be manufactured in France was assembled under their watch. Rousso, "Les paradoxes de Vichy," 76–7.

[19] Kuisel, *Capitalism*, 155.

[20] Rousso, "Les paradoxes de Vichy," 73–4.

[21] "Paradoxes," 41.

[22] Ehrmann, *Organized Business in France*, 87.

between the public and private spheres that would define postwar economic development.

Yet, Vichy's modernizing ambitions and dirigiste and technocratic trappings tell only half the story. As we have seen, these ambitions were counterbalanced by a reactionary political project that sought to re-create a preindustrial social order whose guiding principles derived from the counterrevolutionary France *ante* 1830, if not 1789. Drawing on the ideas of conservative Catholic thinkers such as Joseph de Maistre and the Marquis de la Tour du Pin, Vichy traditionalists sought to restore the hierarchical and organic order of the Ancien Régime through a state-imposed model of corporatism that would replace class by professional identity as the basis of social organization. By institutionalizing and enforcing intersectoral agreements among different groups of producers, Vichy corporatists hoped to minimize the economic competition and class conflicts that paralyzed liberal society, and to which they attributed the nation's collapse in May 1940.[23]

The principal legislative expression of Vichy corporatism was the Labor Charter (Charte du Travail) of October 1941. Following the dissolution of independent workers' and employers' associations in August 1940, the Charte sought to organize these constituencies into a network of compulsory, state-controlled associations representing producers in each economic sector. These corporatist groupings were organized vertically, through the establishment of joint occupational committees (*comités paritaires*) constituted from state-sanctioned professional unions operating at both the level of the enterprise and the sectoral branch as a whole. In turn, social committees (*comités sociaux*) representing mixed councils of workers and employers were constituted in each profession to oversee issues of pay, working conditions, worker training, and the addressing of social needs. Agreement on social and material conditions for each profession was to be arrived at through negotiations within these occupational and social committees. Correspondingly, strikes and lockouts were outlawed and direct government arbitration of labor conflicts suspended. Any dispute that could not be solved within the various corporatist committees was to be submitted to a Labor Tribunal, whose decision was immediately binding and unappealable.[24]

In practice, the Labor Charter failed in achieving a balance among the various producer groups within each sector. At one level, this failure reflected the mutual hostility of sectoral participants and their representatives, as well as the de facto proemployer bias that underlay the charter's implementation. For all intents and purposes, the latter nullified the economic and social power of organized labor and defended the prerogatives of employers under the guise of smoothing the

[23] On the particular origins and forms of corporatism put in place at Vichy, see Paxton, *Vichy France*, 210–20.

[24] For a fuller description of the institutional mechanisms and procedures put in place by the *Charte du travail*, see Ehrmann, *Organized Business in France*, 54, 55, 60; Zdatny, *Politics*, 133–5; and Paxton, *Vichy France*, 217–18.

running of the economy.[25] This proemployer and antiunion bias undermined the regime's pretension of trying to curb the excesses of economic liberalism and impeded the goal of social harmony to which it aspired. On the contrary, the charter drove workers – especially former trade unionists – into increasingly overt opposition to Vichy.[26]

More fundamentally, the Labor Charter was a failure because of ongoing ideological and institutional conflicts within the state apparatus that opposed traditional corporatists who felt it did not go far enough in eliminating independent business organizations on the one hand and representatives of big businesses who resented the dissolution of their associations and opposed the integration of workers and employers in mixed committees on the other. In the end, the latter won out and were able to assert their demand that all economic questions be excluded from the domain of the charter and instead remain the exclusive purview of the COs.[27]

From this standpoint, petty producers also had reason to be upset with the implementation of the charter and, more broadly, with Vichy's corporatist designs. Since the corporatist bodies in which they had been given a say had been precluded from the instances responsible for making economic policy, *petits indépendants* and *petits patrons* grew increasingly wary of the intentions of the regime, some even charging that the Labor Charter had been drafted by *les gros*.[28] Accordingly, when several thousand small businesses were closed by the authorities, this was seen by *petits patrons* as the nefarious handiwork of trusts exerting their influence through the COs.[29] Even the establishment *Journal de la*

---

[25] The representatives of labor found themselves consistently outnumbered in the occupational and social committees in which economic and social policies were agreed – the latter officially recognizing, in addition to employers, the new group of *cadres* as a separate corporative entity. Likewise, membership of the Labor Tribunals that were frequently called upon to resolve sectoral conflicts was heavily stacked in favor of employers and probusiness *fonctionnaires*. As Robert Paxton surmised, "despite its stated concern for labor welfare and its injunctions of charity upon entrepreneurs, the Charter of Labor was clearly designed to break the back of the trade unions in France." *Vichy France*, 217; Luc Boltanski, "Une réussite: La mobilisation des 'cadres,'" in Lavau, Grunberg, and Mayer, *L'univers politique des classes moyennes*, 168; and Zdatny, *Politics*, 133.
[26] Paxton, *Vichy France*, 218.
[27] Ehrmann, *Organized Business in France*, 92.
[28] Zdatny, *Politics*, 135. In this vein, growing numbers of petty producers and traders deplored the gap between Pétain's pronouncements that defended the *artisanat* and *petit commerce* and the domination of the COs by monied and big business interests. The president of the Chamber of Trades for the Haute Garonne, a certain Castéras, reflected this sentiment when he complained that Vichy was perpetuating under a new guise the economic domination of big business that had prevailed before the war, opining that under the Révolution Nationale, "It's the trusts that control things and not the middle classes as we have been promised." Alluding to the enduring and disproportionate influence wielded by the Comité des forges over economic policy, he added: "Take the Comité des forges. This Comité has been, so it would appear, dissolved. Yet we see it revived under the cover of the organization committees. Certainly, we don't see the same people [*sic*], but we see that the activity of these organization committees is directed in the same manner – which is to say, to the advantage of trusts and big business and to the more or less progressive suffocation of the artisanat and of small and medium-sized production." Ibid., 139–40.

Bourse drew attention to the iniquities of the CO system and the farce it made of Vichy's pretension to create a balanced economic and social order. In its 6 December 1941 issue, it denounced "the masquerade [of] incredible proportions" that had permitted the "installation of the trusts under the guise of a revolutionary formula."[30] Consequently, the myth of a Vichy Synarchy gained rapid ground among petty producers: the belief that large-scale financial and industrial interests, in league with the regime's *hauts fonctionnaires*, had subordinated the economic life of the country to their own plutocratic ambitions.[31] Given their deepening disappointment with Vichy's system of economic organization and the ineffectuality of its corporatist measures in dissolving the trusts and other agents of economic *gigantisme*, small businessmen increasingly rejected these new initiatives and resisted the institutions charged with implementing them. Most *petits patrons* resigned from their posts in the CO committees and refused to comply with the new administrative and financial regulations that these had imposed on them.[32]

Perhaps because they presented the strongest corporative identity among *petits indépendants*, artisans grew into a particular hotbed of resistance to the COs. The Assemblée des présidents des chambres de métiers de France (APCMF), the sectoral spokesman for the *artisanat* following the dissolution of the principal artisanal confederations in May 1942, sought from early on to detach artisans from the regulatory purview of the COs by demanding greater control over the registration of new artisans. The regime responded by tightening its grip over the Chambers of Trades and ultimately dissolving the peak association in February 1943. This was followed by the publication of the Statut de l'artisanat (statute of artisans) in August 1943, which replaced the Chambers of Trades with a Chambre nationale des métiers, a state-controlled organization answerable to a newly created Artisanal Service, to preside over the artisanal trades.[33] The suppression of the APCMF and the introduction of the Statut de l'artisanat sounded the death knell of independent artisanal representation and corporative activity under Vichy, signaling instead their virtual encasement by the state. These were authoritarian responses to the resistance of artisans – and more broadly, that of *petits indépendants* as a whole – to what they considered as Vichy's big-business-dominated system of economic organization, as well as the ineffectuality of the corporatist measures introduced to safeguard their interests. This heightened authoritarianism testified to the fact that, by the

---

[29] Ehrmann, *Organized Business in France*, 87.

[30] Ibid., 84.

[31] For an exploration of the objective reality versus mythical status of the Vichy *synarchie*, see ibid., 72–6.

[32] Thus, the Comité overseeing commercial establishments reported in spring 1944 that despite the risk of legal sanction, 200,000 shopkeepers had failed to register with or to pay their yearly dues to their respective COs. And at the Liberation, 80,000 shopkeepers were amnestied for still having not paid their dues. Ibid., 82–3, 87n.

[33] Ibid., 61, and Zdatny, *Politics*, 143–5.

summer of 1943, *petits indépendants* had turned against the regime whose arrival they had so enthusiastically welcomed only three years before.

Petits indépendants' grievances under Vichy were directed not only against the *grand patronat* and high civil servants, however. They also resented the sectoral elevation of the new salaried strata, in particular the increasingly influential class of *cadres* that had emerged during the interwar period, and which contested *petits indépendants'* traditional political primacy among the French middle classes. *Cadres* were granted official recognition as a separate corporative entity under Vichy, and their representatives were commissioned to sit in the occupational and social committees established by the Labor Charter.[34] This affirmation of *cadres* as a distinct occupational group within the regime's corporatist instances, while they themselves were limited to only token representation, cruelly underscored for *petits indépendants* their loss of economic influence and political prestige.

In short, alongside industrial workers, the latter increasingly saw themselves as the victims of Vichy's economic and social policies. They had some reason to believe this because, despite its corporatist rhetoric, the regime did the bidding of the *gros* and of the new middle classes they believed to be in league with the trusts and monopolists. The hollowness of Vichy corporatism was most starkly underlined for *petits indépendants* by the fact that, when the imperative of social reconciliation clashed with the aim of economic rationalization, the latter invariably won out. As Paxton indicates, belying the regime's "verbal hostility to big business, every important decision about establishing corporatism turned in favor of business."[35] For *petits indépendants*, then, the failure to achieve a corporatist order based on traditional small-scale production and commerce underscored the "broken promise" of Vichy.[36] At best, its corporatist designs had been an unattainable goal, "more of a horizon than a reality." At worst it was "social posturing," a "great deception" to advance a modernization program that the regime's staunchest supporters would have surely opposed had it openly pursued it.[37]

In a prefiguration of what would follow, Vichy used the power of the state to, in Zdatny's phrase, "concentrate and rationalize the economy" – a goal diametrically opposed to the interests of petty producers and tradesmen who, as we have seen, constituted one of the regime's greatest initial sources of support.[38] Even when the most fervent modernizers at Vichy – Bouthillier, Lehideux, Pierre Pucheu – had been replaced, economic rationalization and concentration continued apace. In this sense, Vichy's modernization program marked a seminal break from the prewar pattern of economic development. At the same time, the regime was an agent of continuity between the political orders that preceded and succeeded it.

---

[34] Boltanski, "Une réussite," 169.
[35] *Vichy France*, 215.
[36] Zdatny, *Politics*, 128.
[37] Rousso, "Les paradoxes de Vichy," 70, and Zdatny, *Politics*, 146, 151.
[38] Zdatny, *Politics*, 151.

It provided the institutional transition between the National Economic Council (CNE) of the interwar period and the Commissariat général du plan (CGP) of the 1940s and 1950s, in the form of its own planning agency, the DGEN.

Thus, from the standpoint of their economic and political interests, Vichy failed to fulfill *petits indépendants*' hopes. It is not the least of ironies that by overturning the republican order in the name of restoring a traditional society based on rootedness in the land and small-scale property, it in fact hastened the economic and social demise of small producers. Whereas before the war, parliamentary politics had insulated *petits indépendants* from the worst impacts of economic change, the dissolution of the republican regime and the entrusting of economic and social policy to technocratic modernizers exposed these strata to arguably more rapid and far-reaching changes than ever before. As one observer remarked, "the 'anarchy' of the parliamentary system, with its universal manhood suffrage and its weak executive – its benevolent *immobilisme* if you will – was the best guarantee of the survival of independent petty production."[39] Likewise, whereas the hated CGT and independent labor unions had similarly acted as brakes on the modernizing designs of the state during the interwar period, their dissolution by the regime – a development enthusiastically welcomed by most *petits indépendants* – also removed an important impediment to the economic restructuring and rationalization dreaded by the latter. From this standpoint, Jacques Juillard was undoubtedly correct in asserting that, objectively, Vichy corporatism played "an essentially camouflaging role" for the pursuit of economic modernization.[40] As far as shopkeepers and artisans were concerned, this tactic of "modernization by stealth" set an unsettling precedent for subsequent governments of the Liberation and the Fourth Republic. While continuing to affirm their commitment to the defense of *petits indépendants*, the latter would come to pursue a modernizing course favoring growth over stability, innovation over consensus.

PETITS INDÉPENDANTS UNDER THE FOURTH REPUBLIC

State intervention in economic affairs appears necessary in twentieth-century capitalism in order to battle against the forces of restriction and conservatism.
Paul Delouvrier, *Politique économique de la France*, 1953–4[41]

Nous redoutons un État omniprésent et omnipotent, qui assumerait des fonctions pour lesquelles il n'est pas fait. Que l'État contrôle, que l'État dans certains secteurs, exerce une activité, oui! Mais nous croyons qu'un étatisme permanent, un étatisme constant, ne provoquerait pas dans ce pays le redressement que nous souhaitons tous, sans distinction de parti. ... Je crains que votre dirigisme n'aboutisse à un régime où l'État est partout et le gouvernement nulle part.
Radical deputy Gabriel Cudenet before the National Assembly, 1947[42]

---

[39] Ibid., 152.
[40] Quoted in ibid., 153.
[41] Quoted in Kuisel, *Capitalism*, 252.
[42] Quoted in Nordmann, *Histoire des radicaux*, 365.

In many ways, the Fourth Republic consummated the modernizing ambitions of Vichy. Under its stewardship, the country underwent greater structural change than at any time since the Revolution, entailing a fundamental reconstitution of the relations between state and society and "the liquidation," in Hoffmann's lapidary phrase, "of the stalemate society."[43] The republican state established after the Liberation assumed a broad array of functions – many of them traceable to Vichy – that allowed it to reconfigure the economic and social basis of French society. At the same time, it reproduced the parliamentary structures and practices of the Third Republic, marking – on the surface at least – a reversion to the fractured party politics that characterized its predecessor.

As a function of these schizoid foundations, the postwar political order contained the seeds of future conflict between a modernistic technocratic dirigisme and a traditional atavistic liberalism. The new regime presented a potential contradiction between its innate parliamentarism, which was still steeped in the parochial and clientelistic politics of the Third Republic, and a newfound belief in technocracy, whose apostles, imbued with the new spirit of modernization, assumed the levers of executive power. This ambivalence translated into a conflict between "old" and "new" men, pitting "modernizers" against "conservatives," "technocrats" against "Malthusians." Yet, as we shall see, even these restored parliamentary structures adapted to the modernizing vocation of the technocratic state. The streamlining of party and representative organizations, as well as the downgrading of parliamentary influence over economic policy, marked an unmistakable evolution of the regime toward the more nationally representative and cohesive system that would come to characterize de Gaulle's Fifth Republic. In this sense, the Fourth Republic represented an intermediate dispensation between the atomistic Third Republic and the centralized Fifth Republic.

From the vantage point of *petits indépendants*, the Fourth Republic lived up to this ambivalent, intermediate portrayal. On the one hand, it presided to their dismay over the intensification of the state-driven process of modernization launched under Vichy. At the same time, the new regime was also reassuring to *petits indépendants* because it presented many of the institutional and cultural vestiges of the small-producer-friendly Third Republic. Although their economic and social position became more precarious under it, the Fourth Republic's adoption of usages and protections reminiscent of the interwar and even Belle Époque eras maintained the illusion that, given the right political leadership, their economic and social position could still be salvaged. In this sense, the Fourth Republic inspired a false hope among many small producers and traders, which, when it was ultimately punctured, exacerbated their disappointment and frustration with the republican state.

During the opening decade of the Fourth Republic, the French state recast itself as an agent of economic and social modernization. Building on Vichy's

---

[43] "Paradoxes," 60.

technocratic legacy, it adopted proactive, interventionist policies to rationalize the nation's industrial and commercial apparatus and make it more efficient. It pursued three principal strategies to this end. In the first place, a dirigiste program was adopted to encourage economic rationalization and optimize productivity. In order to facilitate its implementation, the postwar state carried over many of the institutions that had been charged with economic management at Vichy. This dirigiste orientation reached its apex in the form of indicative planning, which became the definitive blueprint guiding French economic policy until at least the end of the 1960s. Correlatively, in order to enhance its control over the economy, the state also embarked on a sweeping campaign of nationalization. Assuming either full ownership or a controlling interest in the leading industrial sectors and firms, it assumed direct responsibility for their performance, its agents overseeing their day-to-day operations and taking the strategic and investment decisions for their development. Third and finally, dirigisme was paired with a substantial extension of state intervention in the macroeconomic and social policy spheres. The postwar state pursued activist fiscal and monetary policies to stimulate growth, while setting out ambitious social reforms to mend the class divisions that had torn the country apart in the 1930s and been exacerbated by the war.

Predictably, this intensification of state intervention was badly received by *petits indépendants*. It further isolated the latter from other social and economic groups that accepted these *étatiste* reforms, such as the advanced, larger *patronat*, the new middle-class *cadres* and technicians, and industrial workers.[44] In timeworn fashion, aggrieved small producers and tradesmen turned to the parliamentary system for redress. Yet, even at the level of parliamentary lobbying at which they traditionally enjoyed their greatest influence, *petits indépendants*' sectoral representatives no longer commanded the attention they once did. By throwing up new, politically significant social constituencies, economic modernization broadened the political horizons of the parliamentary parties and forced them to be increasingly attentive to the interests of the sectoral rivals of *petits indépendants*. In this sense, the modernization process doubly hurt *petits indépendants* – first, economically, because rationalization and concentration spelled the ruin of ever-increasing numbers of them and, second, politically, because it downgraded their interests within the centers of legislative and executive power of the French state.

As was previously noted, the postwar dirigiste state was to a great degree a conceptual and structural legacy of Vichy. Many of the Resistance leaders who came to power at the Liberation shared the conviction of Vichy technocrats that the political economy of the Third Republic could not be resurrected.[45]

---

[44] The only group with whom *petits patrons* and especially *petits indépendants* shared a mutual antipathy against this new modernizing statist orientation were marginal small farmers, who would also see their numbers decimated during this period at the hands of concentrated and modern agricultural concerns.

[45] In Hoffmann's phrase, Vichy and the Resistance "cooperated in many ways without wanting or knowing it" to carry the nation "to the threshold of a new social order." "Paradoxes," 58.

Similarly, many of the ideas and institutions identified with the Révolution Nationale served as starting points for the managers of the postwar economy. Postwar leaders were committed to pursuing three modernizing goals they had inherited from Vichy: to free the state and the economy from the domination of the capitalist oligarchy, to eradicate Malthusianism, and to transform the economy into a predominantly industrial and technologically advanced one.[46] In order to preserve social order and disarm class conflict, they substituted the progressive ideals of social and economic democracy for Vichy's corporatist prescriptions.[47] Finally, despite disagreements over the relative emphases to assign to these different goals, postwar economic leaders shared, as Vichy's planners did, a universal belief in deploying the power of the state to achieve them. This dirigiste consensus that emerged at the end of the war – what Richard Kuisel has termed "the spirit of 1944" – was greatly facilitated by the weakness of business, which had been compromised by collaboration, as well as the new productivist orientations of labor.[48] Thus, a mix of modernizing and dirigiste convictions, many of them inherited from the war, solidified among postwar French political and economic elites as the Liberation-era provisional government settled into *Tripartisme* and the Fourth Republic came into being.

Continuities with Vichy are most evident in the institutional holdovers that characterized the postwar French state. Chief among them were the COs – duly renamed *offices professionnels* – which were retained by the provisional government to oversee production in individual branches of industry and, more crucially, distribute raw materials and primary inputs to those sectors most in need of them. Similarly, a new Ministère de l'économie nationale (Ministry of the National Economy, or MEN) was established by the Liberation-era government following the example of Vichy's Ministry of Industrial Production. Put under the authority of Pierre Mendès-France, it was responsible for setting prices, allocating raw materials, compiling economic statistics, and managing newly nationalized public corporations. The new ministry also recast the Vichy-era office of planning, the DGEN, and incorporated certain aspects of its allocation service, the OCRPI, into its competencies. In effect, the MEN became the institutional *fer-de-lance* of the dirigiste state in the immediate postwar period, seeking,

---

[46] Kuisel, *Capitalism*, 157–8. This ideological and programmatic proximity between what were, on the face of it, irreconcilable political enemies was particularly reflected in the area of planning. Indeed, the modernization plans that were issued by the Resistance, such as that drafted by the economic study commission of de Gaulle's London-based French National Committee in 1942, the Courtin report published by the Comité général d'étude in occupied France in November 1943, and the Socialist-inspired Philip report drafted for the Algiers Consultative Assembly in July 1944, all resembled, in both their modernizing objectives and technocratic flavor, the Vichy plans of 1942 and 1944. Ibid., 159–79.

[47] Ibid., 158.

[48] The latter was most clearly enshrined in the productivist drives pursued by the Communist Party from 1944 to 1947, before it left the government and assumed a posture of permanent opposition. Ibid., 178–9, 188, 189, as well as Ehrmann, *Organized Business in France*, 95–6, 103–4.

as Kuisel put it, "to move quickly toward a more modern, planned, democratic economy and a more just society."[49]

The preservation of the COs and the establishment of the MEN was accompanied by the creation of new institutions to support the postwar *dirigisme*. Chief among these was the establishment of the Institut national de la statistique et des études économiques (INSEE) within the MEN to oversee the collection and analysis of statistics for the purpose of indicative planning. Similarly, new state-run scientific and technical research institutes were established in a number of cutting-edge areas deemed paramount for innovation, including communications and electronics, aeronautics and aerospace, and atomic energy. Finally, in 1945 the École nationale d'administration (ENA) was founded to train the *hauts fonctionnaires* who were to be entrusted with running the dirigiste state. Its overarching purpose was to instill in civil servants the technocratic mind-set required to oversee the state-led economic and social renovation envisioned by the nation's leaders at the end of the war.[50]

Last but not least, 1945–6 also saw a sweeping campaign of nationalization on the part of the *tripartite* government formed by the Socialist Félix Gouin following the October 1945 election. The nationalizations targeted the banking system (December 1945), electrical power and gas (March 1946), and the insurance and coal sectors (April 1946).[51] Despite the socialistic rhetoric that accompanied them, these measures were conceived more as a means of reorganizing industry and facilitating its renovation than as a prelude to the socialization of production by the state.[52] In particular, nationalization was seen as essential for overcoming the resistance of Malthusian businesses, reflecting the conviction

[49] Kuisel, *Capitalism*, 191.
[50] On these ancillary reforms, see ibid., 214–15, as well as Hall, *Governing the Economy*, 140.
[51] This spree of nationalizations was followed two years later by the partial nationalization of the transport sector and of Air France. Kuisel, *Capitalism*, 207–8, 212; Hall, *Governing the Economy*, 140; and Patrick Fridenson, "Atouts et limites de la modernisation par en haut: les entreprises publiques face à leurs critiques (1940–1986)," in Fridenson and Straus, *Capitalisme français au XIXe–XXe siècle*, 175–95.
[52] That nationalization served more as a practical corollary of dirigisme than as a stepping-stone to socialism could be seen from its much more limited and selective application than what many of its earliest and most fervent partisans – particularly the Communists – had hoped for. Under the stewardship of Mendès-France, the economy was divided into three components in the hope of enhancing its efficiency and dynamism. First came the nationalized sector, comprising those industries considered most critical for rebuilding and sustaining the economic growth of the country – that is, the capital-intensive heavy industry, communications and transportation, and machine production sectors. The second was a "controlled" sector essentially covering the remaining branches and wholesale trades, in which the state guided private initiative according to guidelines set down by the *offices professionnels* (former COs). Finally, a "free" sector representing the smallest and most marginal enterprises – that is, *petits indépendants* and *petits patrons* – and farmers was left to withstand, unassisted by the state, the full brunt of market competition. The unspoken hope was that, in the face of such competition, many of these firms would disappear, thereby advancing the cause of industrial and commercial rationalization. On this tripartite conceptualization of the French economy by Mendès-France and other economic policy makers at the Ministry of the National Economy, see Kuisel, *Capitalism*, 194.

of postwar leaders that, on its own, the private sector was unable or unwilling to provide sufficient capital to set the country back on a path of growth after nearly two decades of stagnation.[53] It was a powerful lever for rationalizing production, both by imposing controls and efficiency-maximizing measures on the nationalized sectors and through the competition of nationalized enterprises with private firms.[54]

Finally, indicative planning was substantially intensified under the Fourth Republic in comparison to Vichy. Postwar planning was even more explicit and comprehensive in its attempt to, in the words of Peter Hall, "increas[e] the extent to which policies [were] chosen according to rational calculation and improv[e] the degree to which [they were] coordinated with one another."[55] Although planning was first introduced during Mendès-France's stint as minister of the national economy, obstructionist figures within the Provisional Government, notably the orthodox liberal finance minister René Pleven, meant that the first postwar plan could not be launched until 1947. Drawn up by the Commissariat général du plan (CGP), the planning agency that replaced the MEN in January 1946, the goal of this Plan de modernisation et d'équipement or PME was to kick-start growth by improving industrial productivity.[56] In many ways, the PME replicated the renovative priorities of Vichy, particularly as set out in the Tranche de démarrage of summer 1944.[57] However, in stark contrast to its precursors, the CGP sought to enlist the principal economic and social forces of the country in drafting the PME. As such, it established consultative mechanisms so the concerns of the latter would be taken into consideration,[58] creating the basis for what planners called the *économie concertée* (the concerted economy), a pseudocorporatist system of consultation that enlisted – nominally at least – private economic and social interests in the formulation of public policy.[59] At the same time, by securing the participation of

---

[53] Accordingly, the principal reason given by the state in taking control of the largest French banks, starting with the Bank of France, was to ensure that a steady stream of credit continued to flow to the most dynamic sectors of the economy. Since the Bank of France now fell under the control of the Ministry of Finance and in turn French banks were traditionally allowed to rediscount their largest business loans at the bank, the latter – and, through it, the state administrations within the Finance Ministry – would enjoy an enormous influence on the flow of credit to firms. Hall, *Governing the Economy*, 153; Kuisel, *Capitalism*, 214; and Claire Andrieu, "La politique du crédit, frein ou moteur de la modernisation?" in Fridenson and Strauss, *Capitalisme français au XIXe–XXe siècle*, 239–53.

[54] See Kuisel, *Capitalism*, 212–13, 266–7.

[55] *Governing the Economy*, 161.

[56] Kuisel, *Capitalism*, 225.

[57] Notably, the PME replicated the commitments of the latter to renew the nation's capital stock by increasing capital investment, modernize key industrial sectors in order to avoid production bottlenecks, and to expand the production of energy as well as machinery, particularly in the farming sector. Ibid., 225, 200–1.

[58] Ibid., 227; Hall, *Governing the Economy*, 141.

[59] Chief among these consultative structures were the modernization commissions, collegial assemblies composed of "hundreds of businessmen, administrators, trade union officials, farmers, experts and consumers." These were organized into vertical commissions representing particular

these economic and social actors, planners strove to instill in them modern attitudes toward business development and growth in order to facilitate the task of economic renovation. As Peter Hall has observed, "from the outset French planning has been an ideological project" that sought to create "a climate of opinion that emphasized the importance of economic growth and the means to achieving it."[60]

The PME – or Monnet Plan, after the inaugural head of the CGP, Jean Monnet – that was unveiled in January 1947 assigned priority to six sectors in which production bottlenecks were most likely to develop, privileging the fields of steel, coal, transportation, electricity, cement, and agricultural machinery, which were deemed vital to the country's reconstruction and economic expansion.[61] The plan called for increasing the credit available to finance capital improvements in these sectors from 23 to 25 percent of GDP. Depending on whether such improvement was in the public or the private sectors, the CGP deployed different strategies to ensure its objectives were met. On the one hand, it imposed strict production targets on nationalized industries that were enforced by government-appointed managers. On the other, it compelled private firms to adhere to the plan's goals through a variety of controls over foreign exchange, bank loans, prices, and the allocation of scarce materials such as coal and steel. Beginning in 1948, the PME was revised to coordinate the distribution of Marshall Plan aid and its agricultural program recast to rationalize farming and transform the country into a food exporter.[62] Likewise, its focus gradually shifted from overcoming production bottlenecks to promoting potential export industries as planners sought to prepare the country for entry into the European Coal and Steel Community (ECSC) in 1951.[63]

Over its five-year duration (1947–52), the PME proved an unqualified economic success, investment and growth targets for basic sectors either being met or experiencing inconsequential shortfalls. Likewise, the plan spurred renovation in sectors that had previously been reluctant to modernize, such as steel, and drove forward the rationalization in target sectors through industrial concentration. In turn, as domestic and international competition revived, wartime

---

sectors, and horizontal commissions addressing particular issues or problem areas, such as regional policy, manpower, and research and development. As the economy diversified and the purview of planning expanded, the number of modernization commissions substantially grew, increasing from ten in 1946 to thirty-two by 1963. Following consultations with the government, CGP planners synthesized reports of the modernization commissions and then elaborated statements of options that were debated in the Economic and Social Council – the postwar version of the interwar National Economic Council – and National Assembly before being synthesized into an economic plan. On these consultative mechanisms and how they were incorporated in the planning process, see Kuisel, *Capitalism*, 227, and Hall, *Governing the Economy*, 141–2.

[60] Hall, *Governing Economiy*, 151.

[61] For a more complete account of the political debate attending the drafting of the PME and its approval, see Kuisel, *Capitalism*, 233–5.

[62] To this end, state-directed investment was extended to the fertilizer and fuel sectors in 1950. Hall, *Governing the Economy*, 142.

[63] Kuisel, *Capitalism*, 269.

shortages disappeared, and private investment grew, planning increasingly adapted itself to market principles and assumed a less coercive disposition. By the time the PME had run its course, planners sought to coordinate and adapt French firms to the operation of the market rather than directly interfere in it, such that, by the mid-1950s, French planning had assumed a markedly procapitalist bent. As Kuisel has observed, the latter was progressively circumscribed to the "coordination, forecasting, reflection, and exchange of information in a mixed economy," the state acting "more as a guide than as an arbiter among competing interests."[64] Correspondingly, nationalized firms were increasingly run like private enterprises by independent managers, a development that spurred modernization in the private sector by encouraging family-owned firms to break with prewar Malthusian habits and seek external investment to more effectively compete with state-owned enterprises. Thus, as a result of the direct and indirect constraints it wielded over the private sector, it could be said that, in addition to stimulating economic renovation and growth, the PME also presided over the birth of the modern corporation in France.

The Second or Hirsch Plan (1954–8), named after Monnet's successor at the CGP, resumed where its predecessor had left off, by enshrining a more limited, market-friendly form of planning. After the PME had met the urgent imperatives of reconstruction and set the most important sectors on the path of modernization, the Hirsch Plan sought to chart a more balanced course by attempting to improve standards and, more importantly, enhance the competitiveness of French firms as the country prepared its entry in the European Economic Community (EEC).[65] Accordingly, the new plan incorporated fiscal and credit incentives to reconvert obsolescent firms, retrain displaced labor, and promote regional industrial development. It also marked a substantial shift away from the reliance on state credits and foreign aid to fund investment that had characterized the Monnet Plan. Like its predecessor, the Hirsch Plan proved a resounding success, surpassing almost all its targets, in many instances by a substantial margin. By its midpoint in 1956, domestic production had surpassed the level achieved in 1929, the previous high, by 25 to 30 percent. Perhaps more importantly for the country's subsequent development, the Hirsch Plan also presided over a sweeping transformation of the agricultural sector, greatly reducing the number of marginal producers and considerably raising farm exports.[66]

Thus, planning under the Fourth Republic was an indisputable success. The modernization over which it presided, specifically its improvement of the capital stock and rationalization of key industrial sectors, allowed France to attain a

[64] Ibid., 260, 249.
[65] The plan's principal target was to raise national income by 25% compared to 1952, an increase that would be accounted for by a 20% growth in agricultural production, a 30% growth in industrial output, and a 60% rise in construction. Planners estimated that this increase in output would raise the standard of living by 4% annually and restore a balance-of-payments equilibrium through the export surplus that would be generated. Ibid., 260.
[66] Ibid., 264.

mean increase in labor productivity (as measured by output-per-man-hour) of 4.3 percent per annum between 1949 and 1959 – more than twice that of the United States and 1.8 times that of Britain over the same period.[67] This rise in labor productivity in turn translated into high growth, the country averaging a 4.5 percent annual increase in GDP throughout the 1950s, placing it just behind Italy (4.8 percent), but ahead of West Germany (4.3 percent), the United States (3.3 percent), and the United Kingdom (2.4 percent).[68]

Yet, the ultimate significance of the Monnet and Hirsch plans resides less in high productivity and growth rates than in the fact that they institutionalized planning by placing it philosophically and practically beyond debate. They presided over a sea change in the mentality of the principal public and private actors overseeing the nation's economic life, succeeding, as Ehrmann put it, in promoting modernization "not as much as a condition of things as a state of mind that they wished to propagate widely."[69] At a first level, the high civil servants charged with formulating and implementing economic policy became thoroughly imbued by the technocratic modernizing credo underpinning the PME and Hirsch Plan. Taking to heart Monnet's rejoinder to "no longer think of the future in the context of the past," members of the upper state administration embraced his credo that "today the principal idea is that of expansion."[70] Second and perhaps more importantly, by the end of the Hirsch Plan, many formerly skeptical business leaders – particularly in the largest industries and firms – were converted to the new dirigiste mantra. These managers and employers from advanced sectors gave up their prewar insularity and wariness toward the state and accepted the principles of the *économie concertée.*[71] This fraction of the *patronat* was followed by the dynamic constituency of *cadres* tied to the advanced capitalist sector and, to a lesser degree, certain working-class strata employed in the largest and most concentrated firms.[72] In short, by the end of Fourth Republic, *petits patrons* and *indépendants* not only were suffering from the concrete economic impact of dirigisme and planning but, perhaps more significantly, found themselves increasingly marginalized in their opposition to them.

---

[67] Caron, *Economic History*, 193.
[68] Kuisel, *Capitalism*, 264.
[69] Ehrmann, *Organized Business in France*, 285.
[70] Quoted in Kuisel, *Capitalism*, 244.
[71] Ibid., 265, and Ehrmann, *Organized Business in France*, 293.
[72] Although the CGT and its offshoot, Force ouvrière (FO), officially withdrew from the modernization commissions in the early 1950s following the PCF's repudiation of *Tripartisme* and entry into permanent opposition against the regime, and would resume a role in planning only following the election of Mitterrand, the third principal union in the country, the Social Catholic CFTC, and its successor, the secular Confédération française démocratique du travail (CFDT), remained officially involved in planning until the Sixth Plan (1970–5) and the uniting of the Left behind the Common Program. Hall, *Governing the Economy*, 158, 169–70, and Kuisel, *Capitalism*, 259, 262.

The interventionist posture of the postwar state was not limited to dirigisme and economic planning, however. These were accompanied by other forms of intervention, principally in the areas of macroeconomic policy and social reform, in order to facilitate acceptance of the *économie concertée*. Governments of the Fourth Republic embraced Keynesian countercyclical spending policies as a corollary to sustaining state-driven economic growth.[73] This marked the first time since the Popular Front that growth and full employment were favored as economic priorities over preserving monetary stability. In turn, these expansionary policies were accompanied by measures to liberalize trade so as to encourage the rationalization of French firms by exposing them to foreign competition.

There were several arrows to the quiver of Keynesian policies deployed by the governments of the Fourth Republic. At the level of monetary and credit policy, the state increasingly relied on the nationalized banking system to channel funding to dynamic sectors of the economy, even if this meant tolerating moderate inflation due to rising investment and growth.[74] Similarly, though it periodically shut off the monetary spigot when the economy began to overheat – prompting monetary stabilizations in both 1951 and 1958 – it increasingly relied on devaluation rather than austerity as a means of offsetting inflation and the balance-of-payments disequilibria it produced. This loose credit policy, coupled with devaluation and the recourse to discrete deflationary policies – such as those targeting petty shopkeepers in the late 1940s and early 1950s – would set the pattern for monetary policy not only throughout the Fourth Republic but during the first two decades of the Fifth as well.[75]

The state employed fiscal policy to similar ends in order to promote investment in the most productive sectors and encourage the rationalization of the economy. This was the intent behind the *prélèvement* or levy, in the form of new taxes and forced loans, that was imposed by the CGP on the beneficiaries of inflation in 1946–7. An effort to curb the postwar spike in inflation, the measure was also intended to eliminate the most marginal producers and shopkeepers, and thereby unclog the French agricultural, industrial, and, most notably, commercial structures.[76] Starting in the 1950s, changes were made to the tax code to pare down the marginal sector and promote industrial and commercial

---

[73] Although Keynesian policies had been advocated as early as the war, such as in the Philip Report of 1944, and made converts among certain national leaders, including Mendès-France, they were not adopted in earnest until the late 1940s and early 1950s, when the country was overtaken by the global recession following the Korean War. Indeed, in the immediate postwar years, the onus had been on preserving monetary stability and controlling inflation as prices spiraled following the lifting of wartime price controls. As head of the MEN, Mendès-France had been forced to enact an austerity policy that combined a reduction in the money supply with the reimposition of wage and price controls in order to create a stable economic environment in which state planners could operate. However, once price stability was restored, Mendès and his successors proved willing to embrace expansionary policies, even if these generated a certain amount of inflation, provided they resulted in growth. Kuisel, *Capitalism*, 177, 178, 192–3, 268.

[74] Andrieu, "La politique du crédit."

[75] Ibid., 268, and Hall, *Governing the Economy*, 143, 245.

[76] Hall, *Governing the Economy*, 238, 243.

concentration. Successive *patente* increases and the imposition of a self-administered value-added tax (VAT) that forced *petits indépendants* to declare their revenues to the tax authorities left shopkeepers and artisans in a "relatively unfavorable" fiscal situation, particularly after a series of tax deductions and rebates were afforded to wage earners throughout the 1950s and 1960s.[77] The new VAT not only diminished *petits indépendants*' potential for tax fraud but, by reducing the taxes owed by industrial firms on their capital, effectively reduced their capitalization costs. Thus, it benefited the most capital-intensive sectors, serving as a spur to automation and concentration.[78] As with monetary policy, then, the state administration used fiscal policy as a means to further modernization, so that it "conceived," in Kuisel's words, "of public finances... as a means of economic and social action and orientation."[79]

This reliance on monetary and fiscal policy to support its modernizing designs was accompanied by the state's new commitment to trade liberalization. Designed to grow French industry and improve its efficiency by increasing its access to foreign – particularly European – markets, this shift reflected the embrace by state planners of the ideal of European economic integration, conceived as a boon to industrial restructuring and renovation.[80] Accordingly, they welcomed successive European agreements, starting with the Schuman Plan of 1950 and culminating in the creation of the EEC in 1957. By incrementally broadening the purview of trade and expanding the band of industries subjected to foreign competition, these agreements provided substantial impetus to the goal of economic rationalization pursued by the French state since the 1940s.

Alongside these macroeconomic policies, the postwar state also introduced a broad assortment of social reforms to secure the support of certain social segments, notably an increasingly large working class, behind its modernizing agenda and to enlist their participation in the *économie concertée*. In 1945 universal social security was established for all wage earners, guaranteeing them a retirement pension and free health care coverage. Based on compulsory contributions by both employers and wage earners, the new system imposed social obligations on the former for the first time. That same year, the creation of *comités d'entreprise* (plant work committees or CEs) was stipulated in firms of more than one hundred

---

[77] Zdatny, *Politics*, 169, and Maurice Roy, *Les commerçants: entre la révolte et la modernisation* (Paris: Editions du Seuil, 1971), ch. 4.

[78] A 1960 Harvard Law School study concluded that the VAT had been a "major incentive to the modernization and re-equipment of French industry," providing a substantial impetus to the process of rationalization. Quoted in Kuisel, *Capitalism*, 269. On the rationalizing effect of the VAT, see Caron, *Economic History*, 339–40.

[79] Kuisel, *Capitalism*, 257.

[80] The expansion of trade had already been defined as one of the five principal goals of the PME in 1946. When the plan was revised at the end of 1948 to coordinate the distribution of Marshall Plan assistance, the overarching emphasis that had initially been placed on overcoming production bottlenecks was supplanted by a greater focus on export promotion, revealing planners' conceptualization of trade as a vehicle of growth and modernization. Ibid., 224, 238.

employees and, the following year, in firms of more than fifty. Presided over by employers but comprising a majority of worker representatives, the CEs were given considerable authority over the implementation of social policy within the firm. Moreover, the purview of the CEs extended to other areas that had hitherto been the exclusive preserve of employers. For example, each fiscal year employers were compelled to divulge the sum of firms' profits – a potentially troubling development in view of their future contract negotiations with their workers. Similarly, CEs were given the right to voice an opinion regarding the utilization of firm profits.[81] Finally, in February 1950, collective bargaining was introduced as a binding legal basis for employer-employee negotiations, with collective contracts becoming compulsory in certain sectors. Dropping an earlier provision that such contracts be extended nationally, the new law stipulated their implementation at local and regional levels.[82]

In light of these interventionist economic and social policies, it is not surprising that *petits indépendants* strongly opposed the Fourth Republic's dirigiste strategy. At an initial level, they saw the state's new *étatiste* orientation and its commitment to planning as both an ideological and a material threat to their interests.[83] *Petits indépendants* regarded state planning as synonymous with a process of "modernization *à outrance*" that threatened their economic position and even survival in French society. Stephen Zdatny has observed that "such a policy could offer only insecurity to the large number of petty producers whose livelihoods depended on a Malthusian economy."[84] Deploring the inhuman character of technocratic rationalization, small producers couched their critique of dirigisme in the rhetoric of economic liberalism, affirming the sanctity of individual freedom from unwarranted state interference. Correspondingly, they also condemned the automation of production, charging that the latter reinforced the dynamic of dehumanization at work in dirigisme by stripping the

[81] Though in most cases these measures were inadequately enforced or workers failed to take advantage of them, the new CE legislation nevertheless pointed the way toward reshaping employer-employee relations within the firm. In the best case, it intimated the potential for a more equal relationship between workers and management and actually led in a minority of cases to greater democracy within the firm. Ehrmann, *Organized Business in France*, 448–9, 455.
[82] Despite the fact that, as in the case of the CE legislation, many provisions of the new law went unenforced, the fact that it could be passed at all highlighted the strides taken in this period toward social reform. For example, employers often circumscribed its application to wage issues by concluding settlements with workers that stipulated wage scales far below the actual wages prevailing in the workplace. Likewise, its more ambitious objectives, such as the guaranteeing of union rights and introduction of hiring and firing procedures within the firm, the financing of welfare activities under the aegis of the CEs, and the institution of conciliation procedures, vocational training, and other firm-level benefits effectively came to nought. Fournier and Questiaux, *Traité du social*, 279–80, and Ehrmann, *Organized Business in France*, 436.
[83] Accordingly, the Confédération générale des petites et moyennes entreprises (CGPME) established in 1944 in order to defend the prerogatives of small and middling employers, vehemently decried the CGP and the PME from their inception. Ehrmann, *Organized Business in France*, 228.
[84] *Politics*, 178.

productive process of human personality and creativity.[85] *Petits patrons'* opposition to dirigisme reached its paroxysm in response to the nationalizations of the
second half of the 1940s. Viewed as the ultimate expression of the encroachment
by the state on individual freedom, *petits indépendants* condemned nationalization as socialism in another guise.[86]

However, for all their liberal pretensions, *petits indépendants* often attacked
state intervention precisely when it sought to enhance the liberal functioning of
the economy. Thus, they strongly opposed the Laniel-Faure Decrees of August
1953, which called for the "maintenance and reestablishment of industrial and
commercial free competition" and criminalized impediments to the reduction of
wholesale and retail prices.[87] Similarly, the Faure Decrees of May 1955, which
loosened the qualifications for entry into the *artisanat* and opened up the trades
to greater internal competition, were bitterly resisted by master artisans because
they effectively ended their stranglehold over the Chambers of Trade.[88] From
this perspective, their critique of dirigisme dovetailed with a broader repudiation
of modernization. It reflected not only their growing economic unviability but
also their cultural inaptitude to the requirements and processes of industrial
modernity.

Petits indépendants also condemned the macroeconomic policies supporting
the new dirigiste dispensation of the Fourth Republic. First, they rejected the
expansionary monetary policies enacted by the state to stimulate industrial
investment, underscoring their "traditional distrust ... of any expansion as
long as there was no certainty of an increased demand."[89] They refused to
accept that macroeconomic policies should be employed to stimulate expansion,
notably by spurring growth in advanced sectors while downsizing more marginal ones. For example, shopkeepers and artisans resented the austerity plan
introduced by the Provisional Government in 1944–5 to arrest postwar inflation
as well as the *prélèvements* imposed on them in 1946–7 to fund the Monnet Plan,

---

[85] Exemplifying this antitechnocratic and antitechnological bias, Pierre Poujade, the anointed
champion of *petits indépendants* during the 1950s, demanded "a future where technological
service is at the service of men, and not men its slaves" and where "the perfection of labor, the
satisfaction of creative work [is not] crushed by the infernal rhythm of overproduction, by
machines and automation." Similarly, deploring the "disappearance of human liberties" as
a function of the "anonymity" and "depersonalization" of the individual in modern society,
Poujade attacked "lazy and budgetivorous civil servants" and pledged to resist the new *étatisme
envahisseur* (invasive statism). Ibid., 170, 171, and Hoffmann, *Mouvement Poujade*, 210,
212, 213.

[86] Ehrmann, *Organized Business in France*, 352–3.

[87] Specifically, the Laniel-Faure decrees were promulgated in response to the refusal of wholesalers,
acting under the pressure of organized shopkeeper interests, to supply the Leclerc supermarket chain
in Brittany. In June 1958, under pressure from the same shopkeeper groups, the Constitutional
Council even moved to abrogate the decrees, only for them to be restored a week later by the new
provisional government under General de Gaulle. Roy, *Les commerçants*, 117–18.

[88] Zarca, *L'artisanat français*, 94.

[89] Ibid., 307, and also Kuisel, *Capitalism*, 243.

which effectively meant transferring resources from the marginal to the advanced sector.[90] Likewise, *petits indépendants* disapproved of the liberalization of trade, conceived by Fourth Republic planners as a vital corollary to enhancing productive efficiency and sustaining growth. Small business owners viewed such liberalization, first under the auspices of the ECSC and then of the EEC, as a betrayal that would doom a great number of French producers.[91] Thus, the opening of French markets to trade became yet another ingredient fueling the discontent of *petits patrons* with the state's economic orientations under the Fourth Republic. Seeking to harness the economic fears of small business by couching this discontent in the language of patriotic indignation, Pierre Poujade warned in regard to the ECSC: "We are being dragooned against our wills into a German Europe under American direction. The great concentration which Hitler failed to achieve, it is they [the proponents of the ECSC] who will realize it."[92]

Yet, it was the postwar state's fiscal policies that provoked the most resistance among *petits patrons*. Beginning in the early 1950s, *petits indépendants* believed that they were being made to shoulder a proportionately greater tax burden than wage earners because of successive increases in the *patente* and the replacement of the old turnover tax by a steeper *régime forfaitaire*. These increases were felt to be all the more pronounced in that the real value of these taxes rose as a proportion of their incomes as a result of the lessening of inflation during

[90] As a number of contemporary observers have remarked, French business in the immediate postwar period was "hooked" on inflation. This was especially true of the smallest and least efficient enterprises, specifically petty shopkeepers who throve in an environment that allowed them to charge higher prices. Since the sales volume of these firms was so small, their ability to charge more often spelled the difference between solvency and bankruptcy. Similarly, inflation also allowed them to pass on at least some of the costs that they would have to assume themselves under normal circumstances. Finally, inflation was seen by many *petits indépendants* and owners of small and medium-sized enterprises (SMEs) as a necessary price to maintain the costly trade protections without which they were condemned to economic ruin. In turn, the resistance of small business owners most certainly weakened the commitment of the state to pursue anti-inflationary policies. The political difficulty of curbing inflation brought successive governments to adopt a strategy of growth with inflation and to offset its negative external effects through a series of devaluations. Kuisel, *Capitalism*, 267–8, and Caron, *Economic History*, 275. On the inflationary proclivities of French *petits indépendants*, see respectively, John Keeler, "Corporatist Decentralization and Commercial Modernization in France: The Royer Law's Impact on Shopkeepers, Supermarkets and the State," in *Socialism, the State and Public Policy in France*, ed. P. Cerny and M. Schain (London: Frances Pinter, 1985), 268; Hoffmann, *Mouvement Poujade*, 18; and Mayer, "Classes moyennes," 743.

[91] Such sentiments were articulated by the leader of the CGPME, Léon Gingembre, who forcefully exclaimed, in reaction to the ratification of the Schuman Plan, "The first railroad car that crosses the [Franco-German] border after the opening of the common market would be transporting not only European coke, but also a corpse, that of French industry." Quoted in Lefranc, *Les organisations patronales en France*, 155.

[92] Hoffmann, *Mouvement Poujade*, 224.

this period.[93] Correlatively, the new value-added tax was resented by *petits indépendants* because of the unprecedented bureaucratic intrusion it spelled into their affairs.[94] The vigorous manner in which the VAT was applied and enforced afforded *petits indépendants* much less leeway to underdeclare their earnings, subjecting them in effect to a higher turnover tax than they had hitherto paid.[95] More frequent government audits due to the centralization of the tax inspection services, combined with steep increases in penalties for fraud, also fueled their discontent.[96] The new tax legislation left *petits indépendants* with the impression that they were the objects of tax discrimination, particularly relative to wage earners and large employers who, they believed, were unfairly favored by the new *code fiscal*.[97]

Finally, the disquiet of the *petit patronat* over increased state intervention was not simply confined to the economic realm. Small producers also objected to the *économie concertée* and the set of social policies and institutions introduced at war's end to assist the state in formulating economic policy. At one level, the new universal social security legislation of the mid-1940s and new laws regulating employer-employee relations, such as the institution of work plant committees

[93] Concluding that the new tax environment had become "the best of recruiters" for the UDCA, the social scientist Maurice Lauré underscored the relatively unfavorable fiscal situation of *petits indépendants* as compared to wage earners in the department of the Lot, one of the earliest strongholds of Poujadism. The "taxable profits" of the "average" artisan, he wrote, "only increased by 16,000 francs between 1951 and 1953, from 195,000 to 211,000 francs, whereas the taxes he paid in those same years rose from 4,280 francs to 10,400: an increase of 6,120 francs. How is this man, whose business is in decline, not to believe that he is the victim of a greater tax burden, when he sees that he now has to pay two and a half times more on a relatively stable income? It is hardly astonishing, then, that a protest movement of taxpayers has appeared in the Lot at Saint-Céré." Quoted in Borne *Petits bourgeois en révolte?*, 61. See also Roy, *Les commerçants*, ch. 4, and Hoffmann, *Mouvement Poujade*, 18–19.

[94] For example, though it did not impose a greater fiscal burden on shopkeepers, the introduction of the VAT in 1954 saddled them with higher administrative costs since it made them responsible for charging the new tax to their customers. Reflecting the added organizational burden represented by the new tax, Zdatny estimates that fully two-thirds of *petits indépendants* in 1956 needed to resort to the services of an accountant in order to figure out what they owed to the government in terms of sales tax receipts. *Politics*, 169.

[95] From this standpoint, one of the unstated aims of the VAT was to force shopkeepers to more faithfully report their earnings and thereby broaden the tax base represented by this constituency. Roy, *Les commerçants*, 76–87.

[96] For example, under the Pinay government (1950–2), these penalties increased from 100% to 200%. Not to be outdone, the succeeding Laniel government introduced prison sentences for repeat offenders. Hoffmann, *Mouvement Poujade*, 19–20.

[97] In a certain respect, this sense of aggrievement vis-à-vis big business reflected subjective, cultural differences in how these taxes were perceived as well as the objective, material iniquities arising from their application. French small businesses, as expressed through the policy statements of their representative organizations such as the CGPME, clung to a restrictive and instrumental view of taxation, essentially limited to covering the costs of only the most minimal state functions. By contrast, planners and their business allies increasingly advocated treating taxes as a form of collateral against which the state could borrow for the purpose of maximizing investment. Ehrmann, *Organized Business in France*, 311.

(*CEs*) and compulsory collective bargaining within small to medium-sized enterprises (SMEs) carried cost increases that were bound to hurt small producers. More importantly, *petits indépendants* and small employers strongly opposed these laws on the grounds that they represented a significant encroachment on their traditional patronal authority. Far from contributing to a better entente with their workers, these laws – especially those giving workers greater say in the day-to-day running of the workplace – brought many small employers to adopt an obstructionist stance vis-à-vis their employees, heightening contentiousness within the firm. Of particular concern to *petits patrons* was the possibility that these regulations represented the thin end of a wedge by which left-leaning unions would be able to ensconce themselves in the everyday operations of their firms.[98] In this sense, their rejection of these social provisions dovetailed with *petits indépendants'* broader opposition to postwar dirigiste and macroeconomic policy, which they saw not only as threatening economically but also in fundamental conflict with their values and worldview.

If the dirigiste formula occasioned a profound shift in state-society relations, the Fourth Republic marked a no less important political-institutional evolution with respect to the Third Republic. At first sight, this evolution seems minor, since the new regime appeared to restore the prewar parliamentary system and to re-create the prewar political parties. Thus, the postwar Rassemblement des gauches républicaines (RGR) was a compendium of centrist and rightist Radicals who were joined by a moderate wing of the interwar Alliance démocratique, while the Centre national des indépendants (CNI) incorporated the remnants of the latter and the Fédération républicaine into a unified conservative party.[99] Affirming orthodox liberal values and calling for limited state intervention in the economy, these parties became, much like their interwar predecessors, the natural political home for postwar *petits indépendants*.[100] The reestablishment

[98] Thus, marking its protest against the new plant committee law, the Conseil national du patronat français (CNPF), the new peak employers' organization constituted in 1945, affirmed the unquestioned supremacy of patronal authority, asserting that "the law cannot create authority and cannot destroy it." Ehrmann, *Organized Business in France*, 451.

[99] The postwar incarnation of the Radical Party (PR) was more rightist and chauvinistic than its predecessor, principally as a result of the defection of the progressive wing of the party behind the leadership of Mendès-France, combined with the growing influence of its increasingly vociferous, colonialist base in Algeria. In this new guise, the Radicals professed a greater hostility to state intervention in economic affairs and tended to exalt to a much greater degree than had its interwar forerunner the principles of individual liberty, effectively bringing them into the philosophical and programmatic ambit of the postwar *Indépendants*.

[100] According to a survey from 1952, after farmers (who accounted respectively for 28% of the RGR's electorate and 31% of the CNI's), shopkeepers and artisans represented the second-most important socioprofessional constituency within the electorate of each party: 10% for the RGR and 11% for the CNI. When self-employed artisans and pieceworkers are added, it could be said that fully one out of five voters for each of these parties corresponded to the profile of *petits indépendants*. These tallies were followed in decreasing order by industrial workers (9%), *fonctionnaires* (8%), industrialists and *cadres* (4%), and members of the liberal professions and clerical employees (each at 1%) in the case of the RGR, and industrialists and *cadres* (9%),

of prewar parliamentary structures and practices gave small business spokes-men influence over policy, particularly through the parliamentary standing committees in which legislation was drafted and submitted to the National Assembly.[101] Thus, small business advocates were able to push through protective measures, dispensations from fiscal legislation, and social policies favorable to small business that tried to blunt the modernizing thrust of the Administration d'État.

Yet, despite these institutional throwbacks to the past, the constitution that came into force in 1947 substantially limited the influence of *petit indépendant* interests over policy making. In the first place, the new constitution curbed the legislative power of the Senate by stripping it of the faculty to initiate and kill legislation that it had wielded during the Third Republic. Because in the latter the Senate had been the preserve of localized petty producer interests, the downgrad-ing of its legislative prerogatives diminished small business's influence over the

industrial workers (9%), *fonctionnaires* (7%) and clerical employees (4%) in the case of CNI. In short, small proprietors accounted for two voters out of five within each party – approximately 40%, a proportion that rose to approximately half their total electorates when independent workers were included. (In fact, this number may underestimate the proportion of petty pro-prietors within the electorate of these two parties, since it does not account for the number of former farmers and *petits indépendants* who helped make up the sizable constituencies of retirees (fully 19% of the RGR and 18% of the CNI) within the respective electorates of these two parties). Similarly, although they figured less prominently in the Christian Democratic Mouvement républicain populaire (MRP) and the Gaullist Rassemblement du peuple français (RPF), *petits indépendants* remained an important constituency of these new parties. In 1952 *petits indépendants* accounted for 10% of the RPF's electorate, making it alongside clerical workers the third-most important electoral constituency within the new party behind farmers (at 16%) and workers (at 15%). Likewise, with 8% of the party vote, *petits indépendants* repre-sented the third largest constituency within the MRP, after industrial workers (19%) and clerical workers (15%). J.-D. Reynaud and Alain Touraine, "La représentation politique du monde ouvrier"; G. Lavau, "Les classes moyennes et la politique"; Alain Gourdon, "Le Parti radical"; Marcel Merle, "Les modérés"; and Raymond Barillon, "Le rassemblement du peuple français," all in *Partis politiques et classes sociales en France*, ed. M. Duverger (Paris: Cahiers de la FNSP, 1955), 34, 64, 236–9, 252, 280, as well as Nordmann, *Histoire des Radicaux*, 365ff.

[101] Particularly influential in this lobbying capacity was the CGPME, which constituted according to one observer "the purest type of pressure group among all business organizations." Defending an archetypal program built around the themes of budgetary restraint, fiscal conservatism, individ-ual initiative, and minimal state intervention, the CGPME was adept at acting through parlia-mentary study groups in order to influence the standing committees responsible for crafting legislation. Through these mechanisms, it was able to marshal broad political coalitions in support of small business and thus to exert a disproportionate influence over the legislative process. For example, in the early 1950s, the CGPME created a Study and Action Group for Public Enterprise that assembled deputies committed to the principle of free enterprise. The latter included three hundred deputies elected in 1951, representing the virtual totality of the *Indépendant* and RGR parliamentary groups, a majority of the RPF parliamentary group, over a third of MRP deputies, and even four Socialist deputies. When this lobbying effectiveness was combined with its propensity to intervene in elections and endorse candidates across a large number of parliamentary races, the CGPME indisputably came to wield considerable clout within the parliamentary politics of the Fourth Republic, reaching the zenith of its influence in the early 1950s with the accession of the *petite entreprise*-owner and CNI candidate Antoine Pinay to the premiership. Ehrmann, *Organized Business in France*, 172–84.

legislative process.[102] Second, the abandonment of the old *scrutin d'arrondisse-ment* (single majority district) voting system and its replacement with a system based on proportional representation also undercut the ability of parochial inter-ests to sway electoral outcomes. This new system created much larger electoral constituencies, requiring candidates to reach out to broader coalitions of interests than the localized interests that had dominated the single majority districts of the Third Republic. This innovation spurred the emergence of nationally organized and issue-oriented parties. As such, it distinctly worked in favor of financially powerful, nationally organized interests as against locally connected ones.[103]

The cumulative effect of these institutional changes was that, within the new national parties and instances of interest intermediation, advocates for small business and *petits indépendants* were increasingly overridden by the represen-tatives of other, often-competing interests. For example, despite counting a substantial constituency of *petits indépendants* and *petits patrons* in its elector-ate, the Gaullist RPF would nevertheless continue to hew to a program of national modernization and a vision of technocratic partnership between work-ers and employers. That the RPF persisted in pursuing this modernizing agenda despite the significant fraction of its electorate that was composed of *petits indépendants* and small employers testified to the close ties it enjoyed with the most advanced fraction of French business.[104]

This neglect of petty producer interests not only was confined to broadly based parties such as the RPF but also came to characterize parties initially identified with *petits indépendants*, the RGR and the CNI (later CNIP). Despite these historical ties, these parties advanced the interests of social and sectoral constituencies whose interests conflicted with those of petty producers and tradesmen. In the case of the RGR, this was notably true in regard to *fonction-naires* who, as we have seen, represented 8 percent of the party's electorate (compared to 10 percent for *petits indépendants*).[105] In the case of the CNI(P), the rise of a forward-looking constituency of executives attracted by the party's liberal economic message (they represented 9 percent of the Indépendant elec-torate, versus 11 percent for *petits indépendants*) compelled it to embrace modernizing policies at odds with the interests of small employers and petty tradesmen. Accordingly, the CNI(P) found it increasingly difficult to reconcile the old and new fractions of the middle class, an impasse that contributed to its eventual disintegration in the late 1950s.[106]

---

[102] Ibid., 251, and Hoffman, "Paradoxes," 49.
[103] Ehrmann, *Organized Business in France*, 227–8, and Gordon Wright, *France in Modern Times*, 4th ed. (New York: Norton, 1987), 410.
[104] On this theme, see notably Patrick Guiol, "Le RPF ou la difficulté de rassembler," in Lavau, Grunberg, and Mayer, *L'univers politique des classes moyennes*, 219–23.
[105] On the identification of *(petits) fonctionnaires* with the postwar Radical formation, see notably Gourdon, "Le Parti radical," and Michel Crozier, "Les attitudes politiques des employés et des petits fonctionnaires," in Duverger, *Partis politiques et classes sociales en France*, 85–99.
[106] Merle, "Les modérés," 273–6.

More generally, the new national mandates of these traditionally small-producer-based parties forced them to pursue policies that ultimately ran counter to the preferences of *petits indépendants* and their advocates. Thus, the monetary stabilization program implemented in 1950–1 by the Indépendant prime minister Antoine Pinay in order to halt inflation and reestablish an investment-friendly economic environment incurred the wrath of *petits indépendants*, who saw the profits they had reaped due to high postwar inflation disappear. These strata were similarly outraged by the Laniel government's introduction of the VAT in 1954, which, as we saw, limited their ability to underdeclare their earnings and thus minimize their tax obligations. In short, as a result of the centralization of the party system and the subsequent nationalization of interest politics, *petits indépendants* were deprived of the parochial and clientelistic political networks on which they had relied under the Third Republic. As the Fourth Republic evolved, their advocates were more frequently defeated by organizationally and financially stronger interests that were better equipped to marshal their leverage within the newly centralized instances of interest intermediation.

Finally, and perhaps most crucially, the compartmentalization of economic policy making in the executive and administrative branches of the state substantially reduced the influence of parliament in this area. A mixed economy characterized by big nationalized firms and managed through indicative planning "largely escaped parliamentary tutelage," in Kuisel's phrase.[107] This supplanting of the parliament by the state administration as the locus of policy making was starkly demonstrated by the appointment of *hauts fonctionnaires* to preside over the parliamentary committees charged with drafting economic and social legislation. As a result, sectoral opponents of modernization and their parliamentary patrons were prevented from using these committees to block the modernizing initiatives of the technocratic elite.[108] Finally, the parliament's loss of influence was further compounded when new legislative procedures were introduced limiting the financial powers of the Assembly, making the budget the quasi-exclusive preserve of the Finance Ministry. "The drift away from parliament was unmistakable," as Kuisel observed, over the Fourth Republic's short life.[109]

Since it was in the National Assembly that the advocates for small business wielded their greatest influence, the downgrading of its responsibility for economic policy was a significant blow to their capacity to inform decisions in this area. In turn, *petits indépendants* were granted only formal representation in the consultative bodies charged with advising the relevant ministerial administrations on economic policy and planning. Thus, the Economic Council that was established in 1946 differed markedly from the interwar National Economic Council in that its members were limited to the "most representative" economic and social

---

[107] *Capitalism*, 254.
[108] Ehrmann, *Organized Business in France*, 235–6.
[109] Kuisel, *Capitalism*, 255.

organizations. This meant that small business organizations were denied any meaningful advisory role, while big business groups, such as the CNPF and the Assembly of the Presidents of the Chambers of Commerce, were granted preeminent status.[110] Similarly, within the tripartite modernization commissions that consulted with the Commissariat général du plan throughout the planning process, the representatives of *petits indépendants* were also granted only a symbolic role.[111]

At the same time, even though the CGPME, the principal interprofessional organization representing small business, was represented in the modernization commissions from the outset, it was far exceeded by the degree of representation afforded big business and certain trade unions, such as the CFTC/CFTD.[112] The commissions relied primarily on information supplied by the most powerful business associations in order to make recommendations to the CGP, giving big business an active role over planning and in plotting future economic performance. In exchange, it profited from state largesse in the way of investment and subsidies to ensure that performance targets were met. "Rather than regulating the industries for which they ha[d] direct responsibility," as Ezra Suleiman put it, "[administrative] agencies or *directions* ... became the spokesmen or lawyers for the industries."[113]

---

[110] Ehrmann, *Organized Business in France*, 253.

[111] This fact was especially underscored by the dearth of sectoral representatives for small business within the commissions during the earliest and, many would argue, most crucial stage of postwar planning. The Monnet and Hirsch plans, which spanned almost the entire duration of the Fourth Republic, featured no artisanal representation whatever. One would have to wait for the Third Plan (1957–61) for artisans to be consulted in planning following the creation of a special Commission de l'artisanat for them to offer their input. In practice, this body remained largely symbolic, with only nominal importance being accorded to its recommendations. Ibid., 260, and Zdatny, *Politics*, 178.

[112] Stephen Cohen's analysis of the socioprofessional backgrounds of the members of the modernization commissions for the Third Plan captures this imbalance between the representatives of advanced sectors and small business. Whereas businessmen – among whom only a tiny proportion represented SMEs – accounted for 206 of their members, civil servants (136), bankers (13), and "technical experts" (134), all of whom could be safely regarded as proponents of economic growth, accounted for 283. If one added to this tally the 57 trade unionists and 66 persons classified as "miscellaneous" (and among whom artisans featured), it could fairly be concluded that *petits patrons* and *indépendants* were greatly underrepresented in the modernization commissions compared to their actual – if declining – weight in the economy. Zdatny, *Politics*, 178.

[113] *Politics, Power and Bureaucracy in France* (Princeton: Princeton University Press, 1974), 340. Indeed, that the mechanisms of the *économie concertée* and of planning could be thus hijacked is underscored by the organizational muscle exerted by big business organizations over the ministerial administrations that were supposed to watch over them. For example, the Ministry of Industry officially commissioned the National Steel Association and its marketing associate, the Comptoir sidérurgique, to oversee planning for the steel industry. With a combined staff of 750 employees compared to the dozen civil servants manning the ministerial *direction technique* charged with overseeing this sector, it should hardly be surprising that the latter became increasingly dependent on the former in making planning recommendations concerning future steel outputs. Extrapolating from this example, it is easy to imagine that such a symbiotic

In reality, whatever influence was gained by *petits indépendants* from their participation in these consultative bodies was nullified by the downgrading of the latter in the policy-making and planning processes. The fact that, particularly in dirigisme's early stages, the Administration d'État exercised direct control over key nationalized sectors greatly reduced the need for it to consult the various sectoral and social actors. Likewise, its increasing recourse to "controls on bank credit, foreign exchange, trade, raw materials, and prices" to meet planning targets effectively cut the mechanisms of social concertation out of the planning process.[114] In consequence, the most powerful trade association officials came to treat the Economic Council and the modernization commissions with "cool detachment" because the state administration felt increasingly justified in bypassing these bodies to orchestrate its policies.[115]

The fact that the state administration was making its principal planning decisions beyond the purview of the official mechanisms of the *économie concertée* rendered informal forms of interest intermediation essential to the determination of policy. Small business interests found themselves in effect frozen out of this kind of interaction and consultation, their formal "participation in advisory committees [being]," as Ehrmann observed at the time, "usually their only means of expressing their views to the administration."[116] Of particular importance were the personal connections cultivated by business representatives with the *directions techniques* of the ministerial administrations charged with overseeing a particular branch of industry. These connections were almost the exclusive preserve of spokesmen for the most powerful trade associations, representing the largest or most advanced sectors, such as engineering, electrical power, or steel.[117] In turn, these connections bred enduring institutional solidarities and cultural identifications between big business representatives and their contacts in the *haute fonction publique*. At a practical level, the former relied on the latter for setting the planning priorities on which the prosperity of their industries depended, while the latter depended on the former for the information without which planning was impossible. This mutual reliance brought business leaders and *hauts fonctionnaires* to evolve similar perspectives on economic and social questions, resulting in their shared espousal of a technocratic mind-set that shunned Malthusianism and "favor[ed] economic growth, large-scale enterprise, international competitiveness and the pursuit of innovation."[118] Likewise,

relationship between a powerful business organization and its affiliated administrative *direction* could emerge in other important sectors. Ehrmann, *Organized Business in France*, 262.
[114] Kuisel, *Capitalism*, 227–8.
[115] Ehrmann, *Organized Business in France*, 260.
[116] Ibid.
[117] Many of these informal relationships extended all the way back to the First World War and then were greatly strengthened under the Vichy-era *comités d'organisation*. Ibid., 258–62.
[118] Hall, *Governing the Economy*, 162. These institutional and cultural solidarities were reinforced by educational and social affinities shared by the leaders of big business and high civil servants. In particular, the overwhelming majority of the managers from the most advanced firms in the private sector had issued from top state engineering schools such as the École polytechnique and the École des mines, where they internalized the same technocratic mind-set that prevailed at the

it was under the Fourth Republic that the trend of *pantouflage* – the movement of high civil servants from the state administration into managerial posts in leading private firms – emerged in earnest. The crossover of personnel between the public and private sectors reinforced the development of a technocratic mind-set on the part of industry leaders and members of the state administration, accelerating further the impetus toward economic and social modernization.[119]

The emergence of these institutional and cultural affinities between the leaders of big business and the high echelons of the state administration accentuated the widening gap between these two groups on the one hand and traditional employers and *petits indépendants* on the other. It attested to the development of what one author described as a "divided economy" in which small producers found themselves increasingly isolated economically and socially from the rest of French society.[120] The socioprofessional and socioeconomic constituencies – including labor – that made up the latter had a stake in the development of a rationalistic and efficient industrial capitalism, based on the Fordist principles of higher pay for wage earners and greater profits for the firms that employed them. Accordingly, as the Fourth Republic ran its course, *petits indépendants* fell out with the socioeconomic constituencies that had been their erstwhile allies. This growing schism between advanced and backward groups was prominently underscored by the failure to reconstitute the broad middle class and interpatronal alliance that had characterized the interwar period, particularly following the Popular Front. Social and political relations between these groups had become so fraught that they precluded any durable entente between them.

In short, the tensions between the most advanced and backward fractions of the *patronat* – tensions that, as we saw in the previous chapters, had long been latent in French society – assumed a permanent, almost irremediable character under the Fourth Republic, effectively ruling out any return to the modus vivendi that had previously obtained between them. Whereas leading firms had in the past tolerated and even encouraged the Malthusian habits of small enterprises – not least because the higher market prices of the latter meant greater profits for them – by the 1950s these enterprises were generally seen in advanced circles to be a drag on the economy, the costs of which were disproportionately borne by the modern sector.[121] This shift in the attitude of big business in turn led it to disagree with small business over a slew of economic and social issues, attesting to the growing irreconcilability of their respective roles and outlooks.

École nationale d'administration (ÉNA), charged with training the country's *hauts fonctionnaires*. Kuisel, *Capitalism*, 255–6, and Ehrmann, *Organized Business in France*, 263–5.

[119] Underscoring the increased interpenetration between the high civil service and the private sector, a survey of the entering ÉNA class of 1952 found that fully 60% of students in the new *promotion* were preparing to enter the high civil service in order to eventually obtain high managerial posts in the private sector. On the growth of this trend during the Fourth Republic, see Ehrmann, *Organized Business in France*, 263–72.

[120] Ibid., 320.

[121] Cf. Sawyer, "Strains in the Social Structure of Modern France."

Such a rift was most visibly crystallized in the organizational conflicts between the CNPF, as the representative of big business, and the CGPME and ephemeral groups representing *petits patrons* and *petits indépendants*.[122]

Tensions between the CNPF and CGPME emerged in a number of policy areas. In the first place, they disagreed over tax and financial issues, the CNPF advocating equalizing the tax burden between large and small businesses, calling in particular for the repeal of the tax protections afforded to marginal producers historically.[123] Predictably, the CGPME and other small business advocates fought such proposals tooth and nail. As we saw, the introduction of the VAT in 1954 provoked the particular ire of petty producers and tradesmen, convincing many among them to abandon institutionalized political means for Pierre Poujade's UDCA. Similarly, antagonism between large and small business came to a head over other economic matters, such as the CNPF's lobbying to introduce more stringent creditor protections and bankruptcy provisions for French businesses.[124] Officially presented as a way of restoring market competition and improving the overall operation of the economy, the CNPF's real motive in pursuing this initiative was to unclog the nation's commercial and productive apparatus by driving small marginal firms out of business.

Third, disagreement between the advocates of large and small business extended to the area of social legislation. Whereas more advanced firms were willing to tolerate greater worker participation in the running of their firms through the *comités d'entreprises* (CEs), small business representatives, starting with the CGPME, viewed the CEs and the expansion of worker participation as an unacceptable infringement on employers' authority. This conflict over postwar social reforms reflected the stark contrast between the consensus-seeking, technocratic outlook characterizing progressive large employers and

[122] At first sight, this might seem a contradictory development, since the CNPF had been originally created as an inclusive umbrella organization incorporating the diverse factions of French business. In order to guarantee the representation of small business, its bylaws stipulated that 75 out of the 500 seats composing its national council would be reserved for representatives of small business, with the understanding that these would go to delegates from the CGPME. Yet, despite this formal representation within the CNPF, the CGPME remained an organizationally and politically independent entity, free to develop and pursue its own orientations and goals. Consequently, as the interests of the advanced and Malthusian fractions of business progressively diverged, and they began to pursue increasingly conflicting policy agendas, the CNPF evolved into the officious spokesman for big business while the CGPME in effect remained the exclusive representative of *petits patrons*, foreshadowing their formal schism in the late 1960s. Ehrmann, *Organized Business in France*, 451.
[123] Accordingly, the CNPF judged "inadmissible" the fiscal situation that obtained in the early 1950s whereby the tax rates on business profits varied from between 10% for artisans to 34% for large corporations. Ibid., 313.
[124] Specifically, Georges Villiers, the head of the CNPF from 1945 into the 1960s, had called for "a bankruptcy and liquidation mechanism" to be established "which would make possible the rapid elimination of firms that are unable to meet their obligations," a prescription that predictably aroused the hostility of *petits indépendants* throughout the country. Quoted in Hoffmann, *Mouvement Poujade*, 323.

the patrimonial view of employer-employee relations characteristic of *petits patrons*.[125]

Finally, the organizational representatives of big and small business were increasingly divided on the issue of trade liberalization and, in particular, European economic integration. Initially, the CNPF had joined the CGPME in opposing European integration by lobbying against the establishment of the ECSC in 1951.[126] A few years later, both expressed reservations regarding the creation of the EEC, which stipulated the phasing in of free trade among its members. However, the positive experience of trade liberalization, which expanded the market opportunities available to larger firms, caused the CNPF to reverse course and embrace European economic integration. Big business became increasingly convinced that it was economically undesirable to protect all firms within a closed domestic market. In contrast, because of its negative impact on smaller firms, the CGPME remained implacably opposed to European trade liberalization. Because many of the smaller enterprises that went out of business following the establishment of the EEC were bought out and incorporated into larger advanced firms, the CGPME and other small business organizations not only viewed European trade as inimical to the interests of small producers but increasingly suspected big business of supporting it so it could profit from their demise.[127]

The conflicts opposing the representatives of advanced and traditional business on economic and social issues in turn underscored the great divide that separated them regarding the structures and methods of dirigisme that were adopted under the Fourth Republic. The CNPF generally supported greater state control and intervention in the economy if it stimulated growth and economic rationalization. Conversely, small producer groups remained staunchly opposed to *étatisme*. Similarly, the CNPF accepted on the whole the establishment of a "mixed" economy and a comprehensive welfare state, whereas the CGPME persisted in viewing them as socialism in another guise. Thus, by the end of the Fourth Republic, substantial conceptual and policy differences had arisen between small and big business that rendered difficult, if not impossible, a return to the collaborative relations of the past. The worsening antagonism between these interests would henceforth dominate intrasectoral relations within the French business community, eventually coming to a head with the petty producer and shopkeeper revolt of the late 1960s and early 1970s.

At the same time, the Fourth Republic also marked the definitive break between the new and the old middle classes, which only two decades before had united against the Popular Front. New middle-class strata, particularly *cadres* associated

---

[125] Ehrmann, *Organized Business in France*, 450–1.

[126] On French business's debate regarding European economic integration in this early period, see ibid., 401–19.

[127] On the divergence of views that separated the representatives of big and small business regarding the establishment of the EEC, see Jean Bunel and Jean Saglio, *L'action patronale. Du CNPF au petit patron* (Paris: PUF, 1979), 51–2, as well as Lefranc, *Les organisations patronales en France*, 154.

with the most dynamic branches of industry, were increasingly perceived by the traditional middle classes as a threat to their political interests and economic well-being. This antagonism between the new and old fractions of the middle class was starkly underlined by the rapid disintegration of the Comité national de liaison et d'action des classes moyennes (CNCM), which had been established in 1947 to fight for the repeal of the Social Security system introduced in 1945–6. Reminiscent of the Popular Front–era Confédération génerale des syndicats des classes moyennes, the CNCM strove to unify the organizational representatives of *cadres* (CGC), small employers and shopkeepers (CGPME), artisans (Confédération nationale de l'artisanat et des métiers, CNAM), peasants (Fédération française de l'agriculture), and members of the liberal professions (Union nationale des professions libérales) to overturn the new social security law.[128] However, the movement fell apart once exemptions were granted to the *cadres* and individual categories of *indépendants* who would be allowed to establish their own, sectoral social security programs. Thus, far from reproducing the durable and broad-based middle-class alliance of the 1930s, the CNCM was condemned to remain a single-issue movement that, once the issue that gave rise to it was addressed, became unsustainable. Representing the last attempt to create a holistic middle-class movement before the late 1970s, the collapse of the CNCM attested to the insuperable differences that were emerging within the French middle classes as the process of modernization gained momentum and variably impacted their different constituencies.[129]

In sum, by the close of the Fourth Republic, *petits indépendants* were increasingly isolated from their former employer and middle-class allies and found themselves in a much weaker economic and political position than on the eve of World War II. As an indication of their sociopolitical isolation, the only group with whom they consistently made common cause during this period was small agricultural producers, a constituency whose position was even more precarious than theirs. Their economic and political weakness was compounded by the internal divisions among *petits indépendants'* organizational representatives, which diminished even further their ability to influence policy. The artisanal movement was splintered among no less than four ideologically distinct inter-professional confederations, while both artisans and shopkeepers were fractured among a slew of sectoral organizations pursuing divergent economic and social aims.[130] Given this multiplicity of interests and groups, it was hardly surprising that *petits indépendants* were unable to arrive at a cogent economic and political

---

[128] See Mayer, "Classes moyennes," 740.

[129] Indeed, the next such attempt at creating a broad class alliance encompassing both the traditional and the new middle classes would come with the equally short-lived Groupes initiative et responsabilité (GIR) that was constituted in an effort to forestall the victory of the Socialist-Communist coalition in the 1978 parliamentary and 1981 presidential elections. Ibid., 641–2, and S. Berger, "D'une boutique à l'autre," 134–5.

[130] These included the Confédération générale de l'artisanat français, the only artisanal confederation to survive the war and which was close to the Radical Party, the Confédération nationale de

program to present to policy makers. Similarly, conflicts between larger and smaller *petits patrons* – that is, between the owners of small and medium-sized enterprises and self-employed artisans and shopkeepers – also detracted from small business's ability to punch its demographic weight policywise.[131]

With their interests left unaddressed by the state and feeling poorly represented by their traditional parties and organizations, it is no wonder that *petits indépendants* resorted to extrainstitutional forms of action to be heard. From this perspective, the Poujadist explosion of the mid-1950s is revealing of the extent of *petit indépendant* anxiety and frustration under the Fourth Republic. Yet, the cause of this decline was not so much to be traced to explicit policies that targeted this constituency for extinction but rather to the inexorable process of economic and social modernization. Comparing the situation of *petits indépendants* under the Fourth Republic to their relative prosperity under the Third, Zdatny has written:

> The Fourth Republic was nominally less solicitous of *petits indépendants* than the Third Republic had been. The real difference, however, lay less in the political system than in the world around it; that is, in the accelerated development of the French economy. The absence of positive state action in favor of [shopkeepers and] artisans now meant, not Malthusian drift, but modernization.[132]

In this sense, the Fourth Republic proved a critical transition in modern French social and political history because it presided over, in Hoffmann's phrase, "the liquidation of the stalemate society."[133]

At a first and most obvious level, the Fourth Republic oversaw fundamental changes in the country's economic and social system. By the end of its tenure, an increasingly differentiated and specialized economy had emerged, which was managed by technocrats in both the public and private sectors. This new economy was characterized by the spread of an advanced sector that functionally distinguished between management and ownership of the firm. As we saw, the

l'artisanat, the reincarnation of the traditionalist Confédération de l'artisanat familial of the 1930s, the Confédération générale unifiée de l'artisanat, which was close to the PCF and the CGT, and the Confédération nationale de l'artisanat et des métiers, a new interprofessional formation that shunned politics to focus on bread-and-butter issues. The principal sectoral organizations of artisans under the Fourth Republic were the Confédération nationale des artisans ruraux, the Confédération de l'artisanat et des petites entreprises du bâtiment, and the Confédération générale de l'alimentation du détail. Zarca, *L'artisanat français*, 70, and Zdatny, *Politics*, 164–6, 177.

[131] For example, while the value-added tax was virulently opposed by shopkeepers and artisans, larger firms within the small business sector welcomed the latter on the grounds that it instituted greater fairness between them by lessening the potential for tax fraud among the most marginal producers and traders. By the same token, the CGPME's defense of the VAT discredited it in the eyes of many *petits indépendants*, bringing a large number of them to desert the confederation and further diminishing its ability to influence policy. Ehrmann, *Organized Business in France*, 183–4, 312.

[132] *Politics*, 179.

[133] "Paradoxes," 60.

state played a central role in this transformation, forcing the private sector to abandon Malthusianism through incentives and constraints imposed by dirigiste planners, as well as the competition of an increasingly efficient and rationalized public sector.

In the face of this advanced sector, self-employed *petits indépendants* and traditional family firms traumatized by their economic and social demotion remained increasingly marginal and vulnerable. As Hoffmann surmised, the latter experienced "a genuine fall within the value system of the old society to which they ha[d] remained faithful."[134] The trauma of this demotion was exacerbated by the feeling of the traditional middle classes that the strata that they considered inferior to them – industrial workers in particular – had overtaken them as a result of the material and social advantages extended by the postwar state. The new social laws had eroded the socioeconomic standing of *petits indépendants* relative to industrial workers, while reducing their traditional authority as *patrons*. In this sense, the extensive labor unrest that punctuated the immediate postwar period and flared up episodically throughout the course of the Fourth Republic deepened the rift between the advanced state and business sectors, which were often disposed to meet the demands of labor, and patrimonial employers, who equated such concessions with the financial and moral collapse of their firms. Thus, as Hoffmann observed, France in the 1950s experienced "at the same time the quarrels of an industrial society and those of industrialization."[135] It was *petits indépendants* and *petits patrons* who, alongside marginal farmers, principally lost out from this process.

Predictably, these strata blamed their elected representatives and organizational spokesmen for failing to arrest their economic and social decline. Many of them grew consequently ambivalent in their attitude to the republican state, which they accused of betraying the ideal of small producer democracy that underpinned their political worldview. The inevitable result was a weakened commitment of *petits indépendants* to democracy *tout court*. When combined with the misoneistic and authoritarian potentialities of the cultural model of *indépendance*, their ambivalence toward the democratic state made them ready recruits for populist movements of protest that projected the reestablishment of a preindustrial, petty-property-based social order. Ultimately, such a backward-looking vision would be paired, under the aegis of the Front National, with an exclusive conception of national identity, the radical Right providing *petits indépendants* with a scapegoat to blame for their economic and social decline.

[134] Ibid., 65–6.
[135] Ibid., 67.

7

The Age of Decline

Petits Indépendants *under the Fifth Republic*

Notre pays ne peut s'accommoder de lui-même à l'intérieur et compter à l'extérieur que si son activité est accordée à son époque. À l'ère industrielle, il doit être industriel. À l'ère de la compétition, il doit être compétitif. À l'ère de la science et de la technique, il doit cultiver la recherche. Mais, pour produire beaucoup, pour le faire à des conditions qui facilitent les échanges, pour renouveler constamment par l'invention ce qu'il fabrique dans ses usines et récolte dans ses champs, il lui faut se transformer à mesure et profondément.

Comment, étant qui je suis, ne serais-je pas ému et soucieux en voyant s'estomper cette société campagnarde, installée depuis toujours dans ses constantes occupations et encadrée par ses traditions; ce pays des villages immuables, des églises anciennes, des familles solides, de l'éternel retour des labours, des semailles et des moissons...; cette France millénaire, que sa nature, son activité, son génie, avaient faite essentiellement rurale?

Charles de Gaulle, *Mémoires d'espoir. Le renouveau*[1]

The Fifth Republic that was established by General de Gaulle in 1958 saw the intensification and, in a certain sense, the culmination of the process of economic and social development initiated during the Fourth Republic. It presided over the fruition of a modernization strategy whose origins could be traced back to Vichy and the Liberation, but which was fully set in motion under the previous regime. At a first level, the Fifth Republic completed the transformation of the nation's economy into a more rationalized and efficient whole and oversaw the renovation of French industry and commerce. Second, the presidential regime installed by de Gaulle increased the efficiency of the republican state by endowing it with the means to drive the country down the path of modernity and prosperity. Capturing this intensified modernizing vocation, Stanley Hoffmann observed: "Starting from the common aspirations of the Liberation era, what the Fourth Republic set in motion but could not keep on course [was] pursued relentlessly by the Fifth."[2]

---

[1] *Mémoires* (Paris: Gallimard, Coll. de la Pléiade, 2000), 996, 1016.
[2] "Conclusion: The Impact of the Fifth Republic on France," in *The Fifth Republic at Twenty*, ed. W. G. Andrews and S. Hoffmann (Albany: SUNY Press, 1981), 456.

By the same token, the intensification of the process of state-led moderniza-tion and the institutional transformation of the state bred new social and political complications that marred the nation's progression toward a stable and harmonious modernity. Indeed, the changes over which the Fifth Republic presided occasioned new social and political conflicts that unsettled the regime. Perhaps more than any other social stratum, *petits indépendants* were often at the center of these conflicts. Though indisputably the principal losers – along with small farmers – of the modernization process that reached its zenith during the 1960s, they proved more resilient than state planners anticipated and certainly more tenacious than their dwindling numbers suggested. In turn, their temporary political resurgence in the early 1970s prepared the ground for the renewed sociopolitical disillusionment of *petits indépendants* at the end of the decade, thus setting the stage for their embrace of the Front National in the 1980s and 1990s.

PETITS INDÉPENDANTS IN THE RÉPUBLIQUE GAULLIENNE

Ces grands commis du secteur privé appartiennent à des hiérarchies qui sont encore capitalistes, mais qui pourraient, du jour au lendemain, devenir collecti-vistes sans que cela porte atteinte ni à leur autorité ni aux avantages matériels dont ils disposent. Sortis des mêmes écoles, ayant reçu une formation identique à celle des grands cadres de l'administration, ils n'ont plus de véritables préoccupations capitalistes, mais des préoccupations de carrière ou de spéculation. Détenteur essentiellement des formes les plus concentrées de la production ou de la distribution, ils n'ont plus les mêmes réflexes que ceux du "patronat réel" dont ils assurent pourtant la "représentation" en raison même des postes-clés qu'ils occupent dans les secteurs encore privés, mais dont ils remplissent de moins en moins la fonction au fur à mesure que l'on s'éloigne du moment ou l'affaire est passée du "réel" au "financier." ... Ces deux patronats qui doivent coexister dans une société moderne s'attirent et se repoussent. Ils ont l'un et l'autre leurs grandeurs et leurs faiblesses; et il importe pour des raison d'équilibre que le patronat du "management" reste à sa place et que le patronat "réel," en continuant à assurer ses fonctions, garde à la société son caractère humain. Léon Gingembre, President of the Confédération générale des petites et moyennes entreprises[3]

The economic and political reforms introduced during the opening decade of the Fifth Republic held significant implications for *petits indépendants*. In the eco-nomic realm, the advent of the Gaullist regime signaled notable shifts in the state-led modernization program initiated by its predecessor. Foremost among them was an updating of dirigisme that moved away from purely indicative planning toward a more liberal, market-based paradigm in which the state acted to facilitate rather than direct economic concentration and rationalization. In the words of one observer, by the end of the Fifth (1965–70) and Sixth (1970–5)

---

[3] Quoted in Lefranc, *Les organisations patronales en France*, 214.

plans, "the state had abandoned its traditional role of directing the economy, limiting itself to facilitating economic concentration, respect for free competition, and the conquest of external markets."[4]

This evolution also coincided with an expansion in the scope of planning. Throughout the 1960s, the latter came to be seen as the practical *sine qua non* of national modernization.[5] Planning outgrew its narrow purview during the Fourth Republic – where it had been limited to allocating investment and clearing industrial bottlenecks – to preside over more global objectives and processes. By the time the Fifth Plan was being prepared in the early 1960s, the Planning Commission was envisioning increasingly comprehensive programs for allocating resources and stimulating output across a growing array of sectors.[6] This development was facilitated by the growth of INSEE, which began to accumulate substantial time-sequence data and derived increasingly sophisticated economic models from them.[7]

In turn, the province of planning was expanded from overseeing the functioning of the economy to addressing broader infrastructural and social needs. This shift reflected a concern that the previous fifteen years of dirigisme had encouraged rapid growth but not been accompanied by an improvement in the prosperity of the general population.[8] In order to alleviate subsisting material deprivations and reduce wealth inequality, planning in the sixties and seventies

---

[4] Pierre Birnbaum, *Les sommets de l'État: essai sur l'élite du pouvoir en France*, 2nd ed. (Paris: Seuil, 1994), 123. This liberal – or, in Kuisel's terminology, neoliberal – shift in the nature of planning coincided with the replacement of the technocratic modernizer Michel Debré by the more classically liberal Georges Pompidou as de Gaulle's premier and the installation of Valéry Giscard-d'Estaing as finance minister in 1962. Standing in contrast to its domineering role in setting growth targets and allocating investment under the Monnet Plan, this orientation furthered the evolution of the state toward the more supportive and complementary economic role first adumbrated by the Hirsch Plan in the mid-1950s. *Capitalism*, 248–9, 266.

[5] Reflecting the productivist goals that underlay it, de Gaulle himself cast economic expansion as a supreme national duty demanding discipline and abnegation from the French people – a duty enshrined in the "ardent obligation" of the plan. Quoted in Volkmar Lauber, "The Gaullist Model of Economic Modernization," in Andrews and Hoffmann, *The Fifth Republic at Twenty*, 228.

[6] This expansion was reflected in the increase in the number of modernization commissions that assisted planners in defining the priorities and setting the targets within the individual economic sectors. Whereas in 1946, only ten modernization commissions, accounting for 494 persons, had been formed to prepare the Monnet Plan, by 1963 the number of commissions had grown more than threefold to thirty-two, enlisting the participation of 1,950 sectoral and organizational representatives and administrative personnel in preparing the Fifth Plan. Hall, *Governing the Economy*, 141.

[7] Ibid., 145–6.

[8] For example, French workers still endured the longest workweek in Europe, while the country presented the most unequal income distribution on the continent. Similarly, underscoring the persistent material backwardness of much of the population, still only one in every seven French people had a telephone and only half of the housing units in Paris had their own toilets in the early 1960s. De Gaulle himself privileged the imperative of national growth, even if achieved inequitably, over the attainment of individual prosperity for the greatest number of Frenchmen. Thus, he wrote that "the aim of the struggle for prosperity was not so much to make life more comfortable for such and such a category of Frenchmen as to build up the wealth, the power and

increasingly reflected social priorities, incorporating prescriptions to upgrade the nation's social infrastructure as well as improve the welfare safety net. In short, by the end of the 1960s, the focus of planning had shifted away from simply enhancing productivity and increasing output to addressing basic quality-of-life issues that had emerged as the foremost preoccupation of most French people.[9]

Finally, the third goal of planning in the opening decade of the Fifth Republic was to enhance the international competitiveness of French industry. To this end, an activist industrial policy based on a mix of targeted investments and fiscal and monetary measures to build up advanced sectors was adopted, and trade restrictions were lifted to make leading firms competitive in the international marketplace. Reaching its apogee under the Fifth and Sixth plans, the goal of this strategy was "the establishment or reinforcement ... of a small number of firms or groups of international size ... in most industrial sectors. ... The number of these groups [was to] be very small, often even reduced to one or two."[10] The main effect of this "national champions" policy was to streamline the French industrial and commercial structure by encouraging the disappearance of smaller firms or their absorption by larger ones. Accordingly, a significant increase in the number of mergers was recorded after 1958, resulting in the emergence of mammoth enterprises often explicitly supported by the state.[11] This trend peaked between 1962 and 1970 during the Fourth and Fifth plans, when the average number of mergers doubled every year.[12] In the 1960s, then, economic planning became the province of an increasingly insulated technocratic elite that equated its mandate with a superior national interest that

the greatness of France as a whole." Ibid., 147, and Lauber, "The Gaullist Model of Economic Modernization," 228.

[9] Accordingly, the Fourth Plan (1962–5) outlined a school and hospital building program, while the Fifth placed a strong emphasis on rationalizing the social security system, as well as a sweeping overhaul of the university system to refurbish and expand the country's decaying and overcrowded *facultés*. Hall, *Governing the Economy*, 147.

[10] Ibid., 149. The principal sectors targeted by this policy were situated in advanced and heavy industrial fields, including aluminum, steel, mechanical and electrical engineering, electronics, motor cars, aircraft, chemicals, and pharmaceutical products. See also Bela Balassa, "The French Economy under the Fifth Republic, 1958–1978," in Andrews and Hoffmann, *The Fifth Republic at Twenty*, 207.

[11] Foremost among these were Pechiney-Ugine-Kuhlmann, Saint-Gobain-Pont-à-Mousson, Thomson-CSF, Agache-Willot, and Dassault. Hall, *Governing the Economy*, 149.

[12] According to Balassa, the total value of assets accounted for by these mergers grew exponentially from an average of 85 million francs during the 1950s to 1 billion francs in 1965 and 5 billion francs in 1970. This explosion in merger asset values was accompanied by a drastic increase in firm size. Between 1962 and 1968, the average number of workers per plant employing more than fifty workers rose from 215 to 250, with most of this increase attributable to the expansion of the largest firms. In particular, the proportion of firms employing more than 10 workers to those which counted more than 1,000 workers increased by approximately 20%. At the same time, the share of plants numbering between 50 and 100 workers declined as a proportion of total employment, while those employing more than 500 workers increased. For these figures as well as those pertaining to merger asset values, see Balassa, "The French Economy under the Fifth Republic," 207.

transcended particularistic interests and groups within French society. In practice, this rationalizing and productivist agenda increased the size of the most
advanced sectors while driving unprecedented numbers of *petits indépendants*
and *petit patrons* out of business.

At a second level, the dirigisme of the early Fifth Republic attempted to restore
the conditions of market competition throughout the economy. To support this
orientation, the state enacted a number of liberalizing measures, particularly in
the commercial sector.[13] As a first step, in March 1960 it issued the Fontanet
Circular, which made it illegal for commercial establishments to refuse sale to a
customer and criminalized discriminatory pricing.[14] More significantly, this
measure authorized the granting of rebates by suppliers to retailers who took
on large orders, a practice fiercely resisted by shopkeepers because it allowed
large retailers to sell their merchandise at lower prices to theirs and still reap a
profit.[15] In May 1962 the government promulgated the Jeanneney Decree,
which liberalized access to the artisanal trades. Reflecting the desire of planners
to facilitate entry into the "closed" professions, this decree abrogated the long-
standing qualification restrictions that governed artisanal installation.[16] In sum,
by exposing shopkeepers and artisans to greater competition, the Gaullist regime
hoped to force them either to adapt to the demands of the market or to disappear
altogether. In the words of one commentator, it "remained committed to a
forward-looking outlook according to which all the forms of modern commerce
would be free to develop."[17]

Third, the adaptation of planning and use of regulation to promote a more
liberal economy was supported by a complementary set of macroeconomic
policies. At the level of monetary policy, these liberal ambitions became apparent with the Rueff stabilization plan of 1958. Confronted with spiraling
inflation, a bulging balance-of-payments deficit, and unsustainable pressure

---

[13] The Gaullist regime displayed such liberalizing intentions from the start, commissioning a special
committee under the orthodox liberal economists Louis Armand and Jacques Rueff to study how
economic efficiency could be improved and suggest measures for "removing the obstacles to
expansion." Determined to identify and do away with the "rigidities affecting the economy" and
the "factors militating against true costs and prices," the Armand-Rueff committee advocated
lifting commercial restrictions protecting shopkeepers against competition from more concentrated forms of commerce, notably *magasins à prix unique* (nickel and dime stores). Caron,
Economic History, 310, and Birnbaum, *Sommets*, 127–8.

[14] The decree essentially reaffirmed principles previously laid down in the Laniel-Faure circular of
1953 but which had been largely unenforced as a result of pressure from small business groups.

[15] This issue arose when the first supermarkets opened in the 1950s, and traditional commercial
groups successfully pressured wholesalers to refuse to contract with these new large retailers,
arguing that their prices constituted a "source of disorder and disequilibrium." Keeler,
"Corporatist Decentralization," 268.

[16] However, the new decree did allow master artisans to retain their distinct titles of qualification in
order to distinguish themselves from practitioners who had not undergone either an apprenticeship or journeyman training. In addition, the title of master artisan was still required to be able to
train apprentices. Gresle, *Indépendants*, 108, 109, and Zarca, *L'artisanat français*, 104–5.

[17] Roy, *Les commerçants*, 119.

on the franc, the Rueff Plan imposed draconian austerity measures to restore monetary stability and devalued the franc by 20 percent to redress the external balance.[18] Its principal aim was to maintain the conditions of economic stability necessary for the government to pursue its renovation program. The reining in of inflation facilitated planning over the short and medium term by allowing the state and private actors to base their performance projections and investment decisions on the expectation of steady prices. At the same time, by raising the value of foreign exchange revenues and expanding profits, an "overdevalued" currency made more funds available to domestic firms for reinvestment while encouraging them to seek access to broader markets. In this sense, the Rueff Plan was more than just a contingent response to the economic crisis that faced the country at the inception of the Fifth Republic. It set the macroeconomic blueprint for the course of modernization that France was to follow through the 1960s.

Needless to say, the course of development sketched out by the Rueff Plan did not please all quarters of French society. Its restoration of economic competition and stability came at a high cost to certain sectors, foremost among them *petits indépendants* and *petits patrons*. In the short term, these strata were hurt by the curbing of the inflationary conditions from which they had more or less continuously benefited since the war. In the longer term, as a constituency that was, in the phrase of one observer, "nostalgic for an irrational past," they were the principal victims of the process of economic rationalization abetted by the new stabilization policy.[19]

In turn, as the economy settled into a sustained pattern of inflation-free growth, the regime also pursued an activist credit policy geared to encouraging industrial and commercial consolidation. Because the Bank of France frequently rediscounted loans contracted by banks to enterprises, it exerted considerable discretion over lending to firms. Consequently, once the Bank of France fell under the direct supervision of the Finance Ministry, the state was able to effectively control the channeling of credit to particular sectors and firms.[20] At the same time, the state leveraged its control over nationalized banks into investment strategies favoring economic rationalization. For example, under prodding from the regime, the Société Générale and Crédit Lyonnais constituted the Union Immobilière in the early 1960s to fund the construction of supermarkets and other *grandes surfaces*.[21] In effect, by consolidating its influence over the provision of credit, the Gaullist state significantly accelerated the dynamic of industrial and commercial concentration, threatening growing numbers of *petits indépendants* with insolvency.

[18] Chief among these austerity measures were deep cuts in government spending and the temporary abandonment of wage indexation. Balassa, "The French Economy under the Fifth Republic," 211–12.
[19] Lauber, "The Gaullist Model of Economic Modernization," 229.
[20] Hall, *Governing the Economy*, 153.
[21] Birnbaum, *Sommets*, 128.

Likewise, the fiscal policies of the regime also furthered the objective of economic rationalization, particularly in commerce. In the first place, a series of tax initiatives favorable to large retailers and unfavorable to the *petit commerce* were introduced by the government in 1959.[22] The 1960 Fontanet Circular added to these measures, further lightening the tax burden on large enterprises while tightening the guidelines on *petits indépendants*.[23] Finally, *petits indépendants* were subjected throughout the 1960s to a bevy of fiscal reforms that ran counter to their interests. Of particular significance was the tax reform of 1965 that revised the commercial tax code to the benefit of retailers operating on small margins, that is, large retailers, such as supermarkets and department stores, which could afford to charge lower prices because of their higher sales volumes. Likewise, the reform of the VAT meant that all retail outlets paid a nationally set VAT based on their profit margins (i.e., the difference between the supply price paid by the retailer and the selling price charged to the customer), whereas in the past the latter had been locally determined and based on "sales turnover, irrespective of profits."[24] In short, the fiscal burden on larger enterprises and particularly on concentrated retail firms was considerably lightened by the end of the decade, while the opposite was true for *petits commerçants* and artisans.[25] Predictably, this became a source of frustration and resentment for *petits indépendants*. These new tax obligations also contributed to the decline in the number of shopkeepers and artisans in this period, since they spelled economic doom for the most marginal among them.

The updating of dirigisme during the first decade of the Fifth Republic, impressing upon it a broader scope to modernize the country and an increasing recourse to interventionist policy to spur economic rationalization, lay the institutional and regulative foundation for the emergence of a Fordist economic system in France. Deriving its name from the model of industrial organization

---

[22] These included suppressing the higher *patente* regime that applied to chain stores, as well as phasing out the turnover tax based on the *forfait* – a system based on the declaration, and hence substantial underreporting, of earnings by retailers – in favor of a new regime based on the objective estimation of earnings. Similarly, a complementary tax of 9% was levied on industrial and commercial profits (which was subsequently reduced to 8% in 1960 and 6% by 1970), a charge much more easily acquitted by large enterprises than marginal firms operating at a subsistence level. Ibid. and Roy, *Les commerçants*, 93.

[23] Most notably, the circular suspended the "double *patente*" regime based on store size and sales specialties that dated back to the end of the nineteenth century, in effect reducing the *patente* dues owed by larger retailers. By contrast, the extension of the value-added tax (VAT) to all categories of commerce and industry disproportionately affected shopkeepers and artisans by forcing them to maintain accounts for inspection by the authorities, thereby substantially constraining their capacity to underreport their earnings and lessen their tax obligations. Birnbaum, *Sommets*, 128.

[24] Keeler, "Corporatist Decentralization," 268.

[25] According to one estimate, the *patente* rates to which shopkeepers and larger artisans – the smallest artisans still being dispensed from having to pay the *patente* under the regime of the *artisan fiscal* – were increased by 325.5% from 1958 to 1968. Similarly, the revenues attributable to the *patente* shot up dramatically from 1.3 billion francs in 1958 to 5.8 billion francs in 1968. In that year, these were equivalent to 26.4% of the total revenues generated by income taxes, 11.3% of those generated by the VAT, and fully 57% of corporate tax revenues. Ibid.

conceived by Henry Ford during the 1920s, Fordism represented a self-enclosed economic system based on large-scale integrated and rationalized productive units employing a low-skilled work force drawn from a rapidly dwindling rural and *petit indépendant* sector. The system achieved self-sustenance by fueling internal demand for its own goods through a virtuous cycle of cheaper prices made possible by the increasingly efficient organization of production and integration of labor-saving technology and the consistently rising wage levels imputable to rising worker productivity.[26] The trend toward greater concentration implied by this system of industrial organization, combined with the opening of formerly protected sectors to domestic and international competition, condemned unprecedented numbers of petty producers and traders to economic ruin. Accordingly, many *petits indépendants* rejected the new regime incarnated by de Gaulle and blamed him for their rapid socioeconomic decline.

As a corollary to its modernizing agenda, the Gaullist regime also enacted a series of far-reaching institutional reforms that further alienated *petits indépendants* from the political system and elite. Chiefly, these expanded the technocratic core of the state in order to more effectively insulate it from social pressure in determining and implementing policy.[27] The upshot for *petits indépendants* was that they saw their political weight even more diminished than under the Fourth Republic. They became more powerless than ever to inflect the course of modernization and slow the program of rationalization and concentration that would be pursued by the state throughout the 1960s. The institutional reforms that were introduced in the early Fifth Republic were enacted at various levels of organization. First and most obviously, the establishment of a presidential system under the constitution of 1958 marked, under the guise of what one observer termed the "synthesis of democracy with efficiency," the displacement of the legislature by the executive as the fulcrum of national political power and decision making.[28] This shift was particularly evident in the area of economic policy making, the Fifth Republic constituting, as Hoffmann put it, "a regime carefully designed by its constitution to be capable of governing despite the divisions of the nation and [its] representatives."[29]

In turn, the new presidential system presented three innovations that diminished the influence of *petits indépendants* over policy making. First, the reduction of the powers of the parliament eroded the influence of the organizational representatives of small producers and shopkeepers, since it was in the National

---

[26] On the structure and workings of the Fordist model of capitalism, see notably the writings of the French Regulation school, in particular the work of the economic historians Robert Boyer and Michel Aglietta.

[27] According to Stanley Hoffmann, their principal purpose was to "provide France with a state that could pursue economic modernization and handle the resulting social costs with maximum efficiency and minimum friction." Conclusion in Andrews and Hoffmann, *The Fifth Republic at Twenty*, 450.

[28] Philip Cerny, "The Political Balance," in *French Politics and Public Policy*, ed. P. Cerny and M. Schain (London: Frances Pinter, 1980), 9.

[29] "Paradoxes," 93.

Assembly that sectoral and interprofessional groups such as the CGPME and APCMF (association of the presidents of the chambers of trades) wielded their greatest clout. At the same time, the nationalization of political competition under a presidential system, particularly following the popular election of the president beginning in 1965, spelled the end of the traditional, notable-based parties of the Third and Fourth Republics that pandered to *petits indépendants*. In effect, these parties were transformed from loose coalitions of localized interests and notables into highly centralized formations whose deputies were nationally recognized political figures with correlatively "national" prerogatives and concerns.

On the right and center right, the new Gaullist party, the Union pour la nouvelle république (UNR) (subsequently renamed Union des démocrates pour la république, or UDR, in 1968), displaced the old notable-based parties, representing, in the words of one historian, a "centralized, disciplined and well-financed party with the declared aim of consistent support for [de Gaulle's] government."[30] Unlike the former parties of the Right and the center Right, the UNR was so broadly based, drawing support from the "new" middle classes of white-collar workers and midlevel *cadres* as well as – particularly following de Gaulle's withdrawal of France from NATO – from labor, that it no longer needed to pander to traditional middle-class groups to remain in power. Indeed, by the late sixties, the Gaullist party represented a comprehensive cross section of professional and class groups, bringing one contemporary observer to remark that, of all the political formations, it most faithfully reproduced French society as a whole.[31] In short, its broad base of support enabled the UNR to pursue a modernizing agenda without having to worry about antagonizing the traditional middle classes.

Conversely, the institutional downgrading of the legislature and the parliamentary parties was accompanied by a strengthening of the state administration as the principal locus of policy making and implementation within the regime. This shift reinforced *petits indépendants'* political decline in several important respects. First, it signaled a discarding of the ideal of concertation that had characterized economic planning under the Fourth Republic, thus effectively spelling the end of the *économie concertée*. Small producers' already limited ability to inflect the planning process through the old modernization commissions (renamed industrialization commissions under the new regime) was nullified as their recommendations became nonbinding on the *hauts fonctionnaires*

---

[30] M. Anderson, *Conservative Politics*, 321.

[31] Jean Charlot, *Le phénomène Gaulliste* (Paris: Fayard, 1970), 68. In particular, as Charlot points out, the UNR/UDR was not greatly distinguishable from the parties of the Left, since it attracted poorer as well as richer voters, garnering 30% of the working-class vote in the first round of the January 1967 legislative elections (versus 49% for the parties of the Left) and 31% in the first round of the June 1968 legislative elections (versus 51% for the Left). Meanwhile, the UNR/UDR obtained as many votes among white-collar service employees and midlevel executives as the parties of the Left: 35% versus 40% in 1967, and 40% versus 36% in 1968. Ibid., 72. On the catchall social profile of Gaullism, see also Berger and Piore, *Dualism*, 115–16.

charged with planning.[32] When consultation was sought by planners, it was confined to a few oligopolistic firms and their trade associations, such as the department-store-dominated Conseil national du commerce or the organizational arm of the erstwhile Comité des forges, the UIMM. The Commissariat général du plan relied on these trade associations for the information on which to base its projections and decisions, thereby strengthening further the collaborative relationships and mutual dependencies that had developed between the state administration and the most powerful business organizations during the Fourth Republic.[33] In practice, the narrowing of economic consultation to representatives of the most advanced sectors and firms excluded the organizations representing small business from the planning process.

The dilution of parliamentary authority, combined with the circumventing of institutionalized mechanisms of sectoral concertation, heightened the importance of informal contacts and means of access to the Administration d'État in shaping economic policy. Accordingly, the influence of the most powerful business interests and firms increased even further, since such contacts depended most often on social and educational networks connecting firm managers and *hauts fonctionnaires*. As various authors have pointed out, a growing proportion of business leaders passed through *grandes écoles* such as Sciences-Po and l'ÉNA, or studied law, which meant that they underwent the same training and were inculcated with the same outlook as the high civil servants who oversaw the statist apparatus.[34] As Suleiman put it, a "clientele type of relationship" emerged between them "based on an informal system of communication [which] worked to the benefit of both sides."[35]

---

[32] Frank Wilson observes that "the government could, and often did, ignore the advice" of the Industrialization Commissions. *Interest-Group Politics in France* (Cambridge: Cambridge University Press, 1987), 97.

[33] In this respect, Birnbaum has noted that of the eighty-nine members who made up the industrialization commissions that assisted in the preparation of the Fifth and Sixth plans, sixty-four were employers or firm directors (CEOs), a vast majority of them affiliated with the largest or most advanced enterprises. See also Suleiman, *Politics, Power and Bureaucracy*, 339–40, and Birnbaum, *Sommets*, 134–5.

[34] Among leading employers, firm managers, and *hauts fonctionnaires*, we begin to see at this time a marked diminution in the influence of the traditional educational sources of the French economic elite, principally the engineering *grandes écoles* (Polytechnique, l'École des mines, and l'École centrale) in favor of new sources such as Sciences-Po – the stepping-stone to l'ÉNA – the law faculties, and new business schools such as L'École des hautes études commerciales (HEC). Whereas in 1952 the proportion of the heads of the one hundred largest French firms who had issued from the top engineering schools represented 46.5% of the total, this figure fell markedly to 33% in 1972. Conversely, the proportion of *patrons* of the hundred biggest firms who had either gone to Sciences-Po, obtained a law degree, or attended HEC rose from only 9.5% in 1952 to 34% two decades later. Pierre Bourdieu, Luc Boltanski, and Monique de Saint Martin, "Les stratégies de reconversion. Les classes sociales et le système d'enseignement," *Social Science Information*. 12(5) (Oct. 1973), 68–9. On the general schooling and social ties between the French corporate elite and the *haut fonctionnariat*, see Birnbaum, *Sommets*, 140–1.

[35] *Politics, Power and Bureaucracy*, 343.

These informal networks linking the leaders of industry to the administrative elite significantly expanded because of the increased *pantouflage* of members of the *corps d'État* (central state administrations) in the largest firms or business organizations at the nexus of public-private interest intermediation. This "growing interpenetration of the bureaucratic and economic fields," to use Birnbaum's phrase, reinforced the emergence of a common technocratic outlook among *hauts fonctionnaires* and the top managers of the leading French firms.[36] Extolling the goals of modernization, rationalization, and growth, this outlook came to dominate planning and the fashioning of public policy to an extent not seen before or since. As another observer concluded, "to a degree present in few other nations, the management of French industrial strategy became a cooperative endeavor between civil servants and industrialists."[37]

Given this common technocratic mind-set, it should come as no surprise that agents within the state administration who were responsible for economic policy and their allies in the private sector were unsympathetic to the concerns of *petits indépendants*. Viewing the latter as an insupportable drag on economic modernization, they sought to shut out small producers and their organizational spokesmen from the formulation of economic policy.[38] Planners evinced an especial disdain for the CGPME, which they cast as a nefarious impediment to modernization because of its continuous attempts, in the words of one *directeur d'administration*, to pressure civil servants "to take the wrong decisions – that is, to support them in their fight against large-scale business interests."[39] As a function of the interlocking social networks and quasi-clientelistic relations that evolved between them during the Fifth Republic, *hauts fonctionnaires* and their counterparts in advanced business and industry united behind a

---

[36] The following figures highlight the extent of this crossover between the high administration and the upper managerial echelons of the leading French firms: of the 92 persons composing the industrialization commissions charged with elaborating the Sixth Plan (1970–5) during the late 1960s, 89 held the highest managerial posts in French enterprises, overwhelmingly represented by the largest private sector firms. Thirty-seven of these were industrial or commercial firm owners, 23 were CEOs of banks or insurance companies, 8 were managers of state-owned enterprises, 15 were upper-level bank managers, and 5 were high-level managers in the public sector. Among these managers, 53 had served in the *Administration*: 40 within the Corps d'État, of whom 24 came from the Inspectorate of Finance, 3 respectively from the Conseil d'État and the Cour des comptes, and 10 from the corps of state engineers. By extension, 27 of these had at one time or another also served as cabinet secretaries to particular ministers, 14 of them having been tied to the economically paramount minister of finance. Of these 53 former *hauts fonctionnaires*, 39 later became the heads of so-called national champions. Birnbaum, *Sommets*, 135–6.

[37] Hall, *Governing the Economy*, 168.

[38] One *directeur d'administration* evinced the hostile attitude of *hauts fonctionnaires* toward the latter in the following terms: "We've decided to have close contacts with dynamic groups. The others try to oblige us to take Malthusian decisions. It's obvious for example that certain unions defend the large number of unproductive shopkeepers and not the few productive and dynamic ones. We must not therefore be forced to become intoxicated by the non-dynamic groups. This is what the administration has to guard against." Quoted in Suleiman, *Politics, Power and Bureaucracy*, 338.

[39] Ibid., 339.

technocratic agenda of economic rationalization that remained dismissive of *petits indépendants'* concerns.

Throughout the 1960s, then, *petits indépendants* and their sectoral and political representatives were largely powerless to prevent their marginalization from the centers of authority and policy making. To make matters worse, whatever political influence petty producers might have marshaled over the governing Gaullist party and the state bureaucracy was undercut by their own organizational ineffectuality and internal divisions. Associations representing petty producers, such as the Association des Présidents des Chambres de Commerce et de l'Industrie (APCCI) and the APCMF, either were dominated, in the case of the former, by large business interests (i.e., the big department stores) or, in that of the latter, had become formal administrative entities devoid of any real influence.[40]

Similarly, the effectiveness of the petty producer movement was critically undermined by functional competition and political conflicts between the various sectoral and interprofessional organizations representing *petits indépendants*. Occupational differences between shopkeepers and artisans impeded their effective organization and mobilization. Artisans adhered to their own confederations, while various shopkeeper syndicates joined either the APCCI or the CGPME, limiting their ability to pursue an agenda of *petit indépendant* defense. In turn, though it was not as dominated by big department store interests as the former was, the CGPME received a disproportionate amount of support from prosperous *gros commerçants* as well as the owners of middling enterprises, so that the *petits indépendants* felt increasingly unrepresented and ill-served by Gingembre's organization.[41] Third, divisions also became apparent within the principal *petit indépendant* constituencies themselves. These were particularly evident in the case of the *artisanat*, which by the early 1960s was divided between no less than four ideologically and programmatically opposed political formations.[42] Such political fractures were overlaid by even greater fragmentation at a sectoral or occupational level. By the end of the 1960s, artisans were represented by no less than five professional peak associations, which inevitably competed with one another as well as with the more explicitly political organizations.[43] In short, the sectoral and political

[40] Gresle, *Indépendants*, 121, and Zdatny, *Politics*, 177, 179–80.
[41] This was one of the principal factors that enabled Poujade's UDCA to wrest so many *petits indépendants* away from the CGPME and to attract them to its ranks. On the relations between the CGPME and *petits indépendants*, see ibid., 164, and Gresle, *Indépendants*, 114. On the Poujade movement's successful gambit to outflank the CGPME and co-opt its support among shopkeepers and artisans, see Ehrmann, *Organized Business in France*, 183–4, and Hoffmann, *Mouvement Poujade*, 307–14.
[42] These included the center-left CGAF, the Communist and CGT-affiliated CGUA, the traditionalist CNA, and the rump of Poujade's UDCA. Zdatny, *Politics*, 164–5.
[43] These included the CAPEB, specializing in the construction trades, the CNAM, representing various formerly restricted trades, foremost among which were hairdressers, the CNAR, grouping members of the rural *artisanat*, and the CGAD, representing members of the food preparation

divisions that plagued small business reinforced one another both within and across the *petit commerce* and *artisanat*, as well as among *petits patrons* generally. Thus, they diminished the capacity of *petits indépendants* to resist their marginalization from the instances in which the most important policy decisions were taken.

From a general standpoint, the first decade of the Fifth Republic coincided with an unprecedented decline in *petits indépendants*' political influence and socioeconomic prestige. During this period, attention to the interests of small producers and tradesmen by the state even took a back seat to those of labor. The Grenelle Accords of May 1968 were an important if belated recognition of the economic and political prerogatives of organized labor.[44] In turn, the Nouvelle Société program that was introduced by the Chaban-Delmas government in 1969 attempted to institute a tripartite system of collective bargaining whereby workers and employers would negotiate collective contracts under the auspices of the state.[45] Needless to say, the Grenelle Accords and Chaban's collective bargaining initiative added to the consternation of *petits indépendants* and owners of small and medium-sized enterprises (SMEs). The former in particular drew the ire of these groups and their representatives, with the CGPME speaking for most petty producer organizations when it characterized the Grenelle Accords as a new Matignon: another callous betrayal of small business orchestrated by big business and the CGT with the blessing of the state.

The Grenelle Accords and Nouvelle Société initiative drove painfully home for *petits indépendants* the extent to which their capacity for defending their interests in the face of a state intent on pursuing economic modernization had

---

sector. In turn, the CGAF, though it sought a broad mandate to politically represent the *artisanat* as a whole, in fact drew the bulk of its membership from several professional federations, including construction, furniture and furnishings, clothing, shoe repair, and jewelers. Predictably, it found itself weakened by competition from other artisanal associations representing the same professions – particularly the CAPEB and the CNAM. Finally, in 1967 an attempt to coordinate the syndical activities of the CAPEB, the CNAM, and the CNAR was launched under the auspices of an umbrella organization, the Comité interconfédéral de coordination de l'artisanat (CICA). However, this new organization was largely ineffective in bridging the divisions within the *artisanat* and mobilizing it behind a coherent set of demands and program of action. Mayer, "Classes moyennes," 628–9, as well as Zdatny, *Politics*, 177.

[44] The primary concessions wrested by labor included a 33% across-the-board wage increase for all industrial workers, the signing of national wage and collective contract agreements on a branch-by-branch basis, and the legal recognition of the right of trade unions to represent workers within the firm and to contract closed-shop agreements provided they obtain the support of a certain majority of employees on the factory floor. Tim Smith, *France in Crisis: Welfare, Inequality, and Globalization since 1980* (Cambridge: Cambridge University Press, 2004), 92, and Fournier and Questiaux, *Traité du social*, 280, 498.

[45] This system marked a substantial departure from the system of labor relations that had prevailed up to that point in France, where, as a result of the poisonous relations that had subsisted between labor unions and employers, the state had been forced – such as at Grenelle – to unilaterally impose collective contracts on the two rival parties from without. Cf. George Ross, "Gaullism and Organized Labor" and Janice McCormick, "Gaullism and Collective Bargaining: The Effect of the Fifth Republic on French Industrial Relations," in Andrews and Hoffmann, *The Fifth Republic at Twenty*, 330–66.

diminished compared to even a decade earlier. Their political and organizational inability to slow or inflect the process of modernization that reached its apogee in the 1960s was reflected in the dramatic decline in the number of *petits indépendants*.[46] From this point on, despite experiencing a brief resurgence in the 1970s, *petits indépendants* would represent, alongside the peasantry, an increasingly inconsequential quantity within the French economy and society.

PETITS INDÉPENDANTS IN THE POST-GAULLIST FIFTH REPUBLIC

> Notre siècle de production industrielle semble, à priori, étouffer toute tentative de réalisation artisanale. Pourtant, à la pression technique, à la vie conditionnée, aux matériaux de synthèse, l'homme moderne réagit par un instinct naturel de retour aux sources. ... Seul l'artisan peut nous apporter cette parcelle de poésie qui nous sauvera de la sécheresse de notre monde mécanisé. *Contacts*, 1979[47]

> Il est indispensable que la France de l'an 2000 telle que nous la concevons ait toujours des artisans boulangers et des artisans horlogers, et des artisans heureux de l'être. Jacques Chirac before the Conseil économique, May 1976[48]

Yet, the rapid economic and social modernization over which de Gaulle presided held unforeseen political consequences for the ruling coalition that oversaw it. In what is surely an irony of contemporary French political history, modernization eroded the formerly unassailable Gaullist majority that had pursued it and rendered it by the early 1970s increasingly unsustainable. This evolution reflected the contradictory social bases of Gaullism that had been a broadly based movement whose composition mirrored French society as a whole. In this sense, Gaullism represented a potentially unstable alliance between modern and antimodern constituencies: the former comprising social groups that benefited from economic and social modernization, notably the high bourgeoisie of advanced employers and business managers, as well as dynamic middle-class and working-class elements buoyed by industrial rationalization and innovation, the latter largely circumscribed to the traditional middle class of *petits indépendants* and marginal farmers.[49] As a function of the modernization process, however, the Gaullist majority began to lose its broad-based character and eroded as a catchall party. This trend intensified following de Gaulle's

---

[46] See Chapter 3.
[47] Quoted in Gresle, *Indépendants*, 849.
[48] Quoted in ibid., 907.
[49] Despite its modernizing agenda, the UNR/UDR disproportionately benefited from the support of the traditional middle classes and, in particular, *petits indépendants*. As Nonna Mayer has noted, the proportion of the latter who declared their intention to vote for Gaullist candidates rose from 23% before the first round of the 1958 parliamentary election to 47% in 1967 and reached its apogee in the aftermath of May 1968 with 53% of *petits indépendants* declaring they would cast their ballots for Gaullist candidates on the eve of the June parliamentary election. "Classes moyennes," 752.

departure in April 1969, which precipitated a split between the Gaullist Right
(UDR) and a center Right comprising Independent Republicans, erstwhile
Radicals, and former members of the Mouvement Républicain Populaire.[50]
The upshot of this sociopolitical rebalancing was that the Gaullist party in
particular, and the Right in general, shed much of their new middle-class support, particularly among white-collar service employees and middling *cadres*.
These segments were increasingly unhappy with what they saw as the oligopolistic tenor of the Gaullist modernization program, and resented the disregard
shown toward their concerns by firm managers close to the Gaullist state.
Through the late 1960s and early 1970s, many of these new middle strata, and
particularly a growing number of *cadres*, defected to the new Socialist Party
founded by François Mitterrand at the 1971 Épinay Congress.[51] At the same
time, after de Gaulle's departure, the UDR also lost much of its working-class
support to the Left. The widescale defection of new middle-class and working-
class voters heightened the electoral importance of traditional independent
strata for the post–de Gaulle majority.[52]

By the early 1970s, then, the Gaullist majority and the coalition of the Right
and center Right that succeeded it represented an increasingly unstable alliance
between advanced fractions of capital and the traditional middle classes. As a
function of the tension between these bases of support, the leaders of the Gaullist
and succeeding right and center-right coalitions found themselves confronted by,
as Birnbaum has put it, "a dilemma . . .: they need[ed] to conserve the political
support of the middle classes and of the *petit patronat* in order to maintain their
political majority in the parliament," while simultaneously pursuing "an interventionist economic strategy of massive industrialization and concentration,
which [could] only harm the interests of the *petit patronat* and hasten its
disappearance."[53] However, following the defection of a significant part of its
electorate to the Left, the Gaullist party, and subsequent right–center-right
coalitions in general became dependent on the traditional middle classes to
sustain their majority.[54] In this sense, the erosion of the center-right majority

[50] On the repositioning of political forces on the Right and center Right, see Peter Gourevitch,
"Gaullism Abandoned, or the Costs of Success," and William Safran, "Centrism in the Fifth
Republic: An Attitude in Search of an Instrument," both in Andrews and Hoffmann, *The Fifth
Republic at Twenty*, 112–45.
[51] Accordingly, midlevel cadre and white-collar employees went from representing 20% of the UNR's
electorate in 1965 to 16% of the electorate of the right–center-right majority coalition in 1973, to
only 14% of the latter in 1976. Similarly, whereas blue-collar workers had constituted 27% of the
Gaullist electorate in 1965, this proportion fell to only 22% of the right–center-right majority in
1973, and only 17% in 1976. Berger and Piore, *Dualism*, 116. On the turn of the new middle classes
toward the new-style PS, see H. Portelli, "Nouvelles classes moyennes et nouveau Parti Socialiste,"
in Lavau, Grunberg, and Mayer, *L'univers politique des classes moyennes*, 258–73.
[52] Berger and Piore, *Dualism*, 116.
[53] *Sommets de l'État*, 119.
[54] This new vulnerability was brought home by the dramatic fall in traditional middle-class support
for the Gaullist majority in the 1969 referendum, as well as the growing threat posed by the Left
following the conclusion of the Common Program between the PCF and PS in 1972. Indeed, the

had transformed the traditional middle classes into a politically decisive *minorité d'appoint* by the early 1970s whose interests would once again need to be taken into account.[55] It was not the least of paradoxes that, as a result of the political realignments occasioned by the modernization program to which they were opposed, the traditional middle classes would come to enjoy a renewed, if fleeting, influence at the center of the policy-making process.

If the erosion of the sociopolitical foundations of the Gaullist majority provided the context for the political resurgence of *petits indépendants*, its proximate cause was the eruption of small producer and shopkeeper protest in the aftermath of May 1968. The intensity of this protest crystallized the concern of the majority over the allegiance of the traditional middle classes and convinced it of the need to shore up its support among *petits indépendants*. In particular, the CID-UNATI, which was launched in 1969 to protest the social security reform of 1966, quickly morphed into a broad movement of revolt that channeled the anxieties and resentments of *petits indépendants*.[56] Underscoring the extent of their social and political demotion since the 1950s, *petits indépendants*' fear of *déclassement* and sense of economic vulnerability brought many of them to adopt a posture of open defiance against the state. Beginning with an attack on a tax office in a *sous-préfecture* of the Isère in April 1969, the CID-UNATI proceeded to mount, much like Poujade's UDCA before it, a campaign of extralegal actions and violent protest against the state and its representatives.[57] In part, as a result of these spectacular actions, support for the new organization ballooned from 23,000 members in 1970 to 189,000 in 1971, and surpassed 200,000 members in early 1972. Politically capitalizing on these gains, CID-UNATI candidates won 43 percent of the seats in the artisanal *chambres de métiers* in 1971 and 40 percent of the seats the following year for the body overseeing *petit indépendant* and employer pensions.[58]

The CID-UNATI's electrifying spread recalling the Poujade movement's rise in 1953–4 took the former Gaullist majority by surprise. Its leaders, beginning with President Pompidou himself, sought to disarm *petit indépendant* protest by promising to abrogate the general medical insurance law and pledging to defend

latter even managed to make inroads at the expense of the Gaullist party and center Right among *petits indépendants* – the support of shopkeepers and artisans for the Gaullists and their allies falling from 53% in 1968 to 36% in 1973, while their support for the Left rose from 23% to 34%. Keeler, "Corporatist Decentralization," 270.

[55] The phrase is Jeanne Gaillard's. "La petite entreprise," 174.

[56] CID-UNATI stands for *Comité d'information et de défense-Union nationale des travailleurs indépendants*.

[57] Through 1969 and 1970, the CID-UNATI staged tax strikes and sit-ins in tax offices, fought pitched battles with the police, and even went so far as to kidnap tax inspectors – actions that eventually landed many of the movement's activists, including its leader Gérard Nicoud, in prison. Simultaneously, these *opérations ponctuelles* were accompanied by a national speaking tour by Nicoud to garner public support for the *petit indépendant* cause, culminating with a rally in Paris in March 1970 that attracted upward of forty thousand supporters. S. Berger, "D'une boutique à l'autre," 131.

[58] Ibid. and Keeler, "Corporatist Decentralization," 270.

the interests of shopkeepers and artisans.⁵⁹ By the early seventies, these rhetorical commitments were being backed up by legislative action. Successive
governments of the Gaullist–center-right majority reinstituted a raft of protective measures shielding *petits indépendants* from industrial and commercial
modernization in order to win back their allegiance. Beginning with the
January 1970 revision of the health insurance law, more legislative protections
to the benefit of small producers were passed in the ensuing decade than at any
time since the 1930s.⁶⁰ The political momentum behind this legislation built
up during the last two years of the Chaban-Delmas government (June 1969–
July 1972), reached its apogee under the government of Pierre Messmer (July
1972–May 1974), and then was sustained by the inaugural government of
Giscard-d'Estaing's presidency, under the premiership of Jacques Chirac (May
1974–August 1976). It was only in the second half of the 1970s, when inflation,
stagnation, and unemployment reached a critical point, that the campaign to
protect *petits indépendants* lost steam. Beginning with the Barre Plan in August
1976, the concern of the political class for these strata melted away as it
attempted to head off discontent linked to the process of deindustrialization
that hit the country in the late 1970s.

From the middle of 1969 through mid-1972, the Chaban government sought to
reconcile the concerns of *petits indépendants* to the broader imperatives of economic and social modernization. Accordingly, as part of its Nouvelle Société
program to establish a neocorporatist system of industrial relations in France,
Chaban's government instituted a series of reforms specifically concerning *petits
indépendants*. First, their principal demands regarding the reform of the health
insurance and social security system were met. In 1970 shopkeepers, artisans, and
employers were given the right to elect representatives to run their own, sector-
specific health insurance and pension funds, while obtaining a pledge that the costs
of long hospital stays would be reimbursed by the state.⁶¹ This modification paved
the way for a more comprehensive reform in 1972, which introduced a compulsory
system of social security for all shopkeepers, artisans, and small employers, the
provisions of which were to eventually extend to all socioprofessional categories.⁶²

---

⁵⁹ Seeking to placate the fears of *petits indépendants* in a speech from March 1969, Pompidou declared
that the "*artisanat* is assured of a great future, because it represents the personalization – and even
the personality – of an activity, to which its clientele shall always remain attached." In the same vein,
Valéry Giscard-d'Estaing, the minister of finance and of the economy in this period, intoned before
the National Assembly the following May: "The government is convinced of the immense interest
for our country of maintaining in the commercial sector, as in others, an individualistic and familial
business structure, both living and active. ... Our choice is clear: it is to give its chance to
independent commerce in the modern world." Roy, *Les commerçants*, 19, 143.
⁶⁰ For a list of these measures, see Gresle, *Indépendants*, 595ff.
⁶¹ Ibid., 599, and Mayer, "Classes moyennes," 654.
⁶² Chiefly, this new regime mandated an upward revaluation of the contributions and benefits of self-
employed and small business owners so these could be brought into line with those of wage
earners. In exchange for upwardly revising their social security contributions, the state agreed to
cover the deficits anticipated in *petits indépendants'* retirement fund as a result of the disproportionate aging of the shopkeeper and artisanal populations. Gresle, *Indépendants*, 601.

Second, the Chaban government reversed the trend of stripping *petits indépendants* of their fiscal protections on the grounds that, compared to wage earners, they were unfairly penalized by the tax code.[63] This included reducing the complementary tax on *petits indépendants* from 8 to 6 percent, while extending to them the 5 percent general tax allowance and 20 percent allowance on taxable earnings that applied to wage earners.[64] An additional reform in 1972 reduced the *patente* on the smallest shopkeepers, while a simplified method for calculating firm profits – the *bénéfice réel simplifié* – was introduced to bring *petits indépendants* further in line with wage earners' tax schedule.[65] Aligning the tax codes of *petits indépendants* and wage earners meant in practice reducing the tax burden on the former, especially since they continued to underreport their profits under a *forfait*-based system.

Finally, these fiscal reforms were accompanied by a number of explicit protections for *petits indépendants*, many of them throwbacks to regulations discarded at the beginning of the Fifth Republic. In June 1970 Valéry Giscard-d'Estaing, then minister of finance and the economy, issued a joint circular with State Secretary for Commerce Jean Bailly that placed restrictions on competition in the retail sector in order to "correct the excesses to which the most dynamic and powerful enterprises could be tempted to lend themselves."[66] This decree prohibited retailers from selling goods at a loss, forbid those benefiting from a tax break or year-end supply refund from deducting it from their sales price, and banned the sale of certain goods at their supply price while raising the price on other goods. These pricing measures were followed in May 1972 by an initiative to limit rebates by *grandes surfaces* on such staple products as alcohol and gasoline.[67] The general upshot was to restrict large retailers from charging lower prices that would put *petits indépendants* out of business. In turn, these defensive measures were complemented by proactive initiatives designed to help shopkeepers and artisans adapt to the workings of a modern industrial economy, such as the provision of training for prospective and existing *petits indépendants* and the extension of credits to facilitate the conversion of rural *artisans* to factory work. Similarly, in an effort to streamline the *petit indépendant* sector, the government gave older shopkeepers and artisans generous material incentives to withdraw from their respective trades without selling or passing on their businesses to someone else.[68]

---

[63] In this vein, Maurice Roy found that in 1969, the wage-earning head of a family of four would have paid an income tax of 829 francs on a salary of 20,000 francs, whereas a nonsalaried worker – that is, an artisan or a shopkeeper – would have had to pay almost four times (3,126 francs) on the same income. This reflected both the additional levies imposed on *petits indépendants* and tax allowances benefiting salaried workers. *Les commerçants*, 94.

[64] Ibid., 93–7.

[65] Gresle, *Indépendants*, 606.

[66] Roy, *Les commerçants*, 119.

[67] Ibid., 120, and Gresle, *Indépendants*, 604.

[68] As this last set of measures suggests, the attentions lavished by the Chaban-Delmas government on *petits indépendants* fit into a more general modernizing mind-set. This outlook was particularly evident in the government's attempt to build up remaining artisanal firms and *petits commerces*

In the face of continued CID-UNATI pressure, however, the Messmer government that succeeded Chaban's ministry in July 1972 would pursue even more propitiatory policies toward *petits indépendants*.[69] As a first sign of solicitude toward petty shopkeepers and artisans, it elevated to ministerial status the former Secretariat of Commerce and the *Artisanat* and named at its head Jean Royer, a conservative *Indépendant* politician strongly sympathetic to the plight of *petits indépendants*. Under Royer's impetus, the new government enacted in December 1973 the Law on the Orientation of Commerce and the *Artisanat*, or Royer Law, which was nothing less than a comprehensive attempt to improve the position of *petits indépendants* in the fiscal, social, educational, and administrative arenas. First, in the fiscal domain, the new law instituted a tax exemption for the poorest *petits indépendants*, as well as a 15 percent remittance on *patente* obligations for those employing two wage earners or less. The fiscal charges on ceding a small business from one owner to another were also reduced, thereby lowering the cost for an aspiring shopkeeper or artisan to "set up shop" on his own. In the social sphere, the Royer Law imposed the same duration of contributions for *petits indépendants* and for wage earners so that they would both be eligible to receive a pension at the same age. Finally, in the educational sphere, the law sought to halt the slide in the number of people entering the *indépendant* sector by introducing a system of *pré-apprentissage* (preapprenticeship) that guaranteed aspiring artisans training within their respective trades from the age of fourteen (the previous limit had been set at sixteen). At the same time, it stipulated that more on-the-job and professional training be provided to

into small to medium-sized enterprises (SMEs), these being increasingly perceived, with the failure of the national champions policy to achieve the economic efficiency and competitiveness anticipated by 1960s planners, as the microeconomic linchpins of future flexibility and growth. The objective of the Sixth Plan as set out by the Commission of Commerce and Trades Sectors reflected this important shift in emphasis. Its mandate was to encourage greater competition within the small producer and shopkeeper milieu by requiring them to innovate their production methods and technologies, improve their training regimes, and alter their cultural mind-sets. In this context, many of the other policies proposed by the Chaban government pertaining to *petits indépendants* were designed to complement this transition toward an economy based on SMEs. Measures such as offering early retirement to elderly *petits indépendants* and compensating them for not passing on their business to a new set of marginal traders or producers were essentially designed to further the rationalizing aim of unclogging the productive and commercial sectors. Similarly, initiatives to create larger, more efficient retail enterprises by promoting the organization of shopkeepers into store chains or retailer cooperatives could also be read as attempts to further commercial concentration under the guise of shielding *petits indépendants* from competition. At base, then, the Chaban government evinced a fundamental ambivalence toward *petits indépendants*, considering them collectively as a marginal *secteur assisté* that would have to be ultimately eliminated in favor of larger and more dynamic family enterprises. As François Gresle remarked, the government "sacrificed *indépendance* on the altar of the small and middling *patronat*, despite its pretensions to the contrary." In this regard, the Chaban government proved very different from its successor, which, in the face of sustained *petit indépendant* protest, would espouse an unambiguous program of petty producer defense. *Indépendants*, 602–3, 607.

[69] In order to ratchet up the pressure on the new government in the run-up to the legislative elections, the CID-UNATI threatened a tax strike against the *patente* as well as to withhold the health insurance contributions of its members. Ibid., 612.

active *petits indépendants* in order to help them master the new technologies and management techniques coextensive with the modern industrial economy.[70]

However, it was in the administrative sphere that the Royer Law was to have its greatest – and most controversial – impact. Building on previously unsuccessful attempts to restrict the spread of *grandes surfaces*, the new law stipulated the establishment of commercial urbanization commissions (*commissions départementales d'urbanisation commerciale* or *CDUCs*) in each department to approve the construction of new supermarkets. As a function of the rules governing their composition, these commissions were most often staffed by pluralities of delegates sympathetic to petty producers and shopkeepers.[71] The entry into force of the Royer Law substantially slowed commercial concentration, with a 30 percent fall in supermarket openings being recorded in 1974 alone.[72] As such, it proved a real boon to *petits indépendants*, who had been decimated by the breakneck concentration of French commerce since the late 1950s.

The Royer Law marked the high point of the politics of socioeconomic defense that benefited *petits indépendants* during the 1970s. From a bureaucratic standpoint, its passage reflected the first and only instance in the postwar era when modernizing *administrations* saw their policy proposals defeated by the defenders of Malthusian economic and social interests. From this standpoint, the Royer Law underscored the extent to which *petits indépendants* and their organizational representatives had regained some of their former leverage over the political class and state bureaucracy during the first half of the 1970s. Pierre Birnbaum resumed their resurgent political acumen in the following terms:

> The Royer Law demonstrated the extent to which the holders of the apparatus of state, partisans of the process of capitalist modernization and rationalization, needed to stay attentive to the claims of social categories who were fundamentally hostile to large-scale capitalism, but who expressed the expectations of a *France des profondeurs* whose political weight remained electorally decisive.[73]

The election of Valéry Giscard-d'Estaing to the presidency in 1974 seemed to presage an end to this preferential regime favoring *petits indépendants*. Giscard's professed commitment to modernization and neoliberalism flew in the face of the pro–*petit indépendant* stance that had characterized his tenure as Chaban's

---

[70] Ibid., 618–21, and Mayer, "Classes moyennes," 654, 656.

[71] One survey from 1974 found that although *petits indépendants* were entitled by law to occupy only 35% (i.e., 7/20) of the total seats on each *CDUC*, they in fact controlled 39% of the national total because 13% of the seats were assigned to elected local officials, many of whom happened to be *petits indépendants* themselves. Similarly, whereas the law stipulated that at least 22% (2/9) of the elected officials who sat on the commissions needed to come from communes counting fewer than five thousand people, fully 56% of these allotted seats went to the representatives of rural areas, who were generally much more favorably disposed to shopkeepers and artisans. Keeler, "Corporatist Decentralization," 274.

[72] S. Berger, "D'une boutique à l'autre," 132.

[73] *Sommets*, 133.

finance minister.[74] Yet, initially at least, the new government under the steward-ship of Jacques Chirac continued along the same pro-petty-producer lines as its predecessor, a continuity symbolized by its maintenance of a separate Ministry for Individual Enterprise to address the needs of *petits indépendants*.[75] Considering small family-owned enterprises to constitute an essential pillar of French society, the new government pledged to inflect the course of economic development in a direction favorable to small business and *petits indépendants*. As a matter of course, the Royer Law was kept on the books, and its provisions scrupulously applied.[76]

The principal measure enacted by the Chirac government in favor of *petits indépendants* was to replace the old *patente* with a new *taxe professionnelle* or corporate tax that lessened the fiscal obligations on shopkeepers and artisans and shifted the burden of taxation to larger commercial and industrial establish-ments.[77] Similarly, the government's reflationary policies in the wake of the 1973 oil crisis were also generally favorable to *petits indépendants*.[78] At the same time, the growth of unemployment placed downward pressure on wages, a development that benefited the owners of small enterprises. Finally, the govern-ment introduced a series of measures targeting small producers that extended or built on previous legislation. These included the provision of financial assistance to the *artisanat*, the creation of an agency to foster the creation of SMEs, measures to lower the rental costs of commercial spaces, the establishment of preferential bank savings plans to enable young workers to save the funds necessary to set up shop at preferential rates of interest, and the introduction of bankruptcy protection for shopkeepers and artisans.[79]

In short, during the first two years of Giscard's presidency, the economic and social concerns of French *petits indépendants* continued to be systematically addressed. This abruptly changed with the replacement of Chirac by Raymond Barre as prime minister in August 1976 and the austerity program introduced by the latter to rein in the inflationary spiral created by the reflationary policies of

[74] Accordingly, though one of his first acts as president was to sign it, he publicly registered his opposition to the Royer Law when it was presented to the National Assembly. Ibid., 132.
[75] Gresle, *Indépendants*, 626–7.
[76] Reflecting this bias, Chirac unveiled the Seventh Plan (1975–81) by heralding the return to an economy based on small business and even the *petit indépendant* sector, asserting that "the tendency [toward dirigisme] was being reversed to the point of erecting as a national priority the development of small and medium enterprises and the *artisanat*." Ibid., 627, and Birnbaum, *Sommets*, 126.
[77] Analyzing the effects of the new tax, Suzanne Berger estimated that artisans and shopkeepers employing less than three workers respectively paid 53% and 63% less than what they would have done under the old *patente*-based regime. Under the new professional tax, 29% of artisans and 39% of shopkeepers ended up owing less than 25% of the old *patente* in tax obligations. "D'une boutique à l'autre," 133.
[78] Chief among them was the suppression of previously instituted price controls, sparking a rapid rise in retail prices that allowed *petits indépendants* to pad their bottom lines.
[79] C. Ysmal, "Le groupe central Giscardien," in Lavau, Grunberg, and Mayer, *L'univers politique des classes moyennes*, 255; Gresle, *Indépendants*, 627; and S. Berger, *Dualism*, 118.

his predecessor. Likewise, the Barre government reassumed a modernizing stance vis-à-vis small producers and shopkeepers, resurrecting in effect Chaban's old idea of placing the onus of development on SMEs as opposed to the *petit indépendant* sector.[80] In short, Barre's arrival *aux affaires* marked the advent of new ideological and philosophical priorities. It signaled the demotion of *petits indépendants* to a position of secondary importance as policy makers were confronted with stagflation and the challenges of deindustrialization.[81] In this sense, the Barre ministry closed the parenthesis that had lasted from 1969 to 1976 in which successive Gaullist and center-right governments had acceded for political reasons to *petit indépendant* demands.

As a function of this renewed consideration for their concerns, the 1970s also saw a recrudescence of political organization among *petits indépendants* as they sought to capitalize on their greater leverage on the Gaullist and center-right parties. In the first place, the decade marked the return of organized petty producer and commercial interests to the political stage following their estrangement from it during the 1960s.[82] Similarly, this period also ushered in a resumption of more active lobbying on the part of petty producers, reflecting the renewed importance they accorded to parliamentary politics as the Gaullist–center-right majority saw its legislative dominance brought into question by the Left. In this uncertain political context, the organizational representatives of *petits indépendants* attempted from within the system to bring the kind of pressure to bear upon the state that the CID-UNATI had brought against it from without. As Berger put it, they employed their electoral leverage "to force the state to reckon with the prospects of defection of the traditional middle classes on whom it ha[d] always relied."[83]

This consciousness of their renewed political clout translated into a number of political initiatives in the *petit indépendant* sector. In the first place, the renewal

[80] In essence, the new government resumed earlier attempts to spur commercial concentration through the association of small retailers and to further open the trades to virtually all comers. In keeping with this new stance, the Barre government also lauded SMEs as the indispensable microeconomic bases for regenerating the French economy, while increasingly casting *petits indépendants* as a marginal and obsolete "counterculture," the remaining vestiges of which would constitute a living "museum" celebrating the anachronistic virtues of a long-vanished *petite boutique* and traditional *artisanat*. Zarca, *L'artisanat français*, 104–5, and Gresle, *Indépendants*, 631.

[81] The contrary experiences of the Chirac and Barre governments are an apt reminder of the schizoid approach to social and economic affairs that characterized Giscard's presidency. Attempting to reconcile the potentially contradictory imperatives of modernization and stability, Giscard trod a fine line between limiting economic competition and not bringing it fundamentally into question. In a speech delivered in the run-up to the 1974 presidential election, the future president articulated this fundamental ambivalence, averring that "the point is to establish limits to the exercise of free competition that would not be such as to put into question this very right in itself. Failing in this would be to favor a rise in prices and impede the ongoing modernization of the commercial apparatus that is far from complete." Quoted in Birnbaum, *Sommets*, 132.

[82] This dynamic especially gained impetus as support for the CID-UNATI started to level off after 1974. Keeler, "Corporatist Decentralization," 284, and Mayer, "Classes moyennes," 652.

[83] "D'une boutique à l'autre," 134.

of petty producer politics was underscored by the independent candidacy of Jean Royer in the presidential election of 1974.[84] Second, new organizations emerged that sought to harness *petits indépendants'* political vitality. Most notable among them were two formations created under the impulse of the CGPME that testified to its renewed politicization during this period. The first was the Union des chefs et responsables (UNICER), which was constituted in 1975 to mobilize electoral support for the CGPME's message among *petits indépendants* and *petits patrons.* Its goal was to parlay small employers' and business owners' support of the CGPME into electoral leverage by which to force Gaullist and center-right candidates to defend their interests in their political programs.[85] In turn, in 1978 the CGPME attempted to forge a broad middle-class coalition to keep the Left from acceding to power. Emulating previous syncretic movements of the old and the new middle classes, such as the Confédération générale des syndicats des classes moyennes of the 1930s and the Comité national de liaison et d'action des classes moyennes of the late 1940s, the CGPME associated itself with the FNSEA, the Confédération des syndicats médicaux français (Confederation of medical practitioners' unions), the CGC, and the Association permanente des chambres de métiers (successor to the former APCMF) to form the Groupes "Initiative et Responsabilité" or GIR. The purpose of this formation was to unite these various middle-class organizations around a common slogan affirming "the choice of liberty, the willingness to take risks, the taste for work, and the exercise of responsibility and initiative."[86]

The emergence of these new formations, and the substantial support they initially achieved, successfully captured the attention of the mainstream parties of the Right and center Right. The Rassemblement pour la république (RPR) – the successor to the UDR created by Chirac in the early 1970s – tried to co-opt the GIR almost immediately upon its inception. The Giscardiens, meanwhile, lent their support to the rival Comité national de coopération interprofessionnelle, formed in April 1976 and following a similar mandate of middle-class defense to the GIR.[87] The RPR in particular evolved a populist message that was specifically tailored to resonate with *petits indépendants.* In an attempt to capture their support, Chirac embarked on a rhetorical offensive that glorified the national *traditions* represented by the latter and which he claimed had made

---

[84] Though his campaign was largely a failure – Royer falling far short of the 7% projection of some analysts with only 3.2% of the vote in the first round of the election – his candidacy was significant as a symbol of the renewed import of *petit indépendant* issues and concerns following their effective exclusion from the political debate in the 1960s. Ibid.

[85] Highlighting the propitiousness of the political climate toward initiatives targeting small business, within a few days of its inception no less than twenty-five thousand *chefs d'entreprise* had rallied to the UNICER, reflecting their anxiety over the Left's nationalization program as well as their outrage at the prison sentences meted out to *petits patrons* for their refusal to comply with the stricter workplace regulations that had been enacted during this period. Mayer, "Classes moyennes," 640.

[86] Ibid., 641–2.

[87] Ibid., 756.

the country into what it was today.[88] By contrast, Giscardiens and other centrist elements were less comfortable pandering to *petits indépendants*. When push came to shove, they were much closer to advanced, upper-middle-class groups such as *cadres supérieurs* and members of the liberal professions than the traditional middle classes – a fact underscored by the prominence of economic and social modernizers such as Jacques Servan-Schreiber and Jacques Chaban-Delmas within their ranks.[89]

Yet, these various appeals of the Gaullist and center-right parties should not obscure the fact that, in the first half of the 1970s, both had broken with de Gaulle's superlative imperative of "growth at all costs." Each had embraced in varying degrees a "schizophrenic" liberalism that attempted to modernize the French economy while preserving the *petit indépendant* sector. In this sense, the first half of the 1970s marked the resurgence of a backward-looking conservative consensus among the parties of the mainstream Right and center Right that recalled the RGR and Indépendants of the Fourth Republic, and the Radicals and Fédération républicaine of the Third – a consensus that prized stability over innovation, order over growth.

As the 1970s drew to a close, however, economic stagnation became an increasingly urgent preoccupation for the Right and center Right. They were forced to acknowledge the mounting social costs of deindustrialization, particularly the phenomenon of structural unemployment that emerged as a serious problem in the latter part of the decade. These concerns returned the question of structural reform to the center of political debate, as both the Gaullist–center-right coalition and the Left sought new ways to put the country back on the path of growth and full employment it had enjoyed during the Trente glorieuses.

This search for a new productivist paradigm heralded a seminal shift away from the dirigisme that had underpinned French economic policy since World War II. The growth of unemployment during the 1970s and 1980s focused policy makers on crafting social protections that would dampen the social impacts of structural unemployment on the one hand and of structural reform on the other. In particular, the victory of the Left in 1981 displaced the importance accorded by the state to the plight of *petits indépendants* in favor of new priorities. Accordingly, French policy makers on both the left and the right evolved a

---

[88] Gresle, *Indépendants*, 907, and Gaillard, "La petite entreprise," 174.

[89] This variable sectoral appeal is tellingly reflected in the distribution of votes respectively obtained by the RPR and the UDF among *petits patrons* and large employers during this period. In the first round of the 1981 parliamentary election, candidates from the RPR obtained one out of every three votes of shopkeepers and artisans versus only one out of every five for the candidates from the UDF. Similarly, another poll conducted in April 1981 found that 42% of small employers (i.e., those counting fewer than fifty employees) stated that they felt themselves closest to the policy positions espoused by Chirac, whereas only 24% felt closest to those espoused by Giscard. Conversely, however, while only 21% of the largest employers (i.e., those counting more than five hundred workers) claimed to feel closest to the president of the RPR, fully 54% stated that they felt closest to Giscard. Mayer, "Classes moyennes," 761, 763.

schizophrenic discourse toward *petits indépendants* during the closing decades of the century. While rhetorically acknowledging the concerns of the latter, they simultaneously pursued modernization, through liberalizing policies entailing the disengagement of the state from the economy, and followed a strategy of social appeasement to which *petits indépendants* were inherently opposed. Thus, as their numbers dwindled to a new low in this twentieth-century *fin de siècle*, *petits indépendants'* frustration with the mainstream parties finally boiled over, and growing numbers of them cast their political lot with the Front National.

It is ironic that these new efforts at structural reform were being conceived at the very moment when the concerns of *petits indépendants* seemingly ranked highest on policy makers' agendas. It was with the arrival of Raymond Barre as premier in the summer of 1976 that the movement toward structural reform was launched in earnest. Barre took up the premiership with the object of reestablishing the conditions for growth by introducing measures of economic *assainissement* that would restore the balance-of-payments equilibrium, lessen pressure on the franc, and rein in inflation. These measures were part of a broader strategy of market liberalization designed to free the economy from state intervention and control, evincing, as Philip Cerny and Diana Green put it, "a determination to rely progressively on market forces to carry out essential industrial restructuring."[90] In this sense, the Barre Plan represented the first attempt to roll back dirigisme since its advent under the Fourth Republic.

The Barre government set about dismantling the interventionist apparatus of the state in two ways. In the first place, it sought to strengthen the autonomy of French corporations by stripping away the controls and supports of dirigisme and shifting the responsibility for restarting growth and improving competitiveness to private actors. Henceforth, state intervention was to be the exception and not the rule, initiating a process of *déplanification* that would come to a head over the next decade. The state was no longer to oversee the capitalization of firms and industries, but its sphere of influence limited to sustaining favorable macroeconomic conditions. Firms – both large and small – were to be left alone to make their own investment, production, and pricing decisions based on the unfettered operation of the market.[91] The expectation was that, by liberalizing the structural context in which French firms operated, resources would shift to SMEs as the flexible linchpins of the new economy as opposed to inefficient state enterprises.

In turn, the second component of the government's liberalization strategy was to restore a functioning pricing mechanism to efficiently distribute resources and

---

[90] "Economic Policy and the Governing Coalition," in Cerny and Schain, *French Politics and Public Policy*, 164.

[91] As an institutional corollary to this market deregulation, the Barre government established a Competition Commission endowed with extensive powers to ensure the open and fair functioning of the market and, in particular, to root out instances of unfair competition that might interfere with it. Finally, following this pattern of decontrol, the nationalized sector was to be subjected to market prices, and restrictions on overseas investments by French firms were to be removed. On these and other liberalizing measures, see ibid.

prevent bottlenecks or shortages from developing in the economy. Accordingly, the Barre government eliminated price controls, which were abrogated at once in the industrial sector and gradually phased out in services. The resulting spike in inflation and deteriorating balance of payments forced the Barre government to enact a comprehensive austerity program to rein in prices and relieve the pressure on the franc. Thus, as a corollary to price liberalization, the government instituted deep spending cuts and decreed an across-the-board tax hike, while restricting the money supply and deindexing wages from prices.[92]

Among the worst hit by the new inflation-reduction measures were *petits indépendants*, whose profits tend to increase in an inflationary environment.[93] Similarly, though they initially welcomed the proposal to deindex wages, SME owners were quickly disappointed when, in the face of protest from wage earners, this measure was abandoned by the government. The latter sought instead to shift the burden of "paying" for inflation from industrial workers to consumers by raising the prices of electricity, rail transport, and postage – a measure that hit small entrepreneurs doubly hard since it raised their operation and transportation costs, while stripping them of the anticipated windfall on their labor costs.[94]

The Barre Plan proved largely a failure. It was unsuccessful in halting price and wage inflation and similarly failed to halt the rise in the money supply, stanch the budget deficit, and relieve pressure on the franc. Unemployment continued to increase, more than doubling from 3 percent in 1974 to 7 percent in 1981.[95] Meanwhile, the Barre government was only partially able to divest itself from dirigisme and economic planning. Whether it liked it or not, the state still fundamentally determined the extent to which market forces stimulated economic growth. Similarly, despite the government's commitment to end support for certain industries and firms, it continued to pour enormous sums into some sectors to assist erstwhile "national champions" that had turned into "lame ducks."[96] The crucial difference was that, whereas in the past the state had provided such support to promote the rationalization of these industries, now it was giving support to keep them from going under, the costs in terms of

[92] Hall, *Governing the Economy*, 187.
[93] Gresle, *Indépendants*, 629.
[94] At the same time, however, the Barre government maintained existing protections for *petits indépendants*, such as the Royer Law, and oversaw the transition to the *taxe professionnelle* passed by its predecessor, considered more favorable to the latter than the previous *patente*-based regime. Its adherence to such Malthusian measures ran counter to its professed commitment to liberal reform, highlighting the lengths to which a modernizing government of the center Right would still go to placate the traditional middle classes. Hall, *Governing the Economy*, 188.
[95] The only aspect of its program that it was more or less successful in achieving was in righting the nation's balance-of-payments account. Cerny and Green, "Economic Policy and the Governing Coalition," 162, and Smith, *France in Crisis*, 91.
[96] Hall, *Governing the Economy*, 190-1, and Suzanne Berger, "Lame Ducks and National Champions: Industrial Policy in the Fifth Republic," in Andrews and Hoffmann, *Fifth Republic at Twenty*, 304-5. For a specific case study of the evolution of the Barre government's industrial policy and practical compromising on its commitment to *déplanification* in the steel sector, see Cerny and Green, "Economic Policy," 165-8.

unemployment and social and political unrest being too high for the government to contemplate. Most controversially, the Barre government introduced an extremely restrictive labor law requiring firms to obtain the authorization of a Ministry of Labor inspector before being able to lay off more than ten workers at a time. This measure came on the heels of the provision of generous welfare benefits to the unemployed to help cushion the social impact of layoffs occasioned by deindustrialization.[97]

In this sense, the Barre government presided over the inception of a qualitatively novel sociopolitical dynamic that was to have enormous policy and economic repercussions for governments down to the present: the creation of new, compensatory modes of state assistance to address the needs of the actual and prospective victims of deindustrialization – what Jonah Levy has termed the "social-anesthesia state" – in parallel with the gradual extrication of the state from the economy.[98] This new focus on the victims of deindustrialization, combined with the state's realization of the need to disinvest itself from the economy to advance structural reform, underlined the diminishing political significance attached by both the Left and the Right to *petits indépendants* as the economic crisis worsened in the 1980s. From this point forward, the political fortunes of the mainstream parties turned much more on their ability to manage and attenuate the negative impacts of deindustrialization rather than on placating a shrinking constituency of artisans and shopkeepers.

This shift in politicians' attitudes toward *petits indépendants* was paired with an increasingly cynical approach that involved cosmetically addressing their concerns during electoral periods and then reverting to policies of structural reform and social appeasement during nonelectoral ones.[99] Not surprisingly,

---

[97] In a bid to financially tide them over until they could find another job, laid-off workers were to be provided unemployment benefits equivalent to 90% of their previous salaries for a duration of up to one year. S. Berger, "Lame Ducks and National Champions," 304, and also Jonah Levy, *Tocqueville's Revenge: State, Society and Economy in Contemporary France* (Cambridge, MA: Harvard University Press, 1999), 237–8.

[98] "Redeploying the State: Liberalization and Social Policy in France," in *Beyond Continuity: Institutional Change in Advanced Political Economies*, ed. W. Streeck and K. Thelen (New York: Oxford University Press, 2005), 119–22.

[99] This strategy was tellingly revealed in the increasingly political manner in which the Barre government applied the Royer Law to fit the electoral purposes of the Gaullist–center-right coalition. In the run-up to both the 1978 legislative and 1981 presidential elections, an unusually high proportion of CDUC decisions to block the construction of supermarkets was upheld by the Ministry of Commerce in order to secure the *petit indépendant* vote in the forthcoming elections. Conversely, a larger proportion of these decisions was reversed by the ministry – giving in effect the go-ahead for building new supermarkets – outside these election periods. Accordingly, during the politically sensitive years of 1977 and 1980, the Ministry of Commerce authorized an even smaller percentage (-0.4% and -1.6% respectively) of the total proposed supermarket surface area than the CDUCs themselves were willing to authorize, versus authorizing +12.1% and +12.9% more surface area than the CDUCs had initially approved in the less politically sensitive years of 1978 and 1979. As John Keeler points out, by 1979 France had developed the second densest supermarket network in Europe after Germany among the four largest European countries. "Corporatist Decentralization," 281, 275, 284.

such a duplicitous strategy provoked the anger of *petits indépendants* against these politicians and, in particular, their erstwhile advocates on the right and center right. This was reflected in the rapid growth of electoral abstentionism among shopkeepers and artisans, which increased from only 6 percent in the first round of the 1978 parliamentary elections to 25 percent in the first round of the 1981 parliamentary elections and 28 percent in the second round.[100] Although this trend in no way signaled a movement of *petits indépendants* to the left, it suggested a worrisome new electoral availability that presaged the defection of many of them to the FN. Similarly, in 1978 29 percent of shopkeepers and 34 percent of artisans affirmed a belief in the necessity of extraparliamentary action to make themselves heard.[101] This implies that a substantial proportion of these strata was disposed to vote for an antisystem political party and was, as it were, only waiting for the opportunity to do so.

The comprehensive victory of the Left in the 1981 presidential and parliamentary elections signaled the definitive downturn in the political fortunes of *petits indépendants*. The economic policies pursued by Socialist-led governments in the early and mid-1980s were largely inimical to their interests. In the wake of the 1981 elections, the Socialist-Communist coalition tried to end the cycle of economic stagnation by stimulating consumption through a dual strategy of reflation and statist economic management. However, the failure of this strategy to achieve the desired growth forced the government to revert to the joint strategy of *déplanification* and social management first tested by the Barre government in the late 1970s. This dual strategy was in turn adopted by the Right when it resumed power in 1986–8 and 1993–5, and then was alternately pursued by the Right and the Left throughout Chirac's presidency. Once again, each of these governments promised to address the concerns of *petits indépendants* while pursuing in effect economic and social policies that ran counter to their interests and abetted their decline.[102]

During the first two years of Mitterrand's presidency, the Socialist-Communist government under Pierre Mauroy pursued a sweeping reflationary program that amounted to a 12 percent increase in government spending in real terms.[103] Billed as "Keynesianism in one country," this program was accompanied by the most comprehensive nationalization campaign since the Liberation, trenchantly underlining the Socialists' commitment to dirigisme.[104] Accordingly, state aid to industry jumped from 35 billion francs in 1981 to 86 billion in 1985, with public enterprises accounting for 24 percent of the employees, 32 percent of the sales, 30 percent of the exports, and 60 percent of the

---

[100] Mayer, "Classes moyennes," 758–9.
[101] Ibid., 695–6.
[102] See Chapter 3.
[103] Smith, *France in Crisis*, 97, 98, 101.
[104] As a testament to the magnitude of renewed state involvement in the economy, this policy entailed a massive expansion of the public sector in France, covering twelve leading conglomerates and thirty-eight banks and resulting in the creation of 600,000 civil-servant posts in 1982 alone. Levy, *Tocqueville's Revenge*, 44.

annual investment (62 billion francs) in the industrial and energy sectors from 1982 to 1986.[105] This massive reinvestment of the state in the economy went hand in hand with its elaboration of activist industrial policies, including setting production targets for a large contingent of industries, as well as resuming the "national champions" policy that had ostensibly been abandoned in the 1970s, calling for SMEs to be fused into larger, often state-controlled firms.[106]

Second, the Socialist-Communist government's commitment to dirigisme was accompanied by a series of unemployment-reduction measures, which became a staple of French social management in subsequent years. These included reducing the work week from forty to thirty-nine hours and extending paid vacations from four to five weeks, making 500,000 recently laid-off workers between the ages of fifty and fifty-five eligible for retirement, and subsidizing "solidarity contracts" to encourage firms to hire younger workers.[107] In addition, a slew of welfarist policies were promulgated to placate the political base of the left-wing coalition, principally industrial workers and *fonctionnaires*. At one level, these included a reform of labor practices under the Auroux Laws of 1982. Designed to increase democracy in the workplace, these measures sought to give workers and their unions a greater say in running their firms while reinforcing their collective bargaining rights.[108] In turn, the Socialist-Communist government enacted redistributive policies that benefited the most vulnerable socio-economic strata as well as the country's fast-growing population of retirees. The *SMIC* (minimum wage) was immediately increased by 10.6 percent in 1981 (with successive yearly revaluations raising it by 25 percent in real terms by 1983) followed by a 25 percent hike in housing subsidies and a 7 percent rise in pension benefits. Third and finally, the Mauroy government raised taxes on the wealthy – that is, capital owners and businesses – in order to pay for these benefits. Notably, it instituted the highest capital gains tax in the industrialized world, precipitating massive capital flight from France to more investor-friendly markets.[109]

[105] Ibid., and Smith, *France in Crisis*, 98.
[106] Levy, *Tocqueville's Revenge*, 44.
[107] Smith, *France in Crisis*, 98, and Hall, *Governing the Economy*, 194.
[108] Specifically, the Auroux Laws obligated all firms counting more than fifty employees to engage in yearly negotiations on economic and social matters of import to the rank and file, including the organization of production, working hours and conditions, the hiring and firing of employees, and the introduction of new technologies into the workplace, as well as mergers and other major financial decisions envisaged by management. Likewise, the new laws enhanced the protections and grievance procedures available to workers, including the stipulation of stricter rules concerning hiring and firing, and an increase in the severance payments to be extended to laid-off employees. Finally, the Auroux Laws strengthened the health and safety committees, which had ostensibly been established in each plant following the postwar reform of social security, and extended the creation of CEs (plant committees) to almost all firms, thereby generally expanding the access of labor to information and resources. Hall, *Governing the Economy*, 219, and Levy, *Tocqueville's Revenge*, 238–40.
[109] Smith, *France in Crisis*, 99.

These socialistic economic and social reforms enraged business in general and small business in particular. The latter naturally opposed the increases in the corporate tax and the *SMIC*, as well as the shorter workweek and other benefits, which increased their production costs. Most of all, French *patrons* deplored the Auroux labor reforms, which they saw as a frontal attack on their patronal authority to run their firms as they chose.[110] In employer circles and particularly among *petits patrons*, Mitterrand's election, much like the Popular Front's victory in May 1936, was viewed as a political cataclysm. For many among them, the victory of the Left portended the socialization of the means of production, an outcome that they pledged to resist by any means necessary.[111]

The failure of reflation and nationalization to return the economy to a path of growth, however, forced the Socialist government to reappraise its policies and reverse course. In a radical turnabout, it embarked on a more comprehensive course of liberalization and *déplanification* than had hitherto ever been attempted. The proximate causes for this dramatic shift were the spiraling inflation and gaping budget and trade deficits that had been created by the increase in government spending, combined with the contraction of demand for French goods due to the global economic slowdown.[112] These conditions in turn brought unsustainable pressure to bear on the franc, triggering a run on

---

[110] Some employers, for example, even went so far as to compare the strengthening of the CEs under the new laws to the establishment of soviets within their firms. Levy, *Tocqueville's Revenge*, 244.

[111] The opposition of *petits patrons* to the new government and its policies remained pretty much universal despite attempts by the latter to propitiate *petits indépendants* and wean some of them away from the former majority. For example, after the 1981 presidential and legislative elections, André Delelis, minister of commerce and of the artisanat in the Mauroy government, had tried to capitalize on the disillusionment of small shopkeepers and artisans by blocking further commercial development as well as tabling proposals geared to address their foremost grievances. These included broadening the scope of the Royer Law by reducing the threshold surface area of retail spaces subject to *CDUC* approval, introducing higher penalties against violators of the Royer Law in order to "moralize" competition, and further revising the tax laws in favor of *petits indépendants*. Likewise, in an attempt to diminish the corporative influence of the CNPF over French employers and divide their forces, the Mauroy government had recognized the Syndicat national de la petite et moyenne industrie (SNPMI), an upstart organization that sought to break the hold of more traditional organizations over the small *patronat*, as an official interlocutor on par with the CNPF. However, in the face of continued *petit indépendant* hostility as well as the new imperatives guiding the government's U-turn toward a policy of *rigueur*, such proposals were rapidly shelved. Instead, this new course was accompanied by a renewed willingness on the part of the Socialists to "open," as one observer evocatively put it, "the political spigot of commercial development." In this sense, the attempt of the Socialist government to woo petty producers and traders further underlined the extent to which fleeting electoral considerations dictated the attitude of both the mainstream Left and Right toward *petits indépendants*, highlighting the secondary importance that they accorded to their interests versus those of other constituencies. Keeler, "Corporatist Decentralization," 287, and Suzanne Berger, "The Socialists and the *Patronat*: The Dilemmas of Co-existence in a Mixed Economy," in *Economic Policy and Policymaking under the Mitterrand Presidency 1981–1984*, ed. H. Machin and V. Wright (London: Frances Pinter, 1986), 230–1.

[112] Between 1981 and 1982, the budget deficit shot up from 0.4% to 3.0% of GDP, while the trade deficit surged from 56 billion to 93 billion francs. Levy, *Tocqueville's Revenge*, 46.

the French currency that threatened its participation in the European Monetary System.

In short, by March 1983, the Mauroy government, much like the Barre government before it, had been forced to implement an austerity program in order to reduce the budget deficit and rein in inflation on the one hand and redress the external balance and relieve pressure on the franc on the other. Under the stewardship of Finance Minister Jacques Delors, a series of strict price and wage controls, compulsory savings measures and, most significantly, painful spending cuts were instituted to stabilize the deficit at 3 percent of GDP. These austerity measures were intensified under Delors's successor, Pierre Bérégovoy, who did away with the wage indexation system introduced under the Grenelle Accords of 1968, which in turn allowed the government to lift most price controls.[113] As a corollary to this austerity program, Bérégovoy introduced the policy of the *franc fort*, which sought to maintain the franc at a higher exchange parity with the Deutschmark and thereby force French firms to lower their costs in order to remain internationally competitive.[114] Such "competitive disinflation" implied severely tightening the money supply and markedly raising interest rates in order to safeguard the franc and reduce inflation by curbing investment. The real interest rate rose from 5 to 8 percent between 1983 and the early 1990s, leading pundits to coin the term "sado-monetarism" to describe the new policy.[115]

This policy of budgetary austerity and monetary *rigueur* allowed France to achieve one of the lowest inflation rates in Western Europe, while initiating a period of steady balance-of-trade surpluses. However, by crowding out borrowing for investment, penalizing existing business borrowers, and depressing consumer demand, the new policy caused, in the words of one observer, "damage to the economy ... so severe and persistent" that growth was effectively strangled and unemployment climbed to 10 percent.[116] Foremost among the victims of *rigueur* were *petits indépendants*. At one level, high interest rates and sharp cuts in spending trammeled consumption, negatively affecting shopkeepers, who still represented the bulk of French commerce. In turn, high interest rates especially hurt small business debtors while dissuading new borrowing from prospective *petits indépendants* who aspired to set up shop on their own.

At the same time, these restrictive macroeconomic policies were accompanied by microeconomic reforms designed to enhance the flexibility of the economy by disengaging the state from its workings. Accordingly, the government also underwent a U-turn from its reassertion of dirigisme during the first two years of the Mitterrand presidency. This disengagement of the state from the economy, overseen by the new finance minister – and subsequent prime minister – Laurent Fabius, had three key components. First, public enterprises were increasingly

[113] Ibid., 52.
[114] Smith, *France in Crisis*, 104, and Levy, "Redeploying," 105.
[115] Levy, "Redeploying," 105, and Smith, *France in Crisis*, 102.
[116] Smith, *France in Crisis*, 102–3, and Levy, "Redeploying," 105–6.

exposed to market competition and, as such, were no longer held to planning targets but evaluated according to the overarching criterion of profitability. Accordingly, state outlays to nationalized industries were eliminated. In exchange, *étatiste* restrictions on the managerial prerogatives of public firms were lifted, the state no longer interfering with closures or layoffs decreed by their managers in order to render them profitable.[117] Thus, though still effectively owned by the state, nationalized firms were to be run as firms in the private sector. Correlatively, the subjection of state enterprises to market competition was accompanied by the state's abandonment of efforts to steer private industry toward planning targets. As in the public sector, restrictions on hiring and firing workers and raising capital were lifted for private firms in exchange for their no longer receiving government assistance. The fact that both public and private firms were subjected to market forces was starkly highlighted by the elimination of all price controls in 1986, a measure that forced firms to become more competitive and less reliant on state handouts to remain economically viable.[118]

Third, *déplanification* in the public and private sectors was accompanied by comprehensive legislative deregulation. At a first level, the latter targeted the financial system in order to make it more capital responsive and able to channel credit to those sectors most in need of it. Accordingly, a series of measures was implemented that diversified financial markets and facilitated the provision of credit to French businesses. Perhaps the most important among them was enacted in 1984, with the reintroduction of competition in the banking sector in order to lower the costs of borrowing.[119] At the same time, controls on the free movement of capital were lifted, thus making it easier for firms to leave the country if they found conditions not to their liking.[120]

At a second level, the deregulatory campaign also extended to the labor market. First, wage deindexation and the lifting of administrative constraints on managers strengthened the hand of employers to impose their terms on their workers and effect layoffs when they needed to. Similarly, the expansion of workshop bargaining to ostensibly expand democracy in the workplace paradoxically increased the leverage of employers in dealing with their employees.[121] As a result of the

[117] Levy, "Redeploying," 106.
[118] Ibid.
[119] In addition, such measures included authorizing companies to issue nonvoting stock, creating a second market to service the credit needs of SMEs, and establishing markets in commercial paper.
[120] Levy, *Tocqueville's Revenge*, 53.
[121] In particular, they were greatly helped by the principle of *dérogation* stipulating that agreements concluded between employers and workers within the firm were to take precedence over those reached at broader levels of negotiation. This allowed employers to conclude contracts with CEs within their firms that were exempt from collective agreements reached within individual professional branches or even at a regional or national interprofessional level. In some cases, firm-level bargaining agreements even exempted employers from nationally mandated labor regulations such as the SMIC (minimum wage). Ibid., 80–1. For a comprehensive analysis of labor deregulation and specifically the impact of the Auroux Laws on employer-labor relations, see Chris Howell, "The Dilemmas of Post-Fordism: Socialists, Flexibility, and Labor Market Deregulation in France," *Politics and Society* 20(1) (1992), 71–99.

fractured nature and weak implantation of unions in the workplace, combined with a context of high unemployment, French employers were able to achieve much greater labor flexibility within their firms. In this sense, it is no small irony that the Auroux Laws, which had been drafted to enhance the leverage of wage earners in the workplace, ended up benefiting capital instead of labor.

This *déplanification* and deregulation campaign launched by the Fabius government was expanded by the second Chirac ministry of 1986–8 and completed by governments of both the Left and the Right in the early 1990s. In particular, these successive governments reversed the nationalizations undertaken between 1982 and 1984 and returned most public firms to private ownership. In addition, beginning with the ministry of Michel Rocard (1988–91) and lasting through the nineties, measures were introduced to promote the growth of SMEs as the basis of the country's economic revival. These included state subsidies and performance-conditioned loans to integrate modern materials and technologies into the existing product lines of these firms, to encourage them to develop new product lines and computerize their production operations, and to increase their hiring of trained engineers and business managers.[122]

The implementation of these microeconomic reforms from the mid-1980s to the mid-1990s rationalized the structure and liberalized the operation of the French economy. The elimination of subsidies to public and private enterprises resulted in a large number of bankruptcies.[123] Financial deregulation spurred a greater reliance on financial markets by a growing number of French firms.[124] And labor market deregulation enhanced wage flexibility and reduced production costs, substantially increasing firm profits.[125] In short, these reforms ushered in a new economic structure that revealed the profound "decontrol" of the French economy relative to the more selective dirigisme of the 1970s, let alone Socialist-Communist *étatisme* and the nationalizations of 1981–2. The changing face of the French economy reflected a radical evolution in the principles underlying its operation, marking a shift away from direct state oversight and management of public enterprises toward its essential disengagement from the economy, which was almost entirely left to the free operation of the market. As Jonah Levy noted, "French economic policy has been transformed beyond recognition."[126]

From this standpoint, one would have expected that *petits indépendants* and *petits patrons* who claimed to enshrine the tenets of economic liberalism would

[122] Levy, "Redeploying," 112, as well as *Tocqueville's Revenge*, 78–83.
[123] The most spectacular of these, the 1984 bankruptcy of Creusot-Loire, would prove to be the largest in the country's history. Levy, *Tocqueville's Revenge*, 52.
[124] As an indication of this increasing reliance of French firms on the new forms of credit wrought by financial deregulation, the share of external financing provided by banks dropped from 58.6% in 1984 to 33.7% in 1986. Ibid., 53.
[125] Between 1982 and 1989, the share of value-added received by capital rose from 24.0% to 31.7%, surpassing the previous high attained in the early 1970s. As a result of these cost gains going to capital, firm profits rose from 9.8% of value added in 1982 to 17.3% in 1989. Levy, "Redeploying," 107, 106.
[126] *Tocqueville's Revenge*, 20.

rejoice at this disengagement of the state from the economy. Yet, their reaction was tepid at best. In the first place, these measures of deregulation and decontrol overwhelmingly favored large firms, often to the detriment of small employers. For example, financial market liberalization failed to enhance the access of small business to capital and, indeed, may well have impeded it.[127] Similarly, the promotion of SMEs, particularly at the regional and municipal levels, also backfired, in effect benefiting the biggest regional firms and even defunct multinationals to the detriment of small local producers.[128] All in all, the liberalization policies pursued during Mitterrand's presidency were a source of disillusionment for small businessmen. These disproportionately favored *les gros* under the guise of developing small and medium enterprises. In addition, within small business itself, these policies drove a wedge between the advanced SME sector and more marginal family firms and *petits indépendants*, the latter persisting in seeing themselves as the perennial victims of a neglectful, if not malevolent, state.

More fundamentally, the unenthusiastic response of *petits patrons* to the liberal reforms enacted from the mid-1980s on reflected their disquiet over the growing social interventionism that accompanied the decline in state control. Indeed, this retreat from dirigisme did not spell the end of state intervention per se, but instead marked its displacement to the realm of social policy. It is not the least of paradoxes that, despite the abandonment of planning and the decline of state intervention in the economy, overall government spending has continued to increase since the end of the neo-Keynesian experiment of the early 1980s and following the *déplanification* that began in the mid-1980s. Reflecting this trend, total government spending rose from 42.6 percent of GDP in 1983 to fully 46 percent in 1999.[129]

This upsurge in government expenditure is almost wholly attributable to the growth of the welfare state to attenuate the social dislocations attendant upon the retreat from dirigisme and economic liberalization. The growth in welfare spending was geared toward financing social adjustment in two principal areas. First, it underwrote labor market programs designed to dampen the impact of the rise in unemployment caused by economic restructuring and the deflationary policies that accompanied it during the first Mitterrand *septennat*. These mostly took the form of early retirement programs that were intended to allow firms to pare down their workforces without causing a new increase in

[127] Since following deregulation, large multinationals could forsake traditional bank loans and secure credit on the domestic financial market or through foreign borrowing, French banks were forced to offer credit on highly favorable terms if they wished to keep their business. In order to compensate for profits lost from having to make disadvantageous loans to their biggest clients, they substantially stiffened lending conditions for small businesses. The latter were forced to accept these terms since bank loans essentially remained the only form of credit accessible to them, for the most part family-owned firms excluded from the domestic equity market. Ibid., 269–70.

[128] For a microeconomic study of the dysfunctions of SME financing in the Besançon and Saint-Étienne areas, see ibid., ch. 4.

[129] Levy, "Redeploying," 104.

unemployment.[130] By the early 1990s, given their failure to reduce unemployment, successive Socialist and center-right governments supplemented these early retirement programs with various work subsidization measures and business-friendly tax incentives to encourage low-wage hires, particularly among young workers. Finally, in the second half of the 1990s, the Jospin government introduced two further labor market initiatives in the hope of reducing unemployment. These included subsidizing nonprofit and public-sector organizations to encourage youth employment and, most famously, the Aubry Law, which reduced the work week from thirty-nine to thirty-five hours.[131]

Overall, the number of workers affected by these labor-reduction measures increased from 1.2 million in 1984 to 3 million in 1999. Adding this figure to the approximately 2 million unemployed, this meant that by the close of the century, France had one of the lowest labor-force participation rates – particularly among the youngest and oldest workers – and the shortest average duration of employment in the industrialized world.[132] In turn, as a consequence of this upsurge of wage earners enrolled in labor-reducing programs, aggregate spending on labor policy rose from 2 percent of GDP during the mid-1980s to fully 4.2 percent of GDP in 1999. This proportion is comparable to that of Sweden, the national paragon of activist labor-market policy.[133]

The second great area of expenditure increases to offset the effects of *déplanification* is in respect to welfare programs proper. According to Levy, France has evolved the largest welfare state outside of Scandinavia, exceeding even Germany despite the mammoth social costs of reunification. Welfare spending in France increased from 21.3 percent of GDP in 1980 to 26.5 percent in 1990 and 29.5 percent in 1998.[134] This period also saw the launch of

---

[130] Underlying such programs was the belief that following an initially painful period of restructuring, economic growth would resume at a higher clip than before, thus eliminating any further need for them. However, sluggish employment creation despite the resumption of growth in the second half of the 1980s meant the number of people enrolled in early retirement programs did not decline and, in some estimations, even increased. According to one study, this number has remained more or less constant between 450,000 and 600,000 since the mid-eighties. Another study has placed this figure substantially higher, estimating that the number of pre-retirees had quintupled since the late 1970s to a total of about one million people by 1990. Ibid., 107–8, and Smith, *France in Crisis*, 111.

[131] The latter contained a package of incentives to facilitate its implementation by firms, including granting subsidies to those who signed collective contracts reducing workers' work schedules, affording them much greater flexibility in organizing their production, and providing a five-year phase-in period from 1995 to 2000 during which they could adapt to its requirements. Smith, *France in Crisis*, 112–14, and Levy, "Redeploying," 108–9.

[132] In 1985 only 67.8% of men between the ages of fifty-five and fifty-nine still remained employed in France, as compared to 78% in West Germany and 80.1% in the United States. By 2002 only 37% of French men over the age of sixty and under the age of twenty-four were still active in the workforce. Levy, "Redeploying," 109, and Smith, *France in Crisis*, 113.

[133] Levy, "Redeploying," 109.

[134] Within this spending increase, health-care expenditures rose from 7.4% of GDP in 1980 to 9.6% in 1998, while social security expenditures increased from 7.7% of GDP in 1991 to 9.8% in 2000. Ibid., 109–10.

specialized benefit programs to assist those worst affected by deindustrialization and economic restructuring. These included the introduction of the Revenu minimum d'insertion (RMI) in 1988 by the Rocard government, followed by the Couverture maladie universelle and the Aide personnalisée à l'autonomie by the Jospin government in 2000 and 2002.[135]

In short, since the mid-1980s, a vast "social anesthesia state" has emerged to ease the pain of economic restructuring and liberalization. Support for this strategy has not been limited to the Left but extends to the Right as well.[136] Likewise, both Left and Right adhered to common labor-market policies in order to reduce unemployment, particularly by subsidizing new hires.[137] In short, through the course of the 1980s and 1990s, taxes increased under governments of both Left and Right at the same time that the latter were removing statist obstacles to the expansion of the private sector. It was under the stewardship of both political elites that the purview of state intervention was progressively redeployed from the *étatiste* stance it had assumed at the start of Mitterrand's first term to the anesthetizing function it evolved from the mid-eighties on.

Predictably, business and particularly the owners of small enterprises and *petits indépendants* were incensed by the mounting tax burden that was imposed on them to finance this growth in welfare spending. According to one estimate, by 1990 payroll taxes were adding 50 percent to the wages of low-skilled workers.[138] At the same time, the state removed any fiscal exemptions that still applied to SMEs and *petits indépendants*. In many cases, the resulting tax obligations increased their costs beyond a level they could sustain, driving the most marginal among them into bankruptcy – hence, the precipitous fall in the number of French *petits indépendants* that has coincided with the rise in welfare spending since the mid-1980s.

From a political standpoint, then, the experience of *petits indépendants* in the 1980s and 1990s intensified trends that had already been in evidence in the 1960s and, following a brief hiatus in the early 1970s, resumed in the second half of the decade. At one level, these trends reflected the separation of *petits patrons* from the mainstream political parties, particularly on the center right. At the

[135] The RMI provided a monthly allowance of 2,500 francs a month to the long-term unemployed and ostensibly offered them support in finding a job. The Couverture maladie universelle offered free health care to low-income recipients who could not afford the out-of-pocket medical service fee, while the Aide personnalisée à l'autonomie provided coverage for in-home care for the elderly. For various supplemental benefits targeting specific constituencies, see ibid., 110–11.

[136] Hence, for example, Chirac's pledge to heal the nation's social fracture during the 1995 presidential election campaign, implying a joint commitment with the Left to preserve the welfare state.

[137] In this sense, disagreements between the Left and the Right have not been so much over the principle of social intervention or its attendant costs but rather about how such intervention should be paid for. Thus, whereas Jospin elected to fund welfare programs by raising taxes on the wealthy, Chirac and Balladur did so by resorting to more regressive sales and payroll taxes. Smith, *France in Crisis*, 90.

[138] Ibid.

same time, the eighties and nineties saw further fragmentation among *petits patrons* themselves, notably between SME owners, on whom economic recovery was said to depend, and *petits indépendants*, who were cast as throwbacks to an obsolete social and economic order. Accordingly, the latter evinced a renewed willingness to resort to extrainstitutional methods in order to press their interests on the state.

In particular, following Mitterrand's election and the Mauroy government's nationalization and regulatory program, there was a surge of support for the SNPMI, which had taken up the mantle of *petit indépendant* protest following the decline of the CID-UNATI. As a measure of *petit patron* discontent, the SNPMI saw its representation in the labor arbitration court (*prud'homme*) elections jump from 2 percent in 1979 to 14.2 percent in 1982.[139] Shortly thereafter, a SNPMI rally mobilized fifteen thousand small business owners, shopkeepers, and artisans in the streets of Paris. In attendance was Jean-Marie Le Pen, leader of the little-known Front National.[140] This initial demonstration set off a wave of *petit indépendant* protest, culminating in May 1983 in three successive demonstrations by the SNPMI, the CGPME, and the CID-UNATI, the last two bringing respectively twenty thousand and five thousand petty producers, shopkeepers, and small employers out into the Paris streets.[141] It was these marginalized and radicalized small business strata that would bring the FN out of obscurity in the June 1984 European parliamentary elections and then fuel the party's takeoff in the 1986 parliamentary and 1988 presidential elections.

PETITS INDÉPENDANTS AND EXTRAPARLIAMENTARY POLITICS IN THE POSTWAR PERIOD

> Si tous les petits Poujades et tous les tondus de France se donnent la main, ils seront plus puissants que les puissants. *Fraternité française*, 31 December 1955[142]

> Chaban-Delmas et sa clique ont mobilisé tous leurs flics. Pourquoi ce déchainement? Parce que Chaban et toute la mafia capitaliste qui le soutient crèvent de trouille devant la révolte des petits commerçants et artisans. Nous nous battons pour que ça change radicalement, pour liquider les gros, pour survivre le temps que se construise la France du peuple sur la France du fric. CID-UNATI tract, April 1970[143]

> The government knows that beyond the economic power of small business, there is also a political dimension. It remembers the experience of Allende in

---

[139] S. Berger, "Socialists and the *Patronat*," 231.
[140] As several observers have pointed out, the upstart federation enjoyed close ties to the radical Right, its leader, Gérard Deuil, openly professing his admiration for Pétain and Vichy. Mayer, "Classes moyennes," 672, as well as Wilson, *Interest-Group Politics*, 104.
[141] Wilson, *Interest-Group Politics*, 232, and Mayer, "Classes moyennes," 672.
[142] Quoted in Hoffmann, *Mouvement Poujade*, 233.
[143] Quoted in Roy, *Les commerçants*, 7.

Chile. It was not the military that overthrew that regime; it only delivered the final blow. It was really the small entrepreneurs who caused the fall of Allende. The Socialist government here has learned from the Allende failure and wants to avoid our all-out opposition. A senior CGPME leader, 1982[144]

The upsurge of petty producer protest in the wake of Mitterrand's election represents only the latest instance of extraparliamentary revolt by *petits indépendants* in the post–World War II era. The UDCA in the 1950s, the CID-UNATI in the early 1970s, and the SNPMI in the early 1980s shared a common recourse to direct action, verbal excess, and occasional physical violence as means of publicizing their cause and getting the state to recognize their claims. Characteristically, these movements coalesced around a single issue, appealing to shopkeepers and artisans "who could not," in Jeanne Gaillard's phrase, "afford to pay the price of progress."[145] Thus, the strongest support for Poujadism was to be found in poor and rural areas south of the Loire, where the revenues of *petits indépendants* were lower than elsewhere.[146] Similarly, when the CID-UNATI crested in the early 1970s, its greatest level of support (72 percent) was found among shopkeepers and artisans in the food preparation and retail trades, which counted the smallest and most marginal *petits indépendants*. It was no accident that Gérard Nicoud, the movement's leader, presented himself as the defender of the "proletarians" within their ranks.[147] Finally, a socioeconomic analysis of the participants in the SNPMI's rallies revealed that it also appealed mostly to petty shopkeepers and artisans, as well as small family firm owners.[148]

At one level, the appeal of these extraparliamentary movements among *petits indépendants* reflected their loss of faith in institutionalized modes of organization and intermediation within the parliamentary and administrative arenas. Similarly, playing up their antisystem credentials, they engaged in verbal and occasionally physical, violence against political elites and *fonctionnaires* as well as their interlocutors among big business. They relied on extrainstitutional

[144] Quoted in Wilson, *Interest-Group Politics*, 103.
[145] "La petite entreprise," 172. The proximate cause of the Poujade revolt was the tax reform enacted by the Pinay and Laniel governments in 1952–3, that spurring the mobilization of the CID-UNATI was the 1966 health insurance reform, and that driving the SNPMI the profligate spending program put in place by the new Socialist-Communist government. Hoffmann, *Mouvement Poujade*, 17–22; Gresle, *Indépendants*, 100–1, 109; Mayer, "Classes moyennes," 643ff.; Roy, *Les commerçants*, 15; and Wilson, *Interest-Group Politics*, 104.
[146] A report from 1954 on the state of commerce in France found that local tax yields, for the most part *patente* revenues collected from small shopkeepers and artisans, were inferior to the national mean by 39% for the region of Montpellier, 31% for that of Toulouse, 30% for that of Clermont-Ferrand, 28% for that of Limoges, and 15% for that of Marseille. Hoffmann, *Mouvement Poujade*, 11.
[147] Similarly, in 1978, four years after support for the CID-UNATI had begun to erode, the proportion of *petits indépendants* holding a favorable opinion of Gérard Nicoud increased from 32% among those employing three to five salaried workers to 45% among those working alone or relying on family assistance. Mayer, "Classes moyennes," 687, 648–9, 689–90.
[148] S. Berger, "Socialists and *Patronat*," 232, and Mayer, "Classes," 674.

methods such as street protests, tax strikes, sit-ins, the abduction of state officials, and other forms of civil disobedience in order to mark their disapproval and press their demands. Inveighing against the corruption of the political elite, they denounced *la politique politicarde* and called for the ejection of the current political class and its replacement by fresh representatives[149] – hence the perennial appeal of the slogan *Sortez les sortants* (Get rid of the incumbents) that was coined by Poujade in the mid-1950s and then resurrected by Nicoud in the early 1970s.[150] By the same token, they denounced "lazy and budgetivorous" civil servants and "disdainful technocrats" associated with a state bureaucracy perceived to be acting against their interests.[151]

At root, these *petit indépendant*-based extraparliamentary movements grounded their ideology and discourse on a fundamental distinction between the *pays légal* and the *pays réel*. Rather than representing the interests of true Frenchmen, parliamentarians were cast as an obstacle dividing the people from the republican state whose charge it was to protect them.[152] Similarly, the clique of *hauts fonctionnaires* was thought incapable of understanding or empathy for the plight of ordinary Frenchmen.[153] These broadsides against the parliamentary state and bureaucracy in turn opened into a universal condemnation of the structural and conceptual attributes of social and political modernity. These movements attacked the symbols of this modernity and deployed tropes associated with a pristine and harmonious precapitalist order, affirming the ideals of small-scale property and small producer democracy that had underpinned the original republican state.[154] Likewise, they justified their recourse to antiparliamentary methods by appealing to the insurrectionary rhetoric of the French Revolution, incorporating revolutionary imagery and slogans in order to lend moral and historical legitimacy to their actions.[155]

---

[149] Accordingly, they variously excoriated the National Assembly as a "den of debauchees," occupied by "creeps" and "adventurers" (Poujade) who resembled "a clique" or "a mafia" (Nicoud). Hoffmann, *Mouvement Poujade*, 214, 215, and Roy, *Les commerçants*, 7.

[150] Hoffmann, *Mouvement Poujade*, 304.

[151] Ibid., 212, and Roy, *Les commerçants*, 24.

[152] *Fraternité française*, the UDCA's organ, expanded on this theme in February 1955, claiming that "these gentlemen don't give a damn about the people …, they just rake in the bank notes, and they wish for us to accept in exchange for our dough these little pieces of paper called 'electoral ballots,' which aren't even big enough for us to put to another use." Quoted in Hoffmann, *Mouvement Poujade*, 219.

[153] Embroidering on this theme in an interview with *L'Express* in March 1955, Poujade observed that "France is afflicted with an overabundance of people with diplomas, *polytechniciens,* economists, philosophers, and all kinds of other dreamers who have lost all contact with the real people." Quoted in ibid., 220.

[154] On the recurrence of this misoneistic critique among postwar extraparliamentary *petit indépendant* movements, see François Gresle, "Les petits patrons et la tentation activiste," in Lavau, Grunberg, and Mayer, *L'univers politique des classes moyennes*, 308–9, and also Hoffmann, *Mouvement Poujade*, 219–34.

[155] Poujade in particular called for France to be "liberated like in '89," advocating that a new Estates General be convened to overthrow the new "feudalities" and "Bastilles" of large-scale capital and its political defenders. Likewise, reflecting this revolutionary theme, the organism in charge

From this standpoint, the *petit indépendant* protest movements of the post-war era are to be seen less as a repudiation of the republican state than as an attempt to restore the latter to the values and forms of an authentic, primordial liberalism. Much like the interwar Fédération des contribuables, they repre-sented a "radicalism of the Center" to use Seymour Martin Lipset's phrase, rather than an antidemocratic and revolutionary form of petit bourgeois revolt, such as fascism.[156] The primordial Radical filiation of these movements can be seen in the institutional solutions they advocated to restore the republic to its former purity, notably by breaking down the representative divide that was erected between the state and the people. In typically Jacobin fashion, they called for direct democracy in various guises, popular consultation by referendum, and the downgrading or even discarding of parliament, viewed as the seedbed of corruption by which the *gros* exercised undue political influence at the expense of the *petits*.[157] By extension, they called for establishing a kind of corporatist assembly alongside the parliament in order to enlist the various professions in the formulation of economic policy.[158] In this respect, postwar *petit indépendant* revolts reproduced many of the demands of previous Radical oppositional movements, such as Boulangisme, the Parti social français, and even the RPF.

Thus, these postwar *petit indépendant* revolts were the product of the sense of abandonment felt by many shopkeepers and artisans at the hands of a republican state that hitherto had been their greatest protector. The latter was guilty in their eyes of unfairly favoring the interests of large-scale capital, the new middle classes, and even the working class, at their expense. These extraparliamentary revolts reflected *petits indépendants'* angst and frustration at their *déclassement* in respect to these constituencies and their inability to improve their situation from "within the system." In the words of François Gresle, "Their discontent was rooted ... in the feeling of having been abandoned by a state that had formerly protected them ... at the same time that they were being outdistanced by groups ... with whom they believed they could compete, if only they had not been victimized by an 'unjust' fiscal and social security system."[159]

---

of the Poujadist's 1956 parliamentary campaign called itself the Committee of Public Safety. Hoffmann, *Mouvement Poujade*, 233, 234, and Mayer, "Classes," 746–7.

[156] Cf. *Political Man: The Social Bases of Politics* (Baltimore: Johns Hopkins University Press, 1981), ch. 5. See also on this point Hoisington, *Taxpayer Revolt in France*, 168–9, 188–9; Hoffmann, *Mouvement Poujade*, 387–94; and Milza, *Fascisme français*, 306–8.

[157] For example, Poujade continuously inveighed against the parliament for "constantly and out-rageously favoring the trusts, large-scale industry, high finance, and *le grand capitalisme*." A decade and a half later, a CID-UNATI tract demonized "Chaban and the capitalist mafia that support him," and portrayed the new movement as "fighting in order to radically change things, to liquidate *les gros*, and to survive long enough so that the France of the people can be built on the ruins of the France of the rich." Hoffman, *Mouvement Poujade*, 221, and Roy, *Les commerçants*, 7.

[158] Hoffmann, *Mouvement Poujade*, 236, and Gresle, "Petits patrons et la tentation activiste," 307.

[159] Gresle, "Petits patrons et la tentation activiste," 311.

In turn, their success in wrenching concessions from the state following their recourse to extraparliamentary action could not but reinforce *petits indépendants'* conviction of the efficacy of such methods. Many of them became convinced that they stood to secure greater concessions from the state if they revolted against it than if they played by the rules and sought to inform policy through legal institutional channels. In effect, growing numbers of *petits indépendants* concluded that violence, whether rhetorical or physical, "paid" and that the margins of illegality were the best terrain on which to pursue their political ends. It is worth quoting what the leader of the CID-UNATI, Gérard Nicoud, said on the subject in his autobiography:

> Why were we forced to illegality? Of all French social classes, we were the only ones that until 1969 had expressed its discontent only with pious wishes or legal protest. The result as of January 1, 1969: NOTHING, absolutely NOTHING. Now, looking around us, we could see that others were using more direct arguments. Farmers blocked the roads, and the government gave in. Truckers, the same. Employees, when they struck, locked in the bosses and used wildcat strikes. Even the National Police, supposedly the guarantor of legality, threatens to march on Matignon and throw the minister out the window!
>
> And everywhere, public authorities yield and sanction these acts of force. . . . the method obviously is a preferable one. May 1968 was to reveal to us the path we had to take. Not only did the government, though well aware of our serious problems, do nothing for us, but, terrified by the wave that threatened to carry it off, it leaned on us for support; flattering us, invoking "the Flag," "the Republic: . . . What a disillusion! All we got were more supermarkets. . . . Finally, no one can deny the evidence if they compare what our social class obtained up to 1969 and the results since 1969 [i.e., since the start of CID-UNATI violence]. . . . Whose fault is it that concertation takes place in the street? Above all, the Executive.[160]

The growing willingness of their organizational representatives to resort to extrainstitutional, even illegal means reinforced *petits indépendants'* ambivalence toward the parliamentary republic. The extrainstitutional methods employed by these movements and the effectiveness of the latter in helping them achieve their aims inflected the outlook of people who identified with them in an illiberal, even antidemocratic direction. In this sense, these movements were crucibles that shaped the political culture of their participants and, by extension, of the broader social constituencies they claimed to represent.[161] That several such movements emerged in the postwar era appears to confirm

[160] Quoted in S. Berger, "D'une boutique à l'autre," 130.
[161] In this sense, the influence of the civil society organizations represented by these movements did not necessarily coincide with the spread of democratic values and practices, but instead may well have impeded them. This finding would appear to debunk the initial conviction of some civil society theorists and democratization scholars that the existence of an active civil society in a country will somehow automatically translate into the emergence of democratic norms and practices within it. As Philip Nord surmised, "there is good reason to link civic activism and democratic government but at the same time it must be acknowledged that associational

that *petits indépendants* increasingly found these methods acceptable and became more and more disposed to use them.

As in the 1930s, these extrainstitutional dispositions were soon enlisted in the service of the radical Right, and the "radicalism of the Center" they reflected shaded over into support of the latter. This evolution is suggested by the fact that postwar *petit indépendant* protest movements would all develop strong ties to the radical Right. Thus, the Poujade movement was essentially captured by the radical Right after harnessing the civil revolt of *petits indépendants*, while CID-UNATI rallies in the early 1970s and those of the SNPMI a decade later were monitored and attended by figures linked to the Front National.[162] The nostalgia of these movements for a return to a preindustrial society and their attendant vision of small producer democracy betrayed a misoneistic cultural outlook that was readily invested with the exclusionary nationalism of the radical Right. At the same time, such a rapprochement was greatly facilitated by the precarious socioeconomic situation of *petits indépendants* at the end of the twentieth century.

The cumulative sociopolitical experiences of *petits indépendants* since the late nineteenth century, accrued through their interactions with electoral parties and sectoral organizations, parliamentary lobbies and professional associations, state *administrations*, and extrainstitutional groups, imbued in them a fundamental ambivalence toward the principles and processes of representative democracy as enshrined in the French republican state. This ambivalence grew as the country modernized and the state increasingly became implicated in its modernization. At first glance, this ambivalence seems surprising because, at its outset, *petits indépendants* in particular and smallholders in general were among the leading proponents of the democratic principles of the Third Republic. Yet, this initial attachment to the republican state was inextricably bound up in a petty-property-based vision of democracy that predated industrial society. Beginning as early as the turn of the nineteenth century, the social and economic structures supporting this petty producer republicanism began to be eroded by a dynamic of modernization that was inimical to *petits indépendants*' interests and worldview. As the social foundations underlying the republican state superseded the petty producer dispensation that initially had given rise to it, it was only a matter of time before *petits indépendants* brought their initial commitment to that state into question. At the same time, the republican state and its agents did much to disabuse *petits indépendants* of the inexorability of modernization. When the latter was finally foisted on them in the 1950s and 1960s, they saw it as a fundamental betrayal of their interests by their greatest erstwhile protector.

Signs of this betrayal had long been accumulating, however. Already in the interwar period dissident voices had emerged in the mainstream parties,

militancy can take on even anti-democratic forms." Introduction to *Civil Society before Democracy*, xv.
[162] Milza, *Fascisme français*, 308; S. Berger, "Socialists and *Patronat*," 232; and Mayer, "Classes moyennes," 672.

particularly the Alliance démocratique and even the supposed bastion of small producer defense, the Radical Party, which lauded the virtues of modernization. In the postwar period, these voices became amplified in policy circles. Defenders of small property found themselves increasingly isolated as the parliamentary formations that had defended them in the past, such as the Radicals and Conservative Independents, either disappeared or were absorbed into the pro-modernization Gaullist majority.

Similarly, at the level of organization and intermediation, *petits indépendants* saw fairly early on their corporative representatives ignored by elected officials and civil servants in favor of better-organized rival groups, such as advanced employers, *cadres*, industrial workers, and *fonctionnaires*. As *petits indépendants* quickly learned, when push came to shove, organized pressure groups such as the Comité Mascuraud or the UIE before World War I, or peak business organizations such as the CGPF in the 1930s, defended big over small business every time. The same was true in sectoral organizations such as the Chambers of Commerce and Industry, where *petits indépendants* and *petits patrons* invariably took a second seat to more powerful economic interests. In turn, this organizational weakness of *petits indépendants* increased in the post–World War II period. Though pressure groups such as the CGPME continued to lobby on their behalf, the efficacy of these organizations was greatly reduced as the parliament's power to make policy was downgraded and the most advanced sectors gained more and more influence over the Administration d'État.

Because they were unable to influence public policy through the representative and bureaucratic instances of the state, *petits indépendants* increasingly turned to extraparliamentary movements to force the state to address their concerns. The confrontational tactics of Pierre Poujade's UDCA or Gérard Nicoud's CID-UNATI, and the state's inability to co-opt or suppress them, often compelled it to accede to their demands. In this sense, these movements' fleeting success comforted the illusion among *petits indépendants* that a republic of petty producers could be reestablished if only the state recognized their collective aspirations and needs.

From this standpoint, the primordial republican ethos of *morcellement* and petty producer democracy defended by French *petits indépendants* articulated with the misoneism of the radical Right and the organicist conception of society that it presented. As the ideological and sociological foundations of French republicanism shifted to adapt to the changing requirements and conditions of capitalist modernity, the radical Right increasingly stood out as the lone defender of the traditional ideal of *morcellement* and a small-property-based society. In turn, as we have seen, the mythologization of the past by the radical Right, looking back to a social order based on petty rural and artisanal producers, became an increasingly important source of comfort and reassurance for *petits indépendants* as their economic roles and social identities came under threat.

In short, French *petits indépendants* evolved a deep sense of grievance vis-à-vis the republican state. When joined with their traditionalist and authoritarian worldview, this made them potentially receptive to the antimodernist and anti-liberal discourse of the radical Right. Put in another way, *petits indépendants'* commitment to the principles and processes of parliamentary democracy became less and less of a counterweight to the cultural affinities they shared with the radical Right. The model of *indépendance* they had evolved combined with their fraught experience of modernization to instill in *petits indépendants* a distinct political culture that made them increasingly amenable to its prescriptions.

8

Epilogue: French Workers in Crisis and the Entrenchment of the Front National

Il y a tout de même une chose que je voudrais savoir: si la classe ouvrière est foutue, pourquoi êtes vous communistes . . . ou socialistes? . . . comme vous voudrez.

Troppmann in Georges Bataille's *Le bleu du ciel*[1]

Le PC est devenu trop conciliant avec ceux qui foutent la merde, excusez-moi l'expression. Mais quand des petits cons cassent la voiture de ma fille, qui ils emmerdent? Pas les riches. C'est à nous, les ouvriers, qu'ils font du tort.

A retired Marseille longshoreman, July 1995[2]

Je reviens chez moi . . . pour parler de la misère d'où surgissent vos fantasmes, de cette terre aride que n'irrigue plus aucune solidarité, de ce désert où sévit le mirage lepéniste. . . . Si seulement je pouvais forcer les sourds à entendre votre mal de vivre! Avant qu'il ne soit vraiment trop tard. À Sarcelles-sous-Mistral, on courbe les épaules sous les barres de béton, l'horizon est bouché par le chômage. D'année en année, le champ des espoirs se rétrécit. La gauche au pouvoir pas plus que la droite n'a éclairci l'avenir. Sur le terrain, rares sont ceux qui parlent de serrer les coudes, de combattre ensemble. On se bat, on en bave, mais c'est chacun pour soi, quitte à piétiner le voisin. Même une socialiste, ancienne gréviste, prend pour cible aujourd'hui les Arabes et les Juifs. Cette logique de bouc émissaire n'a pas de fin: elle vous, elle nous broiera tous.

Anne Tristan, "Lettre ouverte à Véronique, Denis, Alessandro et les autres . . ."[3]

Up to this point, the analysis has focused on *petits indépendants* as the historic social base of the radical Right. This pattern continued to hold through the 1980s in which, after a decade on the political margins, the Front National chiefly depended on *petits indépendants*' electoral support to emerge onto the national political scene. However, from the early 1990s on, a seminal shift occurred in the composition of the party's electorate: *petits indépendants* were supplanted by industrial workers as its principal source of support.[4] In light of

---

[1] Bataille, *Romans et récits* (Paris: Gallimard, Coll. de la Pléiade, 2004), 146.
[2] Quoted in N. Mayer, "Du communisme au Front National," *L'Histoire*, no. 195 (Jan. 1996), 113.
[3] *Au front* (Paris: Gallimard, 1988), 253–4.
[4] See Introduction.

this development, the resurgence of the radical Right in the form of the FN is not simply reducible to the structural and cultural crisis affecting French *petits indépendants*. The recent surge of working-class support for the party suggests that the analysis also needs to take into account the social situation of French workers over the past quarter century. In particular, we need to explain how the FN came to eclipse the Communist Party (PCF) as the leading political party among French workers during this period.[5]

The radical Right's implantation among the working class cannot just be imputed to the political preferences of conservative workers who, as a function of being employed in smaller, quasi-artisanal firms, displayed many of the same traditionalist attitudes that drew *petits indépendants* to the FN in the 1980s.[6] Indeed, the fact that it was not until very recently that the radical Right made lasting electoral inroads among French workers suggests that much of this support came from properly industrial wage earners. Further, the sheer magnitude of working-class support garnered by the radical Right since the late 1980s – representing according to one survey a full third (33 percent) of working-class voters in the first round of the 2002 presidential election – implies that a radical shift has occurred in the political allegiance of this constituency identified historically with the Left. Accordingly, it was around this time that the term *gaucho-lepénisme* appeared in the French political lexicon to capture this novel phenomenon.[7]

This shift of French workers to the radical Right has gone hand in hand with the profound social crisis that has engulfed the working class as a result of the transformation of the French economy since the late 1970s. As in the case of *petits indépendants* before them, this crisis translates workers' heightened occupational vulnerability and the erosion of their class identity in contemporary French society. In this context, the radical Right made it possible for workers to rationalize their foremost anxieties and offered them a solution for resolving them. They accepted its conspiratorial explanation for their decline and its exclusionary notion of national appurtenance.

As in the case of *petits indépendants*, the crisis that has afflicted French industrial workers presents both structural (occupational and socioeconomic) and cultural (symbolic and psychological) dimensions. At a first level, it reflects

---

[5] See ibid.

[6] On the sociocultural and political-cultural affinities shared by these types of workers with *petits indépendants*, see Capdevielle and Mouriaux, *L'ouvrier conservateur*.

[7] P. Perrineau, "Le vote d'extrême droite en France: adhésion ou protestation?" *Futuribles*, no. 276 (June 2002), 9. The political provenance of working-class support for the FN has been the subject of some debate. Although some have argued that it was mostly constituted of former left-wing voters, others have contended that the proletarianization of the FN vote is the expression of the broader depoliticization of French workers. Both of these views, however, are compatible with the argument that is advanced here: that this upsurge in worker support for the party coincided with the collapse of the Communist Party and union movement as the historic vehicles of political socialization and acculturation of the French working class – regardless of whether these new FN voters had actually voted on the left in the past. For examples of these divergent interpretations, see Perrineau, *Le symptôme Le Pen*, 108–10, 218–19, and Mayer, *Ces Français qui votent Le Pen*, 98–103, 124–6.

the deteriorating socioeconomic situation of French workers over the past quarter century. The material position of the latter was significantly degraded during the 1980s and 1990s as a function of the rapid growth of unemployment in the manufacturing sector and the consequent erosion of workers' wages and standard of living.

Considering the first of these factors, we find that, by the turn of the millennium, the country faced an aggregate unemployment rate of between 9 and 10 percent – after it had peaked at 12.5 percent in 1995 – with workers substantially overrepresented among the unemployed.[8] By the end of the 1990s, unemployment among industrial workers was higher than for any other occupational group (see Table 8.1), having peaked at 16 percent (versus 15 percent for service-sector *employés*, the second-worst afflicted group) in 1999.[9] Most of this rise occurred during the 1980s, when the French economy underwent its most profound structural transformation in thirty years and worker unemployment jumped by almost half from 9.6 percent in 1982 to 14.2 percent in 1990.[10] The hardest-hit category of workers was the unskilled, among whom unemployment levels reached 20 percent in the mid-1990s and 22.6 percent in 1999.[11] These statistics suggest that even as total unemployment receded slightly from the high of the mid-nineties, it continued to progress unabated among industrial workers, particularly the unskilled.[12]

Similarly, industrial workers also represented the social category worst affected by long-term unemployment. In 1982, 15 percent of unemployed workers had been without work for at least two years, accounting for 47 percent of the total long-term unemployed. By 1991, this proportion had risen to 23 percent among out-of-work workers (versus 20 percent for the unemployed as a whole), while the proportion of the total long-term unemployed classified as workers had grown to 51.5 percent.[13] In turn, over the course of the 1990s,

---

[8] Smith, *France in Crisis*, 12, 76.

[9] Amossé, "L'espace des métiers, 1990–1999," 2.

[10] In actual fact, the real unemployment rate among French workers is probably higher because of the failure to account for part-time work, short-term contracts, and other instances of under-employment in the unemployment statistics. According to one study, if one takes into account these various forms of underemployment, the French unemployment rate in fact falls between 15% and 20%. A. Chenu, "Une classe ouvrière en crise," in *Données sociales 1993* (Paris: INSEE, 1993), 482, and Smith, *France in Crisis*, 11.

[11] Amossé and Chardon. "La carte des professions (1982–1999)," 216. Further differentiating within this category of workers, the highest unemployment rate – a staggering 47% – obtained among female workers under the age of twenty-five with no diploma. Mayer, "Du communisme au FN," 112, and Smith, *France in Crisis*, 194.

[12] From 1990 to 1999, the number of unskilled workers declined by 16%, compared to a 10% fall for industrial workers as a whole. Amossé, "L'espace des métiers," 2, and Olivier Chardon, "Les transformations de l'emploi non qualifié depuis vingt ans," *INSEE Première*, no. 796 (July 2001), 1–4.

[13] Older workers in particular suffered from long-term unemployment, representing fully 58% of wage earners between the ages of forty and forty-nine who were without work for at least two years. Chenu, "Une classe ouvrière en crise," 482.

TABLE 8.1. *Employment and Unemployment by Profession, 1982–1999 (in thousands)*

Profession	Employed				Unemployed	
	1982	1990	1999	% Δ 90–99	1990 (%)	1999 (%)
Farmers	1,466	1,005	627	−38	8 (1)	15 (2)
Artisans, shopkeepers, and employers	1,815	1,752	1,525	−13	71 (4)	135 (8)
Artisans	896	827	691	−16	34 (3)	70 (9)
Shopkeepers/family aides	788	756	664	−12	40 (5)	61 (8)
Employers (≥ 10 employees)	132	169	170	+0.1	7 (4)	4 (2)
Management executives/intellectual profs.	1,860	2,603	3,023	+16	90 (3)	139 (4)
Liberal professions	236	308	345	+12	4 (1)	10 (3)
Upper civil servants, intellectual profs.	695	992	1,237	+25	31 (3)	42 (3)
Upper-level management executives	929	1,304	1,441	+10	55 (4)	87 (6)
Intermediary professions	3,784	4,464	5,318	+19	249 (5)	451 (8)
Schoolteachers, health workers, civil servants	1,688	1,916	2,272	+19	69 (3)	128 (5)
Midlevel administrative and sales executives	898	1,279	1,621	+27	113 (8)	217 (12)
Industrial technicians	653	723	880	+22	39 (5)	70 (7)
Foremen/performance-quality control staff	546	546	545	−0.1	28 (5)	36 (6)
Service employees	5,502	5,899	6,655	+13	1,013(15)	1,154(15)
Low-level civil servants	2,038	2,310	2,679	+16	102 (4)	195 (7)
Clerical employees	2,060	1,921	1,749	−9	423 (18)	419 (19)
Sales employees	622	732	865	+18	237 (24)	249 (22)
Home services providers	781	937	1,362	+45	251 (21)	291 (18)
Manual workers	7,044	6,546	5,905	−10	1,077(14)	1,151(16)
Skilled industrial workers	3,686	3,725	3,497	−6	549 (13)	665 (16)
Unskilled industrial workers	3,089	2,586	2,163	−16	482 (16)	434 (17)
Agricultural workers	269	236	245	+3.8	46 (16)	52 (18)
TOTAL	21,472	22,270	23,053	+3.5	2,508(10.1)	3,047(11.7)

Source: Amossé, "L'espace des métiers, 1990–1999," 2.

long-term unemployment among workers only marginally improved due primarily to the spread of temporary contracts and part-time work before falling off again after 2000.[14] While the proportion of long-term unemployed among the unskilled stabilized or even slightly improved after the mid-1990s, a growing proportion of these workers was subjected to increasingly unstable and contingent forms of work. This trend attested to the increasingly tight labor market faced by industrial workers in France and suggested their situation was unlikely to improve in the future.

The second factor feeding the socioeconomic crisis affecting French workers has been their growing material insecurity since the 1980s. First, this development has been reflected by the precipitous growth of income inequality in the country, mostly at the expense of the industrial workforce.[15] If we assume a median income level of 100 for the workforce as a whole, the average yearly salary of French workers fell from 79 in 1983 to 76 in 1991.[16] Despite a slight improvement during the second half of the 1990s – the yearly income of workers rising by 0.5 percent per year on average from 1995 to 2003 as a result of periodic revaluations of the minimum wage – this rise was overshadowed by the fact that from 1998 on, gains at the lower end of the income scale were vastly exceeded by those at the upper end. Likewise, any marginal improvement in

---

[14] The proportion of unskilled unemployed in manufacturing (excluding construction) increased from 10.4% in 1997 to 12.3% in 2004, versus 4.1% and 3.7% respectively for skilled workers. In turn, the share of these workers who had been without work for more than one year fell from 41.3% in 1997 to a low of 35.4% in 2002, before rapidly climbing back to 39.5% in 2004. Among this category of workers, the proportion of job seekers working part-time rose from 27.4% in 1997 to 37.9% in 2004. At the same time, the rate of turnover among unskilled workers rose from 40.3% of the total unskilled manufacturing workforce in 1997 to 47.0% in 2004, testifying to the rapid increase of those hired under short-term contracts. Ministère des affaires sociales, du travail et de la solidarité, "Portrait statistique 1982–2002: Eo – Ouvriers non qualifiés des industries de process," available from http://www.travail-solidarite.gouv.fr/IMG/pdf/ 2002_Eo.pdf; "E1 – Ouvriers qualifiés des industries de process," available from http://www. travail-solidarite.gouv.fr/IMG/pdf/2002_E1.pdf; and "Chômage 1997–2004: Eo – Ouvriers non qualifiés des industries de process," available from http://www.travail-solidarite.gouv.fr/IMG/ pdf/Chomage_1997_-_2004_Eo_Ouvriers_non_ qualifies_des_industries_de_process.pdf; "E1 – Ouvriers qualifiés des industries de process," available from http://www.travail-solidarite.gouv. fr/IMG/pdf/Chomage_1997_-_2004_-_E1_Ouvriers_qualifies_des_industries_de_process.pdf, accessed 30 Sept. 2006.

[15] In 1980 the top decile of the population on the income ladder was approximately 3.1 times better off than the bottom 10%. By 1996, despite the introduction of a tax on "large fortunes" and a massive rise in the government's social spending, the top decile jumped to being 3.35 times better off than the bottom decile, before falling back slightly to 3.23 in 2001. See Smith *France in Crisis*, 136, and Nadine Legendre, "Évolution des niveaux de vie de 1996 à 2001," *INSEE Première*, no. 947 (Jan. 2004), 3. Further underscoring the relatively high levels of wealth inequality that have emerged in France, the latest comparative study of wealth inequality across industrialized countries found that, for the period 1985 to 1989, France presented the second-highest Gini coefficient (29.0) after the United States (31.8). This compared unfavorably with, in descending order, the United Kingdom (27.8), West Germany (24.5), and Finland (20.0), the country with the best score. Smith, *France in Crisis*, 138.

[16] Chenu, "Une classe ouvrière en crise," 482.

workers' standard of living during this period was offset by the loss of earnings occasioned by the steep rise in worker unemployment, particularly among younger workers.[17] At the same time, the increasing material vulnerability of industrial workers was also reflected in their lack of social mobility during the period under study. Since the 1950s, the "social distance" separating industrial workers from members of other social groups has varied little, as measured by indexes of intragenerational professional mobility and intergenerational social mobility.[18] This suggests that the overwhelming majority of workers remained confined to a subaltern position in French society, with little hope of escaping the precarious work and living conditions to which the structural transformation of the economy condemned them.

The rapid rise in unemployment and substantial deterioration in income suffered by French workers over the past quarter century is attributable to a number of macroeconomic and microeconomic factors. From a macroeconomic standpoint, beginning in the 1970s, the country has been exposed to increasing

[17] In 1970 those between the ages of twenty-five and thirty earned 25% less than those between the ages of fifty and fifty-five; in 2000, they earned 50% less. Similarly, by 1996, 60% of the 1.3 million wage earners who qualified as working poor in France were under the age of twenty-five, with almost all of them under forty. Pascal Chevalier, Olivier Guillemin, Aude Lapinte, and Jean-Paul Lorgnet, "Les évolutions de niveau de vie entre 1970 et 2002," and Michel Amar, "Les salaires du secteur privé en France, de 1994 à 2004," both in *Données Sociales 2006* (Paris: INSEE, 2005), 448, 449, 417; and Smith, *France in Crisis*, 194–5. See also Christine Lagarenne and Nadine Legendre, "Les travailleurs pauvres en France: facteurs individuels et familiaux," *Économie et statistique*, no. 335 (2000), 3–25.

[18] An intragenerational analysis of the professional mobility of French workers shows that out of a sample of men working in 1960 who were still factory employed in 1989, 58% of those who had been industrial workers in 1960 were industrial workers thirty years on. Reciprocally, 84% of factory workers in 1989 who had been gainfully employed in 1960 were factory workers at that time. Similarly, out of a representative sample of employed males who reached the age of forty between 1974 and 1989, those who had been industrial workers between the ages of twenty-five and thirty had roughly a one-in-four chance of being promoted to foreman or to set up his own business. For female workers of the same age, the prospects of such intraprofessional mobility fell drastically, to a 6% or 7% chance of promotion or accession to the status of *indépendante*. Finally and most recently, we find that from 1993 to 2003, the incidence of intraprofessional mobility has actually decreased. Whereas one-third of the men between the ages of forty and fifty-nine who started their careers as industrial workers had become *cadres* (executives or technicians) by 1993, this proportion fell to only one-quarter for men in the same age group in 2003.

In terms of intergenerational mobility, 58% of male industrial workers between the ages of forty and fifty-nine were themselves the sons of industrial workers in 2003. This marks a relative increase compared to 1977 (54%) and even 1993 (53%), despite the fact that the proportion of industrial workers within the aggregate workforce fell from 36% to 20% between 1977 and 2003. Conversely, the proportion of the sons of industrial workers who acceded to a "superior" wage-earning or independent profession (*cadre* and liberal professional or artisan, shopkeeper, and firm owner) either barely increased or remained essentially the same throughout the period under study. The sons of workers between the ages of forty and fifty-nine represented only 10% of *cadres* or members of the liberal professions and 8% of artisans, shopkeepers, or firm owners in 2003, versus 9% and 9% of these categories in 1993, and 4% and 8% in 1977. Chenu, "Une classe ouvrière en crise," 483–4, and Stéphanie Dupays, "En un quart de siècle, la mobilité sociale a peu évolué," in *Données Sociales 2006*, 345, 347, 348.

international competition as a function of the liberalization of the global trade and financial regimes and as it prepared for European Monetary Union. Similarly, the upsurge in international capital flows during the 1980s and 1990s precipitated a substantial outsourcing of French manufacturing firms and jobs as the country shifted from a primarily industrial to a service-based economy.[19] In order to meet the challenge posed by intensifying competition and the unprecedented mobility of capital, France needed to make its economy more flexible and efficient. The necessity of reform became all the more evident with the failure of postwar Keynesian and dirigiste policies to sustain growth and employment following the 1970s oil shocks.

As we saw in the preceding chapter, beginning in 1983 the country moved away from dirigisme and state intervention, embarking on a sweeping campaign of *déplanification* and deregulation, which lasted through the first half of the 1990s. At one level, this entailed privatizing the majority of nationally owned firms or, failing that, subjecting them to the market competition faced by their counterparts in the private sector. Correlatively, the shift away from state planning and intervention was accompanied by a reversal in the macroeconomic orientation of the country. The inflationary emphasis on growth and full employment that had obtained in the 1960s and 1970s gave way to a focus on price stability and a strong franc in order to maintain the country in the European Monetary System and make it attractive to foreign investment. Hence, France experienced the turn toward *rigueur* and the adoption of *désinflation compétitive* by the Mauroy government and its successors, the real interest rate spiking at 7 or 8 percent in the late 1980s.[20]

At the same time, the state also introduced reforms that were designed to improve firm competitiveness and flexibility at the microeconomic level. First and most importantly, price, wage, and credit controls were lifted in order to restore market mechanisms, forcing businesses to reduce their costs in order to remain competitive and directing capital to the most efficient sectors of the economy. Second, restrictions on layoffs and temporary and part-time employment were eased in the aim of facilitating wage flexibility within firms. Combined with slack enforcement of existing regulations, such as work safety laws and worker participation rules, these reforms improved the cost competitiveness of French enterprises to the detriment of labor.[21] Likewise, while giving

---

[19] This rapid financialization of the economy is to be seen in the explosion of French financial markets in the 1980s and 1990s, with financial investments (primarily stocks and bonds) expanding exponentially as a percentage of GDP from 29% in 1980 to 204% in 2000. As a testament to the rapid internationalization of finance capital, the Banque de France found that by the end of 2002, foreigners owned 43% of the shares of publicly traded French firms and accounted for 73% of the transactions on the Paris Bourse. Dominique Plihon, "Capitalisme français," in Cordellier and Lau, *L'état de la France 2005–2006*, 202, 203.

[20] Levy, "Redeploying," 105, and Smith, *France in Crisis*, 102.

[21] This slackening enforcement of work-safety laws, combined with the upheaval of production schedules and intensification of work cadences through an increasing recourse by employers to around-the-clock production cycles, resulted in a dramatic increase in the number of work

them unprecedented access to foreign capital, the liberalization of financial markets and lifting of restrictions further exposed French firms to the rigors of international competition and diminished the ability of the state to protect them.

This panoply of macro- and microeconomic reforms exacted a heavy socioeconomic toll on the French industrial workforce. The deindexation of wages from prices and the ensuing efforts of firms to maximize their profits by cutting labor costs quickly translated into a decline in workers' living standards during the 1980s and 1990s. At the same time, greater flexibility in hiring and firing opened the door to mass layoffs of workers and increased the capacity of employers to drive down wages. Finally, the dramatic increase in capital flows, combined with the availability of cheaper labor and less onerous regulative and fiscal environments abroad, accelerated the outsourcing of French industrial production. Coinciding with the country's deindustrialization and its shift to a services-based economy, the *déplanification* and economic liberalization of the 1980s and 1990s were profoundly destabilizing and alarming to French workers because they underscored their functional redundancy in the new postindustrial economy.

As such, these sweeping reforms spelled the end of the Fordist compromise that had underpinned the postwar social contract and presided over rapid economic development and the emergence of French social democracy during the Trente glorieuses. Under the terms of this compromise, in exchange for accepting onerous work roles in increasingly concentrated and rationalized factories, industrial workers were guaranteed lifetime employment, steadily improving living standards, and increasingly comprehensive social benefits and protections. Built on a "virtuous cycle of mass consumption fueling mass production," Fordism co-opted the working class into the workings of the capitalist economy, most often under the stewardship of an ostensibly revolutionary but effectively reformist Communist Party.[22] However, the globalization of product and labor markets and the intensification of international capital flows permanently disrupted the internal equilibrium of Fordism. By directing a growing proportion of domestic demand to foreign goods and allocating a greater fraction of domestic profits to overseas production, global economic integration unsettled the balance between national supply and national demand that had supported the Fordist system. At the same time, the internationalization of capital flows negated the capacity of the state to accumulate and allocate capital in the country. This effectively spelled the demise of dirigisme and rendered obsolete the social democratic institutions that had supported it. In a very real sense, then, the 1980s and 1990s saw the movement from a nationally based global economic model "articulating," as Alain Bihr has put it, "national economic spaces more or less integrated by the regulatory and planning activities of

accidents in the 1980s compared to the 1970s. Stéphane Beaud and Michel Pialoux, *Retour sur la condition ouvrière. Enquête aux usines Peugeot de Sochaux-Montbéliard* (Paris: Fayard, 1999), 423–4; Levy, *Tocqueville's Revenge*, 240; and Michel Cézard and Françoise Dussert, "Le travail ouvrier sous contrainte," in *Données sociales 1993*, 202–11.
[22] Howell, "The Dilemmas of Post-Fordism," 71.

the state" to a properly transnational model "in which the imbrication of the productive structures and the density of trade and capital flows quickly deprived states of their capacity to preserve the coherence and autonomy of the process of national economic development." "Consequently," he concluded, "the possibility of achieving a dynamic equilibrium between supply and demand in the context of a national economic framework escaped the regulative capacity of the [national] state."[23]

   The rupturing of the Fordist economic and social model under the pressures of industrial outsourcing and capital mobility was synonymous with a generalized attack on the material well-being and social *acquis* of the French working class. Entailing the dismantlement of the institutions of *capitalisme social* that had been put in place throughout the Trente glorieuses, this globalization-driven process of economic liberalization has been decried in some quarters as "making the workers pay for the crisis."[24] In turn, this process of liberalization had a further, indirect impact on the employment and wage situation of French workers. As we saw in the preceding chapter, liberalization was accompanied by the growth of an increasingly unaffordable "social anesthesia state" to dampen the social costs that came with it.[25] In order to maintain the social protections and welfare policies that were introduced for this purpose, corporate and payroll taxes were substantially increased, preventing French firms from hiring as many workers as they might have without these new obligations.[26] Similarly, complementary labor market policies that were introduced by the state to help workers often worsened their economic vulnerability.[27] In effect, these "social anesthesia" measures often bore the unintended consequence of deepening worker

---

[23] *Spectre*, 72, 105.
[24] The increasingly skewed distribution of returns from productivity gains away from the owners of labor toward those of capital reinforces this conclusion. From 1982 to 1989, the share of the value added of national production that went to capital increased from 24.0% to a record 31.7%. Likewise, the proportion of the value added that went directly to firm profits nearly doubled from 9.8% to 17.3% over the same period. Conversely, the share of national value added that went to wages declined from a high of around 69% in 1982 to roughly 58% in 1997, a level not seen since 1960–1, years predating the introduction of Fordist wage and Keynesian redistributive policies. Levy, "Redeploying," 106, 107, and Céline Prigent, "La part des salaires dans la valeur ajoutée en France: une approche macroéconomique," *Économie et statistique*, no. 323 (1999), 74.
[25] Levy, "Redeploying," 119.
[26] The following figures put the cost of these "social anesthesia" measures to French firms into stark relief. While 70% of social spending in France by the 1990s was going to people over the age of fifty-nine instead of toward policies to reconvert the unemployed into new sectors, payroll taxes were equivalent to more than 40% of the average cost of labor and 50% of the wages of low-skilled workers. Particularly victimized by the resulting crowding out of workers from the labor market were the unskilled and social constituencies that were disproportionately represented among them: immigrants, women, and the young. Smith, *France in Crisis*, 80, 90, and ch. 7, as well as Beaud and Pialoux, *Retour sur la condition ouvrière*, 420–2.
[27] Perhaps the best case was the thirty-five-hour workweek legislated in 1997 and put into effect in 2002. Conceived as a means of reducing unemployment by sharing jobs among a larger pool of workers, it allowed employers to enhance labor flexibility within their firms. By doing away with previous constraints on production in exchange for reducing the weekly work schedules of

unemployment and insecurity. Thus, they aggravated the causes of workers' discontent, hastening the very social explosion that they were designed to prevent.

However, this crisis of the working class cannot be apprehended purely at a structural, socioeconomic level. It was also, as in the case of *petits indépendants*, cultural in nature, reflecting a profound erosion of identity afflicting French workers. It is this cultural crisis that the Front National has been able to exploit, as evidenced by the rapid increase of its working-class support since the late 1980s. However, before analyzing the cultural crisis of French workers, it is necessary to say something about their culture, as well as the principal loci or institutions by which it was reproduced among them.

At base, this culture derived from a negative process of self-definition and self-affirmation, posited in contradistinction to the onerous material and ecological conditions of industrial labor. As a function of the hardships to which they were exposed in the factory, French workers historically defined themselves "despite" or in opposition to their work. Until most recently, they did not, in contrast to farmers or *petits indépendants*, conceive of that work as a positive marker of social identity.

Specifically, the cultural identity of the industrial worker cannot be separated from his subjection to the repetitive, often sensorily brutal and mentally stultifying processes of factory labor, where his material contribution, as part of a much larger productive chain, is not quantifiable in terms of a palpable output or result. In effect, the worker is transformed into the extension of a machine, reflecting what one author has termed the "paramount constraint of technical necessity" imposed on him as a function of the continuous automation of industrial production. It is not surprising that the industrial worker, serving as a cog in an impersonal, mechanized process whose finality escapes him, should come to place a lower premium on the quality and nature of his labor. Instead, he looks forward to the consumption and leisure possibilities afforded him by the latter. Strictly compartmentalizing between his work life – synonymous with constraint and toil – and his life outside work, seen as synonymous with freedom and leisure, the industrial worker comes to place a greater value on his free time than the members of other socioprofessional categories. In consequence, he has historically organized this freedom from work as a means to escape the constraints of the workplace as well as to make the conditions to which he is subjected within it more supportable.[28] In turn, workers' compartmentalization of the worlds of work and leisure eroded the traditional, economistic conception

employees, the new law made it possible for employers to recast working conditions in the firm in ways that were perceived as detrimental by their workers. For example, as a result of the new law, firms were able to introduce continuous production cycles requiring employees to work the "graveyard" shift more than ever before and considerably shorten, if not altogether eliminate, the break periods available to workers in most industrial firms. Beaud and Pialoux, *Retour sur la condition ouvrière*, 423.

[28] See Michel Verret, *La culture ouvrière*, 2nd ed. (Paris: L'Harmattan, 1996), 169; Vincienne, *Du village à la ville*, 48, 58; and Eizner and Hervieu, *Anciens paysans, nouveaux ouvriers*, 105.

of the family that they had inherited as a function of their artisanal and agricultural origins. For these workers, particularly those employed in the most advanced economic sectors, the family no longer served as a basis of economic and social identity, as in the case of *petits indépendants* and small farmers.[29]

Rejecting the world of work and looking beyond the family as bases of social signification, industrial workers staked out an alternative, class-based identity within capitalist society. They sought to counter the individual alienation and powerlessness deriving from their dehumanizing work environment by fastening onto a positive, collective identity based on a mutually shared sense of class consciousness and solidarity. Reflecting the demand that their productive role be socially recognized and economically valued, this class identity was forged from the dual struggle of industrial workers against their alienating conditions of work on the one hand and the economic exploitation and sociopolitical subjugation that they endured on the other. In the face of these hostile processes and forces, workers resolved to collectively defend their "dignity" and preserve their "honor" as a class in the factory and society at large.[30]

The two institutions that sustained French workers' class consciousness and identity historically were the trade unions – especially the CGT and, to a more limited degree, the Confédération française démocratique du travail (CFDT) – and the Communist Party.[31] These organizations served complementary – and, in the case of the CGT and the PCF, overlapping – roles as socializing agents for the French working class. The unions defended workers' material and social interests in the workplace,[32] while the PCF did so in the political

---

[29] See Vincienne, *Du village à la ville*, 44, 48, 52, as well as Chapter 3.
[30] See Verret, *La culture ouvrière*, 185.
[31] These organizations traditionally enjoyed greater influence over French industrial workers than the Socialist Party (SFIO and then PS), which appealed historically to new middle-class groups – *fonctionnaires* and teachers in the interwar and initial postwar periods and, beginning in the late sixties and early seventies, service-sector *employés* and even low- to midlevel *cadres* – and the Christian Democratic CFTC, which attracted a mix of white-collar workers, *cadres*, as well as workers in more traditional, quasi-artisanal firms, before its *déconfessionalisation* and transformation into the CFDT. See A. Begounioux, "La SFIO ou les classes moyennes impensées"; Boltanski, "Une réussite"; H. Portelli, "Nouvelles classes moyennes et nouveau Parti socialiste," and Gérard Grunberg and Etienne Schweisguth, "Le virage à gauche des couches moyennes salariées," all in Lavau, Grunberg, and Mayer, *L'univers politique des classes moyennes*, 94–112, 156–69, 258–73, and 351–67.
[32] To a greater degree than in most other industrialized countries, the French trade-union movement remained particularly splintered among organizations representing distinct organizational philosophies and political tendencies. Most significant among them has been the CGT, the country's oldest trade union confederation and until recently, indisputably the largest in membership. Of all the union organizations, it has been most strongly represented within the various instances of industrial representation and collective bargaining (*prud'hommes, comités d'entreprise*, paritary commissions in public enterprises, and state administrative bodies). Initially anarchosyndicalist in orientation, the CGT underwent substantial organizational and political changes through the course of its long history. It progressively grew closer to the PCF during the 1930s, before splitting between an effectively procommunist majority, which continued to go by the organization's

sphere.[33] In short, the unions and PCF "sought to occupy" the economic and social space on behalf of French workers, striving in the words of one observer to "render palpable ... visible, tangible, audible not only the presence of the working class, but its strength."[34]

In addition to concretely influencing socioeconomic and political struggles, the unions and the PCF each sought "to conquer, within the public arena, its own space of symbolization."[35] Their object was to counter the dominant capitalist ideology and institutions that it equated with the political-economic subjugation of French workers. Accordingly, the unions and PCF strove to influence the public debate in such a way as to improve the social and political standing of the latter in French capitalist society or, alternatively, for the more radical elements within it, to pave the way for its overthrow and establish the "dictatorship of the proletariat." In this sense, the principal union formations and the PCF occupied economic, social, political, and cultural fields of activity from which its adherents had been formerly excluded. As such, they developed into ideologically and culturally dominant loci of working-class affirmation and empowerment.

In short, the PCF and the unions were crucial agents of socialization responsible for forging the common sense of class consciousness that characterized the economic and social identity of French workers. In particular, they imparted a distinct worldview to the dominant strata of the French working class – the *ouvriers spécialisés* and *ouvriers qualifiés* of the large Fordist factory – imbuing

original name, and a dissident union, Force Ouvrière (FO), which maintained its independence vis-à-vis the PCF after the Liberation. Until the 1980s, the CGT has remained the leading syndical representative among French industrial workers, dominating union membership in the country's established industrial heartlands and traditional heavy industries.

More recently, however, the organizational primacy of the CGT has come under increasing challenge from the CFDT. Initially representing the "secular" wing of the CFTC, from which it had officially broken off in 1964, the CFDT progressively came to contest, particularly starting in the 1980s, the CGT's hold over French wage earners. Since 1990, it has been the sole union organization to see its membership increase, drawing roughly level with the CGT in 2005 with approximately 700,000 members. However, its membership is also more dispersed, much of its support to be found, as in the case of its Christian Democratic predecessor, in the tertiary sector as well as among low- to midlevel managers, technicians, and service employees. In this sense, though the CFDT has grown in influence among wage earners, it is less clear whether it has eroded the CGT's traditional supremacy among industrial workers or, as the economic position of the latter grew increasingly precarious in the 1980s and 1990s, whether it has been any more successful than the CGT in maintaining its membership among them. See Dominique Andolfatto and Dominique Labbé, *Histoire des syndicats* (Paris: Seuil, 2006), as well as D. Andolfatto, "Les principales organisations syndicales de salariés," in Cordellier and Lau, *L'état de la France 2005–2006*, 235–39.

[33] Testifying to the "natural" political affinity many of them felt to the PCF, one worker surveyed in 1966 declared: "For me, any worker who respects himself has to have communist tendencies ... communist ideas. He has to be a communist sympathizer, since he works for a boss. [If you] work for somebody who's getting rich off your back, you've got to be a communist, ... a communist sympathizer, it's as simple as that." Quoted in Mayer, "Du communisme au FN," 111.

[34] Verret, *La culture ouvrière*, 195.

[35] Ibid., 186.

them with an interpretive framework by which to apprehend and relate to the broader society.[36] At the same time, the workers' movement gave rise to a novel popular culture, with its own idiom and myths, ceremonies and rituals, commemorations and heroes. Affirming the primacy of class appurtenance and solidarity, this culture reinforced the identifications that gave French workers an indelible sense of belonging to a historically foreordained and normatively superior collectivity. In this sense, French syndicalism and the PCF came to constitute distinct and self-enclosed *contre-sociétés*, to use Annie Kriegel's term, reflecting their own internally transmitted and reified norms, symbols, and representations.[37]

Yet, in practice, despite its oppositional – and, in the case of the PCF and CGT, ostensibly revolutionary – vocation, the workers' movement reconciled the working class to the workings of French capitalism and liberal democracy. At a first level, the trade unions, including the CGT, facilitated informal, firm-level negotiations and conflict resolution in the workplace. This role was substantially reinforced with the creation of *comités d'entreprise* following the Second World War and the compulsory mandating of union representation in the CEs following the 1968 Grenelle Accords.[38] Unions' stabilizing, conflict-defusing function derived from the corporative model of syndicalism that emerged historically in France and could be traced back to the trade-based identities of French workers and their focus on organization in their individual

---

[36] The inculcation of such a working-class outlook reflected the pedagogical aims of the unions and the PCF to educate French workers and instill in them a distinct set of norms or ideological turn of mind. Writing in respect to the political culture of the Communist Party, Marc Lazar places a particular emphasis on the deliberate nature of this project, which was "put into effect by leaders at all levels of the party ... to diffuse the ideology, mold the imaginary and mythical representations, define the collective beliefs, impose the values, organize the distribution of material and symbolic gratifications, sort what in the past could be useful to the [advancement of] immediate interests, [and] elaborate a representation of [workers'] social and cultural universe, in order to found that which could be properly called a French communist tradition." "L'invention et la désagrégation de la culture communiste," *Vingtième siècle*, no. 44 (Oct.–Dec. 1994), 16. For a detailed analysis of the representational and symbolic system of Communist workers, see G. Michelat and M. Simon, *Classe, religion et comportement politique* (Paris: Presses de la FNSP, 1977).

[37] Not surprisingly, this culture was most pronounced in the oldest and most heavily industrialized areas of the country: the great manufacturing heartlands of north and northeastern France, the southeastern fringe of the Massif Central, and the mythical *ceintures rouges* ringing Paris and other major French cities such as Lyon and Marseille. Fiefdoms of the labor aristocracy, these areas contained the country's largest firms, which were typically concentrated in traditional heavy industrial sectors such as mining, steel, and metallurgy, and which employed the greatest numbers of workers. As a result of ongoing industrial specialization and automation, workers in these firms were subjected to a highly uniform experience of work, greatly facilitating their collective organization and acculturation by trade unions and the Communist Party. Annie Kriegel, *The French Communists: Profile of a People*, trans. E. Halperin (Chicago: University of Chicago Press, 1972). See also M. Lazar, "Forte et fragile, immuable et changeante ... La culture politique communiste," in Berstein, *Les cultures politiques en France*, 215–42.

[38] See Chapters 6 and 7.

firms.[39] By providing tangible services to their members in the workplace and articulating their concerns within the CEs, French unions contributed, as Dominique Labbé put it, to an "original form of regulation of labor relations, which confined the expression of social conflict to the firm and, through informal and formal intermediary mechanisms, addressed and defused its effects within it."[40] In this sense, despite their outward militancy and, in the CGT's case, ostensible revolutionism, individual unions bound their members to the capitalist system.

In turn, the PCF played a similar role by serving, as Georges Lavau has put it, an essential "tribunary function" on behalf of French workers. By offering the latter "a recognized political pulpit from whence to exclaim – loudly but legally – their discontent," the Communist Party co-opted French workers into the processes of parliamentary democracy.[41] Providing a source of political catharsis for this economically and socially frustrated constituency, the PCF fulfilled the need of French workers "for a dream, a utopia, for radical solutions" while limiting its expression to the ballot box.[42] Even at an ideological level, through its recuperation of the discursive and institutional motifs of the French Revolution, the PCF rehabilitated the country's republican tradition and republican state in the eyes of its following.[43] Portraying the French Revolution and its ideal of *liberté, égalité, fraternité* as a precursor for their own emancipatory and leveling political project, French communists portrayed the republic as sufficient to bring about socialism unto itself. Thus, they enlisted – often unwittingly – workers into respecting the principles and

[39] See Andolfatto and Labbé, *Histoire des syndicats*, ch. 3, and D. Labbé, *Syndicats et syndiqués en France depuis 1945* (Paris: L'Harmattan, 1996), 58–70.

[40] Labbé, *Syndicats et syndiqués en France*, 65.

[41] *À quoi sert le Parti communiste français?* (Paris: Fayard, 1981), 36. For a full exposition of this argument, see ibid., 35–44.

[42] For all intents and purposes, the PCF's tribunary function underlined the practical disconnect between the party's revolutionary ideology and rhetoric on the one hand and its willingness to abide by the rules of the democratic game on the other. At one level, by virtue of its respect for the tenets of republican legality, the PCF ensconced the potentially most radical fringe of industrial workers in the camp of democratic legality. Conversely, by playing on the radicalism of its followers, the party was able to extract economic and social concessions from the political elite under the postwar Fordist compromise, thus addressing the worst grievances of French workers and facilitating their acceptance of the capitalist economic and social system. Lazar, "Culture politique communiste," 233.

[43] Chiefly, the PCF co-opted the philosophical antecedents of the Revolution by claiming the scientism and rationalism of the French Enlightenment, as well as radical Jacobin notions of political, social, and economic equality. On the ideological and discursive continuities between the PCF and the revolutionary republican tradition, and the ways these were internalized by Communist activists, see Marie-Claire Lavabre, *Le fil rouge. Sociologie de la mémoire communiste* (Paris: Presses de la FNSP, 1994), ch. 1; Roger Martelli, *Le rouge et le bleu: essai sur le communisme dans l'histoire française* (Paris: Éditions de l'Atelier, 1995), 147–150, 244–5; and Pierre Grémion, "L'idée communiste dans notre histoire nationale: une lecture de François Furet," *Études* 385(3) (Sept. 1996), 207–17.

procedures of French democracy.[44] In short, by "legitimizing the system while constantly decrying its illegitimacy" as Lavau put it, the PCF played a key role in advancing the "social democratization" of French workers. In conjunction with the trade unions, it helped reconcile the working class to the economic and political institutions of French democratic capitalism. In this sense, both the labor movement and the PCF represented, through the end of the Fordist era at least, crucial agents of social and political stability, the benefits of which would be starkly underlined by the consequences of their decline.

At the same time, however, it is important to keep in mind that the stabilizing influence of these institutions remained in constant tension with the affective and symbolic correlates of class struggle that they inculcated among French workers and that came to subtend their cultural outlook and collective consciousness. Despite its legalistic respect for democratic processes and institutions, the revolutionary discourse and communist teleology of the PCF left French workers with only a cursory and provisional commitment to liberal democracy. Similarly, the informal, conflict-defusing role performed by unions within the capitalist firm has coexisted with a long-standing legacy of distrust between workers and their employers that has endured to the present day. In marked contrast to other industrialized countries, workers and employers in France have yet to fully accept one another as legitimate and equal social partners and culturally remain deeply suspicious of each other. This sentiment particularly intensified following May 1968, when unions became official partners in a state-sanctioned process of national collective bargaining.[45] In this sense, as in the case of the PCF, the stabilizing role of unions within French capitalism remained contingent at best. Accordingly, when workers lost their union foothold within the firm and saw their socioeconomic conditions deteriorate, they became a potentially radical and destabilizing political force.

In short, then, the integrative and stabilizing function of the PCF and the union movement within French democratic capitalism remained conditional and ambivalent. At base, these forces always presented a tension between the contradictory impulses of, on the one hand, class struggle and utopian maximalism and, on the other, class conciliation and pragmatic gradualism. When the organizational and political-economic power of these institutions began to erode in the late 1970s and early 1980s, they failed to leave the imprimatur of a durable and innate "democratic" political culture among French workers. Therefore, once their restraining influence over French workers declined, there

[44] Verret, *La culture ouvrière*, 228. This conviction was affirmed by no less a communist stalwart than Maurice Thorez, then first secretary of the party, in an interview given to the *Times* newspaper of London in November 1946, when he asserted that "the progress of democracy across the world makes it possible to envisage the march toward socialism taking different paths from those followed by the Russian Communists. . . . We have always thought and declared that the people of France, so rich in this glorious tradition, would itself find their way toward more democracy, more progress and more social justice." Quoted in Lavau, *À quoi sert le PCF?*, 32.
[45] See, for example, George Ross, "Gaullism and Organized Labor: Two Decades of Failure?" in Andrews and Hoffmann, *The Fifth Republic at Twenty*, 339–44.

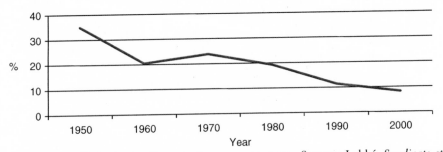

FIGURE 8.1. Unionization Rates in France, 1950–2000. *Sources:* Labbé, *Syndicats et syndiqués*, 132, and D. Andolfatto, "Syndicalisme," in *L'état de la France 2005–2006*, 232.

was no political-cultural impediment to prevent their erstwhile adherents from identifying with the Front National's antiliberal and antidemocratic program.

The structural transformation of the French economy since the 1970s has eroded these socializing institutions that undergird the class identity of French workers in a number of ways. In the first place, it occasioned a precipitous decline in the size and the strength of the syndicalist movement. After falling initially from a peak of 35 percent in 1950 to 20.5 percent in 1960, the rate of unionization slowly climbed back to a level of 23.9 percent in 1969, before resuming its steady decline and falling to 19.3 percent in 1980, 11.4 percent in 1990, and only 8.2 percent in 2003[46] (see Figure 8.1). These figures are not simply the reflection of a relative increase in the size of the workforce. Rather, they mark a decrease in the absolute number of unionized workers, underscoring the failure of unions to compensate for their losses through the recruitment of new members.[47]

Second, the transformation of the French economy has also eroded the political allegiance of French workers to the PCF. In successive parliamentary elections (see Figure 8.2), which are held to represent the most accurate barometer of voters' political allegiances, the percentage of workers who voted Communist fell from close to 50 percent in the early 1950s, to between 30 and 40 percent through the 1960s and 1970s, to 24 percent in 1981, 16 percent in 1988, 14 percent in 1993, 15 percent in 1997, and 6 percent in 2002.[48]

---

[46] Labbé, *Syndicats et syndiqués*, 132, and D. Andolfatto, "Syndicalisme," in Cordellier and Lau, *L'état de la France 2005–2006*, 232.

[47] In this light, the increase in the number of CEs – and hence of the number of union sections – from nine thousand in 1966–7 to twenty-four thousand in 1976–7, combined with the failure of the main union confederations to boost their membership since the mid-1970s, suggests that the latter were hemorrhaging members at the same time that they expanded their activities to almost triple the number of firms. Labbé, *Syndicats et syndiqués*, 82.

[48] It is worth noting this decline occurred in the context of a broader erosion of working-class votes for the Left generally, including the PS, the Greens, and the far-left Trotskyist parties. The proportion of workers who voted for the Left fell from an overwhelming majority of 70% in

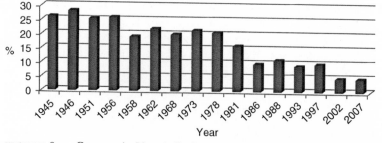

FIGURE 8.2. Communist Vote in Parliamentary Elections, 1945–2007. *Sources:* French Government, Ministère de l'Intérieur.

At a first level, this decline in the unionization rate and communist worker vote reflected an erosion in the demographic weight of industrial workers. As a result of deindustrialization and the shift to a service economy, industrial workers went from representing roughly four in ten members of the total workforce in the late sixties and early seventies (38 percent in 1968–75), to less than one in three in the late nineties (29 percent in 1998). By the end of the nineties, the proportion of industrial workers in the workforce had been surpassed by that of service-sector employees (*employés*).[49] Such a decline in the working-class population deprived trade unions and the PCF of a substantial fraction of their social base. This was particularly the case in areas where these institutions had historically found their greatest reservoir of support, that is, areas where heavy industries were most concentrated and that have been hit hardest by deindustrialization.[50]

Yet, deindustrialization is not the sole or even the principal explanation for the decline of the unions and Communist Party as agents of working-class socialization. Though it shrank in proportion to the total workforce, the industrial labor force remained substantial, accounting for more than 7.6 million individuals in 1998.[51] The fall in unionization and support for the PCF has far outstripped the decline in the size of the working population over the past quarter century, implying that factors other than the structural recomposition

the parliamentary elections of 1978 to a minority of only 43% in the first round of the presidential election of 2002. In other words, less than one worker in two who was eligible to vote did so in favor of the Left, testifying to the generalized collapse of the workers' movement over this period. See Verret, *La culture ouvrière*, 236; Martelli, *Le rouge et le bleu*, 269; Dolez and Laurent, "Marches et marges de la gauche," 256; P. Perrineau and H. Rey, "Classe et comportement politique: retour sur l'électorat ouvrier," in *Aux frontières des attitudes: entre le politique et le religieux*, ed. J.-M. Donegani, S. Duchesne, and F. Haegel (Paris: L'Harmattan, 2002), 19; and Mayer and Cautrès, "Les métamorphoses du vote de classe," 150–2.

49 The latter represented 30% of the total workforce in 1998. Mayer, "Du communisme au FN," 111, and J. Capdevielle, *Modernité du corporatisme* (Paris: Presses de Sciences Po, 2001), 21–2.

50 Bihr, *Spectre*, 77–8; Andolfatto and Labbé, *Histoire des syndicats*, 318–19; and Beaud and Pialoux, *Retour sur la condition ouvrière*, 418.

51 Capdevielle, *Modernité*, 22.

of the French economy were responsible for their erosion. Perhaps more important than this macrolevel shift has been the fundamental transformation of industrial production since the 1970s, which obliterated the sociostructural conditions that previously facilitated the proselytization and organization of workers within the workplace.

The increasing unwieldiness of large productive units in the global economy, combined with the individualization of consumer tastes in advanced industrial society, introduced new conditions of supply and demand that encouraged a movement away from the highly concentrated and rigidly organized factories of the Fordist era.[52] These conditions required new forms of firm organization predicated on maximizing the flexibility of production and the adaptability of capital and labor. Accordingly, they heralded the arrival of what one author has termed the "diffuse" or "flexible" factory featuring unparalleled automation, particularly in the form of robotics and process-directing information technology; organization of the workplace according to a highly adaptable "flow process" model of production; reliance on the "just-in-time" coordination of inputs and outputs; increased subcontracting of productive functions and tasks; and the unprecedented, increasingly sophisticated monitoring of worker performance.[53]

Not surprisingly, these new methods and technologies have profoundly impacted the industrial workforce. The growing recourse to automation and flow process production models has considerably devalued unskilled labor in the new postindustrial factory. As human beings are supplanted by technology in the actual tasks of production, the onus of industrial work shifts to technically proficient employees who can oversee the increasingly sophisticated machines involved in production and supply the complex data parameters that inform it. Correlatively, employers seek to hire and train more versatile workers who are able to perform tasks at various strategic points within this increasingly fluid or adaptive industrial workplace.[54] In turn, this reconfiguration of production stressing flexibility and adaptability has greatly reduced the need for the unskilled

---

[52] Underscoring this trend, the number of workers employed in firms counting over five hundred employees fell by half from 1980 to 2000, whereas the proportion of French workers employed by firms counting less than ten employees rose from 18% to 26%. This movement away from large, concentrated units of production did not herald a return to the small independent enterprises of yesteryear, however. Instead, it coincided with the growth of large multinational groups, with which most of these deconcentrated productive units were affiliated. In 2000 fully half of all French workers were employed by such groups. In this sense, the deconcentration of production reflected the subjection of multinational firms to greater international competition rather than an attempt by these firms to recapture the values of *indépendance*. Ibid., 37.

[53] A. Bihr, "La fragmentation du prolétariat," *L'homme et la société* 24(4) (1990), 8–15; Beaud and Pialoux, *Retour sur la condition ouvrière*, ch. 1; and Capdevielle, *Modernité*, 39–40.

[54] A study from the early 1990s found that, principally as a result of automation, the number of workers employed in industrial sectors (including construction) declined by 2% a year from 1982 to 1990. Conversely, the proportion of managers and members of intermediary professions (foremen, technicians, etc.) in industry grew from one-fifth to one-fourth of the industrial workforce, such that, whereas in 1982 the ratio of workers to *cadres*, technicians, or foremen had been

workers who composed the bulk of the labor force in the Fordist factory. The result is that traditional forms of industrial employment have become much more contingent and insecure. Accordingly, atypical forms of employment have dramatically increased among these workers. Part-time and short-term contracts, internships, and government-subsidized youth employment programs quadrupled between 1982 and 1999, whereas full-time industrial employment increased by only 9 percent.[55]

In effect, the reorganization of production and recourse to more flexible forms of employment has caused a new division of labor to emerge in French industry. At a first level, large factories have been transformed into the principal sites where conceptually and technically complex productive tasks are concentrated. They form the core units in increasingly hierarchic and diffuse production chains employing a nucleus of highly qualified and adaptive technicians. At a second level, alongside these highly automated and process-driven core units, smaller subcontractor units and in-firm affiliates have emerged to supplement the principal productive functions of the former. Specializing in a single or limited number of functions, such as parts supply or maintenance and repair, these subordinate firms overwhelmingly rely on young, unskilled workers who are paid the bare minimum, endure onerous working conditions, and experience the tenuous conditions of employment detailed previously.[56] In short, a two-tiered industrial economy has emerged in France. A first, superior tier oversees the core processes of design and assembly and is populated by a new aristocracy of skilled, technically proficient workers. In turn, a second, subordinate tier of subcontractors and affiliates has emerged that, in order to supply or service the core firms at the lowest cost, subject their unskilled workforces to extreme on-the-job exploitation and wage insecurity.

This fundamental transformation of the structures and processes of production in the workplace has been supported by a juridical framework that has

of 3 to 1, by 1990 it had fallen to 2.34 to 1. This rapid reduction in the size of the industrial workforce disproportionately impacted unskilled labor, as the proportion of workers possessing a technical degree or vocational diploma rose from 29% of the industrial workforce in 1982 to 42% only eight years later. Chenu, "Une classe ouvrière en crise," 478.

[55] By the end of this period, nearly half (47%) of such contingent or provisional contracts were held by industrial workers. This proportion rose to over 80% for the single category of part-time jobs, a majority of which were filled by unskilled workers. Likewise, underscoring the increasingly heavy reliance of industrial producers on these flexible forms of work, in 1999 industrial firms employed only 26% of the full-time wage-earning labor force but 51.5% of total part-time workers in the country. Also in that year, 39% of short-term contracts and 25% of paid internships or government-subsidized jobs were in manufacturing. Another indicator of employers' recourse to these forms of work was the fact that the primary temporary employment firms in France, Adecco and Manpower, had become the largest private employers in the country, having recruited nearly 400,000 people each by 1997. Capdevielle, *Modernité*, 23.

[56] For an instructive account of the organization of these subordinate firms and the forbidding conditions to which their workers are confronted, see Beaud and Pialoux's study of the SMEs subcontracted to produce parts for the French automaker Peugeot in the area of Sochaux-Montbéliard. *Retour sur la condition ouvrière*, particularly 419–22.

codified the shift to more flexible, adaptive modes of production.[57] Legislation such as the Auroux Laws, which gave labor contracts concluded at the firm level priority over branch and even national contracts, and the thirty-five-hour workweek have substantially enhanced the leverage of employers over their workers.[58] Combined with liberalizing measures such as the abrogation of wage indexation and the exemption of firm-level contracts from minimum-wage laws, as well as the lackadaisical enforcement of worker participation and safety laws, the cumulative effect of this legislation was a labor market reform "equivalent," in Howell's phrase, "to a particularly brutal form of flexibility."[59] In short, by revolutionizing production and erecting a legal framework to increase labor market flexibility, French business and political elites considerably weakened the social and professional standing of industrial workers in French society. In so doing, they accelerated the dislocation of the institutions that historically shaped workers' social and political identity.

In turn, the transformation of production at the level of the firm fractured the industrial workforce into multiple strata characterized by divergent, even contradictory interests, thus eroding the solidarities that had bound workers in a shared collective identity and purpose. These strata can be divided into three groups.[60] At a first level is the diminishing segment of workers who, for statutory or economic reasons – *fonctionnaires* and wage earners in competitive or protected sectors – have been unaffected by the implosion of the Fordist productive and social model. They represent a shrinking core of workers whose employment remains secure and who are guaranteed a relatively high and

[57] Bihr, *Spectre*, 76, and "Fragmentation," 14.
[58] Ostensibly designed to increase workplace democracy by strengthening the bargaining and social-monitoring capacity of unions within the firm, the Auroux Laws shifted the onus of collective bargaining away from institutionalized loci of negotiation, notably at the regional or national levels, at which the political and economic power of the unions was strongest. In this sense, the Auroux Laws increased labor-market flexibility without resorting to overtly coercive measures that were bound to provoke the resistance of French workers. As Chris Howell observes, they allowed "employers to sidestep the obstruction and reluctance of unions in national or industry-level bargaining and to achieve a measure of flexibility without prior deregulation." "Dilemmas of Post-Fordism," 87.
[59] In their study of the Peugeot factory and subcontracting firms in the area of Sochaux-Montbéliard, Beaud and Pialoux reported on the impacts of the thirty-five-hour week and of reduced government oversight of safety laws and worker representation within the firm. In the first case, because it substantially reduced the number of breaks available to workers and forced them to work more frequent night and weekend shifts without overtime, the thirty-five-hour law was often perceived as socially regressive by rank-and-file workers. Concurrently, the authors relate that the reduction of labor inspectors for the department of the Doubs, combined with Labor Secretary Martine Aubry's admonition that they "scrupulously observe the principle of restraint" in sanctioning violations, amounted to a green light to firms to cut corners in implementing safety regulations and providing greater firm-level participation to workers as called for by the Auroux Laws. On the contrary, by shirking these preexisting regulatory obligations, the state sought to enhance firm flexibility and reduce production costs, even if this meant degrading safety standards and reducing democracy within the firm. Ibid., 90, and *Retour sur la condition ouvrière*, 422–4.
[60] Bihr, "Fragmentation," 5–8.

stable wage.[61] Second is the growing fraction of workers subjected to mounting occupational instability and material insecurity. Increasingly vulnerable to economic fluctuations and subjected to worsening labor and wage conditions, the majority of these workers engage in atypical, contingent or provisional forms of labor. They include the employees of subcontracting firms who shoulder the brunt of the cost cuts demanded by large primary producers; part-time workers denied the benefits and protections afforded full-time workers; and temporary or short-term workers who, lacking the security of regular employment, are particularly vulnerable to exploitation.[62] As a function of their economic and organizational weakness in the face of employers, these atypical workers find themselves exposed to increasingly onerous and dangerous labor conditions, a fact reflected in the significant rise in the number of work accidents and in the higher levels of job stress reported by French workers.[63] Third and finally, a new *lumpenproletariat* has emerged as a result of the transformation of production and attendant labor-market deregulation and removal of worker protections. Redundant functionally and pauperized materially, members of this new *lumpenproletariat* face extreme exploitation in the "black" or parallel economy when they do not fall into outright criminality or destitution.[64]

This fragmentation of the working class has substantially weakened the traditional socializing institutions of the workers movement. In particular, the last two groups of workers are unable to recognize themselves in trade unions and a Communist Party that historically appealed to the Fordist labor aristocracy, concentrated mostly in large factories and traditional heavy industry.[65] This organizational erosion is reinforced by the fact that, while the largest industrial firms were substantially downsizing jobs, firms counting less than

---

[61] However, even this restricted cohort of wage earners has seen its privileged position increasingly threatened because of high unemployment, technological innovation, and the continued outsourcing of production.

[62] Capturing their worsening condition of economic and social vulnerability, Bihr observed that these workers were at the mercy of "inconsistent employment and revenues, a more or less advanced deregulation of their judicial conditions of employment and work, diminished social rights, a general absence of any form of collective bargaining, an absolute lack of unionization, and a tendency toward an extreme individualization of wage relations." Not surprisingly, a growing proportion of them have come to represent the French equivalent of the working poor. Ibid., 7. On the question of the working poor in France, see notably the article by Lagarenne and Legendre.

[63] Cézard and Dussert, "Le travail ouvrier sous contrainte," as well as Beaud and Pialoux, *Retour sur la condition ouvrière*, 422–4.

[64] Underscoring the tenuous line separating these workers from those in the previous category, Bihr has noted the growing fraction of those who, "caught up in an uninterrupted cycle of part-time work/unemployment or inactivity/unstable jobs" are "forced out of this condition of precarious employment ... into long-term unemployment" and permanent material deprivation. *Spectre*, 76.

[65] In this sense, the decline of these acculturating institutions was bound up in the disappearance of the two stock figures symbolizing the workers' movement in the 1960s and 1970s: the traditional *ouvrier professionnel* and *ouvrier spécialisé* who manned the production line in the typical Fordist factory. Bihr, "Fragmentation," 17.

ten workers – that is, those firms in which unions and support for the Left remained weakest – were creating them. Finally, the fracturing of the working class into functionally and socioeconomically divergent strata has made it extremely difficult for unions to organize them. The ephemeral competencies and identities of these workers, not to mention their general professional and material vulnerability, increasingly precludes their identifying with one another, let alone risk losing what employment they do have by joining a union.

As a function, then, of the new structural and technological modalities governing industrial production and the labor and wage flexibility that has been achieved by employers with the blessing of the state, the changing landscape of French capitalism has "placed a growing mass of workers outside the conditions permitting their organization."[66] The new divisions that have appeared among them due to the transformation of industrial structures and processes have dissolved the unitary class identity that had formerly been impressed on French workers by the union movement and the PCF. On the contrary, these divisions have reactivated and reinforced preexisting status and material inequalities between workers. Similarly, they have also entrenched racist, sexist, even paternalist sentiments among them.[67] In short, the process of capitalist restructuring, viewed in terms of both the macroeconomic structures of the French economy and the microeconomic structures of the firm, induced a major crisis of representation among the traditional syndical and partisan organizations that had sustained the workers' movement through most of the twentieth century. As the socializing institutions that had defined their class identity progressively eroded, workers sought out new sources of identification with which to replace them.[68]

The erosion of workers' sense of class consciousness was abetted by the failure of the union movement and the Communist Party to adapt to the structural transformation of industry and understand its sociopolitical implications. At a first level, French trade unions aggravated the crisis of representation afflicting French workers by abandoning the organization of rank-and-file workers within the firm to concentrate on strengthening their bureaucratic apparatuses. After they had been granted a say in the neocorporatist arrangements that were introduced by the state after May 1968, the principal labor confederations made a strategic decision to discard their traditional model of *syndicalisme industriel* in favor of a new brand of bureaucratic or political syndicalism.[69]

---

[66] Ibid., 19.
[67] Bihr, *Spectre*, 76.
[68] Bihr observes that "the fragmentation of the proletariat weakened the sense of class belonging among workers as a whole, thus opening the way for the reconstitution of their collective identity on a new basis, such as the feeling of national appurtenance." "Fragmentation," 20.
[69] Following the Grenelle Accords and the New Society program introduced by the Chaban-Delmas government, French unions shed their traditional role as "informal social partners" within the firm in order to enhance their organizational clout at the regional and national levels. Accordingly, they sought to represent workers, irrespective of their professional or trade affiliations, in a broader, more explicitly political capacity, deemphasizing the professional identities of the latter

As Andolfatto and Labbé put it, they increasingly "shut themselves in an institutional and bureaucratic logic [which was] detrimental to unionization," spurring
the defection of rank-and-file workers from their local union charters in both the
public and private sectors.[70]

> as a basis for organizing and mobilizing them. This distancing of the unions from the realities of
> the workplace was the perverse result of the financial support extended the principal union
> confederations by the state as part of the neocorporatist dispensation put in place in the late
> 1960s and early 1970s. This institutional shift disposed of the need for firm-level organizing in
> order to sustain unions through the collection of dues. In the past, this function ensured that union
> organizers maintained close contact with rank-and-file workers within the firm and served as
> important intermediaries for conveying their concerns and pressing their demands upon manage-
> ment. The result was that once the functional raison-d'être for the firm-level union organizer
> disappeared, the proximity of union with the workers they represented substantially diminished,
> such that employers themselves often had a better grasp of the realities of the workplace and of the
> needs of their workers than the unions. At the same time, in a certain number of large public
> enterprises, the break between rank-and-file workers and the upper echelons of the union move-
> ment was facilitated by the nomination of the most desirable union delegates on the part of firm
> managers, thus severely limiting the prerogative of the rank and file in selecting its syndical
> representatives. Mirroring the evolution of their counterparts in the private sector, public-sector
> unions shunned the model of a syndicalism of adherents, based on grass-roots organizing, for a
> syndicalism of elections, predicated on strengthening their political-administrative apparatuses. In
> short, in both the private and public sectors, unions eschewed the vital organizing role that had
> underpinned their development since the late nineteenth century. Labbé, *Syndicats et syndiqués*,
> ch. 4, esp. 74–82, 89–90, and Capdevielle, *Modernité*, 48–49.
>
> [70] *Histoire des syndicats*, 321. Reflecting this new onus on building up their bureaucracies, the
> administrative apparatuses of the three main union confederations – the CGT, CFDT, and FO –
> underwent significant growth at the departmental, regional, and national levels at the same time
> that they saw rank-and-file membership decline. In 1965 the CGT's central administrative
> apparatus employed no more than 60 people, composed of 14 confederal secretaries seconded
> by 19 undersecretaries and other *collaborateurs*, and around 25 technical and administrative staff
> (journalists, secretaries, switchboard operators, drivers, etc.). Two decades later, in 1985, the
> number of people in leadership roles had almost quintupled to 150 (18 confederal secretaries and
> 135 *collaborateurs*). To these could be added at least an equivalent number of staff, so that *in toto*
> the CGT's central apparatus had expanded to around 300 people. Thus, the organizational
> structure of the principal union confederations came to resemble an inverted pyramid, depicting
> a weak and ephemeral rank and file, crowned by a bloated bureaucratic apparatus staffed by
> a growing cadre of professional administrators. This administrative cadre was increasingly
> co-opted by the logic of bureaucratic politics and institutional inertia, isolating it further from
> the rank-and-file workers whose interests it claimed to represent.
>
> In turn, it is interesting to note that this movement of unions away from firm-level organization
> toward an overtly bureaucratic role has coincided with the de facto reinvestment of the firm as the
> effective locus of industrial relations, with the state giving primacy to firm-level negotiation and
> contractual agreements. Since the newly federalized unions have often proved unable to address the
> needs of workers at this level, the trend toward defection has continued apace, with many firm-level
> bodies breaking away from the national confederations with which they had been affiliated and
> negotiating with employers on their own terms. Beginning in the 1980s, the growing disillusionment
> of rank-and-file workers with the principal union confederations also inspired the establishment of
> independent unions such as the new Solidaires-Unitaires Démocratiques (SUD) network, which has
> sought to organize workers on the basis of their professional identities. Labbé, *Syndicats et
> syndiqués*, 96–102; Andolfatto and Labbé, *Histoire des syndicats*, 322; Howell, "The Dilemmas
> of Post-Fordism," 86–7; and Guy Groux, "French Industrial Relations: From Crisis to Today," in
> *Contemporary France*, ed. G. Ross and J. Howorth (London: Pinter Publishers, 1989), 58–65.

At the same time, this erosion in membership also reflected the excessive politicization and partisanship of the principal union bodies, especially as the latter began to pursue electoralist agendas in order to gain representation within the neocorporatist instances of the state. Such politicization turned off workers who looked to unions to help them solve the problems they were experiencing within the workplace.[71] As a function of these political rivalries and divisions, French trade unionism developed schizophrenic tendencies during the 1970s. Although it aspired in theory to achieve the social and political unity of the working class, it became embroiled in divisive polemics between the various confederations. The growing disjuncture between the aspirations and practices of the union movement led many unaffiliated workers to tune out the appeals of its representatives and former members to abandon the formations to which they had belonged. In the words of one observer, as a function of "the[ir] internal organization . . ., their politicization, and the manner in which they chose their leaders," French unions became increasingly "tone-deaf" to the demands and aspirations of their constituents, leading workers to desert the confederations *en masse* beginning in the 1970s and continuing up through the 1990s.[72] At base, these widespread defections reflected the unions' strategic incapacity to adapt to the new economic and institutional conditions that shaped French industrial relations from the mid-1970s on. In this sense, they were themselves partly to blame for workers' eroding class consciousness and identity.

In a similar fashion, the erosion of support suffered by the Communist Party among French workers also reflected its inability to adapt to a changing socio-political environment. Specifically, this loss of support stemmed from the discredit cast upon the party by external events as well as by its own political inconsistencies. At a first level, the PCF was hurt by its failure to distance itself from the USSR as the moral and structural bankruptcy of the latter became apparent from the 1970s on.[73] As a result of this strong historical identification, it found it very difficult to recast its image following the collapse of the Soviet Union in 1991. At the same time, however, the growing reformism displayed by the party throughout the 1960s and 1970s – particularly after its conclusion of the Common Program with the new Socialist Party (PS) in 1972 – eroded its political and moral authority for many workers as a credible alternative to the democratic-capitalist status quo. From this standpoint, the PCF presented an increasingly uncredible alternative to the PS on the left and

---

[71] In particular, the political sectarianism that became rife between the CGT and the CFDT in the late 1970s, reflecting the growing tension between the PS and PCF, left a bad taste in the mouth of many workers. Unable to reconcile the revolutionary and gradualist strategies that they respectively advocated, the CGT and the CFDT accused one another of betraying the true interests of the workers, the first by taking the second to task for capitulating to the demands of the capitalist class, the second by impugning the first for advocating an unrealistic program that was doomed to fail. Groux, "French Industrial Relations," 82–5, and Capdevielle, *Modernité*, 28–31.

[72] Labbé, *Syndicats et syndiqués*, 106.

[73] Lavau, *À quoi sert le PCF?* 44, and Lazar, "Culture politique communiste," 244.

consequently proved unable to oppose the neoliberal turn of the latter in the mid-1980s.[74]

In turn, the party's declining stature among French workers was exacerbated by its contradictory attempt to reinvent itself as a social democratic party during the 1990s. From a political-spatial standpoint, there was little room for such a party on the left. As a consequence of this choice, moreover, the PCF abandoned its historic tribunary function with respect to French workers. Instead, this role was assumed to a limited degree by Trotskyist parties on the radical left and, much more significantly, by the Front National on the radical right. In essence, then, by the 1990s the PCF had become just another political entrepreneur within the French party system. As a result, it increasingly found itself caught between two contradictory strategies. On the one hand, when it sought to preserve its traditional working-class bastions of support, it was blamed for neglecting potential recruits – immigrants, the working poor, atypical workers – and failing to serve as an inclusive progressive force.[75] On the other hand, when it tried to broaden its appeal among other social constituencies, it was accused of betraying the labor aristocracy that represented its historical base and had been the worst affected by deindustrialization and economic crisis. In the words of Marc Lazar, "The symbiosis which it had realized between its system of action and forms of communal, notably working class, life [was] in the process of disaggregating and disappearing. ... In short, the PCF [was] less and less a seedbed of [working-class] political culture and identity."[76]

Thus, the precipitous decline of the union movement and PCF heralded the dislocation of the "systems of representation" that had been transmitted to French workers through these agents of working-class organization and socialization, marking the "dissolution of the old collective identities" that had been shared by their members.[77] Thus deprived of these sources of identification, French workers sought out new forms of identity and validation in a world seen to be increasingly lacking in them.

The collapse of these collective agents of class identification caused workers to fall back on more immediate and individual markers of identity. In a period of rising unemployment and occupational uncertainty, one's trade or profession became such a marker, an increasingly important source of recognition for workers threatened with economic redundancy and social *déclassement*.[78] Yet,

---

[74] Bihr, *Spectre*, 262.

[75] Lazar, "Culture politique communiste," 241–2.

[76] Ibid., 241.

[77] Capdevielle, *Modernité*, 40; Labbé, *Syndicats et syndiqués*, 57–8. As Michel Wieviorka observed: "The locus of meaning provided by the workers' movement has been dissolved, emptied of all signification, and the web of social, political, cultural and other organizations for which it served, either directly or symbolically, as the principal referent and impetus, has also disintegrated, at the same time that the old political ideas and debates that it formerly inspired have become exhausted." See "Les bases du national-populisme," 38.

[78] A study conducted in 1995 found that respondents placed their job ahead of any other characteristic or trait as the most important factor of identification according to which they defined themselves.

this occupational basis of identity came itself increasingly under attack during the 1980s and 1990s. The roll-back of the postwar "social *acquis*" in the name of economic flexibility and efficiency broadened into a generalized attack on the very occupations by which French workers increasingly defined themselves. Employers moved away from trade-based qualifications as the principal criterion for hiring new workers in favor of their adaptability to the increasingly fluid and transient processes of industrial production. By debasing their occupations, the introduction of process flow and just-in-time systems of production into the workplace provoked a crisis of identity among ordinary workers. In turn, this erosion in their occupational identities was intensified by rising unemployment during the 1980s and 1990s, which forced industrial workers to compete over a dwindling supply of poorly paid jobs, often with immigrants willing to work for much less.[79] Thus, as more and more of them lost their jobs, they were deprived not only of their means of economic subsistence but, increasingly, of their sole remaining source of identification as well.

The growth of unemployment among industrial workers and their fractionalization along economic, occupational, and ethnic lines resulted in the disintegration of the *quartiers populaires* that had been the incubators of French working-class culture.[80] The abandonment of many these *quartiers* by more affluent blue-collar workers left the most socially and economically vulnerable elements of the working class behind in them, a growing proportion of whom were non-European immigrants. In the words of one analyst, these areas came to be inhabited by strata that

Of those surveyed, 47% put their profession ahead of any other factor, followed by 18% who cited their *quartier* or commune of residency, 15% their region of origin, and 12% their level of professional training or their diploma. However, this new basis of identification reflected not so much the specific pride in one's trade that animated *petits indépendants* but rather satisfaction at holding regular, full-time employment. This valuation of employment for its own sake was highlighted by the fact that, while only 35% of service-sector *employés* and 39% of industrial workers placed their primary marker of identity on their profession versus a high of 51% for management executives and members of the liberal professions, only 21% of workers and 20% of *employés* versus 35% of executives and 32% of the members of *professions intermédiaires* (technicians, foremen, middling executives, teachers, civil servants) disagreed with the statement that work was the most important thing in life. As Jacques Capdevielle has shown, even low-paying, unstable, and mind-numbing jobs – he cites the example of telemarketing – were still a source of social validation for those who held them. This suggests that workers and *employés* ascribed greater importance to holding a job than to the nature of the job held, reflecting the erosion of the craft principle, on the one hand, and the downgrading of the profession as a basis of corporate organization, on the other. Capdevielle, *Modernité*, 66, and Guillaume Lachaise, *Crise de l'emploi et fractures politiques* (Paris: Presses de la FNSP, 1996), 57, 74.

[79] On this point, see S. Beaud and M. Pialoux, "Notes de recherche sur les relations entre Français et immigrés à l'usine et dans le quartier," *Genèses*, no. 30 (March 1998), 101–21, and *Retour sur la condition ouvrière*, ch. 9.

[80] That such *quartiers* remained particularly potent sources of identity for French industrial workers is underscored by the fact that, in the aforementioned study from 1995, 49% of them emphasized territorial identifiers, versus 39% who put forward professional identifiers, as the most important factor defining their social identity. This contrasted with 25% of management executives and members of the liberal professions who put place of origin ahead of other considerations, as opposed to 51% who cited their profession. Lachaise, *Crise de l'emploi*, 57.

were "the most materially, politically, culturally deprived, those who have no chance of 'making it,' in every sense of the word."[81] As a result of the flight of their more prosperous inhabitants, many former working-class neighborhoods were characterized by growing social anomie as the associational fabric that had sustained collective life all but collapsed. To make matters worse, because of their peripheral location on the fringes of cities and dilapidated infrastructures, these *quartiers populaires* were increasingly cut off from the rest of society, reinforcing further the alienation of their inhabitants.[82]

The spread of social alienation and anomie increasingly fueled the animosity of native workers who remained behind against the burgeoning immigrant popula-tions of these areas.[83] Their anti-immigrant feelings were all the more pronounced in that the latter symbolized the very economic and social *déclassement* that they had fought so hard to overcome. The fact that most of them were reduced to competing with immigrants within the workplace and the *quartier* was irrefutable proof, in both a material and symbolic sense, of their socioeconomic decline.[84]

This growth of anti-immigrant feelings represents a *repli identitaire* on the part of a working class increasingly deprived of its cultural and political bases of identity. It testified to the acute cultural crisis that gripped French workers as a result of the disintegration of the traditional habitus they had developed through their interactions in the workplace and in the *quartier*. In turn, this crisis was exacerbated by their perceived betrayal by the Left, particularly following the Socialist government's adoption of *rigueur* in 1983–4. As a result of this shift in policy, many workers grew to despise the PS for sacrificing their interests to the capitalist class and to scorn the PCF for its inability to defend them.[85] Thus, it

---

[81] Bihr, *Spectre*, 78.

[82] From a geographical standpoint, the neighborhoods hardest hit by this process of social disinte-gration have been concentrated in the historic industrial heartlands of the North and Northeast, the lower Massif Central, and the northern and eastern suburbs of Paris. Home to first-wave industrial sectors such as textiles, mining, and metallurgy, they were the first to feel the brunt of deindustrialization as an increasing proportion of these types of industrial jobs were outsourced, and thus the first to see their social fabric progressively dissolve.

[83] Proof of the prevalence of sentiments of "heterophobia" – defined as fear, hatred, and rejection of the other – among French workers as a whole was confirmed by a survey from 1991 that found that fully 32% of Communist voters (a majority of whom were workers) thought that if the population of Arab origin in a given commune was too high, it represented a threat to the security of its inhabitants. Similarly, 34% of these voters expressed the fear that France might one day become an Islamic country. Finally, in an earlier poll from 1989, 26% of Communist voters agreed with the statement that the Jews held too much power in France. Perrineau, *Le symptôme Le Pen*, 161.

[84] As the philosopher Norbert Elias has observed, the tensions between social groups tend to grow when the social distance between in-groups and out-groups is reduced. Quoted in Beaud and Pialoux, "Notes de recherche," 121.

[85] Working-class disenchantment has not simply been directed at the Left. Workers felt similarly let down following the presidential election of 1995, in the run-up to which president-elect Jacques Chirac had campaigned on a pledge to address the social fracture dividing the country. Once elected, however, Chirac and his new prime minister, Alain Juppé, reneged on that pledge, closely hewing to the deflationary program put in place by their predecessors over the previous decade. Capdevielle, *Modernité*, 34.

was only a matter of time before this rejection of the Left broadened into a rejection of the political class as a whole, as well as of the liberal economic and social project with which it was identified. This phenomenon is reflected in the overwhelming opposition of French workers to European economic and political integration, which they view as essentially a lever for the neoliberal transformation of the French economy and society.[86]

Therefore, viewing the Left and the unions as unwilling or unable to defend their social *acquis*, and deprived of their traditional corporative and communal markers of identity, French workers turned in growing numbers to the Front National as a source of political identification. As in the case of the *petits indépendants*, the FN crystallized workers' resentments and fears, identifying ready scapegoats on whom they could blame their social and economic decline – notably, as in the 1880s and 1930s, on recently arrived immigrants. At the same time, the FN offered the countervailing myth of a pure and authentic France in which workers, as *petits indépendants* had done before them, remained secure as producers and vital to the economic and social life of the nation. It strove to restore to workers their sense of collective belonging and worth, while highlighting the unnaturalness and iniquity of their present decline. After having been successively stripped of the identifications of *classe*, *quartier*, and *métier*, then, the attribute of closed national appurtenance cultivated by the FN remained one of the sole bases of identification available to a growing number of French workers on the eve of the twenty-first century.

In turn, this positing of a primordial, ethnically pure France was coupled with concrete policy proposals that were specifically designed to appeal to a working-class audience. Accordingly, the FN advocated a crackdown on petty crime coupled with the repatriation of all recent non-European immigrants who were regarded by many workers as economic and social competitors.[87]

---

[86] Accordingly, fully 78% of French industrial workers voted against ratification in the June 2005 referendum on the European Constitution, compared to the national average of 54.7%. If we further parse these numbers, we find that the most vulnerable categories of wage earners, such as temporary workers (71%) and those on short-term contracts (69%) rejected the European Constitution *en masse*. Similarly, 71% of the unemployed – among whom can be counted a disproportionate number of former industrial workers – rejected the constitution, despite the promise of its advocates that it would contribute to a more favorable business environment and reduce unemployment within the country. These results mirror the social breakdown of the vote of the Maastricht referendum in September 1992, in which the electoral map of the *non* replicated that of the working-class Left, which had voted Communist in the regional elections of March 1992 and for Mitterrand in the second round of the presidential election of 1974. Rémi Barroux, "La précarité de l'emploi a nourri le rejet du traité," *Le Monde* (1 June 2005), 7, and Capdevielle, *Modernité*, 99.

[87] This growing preoccupation with the theme of criminality and security, implicitly overlaid with hostility toward immigrants and the children of immigrants, is brought home particularly forcefully by a formerly Communist industrial worker who first voted for Le Pen in 1995. He declared: "The PC[F] has become too conciliatory toward those who run around stirring up shit, if you'll pardon the expression. But when these little assholes trash my daughter's car, who's left to deal with it? Not the rich. It's us, the workers, whom they're harming." Quoted in Mayer, "Du communisme au FN," 113.

308   *The Resurgence of the Radical Right in France*

Similarly, it advocated measures to improve the material and social situation of French workers, in effect tailoring economic and welfare policies to protect them from the illegitimate competition of immigrants on the one hand and the depredations of rootless corporations on the other.[88] These proposals shrewdly played on the deep-seated insecurities of industrial workers as the principal victims of globalization and of the subsequent transformation of the French economy.[89]

Finally, workers' identification with the FN's program and discourse was greatly facilitated by the erosion of the politically moderating influences of the PCF and traditional syndicalism. As we saw, the sociopolitical restraints deriving from the tradition of firm-level negotiation implicit in traditional French syndicalism, as well as the tribunary function and republican pretensions of the PCF, had effectively bound French workers to the democratic system. As these restraints dissolved with the decline of the unions and the Communist Party, there remained no cultural or political barriers to prevent workers from embracing the antidemocratic politics of the FN. In areas where these syndical and partisan structures continued to exercise a cultural influence over French workers, they had a definite prophylactic effect in limiting the appeal of the FN. Conversely, in places where union or Communist influence was absent or had been eroded, Le Pen and his party received much greater support from workers.[90]

The substantial working-class support garnered by the Front National since the late 1980s marks the first time a radical right-wing party has been able to

[88] Cf. Steve Bastow, "Front National Economic Policy," and "Radicalization."

[89] The flocking *en masse* of French workers to the FN could be said to reflect the declining hold on them of the values of tolerance associated historically with the Left in France. However, as the social-welfarist component of its program suggests, this political identification did not necessarily herald an abandonment by French workers of leftist positions on socioeconomic issues. Hence the term *gaucho-lepénisme* (left-wing Lepenism) to designate their enduring adhesion to left-wing redistributive values in the economic and social arena, colored by the exclusionism of the FN to demarcate the national community to which these values applied. In short, these workers fused their perception of their class-based interests and aspirations with the closed notion of identity advanced by the radical Right. From this standpoint, their growing support for the FN represented not so much the dissolution of class consciousness as a marker of social identity but rather its reinvestment with a racially exclusionary content. Mayer, "Du communisme au FN," 113, and Mayer and Cautrès, "Les métamorphoses du vote de classe," 152.

[90] It is particularly instructive to note that the FN enjoys its strongest support among younger industrial workers, that is, those least likely to have belonged to a trade union or the Communist Party. By contrast, it is the oldest workers who are most likely to have been socialized according to the values of the traditional unions and PCF who consistently evinced the lowest turnout in favor of the FN. This point is borne out by Mayer's analysis of the political preferences expressed by four generational groups of workers or people of working-class background. She found that in the 1988 presidential election, 20% of those born between 1954 and 1970, 14% of those between 1939 and 1953, and 18% of those born before 1939, voted for J.-M. Le Pen. In the 1995 presidential election (which included a new, more recent cohort of voters), 27% of workers or people of working-class descent born between 1971 and 1977, 22% of those born between 1939 and 1970, and 15% of those born before 1939 voted for him. Finally, in the 1997 parliamentary elections, 31% of those born between 1971 and 1977, 26% of those between 1954 and 1970, 19% between 1939 and 1953, and 18% before 1939, voted for FN candidates. *Ces Français qui votent Le Pen*, 441.

achieve a significant following among workers since the late nineteenth century, when large numbers of them turned out for General Boulanger. Yet, whereas Boulangisme amounted to little more than a flash in the pan – its hold on French workers failing to outlast the 1885–90 election cycle – the FN was able to sustain its working-class support throughout the 1990s, largely accounting for Le Pen's accession to the second round of the 2002 presidential elections. In this sense, the FN has shown a remarkable ability to articulate and harness the anxieties and resentments of a working class hard hit by economic change and deprived of its traditional corporative spokesmen. Yet, its success in enlisting French workers' support has not just resided in its ability to give them a voice by which they could air their insecurities and grievances. It also reflected the FN's capacity to offer them a reassuring and reaffirming sense of identity, in much the same manner as previous radical right-wing movements in regard to *petits indépendants*. In this sense, as Alain Bihr has remarked, the FN did not simply resume the tribunary function previously assumed by the PCF. It also "restor[ed] a social and political identity . . . to working-class milieus . . . stripped of their professional, social, and organizational bases of reference."[91]

In sum, the rise and entrenchment of the FN suggest that the breakup of the Fordist economic and social model has had a particularly profound impact in France, where it proved more politically destabilizing and socially traumatic than elsewhere in Europe, let alone the United States. Capitalizing on the fears and uncertainties raised by new post-Fordist economic realities, the FN has managed to combine the age-old appeal of the radical Right among *petits indépendants* with a politics of "welfare chauvinism" directed to the working class. In this sense, it has accomplished what its predecessors on the radical right could only dream of achieving: an alliance between the petite bourgeoisie and the working class against the evils of monopoly capitalism and socialist collectivism, on the one hand, and as a vehicle of social purification and national renewal, on the other.

[91] Bihr, *Spectre*, 94.

9

The Radical Right in France in Comparative Perspective

Within the nations we are witnessing a development under which the economic system ceases to lay down the law to society and the primacy of society over that system is secured. This may happen in a great variety of ways, democratic and aristocratic, constitutionalist and authoritarian, perhaps even in a fashion yet utterly unforeseen. The future in some countries may be already the present in others, while some may still embody the past of the rest. But the outcome is common with them all: the market system will no longer be self-regulating.

Two vital functions of society, the political and the economic, were being used and abused as weapons in a struggle for sectional interests. . . . The one was given by the clash of the organizing principles of economic liberalism and social protection which led to a deep-seated institutional strain; the other by the conflict of classes which, interacting with the first, turned the crisis into a catastrophe.

Karl Polanyi, *The Great Transformation*[1]

The foregoing has important theoretical and heuristic implications not only for understanding the French and European radical Right but also for the analysis of social and political modernization and the avenues of inquiry by which it might best be undertaken. Taking this last aspect first, this study underscores the importance of cultural variables, as brought out in the collective identities of certain constituencies within French society and the dynamics of crisis that came to affect them, in helping to shape social and political developments in the country. Theoretically speaking, by attributing the persistent appeal of the radical Right in France to the cultural proclivities of certain sociopolitical constituencies, this study highlights the inadequacy of political-institutional accounts that rely on an economistic conception of interests in order to explain political outcomes. The fact that, despite the four changes of regime undergone by the country since 1870, the radical Right has continued to appeal to the same antimodern constituencies while evincing essentially the same ideology and program over the past century and a quarter cannot be explained simply in

---

[1] *The Great Transformation* (New York: Farrar and Rinehart, 1944), 251, 133–4.

terms of the institutional structures and processes that characterized the French political system over this period.

Culturalist approaches hold two distinct advantages over political-institutional accounts. First, they offer a much more realistic and robust conception of the interests that animate individual and collective political actors. Whereas political-institutional accounts posit an essentially economistic understanding of political interest, defining the objectives of political agents solely in terms of their own rational self-interest or utility, culturalist explanations take into account the important affective or psychological considerations with which political agents invest their objectives, and which in turn inform how they go about pursuing them. These considerations are related to key forms of social identity – class, ethnic, partisan, occupational – according to which individuals collectively define themselves and, by extension, the symbolic referents by which such identities are expressed and affirmed. According to this view, political interests are inseparable from these broader social identities and the related symbolic meanings with which the latter are invested. They do not exist in isolation or on their own terms but as aggregated bundles of affects and meanings that are bound up in these broader identities and brought into play when any one of these interests is felt to be threatened by those who hold them. This, of course, is not to say that political institutions do not matter. However, it does call for situating the function and influence of such institutions in the broader identity-bound social and cultural contexts that circumscribe how individuals and collective actors will act when confronted by particular institutionally determined situations.

Second, the culturalist approach more readily lends itself to the analysis of historically enduring and recurring political phenomena, such as the French radical Right, within a given society. Because of the autonomy and resilience – what cultural anthropologists have termed the stickiness – of cultural beliefs and orientations beyond the sociostructural conditions that initially gave rise to them, such models are useful for explaining how traditionalist and antimodern political forms continue to survive within advanced capitalist societies that ostensibly present the structural or institutional conditions for their disappearance. In this sense, culturalist approaches such as the one deployed in this study are able to account for the continuity over time of certain forms of politics – such as the French radical Right – in a way that political-institutional accounts, most often limited to a "snapshot" analysis of a particular society or set of societies, cannot. They underscore the primacy of cultural legacies inherited from the past in the determination of political outcomes, as opposed to the purely structural, institutional legacies that command the analytical focus of contemporary political scientists. In turn, because they place greater analytical store by historical inquiry than do standard institutional accounts of politics, culturalist approaches also uncover how structural and institutional processes shape the values and orientations of political agents in particular societies, thus informing political outcomes within them. In short, because it offers, as Shulamit Volkov put it in her study of the *petite bourgeoisie* in Wilhelmine Germany, the "connection between material and social conditions and the shaping of group ideas and action," culture matters as an explanatory variable in political science.[2] As such, it is high time that it be brought back to the center of political analysis.

FRANCE COMPARED: THE BRITISH, GERMAN, AND ITALIAN CASES

Bearing this culturalist focus in mind, it might be useful to deliberate on the historic and contemporary significance of the radical Right in France by comparing the country's social, economic, and political modernization to the experiences of other European societies. Such a comparison should make it possible to adumbrate further avenues of inquiry into what it was about France's sociostructural and class-cultural makeup that distinguished it from countries such as Britain, in which the radical Right has never been an influential political force, and those, such as Germany and Italy, in which fascist regimes rose to power. In France, as we have seen through the course of this study, the radical Right's appeal could be attributed to the illiberal cultural leanings evinced by an enduring traditional middle-class sector and, more recently, by elements of the industrial working class. In Britain, by contrast, these elements, and in particular the lower middle classes – who were never as consequential as in France or, for that matter, in Germany and Italy – conspicuously failed to become a breeding ground for radical right-wing politics.[3] Conversely, in Germany and Italy, from the closing decades of the nineteenth century on, the middle classes plunged headlong into political extremism and, as the tenants of an increasingly antimodernist and antiliberal politics, were strongly represented within the fascist movements that triumphed in those two countries.[4] Likewise, in Germany (though not in Italy), it must be noted that a significant minority of industrial workers – in a dynamic redolent of the

---

[2] *The Rise of Popular Anti-modernism in Germany: The Urban Master Artisans, 1873–1896* (Princeton: Princeton University Press, 1978), 7.

[3] Cf. Geoffrey Crossick, "La petite bourgeoisie britannique au XIXe siècle," *Le mouvement social*, no. 108 (July–Sept., 1979), 21–61; Mayer, "Classes moyennes," 769–79; and Volkov, *Rise of Popular Anti-modernism*,15, 57, 333–4.

[4] On the German case, see respectively Robert Gellately, *The Politics of Economic Despair: Shopkeepers and German Politics, 1890–1914* (London: Sage Publications, 1974), 197–209; Volkov, *Rise of Popular Anti-modernism*, 172–91, 215–29, 297–325, and 343–53; Mayer, "Classes moyennes," 779–85; Conan Fischer, *The Rise of the Nazis* (Manchester: Manchester University Press, 1995), ch. 5; and Bernd Weisbrod, "The Crisis of Bourgeois Society in Interwar Germany," in *Fascist Italy and Nazi Germany: Comparisons and Contrasts*, ed. R. Bessel (Cambridge: Cambridge University Press, 1996), 23–39. On the Italian case, see Alexander De Grand, *Italian Fascism: Its Origins and Development*, 3rd ed. (Lincoln: University of Nebraska Press, 2000), 7–9, 13–14, 25–7, 32–3; and Christopher Seton-Watson, *Italy from Liberalism to Fascism, 1870–1925* (London: Methuen, 1967), 570–4. For a comparison of the roles played by the middle classes in the triumph of fascism in both countries, see Adrian Lyttelton, "The 'Crisis of Bourgeois Society' and the Origins of Fascism," in Bessel, *Fascist Italy and Nazi Germany*, 12–22.

extreme rightward shift of many contemporary French workers – also threw its support behind the Nazi Party in the late 1920s and early 1930s.[5] In this sense, France could be said to represent, as Mayer has put it, an "intermediate" case between Britain, in which the traditional middle classes failed to evolve an illiberal, antimodern political culture, and Germany and Italy, where such a culture, brought out by acute socioeconomic and political crises, contributed to sweeping aside a fragile democratic order and heralded the advent of radical, even revolutionary, radical right-wing regimes.[6]

In order to account for these different national outcomes from a political-cultural standpoint, we need to examine the modalities of social and political modernization within each of these countries, in particular the social structures they evolved and the mechanisms they perfected for managing class conflict. In this vein, it is useful to consider the experience of modernization in each of these countries at three distinct yet interrelated levels of analysis. At a first economic level, it is necessary to examine the nature and timing of the process of industrialization and its sociostructural antecedents and consequences. Particularly important in this regard is the character of the preindustrial social order, notably the economic relations obtaining in the countryside and the size and condition of the peasantry. Second, at a political level, one must look at the pace and character of the process of political liberalization and democratization within a given society, particularly in relation to the dynamics of economic modernization. Third and finally, at a social level, one must take stock of the position of potentially antimodern and illiberal constituencies in relation to other social groups and, in particular, gauge their relative power with respect to the state. Since the petite bourgeoisie and traditional middle classes have historically composed the sectoral backbone for extreme-right parties and movements, the economic and political influence commanded by these groups needs to be analyzed in comparison to the industrial working class on the one hand and the advanced industrial and financial bourgeoisie and managerial middle classes on the other. In this connection, the character and cohesion of the workers' movement, as well as its relationship to economic and political elites and the political system as a whole, take on particular analytical importance. These conditions were crucial in determining whether working-class demands could be peaceably addressed and accommodated under liberal democratic auspices, or whether, in fact, they provoked authoritarian reactions on the part of dominant groups in order to preserve the prevailing economic and social system.

Considering the case of Britain first, the country underwent a slow, incremental process of industrialization in which potentially antimodern social constituencies played a central role. Rather than economically and politically

---

[5] According to a recent study, industrial workers represented approximately 40% of party members and voters from 1925 through 1932. Detlef Mühlberger, *The Social Bases of Nazism, 1919–1933* (Cambridge: Cambridge University Press, 2003), 48–9, 76, as well as Fischer, *Rise of the Nazis*, 168–71.

[6] Mayer, "Classes Moyennes," 785.

marginalizing these groups, the British experience of industrialization in effect served to modernize them. Specifically, it preempted their developing the illiberal cultural traits that would characterize their counterparts in other European countries, rendering them impervious to political extremism and the radical Right.

Several factors account for this gradualist course of modernization that was followed by Britain. In the first place, the early abandonment of feudal arrangements in the countryside and concomitant conversion of the aristocracy, from the sixteenth century on, to commercial agriculture created the ideal economic and social preconditions for the Industrial Revolution. At a financial level, the precocious adoption of commercial agriculture by the landed classes laid the basis for the accumulation of capital necessary to finance the latter. This development spurred the early emergence of a commercial merchant class while, more importantly, breaking the feudal bonds of the peasantry to the land that would constitute a critical impediment to the emergence of economic and political liberalism in other countries. Peasants were cleared from the land as a result of the enclosure movement that swept the country from roughly the mid-sixteenth to the end of the eighteenth century, making it possible for landlords to adopt increasingly intensive methods of cultivation. This meant that by the early 1800s, there effectively remained no peasantry in England in the traditional, feudal sense, thereby removing the demographic reservoir that could sustain a large antimodern small-owner class as in France, or a revolutionary urban or rural proletariat as in Germany and Italy.[7] In turn, the early switch to commercial agriculture encouraged the *embourgeoisement* of the aristocracy, which facilitated its acceptance of industrial capitalism and political liberalism. This process was given fresh impetus by the repeal of the Corn Laws in 1846, which spurred the conversion of growing numbers of commercial landholders to industry, while fueling the emergence of an industrial working class from the ranks of British artisans.[8]

Artisans' involvement in the country's industrialization long antedated this development, however. British craftsmen were drawn into the process of industrialization quite early on, following the spread of the putting-out system in the mid-eighteenth century. Accordingly, industrialization in Britain unfolded not so much in opposition to traditional petty producers but rather by enlisting the latter as key actors within it. Initially, artisans evolved into either capitalist entrepreneurs or home workers. Later on, they developed complementary relationships as subcontractors and suppliers to larger industrial concerns.[9] Similarly, small shopkeepers assumed an auxiliary role in

[7] Moore, *Social Origins of Dictatorship and Democracy*, 9–14, 20–9, and Eric Hobsbawm, *Industry and Empire: From 1750 to the Present Day*, rev. ed. (New York: New Press, 1999), 6–7, 16, 78–81.
[8] Hobsbawm, *Industry and Empire*, 9–10, and Moore, *Social Origins of Dictatorship and Democracy*, 29–39.
[9] Crossick, "La petite bourgeoisie britannique," 28–36; Hobsbawm, *Industry and Empire*, 7, 49; Mayer, "Classes moyennes," 776–7; and Volkov, *Rise of Popular Anti-modernism*, 333.

respect to the concentrated commercial concerns that emerged in Britain from the 1860s on, occupying as a result a broader swathe of the retailing landscape than anywhere else in Europe.[10]

The complementary functions evolved by British petty producers and shop-keepers with respect to large-scale industry and commerce preempted their being marginalized from the process of industrialization. This effectively spared Britain the serious economic and political conflicts that would oppose large-scale industrial and commercial interests to traditional middle-class groups in both France and Germany. In turn, as a result of the important role they played in the industrialization of their country, British petty producers and traders embraced economic liberalism, thereby ceasing early on to represent a potentially antimodern and illiberal force in British society.[11] This experience stands in stark contrast to that of Germany or even France where, as a result of the survival of strong guild or trade-based corporative identities, the conflictive relationship of these constituencies to big business, and the fraught experience of modernization that they endured, shopkeepers and artisans historically evolved strong antimodernist and illiberal cultural proclivities.

In turn, from a political standpoint, British industrialization was accompanied by a gradualistic and controlled process of political liberalization and enfranchisement, so that the country's course of modernization was neither interrupted nor disrupted by the sudden arrival of the industrial "masses" on the political stage. The basis of electoral participation in Britain was only incrementally widened, with successive reforms in 1832, 1867, 1884, and 1918 extending the suffrage first to the petty propertied middle classes and then much later to industrial workers and women.[12] The broadening of the legislative competencies of parliament was even more gradualistic, so that true parliamentary democracy, with the House of Lords demoted to a purely symbolic role, came to Britain only in the years immediately preceding and following the First World War. For example, it was not until 1911 that parliament gained full control over the all-important power of the purse and obtained sole authority to legislate over monetary issues. Likewise, the remaining legislative prerogatives of the House of Lords were not fully discarded until 1928.[13]

This was very different from France, where the introduction of unqualified universal manhood suffrage in 1875 gave the mass of the population – in which small owners figured prominently – considerable political capacity to slow or impede future industrialization and economic modernization. In short, the gradualist course of political liberalization followed by Britain during the nineteenth and early twentieth centuries mirrored the gradualism of its industrialization from the mid-eighteenth century on. And in the same way that

[10] Crossick, "La petite bourgeoisie britannique," 23–7, and Mayer, "Classes moyennes," 777.
[11] Crossick, "La petite bourgeoisie britannique," 38ff.
[12] Hobsbawm, *Industry and Empire*, 103–4, and David Thomson, *Europe since Napoleon*, rev. ed. (London: Penguin Books, 1990), 351.
[13] Thomson, *Europe*, 361.

potentially antagonistic groups within British society were enlisted within the process of industrialization and given their rightful place within it, the country's gradual democratization served to mitigate the most dislocating and destructive effects of industrialization, thereby facilitating its relatively smooth political development.[14]

Perhaps the greatest proof of Britain's gradualistic path to social and political modernity was the consistent shunning of revolutionary socialist parties on the part of the British working class. Beginning in the Victorian era, a corpus of social laws was progressively enacted in order to address the worst blights of worker poverty, improve workplace conditions, and recognize workers' associative rights. This process culminated in the establishment of a comprehensive health and unemployment insurance system and the institution of the minimum wage on the eve of the First World War.[15] More broadly, in stark contrast to France, Germany, or Italy, Britain's gradual industrialization and democratization facilitated the internalization by its workers of liberal economic and political principles. Their experience of modernization inculcated in them a fundamental respect for the democratic state – a conviction reflected in the fact that most workers held Liberal sympathies before turning to the Labour Party during the opening decades of the new century – and, though they frequently resorted to strikes, a general commitment to resolving labor disputes by legal means.[16] In turn, the absence of a revolutionary socialist movement in the country meant that dominant industrial and landed interests, as well as the British middle classes that looked up to them, would not be tempted to resort to authoritarian prescriptions in order to forcibly suppress the working class, as occurred in Germany and Italy or even in the late 1930s in France. Overall, then, Britain's gradualistic experience of industrialization and democratization served to instill among the ruling elites, the middle classes, and the working class alike a deep-seated and durable liberal economic and political culture. This effectively immunized these segments of British society against embracing, even though it too would be confronted by conditions of acute socioeconomic crisis, the radical authoritarian movements that would sweep to power in Italy and Germany and momentarily threatened in France.

Indeed, if we shift our attention to the German and Italian cases, we must begin by remarking that, in contrast to France and Britain, these two countries followed patterns of social and political development under essentially oligarchical and authoritarian auspices. This facilitated the survival of strong culturally antimodern and illiberal elements within their societies, which in turn lay the foundations for the advent of fascism. And though they differed considerably in terms of the relative levels of development that they had achieved on the eve of their respective fascist revolutions, both countries nevertheless presented

[14] Volkov, *Rise of Popular Anti-modernism*, 334.
[15] Hobsbawm, *Industry and Empire*, 103, 132–3, 207, and Thomson, *Europe*, 355–7.
[16] Hobsbawm, *Industry and Empire*, 110–11, 217; Mayer, "Classes moyennes," 778; and Volkov, *Rise of Popular Anti-modernism*, 334.

uncanny political-historical and sociostructural likenesses that make it possible to jointly compare their experiences to those of other European countries.

At a first, sociostructural level of analysis, preindustrial social and political structures were maintained in both countries despite the onset of economic modernization, establishing the class-cultural basis for the antimodernist backlash that would pave the way to fascism within them. Under the auspices of the Bismarckian state in Germany and Savoy monarchy in Italy, deeply conservative landed elites in both countries – the Junkers in Wilhelmine Germany, and the large land owners of the Po Valley and southern *latifundia* in Italy – strove to advance the course of modernization while attempting to preserve the traditional, parafeudal structures that underpinned their economic and political dominance. Having embraced throughout the nineteenth century a form of commercial agriculture that continued to rest on an essentially feudal system of social relations, these landed elites ruthlessly exploited a large mass of landless laborers – increasingly intermixed in some regions, as in the Po Valley, with subsistence sharecroppers – in order to sustain their economic and social power. In a still overwhelmingly agrarian country such as Italy, this peasant mass burgeoned into a large rural proletariat, whereas in rapidly industrializing Germany it represented a deep reservoir for a rapidly growing urban working class.[17] In turn, the process of industrialization that unfolded in each country was overseen and controlled by these large landed interests, principally on the basis of protectionist alliances – such as the "iron and rye pact" in Germany – that were forced by the latter on the nascent industrial and financial bourgeoisie. In 1879 and 1902 in Germany, and 1878 and 1887 in Italy, prohibitive tariffs were imposed on agricultural and industrial products that lay the groundwork for a "solidarity block" uniting these two constituencies. As a result, the landed elites in both countries were able to sustain their agricultural profits despite the fall in world grain prices throughout the 1870s and 1880s, while co-opting the industrial and financial bourgeoisie by ensuring it the windfalls from a state-driven process of industrialization.[18]

This new political-economic dispensation depended largely on disarming middle-class and especially working-class aspirations to share in the returns of industrialization and the exercise of political power. In both countries, the middle classes were rallied by the landed and industrial elites behind chauvinistic imperialist ventures – *Weltpolitik* in Germany, the disastrous Eritrean campaign

---

[17] Alexander Gerschenkron, *Bread and Democracy in Germany*, 3rd ed. (Ithaca, NY: Cornell University Press, 1989), 21–32; Moore, *Social Origins of Dictatorship and Democracy*, 434–6; Seton-Watson, *Italy from Liberalism to Fascism*, 22–6; and De Grand, *Italian Fascism*, 5–11.

[18] On protectionism in Germany, see Gerschenkron, *Bread and Democracy*, 51–80, and Volkov, *Rise of Popular Anti-modernism*, 175–6, 238–9. For Italy, see Frank Coppa, *Planning, Protectionism and Politics in Liberal Italy: Economics and Politics in the Giolittian Age* (Washington DC: Catholic University of America Press, 1971), 32, 34; Vera Zamagni, *The Economic History of Italy, 1860–1990* (New York: Oxford University Press, 1993), 110–17; and Seton-Watson, *Italy from Liberalism to Fascism*, 81–4.

(1895–6) and Libyan War (1911) in Italy – in order to distract them from the fact of their relative political disenfranchisement and, in the case of the traditional middle classes, their rapid decline due to the advance of industrialization.[19] In Germany in particular, jingoistic nationalism was often willfully combined with extreme expressions of antimodernism and anti-Semitism, as the Junkers sought to enlist the support of the traditional middle classes to bring to heel liberal and pro-free-trade forces that questioned the protectionist pact between the Junkers and the industrial bourgeoisie. Specifically, by appealing to such middle-class organizations as the General Union of German Artisans (1882), the Agrarian League (1894), and the German Middle Class Party (1895) during the 1880s and 1890s, they were able to see off the challenges of these economic liberal forces and bring them into line under the auspices of a compromise that reaffirmed the agrarian-industrial protectionist dispensation that had first been introduced in the late 1870s.[20] Likewise, in Italy, where there existed a glut of aspirants to the new middle classes (including lawyers, engineers, and teachers), relative to the undeveloped condition of the economy, the state attempted to propitiate these strata by offering them employment in its administrative apparatus, in effect relying on patronage to limit middle-class dissatisfaction and radicalism.[21]

By contrast, rather than seeking to placate the working class by co-opting its representatives into the political system, the ruling elites in fin-de-siècle Germany and Italy accorded only token representation to it and repressed any independent attempt on the part of workers to organize economically and politically. Thus, in Italy, the Socialist Party (PSI) was forcibly disbanded from 1894 to 1896. In Germany, the antisocialist laws introduced by Bismarck following the establishment of the Social Democratic Party in 1875 prevented the latter from taking an official role in politics until 1890. And, even after it was recognized and permitted to participate in elections, limitations on the powers of the Bundestag continued to stifle meaningful working-class participation in the governance of the country.[22] Likewise, the organizational prerogatives and rights of workers were severely curtailed in both countries, and labor agitation severely dealt with. In consequence, simmering worker discontent that lent itself to radicalism and revolution remained a constant threat in both countries.

In turn, the enlisting of the state behind the process of industrialization under the auspices of a solidarity pact between the landed aristocracy and industrial bourgeoisie spurred an intensive dynamic of industrial development that reached its apex during the 1880s and 1890s in Germany and in the first decade of the twentieth century in Italy. In marked contrast to Britain, this process unfolded so rapidly in both countries that the landed and industrial elites

---

[19] Volkov, Rise of Popular Anti-modernism, 318, 343; Seton-Watson, Italy from Liberalism to Fascism, 138–41, 184–5, 362–5; and De Grand, Italian Fascism, 13.

[20] Volkov, Rise of Popular Anti-modernism, 190–1, 235–6, 266–8; Gellately, Politics of Economic Despair, 149–54; and Moore, Social Origins of Dictatorship and Democracy, 448.

[21] De Grand, Italian Fascism, 7–8.

[22] Seton-Watson, Italy from Liberalism to Fascism, 167–8, and Thomson, Europe, 396–7.

responsible for overseeing it failed to develop the politically liberal and democratizing habits evolved by their British counterparts over two centuries. Thus, when confronted with economic and political challenges from below, they were much more disposed to respond with repression and authoritarian solutions rather than to defuse such challenges by making room for the lower classes within the political system.

At the same time, rapid industrialization proved deeply unsettling to the German and Italian middle classes, and particularly the traditional artisanal and shopkeeper sectors. This was especially the case in Germany, where the historic influence of craftsmen's guilds was strong, and it engendered deeply reactionary antimodernist sentiments among these *Mittelstand* who were hardest hit by industrialization. Exacerbated by the demands of an increasingly radicalized proletariat, these sentiments translated during the 1880s and 1890s into a general sense of "cultural despair" that would ultimately drive the German *Mittelstand* to embrace the antimodernist appeals of the Nazis during the late 1920s and early 1930s.[23] Similar traditional middle-class resentments were also widespread in Italy, especially in the rapidly industrializing areas of the Milan-Turin-Genoa triangle.

The emergence of large and radicalized working classes during the war and its immediate aftermath was seen by economically vulnerable old and new middle-class groups in both countries as an increasingly dangerous threat to their interests and well-being. As before, these strata aligned themselves with dominant agricultural and industrial interests in trying to quell this rising working-class challenge.[24] The aristocratic and oligarchic regimes that had prevailed in both countries had left the middle classes with no tradition of political responsibility and accountability at the national level. In turn, this lack of a liberal or democratic culture among the German and Italian middle classes facilitated their reactionary mobilization as workers gained unprecedented political power following the establishment of democratic institutions in both countries in the immediate wake of World War I. Thus, they became the natural sociological backbones of the Fascist and Nazi parties that swept to power in the 1920s and 1930s.[25]

Finally, this political outcome was abetted in both Germany and Italy by the internal divisions and weaknesses that plagued the workers' movement in the face of the fascist threat. In Italy, the division between the Socialist and Christian Democratic parties and their affiliated labor organizations, as well as the internal

---

[23] Volkov, *Rise of Popular Anti-modernism*, ch. 11, 352–3, and Gellately, *Politics of Economic Despair*, 215–16. See also F. Stern, *The Politics of Cultural Despair: A Study in the Rise of the German Ideology* (Berkeley: University of California Press, 1961).

[24] De Grand, *Italian Fascism*, 13–14, 25–7.

[25] See Fischer, *Rise of the Nazis*, ch. 5; Weisbrod, "The Crisis of Bourgeois Society in Interwar Germany," on Germany; and De Grand, *Italian Fascism*, 31–33, and Lyttelton, "The 'Crisis of Bourgeois Society' and the Origins of Fascism," on Italy. For a localized study of the German middle classes' slide into Nazism, see Benjamin Lapp, *Revolution from the Right: Politics, Class, and the Rise of Nazism in Saxony, 1919–1933* (Atlantic Highlands, NJ: Humanities Press, 1997).

divisions of these parties between a reformist and radical wing in the first case, and a reactionary and democratic wing in the second, sapped the ability of workers to oppose the fascist onslaught.[26] Correlatively, in Germany the bitter divisions that arose between the Social Democratic Party and the newly formed German Communist Party at the national, regional, and even factory levels greatly eroded the working class's capacity to resist the rise of Nazism. In fact, recent studies have shown that these divisions even facilitated Nazi penetration of the workers' movement, to the extent that, after the *Mittelstand*, industrial workers constituted the second most important social constituency in the party's membership and electorate from the mid-1920s up to its assumption of power in January 1933.[27]

In this sense, the Italian and German cases stand in dramatic contrast to the French case where, in the mid-1930s, the unity of the workers' movement and its sociopolitical strength under the Popular Front government forced the industrial bourgeoisie to compose with it. Consequently, the traditional middle classes remained isolated as a potential force of authoritarian reaction in France, thus averting the rise to power of the radical or revolutionary Right as in Italy and Germany. By contrast, it was the concatenation of antiliberal social classes, in the form of oligarchical and illiberal landed and industrial elites, the new managerial middle class, antimodern traditional middle-class strata, and a radicalized agrarian or industrial proletariat, that doomed the fragile democracies established in Italy and Germany after World War I and led to the crushing of the workers' movement under the guise of fascism.

Thus, when we respectively compare the French to the British and the German or Italian cases, we see that the country owes its intermediate historical position to two principal factors: its belated industrialization on the one hand, and early introduction of parliamentary democracy on the other. In terms of its social configuration, France at the end of the nineteenth century was probably closer to Germany and Italy than to Britain, since it presented a significant traditional middle class as well as a large peasantry. Yet, France differed from Germany and Italy in two crucial respects. At a first level, the accession of a large proportion of the peasantry to landownership as a result of the Revolution, and its consequent conversion to commercial agriculture, served to break the quasi-feudal bonds that maintained the peasantry in thrall to landed elites in Germany and Italy. Similarly, the country's early democratization, which preceded that of Britain but, like the latter, was the result of a gradualistic if fitful historical process – the establishment of the Third Republic in 1870 representing the culmination of

---

[26] Seton-Watson, *Italy from Liberalism to Fascism*, 299–306, 511–15, 524–7, and De Grand, *Italian Fascism*, 22–4.

[27] On the Nazi penetration of the German working class, see Mühlberger, *Social Bases of Nazism*, 48–9, 76. On the divisions between Social Democrats and Communists, see Franz Borkenau, *World Communism: A History of the Communist International* (Ann Arbor: University of Michigan Press, 1962), ch. 8, and Conan Fischer, *The German Communists and the Rise of Nazism* (New York: St. Martin's Press, 1991).

abortive democratic experiments in 1793 and again in 1848 – habituated potentially antimodern and illiberal groups to the principles and processes of democracy.

In particular and crucially for this study, the establishment of universal suffrage in a country composed largely of small property holders and petty producers yielded a stable yet inertial sociopolitical dispensation, whereby the *grande bourgeoisie* was able to maintain its grip on power by safeguarding the petty proprietary interests of the traditional middle classes in France. Under the aegis of this republican synthesis, the latter combined a particular cultural mind-set of *indépendance* based on the valuation of the craft and traditional, preindustrial social values with a respect for parliamentary democracy. In this sense, the French traditional middle classes fashioned a peculiar form of archaeoliberalism that was democratic in inspiration (stemming as it did from the Jacobin and Radical political traditions) yet reactionary in content. Inherent in this primordial, small-property-based model of democracy was a fundamental contradiction: the principal social elements on which it depended and staked its legitimacy stood in diametrical opposition to the imperatives of economic modernization and commercial and industrial rationalization. As a result, from essentially the end of Great War to the outbreak of the Second World War, the French state was engaged in a delicate balancing act between preserving the republican synthesis that underlay it and modernizing the country's economic structure.

The radical Right has been the principal political symptom of this contradictory *démarche*. Rather than expressing a traditional middle-class hankering for a predemocratic and premodern social order, its persistent appeal among French *petits indépendants* reflected their mounting anxiety and frustration at the abandonment by the French state of the petty-producer-based conception of democracy that they espoused. Combined with the general cultural disorientation they experienced as a function of the country's economic and social transformation, the radical Right's resurgence might thus be interpreted as the political expression of the cultural tensions resulting from the outstripping of an early preindustrial form of democracy by the norms and institutions of industrial capitalist society. This ironically would suggest that, in contrast to Germany and Italy, where fascism derived from the desire of a large part of the society to undertake industrialization under antidemocratic auspices, or to Britain, where the processes of liberal economic and political development were always "in synch," the persistent appeal of the radical Right in France is an inherent byproduct of the development of French democracy and its ambivalent relationship to the broader processes of social and economic modernization.

In short, by empowering antimodern social groups within the sociopolitical dispensation over which it initially presided and giving them a vital stake within it, the French democratic state sowed the seeds of future resistance against it. As the republican state sought to transcend this initial dispensation and to reach out to more modern or advanced social constituencies and as they were increasingly confronted by culturally disorienting economic and social change, many petty producers turned against the republican state and gravitated to the radical Right. In turn, as the modernization process inexorably progressed, new social strata, notably industrial workers, also found themselves more economically vulnerable and politically marginalized than ever before. Exposed to a cultural crisis similar to that experienced by *petits indépendants* before them, some members of these strata evinced a comparable ambivalence toward the democratic state and the elected leaders who ran it. Consequently, by the end of the twentieth century, they too came to represent an increasingly favorable audience for the radical Right.

10

Conclusion

Throughout the course of this study, we have presented an analytical framework of political supply and political demand in order to account for the periodic resurgence of the radical Right in French society. In Chapter 2, we specified the conditions of political supply that historically fueled this phenomenon. We identified the ideological and discursive attributes of an autochthonous tradition of the radical Right in France and analyzed the rhetorical and symbolic motifs or myths that it employed to appeal to its target audience. Reflecting the synthesis between a revolutionary, national-populist tradition and a counterrevolutionary, elitist tradition, the radical Right posited the establishment – most recently under a pseudorepublican guise – of an ordered, authoritarian, and hierarchical society and polity rooted in a "closed, exclusive and obsidional conception of the nation."[1] In turn, the remainder of the study sought to spell out the conditions of political demand underpinning the enduring appeal of the radical Right in French society. In the first place, *petits indépendants* and the members of culturally similar groups such as the owners of traditional family firms and workers in quasi-artisanal firms proved historically receptive to the radical Right during economic and social crises. More recently, industrial workers, threatened economically and deprived of their traditional sociopolitical bases of identification, have become a significant new source of support for this political current.

In each case, these economically and culturally vulnerable groups gravitated to the radical Right in periods of acute social crisis. At a first level, the latter could be reduced to objective structural factors affecting their material wellbeing and productive capacities, precipitating the decline of these groups in modern French society. In turn, as a function of the economic and social dislocations they reflected, such structural crises precipitated subjective crises of identity or meaning among *petits indépendants* and industrial workers. In short, the proclivity of industrial capitalist society to structural crises due to the inherent instability of its productive and social relations, and the ensuing

---

[1] Winock, "L'action française," in *Histoire de l'extrême droite en France*, ed. M. Winock (Paris: Seuil, 1993), 152.

cultural crises that took hold within it, generated a permanent potential reservoir of support for the radical Right.

Appealing through its discourse to the social categories worst affected by these crises, the latter evinced an uncanny ability to harness the anxieties of these groups and articulate their aspirations. Specifically, the radical Right deployed myths that strongly resonated with crisis-ridden *petits indépendants* and, later, industrial workers. In the case of the former, it affirmed the economic, social, and moral primacy of a society based on the vision of *morcellement* that underpinned their political worldview. In turn, the radical Right invested this *petit indépendant* vision with a strong or primal conception of communal identity, asserting it against alien or foreign agents on whom small producers' decline could be blamed. By replicating the tropes of *indépendance* and casting them in terms of an exclusive collective appurtenance, the radical Right shored up *petits indépendants'* social identity and held out the reassuring – if illusory – prospect of escaping the passage from an early to a modern capitalist economic and social order. Similarly, the closed conception of the nation developed by the radical Right became a ready source of identification for French workers who, in the 1980s and 1990s, were deprived of their traditional partisan, corporative, and ecological markers of class identity. As the trade unions, Communist Party, and *quartiers populaires* that had sustained their class consciousness and identity progressively eroded, workers increasingly embraced the organic and exclusive collective identity offered by the radical Right. Consequently, it is at junctures when movements and leaders of the radical Right have been able to capitalize on the structural and cultural crises afflicting these antimodern groups that it has risen to political prominence. At such moments, the unfolding social crisis and the radical Right's political discourse served to reinforce one another, the latter becoming a source of truth and prescription to action for the victims of the former.

Finally, the erosion of the dominant democratic discourse affirming the values of pluralism, tolerance, and individual rights greatly facilitated the acceptance by *petits indépendants* and workers of the closed nationalism and illiberal prescriptions of the radical Right. As was documented in Chapters 4 through 8, these groups evolved increasingly ambivalent attitudes vis-à-vis the republican state and liberal democracy. For their part, *petits indépendants* were disillusioned by what they saw as the state's betrayal of the petty producer ideal underpinning the original republic and which they continued to equate with the sole authentic form of democracy. Similarly, French workers felt betrayed by the political elite, particularly on the left, whom they accused of abandoning the social and political *acquis* they had fought so hard to achieve since the end of the nineteenth century. Thus, *petits indépendants* and industrial workers were drawn to the radical Right because it respectively promised to return to a petty producer society and, more recently, to restore workers' social *acquis* according to the criterion of "national preference." The inability of these strata to adapt to capitalist modernity ensured that the country's subsequent modernization would provoke their continuing social and political resistance, thereby guaranteeing the radical Right persistent bases of support.

From this standpoint, the current social and cultural crisis affecting French workers and *petits indépendants* could be interpreted as a generalized crisis of identity afflicting antimodern social groups in the era of advanced capitalism, principally to the benefit of the Front National. Yet, this crisis of identity and the resulting identification of both of these groups with the radical Right are a relatively novel development, given the divergent political outlooks that distinguished them historically. From the beginning of the period under study to the present, *petits indépendants'* functional role and cultural worldview brought them into conflict with the structural transformations of the French economy. Beginning in the Belle Époque, these transformations accelerated through the interwar period before coming to a head in the 1950s and 1960s. Conversely, for most of this period, industrial workers had been an ascendant or modern social constituency, representing a forward-looking class in the Marxist sense. In stark contrast to *petits indépendants*, their numbers grew as industrialization progressed during the twentieth century. And, until quite recently, their increasing organizational and political clout made them a dominant sociopolitical force in French society. However, since the 1970s, deindustrialization, the transition to a service-based economy, and the transformation of industrial production gradually forced French workers into the role of economic has-beens that had formerly devolved to *petits indépendants*. Indeed, given their anxiety over the current evolution of the French economy and society, one might even argue that French workers have replaced shopkeepers and artisans as the principal stratum threatened by modernization.

The respective economic and social falls from grace suffered by *petits indépendants* and industrial workers may in turn point to a broader crisis of meaning implicit in capitalist modernity itself. The increasingly rapid pace of structural and social change, impelled by globalization and innovation, may begin to threaten other, formerly unaffected professional and social groups. Such change has disarticulated the workplace and eroded the social identities associated with it, confronting formerly unaffected socioprofessional categories "to the loss of their traditional referents and forc[ing them] to reject a process of modernization whose scope and consequences, most often negative as far as they are concerned, escape them."[2] In effect, the rapid mutations of postindustrial capitalism may be expanding the number of social actors subject to structural and cultural crisis. These include service-sector employees as well as members of the "intermediary" professions – industrial technicians and supervisors, mid-level managers and executives, teachers and clerical *fonctionnaires* – whose economic viability and social status have been progressively undermined by the advance of information technology and outsourcing of their functions.[3]

[2] Capdevielle, *Modernité*, 171.
[3] Reflecting the rising economic and cultural anxiety of service-sector employees, the proportion of voters from this category who voted for Le Pen rose from 13% in the first round of the 1988 presidential election to 19% and 23% in the 1995 and 2002 presidential elections. Perrineau, *Le symptôme Le Pen*, 102, and "La surprise lepéniste et sa suite législative," 210.

Even the heretofore secure category of *cadres* (corporate executives) has come under pressure as their enterprises face intense international competition and strive to cope with the liberalization of services on a global scale. Like *petits indépendants* and industrial workers before them, when confronted by conditions of social crisis, these new "losers" of modernity might also latch onto the forceful and exclusionary forms of identity held out by the radical Right.[4]

As theorists have observed, this broadening erosion of corporative and social identities might be symptomatic of a global crisis of meaning confronting the inhabitants of advanced capitalist societies. As a function of ever more diverse and complex modes of production, consumption possibilities, and experiences of work and leisure, people in advanced capitalist society assume myriad competing roles as producers, consumers, and cultural and social actors. As John Gray has written, they are "abandon[ed] ... to a life of fragments and a proliferation of endless choices ... [i]ntermingling the ephemera of fashion with an ingrained reflex of nihilism."[5] Exacerbated by the collapse of the cultural and religious institutions through which individuals formerly defined themselves, this oversaturation of meanings and identities reflects, as another writer has put it, the growing incapacity "of advanced capitalist societies to develop a stable and coherent symbolic order."[6] The result is that their members are unable to evolve coherent or durable social identities through which they are able to make sense of their interactions in the social world.

In this context, the rise of the FN might be read as a symptom of the symbolic malaise brought on by this *trop-plein de sens* (oversaturation of meaning) within advanced capitalist society. As Jean Viard put it, the current "progression of the radical Right ... appears first and foremost as a response to the collapse of our belief in our capacity to master and organize the world."[7] Like its predecessors, the FN satisfies people's need for a stable collective identity following the

---

[4] This argument was advanced by Louis Chauvel, who contends that the French middle classes have not only seen their material stature eroded by the jettisoning of the Fordist welfare state in the era of globalization but that they are also suffering from a crisis of identity as their status as symbols of social mobility and economic and cultural advancement is brought into question by their growing proletarianization in advanced capitalist society. Cf. *Les classes moyennes à la derive* (Paris: Seuil, Coll. La république des idées, 2006).

　　Correlatively, proof that economic and social crisis was no longer the preserve of established antimodern sectors but also of newly threatened middle-class sectors that had formerly been shielded from competition and restructuring can be seen in the rising incidence of corporative unrest that has wracked the country since the 1990s. Struck in their professional and social identities, people from a widening array of occupational categories demonstrated against a state deemed not to be doing enough to protect them, and a corporate elite accused of betraying their well-being for their own profit. On this "wave of corporative unrest," see Capdevielle, *Modernité*, ch. 3.

[5] *False Dawn*, 38.

[6] *L'actualité d'un archaïsme: la pensée d'extrême droite et la crise de la modernité* (Lausanne: Page deux, 1998), 128, and Lecœur, *Un néo-populisme à la française*, 179.

[7] "Les grandes peurs de l'ère planétaire," in *Aux sources du populisme nationaliste*, ed. J. Viard (La Tour d'Aigues: Éd. de l'Aube, 1996), 20.

dislocation of their old communal identifications as a result of rapid economic and social change. This would suggest that, far from being an anachronism, the radical Right remains an integral feature of social and political modernity in France. As the crisis of meaning engulfing advanced capitalist societies continues to spread and intensify, the radical Right holds out "new ways to construct identifications, a sense of appurtenance, points of reference, and an individual and collective identity."[8] As such, it is an implicitly modern phenomenon, a sociopolitical manifestation of the development of French industrial capitalism rather than, as many would have it, simply a throwback to an irrecoverable past.

THE FRENCH RADICAL RIGHT TODAY: PROSPECTS AND LESSONS

The survival of antimodern sectors in French society, as well as the spread of social crises to new formerly unaffected groups, in turn raises the question of the radical Right's status and prospects in France. The Front National continues to represent the most electorally significant and durable radical right-wing movement in Europe today. In this sense, France differs markedly from Germany and Italy, whose traumatic experience of Nazism and fascism respectively vaccinated their societies against the recrudescence of substantial parties of the radical Right (Chapter 9). Indeed, perhaps it is because it has never been discredited by the exercise of power – Vichy being largely seen as an aberrant product of defeat and occupation – that such a party has once again become a plausible political alternative for significant numbers of French voters.

At first sight, if one were to project into the future the sociological analysis underlying this study, the radical Right's prospects appear mixed at best. The dwindling of the *petit indépendant* sector appears to have stripped it of its traditional base of support within French society. However, as the analysis of its electorate since the early 1990s shows, this evanescent *petit indépendant* base has been augmented by a new constituency that does not look to be depleted any time soon. In this sense, the social and cultural crisis affecting French industrial workers has provided a new and potent source of political demand for the radical Right.

What is particularly worrying is that it is not clear whether anything can be done under the prevailing economic system to halt the social and cultural crisis that has fueled the radical Right's rise. Following from the constraints of heightened global competition and European economic integration, France has continued to pursue liberalizing and monetarist policies so that its firms can remain competitive. The likely outcome is that the economic and social situation of French workers will worsen and that more and more of them will turn to the radical Right. In turn, this process is likely to gain further impetus as the state continues to enact structural reforms while dismantling the "social anesthesia state" that was put in place to mitigate the social effects of *déplanification*.

[8] Lecœur, *Un néo-populisme à la française*, 192.

In this vein, the Fillon government appointed by Nicolas Sarkozy following his election has introduced a number of measures to enhance labor market flexibility, including increasing workers' capacity to derogate from national or branch-level collective agreements, exempting temporary or part-time workers from such agreements, eliminating administrative constraints on layoffs, relaxing the thirty-five-hour workweek by making it easier to work overtime, and reducing the social security tax on firms and offsetting it with an increase in the value-added tax – the so-called *TVA sociale*. At the same time, Sarkozy has sought to further reduce the state's welfare obligations by increasing individual health care liabilities and reducing unemployment benefits for those who refuse to take a job, streamlining the public sector by suppressing sixty thousand civil servant posts since 2007, and, most controversially, increasing the retirement age from sixty to sixty-two to receive partial benefits and sixty-five to sixty-seven for full benefits. Last but not least, in an effort to create a supply-side "confidence shock," the government has accompanied these retrenchment measures with fiscal policies exempting employers and employees from paying social security taxes on overtime work, further reducing corporate and income tax rates – particularly on the highest brackets – and cutting taxes on the wealthy.[9]

In turn, a recourse to protectionism or capital controls so as to safeguard French jobs –notwithstanding the fact that they would require overturning the current European Union trade and financial regimes – would likely backfire in an integrated global marketplace in which French firms are outsourcing their operations to capitalize on cheap foreign labor and French consumers have grown dependent on cheaper consumer goods made outside the EU. Furthermore, protectionism at the EU level – a proposal mooted by President Sarkozy – would be unlikely to have much effect, since the great majority of French trade occurs within the EU. (Two-thirds of French exports are circumscribed to the Eurozone, while the country's trade deficit with Germany [€13 billion] is nearly the same as with China [€13.9 billion].)[10] This would suggest that what France needs is not so much trade protection as policies to make French firms more competitive internationally, that is, more of the very economic and social deregulation that increased the economic and social vulnerability of French workers in the first place, driving many of them to support the radical Right.

The intractable nature of these economic and social problems is reflected in the signal incapacity of French political elites to tackle the challenges posed by globalization and address its social impacts. No longer portraying globalization

---

[9] On these structural and fiscal reforms proposed by Sarkozy, see Jean-Marie Monnier, "Politique fiscale. Une mise en perspective," in *L'état de la France 2009–2010. Un panorama unique et complet de la France*, ed. E. Lau (Paris: La Découverte, 2009), 182–92.

[10] Confirming this trend, French exports outside of the eurozone have fallen by 16% since monetary union, whereas those of Germany have progressed by 11%. Frédéric Lemaître, "Analyse: l'économie rattrape Nicolas Sarkozy," *Le Monde*, 16 August 2007, 2, and François Lenglet, *La crise des années 30 est devant nous* (Paris: Perrin, 2007), 100–1.

as a panacea that needs to be embraced, they now fatalistically cast it as a burden whose costs they are powerless to mitigate. At the same time, these elites have increasingly jettisoned state control and oversight of the economy, reverting to a naturalistic economic discourse that presents the free market as an inalterable law of nature that can be neither impeded nor inflected.[11] This shift has weakened the mainstream political parties, particularly on the left where the PS appears irretrievably fractured between the advocates and the opponents of economic liberalization and European integration. Thus, given the intensification of global competition and the abdication of the French political class before the challenges it poses, life for French workers and a growing proportion of the middle class is likely to worsen – a prospect from which the radical Right stands to benefit over the medium to long term.

From this standpoint, the reversal suffered by the Front National in the 2007 presidential and parliamentary elections may well represent a temporary setback for the radical Right rather than signal its definitive ebb.[12] The working- and lower-middle-class FN voters who flocked *en masse* to Sarkozy in these elections are likely to be hurt by his proposals to further deregulate labor markets and roll back the welfare state.[13] And, as we have seen, his call for a European-level protectionism would – in the improbable event it were adopted – most likely be ineffective in dampening the impact of international competition on French industry. There appears to be little in Sarkozy's program that can ease the crisis afflicting working-class and middle-class voters and keep them from returning to the FN.

In turn, the divergent bases of Sarkozy's electoral coalition will make it exceedingly difficult for him not to disappoint erstwhile FN voters while catering to the other interests that helped to get him elected. On the one hand,

---

[11] Capdevielle, *Modernité*, 34.

[12] Commentators prognosticated the end of the FN following the 2007 presidential and parliamentary elections. See, for example, the headline on the cover of the 7 June 2007 issue of *Libération*, which read "Le Pen, la Fin," and Eric Fottorino, "FN, fin." *Le Monde*, 11 June 2007, 1.

[13] In the first round of the 2007 presidential election, the leader of the FN lost nearly a million votes compared to 2002, from 4.8 million votes (16.86%) to just over 3.8 million (10.51%). The overwhelming majority of these votes were siphoned off by Sarkozy, who overtook Le Pen in regions where the FN leader had come first in 2002, including the Alsace, Provence-Alpes-Côte d'Azur, and the Rhône-Alpes region, as well as other former FN strongholds, such as the Languedoc-Roussillon, Nord-Pas-de-Calais, and the peripheral departments of the Ile-de-France. Among these voters, Sarkozy scored particularly strongly among the FN's middle-class and labor electorate, stealing away 44% of workers and *employés* and 35% of *cadres* and members of the intermediate professions who had voted for Le Pen in 2002 in the first round of the 2007 election. In turn, Sarkozy garnered 82% of the artisanal and shopkeeper vote in the second-round runoff against Ségolène Royal and 46% of the working-class vote. Jean-Baptiste de Montvalon, "Les deux qualifiés ont obtenu deux fois plus de voix que M. Chirac et M. Jospin en 2002," Christiane Chombeau, "Jean-Marie Le Pen perd un million de voix par rapport à 2002," and Dossier Spécial: Présidentielle, Résultats Premier Tour, Evolution 2002–2007, "Les gagnants et les perdants," all in *Le Monde*, 24 April 2007, 4, 7, 43; J. B. de Montvalon, "Mme. Royal a échoué dans sa conquête de l'électorat de M. Bayrou," *Le Monde* 8 May 2007, 8; and Fourquet, "L'échec de Jean-Marie Le Pen à la présidentielle de 2007: les causes d'une hémorragie," 9–10.

second-round Sarkozy voters who first cast their ballots for the centrist François Bayrou tend to be much more culturally liberal and socially tolerant than FN voters, who present the highest indexes for intolerance, ethnocentrism, and repressiveness of any segment of the electorate. On the other hand, potential conflicts loom between many Sarkozy voters and *lepéno-sarkozystes* around economic issues. The economic liberalism of Sarkozy voters who are linked to the advanced sectors of the French economy are likely to clash with the traditional *petits patrons* and working-class voters Sarkozy managed to siphon off from the FN. In particular, the new government's liberalization agenda, which is supported by the former and aims to reduce the fiscal and social burdens on French firms (such as its proposal to shift a part of their social security obligations to consumers through a *TVA sociale*, lowering the maximum rate at which the highest earners are taxed, and raising the retirement age for all workers, regardless of when they joined the workforce), is likely to clash with the welfarist proclivities of many erstwhile FN voters and Bayrouistes.[14] In short, it is not clear how Sarkozy is going to be able to continue to pursue his mandate of economic reform while managing to keep erstwhile Le Pen voters "on side" – a prediction that appears to have been borne out by the March 2010 regional elections, in which the FN recorded its strongest performance since 2004, and again in the March 2011 local elections.[15]

By the same token, speculation that the party would not survive the passing of its founder from the political stage appears to have been equally misguided. In January 2011 the reins of the party leadership were successfully transferred by Jean-Marie Le Pen to his daughter Marine without provoking the destructive internecine divisions that had been widely predicted, and she has shown herself to be a more strategically adroit and media savvy politician than many had anticipated.[16] Indeed, a growing number of French political pundits are starting

---

[14] Nonna Mayer, "Comment Nicolas Sarkozy a rétréci l'électorat Le Pen," *Revue française de science politique* 57(3–4) (2007), 443–4.

[15] After obtaining 11.4% of the vote in the first round of balloting, the FN garnered an average of 17% in the twelve three-way races in which its candidates were involved during the second round, achieving its highest scores in the Provence-Alpes-Côte d'Azur and Nord-Pas-de-Calais where Jean-Marie Le Pen and his daughter Marine Le Pen headed the party list. In turn, in the March 2011 local elections, although the party won only two seats and 12% of the national vote, in the 403 cantons in which its candidates acceded to the second-round runoff, it achieved an average electoral score of 40%. Even more disquieting is that this progression was not limited to the FN's traditional electoral bastions of the Northeast, Rhône-Alpes, and Mediterranean coast but also heralded a substantial breakthrough in the western, more rural areas of the country that had traditionally been impervious to its entreaties. Gilles Perrault, "Le Front national confirme son redressement," *Le Figaro* [online], available from http://www.lefigaro.fr/politique/2010/03/22/01002-20100322ARTFIG00019-le-front-national-confirme-son-redressement-.php, accessed June 2010; "French Politics: Giving the UMP the Hump," *The Economist* [online], available from http://www.economist.com/node/18485957?story_id=18485957, and "Le FN progresse partout, dans ses bastions et au-delà," *Le Monde* [online], available from http://www.lemonde.fr/politique/article/2011/03/21/le-fn-progresse-partout-dans-ses-bastions-et-au-dela_1496462_823448.html, accessed May 2011.

[16] Cf., for example, "France's Far Right: A Respectable Front," *Economist* [online], available from http://www.economist.com/node/17905837?story_id=17905837, accessed Jan. 2011.

to see her as an increasingly viable candidate for the 2012 presidential election, prompting fears in some quarters of a replication of the nightmare scenario of April 2002 whereby she might capitalize on a divided field of candidates on the right in order to accede to the second round runoff.[17]

Yet, in the short term at least, the danger posed by the FN resides less in the possibility that it could win power than in its capacity to turn growing numbers of French people, politicians as well as members of the public, to its way of thinking. That it has been successful in doing this is underscored by the fact that its anti-immigration discourse and the link it draws between criminality and Third World (primarily North African) immigration has effectively been internalized by the mainstream political parties. Thus, when Interior Minister Sarkozy advocated in June 2005 cleaning out the predominantly immigrant northern suburbs of Paris "au Kärcher" (a high-pressure hose used in industrial cleaning) or repeatedly referred to the rioters of November 2005, most of them of North and sub-Saharan African origin, as *racaille* (scum), it revealed the extent to which the terms of acceptable political debate have shifted since the rise of the FN. Similarly, during the presidential campaign, Sarkozy strove to contest the FN's monopoly of the issues of national appurtenance and security by advocating the establishment of a ministry of immigration and national identity – a proposal condemned in some quarters as a throwback to Vichy's Commissariat General of Jewish Affairs – as well as draconian sentences for repeat offenders.[18] In turn, his

[17] The probability of such an outcome would be considerably enhanced by the candidacy of Dominique de Villepin as a direct rival to Sarkozy, as he would certainly slough off a proportion of votes that would otherwise go to the incumbent president. In turn, repeated polls published in the spring of 2011 suggest that Marine Le Pen would not only defeat Nicolas Sarkozy and secure a place in the second round runoff in the 2012 elections, but substantially exceed the 18% of the vote garnered by her father when he reached the second round in 2002. According to one projection, she could take as much of a third of the vote, an outcome that would dramatically reshape the French political landscape. "Marine Le Pen a pris l'ascendant dans l'opinion, selon BVA," *Le Point* [online], available from http://www.lepoint.fr/fil-info-reuters/marine-le-pen-a-pris-l-ascendant-dans-l-opinion-selon-bva-10-12-2010-1273574_240.php, as well as "PS et UMP face au 'piège' Marine Le Pen," *Le Monde* [online], available from http://www.lemonde.fr/politique/article/2010/12/13/ps-et-ump-face-au-piege-de-marine-le-pen_1452594_823448.html, accessed Jan. 2011; "France's Far Right: They Can't Keep Her Down," *The Economist* [online], available from http://www.economist.com/node/18398631?story_id=18398631; Angélique Chrisafis, "Marine Le Pen Emerges from Her Father's Shadow," *The Guardian* [online], available from http://www.guardian.co.uk/world/2011/mar/21/marine-lepen-defends-republic; and "France's National Front: Le Pen, Mightier than the Sword?" *The Economist* [online], available from http://www.economist.com/node/18651184?story_id=18651184, all accessed May 2011.

[18] Though Sarkozy might have gone farther than most in attempting to co-opt the FN's themes, he is hardly the only mainstream politician to have done so. Witness the Socialist Cresson government's recourse to forcibly repatriating immigrants by commissioning special charter flights for this purpose – a measure mooted by the FN only a few years before, which had earned it universal condemnation – or Jacques Chirac's notorious comment about the offputting odors to which French council-estate dwellers were subjected by their immigrant neighbors. Similarly, though she tried to steer clear of explicitly anti-immigrant themes, Ségolène Royal attempted to appear tough on crime by establishing mandatory "boot camps" for underage offenders and to burnish her own nationalist credentials by advocating that all French citizens be made to keep a *tricolore* at home.

government's institution of DNA testing as a precondition for reuniting immigrant families heralded a biologizing of national identity of which the radical Right could only approve.[19]

Most recently, the government has gone even further in drawing a link between immigration and crime by proposing a law that would strip immigrants or their children of their French nationality should they threaten a police officer's life, thus vitiating the republican principle that the state not distinguish between its citizens on the basis of origin. This was followed in September 2010 with the mooting of a proposal to impose a probationary period of ten years for new citizens, during which their nationality could be rescinded if they committed certain crimes. Likewise, the forced deportation of *sans papiers* (undocumented immigrants) has been relentlessly stepped up under Sarkozy's watch.[20] Finally, the banning of the burqa and niqab in all public spaces starting in early 2011, despite the fact that it will concern only several hundred people, is widely viewed as a way of singling out French Muslims for discrimination by implicitly underscoring the incompatibility of Islam with core French values and identity, a theme long developed by the FN.[21]

As these examples suggest, the greatest threat posed by the FN lies not in its accession to power but in the normalization of its discourse and program and their acceptance by the French public and political class.[22] This process of

See C. Chombeau and Philippe Ridet, "M. Sarkozy joue l'électorat FN pour le second tour," *Le Monde*, 14 March 2007, 10; Elaine Sciolino, "Extreme Right Looms over France," *International Herald Tribune*, 29 March 2007, 2; and C. Chombeau, "L'affaiblissement du FN s'est fait au prix d'une reprise de ses thèmes favoris par Sarkozy," *Le Monde* [online], available at http://www.lemonde.fr/societe/chat/2007/04/22/1-affaiblissement-du-fn-s-est-fait-au-prix-d-une-repprise-de-ses-themes-favoris-par-sarkozy 900048 3224.html, accessed 23 Apr. 2007.

[19] Cf. Laetitia Van Eeckhout, "Parlement le texte adopté mardi 23 octobre; une quarantaine de députés de l'UMP n'ont pas voté la loi sur l'immigration," *Le Monde*, 24 October 2007, 14; Mathieu Lindon, "Vox populi: pourquoi tant d'ADN?" *Libération*, 20 October 2007, 29; Patrick Jarreau, "Chronique politique: le prix des voix enlevées à Jean-Marie Le Pen," *Le Monde*, 6 October 2007, 2; Jean-Yves Nau, "Analyse: l'ADN, la biologie et l'éthique," *Le Monde*, 3 October 2007, 2; "Rubrique Société: Test ADN: Le Pen approuve ... et Buffet déplore 'une dérive' ..." *Libération*, 17 September 2007, 11.

[20] Most recently, the expulsion of nearly one thousand Roma in July and August 2010, bringing the total to eight thousand for 2010 alone, elicited an international outcry and led the European Commission to start proceedings against France for violating the EU's free-movement-of-citizens clause.

[21] On these measures, see Patrick Weil, "Les quatre piliers de la nationalité." *Le Monde* [online], available at http://www.lemonde.fr/idees/article/2010/08/23/les-quatre-piliers-de-la-nationalite-par-patrick-weil_1401781_3232.html, and John Lichfield, "France's Highest Legal Authority Removes Last Obstacle to Ban on Burqa." *Independent* [online], available at http://www.independent.co.uk/news/world/europe/%20frances-highest-legal-authority-removes-last-obstacle-to-ban-on-burka-2101002.html, accessed Oct. 2010.

[22] Indeed, changing the terms of the French political debate so as to make the FN appear normal to a growing numbers of voters and creating in essence, as the intellectuals of the Nouvelle Droite had preconized during the 1970s, a discursive and rhetorical basis for the ideological hegemony of the radical Right has been a key part of the party's political strategy from the start. Indirectly alluding to this hegemonic ideological ambition of the FN, Bruno Mégret, Le Pen's principal lieutenant in the party, wrote in September 1991 in *Présent*: "We have seen this summer the manifestations of a

normalization is reflected by the high percentage of French people who, without actually voting for the FN, claim to agree with its ideas.[23] Over time, it appears that the patina of disrepute that kept people from electorally supporting the party has worn off, with increasing numbers of them choosing in Le Pen's favor in each successive presidential election, 2007 excepted. Similarly, that more and more Frenchmen share the FN's ideas is confirmed by the fact that its electorate is no longer simply composed of "one-off" protest voters. According to one study, by the end of the 1990s between two-thirds and three-quarters of FN voters regularly cast their ballots in favor of the party's candidates, no matter who they were or the type of election concerned.[24]

In the short to medium term, then, the FN constitutes an indirect threat to French democracy because of its erosion of the universal principles of tolerance and equality on which the latter was founded. However, given the incapacity of sitting political elites to resolve the unemployment crisis and dispel the social malaise gripping the country – and, on this score, Sarkozy's presidency is likely to be decisive – it is impossible to say for certain how much the radical Right will progress over the next decade. Who knows, perhaps Marx might even be proved right in his prediction, issued in *The Eighteenth Brumaire of Louis Bonaparte*, that the French liberal economic and political order would end up digging its own grave. Should such an outcome come to pass, however, he is very likely to have been mistaken as to what would replace it.

substantial political upheaval. When Madame Cresson [the then Socialist prime minister] begins to take up point by point the analysis of the FN on immigration, going so far as to advocate as a solution the recourse to forced charter flights [of illegal immigrants back to their countries of origin], she is in fact highlighting a new and essential political reality: that it is now the FN that dominates the public debate." In turn, Jean-François Touzé, the national secretary for elected FN officials, made the same point when he argued that Sarkozy's first-round score represented in essence "an ideological victory for the FN." Bihr, *Spectre*, 206, and Chombeau, "Jean-Marie Le Pen," 7.

[23] The percentage of French voters who said that they agreed with the ideas of Jean-Marie Le Pen rose from a low of 16% at the end of 1988 to a peak of 32% in the fall of 1991 before falling back only marginally to 28% in spring 1996, where it has remained more or less constant (29% in winter 2006). Predictably, the strongest expressions of agreement were to be found among *petits indépendants* and small employers – 44% in December 2006 (versus 41% in March 1997) and industrial workers and *employés* – with 35% and 29% respectively in December 2006 (versus a high of 38% and 37% in October 1991). More recently, a TNS-Sofres poll from March 2011 found that 38% of respondents believed the Front National to be a "normal" party of the "patriotic, traditional right" (rather than an extremist or xenophobic one) as compared to 28% in 2006, while the proportion of those who found that the FN did not represent a threat to democracy in France rose from 26% in November 2003 to 37% in January 2011, testifying to the party's growing "acceptability" among French voters. Perrineau, *Le symptôme Le Pen*, 195, and Bruno Cautrès, "Les couches populaires & l'élection présidentielle," in *Baromètre politique français (2006–2007): 3ème vague – Hiver 2006* (Paris: CEVIPOF), 16 Oct. 2007, available from http://www.cevipof.msh-paris.fr/bpf/barometre/vague3/v3-synthese/BC-rapport_BPF_V3.pdf, 10, accessed Sept. 2007; "France's Far Right: They Can't Keep Her Down" and "Baromètre d'image du Front National Janvier 2011," *TNS-Sofres* [online], available from http://www.tns-sofres.com/points-de-vue/F7CBB2C5B11B4B4F893308370D6439A2.aspx, all accessed May 2011.

[24] Bihr, *Spectre*, 210.

Finally, the finding that it is the persistence of antimodern social constituencies that accounts for the resilience of the radical Right in France is important because it suggests that modernization is a country-specific process, the modalities of which are not easily transferred across societies because of the distinct structural and cultural legacies that distinguish them.[25] In this sense, this study brings into question universalistic and teleological conceptions of modernization that project the spread of a liberal economic and political order based on an ostensibly Western experience of development. Rather, it suggests, the introduction of liberal economic and political institutions within socially and culturally distinct national settings is likely to yield divergent outcomes that argue against the validity of a one-size-fits-all conception of modernization.

The French case is particularly instructive on this score because it illustrates that the dynamics of capitalist and democratic development may have consequences that run counter to this standard conception of modernization. Indeed, as in the French case, liberal democracy may end up protecting groups that are functionally ill-adapted and culturally averse to the processes of capitalist development presumed by many modernization theorists to go hand in hand with it.[26] The political empowerment of these strata and the complementary functions they assume in respect to more advanced sectors may sustain or reinforce anachronistic economic structures that in turn impede subsequent modernization. Where such conditions prevail, traditional, economically backward sectors will inevitably continue to play an important role in the economic and political life of the country.[27]

The fact that such structural and cultural agents of resistance can continue to inform a society's long-term development brings into question the positive

---

[25] The currently fashionable prescription that France reform its social model along Scandinavian lines in order to enhance its labor market flexibility while preserving the welfare state appears singularly shortsighted in this respect. This combination evolved in Northern European countries as a result of a model of industrial relations that is distinctly lacking in France. Namely, the voluntary corporatist system of worker and employer consultation that took root in Scandinavia from the late nineteenth century on facilitated the emergence of a culture of collaboration, trust, and respect between the two that never took hold in France. Instead, largely as a function of the paternalistic and authoritarian management model that has prevailed within French firms down to the present, industrial relations have always been acrimonious and conflictive in the country, preventing the kind of consensus from emerging between unions and employers that would permit a simultaneous liberalization of labor markets and expansion of the welfare state as occurred in Scandinavia.

[26] This connection was most famously drawn by Francis Fukuyama in his essay *The End of History and the Last Man* (New York: Free Press, 1992). See also Larry Diamond and Marc Plattner, eds., *Economic Reform and Democracy* (Baltimore: Johns Hopkins University Press, 1995) and *Capitalism, Socialism and Democracy Revisited* (Baltimore: Johns Hopkins University Press, 1993); John Williamson, "Democracy and the 'Washington Consensus,'" *World Development* 21(8) (1993), 1329–36; Joan Nelson, *Intricate Links: Democratization and Market Reforms in Latin America and Eastern Europe* (Washington, DC: Overseas Development Council, 1994); and Henry S. Rowen, "World Wealth Expanding: Why a Rich, Democratic, and (Perhaps) Peaceful Era Is Ahead," in *The Mosaic of Economic Growth*, ed. R. Landau, T. Taylor, and G. Wright (Stanford, CA: Stanford University Press, 1996), 92–125.

[27] Berger and Piore, *Dualism*, ch. 4.

relationship between capitalism and democracy that undergirds liberal theories of modernization. Indeed, at certain times in certain societies, the two may well sit uncomfortably or even at cross-purposes to each other. Echoing a point first made by Karl Polanyi more than sixty years ago, Gray has highlighted this potential incompatibility between capitalism and democracy as a function of the social dislocations and cultural resistances that are generated by the former: "If 'capitalism' means 'the free market,' then no view is more deluded than the belief that the future lies with 'democratic capitalism.' In the normal course of democratic life the free market is always short-lived. Its social costs are such that it cannot for long be legitimated in any democracy."[28] At the very least, this suggests that economic and political modernization is immeasurably complicated and fraught with contradiction – not the least being that, as the French case illustrates, social structures and cultural systems that emerge during the early stages of capitalist and democratic development may hamper their subsequent evolution. By extension, this also implies that the tensions engendered by modernization cannot always be peaceably resolved and that, as Barrington Moore Jr. reminds us, even the most gradualist paths to social and political modernity are paved with extraordinary conflict and violence.[29]

Thus, rather than approaching a universal, teleologically prescribed "end of history" such as communism in the past and democratic capitalism today, the outcome of these processes is likely to be institutionally and culturally manifold. Critiquing the totalizing vision of a global liberal – that is, capitalist and democratic – civilization projected by contemporary theorists of modernization, Gray writes: "The growth of a world economy does not inaugurate a universal civilization, as both Smith and Marx thought it must. Instead it allows the growth of indigenous kinds of capitalism, diverging from the ideal free market and from each other. It creates regimes that achieve modernity by renewing their own cultural traditions. ... There are many modernities, and as many ways of failing to be modern." As such, although "there are evils and goods that are universally human ..., the reality of universal goods and bads does not mean that one political and economic system – 'democratic capitalism,' say – is the best for all humankind. Universal values can be embodied in a variety of regimes."[30]

This study shows that we need to get away from a simplistic "black-box" model of modernization that equates economic and political development with institutions and processes deriving from a monolithic Western or Anglo-Saxon experience of modernity. The differences it suggests even among industrialized countries call for adopting a much more nuanced and humble conception of development, based on a real historical and cultural understanding of the societies concerned. On the contrary, they cry out for our greater appreciation of the complexities – and complications – of modernization, wherever it should unfold.

---

[28] *False Dawn*, 17, and Polanyi, *The Great Transformation*.
[29] Moore, *Social Origins of Dictatorship and Democracy*, 426–30, 505–8.
[30] *False Dawn*, 195, 124.

Index

Union des démocrates pour la république (UDR), 244, 249–51, 258
Union des fédérations régionales de France, 143
Union des industries métallurgiques et minières (UIMM), 125, 142
Union des intérêts économiques (UIE), 125, 127, 144, 147, 180, 192, 278
Union fédérale des commerçants, artisans et petits industriels de la Croix Rousse, 192
Union fraternelle du commerce et de l'industrie, 122
Union Immobilière, 141
Union nationale (government). *See* governments, Poincaré (1926–9)
Union nationale (party), 226
Union nationale des professions libérales, 233
Union pour la démocratie française (UDF), 24, 258–9
Union pour la nouvelle république (UNR), 244, 259
Union textile, 125
urbanization, 32, 165, 204

Vaillant, Édouard, 129
Valéry, Paul, 71
Vallat, Xavier, 193
Valois, Georges, 20, 41
Versailles Treaty (1918), 148
Viard, Jean, 326
Vichy regime (1940–4), 36, 198
  authoritarianism, 194–5, 207–8
  and big business, 203, 204–5, 206–7
  continuities with Third Republic, 36, 194–6, 198
  corporatism, 79, 195, 201–2, 205–9, 212
  dirigisme, 202–5, 211–12
  economic planning, 202–4
  étatisme, 202

and labor, 22, 205–6, 208
  modernizing program, 200–3, 208–9
  and *petits indépendants*, 79, 198, 201–2, 206–9
  and radical Right, 18, 36
  and technocracy, 201–3, 204–5
Vichyisme, 36
Victorian Britain, 316
Victory Bonds, 148
Villiers, Georges, 231
Volkov, Shulamit, 311–12

wage earners, 222–3, 253
wage labor, 135, 305. *See also* industrial workers
wages
  deindexation, 241, 261, 266–7, 286–7, 299
  minimum, 130, 264, 284
Waldeck-Rousseau, Pierre, 121, 124
war veterans, 20, 21, 171, 173, 179
Weber, Eugen, 20
Weil, Simone, 138, 185
Weimar Republic (1919–33), 196
welfare state, 162, 188, 260, 262, 264, 269–71, 288–9, 334
  dismantling of, 326, 327–8, 329
Weltpolitik, 317
white-collar workers, 19, 20, 21, 24–5, 119, 125, 136, 150, 167, 224, 225, 244, 250, 290
Wieviorka, Michel, 7, 304
Wilhelmine Germany, 317
Winock, Michel, 29, 33–4
working class. *See* industrial workers
World War I, 129, 136, 139, 319
World War II, 165
worldviews. *See* cultural systems

xenophobia, 33, 37–8

Zarca, Bernard, 54, 69, 92–3
Zdatny, Stephen, 195, 208, 220, 234